The Top 100

The Fastest Growing Careers for the 21st Century

Ferguson Publishing Company
Chicago, Illinois

Copyright © 1998 Ferguson Publishing Company
ISBN 0-89434-265-7

Library of Congress Cataloging-in-Publication Data

The top 100 : the fastest growing careers for the twenty-first
  century (Revised edition)
        p.   cm.
    ISBN 0-89434-265-7
    1. Occupations--United States--Handbooks, manuals, etc.
    2. Vocational guidance--United States--Handbooks, manuals, etc.
    I. Ferguson Publishing Company.
    HF5382.T59   1998   97-13380
    331.7'02'0973--dc21   CIP

Printed in the United States of America

Published and distributed by:
Ferguson Publishing Company
200 West Madison Street, Suite 300
Chicago, Illinois 60606
312-580-5480
Web: http://www.fergpubco.com

V-6

Table of Contents

Introduction

The world of work today is a lot different from the one your parents first entered years ago. New technology of all types, especially computer technology, has become an important part of nearly every industry. Careers have also become more specialized, and so has the training and education you will need to get a job and move ahead. Continuing education and training is a fact of life for most occupations these days. In order to stay competitive, you will need to expand and update your skills continuously through after-work reading, on-the-job training, and formal college and vocational courses.

The Top 100: The Fastest Growing Careers for the 21st Century presents one hundred careers that are projected by the U.S. Department of Labor and a variety of other sources as the fastest growing careers through the year 2006. Many of these careers, such as Medical Record Technicians, Social Workers, and Webmasters, are part of rapidly growing fields such as Health Care Services, Social Services, and Computer Technology. Many other careers—Service Industry careers such as Cashiers, Janitors and Cleaners, and Secretaries—are "fast growing" because of the sheer number of job openings being created.

You'll discover, as you look at the careers profiled in this book, that we discuss far more than one hundred careers. Many of the Top 100 are broken down into further subspecialties. The training for others allows workers to transfer their skills to related jobs or positions in entirely different fields.

You may feel that any "good" job requires a college education. And while it is often true that careers that require a four-year degree or more offer the highest salaries, there are many lucrative careers in this book that require only a high school diploma or a few years of apprenticeship or technical training. In fact, 33 percent of these jobs, such as Animal Caretakers, Corrections Officers, and Office Clerks require only a high school diploma and on-the-job training. You can get started in many of these fields immediately after graduation or sometimes even while you're still in school. Another 4 percent, such as Carpenters and Electricians, require the completion of a formal apprenticeship program in addition to a high school diploma. Of course, there are many careers available to those who are interested in receiving a one-, two-, or four-year degree or an advanced degree. Twenty-seven percent of these careers, such as Emergency Medical Technicians and Human Services Workers, require some form of postsecondary training, such as a one- or two-year technical program or an associate's degree. A bachelor's degree is required for 28 percent of these careers, such as Computer Programmers, Paralegals, and Special Education Teachers. Finally, 8 percent of these occupations require a Master's degree or higher. They include Chiropractors, Physicians, Speech-Language Pathologists and Audiologists, and Veterinarians.

Trends in the Workplace

Three trends in the future workplace are important to note: the importance of continuing education, the relationship between years of education and earnings, and the increase in number of technician jobs.

Technology is moving at a speed few ever thought possible, making training and skills quickly obsolete. Many now realize that they will be left behind and lose the chance for promotion and better jobs if they fail to keep their skills and training as up-to-date as possible. To offset this, many workers today supplement their knowledge by attending seminars and through after-work reading and on-the-job training. Some workers even return to college or vocational technical schools to receive advanced training and degrees. According to the March 1995 *Occupational Outlook Quarterly,* those with advanced degrees enjoy the lowest unemployment rate of 2.0 percent, while those who have not completed high school suffer the highest average unemployment rate of 11.6 percent. This continuing education trend has created another appealing benefit for many workers—better positions and higher pay.

According to the Bureau of Labor Statistics, jobs that require a bachelor's degree or higher will grow to almost double that of the average for all other occupations. And according to the Winter 1996/97 *Occupational Outlook Quarterly,* those with a bachelor's degree earn average annual salaries of $37,224, while those with only a high school diploma earn annual salaries of $20,248. This statistic can be slightly misleading because there are many fast-growing, good-paying jobs that do not require completion of a four-year degree or higher. Occupations such as Carpenters, Police Officers, and Licensed Practical Nurses, require only a few years of additional training after high school. Other jobs, such as technician careers, are also good-paying, rapidly growing jobs that do not usually require at least a four-year degree.

According to the Bureau of Labor Statistics, over one-fifth of the total workforce will be composed of technicians by 2006. A technician is defined as a highly specialized worker who works with scientists, physicians, engineers, and a variety of other professionals, as well as with clients and customers. The technician can be further defined as a type of middleperson, between the scientist in the laboratory and the worker on the floor; between the physician and the patient; between the engineer and the factory worker. In short, the technician's realm is where the scientific meets the practical application, where theory meets product.

Technician careers are growing as we increasingly rely on technology to solve problems and help us perform our daily work; and this technology continues to change almost as fast as it is introduced. Skilled technicians design, implement, operate, and repair these highly complex systems and machinery. You will see the increasing significance of tech jobs in a variety of fields, but especially in Computers and Health Care, as you page through *The Top 100: The Fastest Growing Careers for the 21st Century.* Cardiovascular Technologists, Computer and Office Machine Service Technicians, Electroneurodiagnostic Technologists, and Laser Technicians are but a few of the tech jobs featured in this book.

The Hottest Growth Fields

Three of the fastest growing fields are Health Care, Computers, and Education. Over 20 percent of the fastest growing jobs in *The Top 100: The Fastest Growing Careers for the 21st Century* relate to health care services. According to the Bureau of Labor Statistics (BLS), 30 percent of all job growth through the year 2006 will occur in Health Care. Many factors are responsible for this rapid growth. The American population is aging; by 2006 the BLS predicts that the American population that is over 70 years of age will grow by more than 10 percent. As the median age of the American population rises, more people will need various types of specialized medical care. A variety of high tech equipment will increasingly be used to diagnose and treat patients. This new technology will improve the survival rates of seriously ill and injured patients and will require trained specialists of all kinds to operate and repair it. The Home Health Care segment of this field will be exceptionally strong as the population ages. Another factor that has caused the field to expand is the increasing focus on wellness. Health Maintenance Organizations (HMOs) are increasingly focusing on preventative medicine and will need trained professionals to monitor patients and administer tests and preventative treatments.

A few factors may affect this rosy outlook for the health care field. Continued industry-wide budget cutting, realignment, and downsizing and mergers may affect growth. In terms of the expanding home care sub-field, many predict that Medicare programs will be reduced, forcing Medicare patients to pay for some home care costs themselves. This may reduce demand slightly for professionals in this segment of the industry. HMOs will continue to compete with hospitals, as well as Preferred Provider Organizations for profits. Most experts predict lucrative opportunities for those employed in HMOs, nursing homes, personal care facilities, and home health agencies. The future outlook for hospitals is less positive, but will still offer many employment opportunities. While the overall outlook for Health Care is good, students will need to carefully study the market to find the best Health Care concentrations and careers.

Computers are becoming as much a part of our culture as televisions, and they serve a significantly more useful purpose, performing tasks that we thought were impossible even a decade ago. Computers are used in almost every field, from the computers Automobile Service Technicians use to diagnose performance problems on cars, to those used by Travel Agents to help customers plan and book their travel plans, to the computer-related technology that allows Radiologic Technicians to properly image and analyze the human body. A grasp of the most basic computer—and Internet—skills is important in almost every field. According to the

Bureau of Labor Statistics, employment for computer professionals will grow 108 percent by the year 2006. Businesses need computer professionals of all types to train their staffs in the latest innovations in technology, to address problems, and to repair and upgrade existing equipment. Furthermore, the cost of computers and related hardware and software has decreased, creating both business and personal opportunities within the home. There is an increased demand for people with data processing, word processing, and desktop publishing skills, as well as people who create the actual systems and software that individuals and businesses use. Finally, the Internet has created a wide variety of opportunities for people with flexible, up-to-date skill training, such as Computer Programmers, Desktop Publishing Specialists, Software Engineers, Technical Support Specialists, and Webmasters.

It is important to note that employment in the computer industry changes almost as continuously as the evolving technology it is based on. Layoffs, mergers, and downsizing occur all of the time, just like in any other fast-growing industry. The key, as always in the new world of work, is education. Workers who continue to upgrade and expand their skills will prosper in any marketplace. There is also an increasing trend toward hiring those with advanced four-year degrees in computer technology.

According to the Bureau of Labor Statistics (BLS), the educational services industry was the largest industry in the economy in 1996, with over 10.7 million jobs. Employment in the professional specialty segment of this industry is projected to grow 19.9 percent by the year 2006. This growth will occur as a result of a marked increase in the school-age population, as well as the increasing number of people going back to school, namely those looking to change careers and retirees looking to expand their educational horizons. This increased enrollment is expected to create a shortage of 300,000 teachers by the year 2006. Other factors that will influence this shortage include the reduction of average class size, teachers leaving the profession for other careers, and the large number of teachers who will reach retirement age in the next decade. Recent reforms to the national educational system—in response to declining test scores and increased global competitiveness—have increased demand for administrative personnel and teachers of all kinds, especially Adult and Vocational Education Teachers, Elementary and Secondary School Teachers, Preschool Teachers and Child Care Workers, Special Education Teachers, and Teacher Aides.

Some factors that may limit growth include budget cuts and school restructuring. Employment for college faculty and administrative staff may be affected by the escalating costs of a college education, which may deter many from returning to school.

How to Use This Book

The following paragraphs describe the major headings used throughout *The Top 100: The Fastest Growing Careers for the 21st Century.*

At the bottom of each page you will find a shaded bar with various types of quick facts pertinent to the career. The bar on the title page of each article contains a listing of codes for three commonly used government classification systems: the Dictionary of Occupational Titles (DOT), The Guide for Occupational Exploration (GOE), and the National Occupational Classification System (NOC, Canada's framework for the classification of occupations). Other bars may feature information on recommended school subjects, personal interests, the minimum education level necessary to work in the field, certification or licensing requirements, and salary ranges for starting, mid-range, and experienced workers.

The Definition section is a brief introductory description of the duties and responsibilities of the career. Oftentimes, a career may be referred to by a variety of job titles. When that is the case, alternate career titles are presented in this section.

The Nature of the Work section describes an average day for a worker in this field, including primary and secondary duties, the types of tools, machinery, or equipment used to perform this job, and other types of workers they interact with. Growing subfields or subspecialties of this career are also discussed in detail in this section.

The Requirements section details the formal educational requirements—from high school diploma to advanced college degree—that are necessary to become employed in this field. It also presents information on how students can receive training if a college degree is not required, via on-the-job training, apprenticeships, the armed forces, or other activities. The section also explains certification, licensing, and continuing-education requirements. Finally, the Requirements section recommends high school and college classes, as well as personal qualities, that will be helpful to someone working in this field.

In the Opportunities for Experience and Exploration section, you will find a variety of ways, such as periodicals, summer jobs and programs, volunteer opportunities, associations, and clubs and hobbies, to explore the field further before you invest time and money in it.

The Methods of Entering section offers tips on how to land your first job, be it through newspaper ads, the Internet, college placement offices, or through personal contacts. It explains how the average person finds employment in this field.

The Advancement section describes the career path for someone in this field and the tools one might need—advanced training or outside education—to proceed in the career.

The Employment Outlook section predicts the potential long-term employment outlook for the field: which areas are growing as a result of technology and which are in decline. When applicable, regional employment trends are presented. Most of this information is obtained from the Bureau of Labor Statistics. Job growth terms follow those used in the *Occupational Outlook Handbook*: growth much faster than the average means an increase of 36 percent or more; growth faster than the average means an increase of 21 to 35 percent; growth about as fast as the average means an increase of 10 to 20 percent.

The Earnings section lists salary ranges for beginning, mid-range, and experienced workers in this field. It also often lists average salaries by educational achievement. Fringe benefits, such as paid vacations and sick days, health insurance, pensions, profit sharing plans, and others are covered. Where applicable, regional salary statistics and trends are presented.

In the Conditions of Work section you will see what a typical day on-the-the job is like. Is indoor or outdoor work required? Are safety measures and equipment such as protective clothing necessary? Is the job in a quiet office or on a noisy assembly line? What are the standard hours of work? Is overtime and weekend work often required? Is travel frequent? If so, to where, and for how long? This is a good place to gauge your true interest in the field.

In the last section, Sources of Additional Information, you'll find the names, addresses, phone numbers, and sometimes email and Web addresses of a variety of associations, government agencies, and unions that can provide further information regarding educational requirements, accreditation and certification, and other general information. This is the section to go to when you've decided to take the next step and want further information about the career you've just read about.

In Conclusion . . .

We hope this book will expand your knowledge and help you to make informed career choices. But this is only the beginning of your career discovery. If you find a career that catches your interest, find out more. Contact the associations listed at the end of each article. Ask your friends and family if they know someone in this field that you can talk to, an expert, a teacher, or someone who is, at least, very experienced in the field. Or, ask your school counselor to arrange a presentation or interview with a worker in this field. Maybe you can take a tour of a job site to see people actually doing the work you're interested in. You'll be surprised at the response you receive. People like to talk about their work, and by listening to someone describe his or her career, the likes and dislikes, and career hopes and dreams, you'll find out more about yourself and your future and if the career is really for you.

No one can be interested in every one of these careers, but browse through the titles and we guarantee that you'll find at least a few careers that match your talents and interests. You may even discover a career that you never knew existed. It's important to note that what is hot today may be only lukewarm tomorrow. That is why your career education must never stop. To survive in this challenging new world of work you will constantly need to analyze the changing marketplace and continue to expand and improve upon your training and skills. That is the only way to guarantee the finding and keeping of a good job.

The Editors

Actors

Definition

Actors play parts or roles in dramatic productions on the stage, in motion pictures, or on television or radio. They impersonate, or portray, characters by speech, gesture, song, and dance.

Nature of the Work

The imitation or basic development of a character for presentation to an audience often seems like a glamorous and fairly easy job. In reality, it is demanding, tiring work requiring a special talent.

The actor must first find a part available in some upcoming production. This may be in a comedy, drama, musical, or opera. Then, having read and studied the part, the actor must audition before the director and other people who have control of the production. This requirement is often waived for established artists. In film and television, actors must also complete screen tests, which are scenes recorded on film, at times performed with other actors, which are later viewed by the director and producer of the film.

If selected for the part, the actor must spend hundreds of hours in rehearsal and must memorize many lines and cues. This is especially true in live theater; in film and television, actors may spend less time in rehearsal and sometimes improvise their lines before the camera, often performing several attempts, or "takes," before the director is satisfied. Actors on television often take advantage of teleprompters, which scroll their lines on a screen in front of them while performing. Radio actors generally read from a script, and therefore rehearsal times are usually shorter.

In addition to such mechanical duties, the actor must determine the essence of the character being portrayed and the relation of that character to the overall scheme of the play. *Radio actors* must be especially skilled in expressing character and emotion through voice alone. In many film and theater roles, actors must also sing and dance and spend additional time rehearsing songs and perfecting the choreography. Some roles require actors to perform various stunts, which can be quite dangerous. Most often, these stunts are performed by specially trained *stuntmen* and *stuntwomen*. Others work as *stand-ins* or *body doubles*. These actors are chosen for specific features and appear on film in place of the lead actor; this is often the case in films requiring nude or seminude scenes. Many television programs, such as game shows, also feature models, who generally assist the host of the program.

Actors in the theater may perform the same part many times a week for weeks, months, and sometimes years. This allows them to develop the role, but it can also become tedious. Actors in films may spend several weeks involved in a production, which often takes place on location—that is, in different parts of the world. *Television actors* involved in a series, such as a soap opera or a situation comedy, also may play the same role for years, generally in thirteen-week cycles. For these actors, however, their lines change from week to week and even from day to day, and much time is spent rehearsing their new lines.

While studying and perfecting their craft, many actors work as extras, the nonspeaking characters who people the background on screen or stage. Many actors also continue their training. A great deal of an actor's time is spent attending auditions.

Requirements

There are no minimum educational requirements to become an actor. However, at least a high school diploma is recommended. As acting becomes more and more involved with the various facets of our society, a college degree will become more important to those who hope to have an acting career. It is assumed that the actor who has completed a liberal arts program is more capable of understanding the wide variety of roles that are available. Therefore, it is strongly recommended that aspiring actors complete at least a bachelor's degree program in theater or the dramatic arts. In addition, graduate degrees in the fine arts or in drama are nearly always required should the individual decide to teach dramatic arts.

College can also serve to provide acting experience for the hopeful actor. More than five-hundred colleges and universities throughout the country offer dramatic arts programs and present theatrical performances. Actors and directors recommend that those interested in acting gain as much experience as possible through acting in plays in high school and college or in those offered by community groups. Training beyond college is recommended, especially for actors interested in entering the theater. Joining acting workshops, such as the Actors Studio, can often be highly competitive.

Prospective actors will be required not only to have a great talent for acting but also a great determination to succeed in the theater and motion pictures. They must be able to memorize hundreds of lines and should have a good speaking voice. The ability to sing and dance is important for increasing the opportunities for the young actor. Almost every actor, even the biggest stars, are required to audition for a part before they receive the role. In film and television, they will generally complete screen tests to see how they will appear on film. In all fields of acting, a love for acting is a must. It might take many years for an actor to achieve any success, if at all.

Performers on the Broadway stages must be members of the Actors' Equity Association before being cast. While union membership may not always be required, many actors find it advantageous to belong to a union that covers their particular field of performing arts. These organizations include the Actors' Equity Association (stage), Screen Actors Guild or Screen Extras Guild (motion pictures and television films), or American Federation of Television and Radio Artists (TV, recording, and radio). In addition, some actors may benefit from membership in the American Guild of Variety Artists (nightclubs, and so on), American Guild of Musical Artists (opera and ballet), or organizations

such as the Hebrew Actors Union or Italian Actors Union for productions in those languages.

Opportunities for Experience & Exploration

The best way to explore this career is to participate in school or local theater productions. Even working on the props or lighting crew will provide insight into the field.

Also, attend as many dramatic productions as possible and try to talk with people who either are currently in the theater or have been at one time. They can offer advice to individuals interested in a career in the theater.

Many books, such as *Beginnings,* by Kenneth Branagh, have been written about acting, not only concerning how to perform but also about the nature of the work, its offerings, advantages, and disadvantages.

Methods of Entering

Probably the best way to enter acting is to start with high school, local, or college productions and to gain as much experience as possible on that level. Very rarely is an inexperienced actor given an opportunity to perform on stage or in film in New York or Hollywood. The field is extremely difficult to enter; the more experience and ability beginners have, however, the greater the possibilities for entrance.

Those venturing to New York or Hollywood are encouraged first to have enough money to support themselves during the long waiting and searching period normally required before a job is found. Most will list themselves with a casting agency that will help them find a part as an extra or a bit player, either in theater or film. These agencies keep names on file along with photographs and a description of the individual's features and experience, and if a part comes along that may be suitable, they contact that person. Very often, however, names are added to their lists only when the number of people in a particular physical category is low. For instance, the agency may not have enough athletic young women on their roster, and if the applicant happens to fit this description, her name is added.

Advancement

New actors will normally start in bit parts and will have only a few lines to speak, if any. The normal procession of advancement would then lead to larger supporting roles and then, in the case of theater, possibly to a role as understudy for one of the main actors. The understudy usually has an opportunity to fill in should the main actor be unable to give a performance. Many film and television actors get their start in commercials or by appearing in government and commercially sponsored public service announcements, films, and programs. Other actors join the afternoon soap operas and continue on to evening programs. Many actors have also gotten their start in on-camera roles such as presenting the weather segment of a local news program. Once an actor has gained experience, he or she may go on to play stronger supporting roles or even leading roles in stage, television, or film productions. From there, an actor may go on to stardom. Only a very small number of actors ever reach that pinnacle, however.

Some actors eventually go into other, related occupations and become dramatic coaches, drama teachers, producers, stage directors, motion picture directors, television directors, radio directors, stage managers, casting directors, or artist and repertoire managers. Others may combine one or more of these functions while continuing their career as an actor.

Employment Outlook

Motion pictures, television, and the stage are the largest fields of employment for actors, with television commercials representing as much as 60 percent of all acting jobs. Most of the opportunities for employment in these fields are either in Los Angeles or in New York. On stage, even the road shows often have their beginning in New York, with the selection of actors conducted there along with rehearsals. However, nearly every city and most communities present local and regional theater productions.

Jobs in acting are expected to grow faster than the average through the year 2006. There are a number of factors for this. The growth of satellite and cable television in the past decade have created a demand for more actors, especially as the cable networks produce more and more of their own programs and films. The rise of home video has also created new acting jobs, as more and more films are made strictly for the home video market. Many resorts have been built in the 1980s and 1990s, and most present their own theatrical productions, providing more job opportunities for actors. Jobs in theater, however, face pressure as the cost of mounting a production rises and as many nonprofit and smaller theaters lose their funding.

Despite the growth in opportunities, there are many more actors than there are roles, and this is likely to remain true for years to come. This is true in all areas of the arts, including radio, television, motion pictures, and theater, and even those who are employed are normally employed during only a small portion of the year. Many actors must supplement their income by working in other areas, such as secretaries, waiters, or taxi drivers, for example. Almost all performers are members of more than one union in order to take advantage of various opportunities as they become available.

It should be recognized that of the 105,000 or so actors in the United States today, an average of only about 16,000 are employed at any one time. Of these, few are able to support themselves on their earnings from acting, and fewer still will ever achieve stardom. Most actors work for many years before becoming known, and most of these do not rise above supporting roles. The vast majority of actors, meanwhile, are still looking for the right break. There are many more applicants in all areas than there are positions. As with most careers in the arts, people enter this career out of a love and desire for acting.

Earnings

The wage scale for actors is largely controlled through bargaining agreements reached by various unions in negotiations with producers. These agreements normally control the minimum salaries, hours of work permitted per week, and other conditions of employment. In addition, each artist enters into a separate contract that may provide for higher salaries.

The 1997 minimum weekly salary for actors in Broadway productions was $1,040, according to the Actors Equity Association. Minimum salaries for those performing in "Off Broadway" productions ranged from $400 to $625 a week, depending on the size of the theater. Smaller capacity theater productions paid about $375 to $600 weekly. Touring shows paid an additional $100 a day. A steady income is not the norm for most stage actors. Less than fifty percent of those belonging to the Actors Equity Association found stage work in 1996; average earnings were $13,700.

According to the Screen Actors Guild, actors appearing in motion pictures or television shows were paid a daily minimum of $559, or $1,942 a week, in 1997. Extras earned a minimum of $99 a day. Motion picture actors may also receive additional payments known as residuals as part of their guaranteed salary. Many motion picture actors receive residuals whenever films, TV shows, and TV commercials in which they appear are rerun, sold for TV exhibition, or put on videocassette. Residuals often exceed the actors' original salary and account for about one-third of all actors' income.

The annual earnings of persons in television and movies are affected by frequent periods of unemployment. Most Guild members earn less than $5,000 a year from acting jobs. Unions offer health, welfare, and pension fund for members working over a set number of weeks a year. Some actors are eligible for paid vacation and sick time, depending on the work contract.

In all fields, well-known actors have salary rates above the minimums, and the salaries of the few top stars are many times higher. Actors in television series may earn tens of thousands of dollars per week, while a few may earn as much as $1 million or more per week. Salaries for these actors vary considerably and are negotiated individually. In film, top stars may earn as much as $20 million per film, and, after receiving a percentage of the gross earned by the film, these stars can earn far, far more.

Until recent years, female film stars tended to earn lower salaries than their male counterparts; the emergence of stars such as Demi Moore, Jodie Foster, and others has started to reverse that trend. The average annual earnings for all motion picture actors, however, are usually low for all but the best-known performers because of the periods of unemployment.

Conditions of Work

Actors work under varying conditions. Those employed in motion pictures may work in air-conditioned studios one week and be on location in a hot desert the next.

Those in stage productions perform under all types of conditions. The number of hours employed per day or week vary, as do the number of weeks employed per year. Stage actors normally perform eight shows per week with any additional performances paid for as overtime. The basic work week after the show opens is about thirty-six hours unless major changes in the play are needed. The number of hours worked per week is considerably more before the opening, because of rehearsals. Evening work is a natural part of a stage actor's life. Rehearsals often are held at night and over holidays and weekends. If the play goes on the road, much traveling will be involved.

A number of actors cannot receive unemployment compensation when they are waiting for their next part, primarily because they have not worked enough to meet the minimum eligibility requirements for compensation. Sick leaves and paid vacations are not usually available to the actor. However, union actors who earn the minimum qualifications now receive full medical and health insurance under all the actors' unions. Those who earn health plan benefits for ten years become eligible for a pension upon retirement. The acting field is very uncertain. Aspirants never know whether they will be able to get into the profession, and, once in, there are uncertainties as to whether the show will be well received and, if not, whether the actors' talent can survive a bad show.

Sources of Additional Information

■■■**Actors' Equity Association**
165 West 46th Street
New York, NY 10036
Tel: 212-869-8530

■■■**American Federation of Television and Radio Artists--Screen Actors Guild**
260 Madison Avenue
New York, NY 10016
Tel: 212-532-0800

American Guild of Musical Artists
1727 Broadway
New York, NY 10019
Tel: 212-265-3687

American Guild of Variety Artists
184 Fifth Avenue
New York, NY 10019
Tel: 212-675-1003

Associated Actors and Artists of America (AFL-CIO)
165 West 46th Street
New York, NY 10036
Tel: 212-869-0358

National Association of Schools of Theater
11250 Roger Bacon Drive, Suite 21
Reston, VA 22090
Tel: 703-437-0700

Screen Actors Guild
5757 Wilshire Boulevard
Los Angeles, CA 90036-3600
Tel: 213-549-6400

Screen Extras Guild
3253 North Knoll Drive
Los Angeles, CA 90068-1517
Tel: 213-851-4301

Adult and Vocational Education Teachers

Definition

Adult and vocational education teachers teach basic academic subjects to adults who did not finish high school or who are new to the language. They help prepare post–high school students and other adults for specific occupations and provide personal enrichment. Adult education teachers offer basic education courses, such as reading and writing, or continuing education courses, such as literature and music. Vocational education teachers offer courses designed to prepare adults for specific occupations, such as data processor or automobile mechanic.

Nature of the Work

Adult and vocational education courses take place in a variety of settings, such as high schools, universities, religious institutions, and businesses. Job responsibilities of an adult or vocational education teacher are similar to those of a school teacher and include planning and conducting lectures, supervising the use of equipment, grading homework, evaluating students, writing and preparing reports, and counseling students.

Adult education is divided into two main areas: basic education and continuing education. Basic education includes reading, writing, and mathematics courses and is designed for students who have not finished high school and who are too old to attend regular high school courses. Many of these students are taking basic education courses to earn the equivalent of a high school diploma (the General Equivalency Diploma, or GED). Some adults who feel that they did poorly in high school and would like to refresh their rudimentary academic skills may also enroll in basic education classes. Finally, recent immigrants may take basic education classes to learn to read, write, and do arithmetic in the language of their new country.

Basic education teachers should be able to deal with students at different skill levels, including some who might not have learned proper study habits or who might have a different first language. These teachers should be able to clearly explain often complex and unfamiliar information. Patience and good communication skills are essential.

Unlike basic education, continuing education for adults is aimed at students who have finished high school or college and are taking courses for personal enrichment. Class topics might include creative writing, art appreciation, photography, history, and a host of other subjects. Often businesses will enroll employees in continuing education courses as part of job training to help them develop computer skills, learn to write grant proposals, or become convincing public speakers, to name just a few. Sometimes, businesses will hire an adult education teacher to come into the business to train employees on-site. These continuing education teachers are called *training representatives*.

Continuing education teachers should be well versed in their field and be able to communicate knowledge and enthusiasm for the subject. Adult education teachers also must be able to teach students who are at different levels of ability and be able to demonstrate techniques if a particular skill, such as painting, is being taught.

Vocational education teachers generally prepare students for specific careers that do not require a college degree, such as cosmetologist, chef, x-ray technician, or welder. Teaching methods usually include demonstrating techniques with the students observing and then attempting these techniques. A vocational education teacher will also need to present effective and appropriate material in lectures and discussion groups.

Besides working for colleges and tech schools, basic education, and continuing and vocational education, teachers are often needed in such institutions as prisons, hospitals, retirement communities, and group homes for disabled adults. Many adult education teachers work part-time.

Requirements

Adult and vocational education teachers usually have professional experience in their area of teaching. Requirements vary according to the subject and level being taught, the organization or institution offering the course, and the state in which the instruction takes place. Many states now require a teacher to have a bachelor's or graduate degree in the subject being taught. To teach vocational education courses, an instructor usually needs several years experience in the particular field as well as any professional certification that is normally required. Teacher certification and course work covering techniques in teaching vocational subjects also may be required to teach in high schools and technical and community colleges. For information on certification, students should contact the department of education in the state in which they are interested in teaching.

Specific skills, however, are often enough to secure a continuing education teaching position. For example, a person well trained in painting may be able to teach a course on painting even without a college degree or teaching certificate.

An adult or vocational teacher should feel comfortable teaching a wide variety of students. Some of these students may have had behavioral patterns that kept them from completing a high school degree. Patience and good communications skills are vital. A teacher should be able to explain sometimes complex information in a variety of ways and with patience and compassion. Many hours of out-of-class preparation may be required, especially when a teacher is just beginning.

Leadership skills are important as a teacher directs and influences a large number of students. A teacher should be comfortable talking in front of a group and be able to counsel students one-on-one. A teacher must also be able to work effectively with other teachers, librarians, office staff, and administrative officials, such as a principal, in the development of course material.

Many states require teacher certification for both adult and vocational education teachers.

Opportunities for Experience & Exploration

High school students have many opportunities to see adult or vocational education teachers at work. Often high schools will be the site of an adult or vocational education class and students may discuss career questions with teachers before or after an actual class. Students may also get the opportunity to observe in one of these classes. Some high school instructors may teach adult or vocational education courses in the evenings, and these instructors may be another good source for career information. Registering for a continuing education or vocational education course is another way of discovering the skills and disciplines needed to succeed in this field.

Students who think they may be interested in becoming adult education instructors might consider volunteering to tutor their peers in high school and college. Also, those with special skills or hobbies might offer to share their knowledge at local community centers, youth group meetings, or retirement homes.

Methods of Entering

Most people entering the field have several years of professional experience in a particular area, a desire to share that knowledge with other adults, and, often, a teaching certificate or academic degree. People with these qualifications should contact colleges, private trade schools, vocational high schools, or other appropriate institutions to receive additional information about employment opportunities. Many colleges, technical schools, and state departments of education offer job lines or bulletin boards that provide a listing of job openings.

Advancement

A skilled adult or vocational education teacher may become a full-time teacher, school administrator, or director of a vocational guidance program. To be an administrator, a master's degree or a doctorate may be required. Advancement also may take the form of higher pay and additional teaching assignments. For example, a person may get a reputation as a skilled ceramics teacher and be hired by other adult education organizations as an instructor.

Employment Outlook

Employment opportunities in the field of adult education are expected to grow faster than average through the year 2006. Adults recognize the importance for further education and training to succeed in today's workplace. In fact, many courses are subsidized by companies who want their employees trained in the latest skills and technology of their field. The biggest growth areas are projected to be in computer technology, automotive mechanics, and medical technology. As demand for adult and vocational education teachers continues to grow, major employers will be vocational high schools, private trade schools, community colleges, and private adult education enterprises. The federal government will also offer opportunities such as the Department of Agriculture's programs that teach farming skills. Labor unions will need teachers, as they offer continuing education opportunities to their members. Changes in immigration policies will create a need for English and American civics classes. Remedial classes in reading, writing, and math, as well as GED courses will result from employers demanding better educated workers.

About half of all employment opportunities are part-time, so many adult and vocational education teachers also have other jobs, often in unrelated areas. Some job openings will result from current teachers retiring from the workforce. Since many adult education programs benefit from State and Federal funding, this occupation's growth is tied to the health of the nation's economy and government budgeting.

Earnings

Full-time adult and vocational education teachers can expect to earn an average of $31,300 a year. In general, full time instructors average between $19,200 and $44,800 a year, with some highly skilled and experienced teachers earning even more. Earnings vary widely according to the subject, the number of courses taught, the

teacher's experience, and the geographic region where the institution is located.

Because many adult and vocational education teachers are employed part-time, they are often paid by the hour or by the course, with no health insurance or other benefits. Hourly rates range from $6 to $50 an hour and, again, depend on the subject being taught, the training and education of the instructor, and the geographic region of the institution.

Conditions of Work

Working conditions vary according to the type of class being taught and the number of students participating. Courses are usually taught in a classroom setting but may also be in a technical shop, laboratory, art studio, music room, or other location depending on the subject matter. Of course, when teaching in such settings as prisons or hospitals, adult education teachers must travel to the students as opposed to the students travelling to the teacher's classroom. Average class size is usually between ten and thirty students, but may vary, ranging from one-on-one instruction to large lectures attended by sixty or more students.

Like many other types of teachers, adult and vocational education teachers may only work nine or ten months a year, with summers off. About half of the adult and vocational education teachers work part-time, averaging anywhere from two to twenty hours of work per week. For those employed full-time, the average work week is between thirty-five and forty hours. Much of the work is in the evening or on weekends, as many adult students work on weekdays.

Sources of Additional Information

American Association for Adult and Continuing Education
1200 19th Street, NW, Suite 300
Washington, DC 20036
Tel: 202-429-5131

American Vocational Association
1410 King Street
Alexandria, VA 22314
Tel: 703-683-3111

Adult Day Care Coordinators

Definition

Adult day care coordinators direct day care programs for adults—usually elderly or disabled—who cannot be left alone all day. They oversee staff members who provide care, meals, and social activities to day care clients and serve as a liaison between the day care center and its clients' families.

Nature of the Work

Adult day care coordinators direct adult day care centers. Although specific duties vary depending upon the size of the center and the services it offers, the coordinator's general responsibility is to ensure that his or her center provides the necessary care for its clients. This may include personal hygiene, meals, medications and therapies, and social activities.

Although coordinators working in small day care centers may actually perform some services for clients, this is not the norm. Instead, coordinators usually oversee various staff members who provide the caregiving. A large center, for example, might have a nurse, a physical therapist, a social worker, a cook, and several aides. The coordinator is responsible for staff hiring, training, and scheduling. He or she may meet with staff members either one-on-one or in group sessions to review and discuss plans for the clients.

Overseeing meal planning and preparation is also the responsibility of the adult day care coordinator. In most centers, clients are given a noon meal, and usually juices and snacks in the mornings and afternoons. Coordinators work with a cook or dietitian to develop well-rounded menus that take into account the nutritional needs of the clients, including any particular restrictions such as a diabetic or low-sodium diet. The coordinator may also oversee the purchasing and inventorying of the center's food supply.

The coordinator schedules daily and weekly activities for the day care clients. Depending upon the particular needs and abilities of the clients, a recreational schedule might include crafts, games, exercises, reading time, or movies. In some centers, clients are taken on outings to shopping centers, parks, or restaurants. The coordinator plans such outings, arranging for transportation and any reservations or special accommodations necessary. Finally, the coordinator also organizes parties for special events, such as holidays or birthdays.

Finding new activities and visitors for the center is also part of the coordinator's job. He or she might recruit volunteers to teach crafts or music to the clients. Oftentimes, church or civic groups also visit such facilities to visit with clients. Some such groups institute "buddy" type programs, in which each group member pairs with a day care client to develop an ongoing relationship. The day care coordinator must authorize and monitor any group visits, activities, or programs.

In addition to planning and overseeing the activities of the center and its clients, the adult day care coordinator also works closely with client family members to make sure that each individual is receiving care that best fits his or her needs. This relationship with the clients' families usually begins before the client is ever actually placed in the day care center.

When a new family is considering placing an elderly person in a day care setting, they often have many questions about the center and its activities. The coordinator meets with family members to show them the center and explain to them how it is run. He or she also gathers information about the potential client, including names and phone numbers of doctors and people to contact in case of emergency; lists of medications taken with instructions on when and how they should be administered; and information on allergies, food choices, and daily habits and routines.

After the client is placed in the center, the coordinator may meet periodically with his or her family to update them on how the client is responding to the day care setting. If necessary, the coordinator may advise the family about social services, such as home health care, and refer them to other providers.

Adult day care coordinators may have other duties, depending upon the center and how it is owned and operated. For example, they may be responsible for developing and adhering to a budget for the center. If the center is licensed or certified by the state, the coordinator may ensure that it remains in compliance with the regulations and necessary documentation. He or she may also be responsible for general bookkeeping, bill payment, and office management.

In addition to supervising the center, the coordinator may also promote and advertise it to members of the community. He or she may help with fund-raising, prepare press releases, and speak to various service clubs.

Requirements

Although the vast majority of employers require at least a high school diploma, there are no definite educational requirements for becoming an adult day care coordinator. Some learn their skills on the job; others have taken courses in home nursing or health care.

Many employers prefer to hire candidates who meet the standards set by the National Institute on Adult Day Care. In order to meet these standards, a coordinator must have a bachelor's degree and one year of full-time experience in a geriatric setting, or an associate's degree and two years' experience in related work. In preparation for such a career, a college student might choose occupational, recreation, or rehabilitation therapy or social work. An increasingly popular major for potential adult day care coordinators is gerontology, or geriatrics.

Over 600 American colleges and universities currently offer a formal program of instruction in gerontology. Although specific courses vary from school to school, most programs consist of classes in social gerontology, biology and physiology of aging, psychology of aging, and sociology of aging. In addition to these four core classes, most pro-

grams offer elective courses in such areas as social policy, community services, nutrition and exercise, diversity in aging, health issues, death and dying, and ethics and life extension.

A practicum or field placement is also a part of most gerontology programs. This allows students to obtain experience working with both well-functioning elderly people and those with age-related disabilities.

High school students who are considering a career as an adult day care coordinator should take classes in psychology, sociology, and home economics. Because communication is an important skill, English and speech classes are also good choices.

No certification or licensing is required to become an adult day care coordinator. In some cases, however, the agency that a coordinator works for may be licensed or certified by the state health department. Any adult day care center that receives payment from Medicare or from other government agencies must be certified by the state Department of Health. In these cases, licensing requirements may include requirements for coordinators and other staff members. The trend is toward stricter standards.

Regardless of what level of education a prospective coordinator has, there are certain personal characteristics that are necessary for success in this field. Compassion and an affinity for the elderly and disabled are vital, as are patience and the desire to help others.

Opportunities for Experience & Exploration

There are several ways for high school students to learn more about the career of adult day care coordinator. The first and easiest way is to visit a nursing home or adult day care center in order to experience firsthand what it is like to spend time with and interact with elderly people. It might even be wise for students to take a volunteer position or part-time job in such a facility. This would allow them to gauge their aptitude for a career in aging.

Students might also check their local libraries for books or articles on aging in order to learn more about this career.

Methods of Entering

It is estimated that there are over 3,000 adult day care centers currently operating in the United States. The great majority are operated on a nonprofit or public basis, and many are affiliated with large organizations such as nursing homes, hospitals, or multi-purpose senior organizations.

In looking for a position as an adult day care coordinator, candidates should first locate and contact all such programs in the area. Checking the local yellow pages under "Nursing Homes," "Residential Care Facilities," "Aging Services," or "Senior Citizens Services" should provide a list of leads. The job seeker might either send a resume and cover letter or call these potential employers directly. Prospective coordinators should also watch for job openings listed in area newspapers.

Another means of finding job leads is to become affiliated with a professional association, such as the American Geriatrics Society, the American Society on Aging, the Gerontological Society of America, or the National Council on the Aging. Many such organizations have monthly or quarterly newsletters that list job opportunities. Some may even have job banks or referral services.

The job seeker who has received an associate's or bachelor's degree should also check with the career placement office at his or her college or university.

Advancement

Because the field of aging-related services continues to grow, the potential for advancement for adult day care coordinators is good. Some coordinators advance by transferring to a larger center which pays better wages. Others may eventually start their own center. Still others advance by moving into management positions in other, similar social service organizations, such as a nursing home, hospice, or government agency on aging.

Finally, an adult day care coordinator might choose to return to school and complete a higher degree—often a master's degree in social work. For those who choose this option, there are many career opportunities in the field of social services. A social worker might, for example, work with individuals and families dealing with AIDS, cancer, or other debilitating illnesses. He or she might also work for agencies offering various types of counseling, rehabilitation, or crisis intervention.

Earnings

Starting salaries for this position depend partly upon the experience and education of the coordinator and partly upon the size and location of the day care center. Larger centers, located in more metropolitan areas, tend to offer the highest wages.

According to the Association for Gerontology in Higher Education, beginning annual salaries range from $18,000 to $31,000 for persons with a bachelor's degree and little experience. Generally, coordinators who do not have a bachelor's degree can expect to earn somewhat less than this. Experienced coordinators with a bachelor's degree employed in large, well-funded centers may earn from $20,000 to $45,000 annually.

In addition to salary, some coordinators are also offered a benefits package, which typically includes health insurance, paid vacation and sick days, and a retirement plan.

Employment Outlook

The career outlook for adult day care coordinators, as for all human services workers, is expected to be excellent through the year 2006. According to the U.S. Department of Labor, the number of human services workers is projected to double between the years 1992 and 2006, with adult day care, specifically, being one of the fastest-growing human service areas.

The main reason for this is that our senior citizen population is growing rapidly. Currently, the number of Americans over 65 stands at 31 million; by 2006, it should exceed 36 million. This rapid growth has led to the development and increased popularity of a number of aging-related services over the last several years. The increase in adult day care centers is one example of this trend. According to the National Institute on Adult Day Care, there were as few as 15 adult day care centers in existence in the 1970s; today, there are over 3,000. This trend should continue, as Americans become increasingly aware of the diverse needs of the elderly and the various service options available to them. Adult day care is expected to be used more frequently as a cost-efficient and preferable alternative to nursing homes.

Conditions of Work

Most adult day care centers have a schedule that corresponds to standard business hours. Most coordinators work a forty-hour week, Monday through Friday with weekends off.

The coordinator's work environment will vary depending upon the size and type of center he or she supervises. Some centers are fairly institutional, resembling children's day care centers or nursing homes. Others have a more residential-feel, carpeted and furnished like a private home. Regardless of the furnishings, the center is typically clean, well-lit, and equipped with ramps, rails, and other devices that ensure the safety of clients.

Part of the coordinator's day may be spent in the center's common areas with clients and staff. He or she may also spend time working in an on-site office. If the staff members take clients on outings, the coordinator may accompany them.

Coordinators are on their feet much of the time, ensuring that meals and activities run smoothly, and helping staff members when necessary. Attire for the job varies from center to center, ranging from very casual to standard office wear. Most coordinators, however, wear clothing that is comfortable and allows them freedom of movement.

Regardless of the size of the center, the coordinator spends the majority of his or her time working with people—both staff members and day care clients. Working with clients is often very trying. Many of them may have had a stroke or have Alzheimer's disease, and may be confused, uncooperative, and even hostile. The job may also be emotionally taxing for the coordinator who becomes attached to his or her clients. Most adults who use a day care center are elderly or permanently disabled; for this reason, day care staff must frequently deal with the decline and eventual death of their clients.

Sources of Additional Information

National Institute on Adult Day Care
National Council on Aging
409 Third Street SW, Suite 200
Washington, DC 20024
Tel: 202-479-1200
WWW: http://www.ncoa.org

American Association of Homes and Services for the Aging
901 E Street NW, Suite 500
Washington, DC 20004
WWW: http://www.aahsa.org

Association for Gerontology in Higher Education
1001 Connecticut Avenue NW, Suite 410
Washington, DC 20036
Tel: 202-429-9277

American Geriatrics Association
600 Maryland Avenue SW, Suite 100 West
Washington, DC 20024
Tel: 202-554-4444

Gerontological Society of America
1275 K Street NW, Suite 350
Washington, DC 20005
Tel: 202-842-1275

National Association of Area Agencies on Aging
1112 16th Street NW, Suite 100
Washington, DC 20036
Tel: 202-296-8130

Alcohol and Drug Abuse Counselors

Definition

Alcohol and drug abuse counselors work with people who abuse or are addicted to drugs or alcohol. Through individual and group counseling sessions, they help their clients understand and change their destructive substance abuse behaviors.

Nature of the Work

The main goal of the alcohol and drug abuse counselor is to help his or her patients stop their destructive behaviors. The counselor may also work with the families of clients to give them support and guidance in dealing with the problem.

The counselor begins by trying to learn about the patient's general background and history of drug or alcohol use. He or she may review patient records, including police reports, employment records, medical records, or reports from other counselors.

He or she also interviews the patient to determine the nature and extent of substance abuse. During an interview, the counselor asks questions about what types of substances the patient uses, how often, and for how long. He or she may also ask the patient about previous attempts to stop using the substance and about how the problem has affected his or her life in various areas.

Using the information they obtain from the patient and their knowledge of substance abuse patterns, counselors formulate a program for treatment and rehabilitation. A substantial part of the rehabilitation process involves either individual, group, or family counseling sessions. During individual sessions, the counselor does a great deal of listening, perhaps asking appropriate questions to guide the patient to insights about him- or herself.

In a group therapy session, the counselor supervises a group of several patients, helping move their discussion in positive ways. In counseling sessions, the counselor also teaches patients methods of overcoming their dependency. For example, he or she might help a patient develop a series of goals for behavioral change.

Counselors monitor and assess the progress of their patients. In most cases, a counselor will be dealing with several different patients in various stages of recovery—some may need help breaking the pattern of substance abuse; some may already have stopped using, but still need support; others may be recovered users who have suffered a relapse. The counselor maintains an ongoing, personal relationship with each patient to help him or her adapt to the different recovery stages.

Working with families is another aspect of many alcohol and drug abuse counselors' jobs. They may ask a patient's family for insight into the patient's behavior. They may also teach the patient's family members how to deal with and support the patient through the recovery process.

Counselors may work with other health professionals and social agencies, including physicians, psychiatrists, psychologists, employment services, and court systems. In some cases, the counselor, with the patient's permission, may serve as a spokesperson for the patient, working with corrections officers, social workers, or employers. In other cases, a patient's needs might exceed the counselor's abilities; when this is the case, the counselor refers the patient to an appropriate medical expert, agency, or social program.

There is a substantial amount of paperwork involved in counseling alcohol and drug abusers. Detailed records must be kept on each patient in order to follow his or her progress. For example, a report must be written after each counseling session. Counselors who work in residential treatment settings are required to participate in regular staff meetings to develop treatment plans and review patient progress. They may also meet periodically with family members or social service agency representatives to discuss patient progress and needs.

In some cases, alcohol and drug abuse counselors specialize in working with certain groups of people. Some work only with children or teenagers; others work with businesses to counsel employees who may have drug and alcohol related problems. In other cases, counselors specialize in treating people who are addicted to specific drugs, such as cocaine, heroin, or alcohol. Special training may be required to work with specific groups.

Counselors are hired by hospitals, private and public treatment centers, government agencies, prisons, colleges and universities, crisis centers, and mental health centers. More and more frequently, large companies are hiring alcohol and drug abuse counselors as well, to deal with employee substance abuse problems.

Requirements

The educational requirements for alcohol and drug abuse counselors vary greatly by state and employer. A high school education may be the minimum requirement for employers who provide on-the-job training, which ranges from six weeks to two years. These jobs, however, are becoming increasingly rare as more states are leaning toward stricter requirements for counselors.

Some employers require an associate's degree in alcohol and drug technology. Most substance abuse counselors, however, have a bachelor's degree in counseling, psychology, health sociology, or social work. Many two- and four-year colleges now offer specific courses for students training to be substance abuse counselors.

Many counselors have a master's degree in counseling with a specialization in substance abuse counseling. Accredited graduate programs in substance abuse counseling are composed of a supervised internship as well as regular class work.

Certification in this field, which is mandatory in some states, is available through state accreditation boards. Currently, thirty-nine states and the District of Columbia have credentialing laws for alcohol and drug abuse counselors. These laws typically require that counselors have a minimum of a master's degree and two to three years of postacademic supervised counseling experience. Candidates must also have passed a written test.

The National Association of Alcoholism and Drug Abuse Counselors also offers a National Certified Addiction Counselor Certification.

High school students who are considering a career in alcohol and drug abuse counseling should choose a curriculum that meets the requirements of the college or university they hope to attend. Typically, four years of English, history, mathematics, a foreign language, and social sciences are necessary. In addition, psychology, sociology, physiology, biology, and anatomy provide a good academic background for potential counselors.

In order to be successful in this job, prospective counselors should enjoy working with people. They must have compassion, good communication and listening skills, and a desire to help others. They should also be emotionally stable and able to deal with the frustrations and failures that are often a part of the job.

Opportunities for Experience & Exploration

Students interested in this career can find a great deal of information on substance abuse and substance abuse counseling at any local library. In addition, by contacting a local hospital, mental health clinic, or treatment center, it might be possible to talk with a counselor about the details of his or her job.

Volunteer work or a part-time job at a residential facility, such as a hospital or treatment center, is another good way of gaining experience and exploring an aptitude for counseling work. Finally, there are a number of professional and government organizations listed at the end of this article which can provide information on alcohol and drug abuse counseling.

Methods of Entering

There are a number of for-profit and not-for-profit organizations that hire alcohol and drug abuse counselors, including hospitals, public school systems, colleges and universities, prisons, health maintenance organizations (HMO's), private and public treatment centers, community mental health agencies, government agencies, and private corporations.

Counselors who have completed a two- or four-year college degree might start a job search by checking with the career placement office or their college or university. Those who plan to look for a position without first attending college might want to start by getting an entry-level or volunteer position in a treatment center or related agency. In this way, they can obtain practical experience and also make connections that might lead to full-time employment as a counselor.

Job seekers should also watch the classified advertisements in local newspapers. Job openings for counselors are often listed under "Alcohol and Drug Counselor," "Substance Abuse Counselor," or "Mental Health Counselor." Finally, one might consider applying directly to the personnel department of various facilities and agencies that treat alcohol and drug abusers.

Advancement

Counselors in this field often advance initially by taking on more responsibilities and earning a higher wage. They may also better themselves by taking a similar position in a more prestigious facility, such as an upscale private treatment center.

As they obtain more experience and perhaps more education, counselors sometimes move into supervisory or administrative positions. They might become directors of substance abuse programs in mental health facilities or executive directors of agencies or clinics.

Career options are more diverse for those counselors who continue their education. They may move into research, consulting, or teaching at the college level.

Employment Outlook

Employment of alcohol and drug abuse counselors is projected to grow much faster than the average for all occupations through the year 2006. There are more than twenty million alcoholics in the United States and an equal, if not greater, number of drug abusers. Because no successful method to significantly reduce drug and alcohol abuse has emerged, these numbers are not

likely to decrease. Overall population growth will also lead to a need for more substance abuse counselors.

Another reason for the expected growth in counselors' jobs is that an increasing number of employers are offering employee assistant programs which provide mental health and alcohol and drug abuse services.

Finally, many job openings will arise as a result of job turnover. Because of the stress levels and the emotional demands involved in this career, there is a high burnout rate. As alcohol and drug abuse counselors leave the field, new counselors are needed to replace them.

Earnings

Salaries of alcohol and drug abuse counselors depend upon their education level, amount of experience, and place of employment. Generally, the more education and experience a counselor has, the higher his or her earnings will be. Counselors who work in private treatment centers also tend to earn more than their public sector counterparts.

According to a 1997 salary study conducted by the Economic Research Institute, substance abuse counselors with less than five years experience earned an average of $27,336 a year. Counselors with five to ten years experience earned an average of $33,740 a year; those with ten or more years earned from $38,807 to $48,742 annually. Directors of treatment programs or centers could earn considerably more. Almost all treatment centers provide employee benefits to their full-time counselors. These usually include paid vacations and sick days, insurance, and pension plans.

Conditions of Work

The hours that an alcohol and drug abuse counselor works depends upon where he or she is employed. Many residential treatment facilities and mental health centers—and all crisis centers—have counselors on duty during evening and weekend hours. Other employers, such as government agencies and universities, are likely to have more conventional working hours.

Work settings for counselors also vary by employer. Counselors may work in private offices, in the rooms or homes of patients, in classrooms, or in meeting rooms. In some cases, they conduct support group sessions in churches, community centers, or schools. For the most part, however, most counselors work at the same work site or sites on a daily basis.

The bulk of a counselor's day is spent dealing with various people—patients, families, social workers, and health care professionals. There may be very little time during a work day for quiet reflection or organization.

Working with alcohol and drug abusers can be an emotionally draining experience. Overcoming addiction is a very hard battle and patients respond to it in various ways. They may be resentful, angry, discouraged, or profoundly depressed. They may talk candidly with their counselors about tragic and upsetting events in their lives. The counselor spends much of his or her time listening to and dealing with very strong, usually negative emotions.

This work can also be discouraging, due to a high failure rate. Many alcoholics and drug addicts do not respond to treatment and return immediately to their addictions. Even after months, and sometimes years, of recovery, many substance abusers suffer relapses. The counselor must learn to cope with the frustration of having his or her patients fail, perhaps repeatedly.

There is a very positive side to drug and alcohol abuse counseling, however. When it is successful, the counselor has the satisfaction of knowing that he or she made a positive impact on someone's life. He or she has the reward of seeing some patients return to happy family lives and productive careers.

Sources of Additional information

■ **National Association of Alcoholism and Drug Abuse Counselors**
1911 North Fort Myer Drive, Suite 900
Arlington, VA 22209
Tel: 703-741-7686
Email: naadac@internetmci.com
WWW: http://www.naadac.org

■ **National Clearinghouse on Alcohol and Drug Abuse**
PO Box 2345
Rockville, MD 20847
Tel: 800-729-6686
Email: webmaster@health.org
WWW: http://www.health.org

■ **American Counseling Association**
5999 Stevenson Avenue
Alexandria, VA 22304
Tel: 800-347-6647
WWW: http://www.counseling.org/

■ **National Institute on Alcohol Abuse and Alcoholism**
Willco Building
6000 Executive Boulevard
Bethesda, MD 20892
Tel:301-443-3860
Email: webmaster@www.niaaa.nih.gov
WWW: http://www.amcom.aspensys.com/nachiv/niaaa.html

■ **National Institute on Drug Abuse**
Email: information@lists.nida.nih.gov
WWW: http://www.nida.nih.gov

Allergists/Immunologists

Definition

An *allergist/immunologist* is a medical doctor that specializes in the treatment of allergic, asthmatic, and immunologic diseases. They work in private offices, hospitals, and research laboratories.

Nature of the Work

Along with the fur of animals, a person may be allergic to certain foods, plants, pollen, air pollution, insects, colognes, chemicals, and cleansers. So, many people seek the aid of an *allergy and immunology specialist*, a doctor who specializes in the treatment of allergic, asthmatic, and immunologic diseases.

Of course, if a person is allergic to dogs or cats, the best solution is to avoid dogs and cats. However, some allergens (the substance that causes the allergic reaction), like grass, dust, or pollinating plants, can be difficult to avoid. When patients see their family doctor with symptoms of an allergy, the doctor will likely refer them to an allergist/immunologist. Hay fever, also called allergic rhinitis, is a common condition treated by an allergist. A person with hay fever may have symptoms such as congestion, sneezing, and a scratchy throat caused by pollens or molds in the air. Asthma, a respiratory disease, can be seriously threatening. An asthma attack, often triggered by an allergic reaction, causes restricted breathing, constricting the air flow to the lungs. Another serious allergic reaction is anaphylaxis. Triggered by a particular food or insect sting, anaphylaxis can quickly restrict breathing, swell the throat, and cause unconsciousness. Other allergies treated by an allergist include skin allergies, such as hives and eczema, and food and drug allergies.

Immunologic diseases are those that affect the immune system. Allergy and immunology specialists treat patients with conditions such as AIDS, rheumatoid arthritis, and lupus. An immunologist will also treat patients who are receiving an organ or bone marrow transplant—to help prevent the patient's body from rejecting the transplanted organ.

The allergist/immunologist, in addition to being a licensed doctor, must also be certified by the American Board of Allergy and Immunology. Allergists/immunologists work in private practice, hospitals, and research laboratories. With their specific knowledge about allergic and immunologic diseases, allergists/immunologists listen carefully to the patient and then develop a treatment plan. The doctor reviews the patient's medical history and background, and may also conduct skin tests and blood tests. Skin tests are often preferred because they are inexpensive and the results are available immediately. Skin tests are also better for identifying more subtle allergies.

Once the diagnosis is made, the doctor will determine a treatment plan. In some cases, the solution may be as simple as avoiding the things that cause the allergic reaction. The allergist will help find ways to limit patients' exposure to the allergen. In other cases, a doctor will prescribe medication. Antihistamines are drugs that relieve allergy symptoms such as nasal congestion, eye burning, and skin rashes. Antihistamines can have side effects such as dizziness, headaches, and nausea. Should these side effects occur, the allergist will treat them and prescribe a new medication. Sometimes a patient can build up a resistance to an antihistamine and the doctor needs to prescribe a stronger variety.

Immunotherapy (a series of allergy shots) is another kind of treatment for asthma and for allergies to pollen, dust, bee venom, and a variety of other substances. Immunotherapy involves injecting the patient with a small amount of the substance that causes the allergic reaction. The immune system then becomes less sensitive to the substances, and reduces the symptoms of allergy. An allergist will give weekly shots over an extended time, gradually increasing the dosage; eventually the shots are only necessary once a month.

Requirements

To become an allergist/immunologist requires several years of intensive study and training. After high school, a premedical college program follows, which usually requires four years of course work. Scholarships and grants are often available from individual institutions, state agencies, and special-interest organizations. Many students finance their medical education through the Armed Forces Health Professions Scholarship Program. Each branch of the military participates in this program, paying students' tuition in exchange for military service. Contact your local recruiting office for more information on this program.

During the second or third year of college, students should arrange to take the Medical College Admission Test (MCAT). The exam covers four areas: verbal facility, quantitative ability, knowledge of the humanities and social sciences, and knowledge of biology, chemistry, and physics. All medical colleges in the country require the test for admission.

The first two years of medical school includes course work in human anatomy, physiology, pharmacology, and microbiology. The last two years are then devoted to clinical training—first-hand experience in a hospital setting. After medical school, doctors must take an examination to be licensed to practice. It is conducted through the board of medical examiners in each state. Training starts with three years of residency training in internal medicine or pediatrics, then a minimum of two years of training in an allergy and immunology fellowship. The American Academy of Allergy, Asthma, and Immunology (AAAAI) publishes a training program directory, which lists accredited training programs and faculty and program information.

Certification from the American Board of Allergy and Immunology (ABAI) requires a valid medical license, proof of residency completion, and written evaluation from the residency director. The evaluation reviews the candidate's clinical judgment, attitude, professional behavior, and other work skills and habits. The certification exam tests the candidate's knowledge of the immune system, human pathology, and the molecular basis of allergic and other immune reactions. The candidate must also show an understanding of diagnostic tests and therapy for immunologic diseases.

Allergists/immunologists should be compassionate, and concerned for the well-being of their patients. They should also be careful listeners—a doctor must have a good understanding of a patient's background, environment, and emotional state to plan the best treatment. An allergist/immunologist must be prepared to deal with the stress of caring for sick patients; some of these patients may have life-threatening diseases such as AIDS, cancer, or severe asthma. Despite the many advances in the treatment of allergic diseases and diseases of the immune system, many of them remain incurable. An allergist/immunologist who deals with severe cases must not become too emotionally involved; a doctor too upset by a patient's illness may not be able to provide the best treatment.

Opportunities for Experience & Exploration

High school students interested in the field of allergy/immunology should take advantage of science courses offered by their schools. Courses such as biology, chemistry, and other health classes will be helpful in preparing students for a college premedical program. Any course that requires lab work will be good experience for the clinical research aspects of allergy/immunology. English composition classes will develop writing skills needed for numerous papers required during college and medical school.

Volunteer work is a great way to become familiar with the medical profession. Volunteering in a hospital or nursing home can give a sense of a doctor's work and responsibilities. Volunteers are often needed to help AIDS and cancer patients in their homes. Part-time work in a retail pharmacy can teach students about the variety of medications prescribed to people with allergies.

Methods of Entering

The only way to become an allergist/immunologist is to attend medical school and receive specialized training through residency and fellowship. Most medical school graduates participate in a match program that best pairs their qualifications and interests to a residency program. Fellowships are great opportunities to get to know the allergy/immunology field from the inside. Besides valuable work experience and training, it's a chance to meet doctors already in the field and establish contacts. Attendance at national association meetings, conferences, and scientific presentations is part of the program. Research done during this time may be published in medical journals giving fellows a competitive edge in the job market. Those interested in this specialty should carefully research different training programs to assure that the fellowship will best serve their long term goals. Since fellowship positions are competitive, knowing about the program, its faculty, and focus, will give the candidate an edge in obtaining one.

Building a private practice can be a slow procedure. Patients are acquired through referrals from hospitals, clinics, or by other patients. Joining a group practice, taking over a retiring doctor's existing practice, or building one from scratch, are different ways to enter in private practice.

Advancement

Most allergists/immunologists work in hospitals, private practice, or in clinical research laboratories. Once allergists/immunologists have begun a practice, they advance by building a strong reputation and a growing list of patients. Continuing education is an important aspect of the job. A doctor must be familiar with new medical findings, medications, and treatments. Some allergists/immunologists, after having a practice for a while, may go into teaching, or clinical research.

Employment Outlook

Employment of physicians will grow faster than average through the year 2006. Over 50 million Americans suffer from some kind of allergy, fueling the demand for allergists/immu-

nologists. This specialty was included in *U.S. News & World Report's* annual feature, "Best Jobs for the Future." Though some doctors remain skeptical about the relationship between allergy and illness, allergy/immunology has become a respected field of medicine. As this field continues to grow, more doctors will refer their patients to these specialists.

Many allergists/immunologists are involved in clinical research that often leads to better treatment for allergies and the causes of allergic reactions. The World Wide Web has shown to be a good forum for promoting the practice and research of allergy/immunology. The Web is inexpensive for doctors to advertise their services and for professional organizations and training schools to publicize the causes and treatment of allergies, and to advertise their programs. People with allergies or diseases of the immune system can also find many support groups on the Web.

Earnings

Physicians are rewarded well for their years of intensive study, for their long hours, and for their level of responsibility. Allergists/immunologists make from about $50,000 to $200,000 a year. Allergists/immunologists who are still in their residencies may make as little as $25,000 a year. The average annual income for all physicians is $160,000.

Though an allergist/immunologist can make a good living, a number of factors, such as geographical location, experience, and reputation of good work, can determine salary.

Conditions of Work

Allergists/immunologists can work in three areas of practice: office based private practice, clinical allergy and immunology in a hospital-based setting, or basic and clinical setting. Some specialists choose to work in all three areas resulting in a six-day work week.

Doctors' offices need to be clean, well lit, and organized facilities. Many doctors employ receptionists, secretaries, and nurses to assist with patients, and the general paperwork associated with running an office. During patient consultations, doctors need to ask questions regarding medical history and symptoms to make a diagnosis. They need to listen to patients carefully to determine the best possible treatment, be it medication or other type of intervention. Skin and blood tests are often necessary to confirm a diagnosis. Many allergies are chronic diseases, sometimes lasting years before they fully present themselves. In such cases, strong doctor-patient relationships are developed as the patient repeatedly seeks medical advice and attention.

Work in a hospital is similar to that in a doctor's office, but more structured. The atmosphere is more formal and impersonal; there is less opportunity to develop patient relationships. Often, the cases seen in a hospital are more complex, the problems more chronic and severe. More than one doctor may be assigned to a patient.

Sources of Additional Information

For career information and a list of accredited training programs, contact:

American Academy of Allergy, Asthma, and Immunology
611 East Wells Street
Milwaukee, WI 53202
Tel: 414-272-6071
WWW: http://www.aaaai.org

American Association of Certified Allergists
85 West Algonquin Road., Suite 550
Arlington Heights, IL 60005
Tel: 847-427-8111

For information on certification, contact:

American Board of Allergy and Immunology University City Science Center
3624 Market Street
Philadelphia, PA 19104
Tel: 215-349-9466

For financial aid, scholarship, and grant information, contact:

Association of American Medical Colleges
2450 N Street, NW
Washington, DC 20037
Tel: 202-828-0400
WWW: http://www.aamc.org/stuapps/finaid

National Health Services Corps Scholarship Program
U.S. Public Health Service
1010 Wayne Avenue, Suite 240
Silver Spring, MD 20910
Tel: 800-638-0824

Animal Caretakers

Definition

Animal caretakers feed, water, nurture, and exercise animals. They monitor the animals' general health, as well as clean and repair cages. Caretakers who work in zoos are responsible for transferring animals needed, arranging exhibits, and setting temperature controls to ensure that the animals are comfortable. Those who work with veterinarians may help treat animals for illness or disease, administer medications, or assist during surgery. Animal caretakers who work in veterinary research are involved in medical testing procedures.

Nature of the Work

Animal caretakers, also referred to as *animal attendants*, perform daily duties that include feeding, grooming, cleaning, and exercising animals. Kennels, pet stores, animal shelters, laboratories, zoos, and veterinary facilities all employ caretakers.

Kennel workers and *shelter workers* generally care for small animals such as cats and dogs. They learn to recognize signs of illness like poor posture, lack of appetite, fatigue, or weakness. They check for sharp edges and other dangerous situations in cages or pens. They take animals to rooms for treatment as well as let them outdoors for exercise. Attendants in an animal shelter screen applicants for animal adoption as well as take care of animals brought in by control officers or other people.

Skilled animal shelter attendants have the unpleasant job of euthanizing (putting to death) animals who are injured, ill, or unwanted. They also administer necessary vaccinations to healthy animals.

Stable workers feed and water horses, saddle and unsaddle them, give them rubdowns, and walk them through cool-offs after riding. Other duties for stable workers include cleaning out stalls, grooming the horses, storing feed and supplies and, with experience, horse training.

Pet shop attendants feed and water animals and clean their cages. Sometimes they bathe cats and dogs and trim their nails. They inspect animals for sores or signs of illness that could spread to other animals. *Groomers* can be part of a pet shop or self-employed and are responsible for maintaining the appearance of animals, usually dogs. They bathe and clip dogs according to different breed standards.

Veterinary technicians have completed formal studies and work in veterinary offices, animal laboratories, and animal hospitals. They prepare animals for surgery and assist during medical procedures. They also keep records. *Veterinary assistants* assist veterinarians or veterinary technicians. They feed and bathe animals and administer medications as well.

Animal laboratory workers are employed wherever live animals are used for research, testing, or educational purposes. Lab workers have various classifications. Entry-level assistant laboratory animal technicians feed animals, clean cages, and help handle the animals. As they gain experience, laboratory animal technicians administer medications, perform lab tests, take specimens, and record daily findings.

Laboratory animal technologists supervise the lab workers. They assist in surgery and oversee the advanced care of animals.

Zookeepers work in zoos or aquariums. They prepare the animals' food and closely monitor the health of the animals. They are often involved with educational projects and other programs dedicated to preserving endangered species.

DOT: 079   GOE: 02.03.03   NOC: 6483

Requirements

Students preparing for animal caretaker careers need a high school diploma. While in high school, classes in biology, English, and mathematics are recommended. Students can obtain valuable knowledge by taking animal science classes. Any knowledge about animal breeds and behavior is helpful, as well as a basic grasp of business and computer skills.

For some caretaking positions, such as in shelters, pet shops, and stables, training occurs on the job. One can also learn about the care of animals through volunteer work

A high school diploma is essential for continuing an education in animal caretaking. There are two-year colleges offering courses in animal health that lead to an associate's degree. This type of program offers courses in anatomy, physiology, chemistry, mathematics, clinical pharmacology, pathology, radiology, animal care and handling, infectious diseases, biology, and current veterinary therapy. Students graduating from programs like this go to work in veterinary practices, humane societies, zoos and marine mammal parks, pharmaceutical companies, and laboratory research institutions. Veterinary technicians should make sure that the programs they select are accredited by the American Veterinary Medical Association.

For students interested in working in zoos, a bachelor's degree in zoology, biology, or an animal-related field is necessary. Experience as a volunteer or paid employee in a small zoo is often required.

Most importantly, animal caretakers should love animals and have great patience and compassion. An animal caretaker should also be self-motivated and hard-working, able to tackle mundane tasks with as much energy as given to exciting ones. A caretaker should also be able to take direction from others as well as being confident and organized.

Opportunities for Experience & Exploration

High school students interested in animal caretaking can volunteer to work in animal shelters, zoos, stables, or veterinary offices, depending on their interests. Volunteering provides hands-on experience and exposes students to a variety of opportunities in the animal care field.

Informational interviews with a shelter worker, veterinary assistant, or zookeeper can be an exciting way to learn more about the field. People are usually interested in talking with someone who demonstrates a serious desire to learn more about a job. Before setting up an informational interview, it is helpful to think about what you'd like to know about the job; for example, how the person entered the field, what the job entails, how to get more information. It is sometimes possible to "shadow" an animal care worker for a day, going around with him or her as tasks are performed, getting an idea of an average day on the job.

Even an informal visit to a shelter or zoo can allow you the opportunity to observe someone at work, or to ask a few quick questions. Career counseling centers usually have resource materials on this career as do public libraries and bookstores.

Methods of Entering

High school students who volunteer at shelters, zoos, or veterinary offices will be able to see whether or not a career as an animal caretaker is truly for them. Volunteer experience is always valuable on a resume or job application, as it demonstrates to prospective employers a serious interest in the job. Volunteers also have opportunities to get to know other people working in the field and to see the type of work they do.

Students who graduate from formal veterinary technology programs have access to their schools' placement office for help finding jobs. The majority of animal caretakers work in veterinary offices or boarding kennels, but there are also jobs in research laboratories, pharmaceutical companies, teaching hospitals, the armed forces, federal and state government agencies, and food production companies.

Advancement

Advancement depends on the job setting. Kennel workers may be promoted to kennel supervisor, assistant manager, or manager. Some animal caretakers go on to open their own kennels. Pet store caretakers may move into management positions. Laboratory assistants may advance to laboratory animal technicians, and then to technologists; however, for the technologist position, a bachelor's degree in the life sciences is required. Shelter caretakers may move into management positions or directing the shelters, or work as an animal control officer. Zookeepers can advance to oversee other keepers in one part of the zoo, then on to administrative positions if they have the necessary qualifications and desire.

Employment Outlook

The animal care field continues to expand. More and more people have pets, whether in city apartments or at houses in the suburbs. As long as the public's love affair with pets continues to grow, there will be a need for more veterinary care, boarding facilities, and grooming and pet shops. There is demand by animal owners for better animal treatment and veterinary care.

Many camps offer horseback riding, requiring people to care for the horses. There is also an increasing need for caretakers at public and private stables.

There is a high turnover rate among animal caretakers. Much of the work is seasonal or part-time, and most job opportunities are a result of the need to replace people leaving the field. Many entry-level positions require little training and offer flexible work schedules. This is ideal for students and others interested in short-term or part-time work.

Positions as animal caretakers in zoos, aquariums, and wildlife rehabilitation centers are the most sought after; aspiring animal caretakers will find few openings in these subfields.

Graduates of veterinary technology programs have the best employment prospects. Laboratory animal technicians and technologists also have good opportunities. Increasing concern for animal welfare means an increase in the need for capable certified laboratory workers.

Another area with favorable prospects is the kennel industry. As owners focus more on the business side of kennels, they will need managers to oversee the various services.

Earnings

Several factors determine salaries for animal caretakers: experience, work performed, level of education, and employer. Entry-level employees earn an average salary of about $11,000.

Dog groomers earn between $12,000 and $30,000 a year. Some groomers work for someone else and make a commission on each dog groomed. Others own their own shops and are able to earn more money.

The highest paid workers in the animal caretaking business are veterinary technicians, laboratory animal technologists, and zookeepers. Licensed veterinary technicians earn an average of $18,500 a year. Zookeepers start at minimum wage and eventually make between $12 and $15 per hour. According to a recent American Association of Zookeepers survey, southern states have a tendency to pay zookeepers less than any other states. The best wages for zookeepers are found in the Pacific Northwest, but the cost of living is higher there.

Many animal caretakers belong to unions and have fairly regulated pay. Examples of weekly earnings are as follows: clerks and kennel persons, $250; attendants, $300; animal care technicians, $320; veterinary technicians, $350.

Fringe benefits vary for animal caretakers. Many full-time workers receive paid vacations. Depending on the employer and the business, many full-time employees receive benefits such as health insurance and sick leave. Pet store employees or shelter workers are seldom given benefits aside from vacation time, often unpaid.

Fringe benefits vary for animal caretakers. Many full-time workers receive paid vacations. Depending on the employer and the business, many full-time employees receive benefits such as health insurance and sick leave. Pet store employees or shelter workers are seldom given benefits aside from vacation time, often unpaid.

Conditions of Work

Animal caretakers are people who love animals and therefore enjoy their work and find it satisfying. It is challenging to work with not only different types of animals, but individual animals. Dealing with the various personalities and quirks of dogs or pigs or elephants keeps attendants on their toes.

Although animal caretakers derive considerable pleasure from their work, there are unpleasant parts of the job. The work is sometimes hard, repetitious, and dirty. Animals constantly need to be fed, watered, and exercised, and to have their living spaces cleaned. The job may involve heavy lifting (moving bags of feed or cages). Workers must bend and stoop to clean animal quarters. Working closely with animals often requires working around strong or foul smells.

While those caretakers who work in pounds and veterinary facilities enjoy close relationships with many of the animals brought in, there are painful moments, too. As much as some animals are affectionate, there are those who bite and scratch. People who form attachments to the lovable, scruffy, or spirited animals they help may later have to watch those animals die. Humane societies euthanize the animals they cannot place in homes.

Many animal care jobs require more than the traditional forty-hour week. Some shelter or veterinary employees arrive early to feed the animals and take care of their cages. At the end of the shift, if an animal still requires care, the caretaker must stay and attend to that animal. Holidays and weekends are not necessarily vacation times for employees, although certain employers have temporary or weekend help. Groomers and kennel workers stay late according to the needs of their employers.

Proper working attire for animal caretakers varies. Groomers wear comfortable clothes that can get dirty. Veterinary technicians and laboratory workers wear lab coats to protect their clothes.

People who work in pet shops dress according to the owners' specifications. Those who work outside wear comfortable, casual clothes.

Sources of Additional Information

For information on careers in animal caretaking, accredited schools, and potential employers, please contact:

■American Association for Laboratory Science
70 Timber Creek Drive
Cordova, TN 38018-4233
Tel: 901-754-8620
Email: info@aalas.org

For a free copy of its Programs in Veterinary Technology, *contact:*

■American Veterinary Medical Association
1931 North Meacham Road
Schaumburg, IL 60173-4360
Tel: 847-925-8070

Automobile Service Technicians

Definition

Automobile service technicians maintain and repair cars, vans, small trucks, and other vehicles. Using both hand tools and specialized diagnostic test equipment, they pinpoint problems and make the necessary repairs or adjustments. In addition to performing complex and difficult repairs, technicians perform a number of routine maintenance procedures, such as oil changes, tire rotation, and battery replacement. Technicians interact frequently with customers to explain repair procedures and discuss maintenance needs.

Nature of the Work

Many automobile service technicians feel that the most exciting part of their work is troubleshooting—locating the source of a problem and successfully fixing it. Diagnosing mechanical, electrical, and computer-related troubles requires a broad knowledge of how cars work, the ability to make accurate observations, and the patience to logically determine what went wrong. Technicians agree that it frequently is more difficult to find the problem than it is to fix it. With experience, knowing where to look for problems becomes second nature.

Generally, there are two types of automobile service technicians: generalists and specialists. Generalists work under a broad umbrella of repair and service duties. They have proficiency in several kinds of light repairs and maintenance of many different types of automobiles. Their work, for the most part, is routine and basic. Specialists concentrate in one or two areas and learn to master them for many different car makes and models. Today, in light of the sophisticated technology common in new cars, there is an increasing demand for specialists. Automotive systems are not as easy or as standard as they used to be, and now require many hours of experience to master. To gain a broad knowledge in auto maintenance and repair, specialists usually begin as generalists.

When a car does not operate properly, the owner brings it to a service technician and describes the problem. At a dealership or larger shop, the customer may talk with a repair service estimator, who writes down the customer's description of the problem and relays it to the service technician. The technician may test-drive the car or use diagnostic equipment, such as motor analyzers, spark plug testers, or compression gauges, to determine the problem. If a customer explains that the car's automatic transmission does not shift gears at the right times, the technician must know how the functioning of the transmission depends on the engine vacuum, the throttle pressure, and, more common in newer cars, the onboard computer. Each factor must be thoroughly checked. With each test, clues help the technician pinpoint the cause of the malfunction. After successfully diagnosing the problem, the technician makes the necessary adjustments or repairs. If a part is too badly damaged or worn to be repaired, he or she replaces it after first consulting the car owner, explaining the problem, and estimating the cost.

Normal use of an automobile inevitably causes wear and deterioration of parts. *Generalist automobile technicians* handle many of the routine maintenance tasks to help keep a car in optimal operating condition. They change oil, lubricate parts, and adjust or replace components of any of the car's systems that might cause a malfunction, including belts, hoses, spark plugs, brakes, filters, and transmission and coolant fluids.

Technicians who specialize in the service of specific parts usually work in large shops with multiple departments, car diagnostic centers, franchised auto service shops, or small independent shops that concentrate on a particular type of repair work.

Tune-up technicians evaluate and correct engine performance and fuel economy. They use diagnostic equipment and other computerized devices to locate malfunctions in fuel, ignition, and emissions-control systems. They adjust ignition timing and valves and may replace spark plugs, points, triggering assemblies in electronic ignitions, and other components to ensure maximum engine efficiency.

Electrical-systems technicians have been in greater demand in recent years. They service and repair the complex electrical and computer circuitry common in today's automobile. They use both sophisticated diagnostic equipment and simpler devices such as ammeters, ohmmeters, and voltmeters to locate system malfunctions. As well as possessing excellent electrical skills, electrical-systems technicians require basic mechanical aptitude to get at electrical and computer circuitry located throughout the automobile .

Front-end technicians are concerned with suspension and steering systems. They inspect, repair, and replace front-end parts such as springs and shock absorbers and linkage parts such as tie rods and ball joints. They also align and balance wheels.

Brake repairers work on drum and disk braking systems, parking brakes, and their hydraulic systems. They inspect, adjust, remove, repair, and reinstall such items as brake shoes, disk pads, drums, rotors, wheel and master cylinders, and hydraulic fluid lines. Some specialize in both brake and front-end work.

Transmission technicians adjust, repair, and maintain gear trains, couplings, hydraulic pumps, valve bodies, clutch assemblies, and other parts of automatic transmission systems. Transmissions have become complex and highly sophisticated mechanisms in newer model automobiles. Technicians require special training to learn how they function.

Automobile-radiator mechanics clean radiators using caustic solutions. They locate and solder leaks and install new radiator cores. In addition, some radiator mechanics repair car heaters and air conditioners and solder leaks in gas tanks.

As more automobiles rely on a variety of electronic components, technicians have become more proficient in the basics of electronics, even if they are not electronic specialists. Electronic controls and instruments are located in nearly all the systems of today's cars. Many previously mechanical functions in automobiles are being replaced by electronics, significantly altering the way repairs are performed. Diagnosing and correcting problems with electronic components often involves the use of specialty tools and computers.

Automobile service technicians use an array of tools in their everyday work, ranging from simple hand tools to computerized diagnostic equipment. Technicians supply their own hand tools at an investment of $6,000 to $25,000 or more, depending upon the technician's specialty. It is usually the employer's responsibility to furnish the larger power tools, engine analyzers, and other test equipment.

To maintain and increase their skills and to keep up with new technology, automobile technicians must regularly read service and repair manuals, shop bulletins, and other publications. They must also be willing to take part in training programs given by manufacturers or at vocational schools. Those who have voluntary certification must periodically retake exams to keep their credentials.

Requirements

In today's competitive job market aspiring automobile service technicians need a high school diploma to land a job that offers growth possibilities, a good salary, and challenges. There is a big demand in the automotive service industry to fill entry-level positions with well-trained, highly skilled persons. Technology demands more from the technician than it did ten years ago. Employers today prefer to hire only those who have completed some kind of formal training program in automobile mechanics—usually a minimum of two years. A wide variety of such programs are offered at community colleges, vocational schools, independent organizations, and manufacturers.

In high school, students should take automotive and shop classes, mathematics, English, and computer classes. Adjustments and repairs to many car components require the technician to make numerous computations, for which good mathematical skills will be essential. Good reading skills are also valuable as a technician must do a lot of reading to stay competitive in today's job market. English classes will prepare the technician to handle the many volumes of repair manuals and trade journals he or she will need to remain informed. Computer skills are also vital as computers are now common in most repair shops. They keep track of customers' histories and parts, and often detail repair procedures. Use of computers in repair shops will only increase in the future.

Many community colleges and vocational schools around the country offer accredited postsecondary education. Postsecondary training programs prepare students through a blend of classroom instruction and hands-on practical experience. They range in length from six months to two years or more, depending on the type of program. Shorter programs usually involve intensive study. Longer programs typically alternate classroom courses with periods of work experience. Some two-year programs include courses on applied mathematics, reading and writing skills, and business practices and lead to an associate's degree.

Some programs are conducted in association with automobile manufacturers. Students combine work experience with hands-on classroom study of up-to-date equipment and new cars provided by manufacturers. In other programs students alternate time in the classroom with internships in dealerships or service departments. These students may take up to four years to finish their training, but they become familiar with the latest technology and also earn a modest salary.

One recognized indicator of quality for entry-level technicians is certification by the National Automotive Technicians Education Foundation (NATEF), an affiliate of the National Institute for Automotive Service Excellence (NIASE). NATEF's goals are to develop, encourage, and improve automotive technical education for students seeking entry-level positions as automobile service technicians. NATEF certifies many postsecondary programs for training throughout the country. Certification is available in the areas of automatic transmission/transaxle, brakes, electrical systems, engine performance, engine repair, heating and air conditioning, manual drive train and axles, and suspension and steering. Certification assures students that the program they enroll in meets the standards employers expect from their entry-level employees.

Automobile service technicians must be patient and thorough in their work—a shoddy repair job may put the driver's life at risk. They must have excellent troubleshooting skills and be able to logically deduce the cause of system malfunctions.

Opportunities for Experience & Exploration

Many community centers offer general auto maintenance and mechanics workshops where students can practice working on real cars and learn from instructors. Trade magazines are excellent sources for learning what's new in the industry and can be found at most public libraries or large bookstores. Many public television stations broadcast automobile maintenance and repair programs that can help beginners to see how various cars differ.

High school auto mechanics and shop courses can help teach students mechanical aptitude and basic auto maintenance. Students learn the proper use of many different tools as they apply to specific auto components. Working on cars as a hobby provides valuable firsthand experience in the work of a technician. An afterschool or weekend part-time job in a repair shop or dealership can give a feel for the general atmosphere and kinds of problems technicians face on the job. Experience with vehicle repair work in the armed forces is another way many pursue their interests in this field.

Methods of Entering

The best way to start out in this field is to attend one of the many postsecondary training programs available throughout the country and obtain accreditation. Trade and technical schools usually provide job placement assistance for their graduates. Schools often have contacts with local employers who need to hire well-trained people. Frequently employers post job openings at nearby trade schools that have accredited programs.

Although postsecondary training programs are considered a better way to learn, a decreasing number of technicians learn the trade on the job as apprentices. Their training consists of working for several years under the guidance of experienced mechanics. Trainees usually begin as helpers, lubrication workers, or service station attendants who gradually acquire the skills and knowledge necessary for the typical service or repair tasks technicians encounter. Fewer employers today are willing to hire apprentices due to the time and cost it takes to train them. Those who do learn their skills on the job will inevitably require some formal training if they wish to advance and stay in step with the changing industry.

Intern programs sponsored by car manufacturers or independent organizations provide students with excellent opportunities to actually work with prospective employers. Internships can provide students with valuable contacts who will be able to recommend future employers once they have completed their training. Many students may even be hired by the company at which they interned.

Advancement

Currently employed technicians may be certified by the National Institute for Automotive Service Excellence. Although certification is voluntary, it is a widely recognized standard of achievement for automobile technicians and is highly valued by many employers. Certification also provides the means and opportunity to advance. To maintain certification, technicians must retake the examination for their specialties every five years. Many employers only hire ASE-accredited technicians and base salaries on the level of the technicians' accreditation.

With today's complex automobile components requiring hundreds of hours of study and practice to master, more repair shops prefer to hire specialists. Generalist automobile technicians advance as they gain experience and become specialists. Other technicians advance to diesel repair, where the pay may be higher. Those with good communications and planning skills may advance to shop foreman or service manager at large repair shops or to sales workers at dealerships. *Master mechanics* (technicians certified in all eight specialty areas) with good business skills often go into business for themselves and open their own shops. Some master mechanics may go on to teach at technical and vocational schools or at community colleges.

Employment Outlook

With an estimated 189 million vehicles in operation today, automobile service technicians should feel confident that a good percentage will require servicing and repair. Skilled and highly trained technicians will be in particular demand. Less skilled workers will face tough competition. The automotive service industry predicts it will need to replace 20 percent of its workforce by the end of the decade due to retirees and people who cannot keep up with the changing technology.

One concern for technicians is the automobile industry's trend toward developing the "maintenance-free" car. Manufactures are producing high-end cars that require no servicing for their first 100,000 miles. In addition, many new cars are equipped with on-board diagnostics (OBD) that detect both wear and failure for many of the car's components, eliminating the need for technicians to perform extensive diagnostic tests. Also, parts that are replaced before they completely wear out prevent further damage from occurring to connected parts that are affected by a malfunction or breakdown. Although this will reduce troubleshooting time and the number of overall repairs, the components that need repair will be more costly and require a more experienced (and hence, more expensive) technician to service.

Fluctuations in the economy have little effect on employment in this field; automobile service technicians generally enjoy the security of steady work. When the economy is bad, people tend to service and repair their cars rather than buy new ones. Conversely, when the economy is good, more people are apt to service their cars regularly and purchase new cars.

Most new jobs for technicians will be at independent service dealers, specialty shops, and franchised new car dealers. Because of the increase of specialty shops, fewer gasoline service stations will hire technicians, and many will eliminate repair services completely. Other opportunities will be available at companies or institutions with private fleets (e.g., cab, delivery, and rental companies, and government agencies and police departments).

Earnings

Salary ranges of automobile service technicians vary depending upon the level of experience, type of shop the technician works in, and geographic location. Technicians with certification earn on average $24,800 per year. Less experienced technicians earn on average $13,000 per year. Since most technicians work on an hourly basis and frequently work overtime, their salaries can vary significantly. Managers of service and repair shops earn between $34,000 and $45,000. In many repair shops and dealerships, technicians can earn higher incomes by working on commission. Typically they earn 40 to 50 percent of the labor costs charged to customers. Employers often guarantee a minimum level of pay in addition to commissions. Some mechanics are members of labor union, which negotiate standard pay scales throughout the country.

Benefit packages vary from business to business. Most technicians can expect health insurance and paid vacations. Additional benefits may include dental, life, and disability insurance and a pension plan. Employers usually cover a technician's work clothes and may pay a percentage of hand tools purchased. An increasing number of employers pay all or most of an employee's certification training, if he or she passes the test. A technician's salary can increase through yearly bonuses or profit sharing if the business does well in the course of a year.

Conditions of Work

Depending on the size of the shop and whether it's an independent or franchised repair shop, dealership, or government or private business, automobile technicians work with anywhere from two to twenty other technicians. Most shops are well lighted and well ventilated. They can frequently be noisy with running cars and power tools.

Minor hand and back injuries are the most common problems of technicians. When reaching in hard-to-get-at places or loosening tight bolts, technicians often bruise, cut, or burn their hands. With caution and experience most technicians learn to avoid hand injuries. Working for long periods of time in cramped or bent positions often results in a stiff back or neck. Technicians also lift many heavy objects that can cause injury if not handled carefully; however, this is becoming less of a problem with new cars, as automakers design smaller and lighter parts to improve fuel economy. Some

technicians may experience allergic reactions to solvents and oils used in cleaning, maintenance, and repair. Shops must comply with strict safety procedures to help employees avoid accidents and injuries.

Most technicians work between forty and forty-eight hours a week but may be required to work longer hours when the shop is busy. Some technicians make emergency repairs to automobiles that are stranded along the roadside.

Sources of Additional Information

For information on accreditation and testing and for general information on the American automobile industry, please contact:

American Automobile Manufacturers Association
1401 H Street, NW, Suite 900
Washington, DC 20005
Tel: 202-326-5500

For more information on the automotive parts industry, please contact:

Automotive Service Industry Association (ASIA)
25 Northwest Point
Elk Grove Village, IL 60007-1035
Tel: 847-228-1310

Automotive Warehouse Distributors Association (AWDA)
9140 Ward Parkway
Kansas City, MO 64114
Tel: 816-444-3500

Motor and Equipment Manufacturers Association (MEMA)
PO Box 13966
10 Laboratory Drive
Research Triangle Park, NC 27709
Tel: 919-549-4800

National Automobile Dealers Association (NADA)
8400 Westpark Drive
McLean, VA 22102
Tel: 703-821-7000

Barbers, Stylists, and Cosmetologists

Definition

Barbers perform the personal services of coloring, bleaching, cutting, trimming, and shampooing hair and of trimming and shaping beards and mustaches.

Cosmetologists, often called *beauty operators*, *beauticians*, or *hairdressers*, work to improve and maintain the personal appearance of their clients. They cut, style, and dye hair, perform facials, apply makeup, and do manicures.

Nature of the Work

In general, the duties of the barber are well defined. Barbers tint, bleach, cut, trim, shape, style, and shampoo hair. They give shaves, facials, scalp treatments, and massages and advise customers on grooming habits and cosmetic aids. They also trim and style beards and mustaches and perform other related personal services for customers.

Barbers use certain tools in their services with trained skill, such as scissors, clippers, razors, combs, brushes, hot towels, tweezers, and razor sharpeners. The barber's tools and working surroundings must be kept in an antiseptic and sterile condition.

In their training, barbers learn some aspects of human physiology and anatomy, including the bone structure of the head and elementary facts about the nervous system. Barbers either cut hair as the customers request or they decide how to cut it by studying the contours of the head, the quality and texture of the hair, and the personal features of the customer. A successful barber recognizes that each customer is an individual and no two possess the same types of personal and physical characteristics.

Barbers may be employed in shops that have as few as one or two operators, or as many as ten or more employees. Some barbers work in combination barber-and-beauty shops, while others are employed in shops in hotels, hospitals, and resort areas. Those who operate their own shops must also take care of the details of business operations. Bills must be paid, orders placed, invoices and supplies checked, equipment serviced, and records and books kept. The selection, hiring, and termination of other workers are also the owner's responsibilities. Barbershop employees may include manicurists, shoe shine attendants, assistant barbers, and custodial help. Like other responsible business people, barber shop owners are likely to be asked to participate in civic and community projects and activities.

Cosmetologists perform personal grooming services for customers that may include styling, cutting, trimming, straightening, permanent waving, coloring, tinting, bleaching, and shampooing hair. Cosmetologists may also give facials, massages, manicures, pedicures, and scalp treatments and may shape and tint eyelashes and eyebrows. They sometimes do makeup analysis, suggest cosmetic aids, and advise customers on what products to use and how to use them for the best results. Many specialize as *hairstylists*. Through advanced training, cosmetologists may specialize in some aspect of their work, such as permanent waving, cutting hair, or setting only the more difficult, high-fashion hairstyles. In small shops the cosmetologist's job duties may also include making appointments for customers, cleaning equipment, and sterilizing instruments.

Cosmetologists use certain tools and equipment in their work, such as scissors, razors, brushes, clippers, cosmetic aids, massage and manicure equipment, hair dryers, towels, and reclining chairs. Most of the equipment and tools are provided by the shop owners.

In some shops, *manicurists* tend to customers' nails, filing and polishing them and trimming the cuticles. Cosmetologists work in close personal contact with the public. They have customers at any age level. Some specialize in children's haircuts.

Barbers and cosmetologists perform similar services in the same type of surroundings. Although some beauty shops may be decorated to appeal to a female clientele, many men now prefer to have their hair cut and styled by cosmetologists. Cosmetologists are employed in privately owned shops throughout the country, many of them small businesses. They may also be employed in beauty shops in large department stores, drugstores, hospitals, nursing homes, and hotels. Cosmetologists may be employed to demonstrate hairstyles and cosmetic products in various retail stores, photographic centers, and television studios. With advanced training, some cosmetologists may qualify to teach in beauty culture colleges and vocational training schools.

Cosmetologists serving the public must have pleasant, friendly, yet professional attitudes, as well as skill, ability, and an interest in their craft. These qualities are necessary to building a following of steady customers. The nature of the work demands that cosmetologists be aware of the psychological aspects of dealing with all types of customers.

Although many of the services performed by cosmetologists are repetitive in nature, the individual personalities of the clients add to the satisfaction and challenge of the occupation. With each new client, cosmetologists are presented with a fresh challenge; they must continually strive for creativity and artistic flair in their jobs through hairstyling, fashion creation, and makeup work for clients.

Requirements

The educational and training requirements for barbers vary among the states. Some states require potential barbers to have the minimum of an eighth-grade education; other states require a high school education. Nearly all states require barbers to be licensed or certified by a state board of examiners. To obtain a license or certification in almost any state, the individual must pass a practical examination and a written test. Most states will not examine anyone younger than sixteen or eighteen who applies for a license. Applicants must also be able to obtain health certificates, and in almost every state they must be graduates of a barber school that is state-approved.

In most states barbers must first be licensed as barber apprentices. After a specified period of employment (usually one to two years), the apprentice may take another written and practical examination to qualify for a license as a journeyman barber. When barbers move from one state to another, they must satisfy the license requirements of the state to which they are moving, but some states will recognize the license from another state.

Training opportunities are available in about four hundred private barber colleges and public vocational training schools. Training periods are generally nine months to one year. Most training institutions require approximately 1,000 to 2,000 hours of formal instruction, including courses in hygiene, anatomy, and skin and scalp diseases. There are lectures, demonstrations, and practice in the art of barbering and the use and care of tools and equipment. Some schools instruct their students in business management and practices, the psychology of sales and advertising, professional ethics, and unionism. Some states have schools that offer advanced coursework for barbers who wish to specialize in such techniques as hair coloring or styling. Students should be careful to select barber schools with training programs that meet at least the minimum requirements of their state. Some schools require students to purchase their basic barbering instruments at a cost of about $450.

A barber needs certain aptitudes to be successful. Finger dexterity is important because it is needed in all aspects of a barber's work. Hand-eye coordination is equally necessary.

A pleasant demeanor and an outgoing personality are very important to the successful barber. Clients look for a tactful, courteous, and friendly barber who is skillful and seems to enjoy the work. Most people place a great deal of importance on how their hair looks, and when they do not like a cut or style, they may become angry or upset. A barber must be aware of the high expectations and do everything to prevent disappointment and frustration. The barber can accomplish this first by listening carefully to what the client wants and observing the specific characteristics of the client's hair and then by explaining his recommendations to the client. Frequently, a client will ask for a particular style or cut that is unsuitable for his features or simply won't work on his type of hair. The barber needs to be able to deal patiently but firmly with such a client, so that he understands perfectly that the end result may not achieve the desired effect.

Almost all cosmetologists learn their craft at an accredited school. The National Association of Cosmetology Schools estimates that more than 3,900 public and private training schools for cosmetologists operate across the country.

As with barbers, most states require that cosmetologists have either a minimum eighth-grade education or a high school diploma.

The majority of private schools offer training programs lasting six to nine months; in some states, however, courses require from twelve to fifteen months for completion. Public training school programs may cover a span of two or three years equal to the last three years of high school, because academic subjects are also a part of the curriculum.

Courses at cosmetology schools may include lectures, demonstrations, and practical work. Classroom training can include such subjects as anatomy, elementary physiology, hygiene, sanitation, applied chemistry, shop planning, applied electricity, and business basics. In practical training, students usually practice their techniques on mannequins with wigs, and on each other. As students gain experience, they may work on customers.

The cost of beauty culture training programs varies among schools. It is determined by such factors as the adequacy of the school's physical plant, training facilities, staff, location, and length of formal training. Tuition may also be affected by the requirements of the state board of examiners.

Cosmetologists in all states must obtain a license. In some states applicants must first pass an examination to qualify as a junior cosmetologist. After passing this exam and practicing for one year, they are eligible to take a second exam for senior cosmetologist. Fees for license examinations and yearly renewals are different in every state.

The number of hours of formal course training students must have before they can apply for a cosmetologist's license with a state board of examiners varies among the states. States may require from 1,000 hours (six months) to 2,500 hours (fifteen months) of combined practical and classroom training. Some states allow completion of this requirement via apprenticeship programs. These programs, however, are decreasing in number as state boards of examiners realize that applicants need more formal and technical training.

Applicants must meet other criteria to be eligible to take the state board examinations for licenses. In the majority of states, the minimum age requirement is sixteen. Because standards and requirements vary from state to state, students are urged to contact the licensing board of the state in which

they plan to be employed to verify the requirements.

Opportunities for Experience & Exploration

Those who are interested in becoming barbers may visit barber colleges and talk to members of the administration, teachers, and students and request permission to visit a class in barbering instruction. Potential students may observe and talk with licensed barbers who are practicing the trade. They may seek summer employment in barbershops as clean-up and errand workers so they can observe the work of the barber.

The occupation of cosmetologist may be explored by visiting various training institutions, such as public training high schools and private beauty colleges. Some schools may permit potential students to visit and observe training classes. Watching and talking with licensed cosmetologists may provide additional information. There is little opportunity to explore this occupation through part-time work experience; however, some individuals may obtain summer or weekend jobs as general shop helpers.

Methods of Entering

Barbering jobs are most frequently obtained by either applying in person or enlisting the aid of barbering unions. The largest union for barbers is the United Food and Commercial Workers International Union. Nearly all barber colleges assist their graduates in locating employment opportunities. Applicants also use the placement services of state or private employment agencies. Newspaper advertisements and personal references are good sources for job opportunities. Some salons have their own training programs from which they hire new employees.

Cosmetologists secure their first jobs in various ways. The majority of beauty colleges and private and public vocational training schools aid their graduates in locating job opportunities. Many schools have formal placement services.

Applicants may also apply directly to beauty shops in which they would like to work. Applicants may hear about openings through newspaper advertisements or through city or state employment services.

Advancement

Barbers usually begin as licensed barber apprentices. Through experience and study, apprentices advance to journeymen barbers. Within small barbershops there is very little opportunity for advancement to the assignment of the "first chair," except by seniority and skill. The first chair is most often the chair nearest the shop entrance. Barbers can change their place of employment and move to bigger, more attractive, and better-equipped shops.

Many barbers aspire to own their own shop. There are many things to consider when contemplating going into business on one's own. It is usually essential to obtain experience and financial capital before seeking to own a shop. The cost of equipping a one-chair shop can be very high. Owning a large shop or even a chain of shops is yet another aspiration for the very ambitious.

Most cosmetologists begin their careers as general beauticians performing a variety of services. In some states a person must begin as a junior operator; after a year of experience at this level, the individual is eligible to take an examination to become licensed as a senior cosmetologist. Some pursue advanced educational training to become specialized in one aspect of beauty culture, such as hairstyling or coloring.

Through skill, training, and seniority, a hairdresser may advance to a position as shop manager. After they have built a loyal clientele, some people may aspire to open their own shop. Cosmetologists may also advance by moving to beauty shops that are located in more affluent areas.

After some years of practical experience and, in many cases, additional academic training, some cosmetologists may become teachers in schools of beauty culture. These opportunities, however, are usually open only to those who possess exceptional skills and abilities.

Cosmetologists may find that their background in beauty culture can help them move into different fields. They may move into jobs such as *representatives of cosmetic companies or equipment firms, beauty editors* for magazines, *makeup artists and stylists* for motion picture and television studios, or *inspectors* on state licensing examination boards. Other related job opportunities include *body makeup artists*, who work with photographers and models, and *mortuary beauticians*.

Employment Outlook

Approximately 59,000 persons were employed as barbers in the United States in 1996. About three out of four own their own shops, while one out of every three works part-time. Future employment opportunities for barbers are not as predictable as those for other occupations. Most openings that present themselves will be to replace barbers who leave the trade for other work, retire, or die. Employment may rise slightly in the coming years as new shopping centers open and suburban areas continue to grow with the expanding population. Barbers who specialize in unisex hairstyling will increase their business opportunities greatly, since men as well as women patronize full-service salons in greater numbers. The competent and well-trained barber should find employment without too much difficulty, but it may not always be in the geographic locality or shop desired.

Most job opportunities through the year 2006 will be for cosmetologists. The market for cosmetologists is expanding as the general population increases, more shops are opened in suburban shopping centers, and working women seek out cosmetic services more frequently. Good employment opportunities are becoming increasingly available to the part-time cosmetologist.

An estimated 586,000 people were employed as cosmetologists and hairstylists in 1996. The number of male workers in this field is increasing steadily. Currently, the demand for cosmetologists far outnumbers the supply.

Earnings

Salaries vary based on a number of factors, including size and location of the business, number of hours worked, and the level of competition from other shops and salons. According to a January 1998 report from the Economic Research Institute, barbers and stylists with less than fifteen years experience earned roughly $16,100 a year; those with fifteen to twenty-nine years of experience, $20,200 annually; and those with thirty or more years experience in the industry, approximately $27,900 annually. Hairstylists and some barbers who own their own shops have incomes of $31,000 a year or more. Most barbers work on a commission basis, receiving from 50 to 70 percent of what they are paid by customers. Others work for set salaries plus a percentage commission. Only a small number of barbers work for a salary without commission.

Tips from customers are considered an important factor in determining a barber's salary. The amount to be earned in tips is unpredictable and depends on the locale of employment, the personality and skill of the barber, individual shop policies, and the income levels of the customers.

Paid vacations, medical insurance, and death benefits are available to some employees, especially those who belong to a union.

Salaries of cosmetologists depend on a number of factors, such as experience, ability, speed of performance, income levels of the shop's clientele, shop location (suburban or urban), and the salary arrangement between the worker and the salon. Most cosmetologists are employed on a commission basis, while others receive a base salary plus 40 percent to 50 percent commission. Tips are also an important factor in the cosmetologist's earnings.

Considering all of these factors, it is difficult to quote exact salary figures for all cosmetologists. Estimated salaries for experienced operators in the late 1990s range from $20,000 to $25,000. Beginning cosmetologists with average skill earn from $13,000 to $14,000. In exclusive city salons, expert operators, specialists, and top stylists earn much more.

Cosmetologists may receive fringe benefits that include group health and life insurance and paid vacations. The availability of fringe benefits varies widely, depending on the employer. Furthermore, these benefits, except for paid vacations, are usually available only to those employed by beauty salon chains and large establishments such as department stores and nursing homes.

Conditions of Work

Barbers usually work a five- or six-day week, which averages forty to fifty hours. Weekends and days preceding holiday seasons may be unusually busy workdays. Some employees have extra days off during slack periods.

Barbers work in shops that must, by law, meet and maintain strict state sanitation codes. Shops are usually comfortably heated, ventilated, and well-lighted. Barbers are usually assigned a chair position and their own work area in a shop. They are required to be on their feet most of their working hours, but little walking is involved. In general, they work in a small space.

Hazards of the trade include nicks and cuts from scissors and razors, minor burns when care is not used in handling hot towels, and occasional skin irritations arising from the constant use of grooming aids that contain chemicals. Some of the chemicals used in hair dyes can be quite abrasive, and plastic gloves are usually required.

Most cosmetologists work a forty-hour week, although some may work forty-four to forty-eight hours weekly. Working hours usually include Saturdays and, very frequently, evening appointments. Some cosmetologists work according to a shift schedule. Holiday seasons and special community events may result in increased business, which would involve overtime work.

The nature of the cosmetologist's job requires standing for most of the workday. The continual use of water, shampoos, lotions, and other solutions with chemical contents may cause skin irritations. Like barbers, cosmetologists wear gloves when working with dyes or chemicals.

Cosmetologists usually work in well-lighted, and comfortably ventilated shops. The level of supervision varies from shop to shop and depends upon the employer's attitude, type of shop, and the skill level and experience of the cosmetologist.

Sources of Additional Information

■■Hair International/Associated Master Barbers and Beauticians of America
PO Box 273, 124-B East Main Street
Palmyra, PA 17078
Tel: 717-838-0795

■■National Accrediting Commission of Cosmetology Arts and Sciences
901 North Stuart Street, Suite 900
Alexandria, VA 22203-1816
Tel: 703-527-7600

■■National Association of Barber Styling Schools
304 South 11th Street
Lincoln, NE 68508
Tel: 402-474-4244

Biologists

Definition

Biologists study the origin, development, anatomy, function, distribution, and other basic principles of living organisms. They are concerned with the nature of life itself—with humans, microorganisms, plants, and animals and with the relationship of each organism to its environment. Biologists perform research in many specialties that advance the fields of medicine, agriculture, and industry.

Nature of the Work

Biology can be divided into many specialties. The biologist, who studies a wide variety of living organisms, has interests that differ from those of the chemist, physicist, and geologist, who are concerned with nonliving matter. Biologists, or life scientists, may be identified by their specialties. Following is a breakdown of the many kinds of biologists and their specific fields of study.

Anatomists study animal bodies from basic cell structure to complex tissues and organs. They determine the ability of body parts to regenerate and investigate the possibility of transplanting organs and skin. Their research is applied to human medicine.

Aquatic biologists study animals and plants that live in water and how they are affected by their environmental conditions, such as the salt, acid, and oxygen content of the water, temperature, light, and other factors.

Biochemists study the chemical composition of living organisms. They attempt to understand the complex reactions involved in reproduction, growth, metabolism, and heredity.

Biophysicists apply physical principles to biological problems. They study the mechanics, heat, light, radiation, sound, electricity, and energetics of living cells and organisms and do research in the areas of vision, hearing, brain function, nerve conduction, muscle reflex, and damaged cells and tissues.

Bio-technicians, or *biological technicians*, assist the cornucopia of biological scientists in their endeavors.

Botanists study plant life. Some specialize in plant biochemistry, the structure and function of plant parts, and identification and classification, among others.

Cytologists, sometimes called *cell biologists*, examine the cells of plants and animals, including those cells involved in reproduction. They use microscopes and other instruments to observe the growth and division of cells and to study the influences of physical and chemical factors on both normal and malignant cells.

Ecologists examine such factors as pollutants, rainfall, altitude, temperature, and population size in order to study the distribution and abundance of organisms and their relation to their environment.

Entomologists study insects and their relation to other life forms.

Geneticists study heredity in various forms of life. They are concerned with how biological traits such as color, size, and resistance to disease originate and are transmitted from one generation to another. They also try to develop ways to alter or produce new traits, using chemicals, heat, light, or other means.

Histopathologists investigate diseased tissue in humans and animals.

Immunologists study the manner in which the human body resists disease.

Limnologists study freshwater organisms and the environment they live in.

Marine biologists specialize in the study of marine species and their environment. They gather specimens at different times and days, taking into account tidal cycles, seasons, and exposure to atmospheric elements, in order to answer a variety of questions concerning the overall health of sea organisms and their environment.

Microbiologists study bacteria, viruses, molds, algae, yeasts, and other organisms of microscopic or submicroscopic size. Some microorganisms can offer positive uses to humans. Some of these are studied and used in the production of foods such as cheese, bread, and tofu. Other microorganisms have been implemented to preserve food and tenderize meat. Other microbiologists work with microorganisms that cause disease. They work to diagnose, treat, and prevent diseases. The world of microbiologists has helped prevent typhoid fever, influenza, measles, polio, whooping cough, and smallpox. Today, they work on cures for AIDS, cancer, cystic fibrosis, and Alzheimer's disease, among others.

Molecular biologists apply their research on animal and bacterial systems with the goal of improving and better understanding human health.

Mycologists study edible, poisonous, and parasitic fungi, such as mushrooms, molds, yeasts, and mildews, to find those useful to medicine, agriculture, and industry. Their research results in benefits such as the development of antibiotics, the propagation of mushrooms, and methods of retarding fabric deterioration.

Nematologists study nematodes (roundworms), which are parasitic in animals and plants, transmit diseases, attack insects, or attack other nematodes that exist in soil or water. They investigate and develop methods of controlling these organisms.

Parasitologists study animal parasites and their effects on humans and other animals.

Pharmacologists may be employed as researchers by pharmaceutical companies and spend most of the time working in the laboratory. They may experiment on the effects of various drugs and medical compounds on mice or rabbits. Working within a controlled environment, pharmacologists precisely note the type, quantity, and timing of medicines administered as a part of their experiments. Periodically, they make blood smears or perform autopsies to study different reactions. They usually work with a team of researchers, headed by one with a doctorate and consisting of several biologists with master's and bachelor's degrees and some laboratory technicians.

Physiologists are biologists who specialize in studying all the life stages of plants or animals. Some specialize in a particular body system or a particular function such as respiration.

Wildlife biologists study the habitats and the conditions necessary for the survival of birds and other wildlife. Their goal is to find ways to ensure continued and healthy wildlife populations, while lessening the impact and growth of civilization around them.

Zoologists study all types of animals to learn their origin, interrelationships, classification, life histories, habits, diseases, relation to environment, growth, genetics, and distribution. Zoologists usually are identified by the animals they study — *ichthyologists* (fish), *mammalogists* (mammals), *ornithologists* (birds), and *herpetologists* (reptiles and amphibians).

Biologists may also work for government agencies concerned with public health. Staff *toxicologists*, for example, study the effects of toxic substances on humans, animals, and plants. The data they gather are used in consumer protection and industrial safety programs to reduce the hazards of accidental exposure or ingestion. *Public-health microbiologists* conduct experiments on water, foods, and the general environment of a community to detect the presence of harmful bacteria so that pollution and contagious diseases can be controlled or eliminated.

Requirements

High school students interested in a career in biology should take English, biology, physics, chemistry, Latin, geometry, and algebra. Prospective biologists should also obtain a broad undergraduate college training. In addition to courses in all phases of biology, useful related courses include organic and inorganic chemistry, physics, and mathematics. Modern languages, English, biometrics (the use of mathematics in biological measurements), and statistics are also useful. Courses in computers will also be extremely beneficial. Students should also take advantage of courses that require laboratory, field, or collecting work.

Nearly all institutions offer undergraduate training in one or more biological sciences. These vary from liberal arts schools that offer basic majors in botany and zoology to large universities that permit specialization in areas such as entomology, bacteriology, and physiology at the undergraduate level.

The best way to become a biologist is to earn a bachelor's degree in biology or one of its specialized fields, such as anatomy, bacteriology, botany, ecology, or microbiology. For the highest professional status, a doctorate is required. This is particularly true of top research positions and most higher level college teaching openings. A large number of colleges and universities offer courses leading to a master's degree and a doctorate. A study made by the National Science Foundation showed that among a group of biologists listed on the National Scientific Manpower Register, 10 percent held a bachelor's degree, 33 percent held a master's or professional medical degree, and the remaining 57 percent had earned a doctorate.

Candidates for a doctorate specialize in one of the subdivisions of biology. A number of sources of financial assistance are available to finance graduate work. Most major universities have a highly developed fellowship (scholarship) or assistantship (part-time teaching or research) program.

Outside organizations, such as the U.S. Public Health Service and the National Science Foundation, make awards to support graduate students. In a recent year, for example, the Public Health Service made 8,000 fellowship and training grants. In addition, major universities often hold research contracts or have their own projects that provide part-time and summer employment for undergraduate and graduate students.

A state license may be required for biologists who are employed as technicians in general service health organizations such as hospitals or clinics. To qualify for this license, proof of suitable educational background is necessary.

Biologists must be systematic in their approach to solving the problems that they face. They should have a probing, inquisitive mind and an aptitude for biology, chemistry, and mathematics. Patience and imagination are also required since they may spend great deals of time in observation and analysis. Biologists must also have good communication skills in order to effectively gather and exchange data and solve various problems that arise in the process of their work.

Opportunities for Experience & Exploration

Students can measure their aptitude and interest in the work of the biologist by taking courses in this area. Laboratory assignments, for example, provide actual informa-

tion on techniques used by the working biologist. Many schools hire students as laboratory assistants to work directly under a teacher and help administer the laboratory sections of courses.

School assemblies, field trips to federal and private laboratories and research centers, and career conferences provide additional insight into career opportunities. Advanced students often are able to attend professional meetings and seminars.

Part-time and summer positions in biology or related areas are particularly helpful. Students with some college courses in biology may find summer positions as laboratory assistants. Graduate students may find work on research projects being conducted by their institution. Beginning college and advanced high school students may find employment as laboratory aides or hospital orderlies or attendants. Despite the menial nature of these positions, they afford a useful insight into careers in biology. High school students often have the opportunity to join volunteer service groups at local hospitals. Student science training programs (SSTPs) allow qualified high school students to spend a summer doing research under the supervision of a scientist.

Methods of Entering

Biologists who are interested in becoming teachers should consult their college placement office. Public and private high schools and an increasing number of colleges hire teachers through the college at which they studied. Private employment agencies also place a significant number of teachers. Some teaching positions are filled through direct application.

Biologists interested in private industry and nonprofit organizations also may apply directly for employment. Major organizations that employ biologists often interview college seniors on campus. Private and public employment offices frequently have listings from these employers. Experienced biologists often change positions on the basis of meeting people at professional seminars and national conventions.

Special application procedures are required for positions with governmental agencies. Civil service applications for federal, state, and municipal positions may be obtained by writing to the agency involved and from high school and college guidance and placement bureaus, from public employment agencies, and at post offices.

Over four hundred firms employ bio-technologists in the United States—mainly in the West, Midwest, and East. Many companies, such as pharmaceutical firms operate throughout the nation. Herpetologists will find employment in zoos or museums and in research laboratories assisting with projects. Those with broader interests may choose to work in local, state, or national parks as park naturalists or for certain companies as environmental specialists. Marine biologists may find employment with the U.S. Department of Interior, the U.S. Fish and Wildlife Service, and the National Oceanic and Atmospheric Administration. They may also find employment in nongovernmental agencies such as the Scripps Institution of Oceanography in California and the Marine Biological Laboratory in Massachusetts. Microbiologists can find employment in government with the U.S. Department of Health and Human Services, the Environmental Protection Agency, and the Department of Agriculture, among others. They may also work for pharmaceutical, food, agricultural, geological, environmental, and pollution control companies. Wildlife biologists can find employment in government, for the U.S. Public Health Service, the U.S. Fish and Wildlife Service, and the Forest Service, among many others.

Advancement

In a field as broad as biology, numerous opportunities for advancement exist. To a great extent, however, advancement depends on the individual's level of education. A doctorate is generally required for college teaching, independent research, and top-level administrative and management jobs. A master's degree is sufficient for some jobs in applied research, and a bachelor's degree may qualify for some entry-level jobs.

With the right qualifications, the biologist may advance to the position of project chief and direct a team of other biologists. Many use their knowledge and experience as background for administrative and management positions. Often, as they develop professional knowledge, biologists move increasingly from strictly technical assignments into positions in which they interpret biological knowledge.

The usual path of advancement in biology, as in other sciences, comes from specialization and the development of the status of an expert in a given field. Biologists may work with professionals in other major fields to explore problems that require an interdisciplinary approach—biochemistry, biophysics, biostatistics (or biometrics). Biochemistry, for example, uses the methods of chemistry to study the composition of biological materials and the molecular mechanisms of biological processes.

Employment Outlook

A faster than average increase in employment of biologists is predicted through the late 1990s, although competition will be stiff for high-paying jobs, and government jobs will be less plentiful.

Advances in genetic research leading to new drugs, improved crops, and medical discoveries should open up some opportunities. Expanded research relating to cancer, AIDS, and the Human Genome project should also offer additional jobs to highly qualified biologists. It is important to note that since many of these projects are funded by the federal government, their growth is not assured. A recession or shift in political power could cause the loss of funding of grants and the growth of research and development endeavors. Private industry will need more biologists to keep up with the advances in biotechnology. Efforts to preserve and clean up the environment will create more job opportunities for the qualified biologist.

Biologists with advanced degrees will be best qualified for the most lucrative and challenging jobs, although this varies by specialty, with genetic, cellular, and biochemical research showing the most promise. Scientists with only a bachelor's degree may find openings as science or engineering technicians or as health technologists and technicians. Many colleges and universities are cutting back on their faculties, but high schools and two-year colleges may have teaching positions available. High school biology teachers are not considered to be biologists, however.

Because biologists are usually employed on long-term research projects or in agriculture, which are not greatly affected by economic fluctuations, they rarely lose their jobs during recessions. In 1996, over 118,000 biologists and medical scientists were employed in the United States. A good many worked at the college and university level. Others worked in research and development laboratories for private industry, mainly in pharmaceutical, chemical, and food companies. About 25 percent were employed by the federal government and by state and local governments. Some held nonteaching positions at colleges or universities; others for nonprofit research organizations or hospitals or were self-employed.

Earnings

Salaries for all biological scientists range from $22,000 to over $66,000, with a median salary of $36,300, as reported by the U.S. Department of Labor. In 1997, biologists with bachelor's degrees who worked for the federal government earned average salaries of $52,100 a year; ecologists averaged $52,700; microbiologists averaged $58,700; and geneticists, $62,700.

According to the National Association of Colleges and Employers, beginning salaries in 1997 in private industry averaged $25,400 a year for people with bachelor's degrees. Those with master's degrees earned $26,900, and doctoral degree recipients earned about $52,400. Most earned an average from $28,400 to $50,900 a year. In general, the highest salaries were earned by biologists in business and industry, followed in turn by those self-employed, working for nonprofit organizations, in military service, and working for the U.S. Public Health Service or other positions in the federal government. The lowest salaries were earned by teachers and by those working for various state and local governments.

Some examples of salaries for specific careers follow. Biotechnologists with a master's degree earn $37,000 a year, while those with a doctorate can earn more than $80,000 a year. Microbiologists employed at educational institutes earn between $16,000 and $30,000 with a bachelor's degree, between $20,000 and $60,000 with a master's degree, and between $30,000 and $100,000 with a Ph.D. Those in industry make very similar amounts on the whole as those in educational institutions. Microbiologists employed by the government and in the private sector with a bachelor's degree earn $17,000 to $33,000 a year; those with a Master's earn from $20,000 to $45,000 a year, and those with a Ph.D earn from $30,000 to $90,000 in yearly compensation. Bio-technicians earn between $13,000 and $50,000 per year, with an average median salary of approximately $26,000 a year.

Biologists are also eligible for health and dental insurance, paid vacations and sick days, and retirement plans. Some employers may offer reimbursement for continuing education, seminars, and travel.

Conditions of Work

The actual work environment of the biologist varies greatly depending upon the position and type of employer. One biologist may work outdoors or travel much of the time. Another wears a white smock and spends years working in a laboratory. Some work with toxic substances and disease cultures—strict safety measures are observed.

Biologists frequently work under some pressure. For example, those employed by pharmaceutical houses work in an atmosphere of keen competition for sales that encourages the development of new drug products and, as they are identified, the rapid testing and early marketing of these products. The work is very exacting, however, and the pharmaceutical biologists must exercise great care to ensure that adequate testing of products has been properly conducted.

Other examples of work conditions for the wide variety of biologists include botanists, ecologists, and zoologists, who may undertake strenuous, sometimes dangerous fieldwork in primitive conditions. Marine biologists may work in the field, on research ships or in laboratories, in tropical seas and ocean areas with considerably cooler climates. They will be required to perform some strenuous work, such as carrying a net, digging, chipping, or hauling equipment or specimens. Marine biologists who work under water must be able to avoid hazards such as razor-sharp coral reefs and other underwater dangers. Wildlife biologists work in all types of weather and in all types of terrain and ecosystems. They may work alone or with a group in inhospitable surroundings in order to gather information.

Sources of Additional Information

■American Society for Investigative Pathology
9650 Rockville Pike
Bethesda, MD 20814-3993
Tel: 301-530-7130

■American Institute of Biological Sciences
1444 I Street, NW, Suite 200
Washington, DC 20005
Tel: 202-628-1500
WWW: http://www.aibs.org

■American Physiological Society
Education Office
9650 Rockville Pike
Bethesda, MD 20814
WWW: http://www.faseb.org/aps

■American Society for Microbiology
Office of Education and Training-Career Information
1325 Massachusetts Avenue, NW
Washington, DC 20005-4171
Tel: 202-737-3600
WWW: http://wwwasmusa.org

■American Society for Biochemistry and Molecular Biology
9650 Rockville Pike
Bethesda, MD 20814-3996
Tel: 301-530-7145

■Biotechnology Industry Organization
1625 K Street, NW, Suite 1100
Washington, DC 20006
Tel: 202-857-0244

■Entomological Society of America
9301 Annapolis Road
Lanham, MD 20706-3115
Tel: 301-731-4535

■Genetics Society of America
9650 Rockville Pike
Bethesda, MD 20814-3998
Tel: 301-571-1825

The following institution operates a job hot line. To access the job hot line, call 410-576-3800 or write to obtain a free information packet concerning a career in the marine sciences.

■National Aquarium
Department of Education and Interpretation, Pier 3
501 East Pratt Street
Baltimore, MD21202-3194
Tel: 410-576-3870

For information on specific careers in biology, contact the following:

■National Institutes of Health
National Center for Research Resources (NCRR)
Building 12A, Room 4003
Bethesda, MD 20892
Tel: 301-496-5605

■National Institutes of Health, Office of Resource Management
Division of Career Resources
9000 Rockville Pike
Building 31, Room B3C15
Bethesda, MD 20892
Tel: 301-496-5979

■National Institutes of Health, Division of Research Grants
6701 Rockledge Drive, Room 3100
Bethesda, MD 20817
Tel: 301-435-1114

The Food and Drug Administration operates a job hot line at 301-443-1969. Contact the agency directly for information on specific careers.

■Food and Drug Administration
4300 Fisher Lane, Room 7B44
Rockville, MD 20857
Tel: 301-443-1970

■National Board for Certified Counselors
3D Terrace Way
Greensboro, NC 27403
Tel: 910-547-0607

Cardiovascular Technologists

Definition

Cardiovascular technologists assist physicians in diagnosing and treating heart and blood vessel ailments. Depending on their specialty, they operate electrocardiograph machines, perform Holter monitor and stress testing, and assist in cardiac catheterization procedures and ultrasound testing. These tasks help the physicians diagnose heart disease and monitor progress during treatment.

Nature of the Work

Technologists who assist physicians in the diagnosis and treatment of heart disease are known as cardiovascular technologists. (*Cardio* means heart; *vascular* refers to the blood vessel/circulatory system.) They include *electrocardiograph (EKG) technologists, Holter monitoring and stress test technologists, cardiology technologists, vascular technologists and echocardiographers* (both ultrasound technologists), *cardiac monitor technicians*, and others. The services of EKG technicians/technologists may be required throughout the hospital, such as in the cancer wards or emergency room; there may be a separate department for these EKG professionals. Increasingly, however, hospitals are centralizing cardiovascular services under one full cardiovascular "service line" overseen by the same administrator.

In addition to cardiovascular technologists, the cardiovascular team at a hospital also may include radiology (X-ray) technologists, nuclear medicine technologists, nurses, physician assistants, respiratory technologists, and respiratory therapists. For their part, the cardiovascular technologists contribute by performing one or more of a wide range of procedures in cardiovascular medicine, including invasive (enters a body cavity or interrupts normal body functions), noninvasive, peripheral vascular or echocardiography (ultrasound) procedures. In most facilities they use equipment that is among the most advanced in the medical field; drug therapies also may be used as part of the diagnostic imaging procedures or in addition to them. Technologists' services may be required when the patient's condition is first being explored, before surgery, during surgery (cardiology technologists primarily), or during rehabilitation of the patient. Some of the work is performed on an outpatient basis.

Depending on their specific area of skill, some cardiovascular technologists are employed in nonhospital health care facilities. For example, EKG technologists may work for clinics, mobile medical services, or private doctors' offices. Their equipment can go just about anywhere. The same is true for the ultrasound technologists.

Some of the specific duties of cardiovascular technologists are described in the following paragraphs. Exact titles of these technologists often vary from medical facility to medical facility because there is no standardized naming system.

Electrocardiograph technologists, or *EKG technologists,* use an electrocardiograph (EKG) machine to detect the electronic impulses that come from a patient's heart during and between a heartbeat. The EKG machine then records these signals on a paper graph called an electrocardiogram. The electronic impulses recorded by the EKG machine can tell the physician about the action of the heart during and between the individual heartbeats. This in turn reveals important information about the condition of the heart, including irregular heartbeats or the presence of blocked arteries, which the physician can use to diagnose heart disease, monitor progress during treatment, or check the patient's condition after recovery.

To use an EKG machine, the technologist attaches electrodes (small, disk-like devices about the size of a silver dollar) to the patient's chest. Wires attached to the electrodes lead to the EKG machine.

Up to twelve leads or more may be attached. To get a better reading from the electrodes, the technologist may first apply an adhesive gel to the patient's skin that helps to conduct the electrical impulses. The technologist then operates controls on the EKG machine or (more commonly) enters commands for the machine into a computer. The electrodes pick up the electronic signals from the heart and transmit them to the EKG machine. The machine registers and makes a printout of the signals, with a stylus (pen) recording their pattern on a long roll of graph paper.

During the test, the technologist may move the electrodes in order to get readings of electrical activity in different parts of the heart muscle. Since EKG equipment can be sensitive to electrical impulses from other sources, such as other parts of the patient's body or equipment in the room where the EKG test is being done, the technologist must watch for false readings.

After the test, the EKG technologist takes the electrocardiogram off the machine, edits it or makes notes on it, and sends it to the physician (usually a cardiologist, or heart specialist). Physicians may have computer assistance to help them use and interpret the electrocardiogram; special software is available to assist them with their diagnoses.

EKG technologists do not have to repair EKG machines, but they do have to keep an eye on them and know when they are malfunctioning so they can call someone for repairs. They also may keep the machines stocked with paper.

Of all the cardiovascular technical positions, EKG technicians/technologists are the most numerous. They comprised about half of all cardiovascular technologists in 1996 (about 16,000 of a total of 32,000). Holter monitoring and stress testing may be performed by *Holter monitor technologists* or *stress test technologists,* respectively, or may be additional duties of some EKG technologists. In Holter monitoring, electrodes are fastened to the patient's chest and a small, portable monitor is strapped to the patient's body, such as at the waist. The small monitor contains a magnetic tape or cassette that records the heart during activity—as the patient moves, sits, stands, sleeps, etc. The patient is required to wear the Holter monitor for up to twenty-four to forty-eight hours while he or she goes about normal daily activities. When the patient returns to the hospital, the technologist removes the magnetic tape or cassette from the monitor and puts it in a scanner to produce audio (sound) and visual representations of heart activity. (Hearing how the heart

sounds during activity helps physicians diagnose a possible heart condition.) The technologist reviews and analyzes the information revealed in the tape. Finally, the technologist may print out the parts of the tape that show abnormal heart patterns or make a full tape for the physician.

Stress tests record the heart's activity during physical activity. In one type of stress test, the technologist connects the patient to the EKG machine, attaching electrodes to the patient's arms, legs, and chest, and obtains a reading of the patient's resting heart activity and blood pressure. Then, the patient is asked to walk on a treadmill for a designated period of time while the technologist and the physician monitor the heart. The treadmill speed is increased so that the technologist physician can see what happens when the heart is put under higher levels of exertion.

Cardiology technologists specialize in providing support for cardiac catheterization (tubing) procedures. These procedures are classified as invasive because they require the physician and attending technologists to enter a body cavity or interrupt normal body functions. In one cardiac catheterization procedure—an angiogram—a catheter (tube) is inserted into the heart (usually by way of a blood vessel in the leg) in order to diagnose the condition of the heart blood vessels, such as whether there is a blockage. In another procedure, known as angioplasty, a catheter with a balloon at the end is inserted into an artery to widen it. Angioplasties are being performed with increasing frequency: approximately 300,000 in 1990, to approximately 6,000 in 1983. Cardiology technologists also perform a variety of other procedures.

Unlike some of the other cardiovascular technologists, cardiology technologists actually assist in surgical procedures. They may help secure the patient to the table, set up a 35mm video camera or other imaging device under the instructions of the physician (to produce images that assist the physician in guiding the catheter through the cardiovascular system), enter information about the surgical procedure (as it is taking place) into a computer, and provide other support. After the procedure, the technologist may process the angiographic film for use by the physician. Cardiology technologists may also assist during open-heart surgery by preparing and monitoring the patient and may participate in placement or monitoring of pacemakers.

This is a specialty that is growing in importance in cardiology care. In 1991, more than 1,300 hospitals had a cardiac catheterization lab and the numbers are expected to significantly expand, according to the American Academy of Medical Administrators.

Vascular technologists and *echocardiographers* are specialists in noninvasive cardiovascular procedures and use ultrasound equipment to obtain and record information about the condition of the heart. Ultrasound equipment is used to send out sound waves to the part of the body being studied; when the sound waves hit the part being studied, they send back an echo to the ultrasound machine. The echoes are "read" by the machine, which creates an image on a monitor, permitting the technologist to get an instant "image" of the part's condition.

Vascular technologists are specialists in the use of ultrasound equipment to study blood flow and circulation problems. Echocardiographers are specialists in the use of ultrasound equipment to evaluate the heart and its structures, such as the valves.

Cardiac monitor technicians are similar to and sometimes perform some of the same duties as EKG technologists. Usually working in the intensive care unit (ICU) or cardio-care unit of the hospital, cardiac monitor technicians keep watch over the patient-monitoring screens to detect any sign that a patient's heart is not beating as it should.

Cardiac monitor technicians begin their shift by reviewing the patient's records to familiarize themselves with what the patient's normal heart rhythms should be, what the current pattern is, and what types of problems have been observed. Throughout the shift, the cardiac monitor technician watches for heart rhythm irregularities that need prompt medical attention. Should there be any, he or she notifies a nurse or doctor immediately so that appropriate care can be given.

In addition to these positions, other cardiovascular technologists specialize in a particular aspect of health care. For example, a *cardiopulmonary technologist* specializes in procedures for diagnosing problems with the heart and lungs. He or she may conduct electrocardiograph, phonocardiograph (sound recordings of the heart's valves and of the blood passing through them), echocardiograph, stress testing, as well as respiratory test procedures.

Cardiopulmonary technologists also may assist on cardiac catheterization procedures, measuring and recording information about the the patient's cardiovascular and pulmonary systems during the procedure and alerting the cardiac catheterization team of any problems.

Nuclear medicine technologists, who use radioactive isotopes in diagnosis, treatment, or studies, assist in the diagnosis or treatment of cardiology problems. Radiology, respiratory, and exercise technicians and therapists also may assist in patient diagnosis, treatment, and/or rehabilitation.

Requirements

In the past, many EKG operators were trained on the job by an EKG supervisor. This still may be true for some EKG technician positions. Increasingly however, EKG technologists get postsecondary schooling before they are hired. Holter monitoring and stress testing may be part of the student's EKG schooling, or they may be learned through additional training. Ultrasound and cardiology technologists tend to have the most postsecondary schooling (up to a four-year bachelor's degree), and have the most extensive academic/experience requirements for credentialing purposes.

People can enter these positions without having had previous health care experience. However, it certainly doesn't hurt to have had some previous exposure to the business or even training in related areas. People with academic training or professional experience in nursing, radiology science, or respiratory science, for example, may be able to move into cardiology technology if they wish.

At a minimum, cardiovascular technologists need a high school diploma or equivalent to enter the field. Although no specific high school classes will directly prepare one to be a technologist, learning how to learn and getting a good grounding in basic high school subjects are important to all technologist positions.

During high school, students should take English, health, biology, and typing. They also might consider courses in social sciences to help them understand the social and psychological needs of patients.

As a rule of thumb, medical employers value postsecondary schooling that gives students actual hands-on experience with patients, in addition to classroom training. At many of the schools that train cardiovascular technologists, students work with patients in a variety of health care settings and train on more than one brand of equipment.

Some employers still train EKG technicians are still simply trained on the job by a physician or EKG department manager. Training generally lasts from one to six months. Trainee learn how to operate the

EKG machine, produce and edit the electrocardiogram, and other related tasks.

Some vocational, technical, and junior colleges have one- or two-year training programs in EKG technology, Holter monitoring, or stress testing, or all three; otherwise, EKG technologists may obtain training in Holter and stress procedures after they've already started working, either on the job or through an additional six months or more of schooling. Formal academic programs give technologists more preparation in the subject than is available with most on-the-job training and allow them to earn a certificate (one-year programs) or associate's degree (two-year programs). The American Medical Association's Allied Health Directory has listings of accredited EKG programs.

Ultrasound technologists usually need a high school diploma or equivalent plus one, two, or four years of postsecondary schooling in a trade school, technical school, or community college. Vascular technologists also may be trained on the job. Again, a list of accredited programs can be found in the AMA's Allied Health Directory; also, a directory of training opportunities in sonography is available from the Society of Diagnostic Medical Sonographers.

Cardiology technologists tend to have the highest academic requirements of all; for example, a four-year bachelor of science degree or two-year associate's degree, or a certificate of completion from a hospital, trade, or technical cardiovascular program for training of varying length. A two-year program at a junior or community college might include one year of core classes (e.g. mathematics, biology, chemistry, and anatomy) and one year of specialized classes in cardiology procedures.

Cardiac monitor technicians need a high school diploma or equivalent, with additional educational requirements similar to those of EKG technicians.

Cardiology is a cutting-edge area of medicine, with constant advancements, and medical equipment relating to the heart is continually being updated. Therefore, keeping up with new developments is vital. In addition, technologists who add to their qualifications through taking part in continuing education tend to earn more money and have more employment opportunities. Major professional societies encourage and provide the opportunities for professionals to continue their education.

Right now, certification or licensing for cardiovascular technologists is voluntary, but the move to state licensing is expected in the near future. Many credentialing bodies for cardiovascular and pulmonary positions exist, including American Registry of Diagnostic Medical Sonographers (ARDMS), Cardiovascular Credentialing International (CCI), and others, and there are more than a dozen possible credentials for cardiovascular technologists. For example, sonographers can take an exam from the ARDMS to receive credentialing in sonography. Their credentials may be registered diagnostic medical sonographer, registered diagnostic cardiac sonographer, or registered vascular technologist.

Credentialing requirements for cardiology technologists or ultrasound technologists may include test taking plus formal academic and on-the-job requirements. Professional experience or academic training in a related field—nursing, radiology science, respiratory science, etc.—may be acceptable as part of these formal academic and professional requirements. As with continuing education, certification is a sign of interest and dedication to the field and is generally favorably regarded by potential employers.

Opportunities for Experience & Exploration

Prospective cardiovascular technologists will find it difficult to gain any direct experience on a part-time basis in electrocardiography. Their first experience with the work generally comes during their on-the-job training sessions. They may, however, be able to gain some exposure to patient-care activities in general by signing up for volunteer work at a local hospital. In addition, they can arrange to visit a hospital, clinic, or physician's office where electrocardiographs are taken. In this way, they may be able to watch a technician at work or at least talk to a technician about what the work is like.

Methods of Entering

Because most cardiovascular technologists receive their initial training on their first job, great care should be taken in finding this first employer. Students should pay close attention not only to the pay and working conditions, but also to the kind of on-the-job training that is provided for each prospective position. High school vocational counselors may be able to tell job seekers which hospitals have good reputations for EKG training programs. Applying directly to hospitals is a common way of entering the field. Information also can be gained by reading the classified ads in the newspaper and from talking with friends and relatives who work in hospitals.

For students who graduate from one- to two-year training programs, finding a first job should be easier. First, employers are always eager to hire people who are already trained. Second, these graduates can be less concerned about the training programs offered by their employers. Third, they should find that their teachers and guidance counselors can be excellent sources of information about job possibilities in the area. If the training program includes practical experience, graduates may find that the hospital in which they trained or worked before graduation would be willing to hire them after graduation.

Advancement

Opportunities for advancement are best for cardiovascular technologists who learn to do or assist with more complex procedures, such as stress testing, Holter monitoring, echocardiography, and cardiac catheterization. With proper training and experience, these technicians may eventually become cardiovascular technologists, echocardiography technologists, cardiopulmonary technicians, cardiology technologists, or other specialty technicians or technologists.

In addition to these kinds of specialty positions, experienced technicians may also be able to advance to various supervisory and training posts.

Employment Outlook

Openings for EKG technicians are expected to decline through the year 2006; although there is an increased demand for EKGs, the equipment and procedures are currently much more efficient than they used to be. One technician can perform far more tests each day than was previously possible, and, because of this, fewer technicians are required. In addition, newer equipment is easier to use, allowing employers to train other personnel, such as respiratory therapists or registered nurses, in its operation. In 1996, there were approximately 16,000 EKG technicians.

Employment of cardiology technologists, on the other hand, is expected to grow faster than the average through the year 2006. Again, growth will be primarily due to the increasing numbers of older people in our population. Most job openings for cardiovascular technologists will be to replace those technicians who are promoted, transferred, or retired.

Earnings

Beginning cardiovascular technologists can expect to receive starting salaries of approximately $15,200 a year, according to the U.S. Department of Labor. Average pay for all EKG technicians was $20,200 in 1996. Experienced technologists earn considerably more, with an average salary of $33,600.

Those with formal training earn more than those who trained on the job, and those who are able to perform more sophisticated tests, such as Holter monitoring and stress testing, are paid more than those who perform only the basic electrocardiograph tests.

EKG technicians working in hospitals receive the same fringe benefits as other hospital workers, including medical insurance, paid vacations, and sick leave. In some cases benefits also include educational assistance, retirement plans, and uniform allowances.

Conditions of Work

Cardiovascular technologists usually work in clean, quiet, well-lighted surroundings. They generally work five-day, forty-hour weeks, although technicians working in small hospitals may be on twenty-four-hour call for emergencies, and all technicians in hospitals, large or small, can expect to do occasional evening or weekend work. With the growing emphasis in health care on cost containment, more jobs are likely to develop in various outpatient settings, so in the future it is likely that cardiovascular technologists will work more often in clinics, cardiologists' offices, HMOs, and other nonhospital locations.

Cardiovascular technologists generally work with patients who either are ill or who have reason to fear they might be ill. With this in mind, there are opportunities for the technicians to do these people some good, but there is also a chance of causing some unintentional harm as well: a well-conducted test can reduce anxieties or make a physician's job easier; a misplaced electrode or an error in record-keeping could cause an incorrect diagnosis. Technicians need to be able to cope with these responsibilities and consistently conduct their work in the best interests of their patients.

Part of the technician's job includes putting patients at ease about the procedure they are to undergo. Toward that end, technicians should be pleasant, patient, alert, and able to understand and sympathize with the feelings of others. In explaining the nature of the procedure to patients, cardiovascular technicians should be able to do so in a calm, reassuring, and confident manner.

Inevitably, some patients will try to get information about their medical situation from the technician. In cases like this, technicians need to be both tactful and firm in explaining that they are only making the electrocardiogram; the interpretation is for the physician to make.

Another large part of a technician's job involves getting along well with other members of the hospital staff. This task is sometimes made more difficult by the fact that in most hospitals there is a formal, often rigid, status structure, and cardiovascular technologists may find themselves in a relatively low position in that structure. In emergency situations or at other moments of frustration, cardiovascular technologists may find themselves dealt with brusquely or angrily. Technicians should not take outbursts or rude treatment personally, but instead should respond with stability and maturity.

Sources of Additional Information

■■■**American Society of Cardiovascular Professionals/Society of Cardiovascular Management (ASCP/SCM)**
120 Falcon Drive, Unit 3
Fredericksburg, VA 22408
Tel: 540-891-0079

For information on credentials, please contact:

■■■**Cardiovascular Credentialing International (CCI)**
4456 Corporation Lane, Suite 110
Virginia Beach, VA 23462
Tel: 800-326-0268

Career and Employment Counselors and Technicians

Definition

Career and employment counselors and technicians, who are also known as *vocational counselors*, provide advice to individuals or groups about occupations, careers, career decision making, career planning, and other career-development related questions or conflicts. Career guidance technicians collect pertinent information to support both the counselor and applicant during the job search.

Nature of the Work

A certified career counselor helps people make decisions and plan life and career directions. Strategies and techniques are tailored to the specific need of the person seeking help. Counselors conduct individual and group counseling sessions to help qualify life and career goals. They administer and interpret tests and inventories to assess abilities and interests and identify career options. They may use career planning and occupational information to help individuals better understand the work world. They assist in developing individualized career plans, teach job-hunting strategies and skills, and help develop resumes. Sometimes this involves resolving personal conflicts on the job. They also provide support for people experiencing job stress, job loss, and career transition.

Vocational-rehabilitation counselors work with disabled individuals to help the counselees understand what skills they have to offer to an employer. A good counselor knows the working world and how to obtain detailed information about specific jobs. To assist with career decisions, counselors must know about the availability of jobs, the probable future of certain jobs, the education or training necessary to enter them, the kinds of salary or other benefits that certain jobs offer, the conditions that certain jobs impose on employees (night work, travel, work outdoors), and the satisfactions that certain jobs provide their employees. Professional career counselors work in both private and public settings and are verified by the National Board for Certified Counselors (NBCC).

College career planning and placement counselors work exclusively with the students of their university or college. They may specialize in some specific area appropriate to the students and graduates of the school, such as law and education, as well as part-time and summer work, internships, and field placements. In a liberal arts college, the students may need more assistance in identifying an appropriate career. To do this, the counselor administers interest and aptitude tests and interviews the student to determine career goals.

The counselor may work with currently enrolled students who are seeking internships and other work programs while still at school. Alumni who wish to make a career change also seek the services of the career counseling and placement office at their former school.

College placement counselors also gather complete job information from prospective employers, and make the information available to interested students and alumni. Just as counselors try to find an applicant for a particular job listing, they also must seek out jobs for specific applicants. To do this, they will call potential employers to encourage them to consider a qualified individual.

College and career planning and placement counselors are responsible for the arrangements and details of on-campus interviews by large corporations and maintain an up-to-date library of vocational guidance material and recruitment literature.

Counselors also give assistance in preparing the actual job search by helping the applicant to write resumes and letters of application, as well as by practicing interview skills through role-playing and other techniques. They also provide information on business procedures and personnel requirements in the applicant's chosen field. At universities with access to the Internet, counselors will set up on-line accounts for students, giving them access to information regarding potential employers.

Some career planning and placement counselors work with secondary school authorities, advising them on the needs of local industries and specific preparation requirements both for employment and for further education. In two-year colleges the counselor may participate in the planning of course content, and in some smaller schools the counselor may be required to teach as well.

The principal duty of career guidance technicians is to help order, catalog, and file materials relating to job opportunities, careers, technical schools, scholarships, careers in the armed forces, and other programs. Guidance technicians also help students and teachers find materials relating to a student's interests and aptitudes. These various materials may be in the form of books, pamphlets, magazine articles, microfiche, videos, computer software, or other media.

Often career guidance technicians help students take and score self-administered tests that determine their aptitude and interest in different careers or job-related activities. If the career guidance center has audiovisual equipment, such as VCRs or film or slide projectors, career guidance technicians are usually responsible for the equipment.

Requirements

Career counselors must have a good background in education, training, employment trends, the current labor market, and career resources. They should be able to provide their clients with information about job tasks, functions, salaries, requirements, and future outlooks related to broad occupational fields.

Knowledge of testing techniques and measures of aptitude, achievement, interests, values, and personality is required. The ability to evaluate job performance and individual effectiveness is helpful. The career counselor must also have management and administrative skills.

In some states the minimum educational program in career and vocational counseling is a graduate degree in counseling or a related field from a regionally accredited higher education institution, and a completed supervised counseling experience, which includes career counseling. A growing number of institutions offer post-master's degrees with training in career development and career counseling. Such programs are highly recommended for people who wish to specialize in vocational and career counseling. These programs are frequently called "Advanced Graduate Specialist Programs" or "Certificates of Advanced Study Programs."

For a career as a college career planning and placement counselor, a master's degree in guidance and counseling, education, college student personnel work, behavioral science, or a related field is commonly the minimum educational requirement. Graduate work includes courses in vocational and aptitude testing, counseling techniques, personnel management and occupational research, industrial relations, and group dynamics and organizational behavior.

As in any profession, there is usually an initial period of training for newly hired counselors and counselor trainees. Some of the skills needed by employment counselors, such as testing procedures skills and interviewing skills, can only be acquired through on-the-job training.

Career guidance technicians need to be high school graduates. In addition, most employers look for applicants who have completed two years of training beyond high school, usually at a junior, community, or technical college. These two-year programs, which usually lead to an associate's degree, may combine classroom instruction with practical or sometimes even on-the-job experience.

Opportunities for Experience & Exploration

Summer employment in an employment agency is a good way to explore the field of employment counseling. Interviewing the director of a public or private agency might give you a better understanding of what the work involves and the qualifications such an organization requires of its counselors.

Interested high school students who enjoy working with others will find helpful experiences in working in the dean's or counselor's office. Many schools offer opportunities in peer tutoring, both in academics and in career guidance–related duties. (If your school does not have such a program in place, consider putting together a proposal to institute one. Your guidance counselor should be able to help you with this.) A student's own experience in seeking summer and part-time work is also valuable in learning what the job seeker must confront in business or industry. You could write a feature story for your school newspaper on your and others' experiences in the workaday world.

People interested in becoming career counselors should seek out professional career counselors and discuss the field with them. Most people are happy to talk about what they do. They also might contact the National Board for Certified Counselors for certification information. They may also consult the National Career Development Association for competency statements and consumer guidelines. Undergraduate students interested in career counseling should take courses in counseling, psychology, sociology, and business management and administration.

High school students interested in becoming career guidance technicians should consider working part time or as a volunteer in a library. Such work can provide students with some of the basic skills for learning about information resources, cataloging, and filing. In addition, assisting schools or clubs with any media presentations, such as video or slide shows, will help familiarize a student with the equipment used by counselors.

Methods of Entering

Journals specializing in information for career counselors frequently have job listings or information on job hotlines and services. School placement centers also are a good source of information, both because of their standard practice of listing job openings from participating firms and because schools are a likely source of jobs for career counselors. Placement officers will be aware of which schools are looking for applicants.

To enter the field of college career planning and placement, interested alumni may consider working for their alma mater as an assistant in the college or university placement office. Other occupational areas that provide an excellent background for college placement work include teaching, business, public relations, previous placement training, positions in employment agencies, and experience in psychological counseling.

Career guidance technicians should receive some form of career placement from schools offering training in that area. Newspapers may list entry-level jobs. One of the best methods, however, is to contact libraries and education centers directly to inquire about their needs for assistance in developing or staffing their career guidance centers.

Advancement

Employment counselors in federal or state employment services or in other vocational counseling agencies are usually considered trainees for the first six months of their employment. During this time, they learn the specific skills that will be expected of them during their career with the agency. The first year of a new counselor's employment is probationary.

Positions of further responsibility include supervisory or administrative work, which may be attained by counselors after several years of experience on the job. Advancement to administrative positions often means giving up the actual counseling work, not an advantage to those who enjoy working with people in need of counseling.

Opportunity for advancement for college counselors—to assistant and associate placement director, director of student personnel services, or similar administrative positions—depends largely upon the type of college or university and the size of the staff. In general, a doctorate is preferred and may be necessary for advancement.

New employees in agencies are frequently considered trainees for the first six months to a year of their employment. During the training period, they acquire the specific skills that will be required of them during their tenure with the agency. Frequently, the first year of employment is probationary. After several years' experience on the job, counselors may reach supervisory or administrative positions.

Employment Outlook

There should be good growth in the field of employment counseling through the year 2006. Although only moderate opportunities are anticipated for employment and rehabilitation counselors in state and local governments, rapid growth is expected in the development of human resource and employment assistance programs in private business and industry, which should produce more jobs.

Libraries and schools have had increasingly limited budgets for staff and resources. Competition for jobs for career guidance technicians is increasingly stiff. The needs of outplacement centers, employment agencies, and armed forces offices are remaining somewhat stagnant. If there is an increased focus on retraining workers or educating students about career options, there may be an increase in the future demand for career guidance technicians.

Earnings

Salaries vary greatly within the career and vocational counseling field. Average salaries for full-time educational and vocational counselors ranged from $18,600 to $60,100 a year in 1996, according to the U.S. Department of Labor. Those in business or industry earn somewhat higher salaries.

In private practice, the range is yet wider. Some practitioners earn as little as $20,000 per year and others earn in excess of $100,000 per year.

Annual earnings of career planning and placement counselors vary greatly among educational institutions, with larger institutions offering the highest salaries. The average salary is approximately $35,000. Earnings are lowest in the Southeast and highest in the Far West. Benefits include holidays and vacations, pension and retirement plans, and in some institutions, reduced tuition.

Salaries for career guidance technicians vary according to education and experience, and the geographical location of the job. In general, career guidance technicians who are graduates of two-year post–high school training programs can expect to receive starting salaries averaging $15,000 to $20,000 a year.

Conditions of Work

Employment counselors usually work about forty hours a week, but some agencies are more flexible. Counseling is done in offices designed to be free from noise and distractions to allow confidential discussions with clients.

College career planning and placement counselors also normally work a forty-hour week, although irregular hours and overtime are frequently required during the peak recruiting period. They generally work on a twelve-month basis.

Career guidance technicians work in very pleasant surroundings, usually in the career guidance office of a college or vocational school. They will interact with a great number of students, some of whom are eagerly looking for work, others who are more tense and anxious. The technician must remain unruffled in order to ease any tension and provide a quiet atmosphere.

Sources of Additional Information

■Career Planning and Adult Development Network
4965 Sierra Road
San Jose, CA 95132
Tel: 408-559-4946

■College Placement Council
62 Highland Avenue
Bethlehem, PA 18017
Tel: 610-868-1421

■Council on Rehabilitation Education
1835 Rohlwing Road, Suite E
Rolling Meadows, IL 60008
Tel: 847-394-1785

■National Career Development Association
5999 Stevenson Avenue
Alexandria, VA 22304
Tel: 703-823-9800

■National Council on Rehabilitation Education
Department of Special Education and Rehabilitation
Utah State University
Logan, UT 84322-2870
Tel: 801-797-3572

Carpenters

Definition

Carpenters cut, shape, level, and fasten together pieces of wood and other construction materials, such as wallboard, plywood, and insulation. Many carpenters work on constructing, remodeling, or repairing houses and other kinds of buildings. Other carpenters work at construction sites where roads, bridges, docks, boats, mining tunnels, and wooden vats are built. A carpenter may specialize in building the rough framing of a structure, and thus be considered a *rough carpenter*, or he or she may specialize in the finishing details of a structure, such as the trim around doors and windows, and thus be considered a *finish carpenter*.

Nature of the Work

Carpenters are the largest group of workers in the building trades. There are about a million carpenters in the United States today. About 80 percent of them work for contractors involved in building, repairing, and remodeling buildings and other structures. Manufacturing firms, schools, stores, and government bodies employ most other carpenters. One third are self-employed.

Carpenters do two basic kinds of work: rough carpentry and finish carpentry. Rough carpenters construct and install temporary structures and supports, wooden structures used in industrial settings, as well as parts of buildings that are usually covered up when the rooms are finished. Among the structures built by such carpenters are scaffolds for other workers to stand on, chutes used as channels for wet concrete, forms for concrete foundations, and timber structures that support machinery. In buildings, they may put up the frame, install rafters, joists, subflooring, wall sheathing, prefabricated wall panels and windows, and many other components.

Finish carpenters install hardwood flooring, staircases, shelves, cabinets, trim on windows and doors, and other woodwork and hardware that make the building look complete, inside and outside. Finish carpentry requires especially careful, precise workmanship as the result must have a good appearance in addition to being sturdy. Many carpenters who are employed by building contractors do both rough and finish work on buildings.

Although they do many different tasks in different settings, carpenters generally follow approximately the same basic steps. First they look over blueprints or plans for information (or get instructions from a supervisor) about the dimensions of the structure to be built and the type of materials to be used. Sometimes local building codes determine how a structure should be built, so carpenters need to know about such regulations. Using rulers, framing squares, chalk lines, and other measuring and marking equipment, they lay out how the work will be done. Using hand and power tools, they cut and shape the wood, plywood, fiberglass, plastic, or other materials. Then they nail, screw, glue, or staple the pieces together. Finally, they use levels, plumb bobs, rulers, and squares to check their work, and they make any necessary adjustments. Sometimes carpenters work with prefabricated units for components such as wall panels or stairs. Installing these is, in many ways, a much less complicated task, because much less layout, cutting, and assembly work is needed.

Carpenters who work outside of the building construction field may do a variety of installation and maintenance jobs, such as repairing furniture, changing locks, and installing ceiling tiles or exterior siding on buildings. Other carpenters specialize in building, repairing, or modifying ships, wooden boats, wooden railroad trestles, timber framing in mine shafts, woodwork inside railcars, storage tanks and vats, or stage sets in theaters.

Requirements

Carpenters can acquire the skills of their trade in various ways, through formal training programs and through informal on-the-job training. Of the different ways to learn, an apprenticeship is considered the best as it provides a more thorough and complete foundation for a career as a carpenter than other kinds of training. However, the limited number of available apprenticeships means that not all carpenters can learn their trade this way.

Many carpenters pick up skills informally on the job while they work as carpenter's helpers. Usually employers prefer applicants who have completed high school. They begin with little or no training and gradually learn as they work under the supervision of experienced carpenters. The skills that helpers develop depend on the jobs that their employers contract to do. Working for a small contracting company, a beginner may learn about relatively few kinds of carpentry tasks. On the other hand, a large contracting company may offer a wider variety of learning opportunities. Becoming a skilled carpenter by this method can take much longer than an apprenticeship, and the completeness of the training varies. Some people who are waiting for an apprenticeship to become available work as helpers to gain experience in the field.

Some people first learn about carpentry while serving in the U.S. armed forces. Other carpenters learn skills in vocational educational programs offered in trade schools and through correspondence courses. Vocational programs can be very good, especially as a supplement to other practical training. But without additional hands-on instruction, vocational school graduates may not be well-enough prepared to get many jobs in the field because some programs do not provide sufficient opportunity for students to practice and perfect their carpentry skills.

Apprenticeships usually last three to four years. They are administered by employer groups and local chapters of labor unions that organize carpenters. Applicants for apprenticeships must meet the specific requirements of local apprenticeship committees. Typically, applicants must be at least seventeen years old, have a high school diploma, and show that they have some aptitude for carpentry.

Apprenticeships combine on-the-job work experience with classroom instruction in a planned, systematic program. Initially, apprentices work at such simple tasks as building concrete forms, doing rough framing, and nailing subflooring. Toward the end of their training apprentices may work on finishing trimwork, fitting hardware, hanging doors, and building stairs. In the course of this experience, they become familiar with the tools, materials, techniques, and equipment of the trade, and they learn how to do layout, framing, finishing, and other basic carpentry jobs.

The work experience is supplemented by about 144 hours of classroom instruction per year. Some of this instruction concerns the correct use and maintenance of tools, safety practices, first aid, building code requirements, and the properties of different construction materials. Other subjects apprentices study include the principles of layout, blueprint reading, shop mathematics, and sketching. Both on the job and in the classroom, carpenters learn how to work effectively with members of other skilled building trades.

A good high school background for prospective carpenters would include carpentry and woodworking courses, as well as other shop classes, applied mathematics, mechanical drawing, and blueprint reading. Carpenters need to have manual dexterity, good eye-hand coordination, and a good sense of balance. They need to be in good physical condition as the work involves a great deal of physical activity. Stamina is much more important than physical strength. On the job, carpenters may have to climb, stoop, kneel, crouch, and reach.

Opportunities for Experience & Exploration

High school students may begin finding out about the work that carpenters do by taking courses such as wood shop, applied mathematics, drafting, and other industrial arts. Simple projects such as building birdhouses or shelving at home can also help people gauge their abilities and interest in the field. In addition, summer employment at a construction site can provide students with a useful overview of the work performed in the construction industry and perhaps the opportunity to talk with carpenters on the job.

Methods of Entering

Two important ways of starting out in carpentry are participating in an apprenticeship program and gradually gaining experience and skills on the job. Information about apprenticeships can be obtained by contacting the local office of the state employment service, area contractors that hire carpenters, or the local offices of the United Brotherhood of Carpenters and Joiners of America, a union that cooperates in sponsoring apprenticeships. Helper jobs that can be filled by beginners without special training in carpentry may be advertised in newspaper classified ads or with the state employment service. Another possibility is contacting potential employers directly.

Advancement

After they have completed and met all the requirements of their apprenticeship training, former apprentices are considered journeymen carpenters. After they have gained enough experience, journeymen carpenters may be promoted to positions where they are responsible for supervising the work of other carpenters. If their background includes exposure to a broad range of construction activities, they may eventually advance to positions as general construction supervisors. Carpenters who are skillful at mathematical computations and have a good knowledge of the construction business may become estimators. Some carpenters go into business for themselves, doing repair or construction work as independent contractors.

Employment Outlook

Overall, the outlook for carpenters through the year 2006 is slower than the average for other occupational fields. Total employment of carpenters is expected to increase moderately as new construction and renovations of existing structures continue. But at any given time,

building activity and thus job opportunities will be better in some geographic areas than in others, reflecting regional and local variations in economic conditions.

Even if construction activity is strong in coming years, several factors will contribute to a slower rate of employment growth than at times in the past. One factor affecting growth is the trend toward increasing the use of prefabricated building components, which are more quickly and easily installed than parts made by traditional construction methods. The use of prefabricated materials is likely to mean that fewer skilled carpenters will be needed. In addition, many new lightweight, cordless tools, such as nailers and drills, are making the work of carpenters easier and faster and thus tending to reduce the total number of workers needed.

Job turnover is relatively high in the carpentry field. Many people prefer to switch to another occupation after working for awhile because they find their skills are too limited to get the best jobs or they don't like the work. As a result, every year thousands of job openings become available. Carpenters with good all-around skills, such as those who have completed apprenticeships, will have the best chances of being hired for the most desirable positions.

Nonetheless, carpenters should expect periods of unemployment. The number of available jobs is always related to various factors, such as economic stability, government spending, and interest rates. During an economic downturn, fewer building projects are started. Carpenters need to plan for the possibility of major ups and downs in their income.

Earnings

In 1996, according to the U.S. Department of Labor, the majority of carpenters who did not own their own businesses earned between $17,900 and $34,300 per year. Some made as little as $13,800, while a few earned around 45,000 or more.

Starting pay for apprentices is approximately 50 percent of the experienced worker's pay scale. It is increased periodically so that by the last phase of training the pay of apprentices is 85 to 90 percent of the journeyman carpenter's rate. Fringe benefits, such as health insurance, pension funds, and paid vacations, are available to most workers in this field and vary with local union contracts.

Conditions of Work

Carpenters may work either indoors or outdoors. If they are engaged in rough carpentry, they probably do most of their work outdoors. They may have to work on high scaffolding or in a basement making cement forms. A construction site can be noisy, dusty, hot, cold, or muddy. Carpenters often must be physically active throughout the day, constantly standing, stooping, climbing, and reaching. Some of the possible hazards of the job include being hit by falling objects, falling off a ladder, straining muscles, and getting cuts and scrapes on fingers and hands. Carpenters who follow recommended safety practices and procedures can minimize these hazards.

Work in the construction industry involves changing from one job location to another, and from time to time being laid off because of poor weather, or shortages of materials, or simply lack of jobs. Workers in this field must thus be able to arrange their finances so that they can make it through sometimes long periods of unemployment. Most carpenters belong to the United Brotherhood of Carpenters and Joiners of America.

Sources of Additional Information

■**Associated General Contractors of America**
1957 E Street, NW
Washington, DC 20006
Tel: 202-393-2040

■**Home Builders Institute**
National Association of Homebuilders
15th and M Streets, NW
Washington, DC 20005
Tel: 202-822-0200

■**Ontario Carpentry Contractors Association**
#305, 1 Greensboro Drive
Rexdale, ON M9W 1C8 Canada
Tel: 416-248-6213

■**United Brotherhood of Carpenters and Joiners of America**
101 Constitution Avenue, NW
Washington, DC 20001
Tel: 202-546-6206

Cartoonists and Animators

Definition

Cartoonists and animators are illustrators who draw pictures and cartoons to amuse, educate, and persuade people.

Nature of the Work

Cartoonists draw illustrations for newspapers, books, magazines, greeting cards, movies, television shows, civic organizations, and private businesses. Cartoons most often are associated with newspaper comics or with children's television, but they are also used to highlight and interpret information in publications as well as in advertising.

Whatever their individual specialty, cartoonists and animators translate ideas onto paper or film in order to communicate these ideas to an audience. Sometimes the ideas are original; other times they are directly related to the news of the day, to the content of a magazine article, or to a new product. After cartoonists come up with ideas, they discuss them with their employers, who include editors, producers, and creative directors at advertising agencies. Next, cartoonists sketch drawings and submit these for approval. Employers may suggest changes, which cartoonists then make. Cartoonists use a variety of art materials including pens, pencils, markers, crayons, paints, transparent washes, and shading sheets. They may draw on paper, acetate, or bristol board.

Animators are relying increasingly on computers in various areas of production. They are color animation art, where every frame used to be painted by hand. Computers also help animators create special effects or even entire films.

Comic strip artists tell jokes or short stories with a series of pictures. Each picture is called a frame, or a panel, and each frame usually includes words as well as drawings. Comic book artists also tell stories with their drawings, but their stories are longer, and they are not necessarily meant to be funny.

Animators, or *motion cartoonists*, also draw individual pictures, but they must draw many more for a moving cartoon. Each picture varies only a little from the ones before and after it in a series. When these drawings are photographed in sequence to make a film and then the film is projected at high speed, the cartoon images appear to be moving. One can achieve a similar effect by drawing stick figures on the pages of a note pad, and then flipping through the pages very quickly. Animators today also work a great deal with computers.

Other people who work in animation are *prop designers*, who create objects used in animated films, and *layout artists*, who visualize and create the world that cartoon characters inhabit.

Editorial cartoonists comment on society by drawing pictures with messages that are usually funny, but which often have a satirical edge. Their drawings often depict famous politicians. *Portraitists* are cartoonists who specialize in drawing caricatures. Caricatures are pictures that exaggerate someone's prominent features, such as a large nose, to make them recognizable to the public. Most editorial cartoonists are also talented portraitists.

Storyboard artists work in film and television production as well as at advertising agencies. They draw cartoons or sketches that give a client an idea of what a scene or television commercial will look like before it is produced. If the director or advertising client likes the idea, the actions represented by cartoons in the storyboard will be reproduced by actors on film.

Requirements

Cartoonists and animators must be creative. In addition to having artistic talent, they must generate ideas, although it is not unusual for cartoonists to collaborate with writers for ideas. Whether they create cartoon strips or advertising campaigns, they must be able to come up with concepts and images that the public will respond to. They must have a good sense of humor and an observant eye to detect people's distinguishing characteristics and society's interesting attributes or incongruities.

Cartoonists and animators need not have a college degree, but some art training is usually expected by employers. To comment insightfully on contemporary life, it is also useful to study political science, history, and social studies. Animators must attend art school to learn specific technical skills. Training in computers in addition to art can be especially valuable.

Cartoonists and animators need to be flexible. Because their art is commercial, they must be willing to accommodate their employers' desires if they are to build a broad clientele and earn a decent living. They must be able to take suggestions and rejections gracefully.

Opportunities for Experience & Exploration

High school students who are interested in becoming cartoonists or animators should submit their drawings to their school paper. They also might want to draw posters to publicize activities, such as sporting events, dances, and meetings.

Scholarship assistance for art students is available from some sources. For example, the Society of Illustrators awards around 125 scholarships annually to artist students from any field. Students do not apply directly; rather, they are selected and given application materials by their instructors. The International Animated Film Society offers scholarships to high school seniors.

Methods of Entering

A few places, such as the Walt Disney studios, offer apprenticeships. To enter these programs, applicants must have attended an accredited art school for two or three years.

Formal entry-level positions for cartoonists and animators are rare, but there are several ways for artists to enter the cartooning field. Most cartoonists and animators begin by working piecemeal, selling cartoons to small publications, like community newspapers, that buy freelance cartoons. Others assemble a portfolio of their best work and apply to publishers or the art departments of advertising agencies. Cartoonists and animators should be willing to work for what equals less than minimum wage to get established.

Advancement

Cartoonists' success, like that of other artists, depends upon how much the public likes their work. Very successful cartoonists and animators work for prestigious clients at the best wages; some become well known to the public.

Employment Outlook

Opportunities in this field are expected to grow faster than average through the year 2006. *U.S. News & World Report* recently included the career of animator in its list of 20 Hot Job Tracks.

Cartoons are not just for children anymore. Much of the animation today is geared for an adult audience. Interactive games, animated films, network and cable television, and the Internet are among the many employment sources for talented cartoonists and animators. Almost two-thirds of all visual artists are self-employed, but freelance work can be hard to come by and many freelancers earn little until they acquire experience and establish a good reputation. Competition for work will be keen; those with an undergraduate or advanced degree in art or film will be in demand. Experience in action drawing and computers a must.

Animation houses, such as Disney, will continue to be good sources of jobs. The growing trend of sophisticated special effects in motion pictures will create many opportunities at industry effects houses such as Sony Pictures Image Works, DreamQuest, Industrial Light & Magic, and Dream-Works.

Earnings

Freelance cartoonists may earn anywhere from $100 to $1,200 or more per drawing, but top dollar generally goes only for big, full-color projects such as magazine cover illustrations. Most cartoonists and animators average from $200 to $1,500 a week, although syndicated cartoonists on commission can earn much more. Salaries depend upon the work performed. Cel painters, as listed in a salary survey conducted by *Animation World,* start at about $750 a week; animation checkers, $930 a week; story sketchers, $1,500 weekly. According to *U.S. News & World Report,* animators, depending on their experience, can earn from $800 to $1,800 a week. Top animators can command weekly fees of about $6,500 or more. Comic strip artists are usually paid according to the number of publications that carry their strip. Self-employed artists do not receive fringe benefits such as paid vacations, sick leave, health insurance, or pension benefits.

Conditions of Work

Most cartoonists and animators work in big cities where employers such as television studios, magazine publishers, and advertising agencies are located. They generally work in comfortable environments, at drafting tables or drawing boards with good light. Staff cartoonists work a regular forty-hour workweek, but may occasionally be expected to work evenings and weekends to meet deadlines. Freelance cartoonists have erratic schedules, and the number of hours they work may depend on how much money they want to earn or how much work they can find. They often work evenings and weekends, but are not required to be at work during regular office hours.

Cartoonists and animators can be frustrated by employers who curtail their creativity, asking them to follow instructions that are contrary to what they would most like to do. Many freelance cartoonists spend a lot of time working alone at home, but cartoonists have more opportunities to interact with other people than most working artists.

Sources of Additional Information

For education and career information, please contact:

■ **National Cartoonists Society**
PO Box 20267
Columbus Circle Station
New York, NY 10023
Tel: 212-627-1550

For an art school directory, a scholarship guide, or general information, please contact:

■ **National Art Education Association**
1916 Association Drive
Reston, VA 22091-1590
Tel: 703-860-8000

For membership and scholarship information, contact:

■ **International Animated Film Society**
725 South Victory
Burbank, CA 91502
Tel: 818-842-8330

For scholarship information for qualified students in art school, have your instructor contact:

■ **Society of Illustrators**
128 East 63rd Street
New York, NY 10021
Tel: 212-838-2560

Cashiers

Definition

Cashiers are employed in many different businesses, including supermarkets, department stores, restaurants, and movie theaters. In general, they are responsible for handling money received from customers.

One of the principal tasks of a cashier is operating a cash register. The cash register records all the monetary transactions going into or out of the cashier's work station. These transactions might involve cash, credit card charges, personal checks, refunds, and exchanges. To assist in inventory control, the machine often tallies the specific products that are sold.

Nature of the Work

Although cashiers are employed in many different types of businesses and establishments, most handle the following tasks: receiving money from customers, making change, and providing customers with a payment receipt. Other duties are dictated by the type of business. In supermarkets, for example, they might be required to bag groceries. Typically cashiers in drug or department stores also package or bag merchandise for customers. In currency exchanges they cash checks, receive utility bill payments, and sell various licenses and permits.

At some businesses cashiers handle tasks not directly related to customers. Some cashiers, for example, prepare bank deposits for the management. In large businesses, where cashiers are often given a lot of responsibility, they may receive and record cash payments made to the firm and handle payment of the firm's bills. Cashiers might even prepare sales tax reports, compute income tax deductions for employees' pay rates, and prepare paychecks and payroll envelopes.

Cashiers usually operate some type of cash register or other business machine. These machines might print out the amount of each purchase, automatically add the total amount, provide a paper receipt for the customer, and open the cash drawer for the cashier. Other, more complex machines, such as those used in hotels, large department stores, and supermarkets, might print out an itemized bill of the customer's purchases. In some cases cashiers use electronic devices called optical scanners, which "read" the price of goods from a bar code printed on the merchandise. As the cashier passes the product over the scanner, the scanner reads the code on the product and transmits the code to the cashier's terminal. The price of the item is then automatically displayed at the terminal and added to the customer's bill. Cashiers generally have their own drawer of money, known as a "bank," which fits into the cash register or terminal. They must keep an accurate record of the amount of money in the drawer. Other machines that are used by cashiers include adding machines and change-dispensing machines.

Job titles vary depending on where the cashier is employed. In supermarkets they might be known as *check-out clerks* or *grocery checkers*; in utility companies they are typically called *bill clerks* or *tellers*; in theaters they are often referred to as *ticket sellers* or *box office cashiers*; and in cafeterias they are frequently called *cashier-checkers, food checkers,* or *food tabulators*. In large businesses they might be given special job titles, such as *disbursement clerks, credit cashiers,* or *cash accounting clerks*.

In addition to handling money, theater box office cashiers might answer telephone inquiries and operate machines that dispense tickets and change. Restaurant cashiers might receive telephone calls for meal reservations and for special parties, keep the reservation book current, type the menu, stock the sales counter with candies and smoking supplies, and seat customers.

Department store or supermarket cashiers typically bag or wrap purchases. During slack periods they might price the merchandise, restock shelves, make out order forms, and perform other duties similar to those of food and beverage order clerks. Those employed as hotel cashiers usually keep accurate records of telephone charges and room-service bills to go on the customer's account. They might also be in charge of overseeing customers' safe deposit boxes, handling credit card billing, and notifying room clerks of customer checkouts.

Cashier supervisors, money-room supervisors, and *money counters* might act as cashiers for other cashiers—receiving and recording cash and sales slips from them and making sure their cash registers contain enough money to make change for customers. Other cashier positions include *gambling cashiers,* who buy and sell chips for cash; *parimutuel ticket cashiers and sellers,* who buy and sell betting tickets at race tracks; *paymasters of purses,* who are responsible for collecting money for and paying money to racehorse owners; and *auction clerks,* who are responsible for collecting money from winning bidders at auctions.

Requirements

Some employers require that cashiers be at least eighteen years old and a high school graduate. Employers might also prefer applicants with previous job experience, an ability to type, or a knowledge of elementary accounting. High school courses useful to cashiers include bookkeeping, typing, business machine operations, and business arithmetic.

Cashiers typically receive on-the-job training from experienced employees. In addition, some businesses have special training programs, providing information on the store's history, for example, as well as instruction on store procedures, security measures, and the use of equipment. For some kinds of more complicated cashier jobs, employers might prefer applicants who are graduates of a two-year community college or business school. Businesses often fill cashier positions by promoting existing employees, such as clerk-typists, baggers, and ushers.

Most cashiers have constant personal contact with the public. A pleasant disposition and a desire to serve the public are thus important qualities of a cashier. Cashiers must also be proficient with numbers and have good hand-eye coordination and finger dexterity. Accuracy is especially important.

Because they handle large sums of money, some cashiers must be able to meet the standards of bonding companies. Bonding companies evaluate applicants for risks and frequently fingerprint applicants for registration and background checks. Not all cashiers are required to be bonded, however.

In some areas cashiers are required to join a union, but fewer than 20 percent of cashiers are union members. Most union cashiers work in grocery stores and supermarkets and belong to the United Food and Commercial Workers International Union.

Opportunities for Experience & Exploration

Students can try to find part-time employment as cashiers, which will enable them to explore their interest and aptitude for this type of work. Related job experience can sometimes be obtained by working in the school bookstore or cafeteria or by participating in community activities, such as raffles and sales drives that require the handling of money. It can also be useful to talk with persons already employed as cashiers.

Methods of Entering

People generally enter this field by applying directly to the personnel directors of large businesses or to the managers or owners of small businesses. Applicants may learn of job openings through newspaper help wanted ads, through friends and business associates, or through school placement agencies. Private or state employment agencies can also help. Employers sometimes require that applicants provide personal references from schools or former employers attesting to their character and personal qualifications.

Advancement

Opportunities for advancement vary depending on the size and type of business, personal initiative, experience, and special training and skills. Cashier positions, for example, can provide people with the business skills to move into other types of clerical jobs or managerial positions. Opportunities for promotion are greater within larger firms than in small businesses or stores. Cashiers sometimes advance to cashier supervisors, shift leaders, division managers, or store managers. In hotels they might be able to advance to room clerks or related positions.

Employment Outlook

There are more than 3.1 million cashiers in the United States, though more than half work part time. Most work in supermarkets and grocery stores. Large numbers are also employed in department, drug, shoe, and other retail stores, and many work in restaurants, hotels, theaters, and hospitals. This occupation is expected to grow as fast as the average through the year 2006. Due to a high turnover rate among cashiers, many job openings will result from the need to replace workers leaving the field. Each year almost one-third of all cashiers leave their jobs for various reasons.

Cashier positions increased greatly during the 1970s and 1980s as businesses turned to modern merchandising methods, such as self-service operations. But most businesses likely to turn to self-service have already done so, and the growth in opportunities resulting from this change is expected to be minor.

Factors that could limit job growth include the increased installation of automatic change-making machines, vending machines, and other types of automatic and electronic equipment, which could decrease the number of cashiers needed in some business operations. Future job opportunities will be available to those experienced in bookkeeping, typing, business machine operations, and general office skills. Many part-time jobs should also be available. Though the majority of cashiers employed are 24 years of age or younger, many businesses have started hiring the elderly or disabled (of all ages) to fill some job openings.

Earnings

New cashiers with no experience are generally paid the minimum wage. Employers can pay workers younger than twenty years old a lower training wage for up to six months.

The median annual salary for cashiers, according to the *1998-99 Occupational Outlook Handbook,* is about $12,844. Most cashiers earn between $10,296 and $17,056 a year. Wages are generally higher for union workers, however. Experienced, full-time cashiers belonging to the United Food and Commercial Workers International Union average about $27,900 a year; beginners make much less, averaging about $5.90 per hour. Cashiers employed in restaurants generally earn less than those in other businesses.

Some cashiers, especially those working for large companies, receive health and life insurance, as well as paid vacations and sick days. Some are also offered employee retirement plans, or stock option plans. Cashiers are sometimes given merchandise discounts. Benefits are usually available only to full-time employees. Some employers try to save money by hiring part-time cashiers and not paying them benefits.

Conditions of Work

Cashiers sometimes work evenings, weekends, and holidays, when many people shop and go out for entertainment. The work of the cashier is usually not too strenuous, but employees often need to stand during most of their working hours. Cashiers must be able to work rapidly and under pressure during rush hours.

Most cashiers work indoors and in rooms that are well ventilated and well lighted. The work area itself, however, can be rather small and confining; cashiers typically work behind counters, in cages or booths, or in other small spaces. Work spaces for cashiers are frequently located near entrances and exits, so cashiers may be exposed to drafts.

Sources of Additional Information

■■■**National Retail Federation**
325 7th Street, NW, Suite 1000
Washington, DC 20004
Tel: 202-783-7971

Chiropractors

Definition

Chiropractors are health care providers who concern themselves with patients' total well-being but who treat mainly conditions of the nerves, muscles, and skeleton. The profession emphasizes prevention of disease through proper nutrition, exercise, stress management, and care of the nervous system.

Nature of the Work

The practice of chiropractic is based on the principle that one cause of many kinds of diseases is the impairment of nerve supply to organs and tissues. The network of nerves originates in the spine, reaching out to every part of the body and transmitting pain, pleasure, heat, cold—indeed, all the senses—to the brain. The core of the central nervous system is the spinal cord, which is protected by the backbone or spinal column, made up of vertebrae. These bones are gently manipulated to relieve pressure on the nerves that emerge between them, thus easing pain and discomfort. Chiropractic is considered preventive health care in that it is believed to increase resistance to disease.

Chiropractors treat orthopedic conditions such as backache, disc problems, sciatica, and whiplash. They also are sought out by patients with headaches, respiratory disorders, allergies, neuralgias, digestive disturbances, and other maladies. Unlike medical doctors who only address particular symptoms, chiropractors take a holistic approach to treatment, considering a patient's way of life. Chiropractors do not prescribe drugs or surgery.

Most chiropractors will take a general history of the patient's health to help determine diagnosis and treatment. Most also use X rays to help locate the source of patients' difficulties in the spine and joints. Chiropractors use their hands to move the spine and other joints while the patient is relaxed. In addition, chiropractors may use light, water, electrical stimulation, massage, heat, ultrasound, and biofeedback to relieve symptoms. They also prescribe diet, rest, exercise, and support of the afflicted body part. The chiropractor may prescribe things for the patient to do at home to maintain and improve the results of the manipulation.

Many people consult a chiropractor because they know someone else who has been successfully treated or because they do not wish to use drugs or have surgery if they can avoid it. About 10 percent of the adult population in the United States has visited chiropractors for treatment.

Often the treatment must be repeated over the course of several visits. On average, chiropractors receive 109 patient visits per week.

Chiropractors are not medical doctors, although general hospitals began accepting chiropractors as staff members in 1983. Most chiropractors, however, maintain offices in a professional building with other specialists or at their own clinics. In addition, they may serve on the staff of a hospital that specializes in chiropractic treatment or in alternative health care centers and clinics.

Requirements

Four years at an accredited chiropractic college, preceded by a minimum of two years undergraduate work, is expected of every prospective chiropractor. Increasingly, however, students of chiropractic are completing four years of undergraduate work instead of two. In preparation for a career in chiropractic, high school students should take math and as many science courses as possible, such as biology, chemistry, and physics.

Chiropractic colleges require undergraduate course work in biology, communications, English, inorganic and organic chemistry, physics, psychology, and social sciences or humanities. Upon completing undergraduate work and enrolling in a chiropractic college, a student can expect to find a vast array of science and medical courses. Students in their junior and senior years train in outpatient clinics affiliated with the college. The degree awarded upon completion of chiropractic training is Doctor of Chiropractic (D.C.).

Chiropractors must pass a state board examination to obtain a license to practice. Educational requirements and types of practice for which a chiropractor may be licensed vary from state to state. Most state boards recognize academic training only in chiropractic colleges accredited by the Council on Chiropractic Education.

Several states require that chiropractors pass a basic science examination. Most state boards will accept the National Board of Chiropractic Examiners' test given to fourth-year chiropractic students in place of a state exam. Chiropractors also must pass an examination for licensure. Most states require chiropractors take continuing education courses each year to keep their license.

The most important requirement in any health care profession is the desire to help people in need and to promote wholeness and health. Other required characteristics include ability to put patients at ease, good business sense, discipline, intelligence, manual skill, patience, professionalism, and sharp powers of observation.

Opportunities for Experience & Exploration

Students may obtain a part-time or summer job in a chiropractic clinic. Work in nursing homes or hospitals is also a valuable way to gain experience working with those in need of medical care.

Methods of Entering

A newly licensed chiropractor might begin working in a clinic or in an established practice with another chiropractor on a salary or income-sharing basis. This allows the chance to start practicing without the major financial investment of equipping an office.

Advancement

A chiropractor who started as a salaried employee in a large practice may eventually set up a new practice or purchase an established one. Chiropractors also may advance their careers by building their client rosters and setting up their own group practices. They also may decide to teach or conduct research.

Employment Outlook

Demand for chiropractors continues to grow as more health conscious people seek alternative forms of maintaining their health. With their holistic and personal approach to health care, chiropractors increasingly are taking the place of family physicians, especially in rural areas. And given chiropractors' preventative approach, more and more insurers are covering their services. Currently, many patients in health maintenance organizations receive insurance coverage of their chiropractic treatment only if they were referred to the chiropractor by another doctor within the HMO. Once HMOs allow direct access to chiropractic care, demand is expected to further increase.

Employment of chiropractors is expected to grow faster than the average rate for all professions through the year 2006. College enrollments are also growing, however, and new chiropractors may find it increasingly difficult to establish a practice where other practitioners already are located. Also, because of the high cost of equipment such as X ray and other diagnostic tools, group practices with other chiropractors or related health care professionals are likely to provide more opportunity for employment or for purchasing a share of a practice. This field sees very little turnover; most chiropractors stay in practice until retirement age.

Earnings

Chiropractors earn an average of $87,072 a year after expenses. New graduates, working as associates, start out earning about $30,000 a year. Experienced chiropractors may earn $200,000 or more per year.

Conditions of Work

According to a survey by the American Chiropractic Association, about 72 percent of chiropractors practice alone. About 25 percent work in a group or a partnership. Only a little over 3 percent are employed by other chiropractors. An even fewer number teach. About half the chiropractors work in communities of over fifty thousand people.

Chiropractors may take an office in a professional building or in their home. They can usually set their own hours. They work, on average, about forty hours per week, fifty weeks a year.

Chiropractic requires a keen sense of observation to diagnose a condition and determine appropriate treatment. Considerable hand dexterity is needed but exceptional strength is not. More important is sureness of movement and a genuine desire to help patients. Chiropractors should be able to work independently, handle responsibility, and be painstaking with detail. Sympathy and understanding are desirable for dealing effectively with patients

Sources of Additional Information

For general information and a career kit contact:

■ **American Chiropractic Association**
1701 Clarendon Boulevard
Arlington, VA 22209
Email: Amerchiro@aol.com
WWW: http://www.amerchiro.org

For information on educational requirements and accredited colleges, contact:

■ **Council on Chiropractic Education**
7975 North Hayden Road, Suite A-210
Scottsdale, AZ 50625

■ **International Chiropractors Association**
1110 North Glebe Road, Suite 1000
Arlington, VA 22201

For a list of chiropractic colleges in Canada, contact:

■ **Canadian Chiropractic Association**
1396 Eglinton Avenue West
Toronto, ON M6C 2E4 Canada

Clergy

Definition

Clergy are religious and spiritual leaders, as well as teachers and interpreters of their faith. They prepare and lead religious services, officiate special ceremonies such as marriage, baptism, and funerals, deliver sermons, read from sacred texts such as the *Bible, Talmud,* or *Koran,* and head religious education programs for their spiritual communities. Clergy members also visit the sick and poor, and offer spiritual and moral counsel to those that seek help. They are responsible for the administrative staff, as well as upkeep and management, of their church or temple.

Nature of the Work

Protestant ministers are the spiritual leaders of Protestant congregations. They interpret the tenets and doctrines of their faith and instruct people who seek conversion. Like other clergy, they lead their congregations in worship, supervise religious educational programs and Bible study, and teach confirmation and adult education courses. They may also play a role in preparing church newsletters and Sunday bulletins. They may answer telephone calls, written requests, or questions, or even counsel walk-in visitors requiring spiritual advice or practical aid such as food or shelter.

Some Protestant denominations or congregations within a denomination have a traditional order of service. Others require that the minister adapt the service to the specific needs of the congregation. Most Protestant services include Bible readings, hymn singing, prayers, and a sermon prepared and delivered by the minister.

Protestant clergy also administer specific church rites, such as baptism, holy communion, and confirmation. They conduct weddings and funerals.

Ministers advise couples concerning the vows and responsibilities of marriage. They may also act as marriage counselors for couples who are having marital difficulties. They visit the sick, comfort the bereaved, and participate in the administration of their parish or congregation.

In smaller churches, ministers may have close personal contact with all the members of the congregation. In larger congregations they may have greater administrative duties and therefore less contact with members of the congregation. Administrative duties may include heading or serving on committees that deal with building programs, fund-raising, member recruitment, event planning, and religious education. In addition, the minister may be involved in interdenominational and interfaith activities in the wider community. They frequently may be asked to give a blessing for a community happening, or make speeches at schools, clubs, or senior centers. Some ministers have become involved in social concerns such as human rights, abortion, poverty, race relations, and nuclear disarmament.

Ministers may share duties with an associate or with an assistant minister as well as other church staff. Some ministers teach in seminaries and other schools. Others write for publications and give speeches within the Protestant community and to those in the community at large. A growing number of ministers are employed only part-time and may serve more than one congregation or have a secular part-time job.

Roman Catholic priests are the spiritual leaders of Roman Catholic congregations. Like other clergy, they conduct services, give sermons, and help and counsel those in need. Priests administer the sacraments, such as baptism and communion. Priests usually begin the day with meditation and mass. They counsel those who are troubled and often visit the sick. Many priests involve themselves in the work of various church committees, civic and charitable organizations, and community projects. Some priests have become involved in concerns such as human rights and other nonliturgical issues. Others may teach in a variety of educational settings.

There are two categories of priests—*diocesan* and *religious*. All priests have the same powers bestowed on them through ordination by a bishop, but their way of life, the type of work they do, and the authority to whom they report depends on whether they are members of a religious order or working in a diocese. Diocesan, or *secular*, priests generally work in parishes to which they are assigned by their bishop. Religious priests, such as Dominicans, Jesuits, or Franciscans, work as members of a religious community, teaching, doing missionary work, or engaging in other specialized activities as assigned by their superiors. Both categories of priests teach and hold administrative positions in Catholic seminaries and educational institutions.

Diocesan priests usually work in parochial schools attached to parish churches and diocesan high schools. Most of the missionary work carried out by the Roman Catholic Church is carried out by members of religious orders.

Roman Catholic clergy do not choose their work assignments; this is done in collaboration with their religious superiors. Work assignments, however, are always made with the interests and abilities of the individual priest in mind. Every effort is made to place a priest in the type of ministry requested. Priests may serve in a wide range of ministries, from counseling full-time and working in social services to being chaplains in the armed forces, prisons, or hospitals.

Rabbis serve congregations affiliated with four movements of American Judaism: Orthodox, Conservative, Reform, and Reconstructionist. Regardless of their affiliation, all rabbis have similar responsibilities. They conduct religious services, officiate at weddings and funerals, help the needy, supervise religious educational programs, and teach confirmation and adult education courses. They also counsel members of their congregation and visit the sick.

Rabbis are the teachers of their community. They help congregants and other interested individuals apply religious teachings to their lives. Within Judaism the rabbi has an elevated status in spiritual matters, but most Jewish synagogues and temples have a relatively democratic form of decision making in which all members participate. Rabbis of large congregations spend much of their time working with their staffs and various committees. They often receive assistance from an associate or assistant rabbi.

The Jewish traditions differ somewhat in their view of God and of history. These differences also extend to such variations in worship as the wearing of head coverings, the amount of Hebrew used during prayer, the use of music, the level of congregational participation, and the status of women. Whatever their particular point of view, all Jewish congregations—Orthodox, Conservative, Reform, or Reconstructionist—preserve the substance of Jewish worship in a manner consistent with their beliefs.

In the Buddhist religion, clergy are referred to as *monks* and *priests*. Monks spend most of their time in meditation and prayer. Priests head temple ceremonies. Monks and priests give religious instruction and pastoral services for laypersons.

In the Hindu religion, *gurus* conduct ceremonies held in temples, and give religious instruction. Monks serve as pastors, and live in monasteries. *Sadhus*, or *sannyasis*, are wandering holy men that travel the country to spread the Hindu faith.

In the religion of Islam there is no ordained ministry or priesthood, although there are religious teachers, called *ulama*, or *mullahs*, and religious orders consisting of *sufis* (mystics) called *dervishes*.

Requirements

Educational requirements for the Protestant ministry vary depending on the denomination, the largest of which include the Baptists, Church of God in Christ, Episcopalians, Lutherans, Presbyterians, and United Methodists. Most denominations require some form of higher education before ordination. In general, the major Protestant denominations have their schools of theological training, but many of these schools admit students of other denominations. Professional study in these theological schools, of which there are about 150 in the United States and Canada, generally lasts about three years and leads to the degree of Master of Divinity. Doctor of Ministry degrees, as offered by some schools, is given after two years of more of additional study, plus two years of service as a minister. There are also several interdenominational colleges and theological schools that give training for the ministry. This may be augmented by training in the denomination in which the student will be ordained.

An undergraduate degree in the liberal arts is the typical college program for prospective clergy, although entrants come from a full range of academic backgrounds. Course work should include English, foreign languages, philosophy, the natural sciences, psychology, history, social sciences, comparative religions, as well as fine arts and music. Many churches encourage prospective candidates to the clergy to spend a few years in the secular world before entering the seminary, to get experience in both worlds.

Seminary curriculum generally covers four areas: history, theology, the *Bible,* and practical ministry techniques. Practical ministry techniques include counseling, preaching, church administration, and religious education. Besides classroom study and examinations, the seminary student serves at least one year as an intern to gain practical experience in leading services and other ministerial duties. Seminary students are eligible for scholarships and loans.

Protestant ministers must meet the requirements of their individual denomination. Both men and women can become ordained ministers in most denominations today. Not all Protestant denominations require seminary training for ordination. Some Evangelical churches, for example, may ordain people with only a high school diploma and *Bible* study.

Some high schools offer preparation for the priesthood, which is similar to that of a college preparatory high school. There are ten such high schools located in the United States, according to the U.S. Bishops Conference. High school seminary studies will focus on English, speech, literature, and social studies. Latin may or may not be required; the study of other foreign languages, such as Spanish, is encouraged. Other recommended high school courses include typing, debating, and music. Eight years of post-high school study are usually required to become an ordained priest. Candidates for the priesthood often choose to enter at the college level or begin their studies in theological seminaries after college graduation. There is a total of 198 seminaries in the United States—72 for diocesan priests; 126 for religious priests. The liberal arts program offered by seminary colleges stresses philosophy, religion, the behavioral sciences, history, the natural sciences, and mathematics. Some priestly formation programs may insist on seminarians majoring in philosophy.

The additional four years of preparation for ordination are given over entirely to the study of theology, including studies in moral (ethics) and pastoral and dogmatic (doctrine) theology. Other areas of study include church history, scripture, homiletics (the art of preaching), liturgy (worship), and canon (church) law. In the third year of advanced training, candidates undertake fieldwork in parishes and the general community. Because the work expected of secular and religious priests differs, they are trained in different major seminaries offering slightly varied programs.

Postgraduate work in theology and other fields is available and encouraged for priests, who may study in American Catholic universities or at ecclesiastical universities in Rome or other places around the world. Continuing education for ordained priests in the last several years has stressed sociology, psychology, and the natural sciences. All Catholic seminaries offer scholarships and grants to qualified students; no one is denied the chance to study for the priesthood because they cannot afford it.

In the Roman Catholic Church only men are ordained. All priests take the vow of celibacy and obedience, as required. Religious priests also take vows of chastity and poverty. Some orders take a special fourth vow, often related to the charism of their community; for example, vow of stability to stay in one place or monastery or the vow of silence for life.

Many aspiring rabbis begin their training early in life in Jewish grade schools and high schools. Others may not choose a rabbinical career until late in college or even later in life after having another career. Completion of a course of study in a seminary is a prerequisite for ordination as a rabbi. Entrance requirements, curriculum, and length of the program vary depending on the particular branch of Judaism. Prospective rabbis normally need to complete an undergraduate degree before entering the seminary. There are about thirty-five Orthodox seminaries in the United States. The two largest are the Rabbi Isaac Elchanan Theological Seminary (an affiliate of Yeshiva University) and the Hebrew Theological College. Both offer a formal four-year program and require a bachelor's degree for entry. Other seminaries have no formal requirements but may require more years of study before ordination. Normally, students entering an Orthodox seminary have had previous course work in Jewish practices and concepts. To be ordained, students must have the approval of an authorized rabbi acting either independently or as a representative of a seminary.

Students admitted to the rabbinical program at the Jewish Theological Seminary of America, which is the seminary for Conservative rabbis, or the Hebrew Union College-Jewish Institute of Religion, which is the seminary for Reform rabbis, not only must have received an undergraduate degree but must have received preparatory training in Jewish studies. The program at the Conservative seminary can be completed in four years by a student with a strong background in Jewish studies; otherwise, ordination may take up to six years. Rabbinical studies at the Reform seminary generally require five years, with an additional year of preparatory work for students lacking sufficient background in Hebrew and Jewish studies. This general training may include field work, internship, or study in Jerusalem. Graduates of seminary schools are given the title Rabbi, along with a Master of Arts in Hebrew Letters. The degree Doctor of Hebrew Letters is awarded after more advanced study.

The program at the Reconstructionist Rabbinical College, Judaism's newest branch of worship, generally lasts five years and, moreover, requires a bachelor's degree for admission. Each year of study emphasizes a different period of Jewish civilization.

The general curriculum of ordination for all branches of Judaism includes courses in the *Bible*, the *Talmud* (post-Biblical writings), rabbinic literature, Hebrew philosophy, Jewish history, and theology. Students should expect to study Hebrew for both verbal and written skills. Many rabbis are fluent in Hebrew. Courses are also offered in education, public speaking, and pastoral psychology. Training for leadership in community service and religious education is also being stressed as an alternative to the pulpit. All Jewish theological seminaries offer scholarships and loans to qualified students.

Those interested in clergyhood should possess a strong religious faith, coupled with the idea that they have received a special call from God to serve and help others. All other interests and potential vocations should be considered secondary to this call. Clergy need to be outgoing and friendly, and have a strong desire to help others. They need to be able to get along with people from a wide variety of backgrounds. They should have patience, sympathy, and open-mindedness to be able to listen to the problems of others, while maintaining a discreet and sincere respect for the problems of others. They need leadership abilities, including self-confidence, decisiveness, and the ability to supervise others. All clergy members must be aware that they will be relied on heavily by their congregation in times of trouble and stress, therefore making it more important they keep the needs of their family balanced with that of the congregation.

Opportunities for Experience & Exploration

People interested in becoming a minister should talk with their own minister and others involved in the work of the church to get a clear idea of the rewards and responsibilities of this profession. Choosing a career as a minister entails much thought. There are numerous opportunities to investigate congregational life. Aspiring ministers would be wise to volunteer at a church or other religious institution to get better acquainted with the type of job responsibilities a minister has. Volunteer work can include teaching Sunday school or running guidance sessions. Essentially, however, there is no single experience that can adequately prepare a person for the demands of being a minister. Seminary training should offer the best opportunity to explore the many facets of the ministry.

People interested in the priesthood, joining a religious order, or becoming involved in religious work should talk with their parish priest and others involved in the work of the church to get a clearer idea of the rewards and responsibilities of this profession. Choosing a career as a priest entails much thought to the demands of this profession. There are numerous opportunities for those interested to investigate parish life.

Aspiring priests may wish to volunteer at a church or other religious institution to get better acquainted with the type of responsibilities a priest has. Those interested in becoming a religious priest may choose to spend considerable amounts of time in a monastery. Many monasteries are open to the public for weekend or even week-long retreats. Post-high school seminary training may also offer an opportunity to explore the many facets of the priesthood. Despite these opportunities, no single experience can adequately prepare a person for the vocation of being a priest. For information on seminaries and religious orders, contact the diocesan office in your area.

Those interested in becoming a rabbi should talk with their own rabbi and others involved in the work of the synagogue or temple to get a clearer idea of the rewards and responsibilities of this profession. Choosing a career as a rabbi requires a good deal of thought as to the demands of this profession. There are numerous opportunities for those interested to investigate congregational life.

Aspiring rabbis may volunteer at a temple or synagogue to get better acquainted with the type of job responsibilities a rabbi has. Seminary training offers the best opportunity to explore many of the facets of a rabbinical career.

Advancement

Newly ordained ministers generally begin their careers as pastors of small congregations or as assistant pastors (curates) in larger congregations. From there, advancement depends on individual interests, abilities, and available positions.

Newly ordained diocesan priests generally begin their ministry as associate pastors, while new priests of religious orders are assigned duties for which they are specially trained, such as missionary work. Priests may also become teachers in seminaries and other educational institutions, or chaplains in the armed forces. The pulpits of large, well-established churches are usually filled by priests of considerable experience. A small number of priests become bishops, archbishops, and cardinals. Only cardinals can be elevated to the position of Pope.

Newly ordained rabbis generally begin their careers as leaders of small congregations, assistants to experienced rabbis, directors of Hillel foundations on college campuses, teachers in seminaries and other educational institutions, or chaplains in the armed forces. With experience, they may acquire their own or larger congregations or choose to remain in their original position. The pulpits of large, well-established synagogues and temples are usually filled by rabbis of considerable experience. They may also choose to open new synagogues in growing communities that require more religious facilities. Others may discover that their talents and abilities are most useful in teaching, fund-raising,

or leadership positions within their particular denomination.

Employment Outlook

Three hundred thousand Protestant clergy were employed in the United States in 1996, according to the National Council of Churches, the majority of which were associated with the five largest Protestant denominations. Employment opportunities for paid Protestant clergy should stay competitive through the year 2006. Slow growth of church membership, and the large number of qualified candidates are factors for this projection. An aging membership, smaller church budgets, and the closing or combining of smaller parishes, have lessened the demand for full time ministers. Graduates of theological schools, or those willing to relocate to rural areas, stand the best chance for employment.

According to the *Official Catholic Directory*, there were 49,000 priests employed in 1996; two-thirds of which were diocesan priests. Most priests were employed in metropolitan areas housing a large Catholic population. Employment opportunities for priests through the year 2006 are favorable. The Catholic Church is currently facing a severe shortage of priests. The Catholic population, currently 50 million, continues to steadily grow, while the number students entering the seminary decreases and more priests reach retirement age. The needs of newly established parishes and Catholic institutions are far greater than the number of ordained priests.

As a result of the continuing shortage of priests, over 10,000 deacons have been ordained to preach, baptize, perform Holy Communion, and other sacraments. Saying mass and hearing confessions are the only duties that deacons may not perform. Lay people, called *Eucharistic Ministers*, give Holy Communion and assist priests and deacons in other ways. As a result, future priests may become less involved in teaching and administrative functions to devote themselves to other duties. There has also been limited debate regarding short-term commitments to the priestly life, as well as women in the priesthood, as a way of attracting more interest in the vocation.

In the past years, slow enrollment figures in Jewish seminaries, more rabbis reaching retirement age, and strong growth within the Jewish community are indications of good employment opportunities for new rabbis. Reconstructionist rabbis should find very good opportunities as membership to this branch expands. In 1996, there were 1,800 Reform rabbis, 1,250 Conservative rabbis, 1,000 Orthodox, and 250 Reconstructionist rabbis. Orthodox seminaries only accept men, but all other denominations accept men and women into the rabbinate. Most rabbis work in states with large Jewish populations, including New York, Florida, New Jersey, Illinois, and Ohio, among others. Opportunities exist in Jewish communities throughout the country. Small communities in the South, Midwest, and Northwest will offer the best opportunities for those rabbis who do not mind receiving less compensation, and working away from large metropolitan areas.

Protestant ministers, Catholic priests, and rabbis, and other religious clergy may choose to serve as chaplains in the Armed Forces, hospitals, colleges, universities, prisons, community service, or homes for the mentally retarded.

Earnings

It should be noted that becoming a member of the clergy is not only a career, but a life choice as well. All clergy enter this profession to spread and teach their faith—reward comes in the form of being able to help others.

Salaries vary substantially for Protestant clergy depending on the individual's experience, as well as the size of the congregation, its denominational branch, location, and financial status. The estimated average income of ministers is about $30,000 per year, though ministers employed in larger, wealthier denominations earn more. Some ministers of smaller congregations may add to their earnings by working at part-time secular jobs.

Religious priests take a vow of poverty and are supported by their religious order. Any salary that they may receive for writing or other activities is usually returned to their religious order. Diocesan priests receive small salaries calculated to cover their basic needs. These salaries vary according to the size of the parish, as well as its location and financial status, and average approximately $11,000 per year. Priests who teach or do specialized work usually receive a small stipend, often referred to as "contributed service," that is equal to that paid to lay persons in similar positions. Priests who serve in the Armed Forces receive the same amount of pay as other officers of equal rank. The Internal Revenue Service recognizes the vow of poverty and does not require priests to pay Federal income tax.

Salaries for rabbis vary according to the size, denominational branch, location, and financial status of the congregation. According to limited information in the *1998-99 Occupational Outlook Handbook,* the earnings of rabbis ranged from $45,000 to $75,000. Smaller congregations pay less, usually between $35,000 and $50,000 a year. Some congregations may allow their rabbi to teach at local universities or other settings to earn additional income.

Additional benefits for ministers, priests and rabbis, usually include a housing stipend, which includes utilities, a monthly transportation allowance, health insurance and retirement fund. Some receive travel stipends for research and rest. Protestant ministers may receive grants for the education of their children. Clergy often are given a monetary gift when they officiate at weddings, funerals, and other ceremonies of life. This is sometimes donated to the church or a charity by clergy. Rabbis often receive gifts for officiating at bar mitzvahs.

Conditions of Work

Clergy spend long hours working under a variety of conditions. There is no such thing as a standard work week. They are on call at any hour of the day or night, sometimes, in the case of ministers and rabbis, interfering with their own family life. They visit the sick, comfort and counsel families in times of crisis, and help raise funds for the church. Much time is also spent reading, studying, writing, attending and chairing meetings, and talking to people. They also must prepare sermons and keep up with religious and secular events. Clergy may also have many administrative responsibilities working with staff and various committees. They also participate in community and interfaith events.

Despite the long hours and sometimes stressful and demanding work conditions, most clergy enjoy their work and find helping and administering to their congregation a satisfying occupation. The public in general and congregations in particular expect clergy members to set high examples of moral and ethical conduct. There is the added pressure of being "on call" twenty-four hours a day, and the need to often comfort people in difficult situations.

Protestant ministers may be reassigned to a new pastorate by a central governing body. Rabbis are generally independent in their positions, responsible only to the board of directors of their congregation rather than to any formal hierarchy. Religious priests are responsible to the superior of their order, the bishop in the diocese that they work, as well as the Supreme Pontiff of the Catholic Church, the Pope.

Sources of Additional Information

For information concerning the work of military chaplains, contact:

■**National Conference on Ministry to the Armed Forces**
4141 North Henderson Road, Suite 13
Arlington, VA 22203
Tel: 703-276-7905

For information regarding a career as a Roman Catholic priest, contact the following organizations:

■**Canadian Conference of Catholic Bishops**
90 Parent Avenue
Ottawa, ON K1N 7B1 Canada

■**National Federation of Priests' Councils**
1337 West Ohio Street
Chicago, IL 60622-6409
Tel: 312-226-3334
Email: nfpc@nfpc.org
WWW: http://www.nfpc.org

■**National Assembly of Religious Brothers**
1337 West Ohio Street
Chicago, IL 60622-6409
Tel: 312-829-8525

The minister or church guidance worker of a denomination in which a person is interested can provide information on requirements for the ministry. Seminaries can give a prospective student information on admission and ordination requirements. Career information about the Protestant ministry is available from:

■**National Council of Churches**
Professional Church Leadership
110 Maryland Avenue, NE
Washington, DC 20002
Tel: 202-544-2350
WWW: http://www.ncl.org/anr/partners/ncounch.htm

For information regarding a career as a rabbi, contact the following organizations:

■**Rabbinical Council of America**
305 Seventh Avenue
New York, NY 10001
Tel: 212-807-7888
WWW: http://www.ou.org/rca

■**American Association of Rabbis**
350 Fifth Avenue, Suite 3304
New York, NY 10118
Tel: 212-244-3350

■**Hebrew Union College-Jewish Institute of Religion**
National Office of Admissions
3101 Clifton Avenue
Cincinnati, OH 45220-2488
Tel: 513-221-1875
WWW: http://www.huc.edu

■**Federation of Reconstructionist Congregations and Havurot (FRCH)**
1299 Church Road
Wyncote, PA 19095
Tel: 215-887-1988

Information about seminary school and career information is available from:

■**Jewish Theological Seminary of America**
3080 Broadway
New York, NY 10027
Tel: 212-678-8000
WWW: http://www.jtsa.edu

College and University Professors

Definition

College or university faculty members instruct undergraduate and graduate students in specific subjects. They are responsible for lecturing classes, leading small seminar groups, and creating and grading examinations. They also may carry on research, write for publication, and aid in administration.

Nature of the Work

College and university faculty members teach at junior colleges or at four-year colleges and universities. At four-year institutions, most faculty members are either *assistant professors, associate professors*, or *full professors*. These three types of professorships differ in regards to status, job responsibilities, and salary. Assistant professors are new faculty members who are working to get tenure—status as a permanent professor.

College and university faculty members have three main functions to perform. Their first and most important job is to teach the students. Most college and university teachers are in class approximately nine to twelve hours each week. However, they may put in two hours of preparation for every hour spent in class so the actual time devoted to teaching responsibilities may be approximately thirty-six to forty hours each week. Depending upon the institution, associate professors and full professors may spend only six to eight hours a week in actual classroom work.

The standard teaching technique for college and university faculty members is the lecture method. Many other methods are also used, however. In some courses, teachers rely heavily on laboratories to transmit course material. Some prefer class discussion or use visual aids to instruct students.

Many combine all methods or go from one to the other.

Another important responsibility of the college and university faculty member is the advising of students. Not all faculty members serve as advisers, but those who do must set aside a large block of time to see the students for whose program they are responsible. *Faculty advisers* may have any number of students assigned to them, from fewer than ten to more than one hundred, depending on the amount of responsibility that the adviser is expected to assume and the administrative policies of the college in which they work. Their responsibility for the student may involve looking over a planned program of studies to make sure that students meet requirements for graduation, or it may involve working intensively with each student on many aspects of college life.

The third responsibility of college and university faculty members is research and publication. Faculty members who are heavily involved in research programs sometimes are assigned a smaller teaching load than those who are not so involved. Most faculty members who do research publish their findings in various scholarly journals. They also write books based on research findings or on their own knowledge and experience in their field. Most textbooks are written by college and university teachers.

Publishing a significant amount of work has been the traditional standard by which assistant professors prove themselves worthy of becoming permanent, tenured faculty, and so typically, pressure to publish is greatest for assistant professors, especially those who work at research universities. Pressure to publish increases again if an associate professor wishes to be considered for a promotion to full professorship.

In recent years, some liberal arts colleges have recognized that the pressure to publish is taking faculty away from their primary duties to the students, and these institutions have begun to place a decreasing emphasis for tenure on publishing and more on performance in the classroom. For the same reason, some larger universities have divided their faculty into research and teaching divisions, thereby keeping up with the research standards of other institutions while maintaining excellence in the classroom. Professors in junior colleges face less pressure to publish than those in four-year institutions.

Some faculty members eventually rise to the position of *department chair,* where they govern the affairs of an entire department, such as English, mathematics, or biological sciences.

Department chairs, faculty, and other professional staff members are aided in their myriad duties by *graduate assistants,* who may help develop teaching materials, conduct research, give examinations, teach lower-level courses, and carry out other activities.

Some college and university faculty members are *extension work instructors.* This means that they conduct classes at times and places other than the normal ones for the benefit of people who otherwise would not be able to take advantage of the institution's resources. They may teach evening or weekend courses. They may travel away from the campus and meet with a group of students at another location. The teacher may work in the extension division entirely and meet all classes off campus, or may divide the time between on-campus and off-campus teaching.

An extension work instructor may give instruction by correspondence to certain students who are unable to come to the campus at that time. Correspondence courses usually are available only to undergraduate students. There may be a standard course of study for the subject, and the teacher's responsibility may be primarily to grade the papers that the student sends in at periodic intervals and to advise the student of progress. The teacher may perform this service in addition to other duties or may be assigned to correspondence work as a major teaching responsibility.

The teacher in the junior college has many of the same kinds of responsibilities as does the teacher in the four-year college or university. Because junior colleges offer only a two-year program, the faculty member will teach only undergraduates and will not be concerned with tutorial methods that must be employed when working with graduate students.

Requirements

At least one advanced degree is required to be a teacher in a college or university. The master's degree is considered the minimum standard, and graduate work beyond the master's is usually desirable. A doctorate is required to advance in academic rank above instructor in most institutions.

The faculty member in a junior college may be employed with only a master's degree. Advancement in responsibility and in salary, however, are more likely to come to those who have earned a doctorate. A number of states that maintain public junior colleges require state certification for teaching in these schools. A faculty member must have completed the master's degree and certain courses in education to qualify.

High school students interested in college teaching should enroll in college-preparatory courses in a wide variety of subjects. This broad background is necessary for students to be able to make an informed decision when selecting a specialty later.

Opportunities for Experience & Exploration

One way for high school students to gain exposure to the field is to visit the campuses of colleges and universities and seek permission to visit classes or to talk with some of the faculty members. Another good means of exploration is to attend college fairs, often held in large cities, where representatives from colleges and universities are available to describe their institutions and teaching programs.

Methods of Entering

Your school's placement office will have a list of teaching vacancies in your field. You may choose from among the positions available and apply to one or to several colleges. For most positions at four-year institutions, job applicants must travel to large conferences where they are interviewed by several professors from the universities to which they have applied.

Professors of the graduate students will often know of vacancies on the faculties of other colleges and universities. Many graduate students find positions because of the professional connections of the faculty members under whom they have studied.

Some professional associations maintain lists of teaching opportunities in their areas. They may also make lists of applicants available to college administrators looking to fill an available position.

Advancement

The usual advancement pattern for the college teacher is from instructor, to assistant professor, to associate professor, to full professor. All four academic ranks are concerned primarily with teaching and research. College faculty members who have an interest in and a talent for administration may be advanced to chair of department, or to dean of their college. A few become college or university presidents or other types of administrators.

The instructor is usually an inexperienced college teacher. He or she may hold a doctorate or may have completed all the requirements for one except for the dissertation. Most colleges look upon the rank of instructor as the period during which the college is trying the teacher out. Instructors usually are advanced to the position of assistant professors within three to four years. Assistant professors are given up to about six years to prove themselves worthy of tenure, and if they do so, they become associate professors. Some professors choose to remain at the associate level. Others strive to become full professors and receive greater status, salary, and responsibilities.

Most colleges have clearly understood promotion policies from rank to rank for faculty members and many have written statements about the number of years in which instructors and assistant professors may remain in grade. Administrators in many colleges hope to encourage younger faculty members to increase their skills and competencies and thus to qualify for the more responsible positions of associate professor and full professor.

Employment Outlook

This occupation is expected to grow about as fast as the average through the year 2006. There were 864,000 faculty members employed in American colleges and universities in 1996. This figure includes instructors and adjunct, or part-time, professors, as well as assistant, associate, and full professors.

In the past, cuts in budgets and grant money caused stiff competition for teaching jobs at the college and university level. However, experts are predicting a large increase in college and university enrollment as the baby boom "echo" generation—the children of baby boomers—will reach college age. Also, more nontraditional students will strive for higher education. These trends will warrant the demand for more qualified instructors.

Many job openings will be created by professors retiring or perhaps leaving the field for non-academic employment. The best employment opportunities for college and university faculty members will be in the departments of engineering, computer science, the health and physical sciences, and mathematics.

Earnings

The average faculty member works for a period of nine or ten months a year, and the stated salary is for that period. Professors may earn additional salary by teaching in summer school or by spending the summer writing for publications, working as a consultant, conducting research projects, or performing other income-producing work.

According to a 1995-96 survey conducted by the American Society of University Professors, full professors earned an average salary of $65,400; associate professors, $48,300; assistant professors, $40,100; and instructors, $30,800. The average salary for the entire field was $51,000. The salaries vary widely according to faculty rank and type of institution. Faculty members in public colleges and universities generally have higher salaries, averaging about $57,500, compared to a yearly average of $45,200 for those employed at a school with a religious affiliation. Private institutions paid their faculty the most—an average of $57,500 a year. Faculty members in four-year schools average higher salaries than those in two-year institutions. Subject matter is another salary factor. Professors who teach courses in the fields of medicine, law, or engineering, for example, earn more than those teaching humanities and education.

Most colleges and universities offer retirement and insurance plans, paid sabbaticals, free tuition for family members, and travel allowances for full time professors. Some also offer faculty housing. Occasionally, this housing is without cost; usually there is a modest rental fee.

Conditions of Work

A college or university is usually a pleasant place in which to work. Campuses bustle with all types of activities and events, stimulating ideas, and a young, energetic population.

The college or university faculty member will often have to share an office with one or more colleagues. Professors seldom have a private secretary, but will share secretarial service with one or several fellow faculty members.

Except for their time in class, the established office hours when they meet with students, and the time needed for their academic meetings, college faculty members' time may be arranged as they see fit. They may spend time in study, in research, or in the laboratory. College faculty members establish their own patterns of work, according to their own special needs and interests. Most college teachers work more than forty hours each week. Although the time spent in class may require only a fraction of the normal working week, college teachers' many additional duties and interests will keep them on the job a great many hours beyond what is generally considered to be an average working period.

Sources of Additional Information

■■**American Federation of Teachers**
555 New Jersey Avenue, NW
Washington, DC 20001
Tel: 202-879-4400

Computer and Office Machine Service Technicians

Definition

Computer and office machine service technicians install, calibrate, maintain, troubleshoot, and repair equipment such as computers, printers, copy machines, adding machines, typewriters, fax machines, mail sorters, VCRs, and monitors. Their primary duty is to diagnose problems caused by mechanical and electronic malfunctions and ensure that computers and machines are running properly at all times.

Nature of the Work

Businesses use computers and office machines in order to perform normal business tasks more efficiently and accurately. Like other machines, computers and office machines require careful installation and regular preventive maintenance to run properly. And, like other machines, computers and office machines sometimes function poorly or break down entirely. Computer or machine "down time" can be extremely expensive for many companies, and a great nuisance to others. Computer and office machine service technicians are responsible for ensuring that machines function well at all times.

Most technicians, or *servicers* as they are sometimes called, perform the same basic duties: they install, calibrate, clean, maintain, troubleshoot, and repair machines. Servicers differ primarily in regard to the kinds of machines they are trained to work on and the nature and scope of their employer.

Service technicians who work in specialized repair shops are usually experts in fixing one or two types of machines. For example, a servicer might specialize in working on color laser printers or color copiers. Or he or she might be trained to work on communications technology products such as fax machines and modems. Other repair specialties include mail-processing equipment servicers and cash register servicers.

As the use of computers, computer peripherals, and computerized office machinery expands at a rapid pace, some technicians are finding they can make more money and have better job security if they are well trained in the installation, maintenance, and repair of these kinds of machines. Many large computer companies, whether manufacturers, servicers, or retailers, provide service contracts with the purchase of their products. They hire computer service technicians to fulfill service contract obligations. Computer service technicians provide a wide range of services. They install and set up computer equipment when it first arrives at the client's office. Later, they follow up installation with a series of preventative maintenance calls to make sure the computers are performing well. In addition, some technicians are always on call in case of emergency breakdown problems. Relying on their background knowledge of the product and diagnostic tests using special instruments, they are able to diagnose the nature and extent of the problem and repair the machines relatively quickly. They are usually trained in replacing semiconductor chips, circuit boards, and other hardware components. If they are unable to fix the computer on site, they bring it back to their employer's service area.

Some technicians are employed in the maintenance department of large companies. Since there are typically many different kinds of machines in such companies, these technicians generally have a very good working knowledge of mechanical as well as electronic equipment. They receive extra training on specific equipment the business uses most often. In addition, they participate in training seminars conducted by the manufacturers of new equipment the business buys or leases.

Field service technicians usually work for specialty repair shops, machine manufacturers, or product-specific service companies. They are technicians who travel to the customer's workplace to do maintenance and repairs. They often follow a predetermined schedule for machine maintenance. For example, they might change the toner, clean the optic parts, and make mechanical adjustments to copiers and printers. They also have to make time each day to respond to incoming requests for emergency service. Even though supervisors prioritize maintenance and repair calls, field service technicians often have a hectic schedule involving a variety and large number of duties. In addition to performing the service, technicians are required to keep detailed written explanations of all service provided so that future problems can be dealt with more effectively.

When machines require service that is too complicated or messy to be dealt with in the customer's office, they are brought back to the repair shop or company service center to be worked on by bench servicers. Bench servicers are technicians that work primarily at their employer's location.

Some very experienced servicers open their own shops. These entrepreneurs often find it necessary to service a wide range of products in order to be successful, particularly when competition is tight. To further supplement their incomes, they might start selling certain products and offering service contracts on them. Business owners have the added responsibility of business duties, such as bookkeeping and advertising.

Requirements

Computer and office machine service technicians must have a strong technical background and an aptitude for learning about new technologies, good communications skills, and superior manual dexterity. A high school diploma is the minimum requirement for pursuing a career in this field. Traditional high school courses such as mathematics, physical sciences, and other laboratory-based sciences can provide a strong foundation for understanding basic mechanical and electronic principles. English and speech classes can help boost both written and verbal communications skills.

More specialized courses offered at the high school level, such as electronics, electricity, automotive/engine repair, or computer applications provide the opportunity to increase understanding of how machines work and gain hands-on experience with them. Any other courses or clubs that make use of flow charts, schematic reading, or audiovisual equipment can also be beneficial.

Since technology changes so quickly, some post-secondary education is recommended for newcomers to this field. Educational requirements vary across employers. Small repair shops, for example, might only require in-depth knowledge and some experience, which an individual could obtain on his or her own. Large corporations or computer companies, however, usually require at least one or two years of courses in mechanics or electronics from a city college or technical/vocational school.

Individuals interested in computer and peripheral repair should choose courses involving the nuts and bolts of computer technology (not just computer software applications), such as microelectronics and computer design. Some technical schools offer two-year degrees in computer technology. While some office machine service technicians can find jobs without a two-year degree, a computer-related two-year degree is required for technicians seeking to specialize in computer repair. The additional educational requirements include courses in elementary computer programming and the physics of heat and light.

Certification is not required by most employers of service technicians, but voluntary certification programs do exist through the International Society of Certified Electronics Technicians and the Institute for Certification of Computing Professionals. Individuals can take exams in order to be certified in fields such as computer, industrial, and commercial equipment. Although not required, voluntary certification can give an individual an edge if job competition is tight.

Regardless of educational background, service technicians receive heavy doses of on-the-job training aimed at familiarizing employees with the machines most often used by the company or its customers. Training programs vary greatly in duration and intensity. Some are self-study while others are conducted in classrooms. Most include both theoretical and more practical, hands-on sessions.

Computer and office machine technicians have to be motivated to keep up with modern computer and office machine technology. Machines rapidly become obsolete, and so does the service technician's training. As soon as new equipment is installed, service technicians must demonstrate the intellectual agility to learn how to handle problems that might arise.

Opportunities for Experience & Exploration

Students interested in a career in computer and office machine service should investigate the possibility of spending a day at a local technical school attending mechanics or electronics courses. This experience might help students develop a better feel for the specific content of the career and determine their interest level in it. Students should also seek the help of a guidance counselor in arranging an on-the-job visit with a working service technician. In this way, students can see firsthand what the ins and outs of a typical day in this career might be. In addition, they might volunteer to tinker around with household machines, such as VCRs or car engines, to test their manual aptitude for such maintenance and repair. Students might decide to take related courses in high school and even at technical schools during summer vacations.

Methods of Entering

Graduates of city colleges or technical/vocational schools often find their first positions through the school's placement center. Employers regularly work directly with placement officers in order to find the best qualified service technicians. Other qualified individuals can identify potential employers by reading the classified ads. They can then write, call, or visit these companies in order to obtain an interview. Voluntary certification, as previously discussed, can boost an individual's chances of obtaining an interview. Prospective servicers should ask friends and family to watch for related job openings in their companies. Individuals already working as servicers can also be good sources of information about job openings.

Experience is an extremely important qualification to have in the job-hunting process. Prospective service technicians should try to gain experience in small, local repair shops by working after school, on weekends, or during summer vacations. Another way to expand technical experience is by volunteering to repair friends' and relatives' household appliances. These kinds of experience round out job applicants' qualifications and make them more attractive to employers.

Advancement

The field of computer and office machine service offers a variety of advancement opportunities, particularly because of the tremendous growth in computer products. Service technicians usually start working on relatively simple maintenance and repair tasks. Over time, they start working on more complicated projects.

Experienced service technicians may advance to positions of increased responsibility. They become supervisors of service crews or managers of service departments or small service companies. This type of promotion is usually reserved for individuals with strong communications skills; supervisors and managers talk at length with both servicers and customers, each of whom understand the products at very different levels. Supervisors and managers also have strong organizational and prioritizing skills and generally have had service experience in a wide range of areas.

Another advancement route a service technician may take is to become a *sales representative* for the manufacturer of a company whose product he or she has had extensive experience with. Technicians develop hands-on knowledge of particular machines and are thus often in the best position to advise potential buyers about important purchasing decisions.

Some entrepreneurial-minded servicers might open their own repair business, which can be risky but can also provide many rewards. Unless they fill a certain market niche, technicians usually find it necessary to service a wide range of computers and office machines.

Employment Outlook

Demand for computer service technicians is expected to increase much faster than average through the year 2006. Employment of office machine repairers is expected to grow about as fast as the average for all occupations through the year 2006.

While demand for computer and office machine service technicians will be higher than the national average, it is predicted that employment growth will not match the expected increase in the amount of equipment produced. This is a result of the increased reliability of the equipment, as well as the ease of its repair.

Large corporations with in-house repair departments will increase their demand for well-rounded servicers, those who can maintain and repair computers as well as office machines. Computer companies and service contractors will look for people with strong computer backgrounds in education or professional experience.

The key for individuals interested in this field: keep up with technology and be flexible.

Earnings

According to the Bureau of Labor Statistics, in 1996, average annual earnings for electronic equipment repairers ranged from a low of $17,108 to $50,908 for technicians who generally have many years of experience.Office machine repairers earned average salaries of $30,264 per year in 1996, according to the 1998-99 Occupational Outlook Handbook. Technicians who develop expertise in certain machinery or product lines may make even more. Within this range, servicers who specialize in computers and computer-related equipment tend to make the most money in this field. Simply put, the highest salaries go to those who work on the most complicated machines.

Service technicians who work for computer companies or large corporations usually enjoy benefits such as health care, sick leave, and paid vacations. The benefits of employees of smaller businesses vary with the employer. In addition, some service technicians have the opportunity to earn bonuses by selling service contracts or for consistently high performance.

Conditions of Work

Working conditions are generally good for computer and office machine service technicians since most equipment is located in air-conditioned, well-lighted, and comfortable environments. However, some of the bigger machinery, such as mail sorters or check-processing units, can be noisy and some maintenance and repair work can be messy, involving grease and oil. In these cases, servicers wear work uniforms, often provided by employers, or their own casual clothes. The most strenuous labor usually involves moving the bigger machines around during installation or overhauls. In some instances, servicers are required to work around extremely high voltages and must know related safety procedures and regulations. Field servicers often travel from one location to another to perform their duties, usually by car. Others work primarily in their service centers.

Many service technicians work during regular business hours. In certain service departments, servicers take turns being on call during off-hours in case of requests for emergency service. When major installation and repair projects are being completed, some servicers may be required to work overtime. On-call hours and overtime are compensated, either by extra paid vacation or increased hourly wages.

Sources of Additional Information

For information about certification in the field of computer and office machine service, contact:

Institute for the Certification of Computing Professionals
2200 East Devon Avenue, Suite 247
Des Plaines, IL 60018
Tel: 847-229-4227

International Society of Certified Electronics Technicians
2708 West Berry Street, Suite 3
Fort Worth, TX 76109-2356
Tel: 817-921-9101
WWW: http://www.iscet.mainland.cc.tx.us

For information about computer and office machine service careers, accredited schools, and employers, contact:

Association for Computing Machinery
1515 Broadway
New York, NY 10036
Tel: 212-869-7440
Email: acmhelp@acm.org
WWW: http://www.info.acm.org/

Electronics Technicians Association, International
602 North Jackson Street
Greencastle, IN 46135
Tel: 317-653-8262
WWW: http://www.serv2.fwi.com/~n9pdt

Computer Programmers

Definition

Computer programmers work in the field of electronic data processing. They write instructions that tell computers what to do in a computer language, or code, that the computer understands. *Systems programmers* specialize in maintaining the general instructions that control an entire computer system. Maintenance tasks include giving computers instructions on how to allocate time to various jobs they receive from computer terminals and making sure that these assignments are performed properly.

Nature of the Work

Broadly speaking, there are two types of computer programmers: systems programmers and *applications programmers*. Systems programmers maintain the instructions, called programs or software, that control the entire computer system, including both the central processing unit and the equipment with which it communicates, such as terminals, printers, and disk drives. Applications programmers write the software to handle specific jobs and may specialize as engineering and scientific programmers or as business programmers. Some of the latter specialists may be designated chief business programmers, who supervise the work of other business programmers.

Programmers are often given program specifications, prepared by systems analysts, which list in detail the steps the computer must follow in order to complete a given task. Programmers then code these instructions in a computer language the computer understands. In smaller companies, analysis and programming may be handled by the same person, called a *programmer-analyst*.

Before actually writing the computer program, a programmer must analyze the work request, understand the current problem and desired resolution, decide on an approach to use in order to attack the problem, and plan what the machine will have to do to produce the required results. Programmers prepare a flow chart to show the steps in sequence that the machine must make. They must pay attention to minute detail and instruct the machine in each step of the process.

These instructions are then coded in one of several programming languages, such as BASIC, COBOL, FORTRAN, PASCAL, RPG, CSP, or C++. When the program is completed, the programmer tests its working practicality by running it on simulated data. If the machine responds according to expectations, actual data will be fed into it and the program will be activated. If the computer does not respond as anticipated, the program will have to be debugged, that is, examined for errors that must be eliminated. Finally, the programmer prepares an instruction sheet for the computer operator who will run the program.

The programmer's job concerns both an overall picture of the problem at hand and the minute detail of potential solutions. Programmers work from two points of view: from that of the people who need certain results and from that of technological problem solving. The work is equally divided between meeting the needs of other people and comprehending the capabilities of the machines.

Electronic data systems do not involve just one machine. Depending upon the kind of system being used, the operation may require other machines such as printers or other peripherals. Introducing a new piece of equipment to an existing system often requires programmers to rewrite many programs.

Programmers may specialize in certain types of work depending on the kind of problem to be solved and the employer. Making a program for a payroll is, for example, very different from programming the study of structures of chemical compounds. Programmers who specialize in a certain field or industry generally have education or experience in that area before they are promoted to senior programming positions. *Information system programmers* specialize in programs for storing and retrieving physical science, engineering, or medical information; text analysis; and language, law, military, or library science data. As the information superhighway continues to grow, information system programmers have increased opportunities in on-line businesses, such as Lexis/Nexis, Westlaw, America On-Line, Microsoft, and so on.

Process control programmers develop programs for systems that control automatic operations for commercial and industrial enterprises, such as steel making, sanitation plants, combustion systems, computerized production testing, or automatic truck loading. Numerical control tool programmers program the tape that controls the machining of automatic machine tools.

Requirements

Most employers prefer their programmers to be college graduates. In the past, as the field was first taking shape, employers were known to hire people with some formal education and little or no experience but determination and aptitude to learn quickly. As the market becomes saturated with individuals wishing to break into this field, however, a college degree is becoming increasingly important. Personal qualifications such as a high degree of reasoning ability, patience, and persistence, as well as an aptitude for mathematics, are important for computer programmers.

Many personnel officers administer aptitude tests to determine potential for programming work. Some employers send new employees to computer schools or in-house training sessions before they are considered qualified to assume programming responsibilities. Training periods may last as long as a few weeks, months, or even a year.

Students should take any computer programming or computer science courses available. They should also concentrate on math, science, and schematic drawing courses, since these subjects directly prepare students for careers in computer programming.

Many junior and community colleges also offer two-year associate's degree programs in data processing, computer programming, and other com-

puter-related technologies. Students who choose to go this route might consider becoming certified by the Institute for the Certification of Computer Professionals, whose address is listed at the end of this article. Though not required, certification may boost an individual's attractiveness to employers during job-hunting.

Most four year colleges and universities have computer science departments with a variety of computer-related majors, any of which could prepare a student for a career in programming.

Some employers whose work is highly technical require that programmers be qualified in the area in which the firm or agency operates. Engineering firms, for example, prefer young people with an engineering background and are willing to train them in some programming techniques. For other firms, like banking, consumer-level knowledge of what banks offer may be sufficient background for in-coming programmers.

Employers who require a college degree often do not express a preference as to major field of study, although mathematics or computer science is highly favored. Other acceptable majors may be business administration, accounting, engineering, or physics. Entrance requirements for jobs with the government are much the same as those in private industry.

Opportunities for Experience & Exploration

Interested high school students might visit a large bank or insurance company in the community and seek an appointment to talk with one of the programmers on the staff. Future programmers may be able to visit the data processing center and see the machines in operation. They might talk with a sales representative from one of the large manufacturers of data processing equipment and request whatever brochures or pamphlets the company publishes.

It is a good idea to start early and get some hands-on experience operating and programming a computer. A trip to the local library or bookstore is likely to turn up countless books on programming; this is one field where the resources to "teach yourself" are highly accessible and available for all levels of competency. Joining a computer club and reading professional magazines are other ways to become more familiar with this career field. In addition, students should start "surfing" the Internet, itself a great source of information about computer-related careers.

High school and college students who can operate a computer may be able to obtain part-time jobs in business computer centers or in some larger companies. Any computer experience will be helpful for future computer training.

Methods of Entering

An entry-level programming position is obtained like most other jobs; there is no special or standard point of entry into the field. Individuals with the necessary qualifications should apply directly to companies, agencies, or industries who have announced job openings either through a school placement office, employment agency, or the classified ads.

Students in two- or four-year degree programs should work closely with their school's placement office since major local employers often list job openings exclusively there.

If the market for programmers is particularly tight, you may want to obtain any entry-level job with a large corporation or computer software firm, even if the job does not include programming. As jobs in the programming department open up, current employees in other departments are often the first to know and are favored over nonemployees during the interviewing process. Getting a foot in the door in this way has proven to be successful for many programmers.

Advancement

Programmers are ranked according to education, experience, and level of responsibility as junior or senior programmers. After the highest programming position as been obtained, programmers can choose to make one of several career moves in order to be promoted still higher.

Some programmers are more interested in the analysis aspect of computing than the actual charting and coding of programming. They often acquire additional training and experience in order to prepare themselves for promotion to a position as a systems programmer or systems analyst. These individuals have the added responsibility of working with upper management to define equipment and cost guidelines for a specific project. They only perform broad programming tasks, leaving most of the detail work to programmers.

Other programmers become more interested in administration and management and may wish to become heads of programming departments. They tend to be more people-oriented and enjoy leading others to excellence. As the level of management responsibilities increase, the amount of technical work performed decreases, so management positions are not for everyone.

Still other programmers may branch out into different technical areas, such as total computer operations, hardware design, and software or network engineering. With experience, they may be placed in charge of the data systems center. Or, they may decide to go to work for a consulting company, work that generally pays extremely well.

Programming provides a solid background in the computer industry. Experienced programmers enjoy a wide variety of possibilities for career advancement; the hardest part for programmers is usually deciding exactly what they want to do.

Employment Outlook

In 1996, there were 568,000 computer programmers employed in the United States. They work for manufacturing companies, data processing service firms, hardware and software companies, banks, insurance companies, credit companies, publishing houses, government agencies, and colleges and universities throughout the country. Many programmers are employed by businesses as consultants, on a temporary or contractual basis.

Employment opportunities for computer programmers should increase faster than the average through 2006 because businesses, scientific organizations, government agencies, and schools continue to look for new applications for computers and to make improvements in software already in use. Also, there is a need to develop complex operating programs that can use higher-level computer languages and can network with other computer equipment and systems.

Job applicants with the best chances of employment will be college graduates with a knowledge of several programming languages, especially newer ones used for computer networking and database management. In addition, the best applicants will have some training or experience in an applied field such as accounting, science, engineering, or management. Competition for jobs will be heavier among graduates of two-year data processing programs and among people with equivalent experience or with less training. Since this field is constantly changing, programmers should stay abreast of the latest technology to remain competitive.

Earnings

According to the National Association of Colleges and Employers, the average 1997 starting salary for college graduates employed in the private sector was about $35,167. Salaries for experienced programmers averaged $40,100 a year; some earned more then $65,200. Programmers employed by the Federal government were paid between $19,520 to $24,180, depending on their academic record. Programmers in the West and the North are generally paid more than those in the South. This is because most big computer companies are located in the Silicon Valley in Northern California or in Seattle, Washington, where Microsoft, a major employer of programmers, has its headquarters. Also, some industries, like the public utilities and data processing service firms, tend to pay their programmers higher wages than other types of firms, like banks and schools.

Most programmers receive the customary paid vacation and sick leave, and are included in such company benefits as group insurance and retirement benefit plans.

Conditions of Work

Most programmers work in pleasant office conditions, since computers require an air-conditioned, dust-free environment. Programmers perform most of their duties in one pri-

mary location, but may be asked to travel to other computing sites on occasion.

The average programmer works between thirty-five to forty hours weekly. In some job situations, the programmer may have to work nights or weekends on short notice. This might happen when a program is going through its trial runs, for example, or when there are many demands for additional services.

Sources of Additional Information

For more information about careers in computer programming, contact

Association for Computing Machinery
1515 Broadway
New York, NY 10036
Tel: 212-869-7440
Email: acmhelp@acm.org
WWW: http://www.info.acm.org/

Data Processing Management Association
505 Busse Highway
Park Ridge, IL 60068
Tel: 847-825-8124
WWW: http://www.negaduck.cc.vt.edu/dpma/

Institute for Certification of Computing Professionals
2200 East Devon Avenue, Suite 268
Des Plaines, IL 60018
Tel: 847-299-4227
WWW: http://www.iccp.org

Data Processing Management Association of Canada
2 Whitehall Boulevard
Winnipeg, MB R2C 0Y2 Canada

Computer Systems Programmer-Analysts

Definition

Computer systems programmer-analysts first analyze the computing needs of a business and then design a new system or upgrade an old system to meet those needs. The position can be split between two different people, the systems programmer and the systems analyst, but is frequently held by just one person who oversees the work from beginning to end.

Nature of the Work

Businesses invest hundreds of thousands of dollars in computer systems to make their operations more efficient and thus more profitable. As older systems become obsolete, businesses are also faced with the task of replacing them or upgrading them with new technology. Computer systems programmer-analysts plan and develop new computer systems or upgrade existing systems to meet changing business needs. They also install, modify, and maintain functioning computer systems. The process of choosing and implementing a computer system is similar for those working for very different employers. However, specific decisions in terms of hardware and software differ depending on the industry.

The first stage of the process involves meeting with management and users in order to discuss the problem at hand. For example, a company's accounting system might be slow, unreliable, and generally outdated. During many hours of meetings, systems programmer-analysts and management discuss various options, including commercial software, hardware upgrades, and customizing possibilities that may solve the problems. At the end of the discussions, which may last as long as several weeks or months, the programmer-analyst defines the specific system goals as agreed upon by participants.

Next, systems programmer-analysts engage in highly analytical and logical activities. They use tools like structural analysis, data modeling, mathematics, and cost accounting to determine which computers, including hardware and software and peripherals, will be required to meet the goals of the project. They must consider the trade-offs between extra efficiency and speed and increased costs. Weighing the pros and cons of each additional system feature is an important factor in system planning. Whatever preliminary decisions they make must be supported by mathematical and financial evidence.

As the final stage of the planning process, systems programmer-analysts prepare reports and formal presentations to be delivered to management. Reports must be written in clear, concise language that business professionals, who are not necessarily technical experts, can understand thoroughly. Formal presentations in front of groups of various sizes are often required as part of the system proposal.

If the system or system upgrades are approved, equipment is purchased and installed. Then, the programmer-analysts get down to the real technical work so that all the different computers and peripherals function well together. They prepare specifications, diagrams, and other programming structures and, perhaps using CASE technology, they write the new (or upgraded) programming code. If they work solely as systems analysts, it is at this point that they hand over all of their information to the systems programmer so that he or she can begin to write the programming code.

Systems design and programming involves defining the files and records to be accessed by the system, outlining the processing steps, and suggesting formats for output that meet the needs of the company. User-friendliness of the front-end applications is extremely important for user productivity. Therefore, programmer-analysts must be able to envision how nontechnical system users view their on-screen work. Systems programmer-analysts might also specify security programs that allow only authorized personnel access to certain files or groups of files.

As the programming is written, programmer-analysts set up test runs of various parts of the system, making sure each step of the way that major goals are reached. Once the system is up and running, problems begin to pop up. Programmer-analysts are responsible for debugging. They must isolate the problem and review the hundreds of lines of programming commands to determine where the mistake is located. Then, they must enter the correct command or code and recheck the program.

Depending on the employer, some systems programmer-analysts might be involved with computer networking. Network communication programs tell two or more computers or peripherals how to work with each other. When a system is composed of equipment from various manufacturers, networking is essential for smooth system functioning. For example, shared printers have to know how to order print jobs as they come in from various terminals. Some programmer-analysts write the code that establishes printing queues. Others might be involved in user training since they know the software applications well. They might also customize commercial software programs to meet the needs of their company.

Many programmer-analysts become specialized in an area of business, science, or engineering. They seek education and further on-the-job training in these areas to develop an expertise. They may therefore attend special seminars, workshops, and classes designed for their needs. This extra knowledge allows them to develop a deeper understanding of the computing problems specific to the business or industry.

Requirements

A bachelor's degree in computer science is a minimum requirement for systems programmer-analysts. Curricula include courses in math, computer programming, science, and logic. Several years of related work experience, including knowledge of programming languages, is often necessary as well. For some very high level positions, an advanced degree in a specific computer subfield may be required. Also, depending on the employer, proficiency in business, science, or engineering may be necessary.

Interested high school students should take as many math, science, and computer classes as pos-

sible. These courses provide a foundation of basic concepts and encourage the development of analytical and logical thinking skills. Since programmer-analysts do a lot of proposal writing that may or may not be technical in nature, English classes are valuable as well. Speech classes help prepare them for making formal presentations to management and clients.

Some programmer-analysts pursue certification through the Institute for Certification of Computer Professionals. In particular, they take classes and exams to become a Certified Systems Professional (CSP). Certification is voluntary and is an added credential for job hunters. CSPs have achieved a recognized level of knowledge and experience in principles and practices related to systems.

Successful systems programmer-analysts demonstrate strong analytical thinking skills and enjoy the challenges of problem solving. They are able to understand problems on many levels, from a very technical problem to a more practical, business-oriented one. They can visualize complicated and abstract relationships between computer hardware and software and are good at matching needs to equipment.

Programmer-analysts have to be flexible as well. They routinely deal with many different kinds of people, from management to data entry clerks. Therefore, they must be knowledgeable in a lot of functional areas of the company. They should be able to talk to management about cost-effective solutions, to programmers about detailed coding, and to clerks about user-friendliness of the applications.

As is true for all computer professionals, systems programmer-analysts must be able to learn about new technologies quickly. They should be naturally curious about keeping up on cutting edge developments because doing so can be time consuming. Furthermore, they are often so busy at their jobs that staying in the know is done largely on their own time.

Opportunities for Experience & Exploration

Interested students have several options to learn more about what it is like to be a computer systems programmer-analyst. They can spend a day with a working professional in this field in order to experience firsthand a typical day. Career days of this type can usually be arranged through school guidance counselors or the public relations manager of local corporations.

Strategy games, including chess, played with friends or school clubs are a good way to put analytical thinking skills to use while having fun. Commercial games range in themes from war simulations to world historical development. When choosing a game, the key is to make sure it relies on qualities similar to those used by programmer-analysts.

Lastly, interested students should become computer "hackers" and learn everything they can about computers by working and playing with them on a daily basis. Surfing the Internet regularly, as well as reading trade magazines, is very informative. Students might also want to try hooking up a mini system at home or school, configuring printers, modems, terminals, etc. into a coherent system. This activity requires a fair amount of knowledge and so should be supervised by a professional.

Methods of Entering

Since systems programmer-analysts typically have at least some experience in a computer-related job, most are hired into these positions from lower-level ones within the same company. For example, programmers, software engineering technicians, and network and database administrators all gain valuable computing experience that can be put to good use at a systems job. Alternatively, individuals who acquire expertise in systems programming and analysis while in a different job may want to work with a head hunter to find the right systems position for them. Also, trade magazines, newspapers, and employment agencies regularly feature job openings in this field. Another source of job information is Career Mosaic on the World Wide Web. Career Mosaic is a service that makes access to various companies' job listings easier and faster.

Students in a four-year degree program should work closely with their school's placement office. Companies regularly work through such offices in order to find the best-qualified graduates. Since it may be difficult to find a job as a programmer-analyst to begin with, it is important for students to consider their long-term potential within a certain company. The chance for promotion into a systems job can make lower-level jobs more appealing, at least in the short-run. The educational reimbursement policy of the company is another important consideration since it can enable individuals to achieve the educational requirements of systems jobs inexpensively.

For those individuals already employed in a computer-related job but wanting to get into systems programming and analysis, additional formal education is a good idea. Some employers without educational policies may be willing to pay for such training if it could directly benefit the business.

Advancement

Systems programmer-analysts already occupy a relatively high level technical job. Promotion, therefore, usually occurs in one of two directions. First of all, programmer-analysts can be put in charge of increasingly larger and more complex systems. Instead of concentrating on a local system, say the corporate services systems, an analyst can oversee all company systems and networks. This kind of technically based promotion can also put systems programmer-analysts into other areas of computing. With the proper experience and additional training, they can get into database or network management and design, software engineering, or even quality assurance.

The other direction programmer-analysts can go is managerial. Depending on the position they seek, formal education, either a bachelor's degree in business or a master's in business administration, may be required. As more administrative duties are added, more technical ones are taken away. Therefore, programmer-analysts who enjoy the technical aspect of their work more than anything else may not want to pursue this advancement track. Excellent computing managers have both a solid background in various forms of computing, as well as a good grasp of what it takes to run a department. Also, having vision for how technology will change in the short- and long-terms and how those changes will affect the industry concerned is a quality of a good manager.

Employment Outlook

The U.S. Department of Labor predicts that the occupation of computer systems programmer-analyst will be one of the three fastest growing careers through 2006. Increases are mainly a product of the growing number of businesses that rely extensively on computers. When businesses automate, their daily operations depend on the capacity of their computer systems to perform at desired levels. The development of new technology, and the necessity of businesses to network their information will add to the demand for qualified programmer-analysts. Businesses will increasing rely on system programmer-analysts to make the right purchasing decisions and to keep systems running smoothly.

Many computer manufacturers are beginning to expand the range of services they offer to business clients. In the years to come, they may hire many systems programmer-analysts to work as consultants on a per project basis with a potential client. They would perform essentially the same duties, except for extensive follow-up maintenance. They would analyze business needs and suggest proper systems to answer them. In addition, more and more independent consulting firms are hiring systems programmer-analysts to perform the same tasks.

Programmer-analysts with advanced degrees in computer science, management information systems, or computer engineering, will be in great demand. MBAs with emphasis in information systems will also be highly desirable.

Earnings

According to the U.S. Department of Labor, annual salaries for systems programmer-analysts averaged about $46,300 in 1996. Fifty percent earned from $34,000 to $59,000 a year. Salaries are slightly higher in geographical areas where many computer companies are clustered, like Northern California and Seattle, Washington. According to the National Association of Colleges and Employers, programmer-analysts with a bachelor's degree earned an average of $39,722 a year; those holding a master's degree or better earned from $44,734 to $63,367 a year.

Most programmer-analysts receive health insurance, paid vacation, and sick leave. Some employers offer tuition reimbursement programs and in-house computer training workshops.

Conditions of Work

Computer systems programmer-analysts work in a comfortable office environment. If they work as consultants, they may travel frequently. Otherwise, travel is limited to trade shows, seminars, and visitations to vendors for demonstrations. They might also visit other businesses to observe their systems in action.

Programmer-analysts usually work forty-hour weeks and enjoy the regular holiday schedule of days off. However, as deadlines for system installation, upgrades, and debugging approach, they are often required to work overtime in order to meet them. Extra compensation for overtime hours may come in the form of time and a half pay or compensatory time off, depending on the precise nature of the employee's duties, company policy, and state law. If the employer operates off-shifts, programmer-analysts may be on-call to address any problems that might arise at any time of the day or night. This is relatively rare in the service sector, but more common in manufacturing, heavy industry, and data processing firms.

Computer systems programming and analysis is very detailed work. The tiniest error can cause major system disruptions, which can be a great source of frustration. Systems programmer-analysts must be prepared to deal with this frustration and be able to work well under pressure.

Sources of Additional Information

For more information about systems programming-analyst positions, contact:

■ **Association for Systems Management**
1433 West Bagley Road
PO Box 38370
Cleveland, OH 44138
Tel: 216-234-2930

■ **Data Processing Management Association**
505 Busse Highway
Park Ridge, IL 60068
Tel: 847-825-8124
WWW: http://www.negaduck.cc.vt.edu/dpma/

For more information on related certification, contact:

■ **Institute for Certification of Computing Professionals**
2200 East Devon Avenue, Suite 268
Des Plaines, IL 60018-4503
Tel: 847-299-4227
WWW: http//www.iccp.org

Cooks, Chefs, and Bakers

Definition

Cooks, chefs, and bakers are employed in the preparation and cooking of food, usually in large quantities, in hotels, restaurants, cafeterias, and other establishments and institutions.

Nature of the Work

Cooks and chefs are primarily responsible for the preparation and cooking of foods. Chefs usually supervise the work of cooks; however, the skills required and the job duties performed by each may vary depending upon the size and type of establishment.

Cooks and chefs begin by planning menus in advance. They estimate the amount of food that will be required for a specified period of time, order it from various suppliers, and check it for quantity and quality when it arrives. Following recipes or their own instincts, they measure and mix ingredients for soups, salads, gravies, sauces, casseroles, and desserts. They prepare meats, poultry, fish, vegetables, and other foods for baking, roasting, broiling, and steaming. They may use blenders, mixers, grinders, slicers, or tenderizers to prepare the food; and ovens, broilers, grills, roasters, or steam kettles to cook it. During the mixing and cooking, cooks and chefs rely on their judgment and experience to add seasonings; they constantly taste and smell food being cooked and must know when it is cooked properly. To fill orders, they carve meat, arrange food portions on serving plates, and add appropriate gravies, sauces, or garnishes.

Some larger establishments employ specialized cooks, such as *banquet cooks, pastry cooks*, and *broiler cooks*. The *Garde-Manger* designs and prepares buffets, and *pantry cooks* prepare cold dishes for lunch and dinner. Other specialists are *raw shellfish preparers* and *carvers*.

In smaller establishments without specialized cooks or kitchen helpers, the general cooks may have to do some of the preliminary work themselves, such as washing, peeling, cutting, and shredding vegetables and fruits; cutting, trimming, and boning meat; cleaning and preparing poultry, fish, and shellfish; and baking bread, rolls, cakes, and pastries.

Commercial cookery is usually done in large quantities, and many cooks, including school cafeteria cooks and mess cooks, are trained in "quantity cookery" methods. Numerous establishments today are noted for their specialties in foods, and some cooks work exclusively in the preparation and cooking of exotic dishes, very elaborate meals, or some particular creation of their own for which they have become famous. Restaurants that feature national cuisines may employ international and regional cuisine specialty cooks.

In the larger commercial kitchens, chefs may be responsible for the work of a number of cooks, each preparing and cooking food in specialized areas. They may, for example, employ expert cooks who specialize in frying, baking, roasting, broiling, or sauce cookery. Cooks are often titled by the kinds of specialized cooking they do, such as fry, vegetable, or pastry. Chefs have the major responsibility for supervising the overall preparation and cooking of the food.

Other duties of chefs may include training cooks on the job, planning menus, pricing food for menus, and purchasing food. Chefs may be responsible for determining portion weights to be prepared and served. Among their other duties they may supervise the work of all members of the kitchen staff. The kitchen staff may assist by washing, cleaning, and preparing foods for cooking; cleaning utensils, dishes, and silverware; and assisting in many ways with the overall order and cleanliness of the kitchen. Most chefs spend part of their time striving to create new recipes that will win the praise of customers and build their reputations as experts.

DOT: 315   GOE: 05.10.08

Many, like *pastry chefs* and *ice-cream chefs* focus their attention on particular kinds of food.

Expert chefs who have a number of years of experience behind them may be employed as *executive chefs*. These chefs do little cooking or food preparation. Their main responsibilities are management and supervision. Executive chefs interview, hire, and dismiss all kitchen personnel, and they are sometimes responsible for the dining room waiters, waitresses, and other employees as well. These chefs consult with the restaurant manager regarding the profit and loss of the food service and ways to increase business and cut costs. A part of their time is spent inspecting equipment. Executive chefs are in charge of all food services for special functions such as banquets and parties, and many hours are spent in the coordination of the work for these activities. They may supervise the special chefs and assist them in planning elaborate arrangements and creations in food preparation. Executive chefs may be assisted by *sous chefs*.

Smaller restaurants may employ only one or two cooks and kitchen helpers to assist them. Cooks and helpers work together to prepare all the food for cooking and keep the kitchen clean. Because smaller restaurants and public eating places usually offer standard menus with little variation, the cook's job becomes standardized. Such establishments may employ *specialty cooks, barbecue cooks, pizza bakers, food order expediters, kitchen food assemblers*, or *counter supply workers*. In some restaurants food is cooked as it is ordered; cooks preparing food in this manner are known as *short-order cooks*.

Regardless of the duties performed, cooks and chefs are largely responsible for the reputation and monetary profit or loss of the eating establishment in which they are employed.

Bakers perform work similar to that of cooks and chefs as they prepare breads, rolls, muffins, biscuits, pies, cakes, cookies, and pastries. Bakers may be supervised by a head baker. In large establishments, second bakers may supervise other bakers who work with a particular type of baked goods. Bakers are often assisted by baker helpers.

Requirements

The occupation of chef, cook, or baker has specific training requirements. Many cooks start out as kitchen helpers and acquire their skills on the job, but the trend today is to obtain training through high schools, vocational schools, or community colleges. Professional associations and trade unions sometimes offer apprenticeship programs; one example is the three-year apprenticeship program administered by the local offices of the American Culinary Federation in cooperation with local employers and community colleges or vocational schools. Some large hotels and restaurants have their own training programs for new employees. The armed forces also offer good training and experience.

The amount of training required varies with the position. It takes only a short time to become an assistant or a *fry cook*, for example, but it requires many years of training and experience to acquire the skills necessary to become an executive chef or cook in a fine restaurant.

Although a high school diploma is not required, it is an asset to job applicants. For those planning a career as a chef or head cook, courses in business mathematics and business administration are useful.

Culinary students spend most of their time learning to prepare food through hands-on practice. At the same time, they learn how to use and care for kitchen equipment. Training programs often include courses in menu planning, determining portion size, food cost control, purchasing food supplies in quantity, selecting and storing food, and using leftovers. Students also learn hotel and restaurant sanitation and public health rules for handling food. Courses offered by private vocational schools, professional associations, and university programs often emphasize training in supervisory and management skills.

A successful chef or cook should have a keen interest in food preparation and cooking and have a desire to experiment in developing new recipes and new food combinations. Cooks, chefs, and bakers should be able to work as part of a team and to work under pressure during rush hours, in close quarters and with a certain amount of noise and confusion. These employees need a mild temperament and patience to contend with the public daily and also to work closely with many other kinds of employees.

Immaculate personal cleanliness and good health are necessities in this trade. Applicants should possess physical stamina and be without serious physical impairments because of the mobility and activity the work requires. These employees spend many working hours standing, walking, and moving about.

Chefs, cooks, and bakers must possess a keen sense of taste and smell. Hand and finger agility, hand-eye coordination, and a good memory are helpful. An artistic flair and creative talents in working with food are definitely strengths in this trade.

The principal union for cooks and chefs is the Hotel Employees and Restaurant Employees International Union (affiliated with the AFL-CIO).

To protect the public's health, chefs, cooks, and bakers are required by law in most states to possess a health certificate and to be examined periodically. These examinations, usually given by the state board of health, make certain that the individual is free from communicable diseases and skin infections.

Opportunities for Experience & Exploration

You may explore your interest in cooking by getting part-time or summer jobs in a fast food or other restaurant, or in an institutional kitchen as a sandwich or salad maker, soda-fountain attendant, kitchen helper, or waitperson where you can observe the work of chefs and cooks.

Practicing and experimenting with cooking at home and in high school home economics courses is another way of testing your interest in becoming a cook, chef, or baker.

Methods of Entering

Apprenticeship programs are one method of entering the trade. These programs usually offer the beginner sound basic training and a regular salary. Upon completion of the apprenticeship, cooks may be hired full time in their place of training or assisted in finding employment with another establishment. Cooks are hired as chefs only after they have acquired a number of years of experience. Cooks who have been formally trained through public or private trade or vocational schools or in culinary institutes may be able to take advantage of school placement services.

In many cases, a cook begins as a kitchen helper or cook's helper and, through experience gained in on-the-job training, is able to move into the job of cook. To do this, the person sometimes starts out in a small restaurant, perhaps as a short-order cook, *grill cook*, or *sandwich or salad maker*, and transfers to larger establishments as he or she gains experience.

School cafeteria workers who want to become cooks may have an opportunity to receive food-services training. Many school districts, with the cooperation of school food-services divisions of the state departments of education, provide on-the-job training and sometimes summer workshops for interested cafeteria employees. Similar programs are offered by some community colleges, state departments of education, and school associations. Cafeteria workers who have completed these training programs are often selected to fill positions as cooks.

Job opportunities may be located through employment bureaus, trade associations, unions, contacts with friends, newspaper want ads, or local offices of the state employment service. Another method is to apply directly to restaurants or hotels. Small restaurants, school cafeterias, and other eating places with simple food preparation will provide the greatest number of starting jobs for cooks. Job applicants who have had courses in commercial food preparation will have an advantage in large restaurants and hotels, where hiring standards are often high.

Advancement

Advancement depends on the skill, training, experience, originality, and ambition of the individual. It also depends somewhat on the general business climate and employment trends.

Cooks with experience can advance by moving to other places of employment for higher wages or to establishments looking for someone with a specialized skill in preparing a particular kind of food. Cooks who have a number of years of successful job experience may find chef positions open to them; however, in some cases it may take ten or fifteen years to obtain such a position, depending on personal qualifications and other employment factors.

Expert cooks who have obtained supervisory responsibilities as head cooks or chefs may advance to positions as executive chefs or to other types of managerial work. Some go into business for themselves as caterers or restaurant owners; others may become instructors in vocational programs in high schools, colleges, or other academic institutions.

Employment Outlook

In 1996, approximately 3.4 million cooks, chefs, and bakers were employed in the United States. Most worked in hotels and restaurants, but many worked in schools, colleges, airports, and hospitals. Still others were employed by government agencies, factories, private clubs, and other organizations.

The employment of chefs, cooks, and bakers is expected to increase as fast as the average for all occupations through the year 2006. The demand will not only grow with the population, but lifestyle changes as well. As people earn higher incomes and have more leisure time, they dine out more often and take more vacations. Working parents and their families will dine out frequently as a convenience. Though some openings will result from job growth, most work opportunities for cooks, chefs, and bakers will result from the need to replace those leaving the workforce for various reasons.

Earnings

The salaries earned by chefs and cooks are widely divergent and depend on many factors, such as the size, type, and location of the establishment, and the skill, experience, training, and specialization of the worker. Salaries are usually pretty standard among the same type of establishment. For example, restaurants and diners serving inexpensive meals and a sandwich-type menu generally pay cooks less than establishments with medium-priced or expensive menus. The highest wages are earned in the West and in large, well-known restaurants and hotels.

As reported in the *1998-99 Occupational Outlook Handbook,* the median salary for short-order cooks is about $6.50 an hour, or $13,520 a year, with most earning between $11,440 and $15,080. The median salary for bread and pastry bakers is also $6.50 hourly or $13,520 annually, with most earning between $12,480 and $16,120. Fast food workers generally earn the minimum wage. Cooks and chefs in famous restaurants, of course, earn much more. The average, according to the National Restaurant Association, was about $38,000, though some renowned executive chefs are paid considerably more. Chefs and cooks usually receive their meals free during working hours and are furnished with any necessary job uniforms.

Conditions of Work

Working conditions vary with the place of employment. Many kitchens are modern, well lighted, well equipped, and air-conditioned, but some older, smaller eating places may be only marginally equipped. The work of cooks can be strenuous, with long hours of standing, lifting heavy pots, and working near hot ovens and ranges. Possible hazards include falls, cuts, and burns, although serious injury is uncommon. Even in the most modern kitchens, cooks, chefs, and bakers usually work amid considerable noise from the operation of equipment and machinery.

Experienced cooks may work with little or no supervision, depending on the size of the food service and the place of employment. Less experienced cooks may work under much more direct supervision from expert cooks or chefs.

Chefs, cooks, and bakers may work a forty- or forty-eight-hour week, depending on the type of food service offered and certain union agreements. Some food establishments are open twenty-four hours a day, while others may be open from the very early morning until late in the evening. Establishments open long hours may have two or three work shifts, with some chefs and cooks working day schedules while others work evenings.

All food-service workers may have to work overtime hours, depending on the amount of business and rush-hour trade. These employees work many weekends and holidays, although they may have a day off every week or rotate with other employees to have alternate weekends free. Many cooks are required to work early morning or late evening shifts. For example, doughnuts, breads, and muffins for breakfast service must be baked by six or seven a.m., which requires bakers to begin work at two or three a.m. Some people will find it very difficult to adjust to working such late and irregular hours.

Sources of Additional Information

■■■**American Culinary Federation**
PO Box 3466
St. Augustine, FL 32085
Tel: 904-824-4468

American Institute of Baking
1213 Bakers Way
Manhattan, KS66502
Tel: 913-537-4750

Bakery Council of Canada
885 Don Mills Road, Suite 301
Don Mills, ON M3C 1V9 Canada

British Columbia Chefs Association
PO Box 2007
Vancouver, BC V6B 3P8 Canada

Chefs de Cuisine Association of America
155 East 55th Street, Suite 302B
New York, NY 10022

Culinary Institute of America
433 Albany Post Road
Hyde Park, NY 12538-1499
Tel: 914-452-9600

Educational Foundation of the National Restaurant Association
250 South Wacker Drive
Chicago, IL 60606
Tel: 312-715-1010

Educational Institute of the American Hotel and Motel Association
PO Box 1240
East Lansing, MI 48826
Tel: 517-353-5500

Corrections Officers

Definition

Corrections officers guard people who have been arrested and are awaiting trial or who have been tried, convicted, and sentenced to serve time in a penal institution. They search prisoners and their cells for weapons, drugs, and other contraband; inspect windows, doors, locks, and gates for signs of tampering; observe the conduct and behavior of inmates to prevent disturbances or escapes; and make verbal or written reports to superior officers. Corrections officers assign work to inmates and supervise their activities. They guard prisoners who are being transported between jails, courthouses, mental institutions, or other destinations, and supervise prisoners receiving visitors. When necessary, these workers use weapons or force to maintain discipline and order.

Nature of the Work

To prevent disturbances or escapes, corrections officers carefully observe the conduct and behavior of the inmates at all times. They watch for forbidden activities and infractions of the rules, as well as for poor attitudes or unsatisfactory adjustment to prison life on the part of the inmates. They try to settle disputes before violence can erupt. They may search the prisoners or their living quarters for weapons or drugs and inspect locks, bars on windows and doors, and gates for any evidence of tampering. The inmates are under guard constantly while eating, sleeping, exercising, bathing, and working. They are counted periodically to be sure all are present. Some officers are stationed on towers and at gates to prevent escapes. All rule violations and anything out of the ordinary are reported to a superior officer such as a *chief jailer*. In case of a major disturbance, corrections officers may use weapons or force to restore order.

Corrections officers give work assignments to prisoners, supervise them as they carry out their duties, and instruct them in unfamiliar tasks. Corrections officers are responsible for the physical needs of the prisoners, such as providing or obtaining meals and medical aid. They assure the health and safety of the inmates by checking the cells for unsanitary conditions and fire hazards.

These workers may escort inmates from their cells to the prison's visiting room, medical office, or chapel. Certain officers, called *patrol conductors*, guard prisoners who are being transported between courthouses, prisons, mental institutions, or other destinations, either by van, car, or public transportation. Officers at a penal institution may also screen visitors at the entrance and accompany them to other areas within the facility. From time to time, they may inspect mail addressed to prisoners, checking for contraband, help investigate crimes committed within the prison, or aid in the search for escapees.

Some police officers specialize in guarding juvenile offenders being held at a police station house or detention room pending a hearing, transfer to a correctional institution, or return to their parents. They often investigate the background of first offenders to check for a criminal history or to make a recommendation to the magistrate regarding disposition of the case. Lost or runaway children are also placed in the care of these officers until their parents or guardians can be located.

Immigration guards guard aliens held by the immigration service awaiting investigation, deportation, or release. *Gate tenders* check the identification of all persons entering and leaving the penal institution.

In most correctional institutions, psychologists and social workers are employed to counsel inmates with mental and emotional problems. It is an important part of a corrections officer's job, however, to supplement this with informal counseling.

Officers may help inmates adjust to prison life, prepare for return to civilian life, and avoid committing crimes in the future. On a more immediate level, they may arrange for an inmate to visit the library, help inmates get in touch with their families, suggest where to look for a job after release from prison, or discuss personal problems. In some institutions, corrections officers may lead more formal group counseling sessions. As they fulfill more rehabilitative roles, corrections officers are increasingly required to possess a college-level education in psychology, criminology, or related areas of study.

Corrections officers keep a daily record of their activities and make regular reports, either verbal or written, to their supervisors. These reports concern the behavior of the inmates and the quality and quantity of work they do, as well as any disturbances, rule violations, and unusual occurrences that may have taken place.

Head corrections officers supervise and coordinate other corrections officers. They perform roll call and assign duties to the officers, direct the activities of groups of inmates, arrange the release and transfer of prisoners in accordance with the instructions on a court order, maintain security and investigate disturbances among the inmates, maintain prison records and prepare reports, and review and evaluate the performance of their subordinates.

In small communities, corrections officers (who are sometimes called *jailers*) may also act as *deputy sheriffs* or *police officers* when they are not occupied with guard duties.

Requirements

To work as a corrections officer, candidates generally must meet the minimum age requirement—usually eighteen or twenty-one—and have a high school diploma or its equivalent. Individuals without a high school education may be considered for employment if they have qualifying work experience, such as probation and parole experience. Many states and correctional facilities prefer or require officers with postsecondary training in psychology, criminology, or related areas of study. Military experience or related work experience is also required by some state governments. On the federal level, applicants should have at least two years of college or two years of work or military experience. Other requirements include good health and physical strength, and many states have set minimum

height, vision, and hearing standards. Sound judgment and the ability to think and act quickly are important qualities for this occupation. All candidates must have a clean arrest record.

Training for corrections officers ranges from the special academy instruction provided by the federal government and some states to the informal, on-the-job training furnished by most states and local governments. The Federal Bureau of Prisons operates a training center in Glynco, Georgia, where new hires generally undergo a three-week program of basic corrections education. Training academies have programs that last from four to eight weeks and instruct trainees on institutional policies, regulations, and procedures; the behavior and custody of inmates; security measures; and report writing. Training in self-defense, the use of firearms and other weapons, and emergency medical techniques is often provided. On-the-job trainees spend two to six months or more under the supervision of an experienced officer. During that period of time, they receive in-house training while gaining actual experience. Periodically, corrections officers may be given additional training as new ideas and procedures in criminal justice are developed.

Some states require applicants to have one or two years of previous experience in corrections or related police work. A few states require passing a written examination. Corrections officers who work for the federal government and most state governments are covered by civil service systems or merit boards and may be required to pass a competitive exam for employment. Many states require random or comprehensive drug testing of their officers, either during hiring procedures or while employed at the facility.

Opportunities for Experience & Exploration

Because of age requirements and the nature of the work, there are no opportunities for high school students to gain actual experience while still in school. Where the minimum age requirement is twenty-one, prospective corrections officers may prepare for employment by taking college courses in criminal justice or police science. Enrollment in a two- or four-year college degree program in a related field is encouraged. Military service may also offer experience and training in corrections. Social work is another way to gain experience. Students may also look into obtaining a civilian job as a clerk or other worker for the police department or other protective service organization. Related part-time, volunteer, or summer work may also be available in psychiatric hospitals and other institutions providing physical and emotional counseling and services.

The ability to speak foreign languages is often a plus when applying for corrections jobs. Many online services also have forums for corrections officers and other public safety employees, and these may provide opportunities to read about and communicate with people active in this career.

Methods of Entering

To apply for a job as a corrections officer, contact federal or state civil service commissions, state departments of correction, or local correctional facilities and ask for information about entrance requirements, training, and job opportunities. Private contractors and other companies are also a growing source of employment opportunities. Many officers enter this field from social work areas and parole and probation positions.

Advancement

With additional education and training, experienced officers may qualify for promotion to head corrections officer or advancement to some other supervisory or administrative position, and eventually may become *prison directors*. Some officers transfer to related fields, such as law, law enforcement, or probation and parole.

Employment Outlook

The prison population has more than doubled in the last ten years, and this growth is expected to be sustained for the near future. The increasing number of prisoners means there will be a strong need for new corrections officers. Of the more than 320,000 corrections officers

employed in the United States, roughly 60 percent work in state-run correctional facilities such as prisons, prison camps, and reformatories. Most of the rest are employed at city and county jails or other institutions, while a few thousand work for the federal government. An increasing number are employed by private corrections contractors.

Employment in this field is expected to increase much faster than the average for all jobs. It is estimated that another 120,000 jobs will be created through the year 2006. The ongoing war on illegal drugs, new tough-on-crime legislation, and increasing mandatory sentencing policies will create a need for more prison beds and more corrections officers. The extremely crowded conditions in today's correctional institutions have created a need for more corrections officers to guard the inmates more closely and relieve the tensions. A greater number of officers will also be required as a result of the expansion or new construction of facilities. As prison sentences become longer through mandatory minimum sentences set by state law, the number of prisons needed will increase. In addition, many job openings will occur from a characteristically high turnover rate, as well as from the need to fill vacancies caused by the death or retirement of older workers. Traditionally, correction agencies have difficulty attracting qualified employees due to job location and salary considerations.

Because security must be maintained at correctional facilities at all times, corrections officers can depend on steady employment. They are not usually affected by poor economic conditions or changes in government spending. Corrections officers are rarely laid off, even when budgets need to be trimmed. Instead, because of high turnovers, staffs can be cut quickly simply by not replacing those officers who leave.

Most jobs will be found in relatively large institutions located near metropolitan areas, although opportunities for corrections officers exist in jails and other smaller facilities throughout the country. The increasing use of private companies and privately run prisons may limit somewhat the growth of jobs in this field as these companies are more likely to keep a close eye on the bottom line. Use of new technologies, such as surveillance equipment, automatic gates, and other devices, may also allow institutions to employ fewer officers.

Earnings

There is a wide variation in wages for corrections officers, depending on which level of government employs them. According to a 1996 national survey in *Correction Compendium*, beginning corrections officers received an average of $20,200. The average salary for all corrections officers was $33,540, but salaries range widely from one state to another. In southern California, for example, corrections officers started at $17,300, while Rhode Island corrections officers could earn $41,000 or more.

Beginning corrections officers at the federal level are generally rated GS-6, with a salary range of $21,000 to $28,000 depending on the location of service. Sergeants and other supervisors generally start at $41,000. The average for all federal corrections officers and sergeants is $30,000 per year, and supervisors average more than $50,000. Overtime, night shift, weekend, and holiday pay differentials are generally available at most institutions.

Benefits may include health, disability, and life insurance; uniforms or a cash allowance to buy their own; and sometimes meals and housing. Officers who work for the federal government and for most state governments are covered by civil service systems or merit boards. Some corrections officers also receive retirement and pension plans, and retirement is often available after twenty years of service.

Conditions of Work

Because prison security must be maintained around the clock, work schedules for corrections officers may include nights, weekends, and holidays. The workweek, however, generally consists of five, eight-hour days, except during emergencies, when many officers work overtime.

Corrections officers may work indoors or outdoors, depending on their duties. Conditions can vary even within an institution: some areas are well lighted, ventilated, and temperature-controlled, while others are overcrowded, hot, and noisy. Officers who work outdoors, of course, are subject to all kinds of weather. Correctional institutions occasionally present unpredictable or even hazardous situations. If violence erupts among the inmates, corrections officers may be in danger of injury or death. Although this risk is higher than for most other occupations, corrections work is usually routine.

Corrections officers need physical and emotional strength to cope with the stress inherent in dealing with criminals, many of whom may be dangerous or incapable of change. A correctional officer has to remain alert and aware of the surroundings, prisoners' movements and attitudes, and any potential for danger or violence. Such continual, heightened levels of alertness often create psychological stress for some workers. Most institutions have stress-reduction programs or seminars for their employees, but if not, insurance usually covers some form of therapy for work-related stress.

Sources of Additional Information

■**The American Correctional Association**
4380 Forbes Boulevard
Lanham, MD 20706
Tel: 301-918-1800

■**The American Probation and Parole Association**
c/o Council of State Governments
Iron Works Pike
PO Box 11910
Lexington, KY 40578
Tel: 606-244-8203
Email: appa@csg.org

■**The International Association of Correctional Officers**
Box 53, 1333 South Wabash Avenue
Chicago, IL 60605
Tel: 312-996-5401

Counter and Retail Clerks

Definition

Counter and retail clerks work as intermediaries between the general public and businesses that provide goods and services. They take orders and receive payments for such services as videotape rentals, automobile rentals, and laundry and dry cleaning. They often assist customers with their purchasing or rental decisions, especially when sales personnel are not available. They might also prepare billing statements, keep records of receipts and sales, and balance money in their cash register.

Nature of the Work

Job duties vary depending on the type of business. In a shoe repair shop, for example, the clerk receives the shoes to be repaired or cleaned from the customer, examines the shoes, gives a price quote and a receipt to the customer, and then sends the shoes to the work department for the necessary repairs or cleaning. The shoes are marked with a tag specifying what work needs to be done and to whom the shoes belong. After the work is completed, the clerk returns the shoes to the customer and collects payment.

In a bicycle store *bicycle-rental clerks* prepare rental forms and quote rates to customers. The clerks answer customer questions about the operation of the bikes. They often take a deposit to cover any accidents or possible damage. Clerks also check the bicycles to be certain they are in good working order and make minor adjustments, if necessary. With long-term rentals, such as storage-facility rentals, clerks notify the customers when the rental period is about to expire and when the rent is overdue. *Video-rental clerks* greet customers, check out tapes, and accept payment. Upon return of the tapes, the clerks check the condition of the tapes and then put them back on the shelves.

In smaller shops with no sales personnel or in situations when the sales personnel are unavailable, counter and retail clerks assist customers with purchases or rentals by demonstrating the merchandise, answering the customers' questions, accepting payment, recording sales, and wrapping the purchases or arranging for their delivery.

In addition to these duties, clerks sometimes prepare billing statements to be sent to customers. They might keep records of receipts and sales throughout the day and balance the money in their registers when their work shift ends. They sometimes are responsible for the display and presentation of products in their store. In supermarkets and grocery stores, clerks stock shelves and bag food purchases for the customers.

Service-establishment attendants work in various types of businesses, such as a laundry, where attendants take clothes to be cleaned or repaired and write down the customer's name and address. *Watch-and-clock-repair clerks* receive clocks and watches for repair and examine the timepieces to estimate repair costs. They might make minor repairs, such as replacing a watch band; otherwise the timepiece is forwarded to the repair shop with a description of needed repairs.

Many clerks have job titles that describe what they do and where they work. These include *laundry-pricing clerks, telegraph-counter clerks, photo-finishing counter clerks, tool-and-equipment-rental clerks, airplane-charter clerks, baby-stroller and wheelchair-rental clerks, storage-facility-rental clerks, boat-rental clerks, hospital-television-rental clerks, trailer-rental clerks, automobile-rental clerks, fur-storage clerks,* and *self-service-laundry and dry-cleaning attendants.*

Counter and retail clerks must be able to adjust to alternating periods of heavy and light activity. No two days—or even customers—are alike. Because some customers can be rude or even hostile, clerks must exercise tact and patience at all times. Some clerks work evening and weekend shifts.

Requirements

Although there are no specific educational requirements for clerk positions, most employers prefer to hire high school graduates. High school courses useful for the job include English, speech, and mathematics, as well as any business-related classes, such as typing and those covering principles in retailing. Legible handwriting and the ability to add and subtract numbers quickly are also a necessity.

Counter and retail clerks should have a pleasant personality and an ability to interact with a variety of people. They should also be neat and well groomed and have a high degree of personal responsibility.

Opportunities for Experience & Exploration

There are numerous opportunities for part-time or temporary work as a clerk, especially during the holiday season. Many high schools have developed work-study programs that combine courses in retailing with part-time work in the field. Store owners cooperating in these programs often hire these students as full-time workers after they complete the course.

Methods of Entering

Those interested in securing an entry-level position as a clerk should contact stores directly. Workers with some experience, such as those who have completed a work-study program in high school, should have the greatest success, but most entry-level positions do not require any previous experience. Jobs are often listed in help wanted advertisements.

Most stores provide new workers with on-the-job training in which experienced clerks explain company policies and procedures and teach new employees how to operate the cash register and other necessary equipment. This training usually continues for several weeks until the new employee feels comfortable on the job.

Advancement

Counter and retail clerks usually begin their employment doing routine tasks, such as checking stock and operating the cash register. With experience they might advance to more complicated assignments and assume some sales responsibilities. Those with the skill and aptitude might become *sales people* or *store managers*, although further education is normally required for management positions.

The high turnover rate in the clerk position increases the opportunities for being promoted. The number and kind of opportunities, however, depend on the place of employment and the ability, training, and experience of the employee.

Employment Outlook

Approximately 374,000 people were employed as retail and counter clerks in the United States in 1996. About half worked part-time. Because of the proliferation of retail outlets, job opportunities for counter and retail clerks are expected to grow faster than average through the year 2006.

As is currently the case, major employers will be laundry or dry cleaning establishments, automobile rental firms, and supermarkets and grocery stores. The continued growth in video rental stores and other rental services will also increase the need for skilled clerks. There should also be an increase in the number of opportunities for temporary or part-time work, especially during busy business periods. However, due to the high turnover rate of this field, most job openings will result from the need to replace workers. Employment opportunities for clerks are plentiful in large metropolitan areas where their services are in great demand.

Earnings

Beginning counter and retail clerks in 1997 generally earned around the minimum wage. Experienced clerks average between $6.00 an hour and $9.50 an hour, with some making as much as $12.85 an hour. The highest wages are paid to those with the greatest number of job responsibilities.

According to the *1998-99 Occupational Outlook Handbook,* full-time clerks averaged about $303 a week, or $15,756 annually. Clerks with considerable work experience earned about $631 weekly, or $32,812 a year. Those workers who have union affiliation (usually those who work for supermarkets) may earn considerably more than their nonunion counterparts. Full-time workers, especially those who are union members, might also receive benefits such as a paid vacation and health insurance, but this is not the industry norm. Some businesses offer merchandise discounts for their employees. Part time workers usually receive less benefits than those working full time.

Conditions of Work

Although a forty-hour workweek is common, many stores operate on a forty-four- to forty-eight-hour workweek. Most stores are open on Saturday and many on Sunday. Most stores are also open one or more weekday evenings, so working hours might vary from week to week and evening and weekend shifts. Many counter and retail clerks work overtime during Christmas and other rush seasons. Part-time clerks generally work during peak business periods.

Most clerks work indoors in well-ventilated and well-lighted environments. The job can be fairly routine and repetitive, and clerks often spend much of their time on their feet.

Sources of Additional Information

■■■**National Retail Federation**
325 7th Street, NW, Suite 1000
Washington, DC 20004
Tel: 202-783-7971

Database Specialists

Definition

Database specialists design, install, update, modify, maintain, and repair computer database systems. They consult with other management officials to discuss computer equipment purchases, determine requirements for various computer programs, and allocate access to the computer system to users. They might also direct training of personnel who use company databases regularly.

Nature of the Work

Database specialists come in many varieties, depending on the needs of the organization that employs them. In large businesses there may be several database specialists who focus on specific aspects of a company's databases. In a smaller organization, one person may wear all the database hats. Database specialists are also known as *database administrators, database managers,* or *information systems managers.* Database specialists rely on their knowledge of database management to code, test, and install new databases. They review proposals for changes in existing database systems and evaluate how well such changes would work on a daily basis. They are also responsible for overseeing the daily operations of the computer systems. These tasks include ensuring that information is being entered and encoded properly by data entry clerks, that various processing programs are retrieving the right information, and that the systems are not experiencing major problems.

Database specialists are responsible for the flow of computer information within an organization. They make major decisions concerning computer purchases, system designs, and personnel training. Their duties combine general management ability with a detailed knowledge of computer programming and systems analysis.

The specific responsibilities of a database specialist are determined by the size and type of employer. For example, a data base manager for a telephone company may develop a system for billing customers while a database manager for a large store may develop a system for keeping track of merchandise in stock. In all cases, most database specialists have a thorough knowledge and understanding of the company's computer operations.

A database specialist's responsibilities can be grouped into three main areas: planning what type of computer system a company needs; implementing and managing the system; and supervising computer room personnel.

To adequately plan a computer system, database specialists must have extensive knowledge of the latest computer technology and the specific needs of their company. Database specialists meet with other high ranking company officials, such as the president or vice president, and together they decide how to apply the available technology to their company's needs. Decisions include what type of hardware and software to order and how the data should be stored. Database specialists must be aware of the cost of the proposed computer system as well as the budget within which the company is operating. Long-term planning is also important. Database managers must ensure that the computer system can not only process the existing level of computer information received, but also the anticipated load and type of information the company could receive in the future. Such planning is vitally important since, even for small companies, computer systems can cost several hundred thousand dollars.

Database managers must be familiar with accounting principles and mathematical formulas in developing proposals. It is not unusual for a database manager to modify an existing computer system or develop a whole new system based on a company's needs and resources.

Implementing and managing a computer system entails a variety of administrative tasks. Database administrators decide how to organize and store the information files so only the appropriate users gain access to them. In addition, program files must be coded for efficient retrieval. Scheduling access to the computer is another vital administrative function. Sometimes, database administrators work with representatives from all the departments to create a schedule. The administrator prioritizes needs and monitors usage so that each department can do its work. All computer usage must be documented and filed away for future reference.

Safeguarding the computer operations is another important responsibility of database specialists. They must make plans in case a computer system fails or malfunctions so that the information stored in the computer is not lost. A duplication of computer files may be a part of this emergency planning. A backup system must also be employed so that the company can continue to process information. Increasingly, database specialists must also safeguard a system so that only authorized personnel have access to certain information. Computerized information may be of vital importance to a company, and database specialists ensure that it does not fall into the wrong hands.

Implementation of a computer operation often involves coordinating the integration of many complex computers into a single system. As an operation grows, this may require the modification of the system.

Database managers must be able to analyze a computer operation and decide if it is operating at top efficiency. They must be able to recognize equipment or personnel problems and adjust the system accordingly. They are often working with an operation that processes millions of bits of information at a huge cost. This demands accuracy and efficiency in decision-making and problem-solving abilities.

Requirements

Prior experience with computers is essential to obtaining a position as a database specialist. High school students interested in this field should take computer programming courses and any electronics or other technical courses that provide understanding of how a computer operates. Mathematics, science, and accounting courses are also desirable. English and speech courses are a good way for students to hone their written and verbal communications skills.

A bachelor's degree is often a prerequisite for most companies hiring a computer professional. Sometimes, if the candidate shows exceptional experience in the computer field, an associate's degree in a computer-related technology from a technical or vocational school is sufficient to fulfill education requirements. Coursework may include classes in electronics, computer hardware and software, physics, mathematics, schematic reading, and basic programming. Many employers prefer their database administrators to have a background in computer science, information science, computer information systems, or data processing.

Promotion from entry-level administrator jobs to managerial positions will require a bachelor's degree in one of the following: computer science, information science, computer information systems, data processing, or business administration. Sometimes, work experience within the company can compensate for the lack of more formal education. Courses in a bachelor's degree program usually include data processing, systems analysis methods, more detailed software and hardware concepts, management principles, and information systems planning. Many businesses, especially larger companies, prefer database managers to have a master's degree in computer science or business administration.

Experience as a computer programmer or systems analyst is also desirable. Those familiar with programming language will be in demand. Individuals interested in working almost exclusively in one industry, such as banking for example, should acquire as much knowledge as possible about that specific field in addition to their extensive computer training. General knowledge in database administration might not prepare an individual for working in a bank unless he or she also understands basic bank operations and goals. With an understanding of both fields of knowledge, individuals are more easily able to apply computer technology to the specific needs of the company.

Some database specialists become certified for jobs in the computer field by passing an examination given by the Institute for Certification of Computer Professionals. The examination is offered in selected cities throughout the United States every year. For further information on certification, contact the above organization at the address given at the end of this article.

Opportunities for Experience & Exploration

High school computer clubs offer a good forum for learning about computers and meeting others interested in the field. Some businesses offer part-time work or summer internships in their computer departments for qualified students. In addition, there are training programs, such as those offered at summer camps, that teach computer literacy during an intensive three- to six-week period. Students might also ask school administrators about databases used by their school and try to interview any database specialists working in or for the school system. Similar attempts could be made with local area charities who make use of computer databases for membership and client records as well as mailing lists.

Methods of Entering

Since at least an associate's degree is needed to obtain a position in this field, most database professionals work closely with their school's placement office to obtain information about job openings and interviews. Interested individuals might also scan the classified ads or work with temporary agencies to find entry- to mid-level positions. Some applicants with extensive on-the-job computer training may be promoted to this position without a degree, but as the field gets more sophisticated, a college degree will continue to be the most dependable means of entering the profession.

College internships or co-op programs are fantastic ways to gain credible work experience and meet valuable contacts for the future. Many businesses favor applicants already familiar with company standards and goals.

Advancement

Skilled database specialists have excellent advancement opportunities. As specialists acquire education and develop solid work experience, advancement will take the form of more responsibilities and higher wages. Database administrators are promoted into database design and management positions. A database specialist at a small company that relies heavily on database technology may move to an upper-level position such as vice president of the firm or may move to a better-paying, more challenging database position at a larger company. Superior database managers at larger companies may also be promoted to executive positions. Some successful database managers become high-paid consultants or start their own businesses.

Database specialists work for investment companies, telecommunications firms, banks, insurance companies, publishing houses, and a host of other large and middle-sized businesses and nonprofit organizations. There are also many opportunities with the federal, state, and city governments. Teaching, whether as a consultant or at a university or community college, is another option for individuals with high levels of experience.

Employment Outlook

We are now firmly rooted in an era often referred to as the "information age." Vast amounts of information about people, places, and events are recorded electronically as databases. Just ten or twenty years ago, the transfer of information from one company to another could be slow and cumbersome; computers now routinely exchange information rapidly through telephone lines and networks twenty-four hours a day. This explosive growth in the computer field has led to increasingly large and complex databases.

The use of computers and database systems in almost all business creates tremendous opportunities for well-qualified database personnel. Database specialists, along with computer support specialists, are predicted by the U.S. Department of Labor to be the two fastest growing occupations through the year 2006. In 1996, there were 212,000 database specialists employed in the United States. By the year 2006, the U.S. Department of Labor expects about 250,000 new jobs in this field—a 115 percent increase. Those with the best education and the most experience in computer systems and personnel management will find the best job prospects.

Employment opportunities for database specialists should be best in large urban areas because of the multitudes of businesses that have computer systems. Since smaller communities are also rapidly developing significant job opportunities, skilled workers can pick from a wide range of jobs throughout the country.

Earnings

Earnings vary with the size and type of organization and a person's experience, education, and job responsibilities. A database administrator with an associate's degree can earn around $17,000 per year. According to Robert Half International, Inc., those with a bachelor's degree earned between $54,000 to $67,500 a year in 1997. However, database administrators, depending on the company and the degree of responsibility, could easily earn more. Consultants working for major computer companies usually earn higher salaries.

Conditions of Work

Database specialists work in modern offices, usually located next to the computer room. Most duties are performed at a computer on the individual's desk. Travel is occasionally required for conferences and visits to affiliated database locations.

Database specialists work a regular forty-hour week, but higher-level positions sometimes require longer hours, especially when major system changes are being implemented. Emergencies may also require specialists to work overtime or long hours without a break, sometimes through the night.

Sources of Additional Information

For general information on career opportunities or information regarding one of their three hundred student chapters, contact:

Association of Information Technology Professionals
505 Busse Highway
Park Ridge, IL 60068
Tel: 847-825-8124

For more information about computer certification, contact:

Institute for Certification of Computing Professionals
2200 East Devon Avenue, Suite 247
Des Plaines, IL 60018
Tel: 847-299-4227
WWW: http://www.iccp.org

Dental Assistants

Definition

Dental assistants perform a variety of duties in the dental office, including helping the dentist examine and treat patients and completing laboratory and office work. They assist the dentist by preparing patients for dental exams, handing the dentist the proper instruments, taking and processing X-rays, preparing materials for making impressions and restorations, and instructing patients in oral health care. They also perform administrative and clerical tasks so that the office runs smoothly and the dentist's time is available for working with patients.

Nature of the Work

Dental assistants help dentists as they examine and treat patients. They usually greet patients, escort them to the examining room, and prepare them by covering their clothing with paper or cloth bibs. They also adjust the headrest of the examination chair and raise the chair to the proper height. Many dental assistants take X-rays of patients' teeth and process the film for the dentist to examine. They also obtain patients' dental records from the office files, so the dentist can review them before the examination.

During dental examinations and operations, dental assistants hand the dentist instruments as they are needed and use suction devices to keep the patient's mouth dry. When the examination or procedure is completed, assistants may give the patient after-care instructions for the teeth and mouth. They also provide instructions on infection-control procedures, preventing plaque buildup, and keeping teeth and gums clean and healthy between office visits.

Dental assistants also help with a variety of other clinical tasks. When a dentist needs a cast of a patient's teeth or mouth—used for diagnosing and planning the correction of dental problems—assistants may mix the necessary materials necessary. They may also pour, trim, and polish these study casts.

Some assistants prepare materials for making dental restorations, and many polish and clean patients' dentures. Some may perform the necessary laboratory work to make temporary dental replacements.

State laws determine which clinical tasks a dental assistant is able to perform. Dental assistants are not the same as *dental hygienists*, who are licensed to perform a wider variety of clinical tasks such as scaling and polishing teeth. Some states allow dental assistants to apply medications to teeth and gums, isolate individual teeth for treatment using rubber dams, and remove excess cement after cavities have been filled. In some states dental assistants can actually put fillings in patients' mouths. Dental assistants may also check patients' vital signs, update and check medical histories, and help the dentist with any medical emergencies that arise during dental procedures.

Many dental assistants also perform clerical and administrative tasks. These include receptionist duties, scheduling appointments, managing patient records, keeping dental supply inventories, preparing bills for services rendered, collecting payments, and issuing receipts. Dental assistants often act as business managers who perform all nonclinical responsibilities such as hiring and firing auxiliary help, scheduling employees, and overseeing office accounting.

Requirements

Most dental assistant positions are entry level. They usually require little or no experience and no education beyond high school. High school students who wish to work as dental assistants should take courses in general science, biology, health, chemistry, and business management. Typing is also an important skill for dental assistants.

Dental assistants commonly acquire their skills on the job. Many, however, go on to receive training after high school at trade schools, technical institutes, and community and junior colleges that offer dental assisting programs. The armed forces also trains some dental assistants.

Students who complete two-year college programs receive associate's degrees, while those who complete one-year trade and technical school programs earn a certificate or diploma. Entrance requirements to these programs require a high school diploma and good grades in high school science, typing, and English. Some postsecondary schools require an interview or written examination, and some require that applicants pass physical and dental examinations. About 240 of these programs are accredited by the American Dental Association's Commission on Dental Accreditation. Some four- to six-month nonaccredited courses in dental assisting are also available from private vocational schools. The University of Kentucky College of Dentistry offers a correspondence course for assistants who cannot participate full time in an accredited, formal program. The course generally takes two years to complete and is equivalent to one year of full-time formal study.

Accredited programs instruct students in dental assisting skills and theory through classes, lectures, and laboratory and preclinical experience. Students take courses in English, speech, and psychology as well as in the biomedical sciences, including anatomy, microbiology, and nutrition. Courses in dental science cover subjects such as oral anatomy and pathology, and dental radiography. Students also gain practical experience in chairside assisting and office management by working in dental schools and local dental clinics that are affiliated with their program. Graduates of such programs may be assigned a greater variety of tasks initially and may receive higher starting salaries than those with high school diplomas alone.

Dental assistants may wish to obtain certification from the Dental Assisting National Board, but this is usually not required for employment. Certified dental assistant (CDA) accreditation shows that an assistant meets certain standards of professional competence. To take the certification examination, assistants must be high school graduates who have taken a course in cardiopulmonary resuscitation and must have either a diploma from a formal train-

ing program accredited by the Commission on Dental Accreditation or two years of full-time work experience with a recommendation from the dentist for whom the work was done.

In twenty-one states dental assistants are allowed to take X-rays (under a dentist's direction) only after completing a precise training program and passing a test. Completing the program for CDA certification fulfills this requirement. To keep their CDA credentials, however, assistants must either prove their skills through retesting or acquire further education.

Dental assistants need a clean, well-groomed appearance and a pleasant personality. Manual dexterity and the ability to follow directions are also important.

Opportunities for Experience & Exploration

Students in formal training programs receive dental assisting experience as part of their training. High school students can learn more about the field by talking with assistants in local dentists' offices. The American Dental Assistants Association, through the ADA SELECT program, can put students in contact with dental assistants in their areas. Part-time, summer, and temporary clerical work may also be available in dentists' offices.

Methods of Entering

High school guidance counselors, family dentists, dental schools, dental placement agencies, and dental associations may provide applicants with leads about job openings. Students in formal training programs often learn of jobs through school placement services.

Most dentists work in private practice, so that's where a dental assistant is most likely to find a job. An office may have a single dentist or it may be a group practice with several dentists, assistants, and hygienists. Other places to work include dental schools, hospitals, public health departments, and U.S. Veterans and Public Health Service hospitals.

Advancement

Dental assistants may advance in their field by moving to larger offices or clinics, where they can take on more responsibility and earn more money. In small offices they may receive higher pay by upgrading their skills through education. Specialists in the dental field, who typically earn higher salaries than general dentists, often pay higher salaries to their assistants.

Further educational training is required for advancing to positions in dental assisting education. Dental assistants who wish to become dental hygienists must enroll in a dental hygiene program. Because many of these programs do not allow students to apply dental assisting courses toward graduation, dental assistants who think they would like to move into hygienist positions should plan their training carefully.

In some cases, dental assistants move into sales jobs with companies that sell dental industry supplies and materials. Other areas that open to dental assistants include office management, placement services, and insurance companies.

Employment Outlook

According to the U.S. Department of Labor, employment for dental assistants is expected to grow much faster than average for all occupations through 2006, with about fifty percent more jobs expected to open in the field. Advances in dental care now allow the general population to maintain better dental health as well as keep their natural teeth longer. Thus, more people will seek dental services for preventative care and cosmetic improvements.

Recent graduates are more likely to hire assistants as compared to older dentists. Dental assistants can handle routine jobs, allowing dentists to perform more difficult and profitable procedures.

Also, as dentists increase their knowledge of innovative techniques such as implantology and periodontal therapy, they generally delegate more routine tasks to assistants so they can make the best use of their time and increase profits. Job openings will also be created through attrition as other assistants leave the field or change jobs.

Earnings

Dental assistants' salaries are determined by specific responsibilities, type of office they work in, and the geographic location of their employer. According to the American Dental Association's 1996 Survey of Dental Practice, the average earnings of full-time dental assistants working for general dentists were between $14,700 and $23,500 a year. Dental assistants working for specialists, such as orthodontists or pediatric dentists, earn slightly more.

About 25 percent of dental assistants work part time. Some offices offer benefits packages such as paid vacations and insurance coverage.

Conditions of Work

Dental assistants work in offices that are generally clean, modern, quiet, and pleasant. They are also well lighted and well ventilated. In small offices, dental assistants may work solely with dentists, while in larger offices and clinics they may work with dentists, other dental assistants, dental hygienists, and laboratory technicians. Although dental assistants may sit at desks to do office work, they spend a large part of the day beside the dentist's chair where they can reach instruments and materials.

About one-third of all dental assistants work forty-hour weeks, sometimes including Saturday hours. About one-half work between thirty-one and thirty-eight hours a week. The remainder work less, but some part-time workers work in more than one dental office.

Taking X-rays poses some risk because regular doses of radiation can be harmful to the body. However, all dental offices must have lead shielding and safety procedures that minimize the risk of exposure to high levels of radiation.

Sources of Additional Information

American Association of Dental Examiners
211 East Chicago Avenue, Suite 760
Chicago, IL 60611
Tel: 312-440-7464

American Association of Dental Schools
1625 Massachusetts Avenue, NW
Washington, DC 20036
Tel: 202-667-9433
Email: aads@aads.jhu.edu

American Dental Assistants Association
203 North LaSalle Street, Suite 1320
Chicago, IL 60601
Tel: 312-541-1320

American Dental Association
211 East Chicago Avenue
Chicago, IL 60611
Tel: 312-440-2500
WWW: http://www.ada.org/prac/careers/dc-menu.html

Dental Assisting National Board, Inc.
216 East Ontario Street
Chicago, IL 60611
Tel: 312-642-3368

National Association of Dental Assistants
900 South Washington Street, Suite G13
Falls Church, VA 22046
Tel: 703-237-8616

Dental Hygienists

Definition

Dental hygienists perform clinical tasks, serve as oral health educators in private dental offices, work in public health agencies, and promote good oral health by educating adults and children. Their main responsibility is to perform oral prophylaxis, a process of cleaning teeth by using sharp dental instruments, such as scalers and prophy angles. With these instruments, they remove stains and calcium deposits, polish teeth, and massage gums.

Nature of the Work

In clinical settings, hygienists help prevent gum diseases and cavities by removing deposits from teeth and applying sealants and fluoride to prevent tooth decay. They remove tartar, stains, and plaque from teeth, take X rays and other diagnostic tests, place and remove temporary fillings, take health histories, remove sutures, polish amalgam restorations, and examine head, neck, and oral regions for disease.

Their tools include hand and rotary instruments to clean teeth, syringes with needles to administer local anesthetic (such as Novocaine), teeth models to explain home care procedures, and X-ray machines to take pictures of the oral cavity that the dentist uses to detect signs of decay or oral disease.

A hygienist also provides nutritional counseling and screens patients for oral cancer and high blood pressure. More extensive dental procedures are done by dentists. The hygienist is also trained and licensed to take and develop X-rays. Other responsibilities depend on the employer.

Private dentists might require that the dental hygienist mix compounds for filling cavities, sterilize instruments, assist in surgical work, or even carry out clerical tasks such as making appoint-ments and filling in insurance forms. The hygienist might well fill the duties of receptionist or office manager, functioning in many ways to assist the dentist in carrying out the day's schedule.

Although some of these tasks might also be done by a *dental assistant*, only the dental hygienist is licensed by the state to clean teeth. Licensed hygienists submit charts of each patient's teeth, noting possible decay or disease. The dentist studies these in making further diagnoses.

The *school hygienist* cleans and examines the teeth of students in a number of schools. The hygienist also gives classroom instruction on correct brushing and flossing of teeth, the importance of good dental care, and the effects of good nutrition. Dental records of students are kept, and parents must be notified of any need for further treatment.

Dental hygienists may be employed by local, state, or federal public health agencies. These hygienists carry out an educational program for adults and children, in public health clinics, schools, and other public facilities. A few dental hygienists may assist in research projects. For those with further education, teaching in a dental hygiene school may be possible.

Like all dental professionals, hygienists must be aware of federal, state, and local laws that govern hygiene practice. In particular, hygienists must know the types of infection control and protective gear that, by law, must be worn in the dental office to protect workers from infection. Dental hygienists, for example, must wear gloves, protective eyewear, and a mask during examinations. As with most health care workers, hygienists must be immunized against contagious diseases, such as hepatitis.

Dental hygienists are required by their state and encouraged by professional organizations to continue learning about trends in dental care, procedures, and regulations by taking continuing education courses. These may be held at large dental society meetings, colleges and universities, or in more intimate settings, such as a nearby dental office.

Requirements

The minimum requirement for admission to a dental hygiene school is graduation from high school. While in high school, students should follow a college preparatory program. Two types of postsecondary training are available to the prospective dental hygienist. One is a four-year college program offering a bachelor's degree. More common is a two-year program leading to a dental hygiene certification. The bachelor's degree is often preferred by employers, and more schools are likely to require completion of such a degree program in the future. In 1997, there were about 230 accredited schools in the United States that offer one or both of these courses.

Aptitude tests sponsored by the American Dental Hygienists' Association are frequently required by dental hygiene schools to help applicants determine whether they will succeed in this field. Skill in handling delicate instruments, a sensitive touch, and depth perception are important attributes that are tested. The hygienist should be neat, clean, and personable.

Classroom work emphasizes general and dental sciences and liberal arts. Lectures are usually combined with laboratory work and clinical experience.

Dental hygienists, after graduation from accredited schools, must pass state licensing examinations, both written and clinical. The American Dental Association Joint Commission on National Dental Examinations administers the written part of the examination. This test is accepted by all states and the District of Columbia. The clinical part of the examination is administered by state or regional testing agencies.

Opportunities for Experience & Exploration

Work as a dental assistant can be a stepping-stone to a dental hygienist's career. As a dental assistant, one could closely observe the work of a dental hygienist. The individual could then assess personal aptitude for this work, discuss any questions with other hygienists, and enroll in a dental hygiene school where experience as a dental assistant would certainly be helpful.

A high school student may be able to find part-time or summer work as a dental assistant or clerical worker in a dentist's office. A prospective dental hygiene student also may be able to arrange to observe a dental hygienist working in a school or a dentist's office or visit an accredited dental hygiene school. The aptitude testing program required by most dental hygiene schools helps students assess their future abilities as dental hygienists.

Methods of Entering

Once dental hygienists have passed the National Board exams and a licensing exam in a particular state, they must decide on an area of work, such as a private dentist's office, school system, or public health agency. Hospitals, industrial plants, and the armed forces employ a small number of dental hygienists. Most dental hygiene schools maintain placement services for the assistance of their graduates, and finding a satisfactory position is usually not too difficult.

Advancement

Opportunities for advancement, other than increases in salary and benefits that accompany experience in the field, usually require additional study and training. Educational advancement may lead to a position as an administrator, teacher, or director in a dental health program or to a more advanced field of practice. With further education and training, some hygienists may choose to go on to become dentists.

Employment Outlook

Dental hygienists are projected to be one of the twenty fastest growing occupations, according to the U.S. Department of Labor. About fifty percent more dental hygiene positions are expected to be created between 1996 and 2006. The demand for dental hygienists is expected to grow as younger generations who grew up receiving better dental care keep their teeth longer.

Population growth, increased public awareness of proper oral home care, and the availability of dental insurance should result in the creation of more dental hygiene jobs. Moreover, as the population ages, there will be a special demand for hygienists to work with older people, especially those who live in nursing homes.

Because of increased awareness about caring for animals in captivity, hygienists are also among a small number of dental professionals who volunteer to help care for animals' teeth and perform annual examinations. Dental professionals are not licensed to treat animals, however, and must work under the supervision of veterinarians.

Earnings

The dental hygienist's income is influenced by such factors as education, experience, locale, and type of employer. Most dental hygienists who work in private dental offices are salaried employees though some are paid a commission for work performed or a combination of salary and commission.

According to the U.S. Department of Labor, in 1996 the average earnings of full-time hygienists ranged between $24,000 and $39,500 a year. The average hourly wage for full-time hygienists was $20.40; the average for part-time hygienists was $24.50. Beginning hygienists earned an average of $15,200 to $17,500 a year. Salaries in large metropolitan areas are generally somewhat higher than in small cities and towns. In addition, dental hygienists in research, education, or administration may earn higher salaries.

A salaried dental hygienist in a private office typically receives a paid two- or three-week vacation. Part-time or commissioned dental hygienists in private offices usually have no paid vacation.

Conditions of Work

Working conditions for dental hygienists are pleasant, with well-lighted, modern, and adequately equipped facilities. Hygienists usually sit while working. State and federal regulations require that hygienists wear masks, protective eyewear, and gloves. Most hygienists don't wear any jewelry, such as earrings or wedding bands. They are required by government infection control procedures to leave their work clothes at work, so many dentists offices now have laundry facilities to properly launder work clothes. They must also follow proper sterilizing techniques on equipment and instruments to guard against passing infection or disease.

Approximately 50 percent of all hygienists work full time, about thirty-five to forty hours a week. It is common practice among part-time and full-time hygienists to work in more than one office because many dentists schedule a hygienist to come in only two or three days a week. Hygienists frequently piece together part-time positions at several dental offices and substitute for other hygienists who take days off. About 88 percent of hygienists see eight or more patients daily, and 68 percent work in only one practice. Many private offices are open on Saturday. Government employees' work hours are regulated by the particular agency.

Sources of Additional Information

American Association of Dental Examiners
211 East Chicago Avenue, Suite 760
Chicago, IL 60611
Tel: 312-440-7464

American Association of Dental Schools
1625 Massachusetts Avenue, NW
Washington, DC 20036
Tel: 202-667-9433
Email: aads@aads.jhu.edu

American Dental Association
211 East Chicago Avenue
Chicago, IL 60611
Tel: 312-440-2500
WWW: http://www.ada.org/prac/careers/dc-menu.html

American Dental Hygienists' Association
444 North Michigan Avenue, Suite 3400
Chicago, IL 60611
Tel: 312-440-8929
WWW: http://www.adha.org

National Dental Hygienists' Association
5506 Connecticut Avenue, NW, Suite 24-25
Washington, DC 20015
Tel: 202-244-7555

Dentists

Definition

Dentists attempt to maintain their clients' teeth through such preventive and reparative practices as extracting, filling, cleaning, or replacing teeth. They perform corrective work, such as straightening teeth, and treat diseased tissue of the gums. They also perform surgical operations on the jaw or mouth, and make and fit false teeth

Nature of the Work

For centuries, the practice of dentistry consisted largely of curing toothaches by extraction or the use of herbs and similar methods to alleviate pain. It was practiced not only by dentists but by barbers and blacksmiths as well. Dental care and correction have become a sophisticated branch of medicine, and dentists are now highly trained professionals of great importance to the public health.

Most dentists are general practitioners, but almost 20 percent practice as specialists. The largest number of these specialists are orthodontists, followed by oral surgeons, pedodontists, periodontists, prosthodontists, endodontists, oral pathologists, and public health dentists.

General practitioners must be proficient in many areas of dentistry. They must not only handle routine treatments, such as cleaning teeth, extracting teeth, and filling cavities but also be on the alert for any condition in the mouth requiring special treatment, such as crooked teeth, diseased gums, and oral cancer. General practitioners must be able to use and understand X rays and be well acquainted with laboratory work.

Specialists devote their time and skills to specific dental problems. *Orthodontists* correct irregularities in the development of teeth and jaws by braces and similar devices. *Oral surgeons* perform difficult tooth extractions, remove tumors from the gums or jaw, and set jaw fractures. *Periodontists* treat diseased gums and other tissues that support the teeth. *Oral pathologists* examine and diagnose tumors and lesions of the mouth. *Public health dentists* work through public health agencies to treat and educate the public on the importance of dental health and care.

Requirements

A high school diploma is required for admission into dental school. In high school, the prospective dental student should be sure to study biology, chemistry, physics, health, and mathematics. Liberal arts courses are also important for meeting college entrance requirements and developing good communications skills. Participation in extracurricular activities is helpful because it provides opportunities to interact with many different people and develop interpersonal skills. The student should also note the importance of manual dexterity and scientific ability. Skilled, steady hands are necessary, as well as good space and shape judgment, and some artistic ability. Good vision is required because of the detailed work.

The dental profession is selective, and standards are high. College grades and the amount of college education are carefully considered in the application process. All dental schools approved by the American Dental Association require applicants to pass the Dental Admissions Test, which gauges a student's ability to succeed or fail in dental school. Information on tests and testing centers may be obtained from the Council on Dental Education of the American Dental Association.

Dental schools require at least two years of college-level predental education. About 80 percent of students entering dental schools have already earned a bachelor's or master's degree. Professional training in a dental school generally requires four academic years. Many dental schools have an inter-disciplinary curriculum in which the dental student studies basic science with medical, pharmacy, and other health profession students. Clinical training is frequently begun in the second year. Most schools now feature a Department of Community Dentistry, which involves a study of communities, urban ghetto problems and sociology, and includes treatment of patients from the community. Generally the degree of doctor of dental surgery (D.D.S.) is granted upon graduation, although some schools give the degree of doctor of dental medicine (D.D.M. or D.M.D.).

Dental students who wish to enter a specialized field should plan on postgraduate study ranging from two to five years. A specialist can only become certified by passing specialty board exams. Further training may be obtained as a dental intern or resident in an approved hospital. Of course, a dentist must continually keep abreast of developments in the profession through reading professional magazines and journals, taking short-term graduate courses, and participating in seminars.

All fifty states and the District of Columbia require dentists to be licensed. To qualify for a license in most states, a candidate must graduate from a dental school accredited by the American Dental Association's Commission on Dental Accreditation and pass written and practical examinations. Candidates may fulfill the written part of the exam by passing the National Board Dental Examinations. Individual states or regional testing agencies give the written or practical examinations. Generally, dentists licensed in one state are required to take another exam to practice in another state. However, twenty states grant licenses to dentists from other states based on their credentials.

Opportunities for Experience & Exploration

A high school student might be able to gain an awareness of the demands of dentistry by observing a dentist at work. Work as a dental hygienist, dental assistant, or dental laboratory technician might lead to continued study in dentistry. Because of the nature of dentistry, developing good manual dexterity through sculpting or metal working would be helpful to the prospective dentist.

Methods of Entering

Once a dentist has graduated from an approved dental school and passed a state licensing examination, there are three common avenues of entry into private practice. A dentist may open a new office, purchase an established practice, or join another dentist or group of dentists to gain further experience. There are, however, other choices for licensed dentists. They may enter the armed forces as a commissioned officer, or through civil service procedures become eligible for work in the U.S. Public Health Service. They may also choose to work in a hospital, clinic, or school. For some, work in the dental laboratory or in teaching dentistry will provide a satisfying career.

Advancement

Advancement for the newly licensed dentist in private practice depends on personal skill in handling patients as well as dental work. Through the years, the successful dentist builds a reputation and thus advances with a growing clientele. The quality of the work depends in part on an ability to keep up with developments in the field. For salaried dentists in the various areas of employment, advancement will also depend on the quality and skill of their work. Advancement may take the form of a step from general practitioner to specialist, a step requiring further study and generally providing higher income. Teachers may look forward to administrative positions or to appointments as professors.

Success may also depend on the location of the practice; people in higher income areas are more likely to request dental care. In small towns and sparsely populated areas a great need exists for dentists, and competition is slight. In cities where there are many dentists, it may be more difficult to establish a practice despite the larger pool of possible patients.

Employment Outlook

Although employment of dentists is expected to grow more slowly than the average for all other occupations, many positions will open as a result of the need to replace the large number of dentists who have reached retirement age or who have opted to stay in practice while reducing their office hours.

Additionally, opportunities for specialists, such as cosmetic dentists, will be very good through the year 2006. This specialty was listed in a recent *US News & World Report* article as of the best jobs for the future. Three-fourths of American adults believe that a winning smile is related to job success. Most adults are unhappy with their teeth, creating a demand for dentists skilled in cosmetic techniques such as bleaching and veneering. People are more concerned about dental health and can better afford dental care, especially because dental insurance is becoming more readily available. Cosmetic dentists will be in demand in large metropolitan areas such as Los Angeles and Chicago.

Scientific advances in the field offer a promising future for specialists. The work, for example, of the oral pathologist or orthodontist will increase as people become more aware of the need for such care. Public health programs, too, can be expected to expand. Dentistry today is focusing more on preventive care than reparative practice.

Interestingly, the number of applicants to dental schools is decreasing, yet standards remain high and admission is competitive. The number of women graduating from dental schools is increasing. High school students must be aware of the importance of maintaining high grades if they wish to qualify. Despite diminishing enrollments, the number of new graduates entering the field each year is larger than the number of openings. Dentists rarely leave the profession except to retire, and many continue to work beyond retirement age, simply reducing the number of hours they work.

One hundred sixty-two thousand dentists were employed in the United States in 1996. Nine out of ten were in private practice. Of the remainder, about half worked in research or teaching, or held administrative positions in dental schools. Some practiced in hospitals and clinics. About 79 percent of all dentists were general practitioners; the remainder were specialists.

The expense of pursuing an education in dentistry and setting up a practice is significant. The prospective dental student should be aware of these financial demands before entering the field. However, in a recent survey reported in *Inc. magazine,*

dental offices were the third highest ranking category of start-up businesses most likely to survive. According to the American Dental Association, among dentists out of dental school less than four years, about 42 percent owned their practice; by six years after graduation 53 percent had their own practice.

Earnings

Beginning dentists, faced with the expense of buying equipment and the problem of establishing a practice, generally earn enough to cover expenses and little more. However, income rises rapidly as the dentist's practice becomes established. According to the American Dental Association, the average net income of the self-employed dentist in 1995 was about $120,000 a year; general practitioners averaged $109,000; specialists, $175,000.

Dentists' earnings are lower during economic downturns when people tend to postpone dental treatment except for emergencies.

Conditions of Work

Because most dentists are in private practice, they are free to set their hours and establish offices and atmospheres suitable to their individual tastes. Most dentists work from four to five days, many times averaging forty or more hours a week. They spend about 89 percent of their time treating patients. The beginning dentist must set aside expensive decorating plans in favor of suitable equipment, but most dentists' offices are designed to be pleasant and comfortable. Dentists may have a dental assistant, hygienist, or laboratory technician, or they may carry out the special duties of each themselves. However, there is a growing trend to leave simpler tasks, teeth cleaning for example, to dental assistants and hygienists, so dentists have more time to perform higher paying procedures, such as root canals.

The dentist in private practice sets individual hours and practices after office hours only in emergencies. Salaried dentists working for a clinic, hospital, or the Public Health Service are subject to conditions set by their employers.

Sources of Additional Information

For admission requirements of U.S. and Canadian dental schools, please contact:

American Association of Dental Schools
1625 Massachusetts Avenue, NW, Suite 600
Washington, DC 20036
Tel: 202-667-9433
WWW: http://www.aads.jhu.edu/

For a list of accredited schools for postgraduate and post-doctoral work, write to:

American Dental Association
Department of Career Guidance
211 East Chicago Avenue
Chicago, IL 60611
Tel: 312-440-2500
WWW: http://www.ada.org/tc-educ.html

Desktop Publishing Specialists

Definition

Desktop publishing specialists use computers to prepare files for printing. They take files that others have created and manipulate the images and text so they will print properly. Desktop publishing specialists also write and edit text, as well as organize and layout the pages of a book.

Nature of the Work

Desktop publishing specialists work on computers, converting and preparing files for printing presses or other mediums. Much of desktop publishing fits into the prepress category, and desktop publishing specialists typeset, or arrange and transform, text and graphics into finished products or products ready to be printed. Typesetting and page layout work entails selecting font types and sizes, arranging column widths, checking for proper spacing between letters, words, and columns, placing graphics and pictures, and more. Editing is also an important duty of a desktop publishing specialist. Articles must be updated, or in some cases rewritten, before it can be arranged on a page.

Desktop publishing specialists also deal with technical issues of files, such as resolution problems, colors that need to be corrected, and software difficulties. Specialists who work for service bureaus handle the technical issues of graphic designers and provide prepress services, including film output. Graphic designers use their creativity and artistic skills to create designs, often from scratch. Some may use computer software programs, while others draw with pencil and paper. They provide the desktop publishing specialists with their designs, and the desktop publishing specialists must convert these designs to the format requested by the designers. A designer may come in with a hand-drawn sketch, a printout of a design, or a file on a diskette, and he or she may want the design to be ready for publication on the World Wide Web, in a high-quality brochure, or in a newspaper or magazine. Each format presents different issues, and the desktop publishing specialist must be familiar with the processes and solutions for each. Service bureaus also provide services such as color scanning, laminating, image manipulation, or poster production.

Desktop publishing specialists at commercial printing houses generally focus less on the technical issues of designs and more on the printing end and prepress operations, although many commercial printers now have in-house service bureaus. Desktop publishing specialists receive disks from customers, check the files for problems, then print the files to film or directly onto printing plates. The process of converting files on disks to film or printing plates is known as digital imaging. The job of the desktop publishing specialist is to ensure that the images on the film or plates will print perfectly and accurately.

One specialization within desktop publishing at the commercial printing house is the *preflight technician*. After a customer brings in a disk, the preflight technician performs an initial check of the files to make sure the files are ready to go into production. This can entail checking the disk contents against a hard copy or printout supplied by the customer and making sure the fonts, colors, resolutions, and all other details are satisfactory. Once the check is complete, the process of printing the files to film can begin.

Desktop publishing specialists can also specialize in scanning. *Scanner operators* focus on color correction, color separation, and image manipulation. They use computerized equipment to output the film that will be used to print the final product. The computer handles the color separation process, which involves producing four-color separation negatives from a print. In printing, photographs must be printed from images consisting of millions of tiny dots. In order to create an accurate reproduction of an original color print, it's necessary to produce separation negatives that will be combined during the printing process. Each scan produces an image of the tiny dots representing one of four colors—cyan, yellow, magenta, and black. Separate printing plates are made for each of these scans and, using transparent color inks, they are printed one at a time. The final result combines all the colors and produces a replica of the original print or photograph. The scanner operator corrects color errors and enhances color where necessary. For instance, the original print may have uneven color or fading problems.

Requirements

Although a college degree is not a prerequisite, many desktop publishing specialists have at least a bachelor's degree, especially those who desire to move into management positions. Areas of study range anywhere from English to communications, to graphic design. Some two-year colleges and technical institutes offer programs in desktop publishing or related fields. A growing number of schools offer programs in technical and visual communications, which may include classes in desktop publishing, layout and design, and computer graphics. Four-year colleges also offer courses in technical communications and graphic design. There are many opportunities to take classes related to desktop publishing through extended education programs offered through universities and colleges. These classes can range from basic desktop publishing techniques to advanced courses in Adobe Photoshop or QuarkXPress and are often taught by professionals working in the industry.

Many of the skills and techniques needed to be a good desktop publishing specialist are actually learned on the job. Work experience may be as important as instruction gained from the classroom. Certification is not mandatory, and currently there is only one certification program offered in desktop publishing. The Association of Graphic Communications has an Electronic Publishing Certificate designed to set industry standards and measure the competency levels of desktop publishing specialists. The examination is divided into a written portion and a hands-on portion. During the practical portion of the examination, candidates receive files on a disk and must manipulate images and text, make color corrections, and perform whatever tasks are necessary to create the final product. Applicants are expected to be knowledgeable in print production, color separation, typography and font management, computer hardware and software, image manipulation, page layout, scanning and color correcting, prepress and preflighting, and output device capabilities.

The Printing Industries of America, Inc. (PIA) is in the process of developing industry standards in the prepress and press industries. PIA may eventually design a certification program in desktop publishing or electronic prepress operation.

A number of professional organizations and schools offer scholarship and grant opportunities. The Graphic Arts Education and Research Foundation (GAERF) and the Education Council of the Graphic Arts Industry, Inc., both divisions of the Association for Suppliers of Printing and Publishing Technologies (NPES), can provide information on scholarship opportunities and research grants (see "Sources of Additional Information"). Other organizations that offer financial awards and information on scholarship opportunities include the Society for Technical Communication, the International Prepress Association, PIA, and the Graphic Arts Technical Foundation, which offers scholarships in graphic communications through the National Scholarship Trust Fund.

Desktop publishing specialists are detail oriented, possess problem-solving skills, and have a sense of design or some artistic skills. A good eye and patience are critical, as well as endurance to see projects through to the finish. They should have an aptitude for computers, the ability to type quickly and accurately, and a natural curiosity. A calm temperament comes in handy when working under pressure and constant deadlines. Desktop publishing specialists should be flexible and be able to handle more than one project at a time.

Opportunities for Experience & Exploration

Classes that will help students develop desktop publishing skills include computer classes and design or art classes. Computer classes should include both hardware and software, since understanding how computers function will help you with troubleshooting and knowing the computers' limits. In photography classes you can learn about composition, color, and design elements. Typing, drafting, and print shop classes, if available, will also provide you with the opportunity to gain some indispensable skills. Working on the school newspaper or yearbook will train you on desktop publishing skills as well, including page layout, typesetting, composition, and working under a deadline.

Joining computer clubs or volunteering at small organizations to produce newsletters or flyers are other activities that will be beneficial, as will experimenting with a home computer. Also, part-time or summer employment with printing shops or companies that have in-house publishing or printing departments are great ways to gain experience and make valuable contacts. Many small businesses and nonprofit organizations need help producing newsletters, brochures, letterhead, flyers, catalogs, and more. Volunteering is an excellent way to try new software and techniques, and to gain experience troubleshooting and creating final products.

Methods of Entering

Most desktop publishing specialists enter the field through the production side, or the editorial side of the industry. Those with training as a designer or artist can easily master the finer techniques of production. Printing houses and design agencies are places to check for production artist opportunities. Writers with experience in editing existing text, or researching new content for a project, are always in demand. Publishing companies often hire such desktop publishing specialists to work in-house or as freelance employees.

The primary employers of desktop publishing specialists are publishing houses, printing shops, service bureaus, newspaper plants, and large companies with in-house graphics or design staffs. Basically, any organization with a printing department will have a need for desktop publishing specialists. Printing shops handle both commercial and business printing. Commercial printing involves catalogs, brochures, and reports, while business printing encompasses products used by businesses, such as sales receipts or forms.

Jobs with the federal government are another option for desktop publishing specialists. The Government Accounting Office (GAO) and the Government Printing Office (GPO) publish a large amount of documents. The GPO even has a Digital Information Technology Support Group (DITS Group) that provides desktop and electronic publishing services to federal agencies.

Advancement

Desktop publishing specialists can move into middle management or sales positions within a printing firm. *Prepress managers* oversee prepress departments and supervise staff members. Prepress managers may be responsible for scheduling, staffing, and the purchasing of equipment, including computer hardware and software. *Sales representatives* work for printing firms or publishing houses. Their job is to find new customers and expand business.

Desktop publishing specialists can also shift into Web design or specialize further in electronic prepress operations. *Web designers*, however, use a different set of tools to accomplish their goals, so some additional training would most likely be necessary. Desktop publishing specialists with a considerable amount of design experience may find work as *art directors* for large companies or advertising agencies. Freelance work is another possibility for desktop publishing specialists.

Employment Outlook

According to the *1998–99 Occupational Outlook Handbook*, the field of desktop publishing is projected to be one of the fastest growing occupations, increasing about 75 percent through the year 2006. In 1996, there were a total of 30,000 desktop publishing specialists employed in the United States. As technology advances, the ability to create and publish documents will become easier and faster, thus influencing more businesses to produce printed materials. Desktop publishing specialists will be needed to satisfy typesetting, page layout, design, and editorial demands. With new equipment, commercial printing shops will be able to shorten the turnaround time on projects and in turn can increase business and accept more jobs. For instance, digital printing presses allow printing shops to print directly to the digital press rather than printing to a piece of film, and then printing from the film to the press. Digital printing presses eliminate an entire step and should appeal to companies who need jobs completed quickly.

Prepress machine operators may notice a decline in employment opportunities as their work becomes more automated. Printing plants may also lose jobs to large companies with in-house printing and preparation capabilities. Desktop publishing specialists are best suited to fill these positions because of their skills with computers and electronic prepress operations.

According to a survey conducted by PIA in 1997, the printing industry is growing, which can be attributed partly to the growth experienced by the North American economy. The electronic prepress segment of the printing market enjoyed the most growth, with an average change from 1996 of 9.3 percent. Traditional prepress, on the other hand, suffered a decline of 5.7 percent. PIA's survey also indicates that printing firms have been experiencing difficulties finding new, qualified employees. This is a good sign for desktop publishing specialists with skills and experience.

QuarkXPress, Adobe PageMaker, Macromedia FreeHand, Adobe Illustrator, and Adobe Photoshop are some programs often used in desktop publishing. Specialists with experience in these and other software, will be demand.

Earnings

There is limited salary information available for desktop publishing specialists, most likely because the job duties of desktop publishing specialists can vary and often overlaps with other jobs. According to a salary survey conducted by PIA in 1997, the average wage of desktop publishing specialists in the prepress department ranged from $11.72 to $14.65 an hour, with the highest rate at $40 an hour. Entry-level desktop publishing specialists with little or no experience generally earn minimum wage. Electronic page makeup system operators earned an average of $13.62 to $16.96, and scanner operators ranged from $14.89 to $17.91.

According to the *1998–99 Occupational Outlook Handbook*, full-time prepress workers in typesetting and composition earned a median wage of $421 a week, or $21,892 annually. Wage rates vary depending on experience, training, region, and size of the company.

Conditions of Work

Desktop publishing specialists spend most of their time working in front of a computer, whether editing text, or laying out pages. They need to be able to work with other prepress operators, and deal with clients. Hours may vary depending on project deadlines at hand. Some projects may take one day to complete, while others may take a week or longer. Projects may range from designing a logo for letterhead, preparing a catalog for the printer, or working on a file that will be published on the World Wide Web.

Sources of Additional Information

The following organizations provide information on schools, scholarship opportunities, careers in desktop publishing, and employment.

Association of Graphic Communications
330 Seventh Avenue, 9th Floor
New York, NY 10001
WWW: http://www.agcomm.org

Association for Suppliers of Printing and Publishing Technologies (NPES)
Education Council of the Graphic Arts Industry, Inc.
Graphic Arts Education and Research Foundation
1899 Preston White Drive
Reston, VA 20191
Tel: 703-264-7200
WWW: http://www.npes.org

Graphic Arts Technical Foundation
PO Box 1020
Sewickley, PA 15143
Tel: 800-662-3916
WWW: http://www.gatf.org

International Digital Imaging Association
84 Park Avenue
Flemington, NJ 08822
Tel: 908-359-3924
WWW: http://www.idia.org

International Prepress Association
7200 France Avenue, Suite 327
Edina, MN 55435
Tel: 612-896-1908
WWW: http://www.ipa.org

National Association of Printers and Lithographers
780 Palisade Avenue
Teaneck, NJ 07666
Tel: 201-342-0700
WWW: http://www.napl.org

Printing Industries of America, Inc.
100 Daingerfield Road
Alexandria, VA 22314-2888
Tel: 703-519-8100
WWW: http://www.printing.org

Society for Technical Communication
901 North Stuart Street, Suite 904
Arlington, VA 22203-1854
Tel: 703-522-4114
WWW: http://www.stc-va.org

Electrical and Electronics Engineers

Definition

Electrical engineers apply their knowledge of the sciences toward working with equipment that produces and distributes electricity, such as generators, transmission lines, and transformers. They also design, develop, and manufacture electric motors, electrical machinery, and ignition systems for automobiles, aircraft, and other engines. *Electronics engineers* are more concerned with devices made up of electronic components such as integrated circuits and microprocessors. They design, develop, and manufacture products such as computers, telephones, and radios. Electronics engineering is a subfield of electrical engineering and both types of engineers are often referred to as electrical engineers.

Nature of the Work

Because electrical and electronics engineering is such a diverse field, there are numerous divisions and departments within which engineers work. The discipline reaches nearly every other field of applied science and technology. In general, electrical and electronics engineers use their knowledge of the sciences in the practical applications of electrical energy. They concern themselves with things as large as atom smashers and as small as microchips. They are involved in the invention, design, construction, and operation of electrical and electronic systems and devices of all kinds.

The work of electrical and electronics engineers touches almost every niche of our lives. Think of the things that have been designed, manufactured, maintained, or in any other way affected by electrical energy: the lights in a room; cars on the road; televisions, stereo systems, telephones; your doctor's blood-pressure reader; computers. Look around you and discover that the electrical engineer has in some way had a hand in science, industry, commerce, entertainment, even art.

The list of specialties that engineers are associated with reads like an alphabet of scientific titles—from acoustics, speech, and signal processing; to electromagnetic compatibility; geoscience and remote sensing; lasers and electro-optics; robotics; ultrasonics, ferroelectrics, and frequency control; to vehicular technology. As evident in this selected list, engineers are apt to specialize in what interests them, such as communications, robotics, or automobiles.

As mentioned earlier, electrical engineers focus on high-power generation of electricity—how it is transmitted for use in lighting homes and powering factories. They are also concerned with how equipment is designed and maintained and how communications are transmitted over wire. Some are involved in the design and construction of power plants and the manufacture and maintenance of industrial machinery.

Electronics engineers work with smaller-scale applications—for example, how computers are wired, how appliances work, or how electrical circuits are used in an endless number of applications. They may specialize in computers, industrial equipment and controls, aerospace equipment, or biomedical equipment.

In both divisions of the field, there are a number of categories in which workers find their niche: research, development and design, production, field service, sales and marketing, and teaching. In addition, even within each category there are divisions of labor.

Researchers concern themselves mainly with issues that pertain to potential applications. They conduct tests and perform studies to evaluate fundamental problems involving such things as new materials and chemical interactions. Those who work in design and development adapt the researchers' findings to actual practical applications. They devise functioning devices and draw up plans for their efficient production, using computer-aided design and engineering (CAD/CAE) tools. For a typical product such as a television, this phase usually takes up to eighteen months to accomplish. For other products, particularly those that utilize developing technology, this phase can take as long as ten years or more.

Production engineers have perhaps the most hands-on tasks in the field. They are responsible for the organization of the actual manufacture of whatever electric product is being made. They take care of materials and machinery, schedule technicians and assembly workers, and make sure that standards are met and products are quality-controlled. These engineers must have access to the best tools for measurement, materials handling, and processing.

After electrical systems are put in place, *field service engineers* must act as the liaison between the manufacturer or distributor and the client. They ensure the correct installation, operation, and maintenance of systems and products for both industry and individuals. In the sales and marketing divisions, engineers stay abreast of customer needs in order to evaluate potential applications, and they advise their companies of orders and effective marketing. A *sales engineer* would contact a client interested in, say, a certain type of microchip for its automobile electrical system controls. He or she would learn about the client's needs and report back to the various engineering teams at his or her company. During the manufacture and distribution of the product, the sales engineer would continue to provide information between company and client until all objectives were met.

All engineers must be taught to be engineers, and so it is important that some remain involved in academia. Professors usually teach a portion of the basic engineering courses as well as classes in the subjects that they are specialized in. Conducting personal research is generally an ongoing task for professors in addition to the supervision of student work and student research. A part of the teacher's time is also devoted to providing career and academic guidance to students.

Requirements

Electrical and electronics engineers must have a solid educational background. The discipline is based on much in the applied sciences but requires a clear understanding of practical applications. To prepare for college, high school students should take classes in algebra, trigonometry, calculus, biology, physics, chemistry, computer science, word processing, English, and social studies. Students who are planning to pursue studies beyond a bachelor of science degree will also need to take a foreign language. Students should aim for honors-level courses.

A bachelor of science degree in electrical, electronics, or computer engineering or another related science is generally required for professional positions. It generally takes four to five years to complete a bachelor of science degree program. Numerous colleges and universities offer electrical, electronics, and computer engineering programs. Programs do vary from one school to another, and high school students should explore as many schools as possible to determine which program is most suited to their academic and personal interests and needs. Most engineering programs have strict admission requirements and require students to have excellent academic records and top scores on national college-entrance examinations. Competition can be fierce for some programs, and high school students are encouraged to apply early.

Many students go on to receive a master of science degree in a specialization of their choice. It usually takes an additional two years of study beyond a bachelor's program to obtain a master's degree. Some students pursue a master's degree immediately upon completion of a bachelor's degree. Other students gain work experience first and then take graduate-level courses on a part-time basis while they are employed. A doctoral degree, or Ph.D., is also available. It generally requires four years of study and research beyond the bachelor's degree and is usually completed by people interested in research or teaching.

By the time one reaches college, it is wise to be considering what specialty and position one might want to work in. In addition to the core engineering curriculum (advanced mathematics, physical science, engineering science, mechanical drawing, computer applications), students will begin to choose from the following types of courses: circuits and electronics; signals and systems; digital electronics and computer architecture; electromagnetic waves, systems, and machinery; communications; and statistical mechanics.

People planning on becoming electrical or electronics engineers should have strong problem-solving abilities, mathematical and scientific aptitudes, and the willingness to learn throughout one's career. Most engineers work on teams with other professionals, and the ability to get along with others is essential. In addition, strong communications skills are needed. Engineers need to be able to write reports and give oral presentations.

Opportunities for Experience & Exploration

People who are interested in the excitement of electricity can tackle experiments such as building a radio or central processing unit of a computer. Special assignments can also be researched and supervised by teachers. Joining a science club, such as the Junior Engineering Technical Society (JETS), can provide hands-on activities and opportunities to explore scientific topics in depth. Student members can join competitions and design structures that exhibit scientific know-how. Reading trade publications, such as the JETS Report, are other ways to learn about the engineering field. This magazine includes articles on engineering-related careers and club activities.

Students can also learn more about electrical and electronics engineering by attending a summer camp or academic program that focuses on scientific projects as well as recreational activities. For example, the Delphian School in Oregon holds summer sessions for high school students. Students are involved in leadership activities and special interests such as computers and electronics. Sports and wilderness activities are also offered. Summer programs such as the one offered by the Michigan Technological University focus on career exploration in computers, electronics, and robotics. This academic program for high school students also offers arts guidance, wilderness events, and other recreational activities. (For further information on clubs and programs, write to the addresses listed at the end of this article.)

Methods of Entering

Most electrical and electronics engineers work in industry, such as with design and manufacturing companies or consulting agencies. Others work for the federal government, as teachers in engineering schools and programs, and in research. Some work as private consultants.

Many students begin to research companies in which they are they are interested during their last two years of college. It is possible to research companies using many resources, such as company directories and annual reports, available at public libraries. General corporate guides such as *Dun's Employment Opportunity Directory*, list companies that are employing people in a wide range of fields, including electrical and electronics engineering. They give brief company profiles, describe possible positions within the company, and provide addresses to which applicants can write.

Employment opportunities can be found through a variety of sources. Students who have participated in an internship, work-study, or cooperative education program may receive job offers through these companies, or they may obtain useful contacts that can lead to a job interview or offer. Many companies recruit on college campuses, hold job fairs, and attend trade shows where they maintain a booth for interested applicants. Some companies use employment agencies and state employment offices. Companies may also advertise positions through advertisements in newspapers and trade publications. In addition, many newsletters and associations post job listings on the Internet.

Interested applicants can also apply directly to a company where they are interested in working. A letter of interest and resume can be sent to the director of engineering or the head of a specific department. One may also apply to the personnel or human resources departments.

Advancement

Engineering careers usually offer many avenues for advancement. An engineer straight out of college will usually take a job as an entry-level engineer and advance to higher positions after acquiring some job experience and technical skills. Engineers with strong technical skills who show leadership ability and good communications and interpersonal skills may advance to a *project engineer* or *managing engineer* position. Both of these positions involve supervising teams of engineers and making sure they are working efficiently. Engineers can advance from these positions to that of *chief engineer*. The chief engineer usually oversees all projects and has authority over project managers and managing engineers.

Many companies provide structured programs to train new employees and prepare them for advancement. These programs usually rely heavily on formal training opportunities such as in-house development programs and seminars. Some companies also provide special programs through colleges, universities, and outside agencies. Engineers usually advance from junior-level engineering positions to more senior-level positions through a series of positions. Engineers may also specialize in a specific area once they have acquired the necessary experience and skills.

Engineers may move into sales and managerial positions, with some engineers leaving the electronics industry to seek top-level management positions with other type of firms. Other engineers set up their own firms in design or consulting. Engineers can also move into the academic field and become teachers at high schools or universities.

The key to advancing in the electronics field is keeping pace with technological changes, which occur rapidly in this field. Electrical and electronics engineers will need to pursue additional training throughout their careers in order to stay up-to-date on new technologies and techniques.

Employment Outlook

More engineers work in the electrical and electronics field than in any other division of engineering. In the United States, there were approximately 367,000 such engineers holding jobs in the industry in 1996. Most engineers work in manufacturing companies that produce electrical and electronic equipment, business machines, computers and data processing companies, and telecommunications parts. Others work for companies that make automotive electronics, scientific equipment, and aircraft parts; consulting firms; public utilities; and government agencies.

The demand for electrical and electronics engineers fluctuates with changes in the economy. In the late 1980s and early 1990s, many companies producing defense products suffered from cutbacks in defense orders and made reductions in their engineering staffs. Current trends now show a high number of skilled engineers are needed to meet demands of increased computer and telecommunications production. The automobile industry is also hiring engineers to help perfect new uses for electronic components. Manufacturing companies need to promote research and development to successfully compete in today's global electronics marketplace; this will create many job openings. Opportunities for electrical and electronics engineers are expected to increase faster than the average for all occupations through the year 2006.

Good job growth and replacement needs should create many positions. However, high numbers of engineering graduates have increased the total number of electrical and electronics engineers in the job market, and competition is increasing for available positions. Successful engineers will need to stay on top of changes within the electronics industry and will need additional training throughout their careers to learn new technologies.

Economic trends and conditions within the worldwide marketplace have become more important. In the past, most electronics production was done in the United States or by American-owned companies. During the 1990s, this has changed, and the electronics industry is entering an era of global production. World economies and production trends will have a larger impact on U.S. production, and companies that cannot compete technologically may not succeed. Lifelong job security is no longer a sure thing, and many engineers can expect to make significant changes in their careers at least once. Engineers with a strong academic foundation, who have acquired technical knowledge and skills, and who stay up-to-date on changing technologies provide themselves with the versatility and flexibility to succeed within the electronics industry.

Earnings

Starting salaries for all engineers are generally much higher than for workers in any other field. According to the National Association of Colleges and Employers, the 1997 average starting salary of electrical engineers was about $39,513. The average salary for experienced electrical and electronics engineers with at least a bachelor's degree was about $51,000 a year. Engineers with a master's degree or Ph.D., earned considerably more.

Most companies offer attractive benefits packages, though the actual benefits vary from company to company. Benefits can include any of the following: paid holidays, paid vacations, personal days, sick leave; medical, health, and life insurance; short- and long-term disability insurance; profit sharing; 401(k) plans; retirement and pension plans; educational assistance; leave time for educational purposes; and credit unions. Some companies also offer computer purchase assistance plans and discounts on company products.

Conditions of Work

In many parts of the country, the five-day, forty-hour work week is still the norm, but it is becoming much less common. Many engineers regularly work ten or twenty hours of overtime a week. Engineers in research and development, or those conducting experiments, often need to work at night or on the weekend. Workers who supervise production activities may need to come in during the evenings or on weekends to handle special production requirements. In addition to the time spent on the job, many engineers also participate in professional associations and pursue additional training during their free time. Many high tech companies allow flex-time, which means that workers can arrange their own schedules within certain time frames.

Most electrical and electronics engineers work in fairly comfortable environments. Engineers involved in research and design may work in specially equipped laboratories. Engineers involved in development and manufacturing work in offices and may spend part of their time in production facilities. Depending on the type of work one does, there may be extensive travel. Engineers involved in field service and sales spend a significant time traveling to see clients. Engineers working for large corporations may travel to other plants and manufacturing companies, both around the country and at foreign locations.

Engineering professors spend part of their time teaching in classrooms, part of it doing research either in laboratories or libraries, and some of the time still connected with industry.

Sources of Additional Information

For information on careers and educational programs, please contact:

Institute of Electrical and Electronics Engineers (IEEE)
1828 L Street, NW, Suite 1202
Washington, DC 20036-5104
Tel: 202-785-0017
WWW: http://www.ieee.org/usab

Electronic Industries Association
2500 Wilson Boulevard
Arlington, VA 22201-3834
Tel: 703-907-7670

For information on careers, educational programs, and student clubs, please contact:

Junior Engineering Technical Society (JETS)
1420 King Street, Suite 405
Alexandria, VA 22314
Tel: 703-548-5387
Email: jets@nas.edu

For information on the Summer at Delphi Youth Program for high school students, please contact:

The Delphian School
20950 SW Rock Creek Road
Sheridan, OR 97378
Tel: 503-843-3521

For information on its summer youth program for high school students, please contact:

Michigan Technological University Summer Youth Program
Youth Programs Office
1400 Townsend Drive
Houghton, MI 49931
Tel: 906-487-1885

Electricians

Definition

Electricians design, lay out, assemble, install, test, and repair electrical fixtures, apparatus, and wiring used in a wide range of electrical, telecommunications, and data communications systems that provide light, heat, refrigeration, air-conditioning, power, and communications.

Nature of the Work

Many electricians specialize in either construction or maintenance work, although some work in both fields. Electricians in construction are usually employed by electrical contractors. Other *construction electricians* work for building contractors or industrial plants, public utilities, state highway commissions, or other large organizations that employ workers directly to build or remodel their properties. A few are self-employed.

Maintenance electricians, also known as *electrical repairers*, may work in large factories, office buildings, small plants, or wherever existing electrical facilities and machinery need regular servicing to keep them in good working order. Many maintenance electricians work in manufacturing industries, such as those that produce automobiles, aircraft, ships, steel, chemicals, and industrial machinery. Some are employed by hospitals, municipalities, housing complexes, or shopping centers to do maintenance, repair, and sometimes installation work. Some work for or operate businesses that contract to repair and update wiring in residences and commercial buildings.

When installing electrical systems, electricians may follow blueprints and specifications or they may be told verbally what is needed. They may prepare sketches showing the intended location of wiring and equipment. Once the plan is clear, they measure, cut, assemble, and install plastic-covered wire or electrical conduit, which is a tube or channel through which heavier grades of electrical wire or cable are run. They strip insulation from wires, splice and solder wires together, and tape or cap the ends. They attach cables and wiring to the incoming electrical service and to various fixtures and machines that use electricity. They install switches, circuit breakers, relays, transformers, grounding leads, signal devices, and other electrical components. After the installation is complete, they test circuits for continuity and safety, adjusting the setup as needed.

Electricians must work according to the National Electrical Code (NEC) and state and local building and electrical codes (electrical codes are standards that electrical systems must meet to ensure safe, reliable functioning). In doing their work, electricians should always try to use materials efficiently, plan for future access to the area for service and maintenance on the system, and avoid hazardous and unsightly wiring arrangements, making their work as neat and orderly as possible.

Electricians use a variety of equipment ranging from simple hand tools such as screwdrivers, pliers, wrenches, and hacksaws to power tools such as drills, hydraulic benders for metal conduit, and electric soldering guns. They also use testing devices such as oscilloscopes, ammeters, and test lamps. Construction electricians often supply their own hand tools. Experienced workers may have hundreds of dollars invested in tools.

Maintenance electricians do many of the same kinds of tasks, but their activities are usually aimed at preventing trouble before it occurs. They periodically inspect equipment and carry out routine service procedures, often according to a predetermined schedule. They repair or replace worn or defective parts and keep management informed about the reliability of the electrical systems. If any breakdowns occur, maintenance electricians return the equipment to full functioning as soon as possible so that the expense and inconvenience are minimal.

A growing number of electricians are involved in activities other than constructing and maintaining electrical systems in buildings. Many are employed to install computer wiring and equipment, telephone wiring, or the coaxial and fiber optics cables used in telecommunications and computer equipment. Electricians also work in power plants, where electric power is generated; in machine shops, where electric motors are repaired and rebuilt; aboard ships, fixing communications and navigation systems; at locations that need large lighting and power installations, such as airports and mines; and in numerous other settings.

Requirements

Some electricians still learn their trade the same way electrical workers did many years ago—informally on the job, while employed as helpers to skilled workers. Especially if that experience is supplemented with vocational or technical school courses, correspondence courses, or training received in the military, electrical helpers may in time become well-qualified craft workers in some area of the field.

However, it is generally accepted that apprenticeship programs provide the best all-around training in this trade. Apprenticeships combine a series of planned, structured, supervised job experiences with classroom instruction in related subjects. Many programs are designed to give apprentices a variety of experiences by having them work for several electrical contractors doing different kinds of jobs. Typically, apprenticeships last four to five years. Completion of an apprenticeship is usually a significant advantage in getting the better jobs in the field.

Applicants for apprenticeships generally need to be high school graduates, at least eighteen years of age, in good health, and with at least average physical strength. Although local requirements vary, many applicants are required to take tests to determine their aptitude for the work.

All prospective electricians, whether they intend to enter an apprenticeship or learn informally on the job, ought to have a high school background that includes such courses as applied mathematics and science, shop classes that teach the use of various tools, and mechanical drawing. Electronics courses are especially important for those who plan

to become maintenance electricians. Good color vision is necessary, because electricians need to be able to distinguish color-coded wires. Agility and manual dexterity are also desirable characteristics.

Most apprenticeship programs are developed and conducted by state and national contractor associations such as the Independent Electrical Contractors, Inc. and the union locals of the International Brotherhood of Electrical Workers. Some programs are conducted as cooperative efforts between such groups and local community colleges and training organizations. In either situation, the apprenticeship program is usually managed by a training committee. An agreement regarding in-class and on-the-job training is usually established between the committee and each apprentice.

Usually apprenticeships involve at least 144 hours of classroom work each year, covering such subjects as electrical theory, electronics, blueprint reading, mathematics, electrical code requirements, and first aid. On the job, apprentices learn how to safely use and care for tools, equipment, and materials commonly encountered in the trade. Over the years of the program, they spend about 8,000 hours working under the supervision of experienced electricians. They begin with simple tasks, such as drilling holes and setting up conduit. As they acquire skills and knowledge, they progress to more difficult tasks, such as diagramming electrical systems and connecting and testing wiring and electrical components.

Many electricians find that after they are working in the field, they still need to take courses to keep abreast of new developments. Unions and employers may sponsor classes introducing new methods and materials or explaining changes in electrical code requirements. By taking skill-improvement courses, electricians may also improve their chances for advancement to better-paying positions.

Electricians may or may not belong to a union. While many electricians belong to such organizations as the International Brotherhood of Electrical Workers; the International Union of Electronic, Electrical, Salaried, Machine, and Furniture Workers; the International Association of Machinists and Aerospace Workers; and other unions, an increasing number of electricians are opting to affiliate with independent (nonunion) electrical contractors.

Some states and municipalities require that electricians be licensed. To obtain a license, electricians usually must pass a written examination on electrical theory, NEC requirements, and local building and electrical codes.

Opportunities for Experience & Exploration

High school students can get an idea about their aptitude for and interest in tasks that come up regularly in the work of electricians by taking such courses as metal and electrical shop, drafting, electronics, and mathematics. Hobbies such as repairing radios, building electronics kits, or working with model electric trains involve skills similar to those needed by electricians. In addition to sampling related activities like these, prospective electricians may benefit by arranging to talk with an electrician about his or her job. With the help of a teacher or guidance counselor, it may be possible to contact a local electrical contracting firm and locate someone willing to give an insider's description of the occupation.

Methods of Entering

People seeking to enter this field may either begin working as helpers with little background in the field, or they may enter an apprenticeship program. Leads for helper jobs may be located by contacting electrical contractors directly and by checking the usual sources for jobs listings, like the local offices of the state employment service and newspaper classified advertising sections. Students taking trade and vocational school courses may be able to find job openings through the placement office of their school.

People who want to become apprentices may start by contacting the union local of the International Brotherhood of Electrical Workers, the local chapter of the Independent Electrical Contractors, Inc., or the local apprenticeship training committee. Information on apprenticeships can also be obtained through the state employment service.

Advancement

The advancement possibilities for skilled, experienced electricians depend partly on their field of activity. Those who work in construction may become supervisors, job site superintendents, or estimators for electrical contractors. Some electricians are able to establish their own contracting businesses, although in many areas contractors must obtain a special license. Another possibility for some electricians is to move, for example, from construction to maintenance work or into jobs in the shipbuilding, automobile, or aircraft industry.

Employment Outlook

Through the year 2006, job opportunities for skilled electricians are expected to be good, although the Bureau of Labor Statistics predicts slower than average growth for electricians as a whole. The growth in this field will be principally related to overall increased levels in construction of buildings for residential and commercial purposes. In addition, growth will be driven by the ever-increasing use of electrical and electronic devices and equipment. Electricians will be called on to upgrade old wiring and to install and maintain more extensive wiring systems than have been necessary in the past. In particular, the increased use of sophisticated telecommunications and data-processing equipment and automated manufacturing systems is expected to lead to many job opportunities for electricians.

While the overall outlook for this occupational field is good, the availability of jobs will vary over time and from place to place. Construction activity fluctuates depending on the state of the local and national economy. Thus, during economic slowdowns, opportunities for construction electricians may not be plentiful. People working in this field need to be prepared for periods of unemployment between construction projects. Openings for apprentices also decline during economic downturns. Maintenance electricians are usually less vulnerable to periodic unemployment because they are more likely to work for one employer that needs electrical services on a steady basis. But if they work in an industry where the economy causes big fluctuations in the level of activity, like automobile manufacturing, they may be laid off during recessions.

Not many electricians switch completely out of their job field because of the time that must be invested in training and the relatively good pay for skilled workers. Nonetheless, many of the job openings that occur each year develop as electricians move into other occupations or leave the labor force altogether. During the coming years, enough electricians are expected to retire that a national shortage of well-qualified workers could develop if training programs don't attract more applicants who can eventually take the place of the retirees.

Earnings

The earnings of electricians vary widely depending on such factors as the industry in which they are employed, their geographic location, union membership, and other factors. In general, the majority of electricians who were employed full-time in 1996 had annual earnings that ranged from $24,300 to $42,300 or more, as reported by the U.S. Bureau of Labor Statistics. One national survey reported that the average wages for electricians who are union members are at least $33,700 a year. Another study has showed that maintenance electricians in metropolitan areas have earnings that average approximately $34,000 a year. Electricians in the West and Midwest tend to make more than those in the Northeast and South.

Wages rates for many electricians are set by agreements between unions and employers. In addition to their regular earnings, electricians may receive fringe benefits such as employer contributions to health insurance and pension plans, paid vacation and sick days, and supplemental unemployment compensation plans.

Wages of apprentices often start at about 30 to 50 percent of the skilled worker's rate and increase every six months until the last period of the apprenticeship, when the pay approaches that of fully qualified electricians.

Conditions of Work

Electricians usually work indoors, although some must do tasks outdoors or in buildings that are still under construction. The standard workweek is approximately forty hours. In many jobs overtime may be required. Maintenance electricians often have to work some weekend, holiday, or night hours because they must service equipment that operates all the time.

Electricians often spend long periods on their feet, sometimes on ladders or scaffolds or in awkward or uncomfortable places. The work can be strenuous. Electricians may have to put up with noise and dirt on the job. They may risk injuries such as falls off ladders, electrical shocks, and cuts and bruises. By following established safety practices, most of these hazards can be avoided.

Sources of Additional Information

For a general brochure on electrical apprenticeship, contact:

■ **National Joint Apprenticeship Training Committee for the Electrical Industry**
16201 Trade Zone Avenue, Suite 105
Upper Marlboro, MD 20774

For information on its electrical apprenticeship curriculum and a list of chapter offices, contact:

■ **Independent Electrical Contractors, Inc.**
507 Wythe Street
Alexandria, VA 22314
Tel: 703-549-7351

For a list of local unions in your area, contact:

■ **International Brotherhood of Electrical Workers**
1125 15th Street, NW
Washington, DC 20005

■ **International Society of Certified Electronics Technicians**
2708 West Berry Street, Suite 3
Fort Worth, TX 76109-2356
Tel: 817-921-9101
WWW: http://www.iscet.org

■ **National Electrical Contractors Association**
3 Bethesda Metro Center, Suite 1100
Bethesda, MD 20814

Electroneurodiagnostic Technologists

Definition

Electroneurodiagnostic technologists, sometimes called *EEG technologists* or *END technologists,* operate electronic instruments called electroencephalographs. These instruments measure and record the brain's electrical activity. The information gathered is used by physicians (usually neurologists) to diagnose and determine the effects of certain diseases and injuries, including brain tumors, cerebral vascular strokes, Alzheimer's disease, epilepsy, some metabolic disorders, and brain injuries caused by accidents or infectious diseases.

Nature of the Work

The basic principle behind electroencephalography (EEG) is that electrical impulses emitted by the brain, often called brain waves, vary according to the brain's age, activity, and condition. Research has established that certain brain conditions correspond to certain brain waves. Therefore, testing EEG can aid the neurologist (a physician specially trained in the study of the brain) in making a diagnosis of a person's illness or injury.

The EEG technologist's first task with a new patient is to take a simplified medical history. This entails asking questions and recording answers about his or her past health status and present illness. These answers provide the technologist with necessary information about the patient's condition. They also provide an opportunity to help the patient relax before the test.

The technologist then applies electrodes to the patient's head. Often, technologists must choose the best combination of instrument controls and placement of electrodes to produce the kind of tracing that has been requested. In some cases, a physician will give special instructions to the technologist regarding the placement of electrodes.

Once in place, the electrodes are connected to the recording equipment. Here, a bank of sensitive electronic amplifiers transmits information. Tracings from each electrode are made on a moving strip of paper or recorded on optical disks in response to the amplified impulses coming from the brain. The resulting graph is a recording of the patient's brain waves.

EEG technologists are not responsible for interpreting the tracings (that is the job of the neurologist); however, they must be able to recognize abnormal brain activity and any readings on the tracing that are coming from somewhere other than the brain, such as readings of eye movement or nearby electrical equipment.

Technologists can make recording changes to better present the abnormal findings for physician interpretation. Stray readings are known as artifacts. Technologists must be able to determine what kinds of artifacts should be expected for an individual patient on the basis of his or her medical history or present illness. They should also be sensitive to these artifacts and be able to identify them if they occur.

Technologists must be able to detect faulty recordings made by technologist error or by machine malfunctions. When mechanical problems occur, technologists should notify their supervisors so that the machine can be repaired by technologist supervisors or trained equipment technicians.

Throughout the procedure, electroneurodiagnostic technicians observe the patient's behavior and make detailed notes about any aspect of the behavior that might be of use to the physician in interpreting the tracing. They also keep watch on the patient's brain, heart, and breathing functions for any signs that the patient is in any immediate danger.

During the testing, the patient may be either asleep or awake. In some cases, the physician may want recordings taken in both states. Sometimes drugs or special procedures are prescribed by the physician to simulate a specific kind of condition. Administering the drugs or procedures is often the technologist's responsibility.

EEG technologists need a basic understanding of any medical emergencies that can occur during this procedure. By being prepared, they can react properly if one of these emergencies should arise. For instance, if a patient suffers an epileptic seizure, technologists must know what to do. They must be flexible and able to handle medical crises should they arise.

EEG technologists may also handle other specialized electroencephalograms. For example, in a procedure called ambulatory monitoring, both heart and brain activity are tracked over a twenty-four-hour period by a small recording device on the patient's side. In evoked potential testing, a special machine is used to measure the brain's response to specific types of stimulus. And electroencephalograms are increasingly used on a routine basis in the operating room to monitor patients during major surgery.

Besides conducting various kinds of electroencephalograms, EEG technologists also maintain the machine, perform minor repairs (major repairs require specially trained repairers), schedule appointments, and order supplies. In some cases they may have some supervisory responsibilities; however, most supervision is done by registered electroencephalographic technologists.

Requirements

Prospective EEG technologists should plan to get a high school diploma, as it is usually a requirement for entry into any kind of EEG technologist training program, whether in school or on the job. In general, students will find it helpful to have three years of mathematics, including algebra, and three years of science, including biology, chemistry, and physics. In addition, students should take courses in English, especially those that help improve their communications skills, and in social sciences so that they can better understand the social and psychological needs of their patients.

There are two main types of postsecondary training available for EEG technologists: on-the-job training and formal classroom training. Many technologists who are currently working received on-the-job training; however, EEG equipment is becoming so sophisticated that many employers prefer to hire EEG technologists with prior formal training.

On-the-job training generally lasts from a few months to one year, depending on the employer's special requirements. Trainees learn how to handle the equipment and carry out procedures by observing and receiving instruction from senior electroencephalographic technicians or technologists.

Formal training consists of both practice in the clinical laboratory and instruction in the classroom. The classroom instruction usually focuses on basic subjects such as human anatomy, physiology, neuroanatomy, clinical neurology, neuropsychiatry, clinical and internal medicine, psychology, electronics, and instrumentation. The postsecondary programs usually last from one to two years and are offered by hospitals, medical centers, and community or technical colleges.

Students who have completed one year of on-the-job training or who have graduated from a formal training program may apply for registration. The American Board of Registration of Electroencephalographic and Evoked Potential Technologists (ABRET) registers technologists at one level of experience and education—that is, as a registered electroencephalographic technologist (REEGT). Technicians who have been in the field for at least one year can earn this registration by passing an exam.

Although registration is not required for employment, it is an acknowledgment of the technologist's training and does make advancement easier. Registration may also provide a salary increase.

EEG technologists need good vision and manual dexterity, an aptitude for working with mechanical and electronic equipment, and the ability to get along well with patients, their families, and members of the hospital staff.

Opportunities for Experience & Exploration

Prospective electroneurodiagnostic technologists will find it difficult to gain any direct experience on a part-time basis in electroencephalography. Their first direct experience with the work will generally come during their on-the-job training sessions or in the practical-experience portion of their formal training.

They may, however, be able to gain some exposure to patient-care activities in general by signing up for volunteer work at a local hospital. In addition, they could arrange to visit a hospital, clinic, or doctor's office where electroencephalograms are taken. In this way, they may be able to watch technicians at work or talk to them about what the work is like.

Methods of Entering

Technologists often obtain permanent employment in the hospital where they received their on-the-job or work-study training.

Prospective technologists can also find employment through classified ads in newspapers and by contacting the personnel offices of hospitals, medical centers, clinics, and government agencies that employ EEG technologists.

Advancement

Opportunities for advancement are good for registered electroneurodiagnostic technologists. EEG technologists who do not take this step will find their opportunities for advancement severely limited.

Usually, technologists are assigned to conduct more difficult or specialized electroencephalograms. They also supervise other electroencephalographic technicians, arrange work schedules, and teach techniques to new trainees. They may also establish procedures, manage a laboratory, keep records, schedule appointments, and order supplies.

EEG technologists may advance to chief electroencephalographic technologist and thus take on even more responsibilities in laboratory management and in teaching new personnel and students. Chief electroencephalographic technologists generally work under the direction of an electroencephalographer, neurologist, or neurosurgeon.

Employment Outlook

The total number of people employed as electroneurodiagnostic technologists is expected to grow much faster than the average for other occupations at least through the year 2006. This is a reflection of the increasing number of neurodiagnostic tests performed in surgery, diagnosing and monitoring patients, and research on the human brain. Though most jobs are currently in hospitals, positions will grow fastest in neurologists' offices and clinics.

Earnings

Starting salaries are approximately $16,000 a year. Experienced EEG technologists average approximately $26,499 a year and may earn as much as $35,000 to $46,000 a year. Salaries for registered EEG technologists tend to be $6,000 to $10,000 a year higher than nonregistered technologists with equivalent experience.

The highest salaries for EEG technologists tend to go to those who work as laboratory supervisors, teachers in training programs, and program directors in schools of electroencephalographic technology.

Electroencephalographic technicians working in hospitals receive the same fringe benefits as other hospital workers. These benefits usually include hospitalization insurance, paid vacations, and sick leave. In some cases the benefits may also include educational assistance, pension plans, and uniform allowances.

Conditions of Work

EEG technologists usually work five-day, forty-hour workweeks, with only occasional overtime required. Some hospitals require them to be on call for emergencies during weekends, evenings, and holidays. Technologists doing sleep studies may work most of their hours at night. EEG technologists work in clean, well-lighted surroundings.

EEG technologists generally work with people who are ill and may be frightened or emotionally disturbed. Successful technologists are the ones who like people, can quickly recognize what others may be feeling, and gear their treatment to the patient's needs. They need to be able to realize that some patients will be very ill; others may be in the process of dying. Work as an EEG technologist can be unpredictable and challenging.

Most EEG technologists work in hospitals, where they work closely with other staff members. This task is sometimes made more difficult by the fact that in most hospitals there is a formal, often rigid, status structure, and EEG technologists often find themselves in a relatively low position in that structure. In emergency situations or at other moments of frustration, EEG technologists can find themselves dealt with brusquely or angrily. Technologists should try not to take these outbursts or rude treatments personally, but instead should respond with stability and maturity. Depending on where the EEG technologist works, the pace can be fast and demanding.

Sources of
Additional Information

American Board of Registration of Electroencephalographic and Evoked Potential Technologists
PO Box 916633
Longwood, FL 32791-6633
Tel: 407-788-6308

American Society of Electroneurodiagnostic Technologists, Incorporated
204 West 7th Street
Carroll, IA 51401
Tel: 712-792-2978

For information and an application to start the EEG or Evoked Potential examination process, contact:

Professional Testing Corporation
1211 Avenue of the Americas, 15th Floor
New York, NY 10036
Tel: 212-852-0400

Elementary and Secondary School Teachers

Definition

Elementary school teachers instruct pupils from the first through sixth grades. They develop teaching outlines and lesson plans, give lectures, facilitate discussions and activities, keep class attendance records, assign homework and evaluate student progress. They usually work with one group of pupils during the entire school day, teaching several subjects and supervising such activities as lunch and recess.

Secondary school teachers teach students in grades seven through twelve. Their overall duties are similar to those of elementary school teachers, but they usually specialize in one subject, such as mathematics or social studies, and work with five or more groups of students during the day. Secondary school teachers usually lecture more than elementary school teachers.

Nature of the Work

Elementary school teachers usually teach a grade between one and six. In some school systems, however, grades seven and eight are also classified as elementary grades. In such school systems, a teacher placed in one of these two grades would also be considered an elementary school teacher. In some smaller schools, grades are combined. The teacher may be assigned to grades one and two, or grades four, five, and six, for example. There are still a few one-room, one-teacher elementary schools in remote rural areas.

In the average school system, the elementary teacher instructs approximately twenty to thirty children who are in the same grade. This person will teach all subjects in the prescribed course of study, including language, science, mathematics, social studies, and sometimes even music, art and physical education. They may also supervise play periods, rest periods, and lunch periods. Some schools have playground and lunchroom supervisors for this purpose. Sometimes elementary school teachers link several subjects under one theme, and then study that theme from the perspective of each subject.

Secondary school teachers teach a specific subject to several groups of students in one day. A high school teacher may specialize in biology, English, or history, just to name a few subjects, and his or her students are usually in grades seven to twelve. Because of this, a secondary school mathematics teacher may teach pre-algebra to a class of seventh graders one period and trigonometry to high school seniors the next.

Most secondary school teachers spend a great deal of time lecturing, but a good teacher must also be able to facilitate discussion and develop projects and activities to interest the students in the subject. Many secondary school teachers also serve as sponsors to student organizations in their field. For example, a French teacher may sponsor the French club and an English teacher may advise the student newspaper. Some secondary school teachers also have the opportunity for extracurricular work as athletic coaches. Secondary school teachers sometimes monitor students during lunch or break times.

Some schools employ *art teachers* who are responsible for developing art projects, procuring supplies, and helping students achieve in drawing, painting, sculpture, mural design, ceramics, and other artistic activities. Some art teachers also teach students about the history of art and lead field trips to local museums. *Music teachers* may teach music appreciation and history. They may direct organized student choruses, bands, or orchestras or simply accompany a classroom of students in singing some songs. With younger students, music teachers often play games that teach children about rhythm and melody, and may help them learn about different music from around the world. They may teach older children to read music or instruct small groups of students in playing a musical instrument. Often, music teachers are responsible for organizing school pageants, musicals, and plays. *Physical education teachers* help students develop physical skills such as coordination, strength, and stamina, and social skills such as self-confidence and good sportsmanship. Physical education teachers often serve as coaches of school teams and are responsible for organizing field days and intramural activities, especially at the high school level. In schools that employ art, music, and physical education teachers, the classroom teachers are not responsible for these duties.

Recent developments in school curricula have led to such concepts as the ungraded or multiage classroom, where one or more teachers work with students within a small age range. Some schools are also turning to bilingual education in which students are instructed throughout the day in two languages, either by one *bilingual teacher* or two teachers who concentrate on different languages.

Teachers are usually responsible for the set-up of their classrooms, including decorating walls and bulletin boards, and designing special work. They may bring plants, fish, or small animals into the classroom and have students help care for them.

Although both elementary and secondary teachers spend only five to seven hours in the classroom each day, their work is not over when the final bell rings. They have to prepare lesson plans for each subject or class they will teach the next day; often they must meet with students or parents before or after school; and they must attend regular faculty meetings at the school. Many teachers average over forty hours of work a week. In addition, all teachers must grade papers, comment on student work, and record these evaluations in a grade book or student file. Secondary teachers, especially, are required to attend conferences and seminars for their specific teaching subject.

Requirements

All fifty states and the District of Columbia public schools require licensure to teach. Though licensure requirements vary by state, four years of accredited college work and completion of a teacher training program are the norms. There are about 500 accredited teacher education programs in the United States. Teachers can be licensed to teach in the following levels: Early childhood grades—nursery school through grade 3; elementary grades—grades 1 through 6 or 8; middle grades—grades 5 through 8; or secondary level—grades 9 through 12. Most states require the elementary education teacher to have majored in elementary education. Secondary level teachers either major in education and take courses in the subject they plan to teach, or they specialize in their subject of interest and take education based classes. Practice teaching, also called student teaching, in an actual school situation is usually required. The student is placed in a school to work with one of the regular teachers there for a specified number of hours, days, or weeks. During the period of practice teaching, the undergraduate student will observe the ways in which lessons are presented and the classroom is managed, learn how to keep records of such details as attendance and grades, and get actual experience in handling the class, both under supervision and alone. Besides licensure and courses in education, prospective high school teachers usually need twenty-four to thirty-six hours of college work in the subject they wish to teach. Some states require a master's degree. Private schools do not require an education degree.

High school students who are interested in becoming teachers should take college-preparatory courses in English, mathematics, science, history, geography, art, and music. A good teacher should work from the broadest base of knowledge possible.

Teachers should enjoy learning and be able to communicate this enjoyment to the young people being taught. Prospective teachers must have a genuine liking for the age-group of students they plan to teach and an ability to get along well with them. They must regard children as individuals, with likes and dislikes, strengths and weaknesses of their own. They must be patient and self-disciplined and have a high standard of personal conduct always.

Public school teachers must be licensed under regulations established by the state department of education in the state in which they are teaching. Not all states require licensure for teachers in private or parochial schools.

When an aspiring teacher receives his or her college degree, they may request that a transcript of their college record be sent to the licensure section of the state department of education. If they have met licensure requirements, they will receive a certificate and thus be eligible to teach in the public schools of the state. If they move to another state, they will have to resubmit college transcripts, as well as comply with any other regulations in the new state to be able to teach there.

Opportunities for Experience & Exploration

High school students interested in exploring the field of elementary or secondary school education may volunteer to teach elementary classes in Sunday School, become an assistant in a Scout troop, act as a counselor or counselor-in-training in a summer camp, or assist a local recreation director in a public park or recreation center. High school students with special knowledge or skills in a field may find volunteer work tutoring younger students or coaching children's athletic teams. High school students interested in become secondary school teachers should talk to their teachers about the field and pay attention to the way their classes are taught and their school is organized.

In college, students may be able to work part-time in a college-related kindergarten; may join a chapter of the Future Teachers of America; or may discuss their interest with professors in the field of education. Summer jobs for college students are often available in summer academic programs such as Upward Bound, tutoring centers, or camps.

Methods of Entering

Most young graduates from colleges and universities who are prepared to teach in elementary or secondary school try to obtain positions through the placement office of their own institution or by direct application to a school principal or district superintendent. Many school systems and state boards of education maintain listings of job openings. Teachers who are unable to find a permanent position in their area might consider registering as a substitute teacher. Teachers who do well in this capacity and are well liked by the school or district may find themselves in line for a permanent position when one becomes available, provided they meet the necessary job requirements.

Advancement

Most teachers advance in the sense that they become more expert in the job that they have chosen. There is usually an increase in salary, also, as teachers acquire experience. Additional training or study usually brings an increase in salary.

A few teachers with administrative ability and interest in administrative work may advance to the position of principal. Others may work into supervisory positions, and some may become helping teachers who are charged with the responsibility of helping other teachers find appropriate instructional materials and develop certain phases of their courses of study. Others may go into teacher education at a college or university. For most of these positions, additional education is required. Some teachers also make lateral moves into other education- related positions such as guidance counselor or resource room teacher.

Employment Outlook

In 1996, there were 3.1 million teachers employed in the United States; almost half taught at the secondary level. Employment opportunities for teachers should grow as fast as the average for all occupations. Secondary level teachers, however, will have faster than average growth. The Bureau of Labor Statistics projects about 350,000 new secondary school jobs due to the expected rise in the number of fourteen through seventeen year olds enrolled in school through the year 2006. Many job openings will also result from the need to replace teachers retiring from the workforce.

Prospects look particularly good in the South and West, as more families relocate to these areas, adding to the school population and creating teacher shortages. Opportunities should be plentiful, also, in the inner-city and rural areas, which traditionally have difficulty attracting teachers.

Those certified by the National Board for Professional Teaching Standards will easily find employment. Teachers who are willing to relocate, and have expertise to teach more than one subject will also be in demand. Minorities and bilingual teachers are being actively recruited for this field to meet the needs of a growing minority and new immigrant population.

Earnings

Most teachers are contracted to work nine months out of the year, though some contracts are made for ten or a full twelve months. (When regular school is not in session, teachers are expected to conduct summer teaching, planning, or other school-related work.) In most cases, teachers have the option of prorating their salary up to fifty-two weeks.

The average annual salary of public secondary school teachers in 1996 was $38,600, according to the National Education Association. Public kindergarten and elementary school teachers earned an average annual salary of $37,300. Private school teachers are usually paid less.

Geographical location plays a great role in salary figures. Connecticut was the highest paying state, with an annual average of $50,045; compared with an annual average of $25,994 earned by teachers in the lowest paying state of South Dakota. Earnings are also affected by how much money a school district has in its budget. Large urban areas and affluent suburbs are able to raise more tax money for schools, which affect teachers' salaries positively.

Experience is also a factor—it would not be unusual for experienced teachers to earn over $50,000 a year in a public high school setting. Teachers can also supplement their earnings through teaching summer classes, coaching sports, sponsoring a club, or other extracurricular work.

On behalf of the teachers, unions bargain with schools over contract conditions such as wages, hours, and benefits. Most teachers join the American Federation of Teachers, or the National Education Association. Depending on the state, teachers usually receive a retirement plan, sick leave, and health and life insurance. Some systems grant teachers sabbatical leave.

Conditions of Work

Most teachers work under generally pleasant conditions. Modern classrooms are usually comfortable. The teacher is usually provided with materials to make the work as effective as possible.

Although the job of the elementary and secondary school teacher is not overtly strenuous, it can be tiring and trying. The teacher must stand for many hours each day, must do a lot of talking, must show energy and enthusiasm, and may have to handle discipline problems.

The number of hours in school each day are often fewer for the elementary teacher than for the secondary teacher. The work of elementary teachers is more confining, because they are often with their pupils constantly throughout the day's activities. School hours are usually 8:00 a.m. until after 3:00 p.m., Monday through Friday. Teachers are usually able to take all school holidays, including the winter and spring vacations.

Many teachers return to college during the summer months to take courses that will help them to do a better job in their present position. Some states require teachers to take courses to renew or upgrade their teaching licenses.

Sources of Additional Information

Send a self-addressed, stamped envelope for information on careers and accredited university programs to:

Association for Childhood Education International
11501 Georgia Avenue, Suite 315
Wheaton, MD 20902-1924
Tel: 301-942-2443

National Council for Accreditation of Teacher Education
2010 Massachusetts Avenue, NW, Suite 500
Washington, DC 20036
Tel: 202-466-7496

For information on certification, contact:

National Board for Professional Teaching Standards
26555 Evergreen Road, Suite 400
Southfield, MI 48076

Emergency Medical Technicians

Definition

Emergency medical technicians, often called *EMTs,* respond to medical emergencies to provide immediate treatment for ill or injured persons both on the scene and during transport to a medical facility. They function as part of an emergency medical team, and the range of medical services they perform varies according to their level of training and certification.

Nature of the Work

EMTs work in fire departments, private ambulance services, police departments, volunteer Emergency Medical Services (EMS) squads, hospitals, industrial plants, or other organizations that provide prehospital emergency care. The goals of this emergency care are to rapidly identify the nature of the emergency, stabilize the patient's condition, and initiate proper procedures at the scene and en route to a hospital. Unfortunately, well-intentioned emergency help from persons who are not trained can be disastrous, especially for automobile accident victims. Communities often take great pride in their emergency medical services, knowing that they are as well prepared as possible and that they can minimize the tragic consequences of mishandling emergencies.

EMTs are sent in an ambulance to the scene of an emergency by the dispatcher, who acts as a communications channel for all aspects of emergency medical services. The dispatcher may also be trained as an EMT. It typically is the dispatcher who receives the call for help, sends out the appropriate medical resource, serves as the continuing link between the emergency vehicle and medical facility throughout the situation, and relays any requests for special assistance at the scene.

EMTs, who often work in two-person teams, must be able to get to an emergency scene in any part of their geographic area quickly and safely. For the protection of the public and themselves, they must obey the traffic laws that apply to emergency vehicles. They must be familiar with the roads and any special conditions affecting the choice of route, such as traffic, weather-related problems, and road construction.

Once at the scene, they must cope immediately and effectively with whatever awaits them. They may find victims who appear to have had heart attacks, are burned, trapped under fallen objects, lacerated, in childbirth, poisoned, or emotionally disturbed—in short, people with any urgent problem for which medical assistance is needed. Because people who have been involved with an emergency are sometimes very upset, EMTs often have to exercise skill in calming both victims and bystanders. They must do their work efficiently and in a reassuring manner.

EMTs are often the first qualified personnel to arrive on the scene, so they must make the initial evaluation of the nature and extent of the medical problem. The accuracy of this early assessment can be crucial. EMTs must be on the lookout for any clues, such as medical identification emblems, indicating that the victim has significant allergies, diabetes, epilepsy, or other conditions that may affect decisions about emergency treatment. EMTs must know what questions to ask bystanders or family members if they need more information about a patient.

Once they have evaluated the situation and the victim's condition, EMTs establish the priorities of required care. They administer emergency treatment under standing orders or in accordance with specific instructions received over the radio from a physician. For example, they may have to open breathing passages, perform cardiac resuscitation, treat shock, or restrain emotionally disturbed patients.

The particular procedures and treatments that EMTs may carry out depend partly on the level of certification they have achieved. A majority of EMTs have only basic certification, which is known as EMT-basic, or EMT-ambulance. EMT-basics can do such things as control bleeding, administer CPR, treat shock victims, apply bandages, and splint fractures. The second level of certification, the EMT-intermediate, allows EMTs to perform somewhat more advanced procedures, such as starting an I.V. A growing number of EMTs have attained the highest level of certification as Registered EMT-paramedics. There are over sixty thousand paramedics in the United States. EMT-paramedics are authorized to administer drugs intravenously and operate complicated life-support equipment—for example, an electric device (defibrillator) to shock a stopped heart into action.

When victims are trapped, EMTs must first assess the medical problem; only after administering suitable medical care and protection do EMTs remove the victims, using specialized equipment. EMTs may have to radio requests for special assistance in order to free victims. During a longer extrication process, it may be necessary for EMTs to help police with crowd control. Sometimes freeing victims involves lifting and carrying them, climbing to high places, or dealing with other difficult or physically demanding situations.

Victims who must be transported to the hospital are put on stretchers or backboards, lifted into the ambulance, and secured for the ride. The choice of hospital is not always up to the EMTs, but when it is they must base the decision on their knowledge of the equipment and staffing needed by the patients. The receiving hospital's emergency department is informed by radio, either directly or through the dispatcher, of details such as the number of persons being transported and the nature of their medical problems. Meanwhile EMTs continue to monitor the patients and administer care as directed by the medical professional with whom they are maintaining radio contact. When necessary, EMTs also try to be sure that contact has been initiated with any utility companies, municipal repair crews, or other services that should be called to correct dangerous problems at the emergency scene, such as fallen power lines or tree limbs.

Once at the hospital, EMTs help the staff bring the victims into the emergency department and may assist with the first steps of in-hospital care. They supply whatever information they can, verbally and in writing, for the hospital's records. In the case of a victim's death, they complete the necessary procedures to ensure that the deceased's property is safeguarded.

After the patient has been delivered to the hospital, EMTs check in with their dispatchers and then prepare the vehicle for another emergency call. This includes replacing used linens and blankets; replenishing supplies of drugs, oxygen, and so forth; sending out equipment to be sterilized; and taking inventory of the contents of the vehicle to ensure adequate supplies. In the case of any special kind of contamination, such as certain contagious diseases or radioactivity, EMTs report the situation to the proper authorities and follow procedures for decontamination.

In addition, EMTs make sure that the ambulance is clean and in good running condition. At least once during the shift, they check the gas, oil, battery, siren, brakes, radio, and other systems.

Requirements

While still in high school, interested students should take courses in health and science, driver education, and English. To be admitted to a basic training program, applicants usually must be at least eighteen years old and have a high school diploma and valid driver's license. Exact requirements vary slightly in different states and in different training courses. Many EMTs first become interested in the field while in the U.S. armed forces, where they may have received training as medics.

The standard basic training program for EMTs was designed by the U.S. Department of Transportation. It is taught in hospitals, community colleges, and police, fire, and health departments across the country. It is approximately 110 hours in length and constitutes the minimum mandatory requirement to become an EMT. In this course, students are taught how to manage common emergencies such as bleeding, cardiac arrest, fractures, and airway obstruction. They also learn how to use equipment such as stretchers, backboards, fracture kits, and oxygen delivery systems.

Successful completion of the basic EMT course opens several opportunities for further training. Among these are a two-day course on removing trapped victims and a five-day course on driving emergency vehicles. Another, somewhat longer course, trains dispatchers. Completion of these recognized training courses may be required for EMTs to be eligible for certain jobs in some areas. In addition, EMTs who have graduated from the basic program may work toward meeting further requirements to become registered at one of the two higher levels recognized by the National Registry of Emergency Medical Technicians: EMT-intermediate and EMT-paramedic.

All fifty states have some certification requirement. Certification is only open to those who have completed the standard basic training course. In some states, EMTs meet the certification requirement by meeting the requirements for basic registration with the National Registry of Emergency Medical Technicians. Some states offer new EMTs the choice of the National Registry examination or the state's own certification examination. A majority of states accept national registration in place of their own examination for EMTs who relocate to their states.

At present, the National Registry of Emergency Medical Technicians recognizes three levels of competency. Although it is not always essential for EMTs to become registered with one of these three ratings, EMTs can expect better prospects for good jobs as they attain higher levels of registration. As time passes, registration requirements may increase, and a larger proportion of EMTs are expected to become registered voluntarily.

Candidates for the basic level of registration, known as EMT-basic, must have completed the standard Department of Transportation training program (or their state's equivalent), have six months of experience, and pass both a state-approved practical examination and a written examination.

Since 1980, the National Registry has recognized the EMT-intermediate level of competency. This registration requires all candidates to have current registration at the basic EMT level. They must also have a certain amount of experience and pass both a written test and a practical examination that assess knowledge and skills above those of basic registered EMTs, but below those of the highest-rated registrants.

EMT-paramedics (or EMT-Ps), the EMTs with the highest levels of registration, must be already registered at least at the basic level. They must have completed a special EMT-paramedic training program, have six months of experience as an EMT-paramedic, and pass both a written and practical examination. Because their training is much more comprehensive and specialized than other EMTs, EMT-Ps are prepared to make more physician-like observations and judgments.

The training programs for EMT-paramedics are currently accredited by the Committee on Allied Health Education and Accreditation of the American Medical Association. They last approximately nine months, although exact course length depends largely on the availability of actual emergency care incidents in which students can gain supervised practical experience. Training is very broad in scope and includes classroom instruction and in-hospital clinical practice, in addition to a field internship.

Once they have attained registration, EMTs must re-register every two years. To re-register, they need to meet certain experience and continuing education requirements. Refresher courses are available to help EMTs stay abreast of new techniques and equipment.

Anyone who is considering becoming an EMT should have a desire to serve people and be emotionally stable and clearheaded. It is important that workers in this field project an impression of confidence and efficiency to both victims and bystanders. Moreover, they must back up the impression of competence with genuine level-headedness and sufficient calmness to let them consistently exercise good judgment in times of stress. They must be efficient, neither wasting time nor working too fast to do a good job. A strong desire to help people, even when it involves difficult work, is essential.

Prospective EMTs need to be in good physical condition. Other requirements include manual dexterity and motor coordination; the ability to lift and carry up to 125 pounds; good visual acuity, with lenses for correction permitted; accurate color vision, enabling safe driving and immediate detection of diagnostic signs; and competence in giving and receiving verbal and written communication.

Opportunities for Experience & Exploration

Students in high school usually have little opportunity for direct experience with the emergency medical field. They may be able to arrange to talk with local EMTs who work for the fire or police department or for a voluntary agency that provides emergency ambulance service to the community. It may be possible to learn a great deal about the health-services field through a part-time, summer, or volunteer job in a hospital or clinic. Such service jobs can provide a chance to observe and talk to staff members concerned with emergency medical services.

High school health courses are a good introduction to some of the concepts and terminology that EMTs use. Students may also be able to take a first-aid class or training in cardiopulmonary resuscitation. Organizations such as the Red Cross can provide information on local training courses.

Methods of Entering

A good source of employment leads for a recent graduate of the basic EMT training program is the school or agency that provided the training. EMTs can also apply directly to local ambulance services, hospitals, fire and police departments, and private and public employment agencies.

In some areas, new EMT graduates may face stiff competition if they are seeking full-time paid employment. Although these EMTs may sometimes qualify for positions with fire and police departments, they are generally more likely to be successful in pursuing positions with private companies.

Volunteer work is another option for EMTs. Volunteer EMTs, who are likely to average eight to twelve hours of work per week, do not face the same competition as those who are seeking full-time work. Beginning EMTs, without prior work experience in the health field, may therefore find it advantageous to start their careers as part-time volunteers. As they gain training and experience, they can work toward registration, which may open new job opportunities.

Flexibility about the location of a job may help new EMTs gain a foothold on the career ladder. In some areas, salaried positions are hard to find because of a strong tradition of volunteer ambulance services. In other areas, the demand for EMTs is much greater. Therefore, if an EMT is willing to relocate to an area where the demand is higher, he or she should have a better chance of finding employment.

Advancement

With experience, EMTs can gain more responsibility while retaining the same job. However, more significant advancement is possible if an EMT moves up through the progression of ratings recognized by the NREMT. These ratings acknowledge increasing qualifications, making higher paying jobs and more responsibility easier to obtain.

An avenue of advancement for some EMTs leads to holding an administrative job, such as supervisor, director, operations manager, or trainer. Communications, safety and risk management, and quality control are other administrative areas that are receiving increasing attention.

Another avenue of advancement might be further training in a different area of the health care field. Some EMTs eventually move out of the health care field entirely and into medical sales, where their familiarity with equipment and terminology can make them valuable employees.

Employment Outlook

The employment outlook for paid EMTs depends partly on the community in which they are seeking employment. Many communities perceive the advantages of high-quality emergency medical services and are willing and able to raise tax dollars to support them. In these communities, which are often larger, the employment outlook should remain favorable. Volunteer services are being phased out in these areas, and well-equipped emergency services operated by salaried EMTs are replacing them.

In some communities, however, particularly smaller ones, the employment outlook is not so favorable. Maintaining a high-quality emergency medical services delivery system can be expensive, and financial strains on some local governments could inhibit the growth of these services. In addition, cutbacks in federal aid to local communities and an overall national effort to contain medical expenditures may lead health care planners to look for ways of controlling or reducing community-based health-related costs. Under such economic conditions, communities may not be able to support the level of emergency medical services that they would otherwise like to, and the employment prospects for EMTs may remain limited.

One general factor that impacts the EMT's employment outlook is the growing number of municipalities that are contracting with private ambulance companies to provide emergency medical services to the community. If this trend continues, job opportunities with private companies should increase.

Another important factor affecting the outlook is that the proportion of older people, who use most emergency medical services, is growing in many communities, placing more demands on the emergency medical services delivery system and increasing the need for EMTs. Many states are starting to give EMTs more responsibility, such as performing primary care on the scene. Turnover is quite high for this occupation due to stressful working conditions, modest salary in the private sector, and the limited growth potential.

Earnings

Earnings of EMTs depend on the type of employer and individual level of training and experience. Those working in the public sector, for police and fire departments, usually receive a higher wage than those in the private sector, working for ambulance companies and hospitals. Salary levels typically rise with increasing levels of skill, training, and certification.

According to a salary survey in the 1996 Journal of Emergency Medical Services, the average salary is $25,000 for those classified as EMT-basic, and $30,400 for EMT-paramedic. To show the disparity in pay between employers, the average pay for an experienced EMT-basic at a private ambulance service is $18,600; at a fire department, it is $29,800.

Benefits vary widely depending on the employer, but generally include paid holidays and vacations, health insurance, and pension plans.

Conditions of Work

EMTs must work under all kinds of conditions, both indoors and outdoors, and sometimes in very trying circumstances. They must do their work regardless of extreme weather conditions and are often required do fairly strenuous physical tasks such as lifting, climbing, and kneeling. They consistently deal with situations that many people would find upsetting and traumatic, such as death, accidents, and serious injury.

EMTs usually work irregular hours, including some nights, weekends, and holidays. Those working for fire departments often put in fifty-six hours a week, while EMTs employed in hospitals, private firms, and police departments typically work a forty-hour week. Volunteer EMTs work much shorter hours. Because the working conditions are so stressful and emotionally exhausting, many EMTs find that they must have a high degree of commitment to the job.

An additional stress factor faced by EMTs is concern over contracting AIDS or other infectious diseases from bleeding patients. The actual risk of exposure is quite small, and emergency medical programs have implemented procedures to protect EMTs from exposure to the greatest possible degree; however, some risk of exposure does exist, and prospective EMTs should be aware of this factor as they consider the career.

In spite of the intensity of their often-demanding job, many EMTs derive enormous satisfaction from knowing that they are able to render such a vital service to the victims of sudden illness or injury.

Sources of Additional Information

For information on EMT education and careers, contact:

National Association of Emergency Medical Technicians
408 Monroe
Clinton, MS 39056

American Ambulance Association
3800 Auburn Boulevard, Suite C
Sacramento, CA 95821
Tel: 916-483-3827

For information on testing for EMT certification, contact:

National Registry of Emergency Medical Technicians
Box 29233
6610 Busch Boulevard
Columbus, OH 43229
Tel: 614-888-4484

American Medical Association
Division of Allied Health Education and Accreditation
515 North State Street
Chicago, IL 60610
Tel: 312-464-5000

Employment Firm Workers

Definition

Employment firm workers help find the right jobs for their clients based on their education, skills, and experience. Employment firm workers also work with companies looking to hire new employees. Using assessment tests and speaking with their clients, employment firm workers try to determine which companies would most likely be a successful match with the applicant.

Nature of the Work

Specific job responsibilities depend on the several types of positions within the employment firm worker field.

Personnel recruiters seek out and recruit qualified applicants for existing job openings with companies. They maintain contacts within the local business community and may travel extensively to find qualified applicants. After interviewing applicants, recruiters recommend those most qualified to fill positions within a company. To aid in the analysis of the applicants, recruiters may arrange skills tests, evaluate the applicant's work history, and check personal references. Much of this work is done by phone or through computer matching services.

Recruiters must be able to present applicants with an accurate picture of companies seeking employees. They need to know about the company's personnel policy in regard to wages and promotional possibilities. They must also be familiar with equal employment opportunity and affirmative action guidelines.

Employment interviewers often have many of the same responsibilities as personnel recruiters but may also have administrative tasks such as giving skills tests or completing a background check on the applicant.

Employment consultants help job seekers find employment and help businesses find workers for existing positions. They interview job seekers and use tests to evaluate the skills and abilities of applicants. They discuss such issues as job responsibilities and benefits. The employment consultant then attempts to find job openings that match the skills and interests of individual applicants. They often put an applicant directly in touch with a potential employer. If a specific opening does not exist, they may contact various firms to see if they need an applicant or suggest that the applicant take additional skills training to qualify for existing positions.

Consultants may also offer suggestions on resume writing, interviewing techniques, and personal appearance to help applicants secure a position. Often, a consultant will have expertise in a particular area, such as accounting or law, and work with applicants interested in jobs in that field.

Employment clerks function as intake workers and interview job seekers to get pertinent information, such as work history, education, and occupational interests. They refer the applicant to an employment consultant or counselor. Employment clerks have administrative duties such as checking applicant references, filing applications, and compiling personnel records.

Employment agency managers supervise the business operations of an employment agency. They establish agency rules and regulations, prepare agency budgets, purchase appropriate equipment and supplies, and resolve client complaints. In general they are responsible for the day-to-day operations of the agency. They are also responsible for hiring and evaluating staff workers and overseeing their training.

Government personnel specialists do essentially the same work as their counterparts in private companies, except they deal with openings that are subject to civil service regulations. Much of government personnel work concentrates on job analysis because civil service jobs are strictly classified according to entry requirements, duties, and wages.

Requirements

Although there are no specific educational requirements for work in this field, most employers require a college education for all employment firm workers. High school graduates occasionally may start as employment clerks and advance with experience to the position of employment consultants. Some employers favor college graduates who have majored in personnel administration while others prefer individuals with a general business background. People interested in personnel work with a government agency may find it an asset to have a degree in personnel administration or public administration.

High school students interested in pursuing a career in the employment firm field should take college-preparatory courses, such as social studies, English, mathematics, and communications. Business courses are also valuable. In college, a combination of courses in the social sciences, behavioral sciences, business, and economics is recommended. Other relevant courses might include principles of management, business administration, psychology, and statistics.

Although most employment firms must be licensed, the workers themselves do not normally need any special license or certificate. Those individuals who plan to work for the government usually must pass a civil service examination.

As a way of attaining increased professional standing, employment workers may become certified by the National Association of Personnel Consultants (NAPC). Employment workers who have at least two years of work experience may receive the title of Certified Personnel Consultant after passing an examination. Further information on the certification process is available from the NAPC at the address given at the end of this article.

Opportunities for Experience & Exploration

Part-time work as a clerk or a personnel assistant are good ways of exploring this field. Large department stores and other large firms usually have personnel departments and are good places to begin looking for part-time or temporary work. High school students may also find part-time work in their school's counsel-

ing department. Discussions with employment firm workers are another good way of learning about the rewards and responsibilities in this field. College students should discuss their career objectives with the career placement counselors at their university.

Methods of Entering

Those with a bachelor's degree in personnel administration or related fields should apply directly to employment firms for a job opening. Colleges and universities have placement offices that can be helpful in supplying possible leads. Those interested in working for a government agency must pass a civil service test. Openings in the government are usually listed with the Office of Personnel Management. High school graduates may apply for entry-level jobs as an employment clerk or personnel assistant, but these positions increasingly require a college degree.

Entry-level workers are usually trained on the job or in formal training programs, where they learn how to classify jobs and interview applicants.

Advancement

After trainees have mastered the basic personnel tasks, they are assigned to specific areas, such as personnel recruitment. In time, skilled workers may become department heads or office managers. A few highly skilled employees may become top executives with employment firms. Advancement may also be achieved by moving into a higher position in another firm. Keep in mind, though, that some types of advancement may require an advanced degree in human resources or a related field.

Employment Outlook

Employment opportunities will be greatest in private industry, especially personnel supply firms. Employers are now more aware of the benefits of using employment firms to find part-time and temporary workers to help fulfill short-term assignments or to launch new projects. Because of the increased used of computerized job matching and budgetary considerations, however, the demand for state employment workers has lessened.

Jobs in the employment field are protected somewhat against changes in the economy. If the economy is growing and businesses are expanding, companies will use employment firms to fill existing positions. If there is a downturn in the economy, more job seekers will use these firms to improve their job prospects. Job opportunities will be greatest in large urban areas, where there are more jobs and a higher degree of job turnover.

Although opportunities in this field will be good, competition for jobs will be keen. An abundance of college graduates and experienced workers is expected for each opening.

Earnings

Earnings vary widely and depend on job responsibilities and the size of the firm. Some employees at employment firms are paid on a commission or a salary plus commission basis, depending on their success rate for finding employment for applicants. Employment clerks usually start between $13,500 and $15,000 per year, and experienced clerks earn between $18,000 and $21,000. Beginning employment consultants, working for a private company, earn between $17,000 and $25,000 per year. Experienced consultants earn $25,000 or more, depending on success in placing workers. State counselors earn less, with salaries ranging from $13,000 to $20,000. Federal employees are usually paid according to civil service grade level, with merit increases. Employment agency managers usually start at between $29,000 and $32,000 per year, with experienced managers earning $50,000 and up depending on specific job responsibilities and the size of the firm. Some managers are also paid a commission on each job they help fill, about 30 percent of what the client is billed. Full-time employment firm workers receive health insurance, vacation, and other benefits.

Conditions of Work

Employment firm workers generally work in pleasant conditions. Their offices are designed to make a good impression on outside visitors and prospective employees, and most are modern, attractive, and nicely furnished.

Employees work a forty-hour week, unless they are working on a special project. There may be some clerical work, such as typing and filing. Many agencies are small, but some can be quite large, sometimes employing over fifty employees.

Some personnel recruiters travel widely. Recruiters visit universities and professional conferences to interview prospective employees.

Workers in this field should have a pleasant personality and enjoy working with people of different levels of education and experience. Much of the day is spent talking to job seekers or prospective employers, either on the phone or in person. Employment firm workers must exercise sensitivity and tact when interviewing potential customers or clients. Good writing and speaking skills are vital, as is attention to detail.

Sources of Additional Information

National Association of Personnel Services
3133 Mount Vernon Avenue
Alexandria, VA 22305
Tel: 703-684-0180

National Employment Counseling Association
Education Office
5999 Stevenson Avenue
Alexandria, VA 22304

International Personnel Management Association
1617 Duke Street
Alexandria, VA 22314
Tel: 703-549-7100

Society for Human Resource Management
606 North Washington Street
Alexandria, VA 22314
Tel: 703-548-3440
Email: shrm@shrm.org

Film and Television Directors

Definition

Lights! Camera! Action! aptly summarize the major responsibilities of the *film and television director*. In ultimate control of the decisions that shape a film or television production, the director is an artist who coordinates the elements of a film or television show and is responsible for its overall style and quality.

Directors are well known for their part in guiding actors, but they are involved in much more—casting, costuming, cinematography, editing, and sound recording. Directors must have insight into the many tasks that go into the creation of a film, and they must have a broad vision of how each part will contribute to the big picture.

Nature of the Work

Motion picture directors, sometimes also called *filmmakers*, are considered ultimately responsible for the tone and quality of the films they work on. They interpret the stories and narratives presented in scripts and coordinate the filming of their interpretations. They are involved in preproduction, production, and postproduction. They audition, select, and rehearse the acting crew; they work on matters regarding set designs, musical scores, and costumes; and they decide on details such as where scenes should be shot, what backgrounds might be needed, and how special effects could be employed.

The director of a film often works with a *casting director*, who is in charge of auditioning performers. The casting director pays close attention to attributes of the performers like physical appearance, quality of voice, and acting ability and experience, then presents to the director a list of suitable candidates for each role.

One of the most important aspects of the film director's job is working with the performers.

Directors each have their own style in extracting accurate emotion and performance from cast members, but they must be dedicated to this goal.

Two common techniques that categorize directors' styles are montage and mise-en-scene. *Montage directors* are concerned with editing techniques to produce desired results; they consider it important to focus on how individual shots will work when pieced together with others. Consider Alfred Hitchcock, who directed the production of one scene in *Psycho*, for example, by filming discrete shots in a bathroom and then editing in dialogue, sound effects, and music to create tremendous suspense. *Mise-en-scene directors* are more concerned with the pre-editing phase, focusing on the elements of angles, movement, and design one shot at a time, as Orson Welles did. Many directors combine elements of both techniques in their work.

The film's *art director* creates set design concepts and chooses shoot locations. He or she meets with the filmmaker and producer to set budgets and schedules and then accordingly coordinates the construction of sets. Research is done on the period in which the film is to take place, and experts are consulted to help create appropriate architectural and environmental styles. The art director also is often involved in design ideas for costumes, makeup and hairstyles, photographic effects, and other elements of the film's production.

The *director of photography*, or *cinematographer*, is responsible for organizing and implementing the actual camera work. Together with the filmmaker, he or she interprets scenes and decides on appropriate camera motion to achieve desired results. The director of photography determines the amounts of natural and artificial lighting required for each shoot and such technical factors as the type of film to be used, camera angles and distance, depth of field, and focus.

Motion pictures are usually filmed out of sequence, meaning that the ending might be shot first and midscenes might not be filmed until the end of production. The director is responsible for scheduling each day's sequence of scenes; he or she coordinates filming so that scenes using the same set and performers will be filmed together. In addition to conferring with the art director and the director of photography, the filmmaker meets with technicians and crew members to advise on and approve final scenery, lighting, props, and other necessary equipment. He or she is also involved with final approval of costumes, choreography, and music.

After all the scenes have been shot, postproduction begins. The director works with picture and sound editors to cut apart and piece together the final reels. The *film editor* shares the director's vision about the picture and assembles shots according to that overall idea, synchronizing film with voice and sound tracks produced by the sound editor and music editor.

While the director supervises all major aspects of film production, various assistants help throughout the process. In a less creative position than the filmmaker, the *first assistant director* organizes various practical matters involved during the shooting of each scene. The *second assistant director* is a coordinator who works as a liaison among the production office, the first assistant director, and the performers. The *second unit director* coordinates sequences such as scenic inserts, and action shots that don't involve the main acting crew.

Requirements

Konstantine Stanislavsky had a passion for his directorial work in the theater, believing that it was an art of immense social importance. Today's motion picture directors must have similar inspiration, if not greater creative strength because of the many more responsibilities involved in directing modern film. Film directors' careers are rather nontraditional. There is no standard training outline involved, no normal progression up a movie industry ladder leading to the director's job.

Dedication, talent, and experience have always been indispensable to a director. No doubt it is beneficial to become aware of one's passion for film as early as possible. Woody Allen, for example, recognized the importance of motion pictures to him early in his life; but he worked as a magician, jazz clarinet player, joke writer, and stand-up comic before ever directing films. Allen took few film courses in his life.

On the other hand, many successful directors such as Francis Ford Coppola and Martha Coolidge have taken the formal film school route. There are more than five hundred film-studies programs offered by schools of higher education throughout the United States, including those considered to be the five most reputable: the American Film Institute (Los Angeles), Columbia University (New York City), New York University, the University of California at Los Angeles (UCLA), and the University of Southern California (USC). These schools have film professionals on their faculties and provide a very visible stage for student talent, being located in the two film-business hot spots—California and New York. (The tuition for film programs offered elsewhere, however, tends to be much less expensive than at these schools.)

Film school offers overall formal training, providing an education in fundamental directing skills by working with student productions. Such education is rigorous, but in addition to teaching skills it provides aspiring directors with peer groups and a network of contacts with students, faculty, and guest speakers that can be of help after graduation.

The debate continues on what is more influential in a directing career: film school or personal experience. Some say that it is always possible for creative people to land directing jobs without having gone through a formal program. Competition is so pervasive in the industry that even film school graduates find jobs scarce (only 5–10 percent of the 26,000 students who graduate from film schools each year find jobs in the industry). Martha Coolidge, for instance, made independent films for ten years before directing a Hollywood movie.

Opportunities for Experience & Exploration

The most obvious opportunity for would-be directors lies in their own imaginations. Being drawn to films and captivated by the process of how they are made is the beginning of the filmmaker's journey.

In high school and beyond, pay attention to motion pictures—watch them at every opportunity, both at the theater and at home. Study your favorite television shows to see what makes them interesting. Be active in school and community drama productions, whether as performer, set designer, or cue card holder. In college and afterward, take film classes and volunteer to work on other students' films. Two major trade publications to read are *Daily Variety* and *Hollywood Reporter*. Also, the book *How to Make It in Hollywood* (Linda Buzzell, 1992) is a very good informal guide that presents insider tips on such factors as "schmoozing" and chutzpah (self-confidence) as well as an extensive list of valuable resources.

During summers, many camps and workshops offer programs for high school students interested in film work. For example, the University of Wisconsin offers its Summer Art Studio for students in grades seven through twelve; in addition to film courses, there are classes in other arts, such as drawing, painting, photography, and TV and video (for information, write to the University of Wisconsin-Green Bay, Office of Outreach, TH 335, Green Bay, WI 54311). UCLA presents its Media Workshops for students aged fourteen to twenty-four. Classes there focus on mass media production, including film, TV/video, and theater; sports activities, such as basketball, swimming, and tennis, are also offered (write to Media Workshops Foundation, UCLA, Rieber Hall, DeNeve Drive, Los Angeles, CA 90024).

Methods of Entering

It is considered difficult to enter a motion picture directorial position. With non-traditional steps to professional status, the occupation poses challenges for those seeking employment. However, there is somewhat solid advice for those who wish to direct motion pictures.

Many current directors began their careers in other film industry professions, such as acting or writing. Consider Jodie Foster, who appeared in thirty films before she went on to direct her first motion picture at the age of twenty-eight. Obviously it helps to grow up near the heart of "tinseltown" and to have the influence of one's family spurring you on. The support of family and friends is often cited as an essential element in shaping the confidence one needs to succeed in the industry.

As mentioned earlier, film school is a breeding ground for making contacts in the industry. Often, contacts are the essential factor in getting a job; many Hollywood insiders agree that it's not what you know but who you know that will get you in. Networking often leads to good opportunities at various types of jobs in the industry. Many professionals recommend that those who want to become directors should go to Los Angeles or New York, find any industry-related job, continue to take classes, and keep eyes and ears open for news of job openings, especially with those professionals who are admired for their talent.

A program to be aware of is the Assistant Directors Training Program of the Directors Guild of America (their address is listed at the end of this article). This program provides an excellent opportunity to those without industry connections to work on film and television productions. Trainees are placed with major studios or on television movies and series. They work for four hundred days and earn between $424 and $521 per week, with the salary increasing every one hundred days. Once they have completed the program, they become freelance second assistant directors and can join the guild. The competition is extremely stiff for these positions; the program accepts only sixteen to twenty trainees from around fifteen hundred applicants each year.

Keep in mind that Hollywood isn't everything. Directors work on documentaries, on television productions, and with various types of video presentations, from music to business. Honing skills at these types of jobs is beneficial for those still intent on directing the big screen.

Advancement

In the motion picture industry, advancement often comes with recognition. Directors who work on well-received movies are given awards as well as further job offers. Probably the most glamorized trophy is the Academy Award of Merit—the Oscar. Sixteen Oscars, including one for Director of the Year, are given annually at a gala to recognize the outstanding accomplishments of those in the field.

Candidates for Oscars are usually judged by peers. Directors who have not worked on films popular enough to have made it in Hollywood should nevertheless seek recognition from reputable organizations. One such group is the National Endowment for the Arts, an independent agency of the U.S. government that supports and awards artists, including those who work in film. The endowment provides financial assistance in the form of fellowships and grants to those seen as contributing to the excellence of arts in the country.

Employment Outlook

According to the U.S. Department of Labor, employment for motion picture and television directors is expected to grow faster than the average for all occupations through the year 2006. This optimistic forecast is based on the increasing global demand for films and television programming made in the United States, as well as continuing U.S. demand for home video rentals. However, competition is extreme and turnover is high. Most positions in the motion picture industry are held on a freelance basis. As is the case with most film industry workers, directors are usually hired to work on one film at a time. After a film is completed, new contacts must be made for further assignments.

Television offers directors a wider variety of employment opportunities such as directing sitcoms, made-for-tv-movies, newscasts, commercials—even music videos. New technology will allow cable companies to offer hundreds of additional stations, and directors will be needed to help create original programming to fill this void. One half of all television directors work as freelancers. This number is predicted to rise as more cable networks and production companies attempt to cut costs by hiring directors on a project-to-project basis.

Earnings

Directors' salaries vary greatly. Most Hollywood film directors are members of the Directors Guild of America, and salaries (as well as hours of work and other employment conditions) are usually negotiated by this union. Generally, contracts provide for minimum weekly salaries and follow a basic trend depending on the cost of the picture being produced: for film budgets over $1.5 million, the weekly salary is about $8,000; for budgets of $500,000 to $1.5 million, $5,800 per week; and for budgets under $500,000, $5,100. Motion picture art directors earn an average weekly salary of about $1,850; directors of photography, $2,000. Keep in mind that because directors are freelancers, they may have no income for many weeks out of the year.

Although contracts usually provide only for the minimum rate of pay, most directors earn more, and they often negotiate extra conditions. Woody Allen, for example, takes the minimum salary required by the union for directing a film but also receives at least 10 percent of the film's gross receipts.

Salaries for directors who work in television vary greatly based on type of project and employer, and whether the director is employed as a freelancer or as a salaried employee. The average annual salary for a director of a television newscast is about $50,000. A director at a small-market station may average as little as $28,000 per year, while a director employed by a larger network affiliate may make up to $120,000 annually.

Conditions of Work

The work of the director is considered glamorous and prestigious, and of course directors have been known to become quite famous. But directors work under great stress—meeting deadlines, staying within budgets, and resolving problems among staff. "Nine-to-five" definitely does not describe a day in the life of a director; sixteen-hour days (and more) are not uncommon. And because directors are ultimately responsible for so much, schedules often dictate that they become immersed in their work around the clock, from preproduction to final cut. Nonetheless, this is the most enjoyable work to be found for those able to make it in the industry.

Sources of Additional Information

For information about colleges with film and television programs of study, please contact:

■ **American Film Institute**
PO Box 27999
2021 North Western Avenue
Los Angeles, CA 90027

■ **Assistant Directors Training Program**
15503 Ventura Boulevard
Encino, CA 91436
Tel: 818-382-1744

■ **Broadcast Education Association**
1771 N Street, NW
Washington, DC 20036-2891
Tel: 202-429-5335

Financial Institution Officers and Managers

Definition

Financial institution officers and managers oversee the activities of banks and personal credit institutions such as credit unions and finance companies. These establishments serve business, government, and individuals. They lend money, keep savings, enable people and businesses to write checks for goods and services, rent safe-deposit boxes for storing valuables, manage trust funds, advise clients on investments and business affairs, issue credit cards and traveler's checks, and take payments for gas and electric bills.

Nature of the Work

Financial institutions include commercial banks, which provide full banking service for business, government, and individuals; investment banks, which offer their clients financial counseling and brokering; Federal Reserve Banks, whose customers are affiliated banks in their districts; or other organizations such as credit unions and finance companies.

These institutions employ many officers and managers whose duties vary depending on the type and size of the firm as well as on their own area of responsibility within it. All financial institutions operate under the direction of a *president*, who is guided by policies set by the board of directors. *Vice presidents* are department heads who are sometimes also responsible for certain key clients. *Controllers* handle bank funds, properties, and equipment. Large institutions may also have *treasurers*, *loan officers*, and officers in charge of departments such as trust, credit, and investment. A number of these positions are described in more detail below.

The financial institution president directs the overall activities of the bank or consumer credit organization, making sure that its objectives are achieved without violating government regulations or overlooking any legal requirements. The officers are responsible for earning as much of a return as possible on the institution's investments within the restrictions demanded by government and sound business practices. They help set policies pertaining to investments, loans, interest, and reserves. They coordinate the activities of the various divisions and delegate authority to subordinate officers, who administer the operation of their own areas of responsibility. Financial institution presidents study financial reports and other data to keep up with changes in the economy that may affect their firm's policies.

The vice president coordinates many of the operations of the institution. This person is responsible for the activities of a regional bank office, branch bank, and often an administrative bank division or department. As designated by the board of directors, the vice president supervises programs such as installment loan, foreign trade, customer service, trust, and investment. The vice president also prepares studies for management and planning, like workload and budget estimates and activity and analysis reports.

The *administrative secretary* usually writes directions for supervisory workers that outline and explain policy. The administrative secretary acts, in effect, as an intermediary between minor supervisory workers and the executive officers.

The financial institution treasurer directs the bank's monetary programs, transactions, and security measures in accordance with banking principles and legislation. Treasurers coordinate program activity and evaluate operating practices to ensure efficient operations. They oversee receipt, disbursement, and expenditure of money and sign documents approving or affecting monetary transactions. They direct the safekeeping and control of assets and securities and maintain specified legal cash reserve. They review financial and operating statements and present reports and recommendations to bank officials or board committees.

Controllers authorize and control the use of funds kept by the treasurer. They also supervise the maintenance of accounts and records and analyze these records so that the directors or other bank officials will know how much the bank is spending for salaries, operating expenses, and other expenses. Controllers often formulate financial policies.

The financial institution manager establishes and maintains relationships with the community. This person's responsibility is to supervise accounting and reporting functions and to establish operating policies and procedures. The manager directs several activities within the bank. The assets, records, collateral, and securities held by the financial institution are in the manager's custody. Managers approve credit and commercial, real estate, and consumer loans and direct personnel in trust activities.

The loan officer and the *credit and collection manager* both deal with customers who are seeking or have obtained loans or credit. The loan officer specializes in examining and evaluating applications for lines of credit, installment credit, or commercial, real estate, and consumer loans and has the authority to approve them within a specified limit or recommend their approval to the loan committee. To determine the feasibility of granting a loan request, the officer analyzes the applicant's financial status, credit, and property evaluation. The job may also include handling foreclosure proceedings. Depending on training and experience, officers may analyze potential loan markets to develop prospects for loans. They negotiate the terms of transaction and draw up the requisite documents to buy and sell contracts, loans, or real estate. Credit and collection managers make up collection notices for customers who already have credit. When the bank has difficulty collecting accounts or receives a worthless check, credit and collection managers take steps to correct the situation. Managers must keep records of all credit and collection transactions.

Loan counselors study the records of the account when payments on a loan are overdue and contact the borrower to discuss payment of the loan. They may analyze the borrower's financial problems and make new arrangements for repayment of the loan. If a loan account is uncollectible, they prepare a report for the bank or thrift institution's files.

Credit card operations managers are responsible for the overall credit card policies and operations of a

bank, commercial establishment, or credit card company. They establish procedures for verifying the information on application forms, determine applicants' creditworthiness, approve the issuance of credit cards, and set a credit limit on each account. These managers coordinate activities involved with reviewing unpaid balances, collecting delinquent accounts, investigating and preventing fraud, voiding lost or stolen credit cards, keeping records, and exchanging information with the company's branches and other credit card companies.

The *letter of credit negotiator* works with clients who hold letters of credit used in international banking. This person contacts foreign banks, suppliers, and other sources to obtain documents needed to authorize the requested loan, then checks the documents to see if they have been completed correctly so that the conditions set forth in the letter of credit meet with policy and code requirements. Before authorizing payment, the negotiator verifies the client's credit rating and may request increasing the collateral or reducing the amount of purchases, amending the contract accordingly. The letter of credit negotiator specifies the method of payment and informs the foreign bank when a loan has gone unpaid for a certain length of time.

The *trust officer* directs operations concerning the administration of private, corporate, and probate trusts. Officers examine or draft trust agreements to ensure compliance with legal requirements and terms creating trusts. They locate, inventory, and evaluate assets of probated accounts. They also direct realization of assets, liquidation of liabilities, payment of bills, preparation of federal and state tax returns on trust income, and collection of earnings. They represent the institution in trust fund negotiations.

Reserve officers maintain the institution's reserve funds according to policy and as required by law. They regulate the flow of money through branches, correspondent banks, and the Federal Reserve Bank. They also consolidate financial statements, calculate the legal reserve, and compile statistical and analytical reports of the reserves.

Foreign-exchange traders maintain the balance that the institution has on deposit in foreign banks to ensure its foreign exchange position and determine the prices at which that exchange will be purchased and sold. Their conclusions are based on an analysis of demand, supply, and the stability of the currency. They establish local rates of exchange based upon money market quotations or the customer's financial standing. They also buy and sell foreign exchange drafts and compute the proceeds.

The *securities trader* performs securities investment and counseling service for the bank and its customers. They study financial background and future trends and advise financial institution officers and customers regarding investments in stocks and bonds. They transmit buy-and-sell orders to a trading desk or broker as directed and recommend purchase, retention, or sale of issues, then notify the customer or the bank of the execution of trading orders. They compute extensions, commissions, and other charges for billing customers and making payments for securities.

The *operations officer* is in charge of the internal operations in a department or branch office of a financial institution. This person is responsible for the smooth and efficient operation of a particular area. Duties include interviewing, hiring, and directing the training of employees, as well as supervising their activities, evaluating their performance, and making certain that they comply with established procedures. Operations officers audit accounts, records, and certifications and verify the count of incoming cash. They prepare reports on the activities of the department or branch, control the supply of money for its needs, and perform other managerial tasks of a general nature.

The *credit union manager* directs the operations of credit unions, which are chartered by the state or federal government to provide savings and loan services to their members. This manager reviews loan applications, arranges automatic payroll deductions for credit union members wishing to make regular savings deposits or loan payments, and assists in collecting delinquent accounts. Managers prepare financial statements, help the government audit credit union records, and supervise bookkeeping and clerical activities. Acting as management representative of the credit union, credit union managers have the power to sign legal documents and checks on behalf of the board of directors. They also oversee control of the credit union's assets and advise the board on how to invest its funds.

Requirements

A bachelor's degree in accounting or finance or in business administration with an emphasis on accounting or finance is the minimum requirement for a position as a finan-

cial institution manager. Increasingly, a master's in business administration is preferred. In high school, students should take classes in business, economics, accounting, and mathematics.

Professional certification is available in specialized fields such as investment and credit management. The Association for Investment Management and Research confers the Chartered Financial Analyst designation to investment professionals who have a bachelor's degree, pass three test levels, and have three or more years of experience in the field. The National Association of Credit Management administers a three-part certification program for business credit professionals. Through a combination of experience and examinations, these financial managers pass through the level of Credit Business Associate, to Credit Business Fellow, to Certified Credit Executive. The Treasury Management Association confers the Certified Cash Manager designation to those who pass an examination and have two years of relevant experience.

In the banking business the ability to get along well with others is essential. Financial institution officers should show tact and should convey a feeling of understanding and confidence in their employees and customers. Honesty is perhaps the most important qualification in financial institution officers. They handle large sums of money and have access to confidential financial information about the individuals and business concerns associated with their institutions. They, therefore, must have a high degree of personal integrity.

Opportunities for Experience & Exploration

Except for high school courses that are business oriented, the average high school student will find few opportunities for experience and exploration during the school year. Teachers may be able to arrange for a class tour through a financial institution so that some knowledge about banking services can be gained. The most valuable experience will be gained through a part-time or a summer job in a bank or other institution that sometimes hires qualified high school students.

Methods of Entering

One way to enter banking as a regular employee is through part-time or summer employment. Anyone can apply for a position by writing to a financial institution officer in charge of personnel or by arranging for an interview appointment. Many institutions advertise in the classified section of local newspapers. The larger banks recruit on college campuses. An officer will visit a campus and conduct interviews at that time. Student placement offices can also arrange for interviews.

Advancement

There is no one method for advancement among financial institution officers. Advancement depends on the size of the institution, the services it offers, and the qualifications of the employee. Usually, the smaller the employer the slower the advancements. Financial institutions often offer special training programs that take place at night, during the summer, and in some special instances during scheduled working hours. People who take advantage of these opportunities usually find that advancement comes more quickly. The American Banking Institute, for example, offers training in every phase of banking through its own facilities or the facilities of the local universities and banking organizations. The length of this training may vary from six months to two years. Years of service and experience are required for a top-level financial institution officer to become acquainted with policy, operations, customers, and the community. Similarly, the National Institute of Credit offers training and instruction through its parent entity, the National Association of Credit Management.

Employment Outlook

In 1996, there were about 800,000 financial officers and managers employed in the United States. The number of job openings for financial institution officers and managers is expected to increase about as fast as the average through the year 2006. The U.S. Department of Labor predicts that 146,000 new jobs will be added between the years 1996 and 2006 as a result of the general expansion of financial services and the more extensive use of computer. The need for skilled professionals will increase primarily as a result of greater domestic and foreign competition, changing laws affecting taxes and other financial matters, and a growing emphasis on accurate reporting of financial data for both financial institutions and other corporations.

Competition for these jobs will be strong, however, for several reasons. Financial institution officers and managers are often promoted from within the ranks of the organization, and, once established in their jobs, they tend to stay for many years. Also, more qualified applicants, many with graduate degrees, are becoming available each year to fill the vacancies that do arise. Chances for employment will be best for people familiar with a range of financial services, such as banking, insurance, real estate, and securities, and for those experienced in computers and data processing systems.

Financial institution officers and managers enjoy job security even during economic downswings, which seem to have little immediate effect on banking.

Earnings

Those who enter banking in the next few years will find the earnings to be dependent on their experience, the size of the institution, and its location. In general, starting salaries in financial institutions are not very high, although among larger financial institutions in big cities, starting salaries often compare favorably with salaries in large corporations. After five to ten years of experience, the salaries of officers usually are slightly higher than those in large corporations for people of comparable experience.

In 1996, financial managers earned a median annual salary of $40,700. The lowest 10 percent, which included those in entry-level and trainee positions, were paid $21,800 or less, while the top 10 percent receive more than $81,100 a year. Those with advanced degrees, master's degree or better, earned about $10,900 more than other workers, according to a 1997 survey conducted by the Treasury Management Association. Group life insurance, paid vacations, profit sharing plans, and hospitalization and retirement plans are some of the benefits offered. Some companies offer year end bonuses.

Conditions of Work

Working conditions in financial institutions are very pleasant. They are usually clean, well maintained, and often air-conditioned. They are generally located throughout cities for the convenience of customers and employees, too. For financial institution officers, hours may be somewhat irregular as many organizations have expanded their hours of business.

Sources of Additional Information

American Bankers Association
1120 Connecticut Avenue, NW
Washington, DC 20036
Tel: 202-663-5221
WWW: http://www.aba.com/aba

Association for Investment Management and Research
5 Boar's Head Lane
PO Box 3668
Charlottesville, VA 22903
Tel: 804-977-6600
WWW: http://www.aimr.com/aimr.html

National Association of Credit Management
8815 Centre Park Drive
Columbia, MD 21045-2117
Tel: 410-740-5560
WWW: http://www.nacm.org

Treasury Management Association
7315 Wisconsin Avenue, Suite 600W
Bethesda, MD 20814
Tel: 301-907-2862
WWW: http://www.tma-net.org

Flight Attendants

Definition

Flight attendants are responsible for the safety and comfort of airline passengers from the initial boarding to the final disembarkment. They are trained to respond in the event of emergencies and passenger illness. Flight attendants are required on almost all national and international commercial flights.

Nature of the Work

Flight attendants perform a variety of preflight and in-flight duties. At least one hour before takeoff, they attend briefing session with the rest of the flight crew; carefully check flight supplies, emergency life jackets, oxygen masks, and other passenger safety equipment; and see that the passenger cabins are neat, orderly, and furnished with pillows and blankets. They also check the plane galley to see that food and beverages to be served are on board and that the galley is secure for takeoff.

Attendants welcome the passengers on the flight and check their tickets as they board the plane. They show the passengers where to store briefcases and other small parcels, direct them to their cabin section for seating, and help them put their coats and carry-on luggage in overhead compartments. They often give special attention to elderly or disabled passengers and those traveling with small children.

Before takeoff, a flight attendant speaks to the passengers as a group, usually over a loudspeaker. He or she welcomes the passengers and gives the names of the crew and flight attendants. The passengers also learn about weather, altitude, and safety information. As required by federal law, flight attendants demonstrate the use of lifesaving equipment and safety procedures and check to

make sure all passenger seatbelts are fastened before takeoff.

Upon takeoff and landing and during any rough weather encountered during the flight, flight attendants routinely check to make sure passengers are wearing their safety belts properly and have their seats in an upright position. They may distribute reading materials to passengers and answer any questions regarding flight schedules, weather, or the geographic terrain over which the plane is passing. Sometimes they call attention to points of interest that can be seen from the plane. They observe passengers during the flight to ensure their personal comfort and assist anyone who becomes airsick or nervous.

During some flights, attendants serve prepared breakfasts, lunches, dinners, or between-meal refreshments. They are responsible for certain clerical duties, such as filling out passenger reports and issuing reboarding passes. They keep the passenger cabins neat and comfortable during flights. Attendants serving on international flights may provide customs and airport information and sometimes translate flight information or passenger instructions into another language.

Most flight attendants work for commercial airlines. A small number, however, work on private airplanes owned and operated by corporations or private companies.

Requirements

Airline companies are very selective in accepting applicants for positions as flight attendants. These employees play a major role in promoting good public relations for the airlines. Attendants are in constant contact with the public, and the impressions they make and the quality of service they render represent a type of advertisement for the airline. Airlines are particularly interested in employing people who are intelligent, poised, resourceful, and able to work in a congenial and tactful manner with the public. Flight attendants must have excellent health, good vision, and the ability to speak clearly.

Flight attendants need to have at least a high school education. Applicants with additional college-level education are often given preference in employment. Business training and experience in working with the public are also considered assets. Attendants employed by international airlines are usually required to be able to converse in a foreign language. Airlines in the United States require flight attendants to be U.S. citizens, have permanent resident status, or have valid work visas. In general, applicants must be at least nineteen to twenty years old, although some airlines have higher minimum age requirements. They should be at least five feet, two inches tall in order to reach overhead compartments, and their weight should be in proportion to their height. Although most flight attendants are women, the number of men in this field is increasing.

Most large airline companies maintain their own training schools for flight attendants. Training programs may last from four to six weeks. Some smaller airlines send their applicants to the schools run by the bigger airlines. A few colleges and schools offer flight attendant training, but these graduates may still be required to complete an airline's own training program.

Airline training programs usually include classes in company operations and schedules, flight regulations and duties, first aid, grooming, emergency operations and evacuation procedures, flight terminology, and other types of job-related instruction. Flight attendants also receive twelve to fourteen hours of additional emergency and passenger procedures training each year. Trainees for international flights are given instruction on customs and visa regulations and are taught procedures for terrorist attacks. Near the end of the training period, trainees are taken on practice flights, in which they perform their duties under supervision.

An on-the-job probationary period, usually six months, follows training school. During this time, experienced attendants pay close attention to the performance, aptitudes, and attitudes of the new attendants. After this period, new attendants serve as reserve personnel and fill in for attendants who are ill or on vacation. While on call, these reserve attendants must be available to work on short notice.

Young people who are interested in this occupation need to have a congenial temperament, a pleasant personality, and the desire to serve the public. They must have the ability to think clearly and logically, even in emergency situations, and they must be able to follow instructions working as team members of flight crews.

Opportunities for Experience & Exploration

Opportunities for experience in this occupation are almost nonexistent until an individual has completed flight training school. Interested persons may explore this occupation by talking with flight attendants or people in airline personnel offices. Airline companies and private training schools publish many brochures describing the work of flight attendants and send them out upon request.

Methods of Entering

Individuals who are interested in becoming flight attendants should apply directly to the personnel divisions of airline companies. The names and locations of these companies may be obtained by writing to the Air Transport Association of America. Addresses of airline personnel division offices can also be obtained from almost any airline office or ticket agency. Some major airlines have personnel recruiting teams that travel throughout the United States interviewing prospective flight attendants. Airline company offices can provide interested people with information regarding these recruitment visits, which are sometimes announced in newspaper advertisements in advance of the actual visit.

Advancement

A number of advancement opportunities are open to flight attendants. They may advance to positions as *first flight attendant* (sometimes known as the *flight purser*), *supervising flight attendant*, *instructor*, or *airline recruitment representative*. They may also have the opportunity to move up to *chief attendant* in a particular division or area. Although the rate of turnover in this field was once high, more people are making careers as flight attendants and competition for available supervisory jobs is very high.

Many flight attendants who no longer qualify for flight duty because of health or other factors move into other jobs with the airlines. These jobs may include *reservation agent*, *ticket agent*, or *personnel recruiter*. They may also work in the public relations, sales, air transportation, dispatch, or communications divisions. Trained flight attendants may also find similar employment in other transportation or hospitality industries such as luxury cruise ship lines.

Employment

Outlook

Nearly 132,000 professionally trained flight attendants are employed in the United States. Commercial airlines employ the vast majority of all flight attendants, most of whom are stationed in the major cities that serve as their airlines' home base.

Employment opportunities for flight attendants are predicted to grow much faster than average in the next decade. More and more people are flying regularly today for business and pleasure, and some estimates predict that the number of flight passengers will increase significantly to accommodate the demand. To meet the needs of the traveling public, airline companies are using larger planes and adding more flights. Because federal regulations require at least one attendant on duty for every fifty passengers aboard a plane, this means there will be many more openings for flight attendants. A large number of jobs will result from current flight attendants leaving the workforce due to a variety of factors, including retirement.

Finding employment as a flight attendant is highly competitive. Even though the number of job openings is expected to grow, airlines receive thousands of applications each year. Students interested in this career will have a competitive advantage if they have at least two years of college and prior work experience in customer relations or public contact. Courses in business, psychology, sociology, geography, speech, communications, first aid and emergency medical techniques such as CPR, and knowledge of foreign languages and cultures

will make the prospective flight attendant more attractive to the airlines.

Earnings

The average income of beginning flight attendants is approximately $12,800 a year. The average salary of all flight attendants was $19,000 per year in 1996, according to the U.S. Department of Labor. Senior flight attendants can earn $35,000 to $40,000 a year. Wage and work schedule requirements are established by union contract. Most flight attendants are members of the Transport Workers Union of America or the Association of Flight Attendants.

Flight attendants are limited to a specific number of flying hours. In general, they work approximately eighty hours of scheduled flying time and an additional thirty-five hours of ground duties each month. They receive extra compensation for overtime and night flights. Flight attendants on international flights customarily earn higher salaries than those on domestic flights. Most airlines give periodic salary increases until a maximum pay ceiling is reached. Flight assignments are often based on seniority, with the most senior flight attendants having their choice of flight times and destinations.

Airlines usually pay flight attendants in training either living expenses or a training salary. Companies usually pay flight attendants' expenses such as food, ground transportation, and overnight accommodations while they are on duty or away from home base. Some airlines may require first-year flight attendants to furnish their own uniforms; however, most companies supply the airline uniform.

Fringe benefits include paid sick leave and vacation time, free or reduced air travel rates for attendants and their families, and, in some cases, group hospitalization and life insurance plans and retirement benefits.

Conditions

of Work

Flight attendants are usually assigned to a home base in a major city or large metropolitan area. These locations include New York, Chicago, Boston, Miami, Los Angeles, San Francisco, St. Louis, and other cities. Some airlines assign attendants on a rotation system to home bases, or they may give preference to the requests of those with rank and seniority on bids for certain home bases. Those with the longest records of service may be given the most desirable flights and schedules.

Flight attendants need to be flexible in their work schedules, mainly because commercial airlines maintain operations twenty-four hours a day throughout the entire year. They may be scheduled to work nights, weekends, and on holidays, and they may find some of their allotted time off occurs away from home between flights. They are often away from home for several days at a time. They work long days, but over a year's time, a flight attendant averages about 156 days off, compared with 96 days off for the average office worker.

The work performed by flight attendants may be physically demanding in some respects. For most of the flight, they are usually on their feet servicing passengers' needs, checking safety precautions, and, in many cases, serving meals and beverages. Working with the public all day can be draining. Flight attendants are the most visible employee of the airline, and they must be courteous to everyone, even passengers who are annoying or demanding. The occupation is not considered a hazardous one; however, there is a certain degree of risk involved in any type of flight work. Flight attendants may suffer minor injuries as they perform their duties in a moving aircraft.

The combination of free time and the opportunity to travel are benefits that many flight attendants enjoy. For those who enjoy helping and working with people, being a flight attendant may be a rewarding career.

Sources of Additional Information

For information on educational and career opportunities, please contact:

Air Line Employees Association
6520 South Cicero Avenue
Bedford Park, IL 60638
Tel: 708-563-9999

Air Transport Association of America
1301 Pennsylvania Avenue, NW
Washington, DC 20004

Federal Aviation Administration
U.S. Department of Transportation
800 Independence Avenue, SW
Washington, DC 20591

Future Aviation Professionals of America
4959 Massachusetts Boulevard
Atlanta, GA 30337
Tel: 800-JET-JOBS

Food Service Workers

Definition

Food service workers include waiters and waitresses of many different types, as well as counter attendants, dining room helpers, fast food workers, kitchen helpers, and others. These workers take customers' orders, serve food and beverages, make out checks, and sometimes take payments. These basic duties, however, may vary greatly depending on the specific kind of food service establishment.

Nature of the Work

Food service workers have a variety of job duties depending on the size and kind of food establishment in which they are employed. In small restaurants, sandwich shops, grills, diners, fast food outlets, and cafeterias, customers are usually looking for hot food and quick service. Informal waiters and waitresses and lunchroom or coffee-shop counter attendants work to satisfy patrons and give them the kind of attention that will make them repeat customers. They take customers' orders, serve food and beverages, calculate bills, and sometimes collect money. Between serving customers, waiters and waitresses in small establishments may clear and clean tables and counters, replenish supplies, and set up table service for future customers. When business is slow, they spend some time cleaning the serving area and equipment such as coffee machines and blenders. Counter attendants often do some simple cooking tasks; make sandwiches, salads, and cold drinks; and prepare ice cream dishes. They also may have to help with such tasks as cleaning kitchen equipment, sweeping and mopping floors, and carrying out trash. Other workers in this category include cafeteria counter attendants, supervisors, canteen operators, and fountain servers.

In larger and fancier restaurants, formal waiters and waitresses perform essentially the same services as those working in smaller establishments, but they usually have extra duties designed to make the dining experience more enjoyable. These duties may include seating the customers, presenting them with menus, suggesting choices from the menu, informing the customers of special preparations and seasonings of food, and sometimes suggesting beverages that would complement the meal. They check to see that the correct dinnerware and utensils are on the table and try to attend to any special requests the customers may have.

Waiters and waitresses in expensive restaurants serve food following more formal and correct procedures. Captains, or headwaiters and headwaitresses, may greet and seat the guests, take reservations over the phone, and supervise the service of the waiters and waitresses. Wine stewards assist customers in selecting wines from the restaurant's available stock.

Dining room attendants, once called bus boys and bus girls, assist the waiters and waitresses in their duties. They may clear and reset tables, carry soiled dishes to the dishwashing area, carry in trays of food, and clean up spilled food and broken dishes. In some restaurants, these attendants also serve water, and bread and butter to customers. During slow periods, they may fill salt and pepper shakers, clean coffee pots, and do various other tasks. Cafeteria attendants clear and set tables, carry trays of dirty dishes to the kitchen, check supplies, and sometimes serve coffee to customers.

While dining room and cafeteria attendants assure clean and attractive table settings in the dining areas, kitchen helpers help maintain an efficient and hygienic kitchen area by cleaning food preparation and storage areas, sweeping and scrubbing floors, and removing garbage. They may also move supplies and equipment from storage to work areas, perform some simple food preparation, and wash the pots and pans used in cooking. To keep the kitchen operating smoothly, they maintain a steady supply of clean dishes by scraping food from plates, stacking them in and removing them from the dishwasher, polishing flatware, and removing water spots from glasses.

In addition to small restaurants, such as grills, sandwich shops, tearooms, soda shops, and diners, and the larger restaurants and hotel dining rooms, food service workers may be employed aboard ships and trains; in hospitals, schools, or factories; and in many other establishments where food is served. Some waiters and waitresses may be designated by the place in which they work or the type of specialized service they perform, such as carhops and bar, dining car, room service, take-out, buffet, and club waiters and waitresses.

Requirements

Applicants for jobs as waiters, waitresses, or food counter workers are usually not required to have a high school diploma. Most employers, however, favor applicants with some high school training, and graduation from high school is generally considered a personal asset. Positions for waiters' assistants, kitchen helpers, and cafeteria counter workers have no educational requirements.

Vocational schools may offer special training courses for waiters and waitresses. Special course training is sometimes offered by restaurant associations in conjunction with schools or food agencies, and many employers seek persons who have had such training.

Smaller, more informal restaurants may hire waiters and waitresses without special training or previous experience. In these situations, the necessary skills are learned on the job. Larger restaurants and those with more formal dining atmospheres usually hire only experienced waiters or waitresses. Almost without exception, food counter workers, waiters' and waitresses' assistants, and kitchen helpers learn their skills on the job.

Food service workers generally must be free from any physical disabilities that would impair their movements on the job. They must possess strong physical stamina, because the work requires many long hours of standing and walking. The job also requires lifting heavy trays of food, dishes, and water glasses, as well as a great deal of bending and stooping. In some cases, employees may work near steam tables or hot ovens.

Food service workers, almost without exception, are required to obtain health certificates from the state Department of Public Health that certify they are free from communicable diseases, as shown by physical examination and blood tests. This is required for the protection of the general public.

The principal union for waiters and waitresses, food counter workers, waiters' assistants, and kitchen helpers is the Hotel Employees and Restaurant Employees International Union (AFL-CIO); however, not all employees are union members.

Waiters, waitresses, and food counter workers need to have a congenial temperament, patience, and the desire to please and be of service to the public. All food service workers must be neat and clean in their personal hygiene and dress. Those who serve the public should present a pleasant appearance, be able to communicate well, and be able to use basic arithmetic skills to compute customers' checks. In some restaurants that specialize in the foods of a certain country, waiters and waitresses might need to speak a foreign language. A good memory and persuasive skills are additional personal assets for this occupation.

Opportunities for Experience & Exploration

Opportunities are especially good in the food service field for people with limited skills or education. Those interested in becoming waiters or waitresses often gain experience by doing part-time or summer work in fast food establishments, small restaurants, grills, and sandwich shops. Many waiters and waitresses started their careers as dining room attendants, carhops, or food counter workers.

Methods of Entering

People interested in entering this field generally do so by applying in person for any open positions. Job openings are frequently listed in newspaper advertisements, or they may be located through local offices of the state employment service or private employment agencies. The private agencies may charge a percentage fee for their placement services. In some areas where food service workers are unionized, potential employees may seek job placement assistance by contacting union offices.

Advancement

Employees may advance to better-paying jobs by transferring to larger and more formal restaurants. They also may gain better positions and higher pay as they obtain more training and experience.

In general, advancement in this field is limited. Nevertheless, waiters and waitresses may earn promotions to positions as headwaiter, *hostess*, captain, or other supervisory position. They may be promoted eventually to *restaurant manager*, depending on their training, experience, and work performance record, as well as on the size and type of food establishment. Food counter workers can advance to *cashier*, *cook*, waiter or waitress, *counter or fountain supervisor*, or *line supervisor* in a cafeteria. Large organizations, such as fast food chains, may have management training programs or less formal on-the-job training for dependable workers who have leadership ability. Promotion opportunities are much more limited for waiters' assistants and kitchen helpers. Some of them become waiters or waitresses, cooks' helpers, or *short-order cooks*; these promotions are more likely to happen in large restaurants and institutions. Some of these higher positions require reading, writing, and arithmetic skills, which employees seeking promotion should keep in mind.

Advancement usually involves greater responsibilities and higher pay. In some cases, a promotion may mean that the employee has the chance to earn more in service tips than in actual salary increases, depending on the size, type, and location of the establishment.

Some individuals may aspire to owning their own businesses or to entering into business partnerships after they have earned and reserved some capital and gained the necessary training and experience. A knowledge of the restaurant and food service business from the inside can be a definite advantage to someone opening or buying a restaurant.

Employment Outlook

An estimated four and a half million people hold jobs as food service workers today. The employment outlook for these workers is expected to be relatively good through the end of the decade, especially in large cities and tourist areas. Thousands of new job opportunities will become available as more restaurants, hotels, motels, and combination business-eating establishments are built. Contributing to the great demand for public food services are a growing population and an increase in discretionary spending for dining and entertainment. Higher incomes and more leisure time encourage people to dine out and travel more frequently. Also, greater numbers of working parents and their families find it convenient to eat out.

This occupation tends to have a high turnover rate; many job openings for this large field will result in the need to replace workers. Jobs for beginning workers will be more plentiful in lower-priced restaurants, where employees usually work only a short time. More expensive and formal restaurants tend to hire only experienced workers. Because of the higher pay, better tips, and other benefits, the job turnover rate is lower in these establishments, which increases the competition for job openings.

Food service workers may find temporary job opportunities in summer or winter resort areas. Some workers prefer to move with the seasonal trade because they can take advantage of the benefits the vacation area offers. Because many of the people in food services do not intend to make it their career choice for life, there are frequent openings throughout the industry, many of which are part time.

Earnings

The earnings of food service workers are determined by a number of factors, such as the type, size, and location of the food establishment, union membership, experience and training of the workers, basic wages paid, and, in some cases, tips earned. Estimating the average wage scale is therefore difficult and has a wide margin of error.

Waiters and waitresses depend a great deal on tips to supplement their basic wages, which in general are relatively small. According to the U.S. Department of Labor, waiters and waitresses earned an average of $14,040 annually in 1996, including tips; half earned between $10,400 and $18,200, and the top 10 percent earned more than $24,440. Tips, usually ranging from 10 to 20 percent of the customers' checks, often amount to more than the actual wages, especially in the larger metropolitan areas. Waiters and waitresses working in busy, expensive restaurants earned the most.

Full-time dining room attendants earned an average annual salary of $13,520. Half earned between $10,400 and $16,640; the top 10 percent earned more than $21,320. Most of their earnings came from wages, while a portion of it came from tip pools that they shared with other members of the wait staff. Kitchen helpers earned higher basic wages than dining room attendants, but they were not in a position to receive tips.

Food counter workers earned an average annual salary of about $11,440. Half earned between $9,880 and $14,040, while the top 10 percent earned more than $18,720. While some counter help in restaurants and diners also received tips, those working in fast food restaurants and cafeterias generally did not. As a benefit, most businesses offered free or discounted meals to workers.

Conditions of Work

Working conditions for food service workers have improved greatly, as more restaurants have been air-conditioned and modernized and many labor-saving techniques have become available. This occupational group is still subject to certain work hazards, however. These may include burns from heat and steam; cuts and injuries from knives, glassware, and other equipment; and sometimes hard falls from rushing on slippery floors.

Working hours will vary with the place of employment. The majority of waiters and waitresses work forty- to forty-eight-hour weeks, while food counter workers, waiters' assistants, and kitchen helpers generally work fewer than thirty hours a week. Split shifts are common to cover rush hours; some employees may work the lunch and dinner shifts, for example, with a few hours off in between. This is good for students, of course, who can then plan their courses around work schedules.

Most food service workers have to work evenings, weekends, and holidays. Some holiday work may be rotated among all the employees. One day off per week is usually in the schedule. Benefits for food service workers usually include free or discounted meals during the hours when they work. Their place of employment often furnishes them with work uniforms.

Work in this field is physically strenuous, requiring long hours of standing and walking, carrying heavy trays or pots and pans, and lifting other types of equipment. Rush hours are hectic for these employees, particularly for those who serve the public, attending to several tables or customers at the same time. Hard-to-please customers can also add to the employee's stress level.

The operation of a restaurant or other food service depends on the teamwork of its employees. An even disposition and a sense of humor, especially under pressure, contribute greatly to the efficiency and pleasantness of the restaurant's operation. The ability to converse easily with customers is a major asset for those working directly with the public.

Sources of Additional Information

■Council on Hotel, Restaurant, and Institutional Education
1200 17th Street NW
Washington, DC 20036-3097
Tel: 202-331-5990
Email: alliance@access.digex.net

■Canadian Society of Nutrition Management
PO Box 948
57 Simcoe Street South
Oshawa, ON L1H 7N1 Canada
Tel: 905-436-0145

■Educational Foundation of the National Restaurant Association
250 South Wacker Drive, Suite 1400
Chicago, IL 60606
Tel: 312-715-1010

General Maintenance Mechanics

Definition

General maintenance mechanics, sometimes called *maintenance technicians*, repair and maintain machines, mechanical equipment, and buildings, and work on plumbing, electrical, air-conditioning, and heating systems. They also do minor construction or carpentry work and routine preventive maintenance to keep the physical structures of businesses, schools, factories, and apartment buildings in good condition. They also maintain and repair specialized equipment and machinery found in cafeterias, laundries, hospitals, offices, and factories.

Nature of the Work

General maintenance mechanics do almost any tasks, other than large and difficult jobs, that may be required to maintain a building or the equipment in it. They may be called on to replace faulty electrical outlets; fix air-conditioning motors; install water lines; build partitions; patch plaster or drywall; open clogged drains; dismantle, clean, and oil machinery; paint windows, doors, and woodwork; repair institutional-size dishwashers or laundry machines; and see to many other problems. Because of the diverse nature of the responsibilities of maintenance mechanics, they have to know how to use a variety of materials and be skilled in the use of most hand tools and ordinary power tools. They also need to be able to recognize when they cannot handle a problem well and a specialized repair person should be called instead.

General maintenance mechanics usually work in many kinds of settings. They work on the machinery and buildings of factories, hospitals, schools, colleges, hotels, offices, stores, malls, gas and electric companies, government agencies, and apart-ment buildings. Those mechanics who work mostly on keeping industrial machines in good condition may be called *factory maintenance workers* or *mill maintenance workers*, while those mechanics who concentrate on the maintenance of a building's physical structure may be called *building maintenance workers*.

Once a problem or defect has been identified and diagnosed, maintenance mechanics must plan the repairs. They may consult blueprints, repair manuals, and parts catalogs to determine what to do. They obtain supplies and new parts from a storeroom or order them from a distributor. They install new parts in place of worn or broken ones, using hand tools, power tools, and sometimes electronic test devices and other specialized equipment. In some situations, maintenance mechanics may fix an old part or even fabricate a new part. To do this, they may need to set up and operate machine tools, such as lathes or milling machines, and operate gas- or arc-welding equipment to join metal parts together. In some cases, it may be impossible or cost-prohibitive to fix the machine, and the mechanic may have to recommend a new purchase.

One of the most important kinds of duties general maintenance mechanics perform is routine preventive maintenance to correct defects before a piece of machinery breaks down or a building begins to deteriorate. This type of maintenance keeps small problems from turning into large, expensive ones. Mechanics often inspect machinery on a regular schedule, perhaps following a checklist that includes such items as inspecting belts, checking fluid levels, replacing filters, oiling moving parts, and so forth. They keep records of the repair work done and the inspection dates. Repair and inspection records can be important evidence of compliance with insurance requirements and government safety regulations.

In small establishments, one mechanic may be the only person working in maintenance, and thus may be responsible for almost any kind of repair.

In large establishments, however, tasks may be divided among several mechanics; for example, one mechanic may be assigned to install and set up new equipment, while another may handle preventive and other maintenance and repairs on the heating, air-conditioning, and ventilation systems.

Requirements

General maintenance mechanics usually start as helpers to experienced mechanics and learn their skills on the job. Beginning helpers are given the simplest jobs, such as changing light bulbs or making minor drywall repairs. As general maintenance mechanics acquire skills, they are assigned more complicated work, such as troubleshooting malfunctioning machinery.

Some mechanics learn their skills by working as helpers to people employed in building trades, such as electricians or carpenters. Other mechanics attend high school shop classes and trade or vocational schools that teach many of the necessary skills. Becoming fully qualified for a mechanic's job usually requires one to four years of on-the-job training or classroom instruction, or some combination of both.

Many employers prefer to hire helpers or mechanics who are high school graduates, but a diploma is not always required. High school courses that offer good preparation for this occupation include mechanical drawing, metal shop, electrical shop, woodworking, blueprint reading, general science, and applied mathematics.

There are some certification programs open to maintenance mechanics. The BOMI Institute, for example, offers the designations of Systems Maintenance Technician (SMT) to applicants who have completed courses in boilers, heating systems, and applied mathematics; refrigeration systems and accessories; air handling, water treatment and plumbing systems; electrical and illumination systems; and building control systems. Technicians who have achieved SMT status can go on and become certified as Systems Maintenance Administrators (SMAs) by taking further classes in building design and maintenance, energy management, and supervision. While not necessarily required for employment, employees with certification may become more valuable assets to their employers and may have better chances at advancement.

Mechanics need to have good manual dexterity and mechanical aptitude. People who enjoy taking things apart and putting them back together are good candidates for this position. Since some of the work, such as reaching, squatting, and lifting, requires physical strength and stamina, reasonably good health is necessary. Mechanics also need the ability to analyze and solve problems and to work effectively on their own, without constant supervision.

Opportunities for Experience & Exploration

Shop classes can give students a good indication of their mechanical aptitude and of whether or not they would enjoy maintenance work. The best way to experience the work these mechanics do, however, is to get a summer or part-time job as a mechanic's helper in a factory, apartment complex, or similar setting. If such a job is not available, it might be possible to talk to a maintenance mechanic to get a fuller, more complete picture of his or her responsibilities.

Methods of Entering

Job seekers in this field usually apply directly to potential employers. Information on job openings for mechanic's helpers can often be found through newspaper classified ads, school placement offices, and the local offices of the state employment service. Graduates of trade or vocational schools may be able to get referrals and information from their school's placement office. Union offices may also be a good place to learn about job opportunities.

Advancement

Some general maintenance mechanics who are employed in large organizations can advance to supervisory positions. Another possibility is moving into one of the traditional building trades and becoming a craftworker, such as a plumber or electrician. In smaller organizations, promotion opportunities are limited, although increases in pay may result from an employee's good performance and increased value to the employer.

Employment Outlook

The job outlook for general maintenance mechanics is good. Through the year 2006, employment of these workers is expected to grow as fast as the the average for all other occupations. There will probably be an increasing number of apartment buildings, office buildings, factories, hotels, schools, and stores; most of these organizations and the machinery they require will need the services of maintenance mechanics. In addition to the newly created jobs for these workers, many openings will arise as experienced mechanics transfer to other occupations or leave the labor force.

About seventeen percent of general maintenance mechanics work for manufacturing companies. They may be subject to layoffs during bad economic times, when their employers are under pressure to cut costs. Most mechanics, however, work in non-manufacturing industries and are not usually as vulnerable to layoffs related to economic conditions.

Earnings

Earnings for general maintenance mechanics vary widely, depending on their skills, their geographical location, and the industry in which they work. According to the *1998-99 Occupational Outlook Handbook*, general maintenance technicians earned an average of $20,550 a year; fifty percent earned from $17,388 to $24,668 a year. Workers who have been in the business for many years and who may have supervisory responsibilities can make $50,000 or more. Those employed in service businesses averaged an annual salary of $19,572; manufacturing businesses offered an average salaries of $20,592.

Almost all maintenance mechanics receive a benefits package that includes health insurance, paid vacation, sick leave, and a pension plan.

Conditions of Work

General maintenance mechanics work in almost every industry. More than one-third are employed in service industries, such as elementary and secondary schools, colleges and universities, hospitals and nursing homes, and hotels. Others are employed in manufacturing industries, office and apartment buildings, government agencies, and utility companies. In most cases, mechanics work a forty-hour week. Some work evening or night shifts or on weekends; they may also be on call for emergency repairs.

In the course of a single day, mechanics may do a variety of tasks in different parts of a building or in several buildings, and they may encounter different conditions in each spot. Sometimes they have to work in hot or cold conditions, on ladders, in awkward or cramped positions, among noisy machines, or in other uncomfortable places. Sometimes they must lift heavy weights. On the job, they must stay aware of potential hazards such as electrical shocks, burns, falls, and cuts and bruises. By following safety regulations and using tools properly, they can keep such risks to a minimum.

The mechanic who works in a small establishment may be the only maintenance worker and is often responsible for doing his or her job with little direct supervision. Those who work in larger establishments usually report to a maintenance supervisor who assigns tasks and directs their activities.

Sources of Additional Information

For more information, contact:

▬BOMI Institute
1521 Ritchie Highway
Arnold, MD 21012
Tel: 410-974-1417

▬Mechanical Service Contractors of America
1385 Piccard Drive
Rockville, MD 20850
Tel: 301-869-5800

Geriatric Social Workers

Definition

Geriatric social workers help elderly people adjust to the challenges of growing older. They develop programs and direct agencies that offer counseling, advocacy, and special services. They evaluate the needs of clients, and help them arrange for meal service, housing, transportation, and legal and medical assistance. Geriatric social workers also develop recreation and educational programs for the elderly.

Approximately one-third of all social workers work with older people. They work in hospitals, nursing homes, and retirement communities; they have offices in human service agencies and senior centers. Geriatric social workers must have a genuine interest in the well-being of older people, and must be sensitive to their concerns and problems. Most full-time social workers have a master's degree in social work; with this degree, they have the best opportunity for advancement.

Nature of the Work

A woman in her late 70s has just lost her husband and now must live alone for the first time in many years. She has decided to move to another town, to live closer to her children, and will need help making the transition. She needs a smaller, more manageable home; she needs help with meals and shopping; she would like to make friends in the community. A number of services are available to her, but she may not find out about them without the aid of a geriatric social worker.

As with any social worker, the geriatric social worker is devoted to helping people and communities solve problems. Social workers are dedicated to empowering people, and helping people to preserve their dignity and worth. This kind of assistance and advocacy is especially important among older people. Because old age can sometimes put a person in poor physical and mental health, as well as cause financial difficulties, older people often need help and protection. They may need help with meals, transportation, and house work. Or they may need assistance moving into a retirement community or nursing home. But the elderly population of any community is diverse; some older people stay in perfectly good health, and rely on social services for recreation, meeting people, educational programs, and grief and loss counseling.

People are living longer these days, and the elderly population is growing. At the beginning of the twentieth century, only one-half of newborns would live past the age of 50; people born at the end of the twentieth century can expect to live past the age of 75. This is why social work will continue to offer many job opportunities.

The social work profession is divided into 2 areas: direct practice and indirect practice. Direct practice is also known as clinical practice. As the name suggests, direct practice involves working directly with the client by offering counseling, advocacy, information and referral, and education. Indirect practice concerns the structures through which the direct practice is offered. Indirect practice (a practice consisting mostly of social workers with Ph.D.s) involves program development and evaluation, administration, and policy analysis. Geriatric social workers may work directly with the elderly population through counseling, advising, and conducting group sessions. They also help clients find services for health, housing, finances, and transportation. Those social workers involved in indirect practice develop and oversee the agencies and departments that provide these social services.

Geriatric social workers work for service agencies, hospitals, nursing homes, senior centers, and for other community organizations. Some also work independently. Their help is needed in every town and city across the country; some social workers in areas with smaller populations may serve a number of small towns within a region. No matter where a geriatric social worker serves, the nature of the work is usually the same. Geriatric social workers will meet with older people individually to determine their needs. Meals-on-wheels, transportation services, and recreational programs are some of the basic services offered by community organizations. Some organizations also offer home health care. With nurses and aides assigned to visit the elderly in their homes and to help them with their housework and medical needs, the elderly clients can continue to live on their own.

The geriatric social worker evaluates the clients by interviewing them and determining their needs; the social worker will then enroll their clients for these services. They will make phone calls and provide the service agencies with client information.

The client may need even more assistance. Adult day care services are available in some cities, as well as adult foster care services which match older people with families. A social worker may also need to help a client arrange to move into a nursing home, and to counsel the client about the transition. These counseling services are also extended to members of the client's family, advising them in how to deal with a parent's or grandparent's aging or illness.

In some cases, an elderly person is neglected, or taken advantage of. A geriatric social worker can look into these cases, and serve as an advocate, stepping in to advise the client in his or her legal rights. In addition to legal services, a geriatric social worker will help a client locate any needed financial services. Social workers help clients make arrangements for the payment of services, through Medicare and other financial aid.

Because of efforts by the government to improve the quality of nursing home care, social workers are becoming more active within these facilities. These geriatric social workers work closely with the elderly and their families in arranging the move into the nursing home. They also counsel families upon the death of an elderly relative, and help with funeral arrangements. Geriatric social workers also protect and promote the rights of the residents, and they may conduct in-services with nursing care staff members on patient rights.

The geriatric social worker is part of the larger field of aging. This field, which works to provide for older people, while researching the process of aging, is composed of hospitals, health care corporations, government agencies, churches, colleges, and other organizations and institutions. A number of varied professions, such as law, psychology, health care, education, and marketing, include specialties in aging, or gerontology.

Requirements

By taking high school courses in sociology and psychology, you can learn something about the study of aging; civics courses will teach you about federal laws such as the Older Americans Act. Though you may be able to work in some levels of geriatric social work with only a high school diploma or associate's degree, most opportunities exist for people with social work degrees. In 1996, the Council on Social Work Education accredited 430 programs granting a bachelor's degree in social work (BSW); 130 Master's of social work (MSW); and 55 programs granting a doctorate's degree in social work (DSW). The Council on Social Work Education requires that five areas be covered in accredited baccalaureate social work programs: human behavior and the social environment; social welfare policy and services; social work practice; research; and field practicum. Most programs require two years of liberal art study, followed by two years of study in the social work major. Also, students must complete a field practicum of at least 400 clock hours.

Though no clear lines of classification are drawn in the social work profession, most supervisory and administrative positions require at least a master's of social work. Master's programs are organized according to fields of practice (such as mental health care), problem areas (substance abuse), population groups (the elderly), and practice roles (practice with individuals, families or communities). They are usually two-year programs, with at least 900 hours of field practice.

In some programs, students of social work may specialize in gerontology. Doctoral degrees are also available and prepare students for research and teaching. Most social workers with doctorates go to work in community organizations.

Licensing, certification, or registration of social workers is required by all states. To receive the necessary licensing, a social worker will typically have to gain a certain amount of experience and also pass an exam. Five voluntary certification programs help to identify those social workers who have gained the knowledge and experience necessary to meet national standards.

To be a successful geriatric social worker, you must care about the needs and problems of older people. Many of these people will be relying on you to help them through crucial and difficult times; you must be completely dedicated to your clients, and devoted to helping them maintain their dignity and sense of self worth.

Most geriatric social workers are involved directly with the people they serve, and they are expected to carefully examine a client's living habits and family relations. A geriatric social worker has to be prepared to occasionally confront depressing situations. In most cases, though, a good geriatric social worker will take pleasure from helping a client through a rough time, and will take pride in seeing the client improve his or her life. It's also important for a geriatric social worker to be good-natured and friendly; clients resistant to change may refuse to cooperate with someone they find unpleasant. A geriatric social worker must be very sensitive to the problems of the elderly, but must also remain supportive and encouraging.

Opportunities for Experience & Exploration

With so many services available for older people, there are many job opportunities for the geriatric social worker. Social workers are needed in hospitals, nursing homes, and in a variety of community and human services. Government agencies also hire geriatric social workers. The field is a diverse one, catering to the interests and needs of very different people. There are some agencies which may only deal with the practical aspects of aiding older people—arranging for services and managing financial and legal issues. Working for other agencies may involve the organization of recreational and educational activities, such as senior theater groups and art classes.

To prepare for work as a geriatric social worker, you should volunteer some time at a local nursing home or senior care center. Part-time work may also be available at a local hospital, or as a home care aide. As a home care aid, you'll have the opportunity to work closely with the elderly, and to get to know their needs and concerns. Also, when enrolled in a social work program, you may have the opportunity to help a faculty member with a gerontological research project.

Methods of Entering

After you've received your social work degree and have had some field experience, you will have made valuable connections among faculty and social service organizations. Your college's job placement service or internship program may also direct you to your first full-time job. You should also become familiar with the local senior centers and agencies for the elderly.

Joining a professional organization can be helpful in entering the field. The American Society on Aging sponsors a job bank, and publishes newsletters. Job opportunities are listed in the newsletters of the National Association of Social Workers, the American Geriatrics Society, the American Counseling Association, and other professional organizations. You should also attend annual meetings, giving you the chance to meet other people working in social work, geriatrics, and gerontology.

Advancement

Most geriatric social workers enter the field focusing on the work, rather than on the promotions and salary raises. However, there are advancement opportunities for dedicated social workers. The first steps in advancing as a social worker involve getting the education; for the higher paid positions in administration, program development, and policy analysis, you must have a Ph.D., or a master's along with practical experience.

To advance, you must be prepared to take on new challenges and roles within your organization. By remaining dedicated to your job, and contributing to the development of the organization or agency for which you work, you can build a good resume and pool of references. You will also have increased responsibilities and more direct involvement with the administrators of geriatric programs. You should also take continuing education courses, either in a social work program or a gerontology program, to supplement your degree.

Within smaller agencies and in smaller towns, advancement opportunities may be few, but there may also be less competition for these jobs. For more advancement opportunities, you may have to look to a service organization in an urban area.

Employment Outlook

The field of social work is expected to grow faster than the average through the year 2006, according to the U.S. Department of Labor. Those specializing in geriatric social work—a career mentioned as a runner-up hot track job in *U.S. News & World Report's* 1998 Career Guide—will be in great demand for several reasons. It is estimated that, as people live longer—over 15 million people in the United States will be over the age of 85 by the middle of the twenty-first century—more geriatric social workers will be needed to create programs and provide services for the growing number of elderly. Rising health care costs are causing many insurance companies to consider alternatives to hospital treatment, so some insurance coverage now includes home stays. In addition, hospitals and nursing homes are trying to balance the demand for their services and their limitations in staff and physical facilities. As home care becomes a viable, affordable option for more older people, more geriatric social workers will be necessary in evaluating the needs of clients and setting up services.

The Omnibus Budget Reconciliation Act (OBRA) passed by the U.S. Congress in 1987 to improve nursing home care requires large nursing care facilities to employ full-time social workers. As the government becomes more involved in providing better care for the elderly, the geriatric social worker will see more full-time job opportunities in nursing homes and hospitals.

Earnings

The more advanced your degree, the more you can make in the social work profession. Typically, work with the elderly has paid less than other areas of social work, such as mental health and community planning. The region of the United States in which you work also determines your salary; you can make more money on the East and West coasts than in the Midwest.

In 1997, social workers with a BSW earned an average annual salary of $25,000; MSWs earned about $35,000. Geriatric social workers, in general, average around $32,500 a year. Social workers employed by the U.S. government tend to earn higher salaries, with the average annual salary at about $39,000. Salaries in Canada are higher, with a median range of $40,000 to $45,000 a year.

Conditions of Work

Though geriatric social workers do spend some time in an office setting, they spend much of their time personally interviewing clients and the directors of programs; they also visit the homes of their clients to evaluate and take notes. They may also visit the homes of the client's family. Though some geriatric social workers may work in hospital and nursing home environments, others have their offices in human service agencies alongside other service providers. Serving as an advocate for the elderly client requires, in addition to phone calls and faxes, personal meetings with directors of agencies, local legislators, and others. In cases of abuse and neglect, it may require testifying in court.

Because poverty and illness afflicts a large number of people over the age of 65, the geriatric social worker is often assigned depressing, seemingly hopeless cases. This may be the situation only temporarily, however, as the social worker introduces the client to the necessary services and assistance.

Sources of Additional Information

For further information, contact:

■ **Council on Social Work Education**
1600 Duke Street
Alexandria, VA 22314
Tel: 703-683-8080

■ **National Association of Social Workers**
Career Information
750 First Street, NE, Suite 700
Washington DC 20002
Tel: 202-408-8600

Graphic Designers

Definition

Graphic designers are practical artists whose creations are intended to express ideas, convey information, or draw attention to a product. They design a wide variety of materials including advertisements, displays, packaging, signs, computer graphics and games, book and magazine covers and interiors, animated characters, and company logos to fit the needs and preferences of their clients.

Nature of the Work

Graphic designers are not primarily fine artists, although they may be highly skilled at drawing or painting. Most designs commissioned to graphic designers involve both artwork and copy. Thus, the designer must not only be familiar with the wide range of art media (photography, drawing, painting, collage, etc.) and styles, but he or she must also be familiar with a wide range of typefaces and know how to manipulate them for the right effect. Because design tends to change in a similar way to fashion, designers must keep up-to-date with the latest trends and hot looks. At the same time, they must be well grounded in more traditional, classic designs.

Graphic designers can work as *in-house designers* for a particular company, as *staff designers* for a graphic design firm, or as *freelance designers* working for themselves. Some designers specialize in designing advertising materials or packaging; others focus on "corporate identity" materials such as company stationery and logos; others work mainly for publishers designing book and magazine covers and page layouts; others work in the area of computer graphics, creating still or animated graphics for computer software, videos, or motion pictures. A highly specialized type of graphic designer, the *environmental graphic designer*, designs large outdoor signs. Some graphic designers design exclusively on the computer, while others may use both the computer and traditional hand drawings or paintings, depending on the project's needs and requirements.

Whatever the specialty and whatever their medium, all graphic designers take a similar approach to a project, whether it is for an entirely new design or for a variation on an existing one. Graphic designers begin by determining as best they can the needs and preferences of the clients and the potential users, buyers, or viewers.

In the case of a graphic designer working on a company logo, for example, he or she will likely meet with company representatives to discuss such points as how and where the company is going to use the logo and what size, color, and shape preferences company executives might have. Project budgets must be carefully respected: a design that may be perfect in every way but that is too costly to reproduce is basically useless. Graphic designers may need to compare their ideas with similar ones from other companies and analyze the image they project. Thus they must have a good knowledge of how various colors, shapes, and layouts affect the viewer psychologically.

After a plan has been conceived and the details worked out, the graphic designer does some preliminary designs (generally two or three) to present to the client for approval. The client may reject the preliminary design entirely and request a new design, or he or she may ask the designer to make alterations to the existing design. The designer then goes "back to the drawing board" to attempt a new design or make the requested changes. This process continues until the client approves the design.

Once a design has been approved, the graphic designer prepares the design for professional reproduction. The printer may require a "mechanical," in which the artwork and copy are arranged on a white board just as it is to be photographed, or the designer may be asked to submit an electronic copy of the design. Either way, designers must have a good understanding of the printing process, including color separation, paper properties, and halftone (i.e., photographs) reproduction.

Requirements

As with all artists, graphic designers need a degree of artistic talent, creativity, and imagination. They must be sensitive to beauty and have an eye for detail and a strong sense of color, balance, and proportion. To a great extent, these qualities are natural, but they can be developed through training, both on the job and in professional schools, colleges, and universities.

More and more graphic designers need solid computer skills and working knowledge of several of the common drawing, image editing, and page layout programs. Graphic design on the computer is more commonly done on a Macintosh system than on a PC system; however many designers have both types of computers.

More graphic designers are recognizing the value of formal training, and at least two out of three people entering the field today have a college degree or some college education. Over one hundred colleges and art schools offer graphic design programs that are accredited by the National Association of Schools of Art and Design. At many schools, graphic design students must take a year of basic art and design courses before being accepted into the bachelor's degree program. In addition, applicants to the bachelor's degree programs in graphic arts may be asked to submit samples of their work to prove artistic ability. Many schools and employers depend on portfolios, or samples, to evaluate the applicant's skills in graphic design. Many programs increasingly emphasize the importance of using computers for design work. Computer proficiency among graphic designers will be very important in the years to come. Interested individuals should select an academic program that incorporates computer training into the curriculum, or train themselves on their own.

A bachelor of fine arts program at a four-year college or university may include courses such as principles of design, art and art history, painting, sculpture, mechanical and architectural drawing, architecture, computerized design, basic engineering, fashion designing and sketching, garment construction, and textiles. Such degrees are desirable but not always necessary for obtaining a position as a graphic designer.

With or without specialized education, graphic designers seeking employment should have a good portfolio containing samples of their best work. The graphic designer's portfolio is extremely important and can make a difference when an employer must choose between two otherwise equally qualified candidates.

A period of on-the-job training is expected for all beginning designers. The length of time it takes to become fully qualified as a graphic designer may run from one to three years, depending on prior education and experience as well as innate talent.

Opportunities for Experience & Exploration

High school students interested in a career in graphic design have a number of ways to find out whether they have the talent, ambition, and perseverance to succeed in the field. Students should take as many art and design courses as possible while still in high school. They should also take any computer courses available in order to become proficient at working on computers. In addition, to get an insider's view of various design occupations, they could enlist the help of art teachers or school guidance counselors to make arrangements to tour design companies and interview designers.

While studying, students interested in graphic design can get practical experience by participating in school and community projects that call for design talents. These might include such activities as building sets for plays, setting up exhibits, planning seasonal and holiday displays, and preparing programs and other printed materials. For those interested in publication design, work on the school newspaper is invaluable.

Part-time and summer jobs offer would-be designers an excellent way to become familiar with the day-to-day requirements of a particular design occupation and to gain some basic related experience. Possible places of employment include design studios, design departments in advertising agencies and manufacturing companies, department and furniture stores, flower shops, workshops that produce ornamental items, and museums. Museums also rely on a number of volunteer workers.

Inexperienced people are often employed as sales, clerical, or general helpers; those with a little more education and experience may qualify for jobs in which they have a chance to develop actual design skills and build portfolios of completed design projects.

Methods of Entering

The best way to enter this field is to have a strong portfolio. Potential employers rely on portfolios to evaluate talent and how that talent might be used to fit the company's special needs. Beginners can assemble a portfolio from work completed at school, in art classes, and in part-time or freelance jobs. The portfolio should continually be updated to reflect the designer's growing skills, so it will always be ready for possible job changes.

Job interviews may be obtained by applying directly to companies that employ designers. Many colleges and professional schools have placement services to help their graduates find positions, and often it is possible to get a referral from a previous part-time employer or volunteer coordinator.

Advancement

As part of their on-the-job training, beginning designers are given the simpler tasks and work under direct supervision. As they gain experience, they move up to more complex work with increasingly less supervision. Experienced graphic designers, especially those with leadership capabilities, may be promoted to chief designer, design department head, or other supervisory positions.

Computer graphic designers can move into other computer-related positions with further education. Some become interested in graphics programming in order to further improve computer design capabilities. Others may want to become involved with multimedia and interactive graphics. Video games, touch-screen displays in stores, and even laser light shows are all products of multimedia graphic designers.

Designers sometimes go into business for themselves. Freelance design work can be erratic, however, so usually only the most experienced designers who have an established client base can count on consistent work.

Employment Outlook

Employment opportunities look very good for qualified graphic designers through the year 2006, especially for those involved with computer graphics. The design field in general is expected to grow at a faster than average rate for all other occupations, according to the U.S. Department of Labor.

As computer graphic technology continues to advance, there will be a need for well-trained computer graphic designers. Companies who have always used graphics will expect their designers to perform work on computers. Companies for whom graphic design was previously too time-consuming or costly are now sprucing up company newsletters and magazines, among other things, and need computer graphic designers to do it.

Because the design field is a popular one, appealing to many talented individuals, competition is expected to be strong in all areas. Beginners and designers with only average talent or without formal education and technical skills may encounter some difficulty in securing employment.

About one-third of all graphic designers are self-employed, a higher proportion than is found in most other occupations. Salaried designers work in many different industries, including the wholesale and retail trade (department stores, furniture and home furnishings stores, apparel stores, florist shops); manufacturing industries (machinery, motor vehicles and aircraft, metal products, instruments, apparel, textiles, printing and publishing); service industries (business services, engineering, architecture); construction firms; and government agencies. Public relations and publicity firms, advertising agencies, commercial printers and mail-order houses all have graphic design departments. The demand for graphic artists is also influenced partly by the level of government funding available from such entities as the National Endowment for the Arts.

Earnings

The range of annual salaries for graphic designers is quite broad. Many earn as little as $15,000, while others receive more than $43,000. Salaries depend primarily on the nature and scope of the employer, with computer graphic designers earning wages on the high end of the scale.

Self-employed designers can earn a lot one year and substantially more or less the next. Their earnings depend on individual talent and business ability, but, in general, are higher than those of salaried designers, although like any self-employed individual, they must pay their own insurance costs and taxes and are not compensated for vacation or sick days.

Salaried designers who advance to the position of design manager or design director earn about $60,000 a year and, at the level of corporate vice-president, make $70,000 and up. The owner of a consulting firm can make $85,000 or more.

Graphic designers who work for large corporations receive full benefits, including health insurance, paid vacation, and sick leave.

Conditions of Work

Most graphic designers work regular hours in clean, comfortable, pleasant offices or studios. Conditions vary depending on the design specialty.

Some graphic designers work in small establishments with few employees; others, in large organizations with large design departments. Some deal mostly with their coworkers; others may have a lot of public contact. Freelance designers are paid by the assignment. To maintain a steady income, they must constantly strive to please their clients and to find new ones.

Computer graphic designers may have to work long, irregular hours in order to complete an especially ambitious project.

Sources of Additional Information

■**American Center for Design**
233 East Ontario, Suite 500
Chicago, IL 60611
Tel: 312-787-2018

For more information about careers in graphic design, contact:

■**American Institute of Graphic Arts**
164 Fifth Avenue
New York, NY 10010
Tel: 800-548-1634
Email: aiganatl@aol.com

■**National Association of Schools of Art and Design**
11250 Roger Bacon Drive, Suite 21
Reston, VA 22090
Tel: 703-437-0700

■**Society for Environmental Graphic Design**
1 Story Street
Cambridge, MA 02138
Tel: 617-868-3381

■**Society of Publication Designers**
60 East 42nd Street, Suite 721
New York, NY 10165
Tel: 212-983-8585

■**Urban Art International**
PO Box 868
Tiburon, CA 94920
Tel: 415-435-5767
WWW: http://www.hite.imagesite.com

Health Care Managers

Definition

Health care managers, also known as *health services managers* and *health services administrators*, direct the operation of hospitals, nursing homes, and other health care organizations. They are responsible for facilities, services, programs, staff, budgets, and relations with other organizations.

Nature of the Work

Health services managers, or *chief executive officers (CEOs) of hospitals and health care facilities*, organize and manage personnel, equipment, and auxiliary services. They are responsible for hiring and supervising personnel, handling budgets and the fee schedule to be charged patients, and establishing billing procedures. They, in addition, assist in planning space needs, purchasing supplies and equipment, overseeing building and equipment maintenance, and providing for mail, phones, laundry, and other services for patients and staff. In some health care institutions, many of these duties are delegated to assistants or to various department heads. These assistants may supervise operations in such clinical areas as surgery, nursing, dietary, or therapy and in such administrative areas as purchasing, finance, housekeeping, and maintenance.

The health services administrator works closely with the institution's governing board in the development of plans and policies. Following the board's directions, the administrator may carry out large projects relating to expanding and developing hospital services. Such services include organizing fund-raising campaigns and planning new research projects.

Health services managers meet regularly with their staffs to discuss achievements and solve the facility's problems. Managers may organize training programs for nurses, interns, and others in cooperation with the medical staff and department heads. Health care executives also represent the health care facility at community or professional meetings.

Requirements

The training required to qualify for this work depends, to a large extent, on the qualifications established by the individual employer or a facility's governing board. Most prefer people with a graduate degree in health services administration. A few require that their chief executives be physicians, while others look for people with formal training in law or general business administration as well as experience in the health care field. The future health care administrator may have a liberal arts foundation with a strong background in the social sciences or business economics. Specialized training in health services administration is offered at both graduate and undergraduate levels. The graduate program is generally a two-year course spent in academic work and with additional months spent as an administrative resident, a full-time on-the-job training post in a facility approved by the university the candidate attends. Successful completion of the course work, the residency, and perhaps a thesis is required to earn the master's degree. An optional third-year fellowship provides additional work experience supervised by a mentor. During this period, the individual may work in various hospital departments as an assistant to department heads.

Much of the work consists of dealing with people— the hospital's governing board, the medical staff, the department heads and other employees, the patients and their families, and community leaders and businesses. Therefore health services managers must be tactful and sympathetic.

Administrators must, in addition, be able to coordinate the facility's many related functions. They need to understand, for instance, financial operations, purchasing, organizational development, and public relations. They must also have the ability to make some decisions with speed and others with considerable study. And, of course, health services executives should have a deep interest in health care and the problems of sick and injured patients.

Special hospitals, such as mental hospitals, often employ administrators who are physicians in the facility's specialty. Usually, facilities which are operated by religious groups employ administrators of the same faith as those of the group operating the hospital. Licensure is not a requirement for health care services executives employed in short-term, general hospitals. However, all states require nursing home administrators to be licensed. Since requirements vary from state to state, those considering careers in nursing home administration should contact the state licensing body for licensure requirements. Also, it should be noted that continuing education is now a condition of licensure in most states.

Opportunities for Experience & Exploration

Young people considering a career as a health services manager should take advantage of opportunities in high school to develop some of the skills required in this occupation. Since administrators and other health care executives should be leaders and talented speakers, participation in clubwork as a leader or active member and in debate and speech clubs is helpful. Working in the school's health center is also useful. Hospitals, nursing homes, and other health service facilities often offer part-time work after school, on weekends, and during the summer. Health services executives are often willing to speak to interested students, but it is suggested that students make an appointment first.

Courses in business law, psychology, and other social sciences, as well as computer science, can also help in evaluating interest in hospital or health services administration.

Methods of Entering

A student in training as an administrative resident or postgraduate fellow may be offered a job as an administrative assistant or a department head by the hospital or health care facility where the residency is served. The hospital's administrator at the place of training also may assist the student in locating a job.

Notice of job openings can often be found by contacting the university's placement bureau or through bulletins of state and national associations. Large professional society meetings often offer on-site notices of job openings; interviews can often be arranged on site. Positions in federal- and state-operated health care institutions are filled by the civil service or by political appointment. Appointments to armed forces hospitals are handled by the various branches of the services.

Although the four-year college program followed by graduate work is becoming the accepted method of entry, it is still possible to gain experience and training in subordinate positions and work up the administrative ladder.

Advancement

It is unusual to finish college and step into a position as an upper-level health services executive. People usually must gain experience that qualifies them for advancement by working in more specialized clinical or administrative areas found in a health care facility. Experience obtained in administration of health care personnel, information systems, budget, patient care, and finance is valuable. Experience and graduate work often leads to promotion as a department head in one of these administrative areas. Those with graduate training can expect to achieve higher-level positions. Assistant administrator or vice president is often the next step and may lead to appointment as the hospital's chief executive.

Employment Outlook

Since every hospital and numerous other health care facilities employ administrators, employment opportunities in health care will be excellent through the year 2006 as the industry continues to diversify and deal with the problems of financing health care for everyone. The U.S. Department of Labor predicts that employment will grow at a rate faster than the average. Not all areas will grow at the same rate, however. Changes in the health care system are taking place because of the need to control escalating costs. This will have the greatest impact on hospitals, traditionally the largest employer of health services executives. The number of hospitals is declining as separate companies are set up to provide services such as ambulatory surgery, alcohol and drug rehabilitation, or home health care. So, while hospitals themselves may offer fewer jobs, many new openings are expected to be available in other health care settings.

The trend toward outpatient care, largely the result of cost containment practices, has created a favorable job outlook in facilities such as HMOs and group medical practices, surgicenters and centers for urgent care, cardiac rehabilitation, diagnostic imaging, and so forth. Also, with Americans living longer than ever before, opportunities should be plentiful in long-term care facilities, such as nursing homes, home health agencies, adult day care programs, life care communities, and other residential facilities.

Colleges and universities are graduating more health services managers than hospitals and other health care facilities can employ. So, competition for administrative jobs will be stiff. However, many starting executives can find jobs working in health care settings other than hospitals, or they may be offered jobs at the department head or staff levels.

With hospitals adopting a more business-like approach aimed at lowering costs and increasing earnings, demand for MBA graduates should remain steady. Those with strong people—as well as business or management—skills will find excellent opportunities as administrators in nursing homes and other long-term facilities, where a graduate degree in health services administration is increasingly required.

Earnings

Salaries of health services executives depend on the type of facility, geographic location, the size of the administrative staff, the budget, and the policy of the governing board. A 1997 survey conducted by *Modern Healthcare* reported average salaries of hospital CEO's to be about $190,500; some CEO's earned more. Salaries varied among clinical department managers—respiratory therapy paid $54,500; ambulatory/outpatient services, $68,500; and nursing services, $97,000.

According to the Buck Survey conducted by the American Health Care Association, nursing home administrators earned a median salary of $49,500 in 1996. Fifty percent earned between $42,100 to $57,300 annually. Assistant nursing home administrators earned a median salary of about $32,000 a year.

Health service administrators managing a small group practice, consisting of seven or fewer physicians, averaged $56,000 annually, as reported by the Medical Group Management Association in 1996. Administrators responsible for practices with more than seven physicians earned an average of $77,000.

Some administrators receive free meals, housing, and laundry service, depending on the facility in which they are employed. They usually receive paid vacations and holidays, sick leave, hospitalization and insurance benefits, and pension programs. The executive benefits package nowadays often includes management incentive bonuses based on job performance ranging from $25,700 to $225,000.

Conditions of Work

To perform efficiently as an executive, health services administrators usually work out of a large office. They must maintain good communication with the staff and members of various departments. Administrators also establish ways to monitor and improve patient care.

Most administrators work five and one half days each week, averaging about fifty-five to sixty hours, but hours can be irregular since hospitals and other health care facilities operate around the clock, and emergencies may require the manager's supervision any time of the day or night.

Sources of Additional Information

American College of Health Care Administrators
325 South Patrick Street
Alexandria, VA 22314
Tel: 703-549-5822

American College of Healthcare Executives
One North Franklin Street, Suite 1700
Chicago, IL 60606-3491
Tel: 312-424-2800
WWW: http://www.ache.org

Association of University Programs in Health Administration
1911 North Fort Myer Drive, Suite 503
Arlington, VA 22209
Tel: 703-524-5500

Healthcare Financial Management Association
2 Westbrook Corporate Center, Suite 700
Westchester, IL 60154
Tel: 708-531-9600

National Health Council
1730 M Street, NW, Suite 500
Washington, DC 20036
Tel: 202-785-3910

HIV/AIDS Counselors

Definition

HIV/AIDS counselors work with people who are infected with HIV (the human immunodeficiency virus) or AIDS (acquired immunodeficiency syndrome), and their families and friends, to help them cope with the physical and emotional results of the disease. They answer questions, offer advice and support, and help HIV/AIDS patients get necessary assistance from medical and social agencies.

Nature of the Work

HIV/AIDS counselors help HIV and AIDS patients deal with their illness in the best way possible. A person who has tested HIV-positive or who has been diagnosed as having AIDS has many issues to deal with. Some of the issues are similar to those faced by anyone diagnosed with a terminal illness—grief, fear, health care, financial planning, and making provisions for children or other family members. Other issues these patients may face are unique to HIV and AIDS sufferers. These may include discrimination, prejudice, and being excluded by family and acquaintances who are afraid of or don't understand the disease. Another special consideration for these patients is how to avoid passing the disease on to others.

HIV/AIDS counselors offer support and assistance in dealing with all the various social, physical, and emotional issues patients face. They work with patients in all stages of the disease—from those who have first tested positive for HIV to those who are in the final stages of the illness. They may work at HIV testing centers, public health clinics, mental health clinics, family planning clinics, and drug treatment facilities.

Counselors who work at testing facilities, sometimes called *test counselors*, work with individuals who are being tested for HIV. These counselors sometimes see clients before they are tested to explain the testing procedure and what the possible test results mean. They also explain how the HIV infection is spread, discuss ways to prevent it, and answer general questions about the disease and its progress.

After the testing, the counselor may give the patient his or her results. If the results are negative, he or she may suggest re-testing if, during the six months before the test, the patient engaged in any behaviors that might have infected him or her. Since the infection does not show up immediately after it is contracted, it is possible to be infected and still test negative.

If the results are positive, counselors talk with patients about their sexual activity and drug use to determine how they might have gotten the disease. They also help them decide who to notify of the test results, such as previous sex partners.

The test counselor is often the first person the HIV-positive patient talks to about his or her illness. A large part of the job, then, is referring the patient to appropriate sources of help, including AIDS-related agencies, social services, and health care providers.

A counselor may also work as a *case manager* for HIV and AIDS patients. Case managers, unlike test counselors, follow patients through the various stages of their illness, helping them coordinate and manage the resources necessary to deal with it. Through letters, phone calls, and contacts with a network of available service providers, counselors help their clients get access to the agencies or organizations that offer the assistance they need. These may be medical care, help with living expenses, or visits by home health aides.

Patients with HIV or AIDS are under severe emotional strain. In addition to coping with the physical effects of the disease, they must also cope with the burden of having a disease that much of society does not understand or accept. They may feel anger, depression, guilt, and shame as they learn to live with their disease.

Counselors help patients deal with these emotional strains. They may conduct AIDS support groups or group counseling sessions in which HIV or AIDS patients discuss their experiences and questions about living with the disease. In these group sessions, the counselor oversees the conversation and tries to move it in a positive direction.

HIV/AIDS counselors may also work with the family members, friends, and partners of AIDS patients in individual or group sessions. They may meet with family members or partners to discuss a patient's progress or to help them understand a patient's needs. Counselors may also set up and oversee grief counseling sessions for those who have lost relatives or partners to the disease.

In order to monitor patients' progress, counselors keep written records on each of their sessions. They may be required to participate in staff meetings to discuss a patient's progress and treatment plan. They may also meet with members of various social service agencies to discuss their patients' needs.

In addition to the primary duty of counseling patients, these counselors may participate in community efforts to increase HIV and AIDS awareness. They may help develop workshops, give speeches to high schools or other groups, or organize and lead public awareness campaigns.

Requirements

Although specific educational requirements for HIV/AIDS counselors vary, most employers require a bachelor's degree in mental health or social work. Some employers may require their counselors to have a master's degree.

High school students considering a career in the field of HIV/AIDS counseling should emphasize sociology and psychology classes in their curriculum. Because this area of counseling requires an understanding of how the human body is affected by the HIV and AIDS viruses, students should also take classes such as biology, physiology, and health.

A college level curriculum for a degree in mental health or social work is likely to include classes in counseling, sociology, psychology, human development, and mental health. To receive a master's degree in social work or counseling, students must complete between 48 and 60 semester hours of classes, including a period of supervised clinical experience.

Most states require some form of credentialing for HIV/AIDS counselors. Many counselors choose to be certified by the National Board for Certified Counselors (NBCC). To become certified by the NBCC, candidates must have completed a master's degree in counseling, have at least two years of professional experience, and pass a national examination. Upon successful completion of these requirements, the candidate is designated as a National Certified Counselor.

Because these diseases receive so much attention from the medical, social, and even governmental arenas, there are often new developments in HIV- and AIDS-related treatments, policies, and services. In order to keep up-to-date, counselors must regularly continue their education by attending seminars or monthly in-service meetings.

For individuals considering a career in HIV/AIDS counseling, certain personal qualifications may be just as important as having the correct educational background. Compassion, sensitivity, and the desire to help others are key qualities for these counselors. They must also be able to communicate effectively and sincerely, and to listen with understanding.

HIV/AIDS counselors must be emotionally stable and resilient in order to keep from becoming depressed and discouraged by the nature of their work. They need to be able to avoid becoming too emotionally involved with their patients by balancing empathy with objectivity.

Opportunities for Experience & Exploration

Students who are interested in a career in HIV/AIDS counseling might contact local hospitals, HIV testing centers, or AIDS service organizations for more information. It may be possible to meet with a counselor to talk about the details of his or her job. Any school or local library should also have a large number of resources both on the AIDS virus and on counseling.

To further explore the career, the interested student may be able to find a volunteer position in a social service agency, health clinic, or hospital. Even if the position does not deal directly with HIV or AIDS patients, it should provide the student with an idea of what it is like to work in such an environment.

Methods of Entering

HIV/AIDS counselors work for hospitals, hospices, HIV testing centers, public health clinics, mental health clinics, social service agencies, Red Cross offices, Planned Parenthood centers, and various AIDS service organizations. They may also work for regional AIDS consortiums organized by health officials, religious leaders, educators, business leaders, and AIDS service representatives.

The newly-graduated counselor might begin a job search at the career placement center of his or her college. He or she might also apply directly to any area social service, health, or AIDS service organizations.

Some openings for HIV/AIDS counselors might be advertised in the classified sections of local newspapers. Membership in a professional organization for counselors, such as the American Counseling Association, might also provide the job seeker with leads through publications, meetings, or job banks.

Advancement

Counselors who work for large organizations will have more opportunity for advancement than those who work for smaller ones. In a large organization, for example, the counselor with education and experience might move into an administrative position, such as program director. Because smaller organizations—especially not-for-profits—usually have small staffs, advancement is often slow and limited.

Counselors who continue their education may have a wider range of possibilities for advancement. Those who complete a master's degree in social work or rehabilitative counseling, for example, might be employed by social welfare agencies as medical or psychiatric social workers, child protective workers, rehabilitative counselors, or parole or probation officers. These fields have a broader scope of advancement opportunities.

Finally, some counselors who continue their education elect to go into research or teaching at the college level.

Employment Outlook

The employment of all types of counselors is expected to grow about as fast as the average for occupations through the year 2006. For HIV/AIDS counselors specifically, employment trends are likely to depend upon government funding for AIDS-related programs, since private funding for such programs is usually limited. Because AIDS sometimes becomes a political issue, rather than merely a medical one, government spending may be negatively influenced by resistance from special interest groups or policy makers. Because of funding issues, many AIDS programs rely on volunteers, rather than paid counselors. This, obviously, decreases the number of job openings for counselors.

However, as the number of AIDS patients increases, the need for AIDS-related services—including counseling—will inevitably grow. Counselors can play an especially important role in educating HIV and AIDS victims on how to avoid spreading the disease.

Jobs for HIV/AIDS counselors will probably be most plentiful in urban areas, where there is a higher concentration of AIDS cases.

Earnings

Generally, earnings for HIV/AIDS counselors are similar to those for other counselors and social workers. Salaries can vary, however, depending upon the experience and education of the individual and the location, size, and funding source of the employer. In not-for-profit agencies or clinics where funding is limited, beginning counselors may make around $19,000 per year. Counselors working for private, prestigious clinics may earn an average of up to $36,000 annually.

In addition to salary, most HIV/AIDS counselors receive a benefits package which includes paid vacations, holidays, and sick time, medical insurance, and sometimes a retirement plan.

Conditions of Work

HIV/AIDS counselors usually work regular eight-hour days, five days a week. Occasionally, however, they may have appointments with health care providers, social service agencies, or patients that are not during regular office hours.

Counselors who work in HIV testing centers and health clinics usually have an office on-site, where they can talk privately with patients. Those who work as case coordinators may visit patients in their homes, or in hospitals or other long-range care facilities. They may conduct group sessions in classrooms or conference rooms of hospitals or social service agencies.

Regardless of the setting, the majority of an HIV/AIDS counselor's day is spent meeting with people—either patients or representatives from social service or health care agencies.

Counseling HIV and AIDS patients is stressful and often depressing work. In most cases, patients are preparing for eventual death and they turn to the counselor for help and support in facing it. Counselors often watch their patients become very sick as the virus progresses; frequently, they must deal with a patient's death. Dealing with this sickness, death, and accompanying emotional distress on a daily basis may be difficult.

Sources of Additional Information

■■Centers for Disease Control National AIDS Hotline
PO Box 13827
Research Triangle Park, NC 27709
Tel: 800-342-2437

■■American Counseling Association
5999 Stevenson Avenue
Alexandria, VA 22304
Tel: 800-347-6647
Email: sniseoff@counseling.org
WWW: http://www.counseling.org/

■■National Board for Certified Counselors
3 Terrace Way, Suite D
Greensboro, NC 27403

■■National Association of Social Workers
750 1st Street NE, Suite 700
Washington, DC 20002
Tel: 202-408-8600
WWW: http://www.naswdc.org/main.htm

Home Care Aides

Definition

Home care aides, also known as *homemaker-home health aides* or *home attendants*, serve elderly and infirm persons by visiting them in their homes and caring for them. Working under the supervision of nurses or social workers, they perform various household chores that clients are unable to perform for themselves, as well as attend to patients' personal needs. Although they work primarily with the elderly, home care aides also attend to clients with disabilities or those needing help with small children.

Nature of the Work

Home care aides enable elderly persons to stay in their own homes. For some clients, just a few visits a week are enough to help them look after themselves. Although physically demanding, the work is often emotionally rewarding. Home care aides may not have access to equipment and facilities such as those found in hospitals, but they also don't have the hospital's frantic pace. Home care aides are expected to take the time to get to know their clients and their individual needs. They perform their duties within the client's home environment, which often is a much better atmosphere than the impersonal rooms of a hospital.

In addition to the elderly, home care aides assist people of any age who are recovering at home following hospitalization. They also help children whose parents are ill, disabled, or neglectful. Aides may be trained to supply care to people suffering from specific illnesses such as AIDS, Alzheimer's disease, or cancer, or patients who are developmentally disabled and lack sufficient daily living skills.

Clients unable to feed themselves may depend on home care aides to shop for food, prepare their meals, feed them, and clean up after meals. Likewise, home care aides may assist clients in dressing and grooming, including washing, bathing, cleaning teeth and nails, and fixing the clients' hair.

Massages, alcohol rubs, whirlpool baths, and other therapies and treatments may be a part of a client's required care. Home care aides may work closely with a physician or home nurse in giving medications and dietary supplements and helping with exercises and other therapies. They may check pulses, temperatures, and respiration rates. Occasionally, they may change nonsterile dressings, use special equipment such as a hydraulic lift, or assist with braces or artificial limbs.

Home care aides working in home care agencies are supervised by a registered nurse, physical therapist, or social worker who assigns them specific duties. Aides report changes in patients' conditions to the supervisor or case manager.

Household chores are often another aspect of the home care aide's responsibilities. Light housekeeping such as changing and washing bed linens, doing the laundry and ironing, and dusting may be necessary. When a home care aide looks after the children of a disabled or neglectful parent, work may include making lunches for the children, helping them with their homework, or providing companionship and adult supervision in the evening.

Personal attention and comfort are important aspects of an aide's care. Home care aides can provide this support by reading to children, playing checkers, or visiting with an elderly client. Often just listening to clients' personal problems will help the client through the day. Because elderly people do not always have the means to venture out alone, a home care aide may accompany an ambulatory patient to the park for an afternoon stroll or to the physician's office for an appointment.

Requirements

Caring for people in their own homes can be physically demanding work. Lifting a client for baths and exercise, helping a client up and down stairs, performing housework, and aiding with physical therapy all require that an aide is in good physical condition. The aide does not have the equipment and facilities of a hospital to help them with their work, and this requires adaptability and ingenuity. Oftentimes they must make do with the resources available in an average home.

An even temperament and a willingness to serve others are important characteristics for home care aides. People in this occupation should be friendly, patient, sensitive to others' needs, and tactful. At times an aide will have to be stern in dealing with uncooperative patients or calm and understanding with those who are angry, confused, despondent, or in pain. Genuine warmth and respect for others are important attributes. Cheerfulness and a sense of humor can go a long way in establishing a good relationship with a client, and a good relationship can make working with the client much easier.

In states where certification is required, home care aides need special training. Most agencies will offer free training to prospective employees. Such training may include instruction on how to deal with depressed or reluctant patients, how to prepare easy and nutritious meals, and tips on housekeeping. Specific course work on health and sanitation may also be required.

Homemaker-home health aides must be willing to follow instructions and abide by the health plan created for each patient. Aides provide an important outreach service, supporting the care administered by the patient's physician, therapist, or social worker. They are not trained medical personnel, however, and must know the limits of their authority.

A Model Curriculum and Teaching Guide for the Instruction of the Homemaker-Home Health Aide was developed by the National Homecaring Council. The training set forth in this curriculum combines classroom study and hands-on experience, with sixty hours of class instruction supplemented by an additional fifteen hours of field work. It reflects the widespread desire to upgrade training for people in this field.

Many programs require only a high school diploma for entry-level positions. Previous or additional coursework in home economics, cooking, sewing, and meal planning are very helpful, as are courses that focus on family living and home nursing.

Health care agencies usually focus their training on first aid, hygiene, and the principles of health care. Cooking and nutrition, including meal preparation for patients with specific dietary needs, are often included in the program. Home care aides may take courses in psychology and child development as well as family living. Because of the need for hands-on work, aides usually learn how to bathe, dress, and feed patients, as well as how to help them walk upstairs or get up from bed. The more specific the skill required for certain patients, the more an agency is likely to have more comprehensive instruction.

Opportunities for Experience & Exploration

Home care aides are employed in many different areas. Interested students can learn more about the work by contacting local agencies and programs that provide home care services and requesting information on the organization's employment guidelines or training programs. Visiting the county or city health department and contacting the personnel director may provide useful information as well. Often, local organizations sponsor open houses to enlighten the community to the services they provide. This could serve as an excellent opportunity to meet the staff involved in hiring and program development and to learn about job opportunities. In addition, it may be possible to arrange to accompany a home care aide on a home visit.

Methods of Entering

Some social service agencies enlist the aid of volunteers. By contacting agencies and inquiring about such openings, aspiring home care aides can get an introduction to the type of work this profession requires. Also, many agencies or nursing care facilities offer free training to prospective employees.

Checking the local yellow pages for agencies that provide health care to the aged and disabled or family-service organizations can provide a list of employment prospects. Nursing homes, public and private health care facilities, and local chapters of the Red Cross and United Way are likely to hire entry-level employees. The National Homecaring Council can also supply information on reputable agencies and departments that employ home care aides.

Advancement

As home care aides develop their skills and deepen their experience, they may advance to management or supervisory positions. Those who find greater enjoyment working with clients may branch into more specialized care and pursue additional training. Additional experience and education often bring higher pay and increased responsibility.

Aides who wish to work in a clinic or hospital setting may return to school to complete a nursing degree. Other related occupations include social worker, therapist, and registered dietitian. Along with a desire for advancement, however, must come the willingness to meet additional education and experience requirements.

Employment Outlook

As government and private agencies develop more programs to assist the dependent, the need for home care aides will continue to grow. Because of the physical and emotional demands of the job, there is high turnover and, therefore, frequent job openings for home care aides.

Also, the number of people seventy years of age and older is expected to increase substantially, and many of them will require at least some home care. Rising health care costs are causing many insurance companies to consider alternatives to hospital treatment, so many insurance providers now cover home care services. In addition, hospitals and nursing homes are trying to balance the demand for their services and their limitations in staff and physical facilities. The availability of home care aides can allow such institutions as hospitals and nursing homes to offer quality care to more people.

Earnings

Earnings for home care aides are commensurate with salaries in related health care positions. Depending on the agency, considerable flexibility exists in working hours and patient load. For many aides who begin as part-time employees, the starting salary is usually the minimum hourly wage. For full-time aides with significant training or experience, earnings may be around $6.00 to $8.00 per hour. According to the U.S. Department of Labor, Medicare-certified aides earned an hourly average of $6.00 in 1996. Aides are usually paid only for the time worked in the home. They normally are not paid for travel time between jobs.

Conditions of Work

Health aides in a hospital or nursing home setting work at a much different pace and in a much different environment than the home care aide. With home care, aides can take the time to sit with their clients and get to know them. Aides spend a certain amount of time with each client and can perform their responsibilities without the frequent distractions and demands of a hospital. Home surroundings differ from situation to situation. Some homes are neat and pleasant, while others are untidy and depressing. Some patients are angry, abusive, depressed, or otherwise difficult; others are pleasant and cooperative.

Because home care aides usually have more than one patient, the hours an aide works can fluctuate based on the number of clients and types of services needed. Many clients may be ill or disabled. Some may be elderly and have no one else to assist them with light housekeeping or daily errands. These differences can dictate the type of responsibilities a home care aide has for each patient.

Vacation policies and benefits packages vary with the type and size of the employing agency. Many full-time home care aides receive one week of paid vacation following their first year of employment and often receive two weeks of paid vacation for each successive year. Full-time aides may also be eligible for health insurance and retirement benefits. Some agencies also offer holiday or overtime compensation.

Working with the infirm or disabled can be a rewarding experience, as aides enhance the quality of their clients' lives with their help and company. However, the personal strains—on the clients as well as the aides—can make the work challenging and occasionally frustrating. There can be difficult emotional demands that aides may find exhausting. Considerable physical activity is involved in this line of work, such as helping patients to walk, dress, or take care of themselves. Traveling from one home to another and running various errands for patients can also be tiring and time-consuming or can be a pleasant break.

Sources of Additional Information

For career and certification information, contact:

National Association for Home Care
228 7th Street, SE
Washington, DC 20003
Tel: 202-547-7424
WWW: http://www.nahc.org

Hotel and Motel Managers

Definition

Hotel and motel managers are responsible for personnel, the financial operation of the hotel or motel, and promotional activities. Managers are also responsible for operating matters such as rates of the rooms, use of guests' credit, and the assignment of personnel. They must provide the best possible services for guests while still maintaining a profit.

Nature of the Work

The manager's duties include housing, feeding, and entertaining customers. In small hotels, the manager may also be the owner. In such cases, their responsibilities may include the operation of the front office and overseeing all other functions of the hotel. For example, the manager may personally greet guests, assign rooms, handle their mail, and perform many other duties. Small hotel managers usually spend a good deal of time performing clerical tasks and bookkeeping.

There are differences in the size of hotels and the services provided by them. Large establishments are highly specialized and have a wide variety of facilities for their guests. Larger hotels and motels are sometimes owned and operated by hotel chains and are controlled by a board of directors that establishes the general policy and hires the manager. Chains employ branch operation evaluation managers to travel to various branches periodically and examine the facilities to make sure they are being operated and maintained according to company standards. Nevertheless, the hotel manager has complete charge of the hotel, is responsible for the operation of the hotel, and sees to the administration of policy. Managers of large hotels with many employees must delegate responsibilities to department heads who supervise other workers. Department managers may include the following:

Promotion managers publicize the establishment and plan sales and marketing programs to solicit business from conventions, social and business functions, and travel bureaus.

Convention managers work with hotel guests to direct the actual arrangements for conventions and group meetings scheduled to be held in the hotel.

Food service managers coordinate the planning, purchase, preparation, and serving of food and beverages in the hotel dining rooms and coffee shops, as well as for room service and banquets.

Liquor establishment managers run the cocktail lounges, nightclubs, or other rooms in a hotel where alcoholic beverages are sold.

Front office managers are concerned with room reservations and assignments, greeting guests, answering their inquiries, and handling their requests and complaints.

Hotel recreational facilities managers are in charge of making available for guests such activities as swimming, boating, skating, and other sports. Particularly for hotels accommodating corporate clientele, on-premises workout rooms, swimming pools, and other athletic facilities are becoming more prominent.

Executive housekeepers are responsible for keeping the establishment clean, orderly, and attractive and for maintaining an inventory of housekeeping supplies and equipment.

Routine work does not require much supervision, but the hotel manager must be available at any time to deal with emergencies or problems that might arise. A major responsibility of the manager is community relations and marketing. Conventions, training seminars, and workshops often are held at hotels and motels. In addition, hotels often are used as campaign headquarters and as meeting places for union negotiations. The manager must carefully select the people who meet the general public in an effort to present the hotel's services in a favorable way.

Requirements

In the past, hotel executives tended to favor promotion of capable employees from the ranks of their staffs. While this remains true to an extent, a high school education is essential, and serious candidates for hotel or motel management positions are advised to complete postsecondary education and training specialized in business, especially in hotel management and related programs. Bachelor's degrees and advanced degrees are becoming more necessary for advancement even in smaller establishments and resorts.

Many large hotel chains hire managers who have trained at such well-established schools as the Cornell School of Hotel Administration in New York State. More than one hundred colleges in the nation offer a specialized four-year curriculum in hotel administration and food management. Several junior colleges offer specialized courses in hotel work, and the Educational Institute of the American Hotel and Motel Association offers home study courses in this field.

Hotel managers must understand hotel administration, hotel accounting, the economics of food service, and general hotel engineering. A background in history, psychology, and languages is also helpful. Even college-trained people will usually be required to start in the front office as desk clerks, registration clerks, or department heads.

Successful hotel managers must be able to get along with guests as well as with hotel employees. The ability to make quick decisions while maintaining composure is vital. Patience and tact as well as a good sense of humor are necessary in dealing with all types of people. In large establishments, the ability to coordinate the operations of various departments with a minimum of friction among staff members is a most important requirement. While education is essential, many of the skills necessary to conduct hotel business are best gained by experience and training on the job.

Opportunities for Experience & Exploration

There are a number of hotel jobs interested students can take to obtain experience in hotel work. Most resort hotels will hire students as seasonal workers, and commercial establishments usually have part-time openings. Entry-level jobs offer an opportunity to deal with the hotel public and to see the operation of the hotel from all perspectives. These service positions include work as a *bellhop, desk clerk, night clerk, baggage porter, elevator operator, doorkeeper, waiter, bartender, cook,* and *housekeeper.*

Some large hotels in major cities offer paid work-study programs to high school students. The goal of the program is to expose students to hotel management positions that they may not have considered for their careers.

Methods of Entering

The most direct method of entering the hotel business is by taking an entry-level job such as those mentioned above. Most hotel managers are eager to promote hardworking employees.

College graduates who have majored in hotel administration have a good opportunity for advancement, but they usually are required to gain experience while employed in service positions in hotels or restaurants.

Advancement

After trainees successfully complete an on-the-job assignment, they are often moved to another interdepartmental job for the broadest possible experiences. For example, a bellhop may be promoted to bell captain. A desk clerk may be put in charge of the front office. On occasion, a trainee may be rotated to other departments for more varied experience. Many large hotels offer special programs for management trainees.

More and more employers require their employees to have a college education, but a degree does not assure advancement. In any event, several years of experience is usually necessary before advancement into the top management level. Most managers of large hotels have worked in a great variety of departments and are familiar with all aspects of a hotel's operations.

Employment Outlook

The overbuilding of hotels and motels in the 1980s caused a glutted market and many hotels and motels to fail. The improved economy of the mid- to late 1990s, however, has restored growth to the industry. Nonetheless, management positions are expected to grow only about as fast as the average through the year 2006. Consolidation of hotels by franchises and chains have reduced the need for managers since many job responsibilities were merged, or taken over by departmental managers. Front desk clerks have increasingly assumed some managerial duties. Another reason for this has been a shift in the type of hotel being operated. Economy hotels have become increasingly popular, both with the customer and with the large hotel and motel chains. These hotels offer a limited range of services and amenities and therefore require fewer managers to oversee their operations.

There is high turnover in this field. Long hours and sometimes stressful work conditions cause many to leave the field for other hospitality positions or other occupations. Others leave the field for retirement or for other reasons. As a result, there will be a large number of positions available to well-trained, motivated individuals.

Full-service hotels, especially those catering to the convention and business customers, continue to require managers for the different services they provide. More resort-style hotels are being built, and these too will require a diverse array of employees. Managerial openings will be most available to those with college-level hotel or restaurant management degrees.

Earnings

The size and location of a hotel are major factors in determining the earnings of an owner or manager. Profits depend greatly upon the size of the facility, the investment, the services rendered, the length of the season, the wages paid the staff, and a great variety of miscellaneous charges and general maintenance expenses.

In 1996, the average salaries for all hotel and motel managers was $54,000 per year. Earnings varied greatly and ranged from about $39,000 for those employed in hotels and motels with fewer than 150 rooms to about $81,000 in large hotels with 350 rooms or more. The overall average for assistant hotel and motel managers was $40,000 a year. General managers earned considerably more, an average of $111,000 per year, excluding bonuses, which often add an additional 25 percent to their salaries.

Salaries of departmental managers varied greatly depending on their level of experience and the scope of their responsibilities. For example, front office managers had average salaries of about $28,000, whereas food and beverage managers averaged around $43,000 a year. Executive housekeepers, according to a 1997 salary survey by *Executive Housekeeping Today*, earned an average of $36,974 annually. Top earning executive housekeepers at larger hotels earned over $110,000 year.

Many hotels provide managers and their families with living quarters, meals, and use of the hotel facilities as part of their remuneration. In some cases managers also share in profits or receive a yearly bonus of up to 25 percent or more of their annual salary, depending upon the successful operation of the establishment. Other benefits such as paid vacations, insurance, hospitalization, and hotel discounts are also usually offered.

Conditions of Work

The working conditions in hotels are as varied as are hotels themselves. Because professional managers usually live in the hotel, they enjoy the same facilities as do the guests. The manager who trains a staff well will be able to enjoy more leisure time. The general atmosphere and decor of the surroundings are just as restful or exciting as managers wish to make them. Managers usually work a regular work week, but because many managers live in the hotel they remain on call twenty-four hours a day, seven days a week.

Sources of Additional Information

■ **Council on Hotel, Restaurant and Institutional Education**
1200 17th Street, NW
Washington, DC 20036

■ **Educational Institute of the American Hotel and Motel Association**
1407 Harrison Road, Third Floor
East Lansing, MI 48823
Tel: 517-353-5500

Human Services Workers

Definition

Under the supervision of social workers, psychologists, sociologists, and other professionals, *human services workers* offer support to families, the elderly, the poor, and others in need. They teach life and communication skills to people in mental health facilities or substance abuse programs. Employed by agencies, shelters, halfway houses, and hospitals, they work individually with clients or in group counseling. They also direct clients to social services and benefits.

Nature of the Work

A group of teenagers in a large high school are concerned about the violence that threatens them every day. They've seen their friends and classmates hurt in the school's hallways, on the basketball court, in the parking lot. In a place built for their education, they fear for their safety, and they each have something to say about it. They have something to say to the administration, to the parents, and, most of all, to the kids who carry guns and knives to school. Human services workers come to their aid. Human services workers step in to support the efforts of social workers, psychologists, and other professional agencies or programs. Human services workers may work in a school, a community center, a housing project, or a hospital. They may work as an aide, an assistant, a technician, or a counselor. In this case, under the supervision of a school social worker, they serve as group leader, meeting with some of the students to discuss their fears and concerns. They also meet with administrators, faculty, and parents. Eventually, they conduct a schoolwide series of group discussions, listening, taking notes, offering advice, and, most importantly, empowering people to better their community and their lives.

"Human services" covers a wide range of careers, from counseling prison inmates to counseling the families of murder victims; from helping someone with a disability find a job to caring for the child of a teen mother during the school day. From one-on-one interaction to group interaction, from paperwork to footwork, the human services worker is focused on improving the lives of others.

As society changes, so do the concerns of human services workers. New societal problems (such as the rapid spread of AIDS among teens and the threat of gang violence) require special attention, as do changes in the population (such as the increasing number of elderly people living on their own and the increasing number of minimum-wage workers unable to fully provide for their families). New laws and political movements also affect human services workers, because many social service programs rely heavily on federal and state aid. And though our government policy makers are more educated than the policy makers of years past, social service programs are more threatened than ever before. Despite all these changes in society and the changes in the theories of social work, some things stay the same—human services workers care about the well-being of individuals and communities. They're sensitive to the needs of diverse groups of people, and they're actively involved in meeting the needs of the public.

Many of the responsibilities of human services workers have also remained the same throughout the years. They offer their clients counseling, representation, emotional support, and the services they need. Though some human services workers assist professionals with the development and evaluation of social programs, policy analysis, and other administrative duties, most work directly with clients.

This direct work can involve aid to specific populations, such as cultural groups, women, and the poor. Many human services workers assist poor people in numerous ways. They interview clients to identify needed services. They care for the client's children during job or medical appointments and offer the client emotional support. They determine whether a client is eligible for food stamps, Medicaid, or other welfare programs. In some food stamp programs, aides advise low-income family members how to plan, budget, shop for, and prepare balanced meals, often accompanying or driving the client to the store and offering suggestions on the most nutritious and economical food to purchase.

Some aides serve tenants in public housing projects. They are employed by housing agencies or other groups to help tenants relocate. They inform tenants of the use of facilities and the location of community services such as recreation centers and clinics. They also explain the management's rules about sanitation and maintenance. They may at times help resolve disagreements between tenants and landlords.

Members of specific populations call on the aid of human services workers for support, information, and representation. The human services worker can provide these clients with counseling and emotional support and direct them to support groups and services. Social workers work with human services workers to reach out to the people; together, they visit individuals, families, and neighborhood groups to publicize the supportive services available.

Other clients of human services workers are those experiencing life-cycle changes. Children, adolescents, and the elderly can require assistance in making transitions. Human services workers help parents find proper day-care for their children. They educate young mothers in how to best care for an infant. They counsel children struggling with family problems or peer pressure. They offer emotional support to gay and lesbian teens and involve them in support groups. Some programs help the elderly stay active and help them to prepare meals and clean their homes. They also assist the elderly to and from hospitals and community centers and stay in touch with these clients through home visits and telephone calls.

Some human services workers focus on specific problems, such as drug and alcohol abuse. Human services workers assist in developing, organizing, and conducting programs dealing with the causes of and remedies for substance abuse. Workers may help individuals trying to overcome drug or alcohol addiction master practical skills such as cook-

ing and doing laundry, and teach them ways to communicate more effectively with others. Domestic violence is also a problem receiving more attention, as more and more people leave abusive situations. Shelters for victims require counselors, assistants, tutors, and day-care personnel for their children. Human services workers may also teach living and communication skills in homeless shelters and mental health facilities.

Record keeping is an important part of the duties of human services workers, since records may affect a client's eligibility for future benefits, the proper assessment of a program's success, and the prospect of future funding. Workers prepare and maintain records and case files of every person with whom they work. They record the client's responses to the various programs and treatment. They must also track costs in group homes in order to stay within budget.

Requirements

Many people perform human services work because they want to make a difference in their community. Or they may like connecting on a personal level with other people, offering them emotional support, helping them sort out problems, and teaching them how to care for themselves and their families. A genuine interest in the lives and concerns of others and a sensitivity to their situations is important to a human services worker. An artistic background can also be valuable in human services. Some programs in mental health facilities, domestic violence shelters, and other group homes use art therapy. Painting, music, dance, and creative writing are sometimes incorporated into counseling sessions, providing a client with alternative modes of expression.

In addition to the rewarding aspects of the job, a human services worker must be prepared to take on difficult responsibilities. The work can be very stressful. The problems of some populations, such as prison inmates, battered women and children, substance abusers, and the poor, can seem insurmountable. Their stories and day-to-day lives can seem tragic. Even if you're not counseling the clients, you'll be working directly with clients on some level. Just helping a person fill out an application or prepare a household budget requires a good disposition and the ability to be supportive. Clients may not welcome your help and may not even care about their own well-being. In these cases, a human services worker must remain firm but supportive and encouraging. Patience is very important, whatever the area of human service.

The work load for a human services worker can also be overwhelming. An agency with limited funding can't always afford to hire the number of employees it needs. A human services worker employed by an understaffed agency will probably be overworked. This can sometimes result in employee burn-out.

Some employers will hire people with only a high school education, but these people might find it hard to move beyond clerical positions. Interested high school students should plan to attend a college or university by taking classes in English, mathematics, political science, psychology, and sociology.

Certificate and associate degree programs in human services or mental health are offered at community and junior colleges, vocational-technical institutes, and other postsecondary institutions. Or it's also possible to pursue a bachelor's degree in human services. Almost five hundred human services education programs exist. Academic programs such as these prepare students for occupations in the human services. Because the educators at these colleges and universities stay in regular contact with the social work employers in their area, the programs are continually revised to meet the changing needs of the field. Students are exposed early and often to the kinds of situations they may encounter on the job.

Undergraduate and graduate programs typically include courses in psychology, sociology, crisis intervention, family dynamics, therapeutic interviewing, rehabilitation, and gerontology.

Opportunities for Experience & Exploration

To get an idea of the requirements of human service, students can volunteer their time to a local human services agency or institution. Church organizations also involve young people in volunteer work, as do the Red Cross, the Boy Scouts, and the Girl Scouts. Volunteer work could include reading to blind or elderly people and visiting nursing homes and halfway homes. You could get involved organizing group recreation programs at the YMCA or YWCA, or performing light clerical duties in an office. And you could encourage the high school organizations to which you belong to become actively involved in charity work.

Some members of high school organizations also perform social services within their own school, educating classmates on the dangers of gangs, unsafe sex, and substance abuse. By being actively involved in your community, you can gain experience in human services, as well as build-up a history of volunteer service that will impress future employers.

Methods of Entering

Students may find jobs through their high school counselor or local and state human services agencies. Sometimes summer jobs and volunteer work can develop into full-time employment upon graduation. Employers try to be selective in their hiring, because so many human services jobs involve direct contact with people who are impaired and therefore vulnerable to exploitation. Evidence of helping others is a definite advantage.

Advancement

Job performance has some bearing on pay raises and advancement for human services workers. However, career advancement almost always depends on formal education, such as a bachelor's or master's degree in social work, counseling, rehabilitation, or some other related field. Many employers encourage their workers to further their education, and some may even reimburse part of the costs of school. In addition, many employers provide in-service training such as seminars and workshops.

Employment Outlook

Employment for human services workers will grow much faster than the average through the year 2006. Much of this growth is expected to occur in homes for the mentally impaired and developmentally disabled. Also, the life expectancy for people in the United States continues to rise, requiring more assistance for the elderly such as adult daycare and meal delivery. Correctional facilities are also expected to employ many more human services workers. Because counseling inmates and offenders can be undesirable work, there are a number of high-paying jobs available in this area.

New ideas in treating disabled or mentally ill people also influence employment growth in group homes and residential care facilities. Public concern for the homeless—many of whom are former mental patients who were released under service reductions in the 1980s—as well as troubled teenagers, and those with substance abuse problems, will likely bring about new community-based programs and group residences.

Job prospects in public agencies are not as bright as they once were because of fiscal policies that tighten eligibility requirements for federal welfare and other payments. State and local governments are expected to remain major employers, however, as the burden of providing social services such as welfare, child support, and nutrition programs is shifted from the federal government to the state and local level. In a larger city, such as New York or Washington, DC, jobs in the public sector will be more plentiful than in a smaller city because of the higher demand. There is also a higher burn-out rate in the larger cities, resulting in more job opportunities as people vacate their positions for other careers.

Earnings

Salaries of human services workers depend in part on their employer and amount of experience. According to the *1998-99 Occupational Outlook Handbook*, starting salaries for human services workers ranged from $15,000 to $24,000 a year. Experienced workers can earn from $20,000 to $30,000 annually.

Conditions of Work

Human services workers are employed in a variety of settings, including agency offices, community centers, group homes, hospitals, shelters, and the private homes of clients. Most human services workers work a standard forty-hour week, spending time both in the office and in the field interviewing clients and performing other support services. Some weekend and evening work may be required, but compensatory time off is usually granted. Workers in residential settings generally work in shifts. Because of the twenty-four-hour staffing needs of group homes, workers usually work some evenings and weekends.

Work conditions are affected by the size and location of the town in which you work. The societal problems of large, urban areas are different from those of small, rural areas. In a city, you'll be dealing with issues of crime, racism, gang warfare, and violence in the schools. These problems can exist in smaller communities as well, but the human services workers of rural areas focus more on work with the elderly and the poor. Rural communities typically have an older population, with people living deeper in the country and farther from public and private services. This can require more transportation time. The social services in rural areas, because of lower salaries and poorer facilities, typically have trouble attracting workers.

Offices and facilities may be clean and cheerful, or they may be dismal, cramped, and inadequately equipped. While out in the field with clients, workers may also find themselves in dangerous, squalid areas. In a large city, workers can rely on public transportation, while workers in a rural community must often drive long distances.

Sources of Additional Information

For job and education information , contact:

■ **American Association for Counseling and Development**
5999 Stevenson Avenue
Alexandria, VA 22304
Tel: 800-545-2223

■ **Counsel for Standards in Human Service Education**
Northern Essex
Haverhill, MA 01830

■ **National Organization for Human Service Education**
Brookdale Community College
Lyncroft, NJ 07738

Insurance Claims Representatives

Definition

Insurance claims representatives, or *claims adjusters*, investigate claims for personal, casualty, or property loss or damages. They determine the extent of the insurance company's liability and try to negotiate an out-of-court settlement with the claimant.

Nature of the Work

An insurance company's reputation and success is dependent upon its ability to quickly and effectively investigate claims, negotiate equitable settlements, and authorize prompt payments to policyholders. Claims representatives perform these duties.

Claims clerks review insurance forms for accuracy and completeness. Frequently, this involves calling or writing the insured party or other people involved to secure missing information. After placing this data in a claim file, the clerk reviews the insurance policy to determine coverage. Routine claims are transmitted for payment; if further investigation is needed, the clerk informs the claims supervisor.

In companies specializing in property and casualty insurance, claims adjusters may perform some or all of the duties of claims clerks. They can determine whether the policy covers the loss and amount claimed. Through investigation of physical evidence, the securing of testimony from relevant parties, including the claimant, witnesses, police, and, if necessary, hospital personnel, and the examination of reports, they promptly negotiate a settlement. Adjusters make sure that the settlement reflects the actual claimant losses while making certain the insurer is protected from invalid claims.

Adjusters may issue payment checks or submit their findings to claims examiners for payment. If litigation is necessary, adjusters recommend this action to legal counsel, and they may attend court hearings.

Some claims adjusters do not specialize in one type of insurance, but most do. They act exclusively in one field, such as fire, marine, automobile, or product liability. A special classification is the claims agent for petroleum, who handles activities connected with the locating, drilling, and producing of oil or gas on private property. In states with "no fault" insurance, adjusters are not concerned with responsibilities, but they still must determine the amount of payment. To help settle automobile insurance claims, an *automobile damage appraiser* examines damaged cars and other vehicles, estimates the cost of labor and parts, and determines whether it is more practical to make the repairs on the damaged car or to pay the claimant the precollision market value of the vehicle.

For minor or routine claims, the trend among property and casualty insurers is to employ *telephone or inside adjusters*. They use the telephone and written correspondence to gather information, including loss estimates, from the claimant. Drive-in claim centers have developed to provide on-the-spot settlement for minor claims. After determining the loss, the adjuster issues a check immediately.

More complex claims are handled by outside adjusters. *Outside adjusters* spend more time in the field investigating the claim and gathering relevant information.

In life and health insurance companies, *claims examiners* perform all the functions of claims adjusters. Examiners in these companies, and in others where adjusters are employed, review settled claims to make sure the settlements and payments adhere to company procedures and policies. They report on any irregularities. In cases involving litigation, they confer with attorneys. Where large claims are involved, a *senior examiner* frequently handles the case.

Requirements

College graduates generally are preferred for insurance claims jobs, but persons with special experience may not need a degree. No specific college major is preferred, but certain ones may indicate a possible specialty. For example, an engineering degree would be valuable in industrial claims, and a legal background would be helpful in ones involving workers' compensation and product liability. In most companies, on-the-job training is usually provided.

Supplementary professional education is encouraged by insurance companies. A number of options are available. The Insurance Institute of America offers a series of courses culminating in a comprehensive examination. Passing the exam earns the examinee an Associate in Claims (AIC) designation. The College of Insurance in New York City offers a program leading to a professional certificate in insurance adjusting. In addition, life and health claims examining programs for people interested in working as claims examiners are offered by both the Life Office Management Association (LOMA) and the International Claim Association (ICA), both of which lead to a professional designation.

Claims representatives must have good communication skills in order to be able to gain the respect and confidence of all involved parties. They should be mathematically adept and have a good memory. Knowledge of legal and medical terms and practice, as well as state and federal insurance laws and regulations, is required in this profession. Some companies require applicants to take aptitude tests designed to measure mathematical, analytical, and communications skills. Increasingly, a knowledge of computers is important.

Most states require licensing of claims representatives. Licensing requirements vary and may include age restrictions, state residency, education in such subjects as loss adjusting or insurance, character references, and written examinations.

Opportunities for Experience & Exploration

There are vast opportunities for career exploration, ranging from getting a job with an insurance company to taking relevant coursework and interviewing people in the field.

You might consider asking a teacher, guidance counselor, or even your parents to arrange a meeting with an insurance claims representative or someone else that works in the insurance field.

Methods of Entering

A person can enter this occupation by applying directly to an employer, answering a newspaper ad, or using the local office of the U.S. Employment Service Office.

Advancement

Depending upon the individual, advancement prospects are good. As trainees demonstrate competence and advance in coursework, they are assigned higher and more challenging claims. Promotions are possible to department supervisor in a field office or a managerial position in the home office. Sometimes claims workers transfer to underwriting and sales departments.

Employment Outlook

Growth for this field will be faster than the national average for all occupations through the year 2006. Most of the new jobs will be created as a result of increased insurance sales, resulting in a larger number of insurance claims, as well as of changes in the population, economics, trends in insurance settlement procedures, and opportunities arising from employees who change jobs or retire.

The predominance of the group most in need of protection, individuals between twenty-five and fifty-four, indicates the need for more claims jobs. Also, as the number of working women rises, so will their demand for increased insurance coverage. New and expanding businesses will require insurance for production plants and equipment, as well as employees.

Claims representatives who specialize in complex business insurance such as marine cargo, workers' compensation, and product and pollution liability insurance will be in demand. Insurance claims representatives will always be in demand since their work requires significant interpersonal contact, and does not lend itself to automation.

Earnings

According to the U.S. Department of Labor, claims representatives earned an average of about $22,800 a year in 1996. Adjusters are furnished a company car or reimbursed for business travel.

Claims examiners make about $31,000 a year; claims supervisors, $44,000; and claims managers, $55,000. Insurance companies have liberal vacation policies and employee-financed life and retirement programs.

Conditions of Work

Inside adjusters work in offices, as do clerks and examiners. They work thirty-five to forty hours a week and occasionally travel. They may work additional hours during peak claim periods or when quarterly or annual reports are due. Outside claims adjusters may travel extensively. An adjuster may be on call twenty-four hours a day.

Sources of Additional Information

General information about claims representative careers is available from many insurance companies, as well as the following:

■**Alliance of American Insurers**
1501 Woodfield Road, Suite 400 West
Schaumburg, IL 60173
Tel: 847-330-8500

Information on health insurance adjusting can be obtained from:

■**Health Insurance Association of America**
555 13th Street, NW, Suite 600 East
Washington, DC 20004
Tel: 202-824-1600

■**Insurance Information Institute**
110 William Street
New York, NY 10038
Tel: 212-669-9200
WWW: http://www.iii.org

■**National Association of Independent Insurers**
2600 River Road
Des Plaines, IL 60018
Tel: 847-297-7800
WWW: http://www.naii.org

Information on public insurance adjusting can be obtained from:

■**National Association of Public Insurance Adjusters**
300 Water Street, Suite 400
Baltimore, MD 21202
Tel: 410-539-4141

■**Insurance Institute of Canada**
18 King Street East, 6th Floor
Toronto, ON M5C 1C4 Canada
Tel: 416-362-8586

■**National Association of Independent Insurers**
2600 River Road
Des Plaines, IL 60018
Tel: 847-297-7800
WWW: http://www.naii.org

Information on public insurance adjusting can be obtained from:

■**National Association of Public Insurance Adjusters**
300 Water Street, Suite 400
Baltimore, MD 21202
Tel: 410-539-4141

■**Insurance Institute of Canada**
18 King Street East, 6th Floor
Toronto, ON M5C 1C4 Canada
Tel: 416-362-8586

Janitors and Cleaners

Definition

Janitors or *cleaners*, sometimes known as *building custodians,* are responsible for the cleaning and maintenance of schools, apartments, hospitals, office buildings, manufacturing plants, and other public structures. In addition to daily cleaning duties, they may be responsible for performing light repair work when needed, and for making sure heating and cooling systems are in proper working order.

Nature of the Work

Janitors perform a wide range of jobs, using equipment that varies from simple mops to power tools for making minor repairs. They are responsible for selecting the proper methods and equipment to clean and maintain the structure in which they work, be it a school, shopping mall, hospital, or hotel. Their specific duties may vary somewhat, depending upon the type of building they are responsible for.

Their job description may include sweeping, mopping, waxing, and buffing floors, vacuuming carpets, dusting furniture and handrails, washing walls and windows, cleaning bathrooms, and collecting and disposing of trash. They may also be responsible for some low-level maintenance and repair work, such as fixing leaky faucets, monitoring heating, cooling, and electrical systems, and exterminating pests or arranging for a pest control worker to do so.

In some cases, janitors perform outdoor maintenance. They may repaint units, repair broken signs or landscaping, recaulk windows, fix holes in parking lots or sidewalks, or replace locks. They may also shovel snow or apply salt or sand to sidewalks in the winter, and mow lawns and trim shrubs in the spring.

Some janitors have duties that are particular to their workplace. For example, when schools close for the summer, their janitors work on the grounds, make minor repairs, and sanitize the building to prepare it for the next year. They also maintain and repair the gymnasium floors, and test and service the heating and cooling systems. Janitors who work for apartment buildings or complexes may be responsible for dealing with residents' complaints or needs and, in some cases, collecting rent. Those who work in hotels and motels change linens and make beds, in addition to performing regular cleaning tasks.

Janitorial workers in hospitals, often called *central supply workers,* clean, sterilize, and assemble hospital equipment, supplies, and instruments. Similar duties are performed by *laboratory equipment cleaners* in other industries.

Requirements

No special educational requirements exist for this position, although employers prefer to hire applicants with a high school diploma. High school classes that are helpful to prospective janitorial workers are home economics, mathematics, and chemistry. Because understanding and following directions is very important, English or communication classes might be beneficial. Finally, shop classes can be helpful by teaching minor plumbing or carpentry work.

Janitors should also be good with their hands and be able to operate tools and equipment. A certain level of stamina and energy is essential, since the job does require physical labor. Finally, tact and courtesy in dealing with people are important assets. Employers usually look for dependable, hardworking individuals who are in good health, follow directions well, and get along with other people.

Although not a requirement for finding a job, some janitors opt to become certified by the

National Executive Housekeepers Association (NEHA). The NEHA offers two levels of certification, which indicate a certain degree of professionalism and training and may be beneficial in finding a job or in moving to better positions. The first level of certification, the Certified Executive Housekeeper, requires that the applicant be a high school graduate and complete a prescribed number of classroom or self-study hours in the NEHA program. The Registered Executive Housekeeper designation, which is the highest offered, can be obtained by completing a collegiate degree program, consisting of sixty semester credit hours.

Opportunities for Experience & Exploration

In many cases, interested high school student can find summer or part-time employment in the janitorial trades. High schools, college dormitories, and apartment complexes often hire extra custodial help during the summer months.

Another source of learning about janitorial and maintenance jobs is high school shop courses, which help students prepare for the variety of maintenance tasks that custodians perform in their jobs. A familiarity with cleaning tools and materials, whether gained through part-time employment or through maintaining one's own home, should prove helpful, as well. Finally, students might talk with a janitor at their school or apartment building in order to find out more about the job.

Methods of Entering

Entry into janitorial or custodial jobs may be obtained by filing applications with state employment offices or private companies. Positions are sometimes also advertised in newspaper want ads. Applying to building management firms, building service contract firms, or building owners are possibilities for those who desire jobs in apartment or office buildings. Hotels and motels typically have a personnel office that does the hiring, so job seekers should check with them for openings and applications.

Advancement

More complex tasks and higher pay are usually given to those who have gained experience and have proven themselves to be efficient and dependable workers. If the custodian is the only maintenance employee in a building, advancement opportunities are limited. Supervisory positions are possible, on the other hand, for those who work on a large maintenance staff, especially for those who hold a high school diploma. Janitors may become building superintendents, janitorial services supervisors, or custodial supervisors. With additional training in real estate and managerial skills, the ambitious custodian may eventually move into property management. Some experienced custodians establish their own contract cleaning and maintenance businesses, providing services to a number of clients. This requires some administrative and supervisory skills, as well as the ability and resources needed to start and grow a new business.

Employment Outlook

There were about 3.2 million janitors and cleaners employed in the United States in 1996, one third of which were employed part time. Though employment opportunities will be plentiful as the number of office buildings, apartments, schools, hotels, hospitals and factories increase, growth for this occupations is expected to be slower than the average through the year 2006. The janitorial field is an easy one to enter since little training or education is required. Relatively high turnover is expected. The need to replace existing janitors and cleaners leaving the workforce for retirement or other reasons will create many full and part-time jobs, many of which will be located in busy urban areas.

Independent cleaning contractors will offer many janitorial, cleaning and supervisory positions; about twenty four percent of all janitors and cleaners work for this type of employer.

Earnings

Earnings vary widely, depending on employer, geographical location, and experience and training level. According to the U.S. Department of Labor, the median salary for janitors in 1996 was $15,600 a year. Fifty percent of janitors earned from $12,480 to $21,840 a year; the top ten percent earned over $29,120. Comparatively, maids earn less. In 1996, maids averaged 14,040 a year, with the top ten percent averaging only $21,320 a year.

Cleaning supervisors averaged $20,800 annually; top earners made about $39,500 a year. Certification does make a difference in salary. According to a survey done by the International Executive Housekeepers Association, certified housekeeping managers earned an average of $37,000 or more a year.

Most janitorial workers who are employed by building service firms, property management firms, or schools receive paid holidays and vacations and health insurance.

Conditions of Work

Working conditions for employees in this field vary depending upon the establishment they are responsible for. Because most office buildings are cleaned while they are empty, janitors for these establishments often work evening hours. Others, such as school and hospital custodians, work in the daytime. In places with a need for twenty-four-hour maintenance, such as factories, janitors may be assigned to work shifts. Part-time custodians usually work in the evenings or on weekends.

Janitors and custodians usually work inside heated, well-lit buildings. However, sometimes they work outdoors sweeping walkways, mowing lawns, or shoveling snow. Some tasks, such as cleaning bathrooms and trash rooms, can be dirty and unpleasant. Because they spend most of the day on their feet, some workers may find the job physically demanding and tiring. Custodians who are required to move a great deal of furniture or are continually bending, lifting, and reaching may develop back and neck strain or other problems.

The use of hazardous tools and machines may result in a variety of minor cuts, bruises, and burns. Many cleaners and chemical solvents may also be caustic to the skin or dangerous to inhale. Janitors who work with machinery maintenance and heating systems need to adjust to the noise, grease, and general physical strain.

Sources of Additional Information

For information on careers and training in the janitorial services field, contact:

Cleaning Management Institute
13 Century Hill Drive
Latham, NY 12110
Tel: 518-783-1281

For information about certification programs in housekeeping, contact:

National Executive Housekeepers Association, Inc.
1001 Eastwind Drive, Suite 301
Westerville, OH 43081
Tel: 800-200-6342

Landscapers and Grounds Managers

Definition

Landscapers and grounds managers plan, design, and maintain gardens, parks, lawns, and other landscaped areas and supervise the care of the trees, plants, and shrubs that are part of these areas. Specific job responsibilities depend on the type of area involved. Landscapers and grounds managers direct projects at private homes, parks, schools, arboretums, office parks, shopping malls, government offices, and botanical gardens. They are responsible for purchasing material and supplies and for training, directing, and supervising employees. Grounds managers maintain the land after the landscaping designs have been implemented. They may work alone or supervise a grounds staff. They may have their own business or be employed by a landscaping firm.

Nature of the Work

There are many different types of landscapers and grounds managers, and their specific job titles depend on the duties involved. One specialist in this field is the *landscape contractor*, who performs landscaping work on a contract basis for homeowners, highway departments, operators of industrial parks, and others. They confer with prospective clients and study the landscape design, drawings, and bills of material to determine the amount of landscape work required. They plan the installation of lighting or sprinkler systems, erection of fences, and the types of trees, shrubs, or ornamental plants required. They inspect the grounds and calculate labor, equipment, and materials costs. They also prepare and submit bids, draw up contracts, and direct and coordinate the activities of landscape laborers who mow lawns, plant shrubbery, dig holes, move topsoil, and perform other related tasks.

On golf courses, landscapers and grounds managers are employed as *greenskeepers*. There are two types of greenskeepers: *Greenskeepers I* supervise and coordinate the activities of workers engaged in keeping the grounds and turf of a golf course in good playing condition. They consult with the greens superintendent to plan and review work projects; they determine work assignments, such as fertilizing, irrigating, seeding, mowing, raking, and spraying; and they mix and prepare spraying and dusting solutions. They may also repair and maintain mechanical equipment.

Greenskeepers II follow the instructions of greenskeepers I as they maintain the grounds of golf courses. They cut the turf on green and tee areas; dig and rake grounds to prepare and cultivate new greens; connect hose and sprinkler systems; plant trees and shrubs; and operate tractors as they apply fertilizer, insecticide, and other substances to the fairways or other designated areas.

Greens superintendents supervise and coordinate the activities of greenskeepers and other workers engaged in constructing and maintaining golf course areas. They review test results of soil and turf samples, and they direct the application of fertilizer, lime, insecticide, or fungicide. Their other duties include monitoring the course grounds to determine the need for irrigation or better care, keeping and reviewing maintenance records, and interviewing and hiring workers.

Industrial-commercial grounds managers maintain areas in and around industrial or commercial properties by cutting lawns, pruning trees, raking leaves, and shoveling snow. They also plant grass and flowers and are responsible for the upkeep of flower beds and public passageways. These types of groundskeepers may repair and maintain fences and gates and also operate sprinkler systems and other equipment.

Parks-and-grounds grounds managers maintain city, state, or national parks and playgrounds. They plant and prune trees; haul away garbage; repair driveways, walks, swings, and other equipment; and clean comfort stations.

Landscape supervisors supervise and direct the activities of landscape workers who are engaged in pruning trees and shrubs, caring for lawns, and performing related tasks. They coordinate work schedules, prepare job cost estimates, and deal with customer questions and concerns.

Landscapers maintain the grounds of private or business establishments. They care for hedges, gardens, and other landscaped areas. They mow and trim lawns, plant trees and shrubs, apply fertilizers and other chemicals, and repair walks and driveways.

Many *arboriculture technicians* work as landscapers or grounds managers. Below is a listing of some careers in this area.

Tree surgeons prune and treat ornamental and shade trees to improve their health and appearance. This may involve climbing with ropes, working in buckets high off the ground, spraying fertilizers and pesticides, or injecting chemicals into the tree trunk or root zone in the ground. *Tree-trimming supervisors* coordinate and direct the activities of workers engaged in cutting away tree limbs or removing trees that interfere with electric power lines. They inspect power lines and direct the placement of removal equipment. Tree-trimming supervisors answer consumer questions when trees are located on private property.

Pest management scouts survey landscapes and nurseries regularly to locate potential pest problems including insects, diseases, and weeds before they become hard to control in an effective, safe manner. Scouts may specialize in the treatment of a particular type of infestation, such as gypsy moths or boll weevils.

Lawn-service workers plant and maintain lawns. They remove leaves and dead grass and apply insecticides, fertilizers, and weed killers as necessary. Lawn-service workers also use aerators and other tools to pierce the soil to make holes for the fertilizer and de-thatchers to remove built-up thatch.

Related jobs include the *horticulturist* who conducts experiments and investigations into the problems of breeding, production, storage, processing, and transit of fruits, nuts, berries, flowers, and trees. Horticulturists also develop new plant varieties and determine methods of planting, spraying, cultivating, and harvesting. A *city forester* advises communities on the selection, planting schedules, and

proper care of trees. They also plant, feed, spray, and prune trees and may supervise other workers in these activities. Depending on the situation, landscapers and groundskeepers may perform these functions alone or with city foresters. *Turf grass consultants* analyze turf grass problems and recommend solutions. They also determine growing techniques, mowing schedules, and the best type of turf grass to use for specified areas. Depending on the geographic area of the country, lawn-service companies regularly use such consultants.

Requirements

In general, a high school diploma is necessary for most positions, and at least some college training is needed for those with supervisory or specialized responsibilities. Aspiring landscapers and grounds managers should have "green thumbs," and an interest in preserving and maintaining natural areas. They should also be reasonably physically fit, have an aptitude for working with machines, and display good manual dexterity.

High school students interested in this career should take classes in English, mathematics, chemistry, biology, and as many courses as possible in horticulture and botany. Those interested in college training should enroll in a two or four-year program in horticulture, landscape management, or agronomy. Classes might include landscape maintenance and design, turf grass management, botany, and plant pathology. Course work should be selected with an area of specialization in mind. Those wishing to have managerial responsibilities should take courses in personnel management, communications, and business-related courses such as accounting and economics.

Many trade and vocational schools offer landscaping, horticulture, and related programs. Several extension programs are also available that allow students to take courses at home.

Licensing and certification differ by state and vary according to specific job responsibilities. For example, in most states landscapers and grounds managers need a certificate to spray insecticides or other chemicals. Contractors and other self-employed people may also need a license to operate their business.

All managerial personnel must carefully supervise their workers to ensure that they adhere to environmental regulations as specified by the Environmental Protection Agency (EPA) and other local and national governmental agencies.

Opportunities for Experience & Exploration

Part-time work at a golf course, lawn-service company, greenhouse, botanical garden, or other similar enterprise is an excellent way of learning about this field. Many companies gladly hire part-time help, especially during the busy summer months. In addition, there are numerous opportunities mowing lawns, growing flowers, and tending gardens. Interested students can also join garden clubs, visit local flower shops, and attend botanical shows.

The American Association of Botanical Gardens and Arboreta (AABGA) has a very strong internship program and offers a directory of internships in over one hundred public gardens throughout the United States. AABGA is a valuable resource to those individuals interested in gaining practical experience. Finally, a summer job mowing lawns and caring for a neighbor's garden is an easy, simple introduction to the field.

Methods of Entering

Summer or part-time jobs often lead to full-time employment with the same employer. Those who enroll in a college or other training programs can receive help in finding work from the school's job placement office. In addition, directly applying to botanical gardens, nurseries, or golf courses is common practice. Jobs may also be listed in newspaper want ads. Most landscaping and related companies provide on-the-job training for entry-level personnel.

Advancement

In general, landscapers and grounds managers can expect to advance as they gain experience and additional educational training. For example, a greenskeeper with a high school diploma usually must have at least some college training to become a greens superintendent. It is also possible to go into a related field, such as

selling equipment used in maintaining lawns and other natural areas.

Those in managerial positions may wish to advance to a larger establishment or go into consulting work. In some instances, skilled landscapers and grounds managers may start their own consulting or contracting businesses.

Employment Outlook

Job growth for this field is expected to grow as fast as the average for all occupations through the year 2006. Landscapers and their services will be in strong demand due to increased construction of buildings, shopping malls, homes, and other structures. Upkeep and renovation of existing landscapes will create jobs as well. There is also a high degree of turnover in this field as many workers transfer to better-paying occupations, retire, or leave the field for other reasons.

Another factor for job growth is the increase in amount of disposable incomes. In order to have more leisure time, people are beginning to contract out for lawn care and maintenance. The popularity of home gardening will create jobs with local nurseries and garden centers. Jobs should be available with governmental agencies as well as in the private sector.

Non-seasonal work will be more prevalent in states such as California, Arizona, and Florida, where mild climates warrant landscaping and lawn maintenance year round.

Earnings

Salaries depend on the experience and education level of the worker, the type of work being done, and geographic location. According to the *1998-99 Occupational Outlook Handbook*, the median starting salary for landscapers and groundskeepers in 1996 was $15,600 a year. Fifty percent earned from $11,440 to $21,320 a year. Top landscape workers earned about $29,120 a year. Landscape contractors and others who run their own businesses earn between $23,000 and $50,000 per year, with those with a greater ability to locate customers earning even more.

A readership salary survey conducted by the *Grounds Maintenance Magazine* found the average golf course superintendent earned $38,600 a year; company grounds manager, $38,900; and lawn care contractor, $32,500.

Conditions of Work

Landscapers and grounds managers spend much of their time outside. Those with administrative or managerial responsibilities spend at least a portion of their workday in an office. Most of the outdoor work is done during daylight hours, but work takes place all year round in all types of weather conditions. Most people in the field work thirty-seven to forty hours a week, but overtime is especially likely during the summer months when landscapers and grounds managers take advantage of the longer days and warmer weather. Work weeks may be shorter during the winter. Weekend work is highly likely. Fringe benefits vary from employer to employer but generally include medical insurance and some paid vacation.

Much of the work can be physically demanding and most of it is performed outdoors in one extreme or another. Workers shovel dirt, trim bushes and trees, constantly bend down to plant flowers and shrubbery, and may have to climb ladders or the tree itself to prune branches or diagnose a problem. There is some risk of injury using planting and pruning machinery and some risk of illness from handling and breathing pesticides, but proper precautions should limit any job-related hazards. Managerial personnel should be willing to work overtime updating financial records and making sure the business accounts are in order.

Sources of Additional Information

American Association of Botanical Gardens and Arboreta
786 Church Road
Wayne, PA 19087
Tel: 610-688-1120

For information on career opportunities and educational training, contact:

American Society for Horticultural Sciences
113 South West Street, Suite 400
Alexandria, VA 22314-2824
Tel: 703-836-4606

Associated Landscape Contractors of America
12200 Sunrise Valley Drive, Suite 150
Reston, VA 22091
Tel: 703-620-6363

National Landscape Association
1250 I Street, NW, Suite 500
Washington, DC 20005
Tel: 202-789-2900

Professional Grounds Management Society
120 Cockeysville Road, Suite 104
Hunt Valley, MD 21031
Tel: 410-584-9754

Laser Technicians

Definition

Laser technicians produce, install, operate, service, and test laser systems and fiber optics equipment in industrial, medical, or research settings. They work under the direction of engineers or physicists who conduct laboratory activities in laser research and development or design. Depending upon the type of laser system—gas or solid state—a technician generally works either with information systems or with robotics, manufacturing, or medical equipment.

Nature of the Work

There are basically two types of laser systems with which laser technicians work. Those who work with semiconductor laser systems, which are the most compact and reliable, work mainly with computer and telephone systems. In addition to helping test, install, and maintain these systems, technicians work with engineers in their design and improvement.

Technicians who work with gas-type laser systems, which are larger and more expensive, usually assist scientists, engineers, or doctors. These systems are used primarily in the fields of robotics, manufacturing, and medical equipment.

Not all laser technicians are responsible for the same types of tasks. Much depends upon their positions and places of employment. For example, some repair lasers and instruct different companies on their use, while others work as technicians for very specific applications, such as optical surgery or welding parts in a manufacturing process. In general, most technicians are employed in one of five areas: materials processing, communications, military, medical, and research.

In any one of these areas, technicians may be involved in the process of building laser devices. To build a solid-state laser, they may construct, cut, and polish a crystal rod to be used in the laser. They put a flash tube around the crystal and place the unit in a container with a mirror at each end. Using precision instruments, they position the mirrors so that all emitted or reflected light passes through the crystal. Finally, they put the laser body in a chassis, install tubing and wiring to the controls, and place a jacket round the assembly.

In addition, there are other duties that all technicians perform, no matter what application they work in. Taking measurements, cleaning, aligning, inspecting, and operating lasers, and collecting data are standard duties in almost all areas. Since the field of lasers is very technologically advanced, computers are used in many tasks and applications. Technicians may be responsible for programming the computers that control the lasers, inputting data, or outputting computer generated reports.

Lasers are used in the area of materials processing for machining, production, measurement, construction, excavation, and photo-optics. Technicians in this area often read and interpret diagrams, schematics, and shop drawings in order to assemble components themselves or oversee the assembly process. They may operate lasers for welding, precision drilling, cutting, and grinding of metal parts or for trimming and slicing electronic components and circuit elements. They may use lasers to measure parts to verify that they are the precise size needed. Finally, technicians may be involved in part marking—using a laser to mark an identifying number or letter on each component manufactured. If working in construction, they may use a laser as a surveying guideline or an aligning tool because of its ability to travel in a straight, or coherent, beam.

Laser technicians in communications use lasers to generate light impulses transmitted through optical fibers. They work to develop, manufacture, and test optical equipment, and they may design, set up, monitor, and maintain fiber fabrication facilities. This field also uses lasers for data storage and retrieval.

In military and space projects, lasers are frequently used for target-finding, tracking, ranging, identification, and communications. Technicians repair and adapt low-power lasers, which are widely used for these applications.

Technicians who work in the medical field serve as technical equipment experts and assist the physicians and surgeons who use the laser system. They advise the surgeons on which type of laser to use and which method of delivery to use, such as through a microscope, fiber optic tube, or contact tip that transfers the energy to tissue in the form of heat. They must be on hand during laser surgical procedures to offer recommendations, fine-tune attachments and machines, and troubleshoot should a technical problem occur. In addition, technicians help set up the reflection devices that are used to aim the laser beam into hard-to-reach spots.

There are many areas of research and development in laser technology. For example, lasers are being studied as a source to produce the multimillion degree temperatures needed to cause elements to develop controlled nuclear fusion. These studies are part of the continuing research to produce inexpensive electrical power for the nation's energy needs. Technicians on a research and development team use lasers and electronic devices to perform tests, take measurements, gather data, and make calculations. They may use the data to prepare reports for engineers, doctors, scientists, production managers, or lab workers.

Requirements

Most laser technicians enter the field by attending a two-year program in laser technology at a vocational, technical, or community college. The prospective technician can begin to prepare for the career while still in high school by taking certain classes. Important courses include four years of English and at least two years of mathematics, one of which should be algebra. At least one year of physical science, preferably physics, should be included, as should a class in basic computer programming. Machine shop, basic electronics, and blueprint reading classes are also useful.

The average course of study leading to an associate's degree in laser technology includes intensive technical and scientific study, with more hours

spent in a laboratory or work situation than in the actual classroom. This hands-on experience is supplemented in the first year by courses in mathematics, physics, drafting, diagramming and sketching, basic electronics, electronic instrumentation and calibration, introduction to solid-state devices, electromechanical controls, computer programming, and English composition.

A second year's study might include courses in geometrical optics, digital circuits, microwaves, laser and electro-optic components, devices and measurements, vacuum techniques, technical report writing, microcomputers, and computer hardware. Special laser projects are often a part of the second year and can help students decide upon the specific field in which they want to work.

Even after completing their education, technicians typically require further training in the specific practices of their employers. This training is usually paid for by employers to help employees adapt their general knowledge to their specific positions.

There are several personal characteristics that are needed to ensure success as a laser technician. A reasonable degree of intelligence and a strong motivation to learn are important. An interest in instruments, laboratory apparatus, and how devices and systems work is also highly appropriate. Written and spoken communications are very important in the majority of positions for laser technicians, since they often have to work closely with many people of varied technological backgrounds.

Physical strength is not usually required for laser technicians, but good manual dexterity and hand-eye and body coordination are quite important. Because lasers can be extremely dangerous, it is necessary that technicians be careful and attentive and willing to follow safety precautions closely. The ability to work efficiently, patiently, and consistently is extremely important for laser technicians, as is a strong ability to solve problems and to do careful, detailed work.

Opportunities for Experience & Exploration

For high school students and others interested in a career as a laser technician, the high school vocational guidance counselor is a valuable resource person. If a community or technical college is nearby, its occupational information center and counseling staff can also be very helpful. In addition, there are several periodicals that are devoted to the field of lasers. Periodicals such as the Journal of Laser Applications, Laser Bulletin, and Laser Focus World may offer valuable insight into the field.

Lasers are used in so many places that it should be fairly easy to find a local laser technician, operator, or engineer in the community who can share knowledge about his or her job. It might be possible to find summer or part-time work in construction, manufacturing, or mining where lasers are used in measuring, cutting and welding, and surveying. This type of work can provide the interested student with exposure to jobs in laser technology.

Methods of Entering

Colleges that offer associate's degrees in laser technology usually work closely with industry, providing their graduating students with placement services and lists of potential employers. Most laser technicians graduating from a two-year program, in fact, are interviewed and recruited while still in school by representatives of companies who need laser technicians. If hired, they begin working soon after graduation.

Another way to enter the career is to join a branch of the U.S. armed forces under a technical training program for laser technicians. Military laser training is not always compatible to civilian training, however, and further study of theory and applications is needed to enter the field as a civilian.

Advancement

Opportunities for advancement in laser technology are excellent for technicians who keep abreast of advances in the field. In a relatively new technology such as that of the laser, new developments occur very rapidly; those workers who investigate and adapt to these changes become more valuable to their employers and advance to greater responsibilities.

Many employers designate various levels of employment for laser technicians, according to experience, education, and job performance. By being promoted through these levels, technicians

can advance to supervisory or managerial positions. Supervisors manage a department, supervise other technicians, and conduct training of new or current employees.

Mature, experienced, and highly successful laser technicians may decide to become consultants or specialists for individual firms. A consulting position entails working closely with clients, conducting studies and surveys, and proposing improvements, changes, and solutions to problems.

Some technicians move into positions in sales or technical writing. Others become instructors in vocational programs, teaching intermediate or advanced laser and fiber optics technology courses.

Employment Outlook

Employment opportunities for laser technicians are expected to be very good through the year 2006. Rapid changes in technology and continued growth in the industry will almost certainly lead to an increase in the number of technicians employed.

One of the fastest growing areas for laser technicians is the area of fiber optic systems used in communications. Optical fiber is replacing wire cables in communication lines and in many electronic products. This trend is expected to continue, so the demand for technicians in the fiber optics field should be especially strong. Growth is also expected to be strong in production, defense, medicine, construction, and entertainment.

Technicians interested in the area of research and development, however, should keep in mind that growth in opportunities for jobs such as these often slows in the face of economic downturns.

Earnings

According to a survey done by the Laser Institute of America, the overall average starting salary for laser technicians is between $21,000 and $25,000 per year. Salaries for technicians with at least five years of experience average approximately $30,000 per year, depending on background, experience, and the industry where they are employed. Those in advanced supervisory positions, advanced sales and service, or in private consulting work earn between $35,000 and $38,000 a year or more.

In addition to salary, technicians usually receive benefits such as insurance, paid holidays and vacations, and retirement plans. Many employers have liberal policies of paying for professional improvement through continued study in school or at work.

Conditions of Work

Working conditions for laser technicians vary. They may spend their workday in a wide variety of environments, including laboratories, hospital operating rooms, offices, or manufacturing plants. In most cases, however, work areas are kept clean and temperature-controlled in order to protect the laser equipment.

Laser technicians may work at relatively stationary jobs, assembling or operating lasers in the same environment every day, or they may be required to move around frequently, in and out of laboratory areas, production sites, or offices. Some are office- or laboratory-based; others, especially those in sales and service positions, may travel the country.

Laser technicians typically work regular hours. Five eight-hour days per week is the standard, although certain projects may occasionally require overtime.

There are possible dangers present in most areas where lasers are used. Because the power sup-plies for many lasers involve high voltages, the technician frequently works around potentially deadly amounts of electricity. The laser beam itself is also a possible source of serious injury to users and bystanders, either through direct exposure to the beam or by reflected light from the laser. Close adherence to safety precautions, such as wearing protective glasses, reduces the danger of injury, however.

In addition to the pressure of working in potentially dangerous conditions, there is the stress of handling extremely valuable instruments. The parts used to make lasers are almost always costly. Mistakes that damage lasers or errors in applying lasers can be very costly, running into the thousands of dollars.

The laser technician often works as part of a production team or supervisory group, sometimes with scientists and engineers, sometimes as a member of a production team or supervisory group. Some technicians work alone but usually report directly to an engineer, scientist, or manager.

Among the greatest sources of satisfaction that laser technicians experience is the feeling of success whenever they meet a challenge and see their laser systems perform correctly. This is especially true in sales and service where new users are taught to use this complicated technology and where the technician can actually see customers discovering the effectiveness of lasers. The same satisfaction is felt in research when a new development is proved to be a success.

Sources of Additional Information

For information on becoming a laser technician, contact:

Institute of Electrical and Electronics Engineers/LEOS
445 Hoes Lane
Piscataway, NJ 08854
Tel: 908-562-3892

For information on colleges and universities that offer programs in laser technology and optics education, as well as general career information, contact:

Laser Institute of America
12424 Research Parkway, Suite 125
Orlando, FL 32826
Tel: 407-380-1553
Email: lia@laserinstitute.org
WWW: http://www.creol.ucf.edu/~lia/

Lawyers and Judges

Definition

Lawyers serve a dual role in our society: as advocates, they represent the rights of their clients in legal forums such as trials and depositions or in front of various administrative and government bodies; as advisors, attorneys counsel clients on the ramifications of the law and how it might affect any number of business or personal decisions, such as the purchase of property or the creation of a will. Lawyers may represent individuals, businesses, and corporations.

Judges are elected or appointed officials who preside over federal, state, county, and municipal courts. They administer court proceedings according to legal precedent and establish new rulings on issues not previously decided.

Nature of the Work

All lawyers may give legal advice and represent clients in court when necessary. No matter what their specialty, their job is to help clients know their rights under the law and then help them achieve these rights before a judge, jury, government agency, or other legal forum, such as an arbitration panel. Lawyers may represent businesses and individuals. For businesses, they handle tax matters, arrange for issuance of stock, handle claims cases, represent the firm in real estate dealings, and, in general, advise on all legal matters. For individuals they may be trustees, guardians, or executors; they may draw up wills or contracts or advise on income taxes or on the purchase or sale of a home. Some work solely in the courts; others carry on most of their business outside of court, doing such tasks as drawing up mortgages, deeds, contracts, and other legal documents or by handling the background work necessary for court cases, which might include researching cases in a law library or interviewing witnesses. A number of lawyers work to establish and enforce laws for the federal and state governments by drafting legislation, representing the government in court, or serving as judges.

There are also positions for *professors in law schools*. Administrators, research workers, and writers are also important to the profession. Administrative positions in business or government may be of a nonlegal nature, but the qualities, background, and experience of a lawyer are often helpful in such positions.

Other individuals with legal training may choose not to practice but instead opt for careers in which their background and knowledge of law are important, including tax collectors, credit investigators, FBI agents, insurance adjusters, process servers, and probation officers.

Some of the specialized fields for lawyers are as follows:

Civil lawyers work in a field also known as private law. They handle damage suits and breach-of-contract suits; prepare and draw up deeds, leases, wills, mortgages, and contracts; and can act as trustees, guardians, or executors of an estate when necessary.

Criminal lawyers, also known as *defense lawyers*, specialize in cases dealing with offenses such as theft, murder, or arson committed against society or the state. They interview clients and witnesses to ascertain facts in a case, correlate their findings with known cases, and prepare a case to defend a client against the charges made. They conduct a defense at the trial, examine witnesses, and summarize the case with a closing argument to a jury.

District attorneys, also known as *prosecuting attorneys,* represent the city, county, state, or federal government in court proceedings. They gather and analyze evidence and review legal material relevant to a lawsuit. Then they present their case to the grand jury, which decides whether the evidence is sufficient for an indictment. If it is not, the suit is dismissed and there is no trial. If the grand jury decides to indict the accused, however, the case goes to court, where the district attorney appears before the judge and jury to present evidence against the defendant.

Probate lawyers specialize in planning and settling estates. They draw up wills, deeds of trust, and similar documents for clients who want to plan for the eventual disposition of their assets to designated heirs. Upon a client's death, probate lawyers vouch for the validity of the will and represent the executors and administrators of the estate.

Bankruptcy attorneys assist their clients, both individuals and corporations, in obtaining protection from creditors under existing bankruptcy laws and with financial reorganization and debt repayment.

Corporation lawyers advise corporations concerning their legal rights, obligations, or privileges. They study constitutions, statutes, previous decisions, ordinances, and decisions of quasi-judicial bodies that are applicable to corporations. They advise corporations on the pros and cons of prosecuting or defending a lawsuit. They act as agent of the corporation in various transactions and seek to keep clients from expensive litigation.

Maritime lawyers, sometimes referred to as *admiralty lawyers*, specialize in laws regulating commerce and navigation on the high seas and any navigable waters, including inland lakes and rivers. Although there is a general maritime law, it operates in each country according to that country's courts, laws, and customs. Maritime law covers contracts, insurance, property damage, and personal injuries.

Patent lawyers specialize in securing patents for inventors from the U.S. Patent Office and prosecuting or defending suits of patent infringements. They prepare detailed specifications for the patent, may organize a corporation, or advise an existing corporation to commercialize on a patent.

Tax attorneys handle cases resulting from problems of inheritance, income tax, estate tax, franchises, and real estate tax, among other things.

Insurance attorneys advise insurance companies about legal matters pertaining to insurance transactions. They approve the wording of insurance policies, review the legality of claims against the company, and draw up legal documents.

An *international lawyer* specializes in the body of rules that are observed by nations in their relations with one another. Some of these laws have been agreed to in treaties, some have evolved from long-standing customs and traditions.

Securities and exchange lawyers monitor individuals and corporations involved in trading and oversee their activities to make sure they comply with applicable laws. When corporations undergo takeovers and mergers, securities and exchange lawyers are there to represent the corporation's interests and fulfill all legal obligations involved in the transaction.

Real estate lawyers handle the conveyance of property and perform such duties as searching into public records and deeds to establish titles of property, holding funds for investment in escrow accounts, and acting as trustees of property. They draw up legal documents and act as agents in various real estate transactions.

Title attorneys deal with titles, leases, contracts, and other legal documents pertaining to the ownership of land, and gas, oil, and mineral rights. They prepare documents to cover the purchase or sale of such property and rights, examine documents to determine ownership, advise organizations about legal requirements with respect to titles, and participate in the trial or lawsuits in connection with titles.

It is important to note that once one is licensed to practice law, one is legally qualified to practice any one or more of these and many other specialties. Some general practitioners handle both criminal and civil matters of all sorts. To become licensed, graduates must be admitted to the bar of that state. Bar examiners test the qualifications of applicants. They prepare and administer written exams covering legal subjects, examine candidates orally, and recommend admission of those who meet the prescribed standards.

Lawyers become judges by either being elected or appointed to preside over federal, state, county, or municipal courts. Judges administer court procedures during trials and hearings and establish new rules on questions where standard procedures have not previously been set. They read or listen to claims made by parties involved in civil suits and make decisions based on facts, applicable statutes, and prior court decisions. They examine evidence in criminal cases to see if it will support the charges. Judges listen to the presentation of cases, rule on the admission of evidence and testimony, and settle disputes between attorneys. They instruct juries on their duties and advise them of laws that apply to the case. They sentence defendants found guilty of criminal charges and decide who is responsible in non-jury civil cases. Besides their work in the courtroom, judges also research legal matters, study prior rulings, write opinions, and keep abreast of legislation that may affect their own rulings.

Some judges have other titles such as *magistrate*, or *justice*, and are not subject to constitutional and state regulations. Magistrates hear civil cases in which damages do not exceed a prescribed maximum, as well as minor misdemeanor cases that do not involve penitentiary sentences or fines that exceed a certain specified amount.

Requirements

A high school diploma, a college degree, and three years of law school are minimum requirements for a law degree. To enter any law school approved by the American Bar Association, a student must satisfactorily complete at least three, and usually four, years of college work.

Most law schools do not specify any particular courses for prelaw education. Usually a liberal arts course is most advisable, with courses in English, history, economics, social sciences, logic, and public speaking. The same general requirements would apply to the high school student considering a career in law. Such a student should plan on a strong college preparatory course—specialized training will come later—while high school and college education should be devoted to an understanding of society and the way it functions. A college student planning on specialization in a particular area of law, however, might also take courses significantly related to that area, such as economics, agriculture, or political science. Those interested should write to several law schools to find out about any requirements and to see if they will accept credits from the college the student is planning to attend.

Currently, 177 law schools in the United States are approved by the American Bar Association; others, many of them night schools, are approved by state authorities only. Most of the approved law schools, however, do have night sessions to accommodate part-time students. Such a course usually takes four years.

Law school training itself consists of required courses such as legal writing and research, contracts, criminal law, constitutional law, torts, and property. The second and third years may be devoted to specialized courses of interest to the student, such as evidence, business transactions and corporations, or admiralty. The study of cases and decisions is of basic importance to the law student, who will be required to read and study thousands of these cases. A degree of juris doctor (J.D.) or bachelor of laws (LL.B.) is usually granted upon graduation. Some law students considering specialization, research, or teaching may go on for advanced study.

Most law schools require that applicants take the Law School Admission Test, where prospective law students are tested on their critical thinking, writing, and reasoning abilities.

Every state requires that lawyers be admitted to the bar of that state before they can practice. They require that applicants graduate from an approved law school and that they pass a written examination in the state in which they intend to practice. In a few states, graduates of law schools within the state are excused from these written examinations. Once lawyers have been admitted to the bar in one state, they can practice in another state without taking a written examination if the states have reciprocity agreements; however, they will be required to meet certain state standards of good character and legal experience and pay any applicable fees.

Federal courts and agencies have their own rules regulating admission to practice. Other requirements vary among the states. For example, a few states will allow a person who has spent several years reading law in a law office but has no college training or who has a combination of reading and law school experience to take the state bar examination. Few people now enter law practice in this manner.

A few states will accept the study of law by correspondence. Some states require that newly graduated lawyers serve a period of clerkship in an established law firm before they are eligible to take the bar examination.

Almost all judges appointed or elected to any court must be lawyers and members of the bar, usually with many years of experience.

Opportunities for Experience & Exploration

Interested high school students can select several ways to learn about the law profession, although they may not actively participate in the field until licensed to do so. Students may find it helpful to talk to lawyers about their profession and its demands, observe lawyers working, or attend court sessions, which are often open to the public. The prospective lawyer can also learn a great deal by reading and possibly obtaining a summer or part-time job in a law office.

High school guidance counselors may be able to help students assess their interests and abilities in relation to a law career. The aptitude tests required by law schools will also help the prospective lawyer make a decision. A student with an interest in abstract subjects in school is likely to find a lawyer's work satisfying.

Methods of Entering

The first steps in entering the law profession are graduation from an approved law school and passing a state bar examination. Usually beginning lawyers do not go into solo practice right away. It is often difficult to become established, and additional experience is helpful to the beginning lawyer. Also, most lawyers do not specialize in a particular branch of law without first gaining experience. Beginning lawyers usually work as assistants to experienced lawyers. At first they do mainly research and routine work. After a few years of successful experience, they may be ready to go out on their own. Another choice open to the beginning lawyer is to join an established law firm. Or one may enter into partnership with another lawyer. There are also positions with banks, business corporations, insurance companies and private utilities and with a number of government agencies at different levels.

Advancement

Lawyers with outstanding ability may expect to go a long way in their profession. Novice lawyers generally start as law clerks, but as they prove themselves and develop their abilities, many opportunities for advancement will arise. They may be promoted to junior partner in a law firm or establish their own practice. The lawyer may enter politics and become a judge, mayor, congressman, or other governmental leader. Top positions are available in business, too, for the qualified lawyer. Lawyers working for the federal government advance according to the civil service system.

Employment Outlook

About seventy percent of the 699,000 practicing lawyers in the United States in 1996 were in private practice, either in law firms or alone. The rest were employed in government, mostly at the local level. The majority of the lawyers worked for the federal government held positions in the Departments of Justice, Treasury, and Defense. Lawyers also held positions as house counsel for public utilities, transportation companies, banks, insurance companies, real estate agencies, manufacturing firms, welfare and religious organizations, and other businesses and nonprofit organizations.

The demand for lawyers is expected to grow as fast as the average through the year 2006, but record numbers of law school graduates have created strong competition for jobs, even though the number of graduates has begun to level off. Continued population growth, typical business activities, and increased numbers of legal cases involving healthcare, environmental, and sexual harassment issues, among others, will create a steady demand for lawyers. Law services will be more accessible to the middle income public with the popularity of prepaid legal services and clinics. While employment growth is expected to be only average, the U.S. Department of Labor predicts that 120,000 new positions will be added between the years 1996 and 2006—a 17 percent increase in employment.

The top 10 percent of the graduating seniors of the country's best law schools will have no trouble finding salaried positions in well-known law firms and jobs on legal staffs of corporations, in government agencies, and in law schools in the next few decades. Lawyers in solo practice will find it hard to earn a living until their practice is fully established. The best opportunities exist in small towns or suburbs of large cities, where there is less competition.

Graduates with lower class standings and from lesser known schools may have difficulty in obtaining the most desirable positions. Banks, insurance companies, real estate firms, government agencies, and other organizations often hire law graduates for administrative, managerial, and business work. Legal positions in the armed forces are also available.

Employment of judges employed is expected to grow more slowly through the year 2006. Judges who retire, however, will need to be replaced. There may be an increase in judges in cities with large population growth, but competition will be high for any openings.

Earnings

Incomes generally increase as the lawyer gains experience and becomes better known in the field. The beginning lawyer in solo practice may barely make ends meet for the first few years.

In 1996, according to the National Association for Law Placement, the starting salary for federal government lawyers was approximately $34,500. Average starting salaries for lawyers in business was nearly $45,000. The top graduates from the best law schools earned over $80,000 a year.

Experienced lawyers earn salaries that vary widely depending on the type, size, and location of their employers. The 1996 average for lawyers in private industry was about $60,000 annually, though some senior partners earned well over one million dollars a year. General attorneys in the federal government received an average of about $72,000. Patent attorneys in the federal government averaged around $81,600.

Judges generally earn less than lawyers, although their incomes overall are good. According the Administrative Office of the U.S. Courts, in 1996, Federal district court judges averaged $133,600; Federal circuit court judges, $141,700. The Chief Justice of the United States earned $171,500, while Associate Justices of the Supreme Court earned $164,100. A survey conducted by the National Center for State Courts reports the 1997 salary average for State intermediate appellate court judges was $91,000; State associate justices earned $101,800 a year.

Conditions of Work

Offices and courtrooms are usually pleasant. Lawyers also spend significant amounts of time in law libraries or record rooms, in the homes and offices of clients, and sometimes in jail cells. Many lawyers never work in a courtroom. Unless they are directly involved in litigation, they may never perform at a trial.

Some courts, such as small claims, family, or surrogate, may have evening hours to provide flexibility to the community. Criminal arraignments may be held at any time of the day or night. Court hours for most lawyers and judges are usually regular business hours, with a one-hour lunch break. Often lawyers have to work long hours, spending evenings and weekends preparing cases and materials and working with clients. In addition to the work, the lawyer must always keep up with the latest developments in the profession. Also, it takes a long time to become a qualified lawyer, and it may be difficult to earn an adequate living until one becomes established as a solo practitioner.

Sources of Additional Information

American Bar Association
Information Services
750 North Lake Shore Drive
Chicago, IL 60611
Tel: 312-988-5000
WWW: http://www.abanet.org

Association of American Law Schools
1201 Connecticut Avenue, NW, Suite 800
Washington, DC 20036
Tel: 202-296-8851
Email: aals@aals.org.com

Licensed Practical Nurses

Definition

Licensed practical nurses (LPNs), a specialty of the nursing profession, are sometimes called licensed vocational nurses. LPNs are trained to assist in the care and treatment of patients. They may assist registered nurses and physicians or work under various other circumstances. They perform many of the general duties of nursing and may be responsible for some clerical duties. LPNs work in hospitals, public health agencies, nursing homes, or home health.

Nature of the Work

Licensed practical nurses work under the supervision of a registered nurse, or a physician. They are responsible for many general duties of nursing such as administering prescribed drugs and medical treatments to patients, taking patients' temperature and blood pressure, assisting in the preparation of medical examination, surgery, and performing routine laboratory tests. LPNs help with therapeutic and rehabilitation sessions; they may also participate in the planning, practice and evaluation of a patient's nursing care.

A main duty of an LPN is to ensure that patients are clean and comfortable, and their needs, both physical and emotional, are met. They sometimes assist patients with daily hygiene such as bathing, brushing teeth, and dressing. Many times they provide emotional comfort by simply talking with the patient.

LPNs working in nursing homes have duties similar to those employed by hospitals. They provide bedside care, administer medications, develop care plans, and supervise nursing attendants. Those working in doctors' offices and clinics are sometimes required to perform clerical duties such as keeping records, maintaining files and paperwork, as well as answering phones and tending the appointment book. Home health LPNs, in addition to their nursing duties, may sometimes prepare and serve meals to their patients.

Requirements

Those interested in a career as an LPN usually enroll in a practical nursing program after graduating from high school (However, some programs do not require a high school diploma.) There were about 1,100 state approved programs in the United States in 1997 providing practical nursing training. According to the U.S. Department of Labor, sixty percent of all LPNs graduate from a technical or vocational school and thirty percent from a community or junior college. The remainder were enrolled in colleges, hospital programs, or high schools. Most programs last from twelve to eighteen months, with time spent for both classroom study and supervised clinical care. Courses include basic nursing concepts, anatomy, physiology, medical-surgical nursing, pediatrics, obstetrics, nutrition and first aid. Clinical practice is most often in a hospital setting. A licensing examination is required by all fifty states upon graduation.

Opportunities for Experience & Exploration

To prepare for a career as an LPN, students should study biology, chemistry, physics, and science, while in high school. English and mathematics courses are also helpful.

High school students can explore this interest by reading books or by checking out Web sites devoted to the nursing field. They should also take advantage of any information available in their school career center. An excellent way to learn more about this career first hand is by speaking with the school nurse or local public health nurse. Visits to the local hospital can give students a feel for the work environment. Volunteer work at a hospital, community health center, or even the local Red Cross chapter can provide valuable experience for the student. Some high schools offer membership in Future Nurses organizations.

Methods of Entering

After licensing requirements are fulfilled, LPNs should check with human resource departments of hospitals, nursing homes, and clinics for openings. Employment agencies that specialize in health professions, and state employment agencies are other ways to gain employment, as are school placement centers. Newspaper classified ads, nurses associations, and professional journals are great sources of job opportunities.

Advancement

About forty percent of LPNs use their license and experience as a stepping stone for other occupations in the health fields, many of which offer more responsibility and higher salaries. Some LPNs, for example, with additional training, become medical technicians, surgical attendants, optometric assistants, or psychiatric technicians. Many LPNs return to school to become registered nurses. Hospitals often offer LPNs the opportunity for more training, seminars, workshops, and clinical sessions to sharpen their nursing skills.

Employment Outlook

There were over 699,000 LPNs employed in the United States in 1996. Thirty-two percent worked in hospitals; twenty-seven percent were employed in nursing homes; and thirteen percent treated patients in doctors' offices and clinics. The remainder of LPNs worked for home health or temporary agencies.

Employment prospects for LPNs are expected to grow faster than the average for all occupations through the year 2006. A growing elderly population requiring long term health care is the primary factor for the demand of qualified LPNs. Traditionally, hospitals provide the most job opportunities for LPNs. However, this source will only provide a moderate number of openings in the future. Inpatient population is not expected to increase significantly. Also, in many hospitals, certified nursing attendants (CNAs) are increasingly taking over many of the duties of LPNs.

Demand for LPNs will be greatest in nursing home settings and home health care agencies. Due to advanced medical technology, people are able to live longer, though many will require medical assistance. Private medical practices will also be good job sources since many medical procedures are now being performed on an outpatient basis in doctors' offices.

Earnings

According to the *1998-99 Occupational Outlook Handbook,* LPNs earned an average of $24,336 annually in 1996. Fifty percent earned between $20,176 and $29,276; the top ten percent earned over $34,996. A recent Buck Survey listed average earnings for LPNs employed at national chain nursing homes in 1996 at $12 an hour, or $480 weekly. Many LPNs are able to supplement their salaries with overtime pay and shift differentials. One-third of all LPNs work part time.

Conditions of Work

Most LPNs work forty-hour weeks, less if part time. As with other health professionals, they may be asked to work during nights, weekends, or holidays to provide twenty-four hour care for their patients. Nurses are usually given pay differentials for these shifts.

LPNs employed in hospitals and nursing homes, as well as in clinics, enjoy clean, well lighted and generally comfortable work environments. The nature of their work calls for LPNs to be on their feet for most of the shift—providing patient care, dispensing medication, or assisting other health personnel. Stamina, both physical and mental, is a must for this occupation. LPNs may be assigned to care for heavy or immobile patients, or patients confused with dementia. Patience, and a caring, nurturing attitude, are valuable qualities to possess in order to be a successful LPN.

Sources of Additional Information

American Association of Colleges of Nursing
1 Dupont Circle, Suite 530
Washington, DC 20036
Tel: 202-463-6930
Email: webmaster@aacn.nche.edu
WWW: http://www.aacn.nche.edu

National Association for Practical Nurse Education and Service, Inc.
1400 Spring Street, Suite 310
Silver Spring, MD 20910
Email: napnes@aol.com

National Federation of Licensed Practical Nurses, Inc.
1418 Aversboro Road
Garner, NC 27529
Tel: 919-779-0046
WWW: http://www.social.com/health/nhic

National League for Nursing
Communications Department
350 Hudson Street
New York, NY 10014
Tel: 212-989-9393
Email: nlnweb@nln.org
WWW: http://www.nln.org

Management Analysts and Consultants

Definition

Management analysts and consultants analyze business or operating procedures to devise the most efficient methods of accomplishing work. They gather and organize information about operating problems and procedures and prepare recommendations for implementing new systems or changes. They may update manuals outlining established methods of performing work and train personnel in new applications.

Nature of the Work

Management analysts and consultants are called in to solve any of a vast array of organizational problems. They are often needed when a rapidly growing small company needs a better system of control over inventories and expenses.

The role of the consultant is to come into a situation in which a client is unsure or inexpert and to recommend actions or provide assessments. There are many different types of management analysts and consultants. In general, they all require knowledge of general management, operations, marketing, logistics, materials management and physical distribution, finance and accounting, human resources, electronic data processing and systems, and management science.

Management analysts and consultants may be called in when a major manufacturer must reorganize its corporate structure when acquiring a new division. For example, they assist when a company relocates to another state by coordinating the move, planning the new facility, and training new workers.

The work of management analysts and consultants is quite flexible—it varies from job to job. In general, management analysts and consultants collect, review, and analyze data, make recommendations, and assist in the implementation of their proposals. Some projects require several consultants to work together, each specializing in a different area. Other jobs require the analysts to work independently.

Public and private organizations use management analysts for a variety of reasons. Some don't have adequate resources to handle a project. Others, before they pursue a particular course of action, will consult an analyst to determine what resources will be required or what problems will be encountered. Some organizations are seeking outside advice on how to resolve organizational problems that have already been identified or to avoid troublesome problems that could arise.

Firms providing consulting practitioners range in size from solo practitioners to large international organizations employing hundreds of people. The services are generally provided on a contract basis. A company will choose a consulting firm that specializes in the area that needs assistance, and then the two firms negotiate the conditions of the contract. Contract variables include the proposed cost of the project, staffing requirements, and deadline.

After getting a contract, the analyst's first job is to define the nature and extent of the project. He or she analyzes statistics, such as annual revenues, employment, or expenditures. He or she may also interview employees and observe the operations of the organization on a day-to-day basis.

The next step for the analyst is to use his or her knowledge of management systems to develop solutions. While preparing recommendations, he or she must take into account the general nature of the business, the relationship of the firm to others in its industry, the firm's internal organization, and the information gained through their data collection and analysis.

Once they have decided on a course of action, management analysts and consultants usually write reports of their findings and recommendations and present them to the client. They often make formal oral presentations about their findings as well. Some projects require only reports; others require assistance in implementing the suggestions.

Requirements

Employers generally prefer to hire management analysts and consultants with a master's degree in business or public administration, or at least a bachelor's degree and several years of appropriate work experience. Most government agencies offer entry-level analyst and consultant positions to people with bachelor's degrees and no work experience. Many entrants are also career changers who were formerly mid- and upper-level managers. With half the practicing management consultants self-employed, career changing is a common route into the field.

Many fields of study provide a suitable formal educational background for this occupation because of the diversity of problem areas addressed by management analysts and consultants. These include many areas in the computer and information sciences, engineering, business and management, education, communications, marketing and distribution, and architecture and environmental design.

When hired directly from school, management analysts and consultants often participate in formal company training programs. These programs may include instruction on policies and procedures, computer systems and software, and management practices and principles. Regardless of background, most management analysts and consultants routinely attend conferences to keep abreast of current developments in the field.

Opportunities for Experience & Exploration

The reference departments of most libraries include business areas that will have valuable research tools such as encyclopedias of business consultants and "who's who" of business consultants. These books should list management analysis and consulting firms across the country, describing their annual sales and areas of specialization, like industrial, high tech, small business, and retail. Interested students can call or write to these firms and ask for more information.

Methods of Entering

Anyone with some degree of business expertise or an expert field can begin to work as a consultant. The number of one- and two-person consulting firms in this country is well over one hundred thousand. Establishing a wide range of appropriate personal contacts is by far the most effective way to get started in this field. Consultants have to sell themselves and their expertise, a task far tougher than selling a tangible product the customer can see and handle. Many consultants get their first clients by advertising in newspapers, magazines, and trade or professional periodicals. After some time in the field, word-of-mouth advertising is often the primary force.

Thousands of business school professors work part-time as management analysts or consultants, entering on the basis of their academic achievement.

Others enter the field through accounting firms known as management consulting services. Others begin as in-house consultants, working for organizations that have their own management consulting operations.

Advancement

A new consultant in a large firm may be referred to as an associate for the first couple of years. The next progression is to senior associate, a title that indicates three to five years experience and the ability to supervise others and do more complex and independent work. After about five years, the analyst who is progressing well may become an engagement manager with the responsibility to lead a consulting team on a particular client project. The best managers become senior engagement managers, leading several study teams or a very large project team. After about seven years, those who excel will be considered for appointment as junior partners or principals. Partnership involves responsibility for marketing the firm and leading client projects. Some may be promoted to senior partnership or director, but few people successfully run this full course. Management analysts and consultants with entrepreneurial ambition may open their own firms.

Employment
Outlook

In 1996, management analysts and consultants held about 244,000 jobs in the United States. About half of these people were self-employed. Federal, state, and local governments employed many of the others. The Department of Defense employed the majority of those working for the federal government. The remainder worked in the private sector for companies providing consulting services.

Although management analysts and consultants are found throughout the country, the majority are concentrated in major metropolitan areas.

Through the year 2006, employment of management analysts is expected to grow faster than the average for all occupations. Industry and government agencies are expected to rely more and more on the expertise of these professionals to improve and streamline the performance of their organizations. Many job openings will result from the need to replace personnel who transfer to other fields or leave the labor force.

The challenging nature of this job, coupled with high salary potential, attracts many. A graduate degree, experience and expertise in the industry, as well as a knack for public relations, are needed to stay competitive.

Earnings

Salaries and hourly rates for management analysts and consultants vary widely, according to experience, specialization, education, and employer. A 1996 survey conducted by the Association of Management Consulting Firms showed the average salary (including bonuses and other perks) for management firm employees to be about $35,200 in an entry-level position; senior consultants earned $74,300; junior partners, $91,100; and senior partners, $167,100. The median annual earnings were about $39,500, with the middle 50 percent of these workers earning between $30,200 and $81,500.

Many consultants can demand between $400 and $1,000 per day. Their fees are often well over $40 per hour. Self-employed management consultants

receive no fringe benefits and generally have to maintain their own office, but their pay is usually much higher than salaried consultants. They can make more than $2,000 per day or $250,000 in one year from consulting just two days per week.

In 1997, according to the U.S. Department of Labor, management analysts with a college degree earned an average starting salary of $55,240 a year while working for the Federal government.

Typical benefits for salaried analysts and consultants include health and life insurance, retirement plans, vacation and sick leave, profit sharing, and bonuses for outstanding work. All travel expenses are generally reimbursed by the employer.

Conditions
of Work

Management analysts and consultants generally divide their time between their own offices and the client's office or production facility. They can spend a great deal of time on the road.

Most management analysts and consultants work at least forty hours per week plus overtime depending on the project. The nature of consulting projects—working on location with a single client toward a specific goal—allows these professionals to totally immerse themselves in their work. They sometimes work fourteen- to sixteen-hour days, and six- or seven-day workweeks can be fairly common.

While self-employed, consultants may enjoy the luxury of setting their own hours and doing a great deal of their work at home; the trade-off is sacrificing the benefits provided by the large firms. Their livelihood depends on the additional responsibility of maintaining and expanding their clientele on their own.

Although those in this career usually avoid much of the potential tedium of working for one company all day, every day, they face many pressures resulting from deadlines and client expectations. Because the clients are generally paying generous fees, they want to see dramatic results, and the management analyst can feel the weight of this.

Management analysts and consultants are often responsible for recommending layoffs of staff, so it is important that they learn to deal with people diplomatically. Their job requires a great deal of tact, enlisting cooperation while exerting leadership, debating their points, and pointing out errors. Consultants must be quick thinkers, able to refute objections with finality. They also must be able to make excellent presentations.

A management analyst must be unbiased and analytical, with a disposition toward the intellectual side of business and a natural curiosity about the way things work best.

Sources of Additional Information

American Management Association
135 West 50th Street
New York, NY 10020
Tel: 212-586-8100

American Institute of Certified Public Accountants
Management Consulting Services Division
Harborside Financial Plaza
201 Plaza Three
Jersey City, NJ 07311-3881
Tel: 201-938-3000

For industry information, please contact:

Association of Internal Management Consultants
7960-B Soquel Drive, Suite 298
Aptos, CA 95003
Tel: 408-662-9890
WWW: http://www.benchnet.com1/aimc

Association of Management Consulting Firms
521 Fifth Avenue, 35th floor
New York, NY 10175
Tel: 212-697-9693

Mechanical Engineers

Definition

Mechanical engineers plan and design tools, engines, machines, and other mechanical systems that produce, transmit, or use power. Their work varies by industry and function. They may work in design, instrumentation, testing, robotics, transportation, or bioengineering, among other areas. As in all engineering professions, the goal of the mechanical engineer is to make sure that the mechanical systems he or she develops are as efficient as possible.

Nature of the Work

Mechanical engineering is the broadest engineering discipline. Most mechanical engineers work in manufacturing, and are employed by a wide variety of industries. For example, manufacturers of industrial and office machinery, farm equipment, automobiles, petroleum, pharmaceuticals, fabricated metal products, pulp and paper, electronics, utilities, computers, soap and cosmetics, and heating, ventilating, and air-conditioning systems employ mechanical engineers. Others are self-employed or work for consulting firms, government agencies, or colleges and universities. Despite the variety of settings, the goal of most mechanical engineers is the same: to develop machines and mechanical systems that are reliable, efficient, and safe.

The work of mechanical engineering begins with research and development. A company may need to develop a more fuel-efficient automobile engine, for example, or a cooling system for air-conditioning and refrigeration that does not use materials that harm the earth's atmosphere. The *research engineer* explores the project's theoretical, mechanical, and material problems. He or she performs experiments to gather necessary data and acquire new knowledge. Often, an experimental device or system is developed.

The *design engineer* takes information gained from research and development and uses it to plan a commercially useful product. To prevent rotting in a grain storage system, for example, a design engineer might use research on a new method of circulating air through grain. He or she would be responsible for specifying every detail of the machine or mechanical system. Since the introduction of sophisticated software programs, mechanical engineers have increasingly used computers in the design process.

After the product has been designed and a prototype developed, the product is analyzed by *testing engineers*. A tractor transmission, for example, would need to be tested for temperature, vibration, dust, and performance under the required loads, as well as for any government safety regulations. If dust is penetrating a bearing, the testing engineer would refer the problem to the design engineer, who would then adjust the design of the transmission. Design and testing engineers continue to work together until the product meets the necessary criteria.

Once the final design is set, it is the job of the *manufacturing engineer* to come up with the most time-efficient and cost-efficient way of making the product, without sacrificing quality. The amount of factory floor space, the type of manufacturing equipment and machinery, and the cost of labor and materials are some of the factors that must be considered. Engineers select the necessary equipment and machines and oversee their arrangement and safe operation. Other engineering specialists, such as chemical, electrical, and industrial engineers, may provide assistance.

Some types of mechanical systems—from machinery on a factory floor to a nuclear power plant—are so sophisticated that mechanical engineers are needed to oversee operation and ongoing maintenance. With the help of computers, *mainte-*

nance and *operations engineers* use their specialized knowledge to monitor these complex systems and to make necessary adjustments.

Mechanical engineers also work in marketing, sales, and administration. Because of their training in mechanical engineering, *sales engineers* can give customers a detailed explanation of how a machine or system works. They may also be able to alter its design to meet a customer's needs.

In a small company, a mechanical engineer may need to perform many, if not most, of the above responsibilities. Some tasks might be assigned to *consulting engineers,* who are either self-employed or work for a consulting firm.

Other mechanical engineers may work in a number of specialized areas. *Energy specialists* work with power production machines to supply clean and efficient energy to individuals and industries. *Application engineers* specialize in computer-aided design and manufacturing (CAD/CAM) systems. *Process engineers* work in environmental sciences to reduce air pollution levels without sacrificing essential services such as those provided by power stations or utility companies

Requirements

A bachelor's degree in mechanical engineering is usually the minimum educational requirement for entering this field. A master's degree, or even a Ph.D., may be necessary to qualify for some positions, such as those in research, teaching, and administration.

In the United States, there are about 350 colleges and universities where engineering programs have been approved by the Accreditation Board for Engineering and Technology (ABET). Most of these institutions offer programs in mechanical engineering. Engineering technology is offered at about 250 of these colleges and universities.

Although admissions requirements vary slightly from school to school, most require a solid background in mathematics and science. High school students interested in mechanical engineering should take courses in algebra, geometry, trigonometry, and calculus. One year of physics, and one of chemistry is recommended. As reading and writing are important skills for mechanical engineers, four years of English should be taken. Finally, because computers are such an important part of today's engineering, computer science courses are also good choices.

In a four-year undergraduate program, students typically begin by studying essential mathematics and science subjects, such as calculus, differential equations, physics, and chemistry. Course work in liberal arts and elementary mechanical engineering is also taken. By the third year, students begin to study the technical core subjects of mechanical engineering—mechanics, thermodynamics, fluid mechanics, design manufacturing, and heat transfer—as well as such specialized topics as power generation and transmission, computer-aided design (CAD), and the properties of materials.

At some schools, there is a five- or six-year program that combines classroom study of mechanical engineering with practical experience working for an engineering firm. Although these cooperative, or work-study, programs take longer, they offer significant advantages. Not only does the salary help pay for educational expenses, but the student has the opportunity to apply theoretical knowledge to actual work problems in mechanical engineering; in addition, he or she graduates with valuable work experience, which is often sought by employers. In some cases, the company may offer full-time employment to its co-op workers after graduation.

There are more than one hundred accredited graduate mechanical engineering programs in the United States. In graduate school, students are required to specialize in one area of mechanical engineering. A master's degree takes one to two years of full-time study beyond the undergraduate degree. A Ph.D. program lasts considerably longer, often taking four to six years.

A graduate degree is a prerequisite for becoming a university professor or researcher. It may also lead to a higher-level job and promotion within an engineering department or firm. Some companies encourage their employees to pursue graduate education by offering tuition-reimbursement programs. Because technology is rapidly developing, mechanical engineers need to continue their education, formally or informally, throughout their careers. Conferences, seminars, and professional journals serve to educate engineers about developments in the field.

Personal qualities essential for mechanical engineers include the ability to think analytically, to problem solve, and to work with abstract ideas. Attention to detail is also important, as are good oral and written communications skills and the ability to work well in groups. Computer literacy is essential.

All fifty states and the District of Columbia require the registration of engineers whose work may affect the life, health, or safety of the public. Applicants for registration must have received a degree from an engineering program accredited by ABET and have four years of experience. They must also pass a written examination.

Many mechanical engineers also become certified. Certification is a status conferred by a professional or technical society for the purpose of recognizing and documenting an individual's abilities in a specific engineering field.

Opportunities for Experience & Exploration

One of the best ways to learn about the field is to talk with a mechanical engineer. It might also be helpful to tour an industrial plant or visit a local museum specializing in science and industry. Public libraries usually have books on mechanical engineering that might be enlightening. Finally, some high schools offer engineering clubs or organizations. Membership in the Junior Engineering Technical Society (JETS), a national organization, is recommended for prospective mechanical engineers.

Methods of Entering

Many mechanical engineers find their first job through their college or university placement office. Many companies send recruiters to college campuses to interview and sign up engineering graduates. Other students may find a position in the company where they had summer or part-time employment.

Newspapers and professional journals often list job openings for engineers. Job seekers who wish to work for the federal government should contact the nearest branch of the Office of Personnel Management.

Advancement

As engineers gain experience, they can advance to jobs with a wider scope of responsibility and higher pay. Some of these higher-level jobs include technical service and development officers, team leaders, research directors, and managers. Some mechanical engineers use their technical knowledge in sales and marketing positions, while others form their own engineering business or consulting firm.

Many engineers advance by furthering their education. A master's degree in business administration, besides an engineering degree, is sometimes helpful in obtaining an administrative position. A master's or doctoral degree in an engineering specialty may also lead to executive work. In addition, those with graduate degrees often have the option of research or teaching positions.

Employment Outlook

There were approximately 228,000 mechanical engineers employed in the United States in 1996. Six out of ten mechanical engineers worked in manufacturing fields, such as machinery, transportation (including automotive) equipment, electrical equipment, instruments, and fabricated metal products. The remainder were largely found in government agencies and consulting firms.

The employment of mechanical engineers is expected to grow about as fast as average through the year 2006. This specialty was recently included in *U.S. News & World Report's* article, "Best Jobs for the Future." Engineers will be needed in response to the demand for more efficient industrial machinery and machine tools. Industries involved in transportation, environmental controls, bioengineering, energy conversion, and robotics are particularly expected to have increasing needs for mechanical engineers to meet the technological requirements of the future. Many job openings will also result from older engineers retiring from the workforce.

It should be noted, however, that reductions in defense spending may adversely affect the employment outlook for engineers within the federal government.

Earnings

Engineers enjoy higher than average salaried compared to other fields. According to the National Association of Colleges and Employers, starting salaries in 1997 for mechanical engineers average around $38,113 a year. Typically, compensation is considerably higher for those with a graduate degree or more experience. Mid-level engineers earned about $49,700 in 1996. Those with a great deal of experience can earn salaries in the upper $60,000s to the mid $70,000s, and those in top management positions might earn $90,000 or more. Level VIII engineers, the highest ranking, averaged $117,000 a year in 1996. Experienced engineers employed by the federal government average about $61,950 a year.

Like most professionals, mechanical engineers who work for a company usually receive a generous benefits package, including vacation days, sick leave, health and life insurance, and savings and pension programs. Self-employed mechanical engineers must provide their own benefits.

Conditions of Work

The working conditions of mechanical engineers vary. Most engineers work indoors in offices, research laboratories, or production departments of factories. Depending on the job, however, a significant amount of work time may be spent on a noisy factory floor, at a construction site, or at another field operation. Mechanical engineers have traditionally designed systems on drafting boards, but, since the introduction of sophisticated software programs, design has increasingly been done on computers.

Engineering is, for the most part, a cooperative effort. While the specific duties of an engineer may require him or her to work individually, each project is typically the job of an engineering team. Such a team might include other engineers, engineering technicians, and engineering technologists.

Mechanical engineers generally have a forty-hour workweek. However, their working hours are often dictated by the projects they are assigned to and the deadlines they must meet. They may work long hours to meet a deadline, or show up on second or third shifts to check production at a factory or a construction project.

Mechanical engineering can be a very satisfying occupation. Engineers often get the pleasure of seeing their designs or modifications put into actual, tangible form. Conversely, it can be frustrating when a project is stalled, full of errors, or even abandoned completely.

Sources of Additional Information

For information on colleges and universities offering accredited engineering programs, contact:

Accreditation Board for Engineering and Technology
111 Market Place, Suite 1050
Baltimore, MD 21202
Tel: 410-347-7700
Email: abet@tardis.union.edu
WWW: http://www.tardis.union.edu/ABET/

For information on mechanical engineering and mechanical engineering technology, contact:

American Society of Mechanical Engineers
345 East 47th Street
New York, NY 10017
Tel: 212-705-7158
WWW: http://www.asme.org

For information on high school programs that allow students to learn more about engineering, contact:

Junior Engineering Technical Society (JETS)
1420 King Street, Suite 405
Alexandria, VA 22314
Tel: 703-548-5387
Email: jets@nas.edu
WWW: http://www.sol.asee.org/jets/

Medical Assistants

Definition

Medical assistants help physicians in offices, hospitals, and clinics. They keep medical records, help examine and treat patients, and perform routine office duties to allow physicians to spend their time working directly with patients. Medical assistants are vitally important to the smooth and efficient operation of medical offices.

Nature of the Work

Depending on the size of the office, medical assistants may perform clerical or clinical duties, or both. The larger the office, the greater the chance that the assistant will specialize in one type of work.

In their clinical duties, medical assistants help physicians by preparing patients for examination or treatment. They may check and record a patient's blood pressure, pulse, temperature, height, and weight. Medical assistants often ask patients questions about their medical histories and record the answers in the patient's file. In the examining room the medical assistant may be responsible for arranging medical instruments and handing them to the physician as requested during the examination. Medical assistants may prepare patients for X-rays and laboratory examinations, as well as administer electrocardiograms. They may apply dressings, draw blood, and give injections. Medical assistants also may give patients instructions about taking medications, watching their diet, or restricting their activities before laboratory tests or surgery. In addition, medical assistants may collect specimens such as throat cultures for laboratory tests and may be responsible for sterilizing examining room instruments and equipment.

Medical assistants are responsible for preparing examining rooms for patients and keeping examining and waiting rooms clean and orderly. After each examination, they straighten the examination room and dispose of used linens and medical supplies. Sometimes medical assistants keep track of office and medical supply inventories and order necessary supplies. They may deal with pharmaceutical and medical supply company representatives when ordering supplies.

At other times medical assistants may perform a wide range of administrative tasks. *Medical secretaries* and *medical receptionists* also perform administrative activities in medical offices, but these workers are distinguished from medical assistants by the fact that they rarely perform clinical functions. The administrative and clerical tasks that medical assistants may complete include typing case histories and operation reports; keeping office files, X-rays, and other medical records up-to-date; keeping the office's financial records; preparing and sending bills and receiving payments; and transcribing dictation from the physician. Assistants may also answer the telephone, greet patients, fill out insurance forms, schedule appointments, take care of correspondence, and arrange for patients to be admitted to the hospital. Most medical assistants use word processors and computers for most recordkeeping tasks.

Some medical assistants work in ophthalmologists' offices, where their clinical duties involve helping with eye exams and treatments. They use special equipment to test and measure patients' eyes and check for disease. They administer eye drops and dressings and teach patients how to insert and care for contact lenses. They may maintain surgical instruments and help physicians during eye surgery. Other medical assistants work as *optometric assistants*, who may be required to prepare patients for examination and assist them in eyewear selection. Others work as *chiropractor assistants*, whose duties may include treatment and examination of patients' muscular and skeletal problems.

Requirements

Medical assistants usually need a high school diploma, but in many cases they receive their specific training on the job. High school courses in the sciences, especially biology, are helpful to the prospective medical assistant, as are courses in algebra, English, bookkeeping, typing, computers, and office practices.

Formal training for medical assistants is available at many trade schools, community and junior colleges, and universities. College programs generally award an associate's degree and take two years to complete. Other programs can last as long as a year and award a diploma or certificate. Prior to enrolling in any school program, students should check its curriculum and verify its accreditation.

Schools for medical assistants may be accredited by either the Commission on Accreditation of Allied Health Education Programs, which has approved more than 200 medical and ophthalmic programs, or the Accrediting Bureau of Health Education Schools, which accredits over 150 medical assisting programs. Students in these programs do coursework in biology, anatomy, physiology, and medical terminology, as well as typing, transcribing, shorthand, recordkeeping, and computer skills. Perhaps most important, these programs provide supervised, hands-on clinical experience in which students learn laboratory techniques, first-aid procedures, proper use of medical equipment, and clinical procedures. They also learn about administrative duties and procedures in medical offices and receive training in interpersonal communications and medical ethics.

Medical assistants generally do not need be licensed. However, they may voluntarily take examinations for credentials awarded by certain professional organizations. The registered medical assistant (RMA) credential is awarded by American Medical Technologists and the American Registry of Medical Assistants, and the American Association of Medical Assistants (AAMA) awards a credential for certified medical assistant (CMA). Ophthalmic assistants can be certified at three levels by the Joint Commission on Allied Health Personnel in Ophthalmology: certified ophthalmic assistant, certified ophthalmic technician, and certified ophthalmic technologist.

Medical assistants must be able to interact with patients and other medical personnel, and they must be able to follow detailed directions. In addition, they must be dependable and compassionate and have the desire to help people. Medical assistants must also respect patients privacy by keeping medical information confidential. Overall, medical assistants who help patients feel at ease in the doctor's office and have good communications skills and a desire to serve should do well in this job.

Opportunities for Experience & Exploration

Students in post–high school medical assistant programs will have the chance to explore the field through the supervised clinical experience required by the various programs. Others may wish to gain additional experience by volunteering at hospitals, nursing homes, or clinics to get a feel for the work involved in a medical environment. People interested in this field may want to talk with the medical assistants in their own or other local physicians' offices to find out more about the work they do.

Methods of Entering

Students enrolled in college or other post–high school medical assistant programs may learn of available positions through their school placement offices. High school guidance counselors may have information about positions for students about to graduate. Newspaper want ads and state employment offices are other good places to look for leads. Workers may also wish to call local physicians' offices to find out about unadvertised openings.

Advancement

To advance, many medical assistants must change occupations. Medical assistants may be able to move into managerial or administrative positions without further education, but moving into a more advanced clinical position such as nursing requires more education. As more and more clinics and group practices open, more office managers will be needed, and these are positions that well-qualified, experienced medical assistants may be able to fill. As with most occupations, today's job market gives medical assistants with computer skills more opportunities for advancement.

Employment Outlook

In 1996, about 225,000 medical assistants worked in physicians' offices, clinics, hospitals, health maintenance organizations, and other medical facilities. Over 70 percent work in private doctors' offices. Another 10 percent work in optometrists' and chiropractors' offices and other health care facilities. The ratio of medical assistant personnel to physicians is about seven to one.

The employment outlook for medical assistants is expected to be exceptionally good through the year 2006. Most openings will arise to replace workers who leave their jobs, but many will be the result of a predicted surge in the number of physicians' offices and outpatient care facilities. Technological advances and the growing number of elderly Americans who need medical treatment is also a factor in this increased demand for health services. In addition, new and more complex paperwork for medical insurance, malpractice insurance, government programs, and other purposes will create a growing need for assistants in medical offices.

Experienced and formally trained medical assistants are preferred by many physicians, so these workers have the best employment outlook. Word-processing skills, other computer skills, and formal certification are all definite assets.

Earnings

The earnings of medical assistants vary widely, depending on experience, skill level, and location. According to a 1997 Staff Salary Survey, published by the Health Care Group, the average starting salary for graduates of the medical assistant programs they accredit is about $14,500. With experience, medical assistants may eventually earn an average of $24,793 a year. Earnings are higher in the Northeast and the West as compared to other regions of the United States.

Conditions of Work

Most medical assistants work in pleasant, modern surroundings, although older hospitals and clinics may be less well-ventilated. Sterilizing equipment and handling medical instruments require care and attentiveness. As most professionals in the health sciences will attest, working with people who are ill may be upsetting at times, but it can also have many personal rewards.

Most medical assistants work forty hours a week, frequently including some Saturday and evening hours. They are usually given six or seven paid holidays a year, as well as annual paid vacation days. They often receive health and life insurance, a retirement plan, sick leave, and uniform allowances.

Sources of Additional Information

■**American Registry of Medical Assistants**
69 Southwick Road, Suite A
Westfield, MA 01085-4729
Tel: 413-562-7336

For information on accreditation and testing, please contact:

■**Accrediting Bureau of Health Education Schools**
Oak Manor Office, 29089 US 20 West
Elkhart, IN 46514
Tel: 219-293-0124

For an information packet on a career as a medical assistant, please contact:

■**American Association of Medical Assistants**
20 North Wacker Drive, Suite 1575
Chicago, IL 60606
Tel: 312-899-1500

■**American Medical Technologists**
710 Higgins Road
Park Ridge, IL 60068
Tel: 847-823-5169

Medical Record Technicians

Definition

In any hospital, clinic, or other health care facility, permanent records are created and maintained for all the patients treated by the staff. Each patient's medical record describes in detail his or her condition over time; entries include illness and injuries, operations, treatments, outpatient visits, and the progress of hospital stays. *Medical record technicians* compile, code, and maintain these records. They also tabulate and analyze data from groups of records in order to assemble reports. They review records for completeness and accuracy; assign codes to the diseases, operations, diagnoses, and treatments according to detailed standardized classification systems; and post the codes on the medical record, thus making the information on the record easier to retrieve and analyze. They transcribe medical reports; maintain indices of patients, diseases, operations, and other categories of information; compile patient census data; and file records or supervise others who do so. In addition, they may direct the day-to-day operations of the medical records department. They maintain the flow of records and reports to and from other departments, and sometimes assist medical staff in special studies or research that draws on information in the records.

Nature of the Work

A patient's medical record consists of all relevant information and observations of any health care workers who have dealt with the patient. It may contain, for example, several diagnoses, X-ray and laboratory reports, electrocardiogram tracings, test results, and drugs prescribed. This summary of the patient's medical history is very important to the physician in making speedy and correct decisions about care. Later, information from the record is often needed in authenticating legal forms and insurance claims. The medical record documents the adequacy and appropriateness of the care received by the patient and is the basis of any investigation when the care is questioned in any way.

Patterns and trends can be traced when data from many records are considered together. These types of statistical reports are used by many different groups. Hospital administrators, scientists, public health agencies, accrediting and licensing bodies, people who evaluate the effectiveness of current programs or plan future ones, and medical reimbursement organizations are examples of some groups that rely on health care statistics. Medical records can provide the data to show whether a new treatment or medication really works, the relative effectiveness of alternative treatments or medications, or patterns that yield clues about the causes or methods of preventing certain kinds of disease.

Medical record technicians are involved in the routine preparation, handling, and safeguarding of individual records as well as the statistical information extracted from groups of records. Their specific tasks and the scope of their responsibilities depend a great deal on the size and type of the employing institution. In large organizations, there may be a number of technicians and other employees working with medical records. The technicians may serve as assistants to the *medical record administrator* as needed or may regularly specialize in some particular phase of the work done by the department. In small facilities, however, technicians often carry out the whole range of activities and may function fairly independently, perhaps bearing the full responsibility for all day-to-day operations of the department. A technician in a small facility may even be a department director. Sometimes technicians handle medical records and also spend part of their time helping out in the business or admitting office.

Although most medical record technicians work in hospitals, many work in other health care settings, including health maintenance organizations (HMOs), industrial clinics, skilled nursing facilities, rehabilitation centers, large group medical practices, ambulatory care centers, and state and local government health agencies. Records are maintained in all these facilities, although record-keeping procedures vary.

Whether they work in hospitals or other settings, medical record technicians must organize, transfer, analyze, preserve, and locate vast quantities of detailed information when needed. The sources of this information include physicians, nurses, laboratory workers, and other members of the health care team.

In a hospital, a patient's cumulative record goes to the medical record department at the end of the hospital stay. A technician checks over the information in the file to be sure that all the essential reports and data are included and appear accurate. Certain specific items must be supplied in any record, such as signatures, dates, the patient's physical and social history, the results of physical examinations, provisional and final diagnoses, periodic progress notes on the patient's condition during the hospital stay, medications prescribed and administered, therapeutic treatments, surgical procedures, and an assessment of the outcome or the condition at the time of discharge. If any item is missing, the technician sends the record to the person who is responsible for supplying the information. After all necessary information has been received and the record has passed the review, it is considered the official document describing the patient's case.

The record is then passed to a *medical record coder*. Coders are responsible for assigning a numeric code to every diagnosis and procedure listed in a patient's file. Most hospitals in the United States use a nationally accepted system for coding. The lists of diseases, procedures, and conditions are published in classification manuals that medical records personnel refer to frequently. By reducing information in different forms to a single consistent coding system, the data contained in the record is rendered much easier to handle, tabulate, and analyze. It can be indexed under any suitable heading; for example, under patient, disease, type of surgery, physician attending the case, and so forth. Cross-indexing is likely to be an important part of the medical record technician's job. Because the

same coding systems are used nearly everywhere in the United States, the data may be used not only by people working inside the hospital, but may also be submitted to one of the various programs that pool information obtained from many institutions.

After the information on the medical record has been coded, technicians may use a packaged computer program to assign the patient to one of several hundred "diagnosis-related groupings," or DRGs. The DRG for the patient's stay determines the amount of money the hospital will receive if the patient is covered by Medicare or one of the other insurance programs that base their reimbursement on DRGs.

A vital part of the job concerns filing. Regardless of how accurately and completely information is gathered and stored, it is worthless unless it can be retrieved promptly. If paper records are kept, technicians are usually responsible for preparing records for storage, filing them, and getting them out of storage when needed. In some organizations, technicians supervise other personnel who carry out these tasks.

In many health care facilities, computers, rather than paper, are used for nearly all the medical record-keeping. In such cases, medical and nursing staff make notes on an electronic "chart." They enter patient care information into computer files, and medical record technicians access the information using their own terminals. Computers have greatly simplified many traditional routine tasks of the medical records department, such as generating daily hospital census figures, tabulating data for research purposes, and updating special registries of certain types of diseases, such as cancer and stroke.

Confidentiality and privacy laws have a major bearing on the medical records field. The laws vary in different states, but in all cases, maintaining the confidentiality of individual records is a major concern of medical records workers. All individual records must be in secure storage but also available for retrieval and authorized use. Technicians may be responsible for retrieving and releasing this information. They may prepare records to be released in response to a patient's written authorization, a subpoena, or a court order. This requires special knowledge of legal statutes and often requires consultation with attorneys, judges, insurance agents, and other parties with legitimate rights access information about a person's health and medical treatment.

Medical record technicians may participate in the quality assurance, risk management, and utilization review activities of a health care facility. In these cases, he or she may serve as a data abstractor and analyst, reviewing records against established standards to ensure quality of care. He or she may also prepare statistical reports for the medical or administrative staff that reviews appropriateness of care.

With more specialized training, medical record technicians may participate in medical research activities by maintaining special records, called registries, related to such areas as cancer, heart disease, transplants, or adverse outcomes of pregnancies. In some cases, they are required to abstract and code information from records of patients with certain medical conditions. These technicians also may prepare statistical reports and trend analysis for the use of medical researchers.

Not all medical record technicians are employed in a single health care facility; some serve as consultants to several small facilities. Other technicians do not work in health care settings at all. They may be employed by health and property liability insurance companies to collect and review information on medical claims. Government agencies also hire some medical record technicians, as do manufacturers of medical records systems and equipment. A few are self-employed, providing medical transcription services.

Requirements

Most employers prefer to hire medical record technicians who have completed a two-year associate's degree program accredited by the American Medical Association's Commission on Accreditation of Allied Health Professions (CAAHP) and the American Health Information Management Association (AHIMA). There are approximately 150 of these accredited programs available throughout the United States, mostly offered in junior and community colleges. They usually include classroom instruction in such subjects as anatomy, physiology, medical terminology, medical record science, word processing, medical aspects of recordkeeping, statistics, computers in health care, personnel supervision, business management, English, and office skills.

In addition to classroom instruction, the student is given supervised clinical experience in the medical records departments of local health care facilities. This provides the student with practical experience in performing many of the functions learned in the classroom and with the opportunity to interact with health care professionals.

An alternative educational method is open to individuals with experience in certain related activities. It requires completion of an independent study program offered by the AHIMA. Students in this program must successfully complete a lesson series and clinical experience internship in a health care institution. They must also earn thirty semester hours of credit in prescribed subjects at a college or university.

For either entry method, a high school diploma is required. Students contemplating a career in medical records should take as many high school English classes as possible, because technicians need both written and verbal communication skills to prepare reports and communicate with other health care personnel. Basic math or business math is very desirable because statistical skills are important in some job functions. Biology courses help by familiarizing the student with the terminology that medical record technicians use. Other science courses, computer training, typing, and office procedures are also helpful.

Medical record technicians who have completed an accredited training program are eligible to take a national qualifying examination to earn the credential of *accredited record technician* (ART). Most health care institutions prefer to hire individuals with an ART credential as it signifies that they have met the standards established by the AHIMA as the mark of a qualified health professional.

Technicians who have achieved the ART credential are required to obtain twenty hours of continuing education credits every two years in order to retain their ART status. These credits may be obtained by attending educational programs, participating in further academic study, or pursuing independent study activities approved by the AHIMA.

Medical records are extremely detailed and precise. Sloppy work could have serious consequences in terms of payment to the hospital or physician, validity of the patient records for later use, and validity of research based on data from medical records. Therefore, a prospective technician must have the capacity to do consistently reliable and accurate routine work. Records must be completed and maintained with care and attention to detail. The medical record technician may be the only person who checks the entire record, and he or she must understand the responsibility that accompanies this task.

The technician needs to be able to work rapidly as well as accurately. In many medical record departments, the work load is very heavy, and technicians must be well organized and efficient in order to stay on top of the job. They must be able to complete their work in spite of interruptions, such as phone calls and requests for assistance. These workers also need to be discrete as they deal with records that are private and sometimes sensitive. Computer skills also are essential, and experience in transcribing dictated reports may be useful.

Opportunities for Experience & Exploration

Interested high school students may be able to find summer, part-time, or volunteer work in a hospital or other health care facility. Sometimes such jobs are available in the medical records area of an organization. This experience could provide an ideal chance to measure aptitude and interests against those of people already employed in the medical records field.

Students may also be able to arrange to talk with someone working as a medical record technician or administrator. Faculty and counselors at schools that offer medical record technician training programs may also be good sources of information. Interested students also can learn more about this profession by reading journals and other literature available at a public library.

Methods of Entering

Most successful medical record technicians are graduates of two-year accredited programs. Graduates of these programs should check with school placement offices for job leads. For those who have taken the accrediting exam and become ARTs, the AHIMA offers a resume referral service.

Individuals may also apply directly to the personnel departments of hospitals, nursing homes, outpatient clinics, and surgery centers. Many job openings are also listed in the classified sections of local newspapers and with private and public employment agencies.

Advancement

Medical record technicians may be able to achieve some advancement and salary increase without additional training simply by taking on greater responsibility in their job function. With experience, they may move to supervisory or department head positions, depending on the type and structure of the employing organization.

Another means of advancing is through specialization in a certain area of the job. Some technicians specialize in coding, particularly Medicare coding or tumor registry. With a broad range of experience, some technicians may be able to establish themselves as independent consultants. Generally, technicians with an associate's degree and the ART designation are most likely to advance.

More assured job advancement and salary increase come with the completion of a bachelor's degree in medical record administration. The bachelor's degree, along with AHIMA accreditation, makes the technician eligible for a supervisory position, such as department director. Because of a general shortage of medical record administrators, hospitals often assist technicians who are working toward a bachelor's degree by providing flexible scheduling and financial aid or tuition reimbursement.

Employment Outlook

Most employment opportunities exist in hospitals; however, opportunities can be found in extended-care facilities, ambulatory-care facilities, HMOs, medical group practices, nursing homes, and home-health agencies. Technicians also work for computer firms, consulting firms, and government agencies.

Employment prospects for this field are excellent. The demand for well-trained medical record technicians will grow rapidly and will continue to exceed the supply. It is estimated that 47,000 new medical tech jobs will be created by the year 2006, according to the U.S. Department of Labor's Bureau of Labor Statistics. This forecast is related to the health care needs of a population that is both growing and aging and the trend toward more technologically sophisticated medicine and greater use of diagnostic procedures. It is also related to the increased requirements of regulatory bodies that scrutinize both costs and quality of care of health care providers. Because of the fear of medical malpractice lawsuits, doctors and other health care providers are documenting their diagnoses and treatments in greater detail. Also, because of the high cost of health care, insurance companies, government agencies, and courts are examining medical records with a more critical eye. These factors combine to ensure a healthy job outlook for medical record technicians.

Technicians with two-year associate's degrees and ART status will have the best prospects, and the importance of such qualifications is likely to increase.

Earnings

The salaries of medical record technicians are greatly influenced by the location, size, and type of employing institution, as well as the technician's training and experience. Beginning technicians who have earned their ART status can expect to earn between $20,000 and $25,000 a year. The average salary for all ARTs is between $35,000 and $36,000. With experience and, perhaps, specialization in a particular area, technicians may earn as much as $47,000 annually. Technicians who are not accredited typically earn somewhat less.

By earning a bachelor's degree or other advanced degree, the technician becomes more valuable to an employer and can expect higher wages. These technicians eventually can reach salary levels in the high $70,000s or the low $80,000s.

In general, medical record technicians working in large urban hospitals make the most money, and those in rural areas make the least. Like most hospital employees, medical record technicians usually receive paid vacations and holidays, life and health insurance, and retirement benefits.

Conditions of Work

Medical records departments are usually pleasantly clean, well-lighted, and air-conditioned areas. Sometimes, however, paper or microfilm records are kept in cramped, out-of-the-way quarters. Although the work requires thorough and careful attention to detail, there may be a constant bustle of activity in the technician's work area, which can be disruptive. The job is likely to involve frequent routine contact with nurses, physicians, hospital administrators, other health care professionals, attorneys, and insurance agents. On occasion, individuals who the technicians may interact with are demanding or difficult. In such cases, technicians may find that the job carries a high level of frustration.

A forty-hour workweek is the norm, but because hospitals must operate on a twenty-four-hour basis, the job may regularly include night or weekend hours. Part-time work is sometimes available.

The work is extremely detailed and may be tedious. Some technicians spend the majority of their day sitting at a desk, working on a computer. Others may spend hours filing paper records or retrieving them from storage.

In many hospital settings, the medical record technician experiences pressure caused by a heavy workload. As the demands for health care cost containment and productivity increases, medical record technicians may be required to produce a significantly greater volume of high-quality work in shorter periods of time.

Nonetheless, the knowledge that their work is significant for patients and medical research can be personally very satisfying for medical record technicians.

Sources of Additional Information

For information on careers in health information management and ART accreditation, contact:

American Health Information Management Association
919 North Michigan Avenue, Suite 1400
Chicago, IL 60611
Tel: 312-787-2672
WWW: http://www.ahima.org

For a list of schools offering accredited programs in health information management, contact:

Commission on Accreditation of Allied Health Education Professions
American Medical Association
515 North State Street, Suite 7530
Chicago, IL 60610
Tel: 312-464-5000

Musicians

Definition

Musicians perform, compose, conduct, arrange, and teach music. Performers of music would include singers as well as instrumental musicians. Performing musicians may work alone or as part of a group, or ensemble. They may play before live audiences in clubs or auditoriums, or they may perform on television or radio, in motion pictures, or in a recording studio. Musicians usually play either classical, popular (including country and western), jazz or folk music, but many musicians play in several musical styles.

Nature of the Work

Instrumental musicians play one or more musical instruments, usually in a group and in some cases as featured soloists. Musical instruments are usually classified in several distinct categories according to the method by which they produce sound: strings (violins, cellos, basses, etc.), which make sounds by vibrations from bowing or plucking; woodwinds (oboes, clarinets, saxophones), which make sounds by air vibrations; brass (trumpets, French horns, trombones, etc.), which also make sounds by air vibrations, but differ from the woodwinds in shape and operation; and percussion (drums, pianos, triangles), which produce sound by striking. Instruments can also be classified as electric or acoustic, especially in popular music. Synthesizers are another common form of music, and computer and other electronic technology is increasingly used for creating music.

Musicians may play in symphony orchestras, dance bands, jazz bands, rock bands, country and western bands, or other groups or alone. Some of them may play in recording studios either with their group or as a session player for a particular recording. Recordings are in the form of records, tapes, compact discs, and videotape cassettes. *Classical musicians* perform in concerts, opera performances, and chamber music concerts, and they may also play in theater orchestras, although theater music is not normally classical. The most talented ones may work as soloists with orchestras or alone in recital. Some classical musicians accompany singers and choirs, and they may also perform in churches and temples.

Musicians who play popular music make heavy use of such rhythm instruments as piano, bass, drums, and guitar. *Jazz musicians* also feature woodwind and brass instruments, especially the saxophone and trumpet, and they extensively utilize the bass. Synthesizers are also commonly used instruments; some music is performed entirely on synthesizers, which can be programmed to imitate a variety of instruments and sounds. Musicians in jazz, blues, country western, and rock groups play clubs, festivals, and concert halls and may perform music for recordings, television, and motion picture sound tracks. Occasionally they appear in a movie themselves. Other musicians compose, record, and perform entirely with electronic instruments, such as synthesizers and other devices. In the late 1970s, *rap artists* began using turntables as musical instruments, and later, samplers, which record a snippet of other songs and sounds, as part of their music.

Instrumental musicians and *singers* use their skills to convey the form and meaning of written music. Instrumentalists and *vocalists* work to achieve precision, fluency, and clarity of tone; vocalists attempt to express emotion through phrasing and characterization. Musicians practice constantly to perfect their techniques.

Many musicians supplement their incomes through teaching, while others teach as their full-time occupation, perhaps playing jobs occasionally. *Voice* and *instrumental music teachers* work in colleges, high schools, elementary schools, conservatories, and in their own studios; often they give concerts and recitals featuring their students.

Many professional musicians give private lessons. Students learn to read music, develop their voices, breathe correctly, and hold their instruments properly.

Choral directors lead groups of singers in schools and other organizations. Church choirs, community oratorio societies, and professional symphony choruses are among the groups that employ choral directors outside of school settings. Choral directors audition singers, select music, and direct singers in achieving the tone, variety, intensity, and phrasing that they feel is required. *Orchestra conductors* do the same with instrumental musicians. Many work in schools and smaller communities, but the best conduct large orchestras in major cities. Some are resident instructors, while others travel constantly, making guest appearances with major national and foreign orchestras. They are responsible for the overall sound and quality of their orchestras.

Musicians may also spend part or all of their time as *composers, arrangers, orchestrators, copyists, librettists,* and *lyricists.* The people in these occupations write and prepare the music that musicians play and sing. Composers write the original music symphonies, songs, or operas using musical notation to express their ideas through melody, rhythm, and harmony. Arrangers and orchestrators take a composer's work and transcribe it for the various orchestra sections or individual instrumentalists and singers to perform; they prepare music for film scores, musical theater, television, or recordings. Copyists assist composers and arrangers by copying down the various parts of a composition, each of which is played by a different section of the orchestra. Librettists write words to opera and musical theater scores, and lyricists write words to songs and other short musical pieces. Most songwriters compose both music and lyrics, and many are musicians who perform their own songs.

Requirements

Many musicians begin learning their musical skills at an early age, sometimes before they even enter elementary school. From that point on, the development of musical skills requires long hours of practice and study. Even after high school few students are prepared to take their place as professional musicians; more practice and study are needed. Further institutional study is not required, though, particularly for those

seeking a career in the popular music field. College or conservatory degrees would only be required for those who plan to teach in institutions. However, it is probably a good idea for anyone going into music to acquire a degree, just to have a more versatile background in case of a career switch. Some musicians learn to play by ear, but for most, learning musical notation is a requirement.

Scores of colleges and universities have excellent music schools, and there are numerous conservatories that offer degrees in music. Many schools have noted musicians on their staff, and music students often have the advantage of studying under a professor who has a distinguished career in music. Having the means and a high grade average does not always assure entry into the top music schools. More than likely an audition is required and only the most talented are accepted. College undergraduates in music school will generally take courses in music theory, harmony, counterpoint, rhythm, melody, ear training, applied music, and music history. Courses in composing, arranging, and conducting are available in most comprehensive music schools. Students will also have to take courses such as English and psychology along with a regular academic program.

Hard work and dedication are key factors in a musical career, but music is an art form, and like those who practice any of the fine arts, musicians will succeed according to the amount of musical talent they have. Those who have talent and are willing to make sacrifices to develop it are the ones most likely to succeed. How much talent and ability one has is always open to speculation and opinion, and it may take years of studying and practice before musicians can assess their own degree of limitation.

There are other requirements necessary to becoming a professional musician that are just as important as training, education, and study. Foremost among these is a love of music strong enough to endure the arduous training and working life of a musician. To become an accomplished musician and to be recognized in the field requires an uncommon degree of dedication, self-discipline, and drive. Musicians who would move ahead must practice constantly with a determination to improve their technique and quality of performance. Musicians also need to develop an emotional toughness that will help them deal with rejection, indifference to their work, and ridicule from critics which will be especially prevalent early in their careers. There is also praise and adulation along the way, which is easier to take, but also requires a certain psychological handling.

Musicians who want to teach in state elementary and high schools must be state certified. To obtain a state certificate, musicians must satisfactorily complete a degree-granting course in music education at an institution of higher learning. About six hundred institutions in the United States offer programs in music education that qualify students for state certificates. Music education programs include many of the same courses mentioned earlier for musicians in general. They also would include education courses and supervised practice teaching. To teach in colleges and universities or in conservatories generally requires a graduate degree in music. Widely recognized musicians, however, sometimes receive positions in higher education without having obtained a degree.

For musicians interested in careers in popular music, however, little to no formal training is necessary. Many popular musicians teach themselves to play their instruments, which often results in the creation of new and exciting playing styles. Quite often, popular musicians do not even know how to read music. Some would say that many rock musicians do not even know how to play their instruments—this was especially true in the early days of the punk era. Most musicians, however, have a natural talent for rhythm and melody.

Musicians playing popular music, such as rock, jazz, or blues, often go through years of "paying their dues"—that is, receiving little money, respect, or attention for their efforts. They must have a strong sense of commitment to their careers and to their creative ideas.

Opportunities for Experience & Exploration

Opportunities for aspiring musicians to explore the field and find early musical experiences are fairly plentiful. Elementary schools, high schools, and institutes of higher education all present students with a number of options for musical training and performance, including choirs, ensembles, bands, and orchestras. Musicians may also have chances to perform in school musicals and talent shows as well. Music students taking private lessons usually are able to display their talents in recitals arranged by their teachers. College, university, and conservatory students also gain valuable performance experience by appearing in recitals and playing in bands, orchestras, and school shows. The more enterprising students in high school and in college form their own bands and begin earning money by playing while still in school.

It is important for aspiring musicians to take advantage of every opportunity to audition as they present themselves. There are numerous community amateur and semi-professional theater groups throughout the United States that produce musical plays and operettas, in which beginning musicians can gain playing experience. Churches provide numerous opportunities for singers, instrumentalists, and directors to perform and learn. Musical summer camps give young music students a chance to perform with others, gain experience on stage, and begin to find out if they have what it takes to become a professional musician.

Methods of Entering

Young musicians need to enter as many playing situations as they can in their school and community musical groups. They should audition as often as possible, because experience at auditioning is very important. Whenever possible they should take part in seminars and internships offered by orchestras, colleges, and associations. The National Orchestral Association offers training programs for musicians who want a career in the orchestral field.

Musicians who want to perform in established groups, such as choirs and symphony orchestras, enter the field by auditioning. Recommendations from teachers and other musicians often help would-be musicians obtain the opportunity to audition. Concert and opera soloists are also required to audition. Musicians must prepare themselves thoroughly for these auditions, which are demanding and stressful. A bad audition can be very discouraging for the young musician.

Popular musicians often begin playing at low-paying social functions and at small clubs or restaurants. If people like their performances, they usually move on to bookings at larger rooms in better clubs. Continued success leads to a national reputation and possible recording contracts. Jazz musicians tend to operate in the same way, taking every opportunity to audition with established jazz musicians.

Music teachers enter the field by applying directly to schools. College and university placement offices often have listings of positions. Professional associations, in their newsletters and journals, also frequently list teaching openings, as do newspapers. An excellent source to check for instrumental jobs is The International Musician, the newsletter of The American Federation of Musicians. Other music-oriented journals and associations, such as the American Symphony Orchestra League, can also be contacted for leads and information.

Advancement

Advancement is not easy to define. Popular musicians, once they have become established with a band, advance by moving up to more famous bands or by taking leadership of their own group. Bands may advance from playing small clubs to larger halls and even stadiums and festivals. They may receive a recording contract; if their songs or recordings prove successful, they can command higher fees for their contracts. Symphony orchestra musicians advance by moving to the head of their section of the orchestra. They can also move up to a position such as assistant or associate conductor. Once instrumental musicians acquire a reputation as accomplished artists, they receive engagements that are of higher status and remuneration, and they may come into demand as soloists. As their reputations develop, both classical and popular musicians may receive attractive offers to make recordings and personal appearances.

Popular and opera singers move up to better and more lucrative jobs through recognition of their talent by the public or by music producers and directors and agents. Their advancement is directly related to the demand for their talent and their own ability to promote themselves.

Music teachers in elementary and secondary schools may, with further training, aspire to careers as supervisors of music of a school system, a school district, or an entire state. With further graduate training, teachers can qualify for positions in colleges, universities, and music conservatories, where they can advance to become department heads. Well-known musicians can become artists-in-resi-

dence in the music departments of institutions of higher learning.

Employment Outlook

It is difficult to make a living solely as a musician, and this will continue because competition for jobs will be as intense as it has been in the past. Most musicians must hold down other jobs while pursuing their music career. Many thousands of musicians are all trying to "make it" in the music industry. Musicians are advised to be as versatile as possible, playing various kinds of music and more than one instrument. More importantly, they must be committed to pursuing their craft.

A variety of factors will affect musician employment through the year 2006, which the U.S. Bureau of Labor Statistics predicts will grow faster than the average for all other occupations. The demand for musicians will be greatest in bands, orchestras, and religious organizations. The outlook is less favorable in bars and restaurants. Bars—regular employers of musicians—are predicted to grow more slowly in the next decade; the number of musicians employed by restaurants that also feature live entertainment will decrease as the consumption of alcoholic beverages outside the home continues to decline. The increasing numbers of cable television networks, and increasing numbers of new television programs, will likely see an increase in employment for musicians. The number of record companies has grown dramatically over the last decade, particularly among small, independent houses. Digital recording technology has also made it easier and less expensive for musicians to produce and distribute their own recordings. However, few musicians will earn substantial incomes from these efforts. Popular musicians may receive many short-term engagements in nightclubs, restaurants, and theaters, but these engagements offer little job stability.

The opportunities for careers in teaching music are expected to grow at an average rate in elementary schools and in colleges and universities but at a slower rate in secondary schools. Although increasing numbers of colleges and universities have begun to offer music programs, enrollments in schools at all levels have been depressed and are not expected to increase until early in the next century. Some public schools, facing severe budget problems, have had to eliminate music programs altogether, making competition for jobs at that level even keener. In addition to these, private music teachers are facing greater competition from instrumental musicians who increasingly must turn to teaching because of the oversupply of musicians seeking playing jobs. The job supply is also diminishing because of the advent of electronic instruments such as synthesizers, which can replace a whole band, and the increasing trend to use recorded music.

Earnings

It is difficult to estimate the earnings of the average musician, because what they can earn is dependent upon the performer's skill, reputation, geographic location, type of music, and number of engagements per year.

Musicians in the major U.S. symphony orchestras earn minimum salaries of between $140 and $1,200 a week. The season for these major orchestras, generally located in the largest U.S. cities, ranges from twenty-nine to fifty-two weeks. In major orchestras during the 1996-97 performing season, musicians earned annual salaries that ranged from $22,000 to $90,000, according to the American Federation of Musicians. Featured musicians and soloists can earn much more, especially those with an international reputation.

Popular musicians are usually paid per concert or "gig." A band just starting out playing a small bar or club may be required to play three sets a night, and each musician may receive next to nothing for the entire evening. Often, bands receive a percentage of the cover charge at the door. Some musicians play for drinks alone. On average, however, pay per musician ranges from $30 to $300 or more per night. Bands that have gained national recognition and a following may earn far more, because a club owner can usually be assured that many people will come to see the band play. The most successful popular musicians, of course, can earn millions of dollars each year. In the late-1990s, some artists have signed recording contracts worth $20 million and more.

Musicians are well paid for studio recording work, when they can get it. For recording film and television background music, musicians are paid a minimum of about $185 for a three-hour session; for record company recordings they receive a minimum of about $234 for three hours. Instrumentalists performing live earn anywhere from $30 to $300 per engagement, depending on their degree of popularity, talent, and the size of the room they play.

Church organists, choir directors, and soloists make an average of $40 to $100 each week, but this is often part-time work supplemented by pay from other jobs.

The salaries received by music teachers in public elementary and secondary schools are the same as for other teachers. In public elementary schools the salary received by teachers in the 1990s is about $25,000 per year. The figure for public secondary school teachers is about $27,000. Music teachers in colleges and universities have widely ranging salaries. Most teachers supplement their incomes through private instruction and by performing in their off hours.

Most musicians do not, as a rule, work steadily for one employer, and they often undergo long periods of unemployment between engagements. Because of these factors, few musicians can qualify for unemployment compensation. Unlike other workers, most musicians also do not enjoy such benefits as sick leave or paid vacations. Some musicians, on the other hand, who work under contractual agreements do receive benefits, which usually have been negotiated by artists unions, such as the American Federation of Musicians.

Conditions of Work

Work conditions for musicians vary greatly. Performing musicians generally work in the evenings and on weekends. They also spend much time practicing and rehearsing for performances. Their workplace can be almost anywhere, from a swanky club to a high school gymnasium to a dark, dingy bar. Many concerts are given outdoors and in a variety of weather conditions. Performers may be given a star's dressing room or share a mirror in a church basement or find themselves changing in a bar's storeroom. They may work under the hot camera lights of film or television sets or tour with a troupe in subzero temperatures. They may work amid the noise and confusion of a large rehearsal of a Broadway show or in the relative peace and quiet of a small recording studio. Seldom are two days in a performer's life just alike.

Many musicians and singers travel a great deal. More prominent musicians may travel with staffs who make their arrangements and take care of wardrobes and equipment. Their accommodations are usually quite comfortable, if not luxurious, and they are generally playing in major urban centers. Lesser known musicians may have to take care of all their own arrangements and put up with lesser accommodations in relatively remote places. Some musicians perform on the streets or in subway tunnels and other places likely to have a great deal of passersby. Symphony orchestra musicians probably travel less than most, but those of major orchestras travel largely under first-class conditions.

The chief characteristic of musical employment is its lack of continuity. Few musicians work full-time and most experience periods of unemployment between engagements. Most work day jobs to supplement their incomes. Those who are in great demand generally have agents and managers to help direct their careers.

Music teachers affiliated with institutions work the same hours as other classroom teachers. Many of these teachers, however, spend time after school and on weekends directing and instructing school vocal and instrumental groups. Teachers may also have varied working conditions. They may teach in a large urban school, conducting five different choruses each day, or they may work with rural elementary schools and spend much time driving from school to school.

College or university instructors may divide their time between group and individual instruction. They may teach several musical subjects and may be involved with planning and producing school musical events. They may also supervise student music teachers when they do their practice teaching.

Private music teachers work part- or full-time out of their own homes or in separate studios. The ambiance of their work place would be in accordance with the size and nature of their clientele.

Most musicians work in large urban areas and are particularly drawn to the major recording centers, such as Chicago, New York City, Los Angeles, Nashville, and Miami Beach. Most musicians find work in churches, temples, clubs and restaurants, at weddings, in opera and ballet productions, and on television and radio. Religious organizations are the largest single source of work for musicians.

Professional musicians generally hold membership in the American Federation of Musicians (AFL-CIO), and concert soloists also hold membership in the American Guild of Musical Artists, Inc. (AFL-CIO). Singers can belong to a branch of Associated Actors and Artistes of America (AFL-CIO). Music teachers in schools often hold membership in the Music Educators National Conference, a department of the National Education Association.

Sources of Additional Information

■ **American Federation of Musicians of the United States and Canada**
Paramount Building
1501 Broadway, Suite 600
New York, NY 10036
Tel: 212-869-1330
Email: info@afm.org

■ **American Guild of Musical Artists**
1727 Broadway
New York, NY 10019
Tel: 212-265-3687

■ **International Guild of Symphony, Opera, and Ballet Musicians**
5802 16th, NE
Seattle, WA 98105
Tel: 206-524-7050

■ **Music Teachers National Association**
Carew Tower
441 Vine Street, Suite 505
Cincinnati, OH 45202
Tel: 513-421-1420
Email: smcray@mtna.org
WWW: http://www.mtna.org

■ **National Association of Schools of Music**
11250 Roger Bacon Drive, Suite 21
Reston, VA 22091
Tel: 703-437-0700
Email: kpmnasm@aol.com
WWW: http://www.arts-accredit.org/nosm

■ **Women In Music**
31121 Mission Boulevard, Suite 300
Hayward, CA 94544
Tel: 510-232-3897
Email: womeninmusic@pacbell.net
WWW: http://www.womeninmusic.com

Nursing Aides

Definition

Nursing aides care for patients in hospitals and nursing homes under the supervision of nurses.

Nature of the Work

Though the job title suggests someone who assists nurses, nursing aides actually perform many duties independently; in some cases, they become more closely involved with patients or nursing home residents than do registered nurses. Nursing aides work under the supervision of nurses and perform tasks that allow the nursing staff to perform their primary duties effectively and efficiently.

Nursing aides perform basic nursing care in hospitals and nursing homes. Male nursing aides are perhaps better known as *orderlies*. Working independently and alongside nurses and doctors, nursing aides help move patients, assist in patients' exercise and nutrition, and see to the patients' personal hygiene. They bring the patients their meal trays and help them to eat. They push the patients on stretchers and in wheelchairs to operating and X-ray rooms. They also help to admit and discharge patients. Nursing aides must keep charts of their work for review by nurses.

About half of the nursing aides today work in nursing homes, tending to the daily care of elderly residents. They help residents with baths and showers, meals, and exercise. They help them in and out of their beds and to and from the bathroom. They also record the health of residents by taking body temperatures, blood pressures, and other vital signs.

Because the residents are living within such close proximity to each other, and because they need help with personal hygiene and health care, a nursing aide also takes care to protect the privacy of the resident. It is the responsibility of a nursing aide to make the resident feel as comfortable as possible. Nursing aides may also work with patients who are not fully functional, teaching them how to care for themselves, educating them in personal hygiene and health care.

Nursing aides may be called upon by nurses and physicians to perform the more menial and unappealing tasks, but they also have the opportunity to develop meaningful relationships with residents. Nursing aides work closely with residents, often gaining their trust and admiration. When residents are having personal problems, or problems with the staff, they may turn to the nursing aide for help.

Requirements

Communication skills are valuable for a nursing aide, so high school students should take English, speech, and writing courses. Science courses, such as biology and anatomy, will also prepare you for future training. Nursing aides are not required to have a college degree but may have to complete a short training course at a community college or vocational school. These training courses, usually instructed by a registered nurse, teach basic nursing skills and prepare students for the state certification exam. Nursing aides typically begin the training courses after getting their first job as an aides, and the course work is incorporated into their on-the-job training.

Many people work as nursing aides as they pursue other medical professions; someone interested in becoming a nurse or a paramedic may work as an aide while taking courses. A high school student or a student in a premedical program may work as a nursing aide part-time before going on to medical school.

Nursing aides in hospitals are not required to be certified but those working in nursing homes must pass a state exam. The Omnibus Budget Reconciliation Act (OBRA) passed by Congress in 1987 requires nursing homes to hire only certified nursing aides. OBRA also requires continuing education for nursing aides, and periodic evaluations.

A nursing aide must care about their work and show a general understanding and compassion for the ill, disabled, and the elderly. Because of the rigorous physical demands placed on a nursing aide, you should be in good health. Also, the hours and responsibilities of the job won't allow you to take many sick days. Along with this good physical health, you should have good mental health, as well. The job can be emotionally demanding, requiring your patience and stability. You should also be able to take orders and to work as part of a team.

Opportunities for Experience & Exploration

Because a high school diploma is not required of nursing aides, many high school students are hired by nursing homes and hospitals for part-time work. Job opportunities may also exist in a hospital or nursing home kitchen, introducing you to diet and nutrition. Also, volunteer work can familiarize you with the work nurses and nursing aides perform, as well as introduce you to some medical terminology.

Methods of Entering

One-half of all nursing aides work in nursing homes. Other places where they are employed include hospitals, halfway houses, retirement centers, and private homes. Because of the high demand for nursing aides, you can apply directly to the health care facilities in your area. Most will probably have a human resources department that advertises positions in the newspaper and interviews applicants.

Advancement

For the most part, there is not much opportunity for advancement within the job of nursing aide. To move up in a health care

facility requires additional training. Some nursing aides, after gaining experience and learning medical technology, enroll in nursing programs, or may even decide to pursue medical degrees.

A nursing home requires a lot of hard work and dedication so nursing aides frequently burn out, or quit before completing their training. Others may choose another aspect of the job, such as working as a *home health aide*. Helping patients in their homes, these aides see to the client's personal health, hygiene, and home care.

Employment Outlook

There will continue to be many job opportunities for nursing aides. Because of the physical and emotional demands of the job, and because of the lack of advancement opportunities, there is a high turnover rate in this field. Also, health care is constantly changing; more opportunities open for nursing aides as different kinds of health care facilities are developed. Business-based health organizations are limiting the services of health care professionals and looking for cheaper ways to provide care. This may provide opportunities for those looking for work as nursing aides.

Government and private agencies are also developing more programs to assist dependent people. And as the number of people seventy years of age and older continues to rise, new and larger nursing care facilities will be needed.

Earnings

Although the salaries for most health care professionals vary by region and population, the average hourly wage of nursing aides is about the same across the country. Midwestern states and less populated areas, where a large staff of nursing aides may be needed to make up for a smaller staff of nurses and therapists, may pay a little more per hour.

Median weekly earnings of full-time salaried nursing aides were $292 in 1996. According to the Buck Survey conducted by the American Health Care Association, nursing aides in chain nursing homes had median hourly earnings of about $6.00 in 1996. The middle 50 percent earned between $5.95 and $7.50 per hour.

Conditions of Work

Nursing aides generally work a forty-hour work week, with some overtime. The hours and weekly schedule may be irregular, however, depending on the needs of the care institution. An aides may have one day off in the middle of the week, followed by three days of work, then another day off. Nursing aides are needed around the clock, so beginning aides may be required to work late at night or very early in the morning.

The work can be strenuous, requiring the lifting and moving of patients. Nursing aides must work with partners, or in groups, when performing the more strenuous tasks, so that neither the nursing aide nor the resident is injured. Some requirements of the job can be as routine as changing sheets and helping a resident with phone calls, while other requirements can be as difficult and unattractive as assisting a resident with elimination and cleaning up a resident who has vomited.

Sources of Additional Information

For information on schools that offer training, contact:

■■■**National Association of Health Career Schools**
750 First Street, NE, Suite 940
Washington, DC 20002
Email: NAHCS@aol.com

Occupational Therapists

Definition

Occupational therapists select and direct therapeutic activities designed to develop or restore maximum function to individuals with disabilities.

Nature of the Work

Occupational therapists use a wide variety of activities to aid clients in attaining their goals for productive, independent living. These goals include developing maximum self-sufficiency in activities of daily living, such as eating, dressing, writing, and using a telephone and other communication resources, and helping patients to develop and employ skills that will help them in the community and in the workplace.

In developing a therapeutic program for a client, the occupational therapist often works as a member of a team that can include physicians, nurses, psychiatrists, physical therapists, speech therapists, rehabilitation counselors, social workers, and any other required specialists. Occupational therapists use creative, educational, and recreational activities, as well as human ingenuity, in helping people achieve their full potential, regardless of their disabilities. Each therapy program is designed specifically for the individual client.

Occupational therapists help clients explore their likes and dislikes, their abilities, and their creative, educational, and recreational experiences. Therapists help people choose activities that have the most appeal and value for them. For example, an activity may be designed to promote greater dexterity for someone with arthritic fingers. Learning to use an adapted computer might help a young person with a spinal cord injury to succeed in school and career goals. The therapist works with the clients' interests and helps them develop practical skills and functional independence.

The occupational therapist may work with a wide range of clients. They may assist a client in learning to use an artificial limb. Another client may have suffered a stroke or other neurological disability, and the therapist works with the client to redevelop their motor functions or reeducate their muscle function. Therapists may assist in the growth and development of premature infants, or they may work with disabled children, helping them learn motor skills or develop skills and tools that will aid them in their education and social interaction. Some therapists also conduct research projects in developing new types of therapies and activities and in measuring the effectiveness of a program of therapy. They may also design and make special equipment or splints to aid a client in performing his or her activities.

Other duties may include supervision of volunteer workers, student therapists, and occupational therapy assistants who give instruction in a particular skill. A duty of therapists is to prepare reports to keep members of the professional team informed.

Chief occupational therapists in a hospital may teach medical and nursing students the principles of occupational therapy. Many occupational therapists have administrative duties such as directing different kinds of occupational therapy programs, coordinating patient activities, and acting as consultants or advisors to local and state health departments, mental health authorities, and the Division of Vocational Rehabilitation.

Requirements

Preparation for occupational therapy requires the completion of an accredited program in occupational therapy, either at the bachelor's degree or master's degree level. More than one hundred colleges and universities offer training in occupational therapy that has been accredited by the Council on Medical Education and Hospitals of the American Medical Association and the American Occupational Therapy Association. High school students can best prepare for this career by following a college-preparatory program.

Graduates of a bachelor's degree program in occupational therapy are required to fulfill a clinical training period of six months in order to qualify for professional registration. The Armed Forces also offers programs whereby graduates of approved schools of occupational therapy who meet the requirements to become commissioned officers may receive the clinical part of their training while in the service.

College graduates with training in other fields may apply for entry into a master's program or for a limited number of certificate programs. These advanced programs generally last from two to two-and-a-half years and include both academic and clinical work.

In college preparation for occupational therapy, the emphasis is on biological and behavioral sciences. Courses include anatomy, physiology, neurology, psychology, human growth and development, and sociology. Clinical subjects cover general medical and surgical conditions, interpretation of the principles and practice of occupational therapy in pediatrics, psychiatry, orthopedics, and general medicine and surgery. Many bachelor's degree programs require students to fulfill two years of general study before specializing in the last two years in occupational therapy.

Occupational therapists with bachelor's degrees may decide to continue their education in an advanced degree program. Master's and doctoral programs are advised for occupational therapists seeking careers in teaching, administration, and research.

In addition to these full-time study options, there are a limited number of part-time and evening programs that will allow prospective occupational therapists to work in another field while completing their requirements in occupational therapy.

Upon graduation and completion of the clinical practice period, therapists are eligible to take the examination administered by the American Occupational Therapy Certification Board. Those who pass this examination may use the initials OTR (Occupational Therapist, Registered) after their names. Many hospitals require that their occupational therapists be registered. A license to practice occupational therapy is required by all states and the District of Columbia. Applicants for a license must have a degree or certificate from an accredited educational program and pass the national certification examination.

In addition, prospective occupational therapists should enjoy working with people. They should have a patient, calm, and compassionate temperament and have the ability to encourage and inspire their clients.

Opportunities for Experience & Exploration

While in high school, students interested in a career in occupational therapy should meet with occupational therapists, visit the facilities where they work, and gain an understanding of the types of equipment and skills they use. Many hospitals and occupational therapy facilities and departments also have volunteer opportunities, which will give students strong insight into this career.

Methods of Entering

A school's placement office is usually the best place to start a job search for a newly graduated occupational therapist. Individuals may also apply directly to government agencies, such as the U.S. Public Health Service, private hospitals, and clinics. In addition, the American Occupational Therapy Association can provide job seekers with assistance through their employment bulletins.

Advancement

Newly graduated occupational therapists usually begin as staff therapists and may qualify as senior therapists after several years on the job. The Army, Navy, Air Force, and the U.S. Public Health Service commission occupational therapists; other branches of the federal service give civil service ratings. Experienced therapists may become directors of occupational therapy programs in large hospitals, clinics, or workshops or may become teachers. Some positions are available as program coordinators and as consultants with large institutions and agencies.

A few colleges and health agencies offer advanced courses in the treatment of special disabilities, such as those resulting from cerebral palsy, for graduates of approved curriculums. Some institutions provide in-service programs for therapists.

Employment Outlook

In 1996, there were approximately 57,000 occupational therapists at work in hospitals, schools, nursing homes, home health agencies, mental health centers, adult day care programs, outpatient clinics, and residential care facilities. A growing number are self-employed, in either solo or group practice or in consulting firms.

Opportunities for occupational therapists are expected to be highly favorable through the year 2006 and will grow much faster than the average for all careers. This growth will occur as a result of the increasing number of middle-aged and elderly people that require therapeutic services. The demand for occupational therapists is also increasing because of growing public interest in and governmental support for people with disabilities and for occupational therapy programs helping people attain the fullest possible functional status. The demand for rehabilitative and long-term care services is expected to grow strongly over the next decade. There will be numerous opportunities for work with mental health clients, children, and the elderly, as well as with those with disabling conditions.

As the health care industry continues to be restructured, there should be many more opportunities for occupational therapists in nontraditional settings. This factor and proposed changes in the laws should create an excellent climate for therapists wishing to enter private practice. Home health care may experience the greatest growth in the next decade.

Earnings

According to the U.S. Department of Labor, beginning salaries for occupational therapists in 1996 averaged about $40,560 and can range from $24,900 to $35,600 a year. Experienced therapists average about $42,000 to about $51,000 per year. Administrators earn an average of $55,000 per year.

Salaries for occupational therapists often vary according to where they are located. In areas where the cost of living is higher, occupational therapists generally receive higher pay. Occupational therapists employed in public schools earn salaries that vary by school district. In some states, they are classified as teachers and are paid accordingly.

Therapists employed at hospitals, government and public agencies, and the like generally receive full benefit packages that include vacation and sick pay, health insurance, and retirement benefits. Self-employed therapists and those who run their own businesses must provide their own benefits.

Conditions of Work

Occupational therapists work in occupational therapy workshops or clinics. Such places are usually well-lighted, pleasant settings. Generally, they work an eight-hour day, forty-hour week, with some evening work required in a few organizations.

Sources of Additional Information

Contact the following organization for further information on a career in occupational therapy:

American Occupational Therapy Association
4720 Montgomery Lane
PO Box 31220
Bethesda, MD 20824-1220
Tel: 301-652-2682
WWW: http://www.aota.org

Ontario Society of Occupational Therapists
55 Eglinton Avenue East, Suite 210
Toronto, ON M4P 1G8 Canada
Tel: 416-322-3011

Occupational Therapy Assistants

Definition

Occupational therapy assistants help people with mental, physical, developmental, or emotional limitations using a variety of activities to improve basic motor functions and reasoning abilities. They work under the direct supervision of an occupational therapist to help plan, implement, and evaluate rehabilitation programs designed to regain patients' self sufficiency and to restore their physical and mental functions.

Nature of the Work

Occupational therapy is used to help provide rehabilitation services to persons with mental, physical, emotional, or developmental disabilities. The goal of the occupational therapy department is to improve a patient's quality of life by compensating for limitations caused by age, illness, or accident. It differs from physical therapy because it not only centers on physical rehabilitation, but also psychological well being. Occupational therapy emphasizes improvement of the activities of daily living (ADL)—including such functions as daily personal hygiene, dressing, eating, and cooking.

Occupational therapists plan patient care plans and activities. They are in charge of the occupational therapy department. Occupational therapy assistants, under the supervision of the therapist, implement the plans. Assistants help patients improve mobility and productivity using a variety of activities and exercises. They may use adaptive techniques and equipment to help patients perform tasks many take for granted. A reacher, a long handled device that pinches and grabs small items, may be used to pick up keys from the floor, or a book from the shelf. Therapy assistants may have patients mix ingredients for a cake, or flip a grilled cheese sandwich using a special spatula. Activities such as dancing, playing cards, or throwing a ball are fun, yet they help improve mobility, and give the patient's a sense of self esteem. Therapists evaluate an activity, minimize the number of steps, and streamline movement so the patient will be less fatigued.

Assistants may also help therapists evaluate a patient's progress, change care plans as needed, make therapy appointments, and office paperwork.

Occupational therapy aides are responsible for materials and equipment used during therapy. They assemble and clean equipment, and make certain the therapists and assistants have what they need for a patient's therapy session. A therapy aide's duties are more clerical in nature. They answer telephones, schedule appointments, order supplies and equipment, and complete insurance forms and other paperwork.

Requirements

All occupational therapy assistants have either an associate's degree or certificate from an accredited community college or technical school. There were 117 such programs located in the United States in 1996. The first year of study focuses on basic health care, medical terminology, and anatomy and physiology. Second year coursework includes occupational therapy classes, mental health, gerontology, and pediatrics. A supervised apprenticeship in a clinic or community setting is also required. Assistants must pass a national certification examination upon graduation.

Aides are not required to have any formal education apart a high school diploma and on the job training. Assistants and aides must be able to take directions. They should have a pleasant disposition, patience, responsibility, strong people skills, and a desire to help those in need. It is important for assistants and aides to work well as a team.

Opportunities for Experience and Exploration

A visit to the local hospital's occupational therapy department is the best way to learn about this field. Interest students should speak with occupational therapists, assistants, and aides to gain an understanding of the work they do. Also, organizations, such as the American Occupational Therapy Association, may be able to provide career information. School guidance and job centers, and the library, may be good information sources.

Methods of Entering

The placement center of the community college or technical school can provide a listing of jobs available in the occupational therapy field. Job openings are usually posted in hospital human resource departments. Also, the American Occupational Therapy Association, can help graduates with help through their Web site's employment page.

Advancement

Occupational therapy assistants, after some experience, can be promoted to lead assistant. Lead assistants are responsible for making work schedules of other assistants, and the training of occupational therapy students. Since occupational therapy assistants work under the supervision of an occupational therapist, there is little room for advancement. Some assistants and aides return to school to become occupational therapists. Some shift to other health field careers.

Employment Outlook

According to the *1998-99 Occupational Outlook Handbook*, occupational therapy assistants will be one of the fastest growing fields—an increase of about seventy percent through the year 2006. However, only a small number of new jobs will actually be available due to the size of this occupation—about 16,000 occupational therapy assistants were employed in 1996. One-third of all occupational therapy assistants worked in a hospital setting; one-fourth were employed by nursing homes or personal care agencies. They rest were employed by residential care facilities, outpatient rehabilitation centers, and home health services.

Occupational growth will stem from an increased number of elderly people. Though more people are living well into their seventies, eighties, and in some cases, nineties, they often need the kind of services occupational therapy provides. Medical technology has greatly improved, saving many lives that would, in the past, be lost through accidents, stroke, or other illnesses. Such people need rehabilitation therapy as they recuperate.

Hospitals and employers, to reduce costs, are hiring more therapy assistants to help with the work load. Traditionally, assistants are paid less than occupational therapists.

Earnings

The average annual salary of occupational therapy assistants is about $27,442, according to a membership survey conducted by the American Occupational Therapy Association. Occupational therapy assistants with experience can earn considerably more. Starting pay for therapy aides is about $6.50 to $7.50 an hour, or $13,520 to $15,600 annually. Those working in day care programs in school systems earn less than those employed by nursing homes.

Benefits for full time assistants and aides include health and life insurance, paid sick and vacation time, holiday pay, and retirement fund.

Conditions of Work

Most occupational therapy assistants and aides work during the day, though depending on the place of employment, some evening or weekend work is required. Most therapy is done in a hospital or clinic setting that is clean, well lighted and generally comfortable.

Occupational therapy assistants often use every day items, settings, and activities to help rehabilitate their patients. Such props include kitchen settings, card games, dancing, or exercises. Therapy assistants should be in good physical shape since heavy lifting—patients as well as equipment—is a daily part of the job. They should also have stamina, since therapy assistants are on their feet for much of the day.

Sources of Additional Information

For career information, contact:

American Occupational Therapy Association
4720 Montgomery Lane
PO Box 31220
Bethesda, MD 20824
Tel: 301-652-2682
WWW: http://www.aota.org

For information on certification requirements, contact:

American Occupational Therapy Certification Board
4 Research Place, Suite 160
Rockville, MD 20850
Tel: 301-990-7979

Office Administrators

Definition

Office administrators direct and coordinate the work activities of office workers within an office. They supervise office clerks and other workers in their tasks and confer with other supervisory personnel in planning department activities. Office administrators often define job duties and develop training programs for new workers. They evaluate the progress of their clerks and work with upper management officials to ensure that the office staff meets productivity and quality goals. Office administrators often meet with office personnel to discuss job-related issues or problems, and they are responsible for maintaining a positive office environment.

Nature of the Work

As modern technology and an increased volume of business communications become a normal part of daily business, offices are becoming more complicated places in which to work. By directing and coordinating the activities of clerks and other office workers, office administrators are an integral part of an effective organization.

The day-to-day work of office administrators, who are also known as *office managers,* involves organizing and overseeing many different activities. Although specific duties vary with the type and size of the particular office, all supervisors and managers have several basic job responsibilities. Essentially, the primary responsibility of the office administrator is to "run the office," that is, whatever the nature of the office's business, the office administrator must see to it that all workers have what they need to do their work.

Office administrators are usually responsible for interviewing prospective employees and making recommendations on hiring. They train new workers, explain office policies, and explain performance criteria. Office administrators are also responsible for delegating work responsibilities. This requires a keen understanding of the strengths and weaknesses of each worker, as well as the ability to determine what needs to be done and when it must be completed. For example, if a supervisor knows that one worker is especially good at filing business correspondence, that person will probably be assigned to any important filing tasks. Office administrators often know how to do many of the tasks done by their subordinates and assist or relieve them whenever necessary.

Office administrators not only train clerical workers and assign them job duties but also recommend increases in salaries, promote workers when approved, and occasionally fire them. Therefore, they must carefully observe clerical workers performing their jobs (whether answering the telephones, opening and sorting mail, or inputting computer data) and make positive suggestions for any necessary improvements. Managers who can communicate effectively both verbally and in writing will be better able to carry out this kind of work. Motivating employees to do their best work is another important component of an office administrator's responsibilities.

Office administrators must be very good at human relations. Difference of opinion and personality clashes among employees are inevitable in almost any office, and the administrator must be able to deal with grievances and restore good feelings among the staff. Office administrators meet regularly with their staff, alone and in groups, to discuss and solve any problems that might affect people's job performance.

Planning is a vital and time-consuming portion of the job responsibilities of office administrators. Not only do they plan the work of subordinates, they also assist in planning current and future office space needs, work schedules, and the types of office equipment and supplies that need to be purchased.

Office administrators must always keep their superiors informed as to the overall situation in the clerical area. If there is a delay on an important project, for example, upper management must know the cause and the steps being taken to expedite the matter.

Requirements

A high school diploma is essential for this position, and a college degree is highly recommended. Since many offices promote office administrators from clerical work positions within their organization, relevant work experience is also helpful. High school students should take courses in English, speech and communications, mathematics, sociology, history, and as many business-related courses, such as typing and bookkeeping, as possible. Knowledge of a wide variety of computer software programs is also very important.

In college, a student should pursue a degree in business administration or at least take several courses in business management and operations. In some cases, an associate's degree is considered sufficient for a supervisory position. Many community colleges and vocational schools offer business education courses that help train office administrators.

Offices can be hectic places. Deadlines on major projects can create tension, especially if some workers are sick or overburdened. Office administrators must constantly juggle the demands of their superiors with the capabilities of their subordinates. Thus, they need an even temperament and the ability to work well with others. Additional attributes that are important include organizational ability, attention to detail, dependability, and trustworthiness.

Opportunities for Experience & Exploration

Interested students may get experience by taking on clerical or bookkeeping responsibilities with a school club or other organization. (Volunteering in your school office is an ideal introduction to office work.) This type of volunteer work allows people to practice office skills such as opening and sorting mail, answering telephones, and filing business documents.

Individuals may have the opportunity to get training in the operation of business machinery (computers, fax machines, and so on) through evening courses that are offered by business schools. In addition, some school work-study programs may have opportunities for part-time, on-the-job training with local businesses.

Methods of Entering

Qualified persons should contact the personnel offices of individual firms directly. This is especially appropriate if the candidate already has previous clerical experience. College placement offices or other job placement offices may also know of openings. Jobs may also be located through help wanted advertisements. Another option is to sign up with a temporary employment service. By working as a "temp," you have the advantage of getting a firsthand look at a variety of office settings and making many contacts.

Often, a firm will recruit office administrators from its own clerical staff. A clerk with potential supervisory abilities may be given periodic supervisory responsibilities. Later, when an opening occurs for an administrator, that person may be promoted to a full-time position.

Advancement

Skilled administrators may be promoted to a group manager position. Promotions, however, often depend on the administrator getting a college degree or other appropriate training, often including full training in the company's computer system. Supervisory and management training can be obtained through company training or community colleges and local vocational schools. Firms usually encourage their employees to pursue more education and may even pay for some tuition costs.

Some companies will prepare office clerks for advancement to an administrative position by having them work in a number of company departments. This broad experience allows the administrator to better coordinate numerous activities and make more knowledgeable decisions.

Employment Outlook

Although the increased use of data processing machines and other types of automated equipment may reduce the number of administrators, this profession will still offer good employment prospects because of its sheer size. A large number of job openings will occur as administrators transfer to other industries or leave the workforce for other reasons. Therefore, employment of office administrators is expected to grow about as fast as the average for all occupations. Since some clerical occupations will be affected by increased automation, some office administrators may have smaller staffs and be asked to perform more professional tasks.

More than 1.4 million office administrators were employed in the United States in 1996. According to the U.S. Department of Labor, office administrators will enjoy large numerical growth, with a projected increase of about 280,000 jobs through the year 2006.

The federal government should continue to be a good source for job opportunities. Private companies, particularly those with large clerical staffs such as hospitals, banks, and telecommunications companies, should also have numerous openings. Employment opportunities will be especially good for those trained to operate computers and other types of modern office machinery.

Earnings

According to the *1998-99 Occupational Outlook Handbook,* office administrators earned an average of about $28,900 a year in 1996. Fifty percent earned between $21,500 to $38,900 a year, with the top ten percent earning over $50,600. The size and geographic location of the company and the person's individual skills can be key determinants of earnings. Higher wages will be paid to those who work for larger private companies located in and around major metropolitan areas. Full-time workers also receive paid vacations, health and life insurance. Some companies offer year-end bonuses and stock options.

Conditions of Work

As is the case with most office workers, office administrators work an average of thirty-five- to forty-hours a week, although overtime is not unusual. Depending on the company, night, weekend, holiday, or shift work may be expected. Most offices are pleasant places to work. The environment is usually well ventilated and well lighted, and the work is not physically strenuous. The administrator's job can be stressful, however, as it entails supervising a variety of employees with different personalities, temperaments, and work habits.

Sources of Additional Information

■**American Management Association**
1601 Broadway
New York, NY 10019-7420
Tel: 212-586-8100
WWW: http://www.amanet.org

For information on careers and related education, please contact:

■**National Association of Executive Secretaries**
900 South Washington Street, Suite G-13
Falls Church, VA 22046
Tel: 703-237-8616

■**Canadian Management Centre of AMA International**
150 York Street, 5th Floor
Toronto, ON M5H 3S5 Canada
Tel: 416-214-5678
Email: cmcinfo@amanet.org
WWW: http://www.cmcamai.org

For a career brochure, please contact:

■**National Management Association**
2210 Arbor Boulevard
Dayton, OH 45439
Tel: 937-294-0421
Email: sue@nma1.org
WWW: http://www.nma1.org

Office Clerks

Definition

Office clerks perform a variety of clerical tasks that help an office run smoothly, including file maintenance, mail sorting, and record keeping. In large companies, office clerks might have specialized tasks such as inputting data into a computer, but in most cases clerks are flexible and have many duties, such as typing, answering telephones, taking messages, making photocopies, and preparing mailings. Office clerks usually work under close supervision, often with experienced clerks directing their activities.

Nature of the Work

Office clerks usually perform a variety of tasks as part of their overall job responsibility. They may type or file bills, statements, and business correspondence. They may stuff envelopes, answer telephones, and sort mail. Office clerks also enter data into computers, run errands, and operate office equipment such as photocopiers, fax machines, and switchboards. In the course of an average day, an office clerk usually performs a combination of these and other clerical tasks, spending an hour or so on one task and then moving on to another as directed by an office manager or other supervisor.

An office clerk may work with other office personnel, such as a bookkeeper or accountant, to maintain a company's financial records. The clerk may type and mail invoices and sort payments as they come in, keep payroll records, or take inventories. With more experience, the clerk may be asked to update customer files to reflect receipt of payments and verify records for accuracy.

Office clerks often deliver messages from one office worker to another, an especially important responsibility in larger companies. Clerks may relay questions and answers from one department head to another. Similarly, clerks may relay messages from people outside the company or employees who are outside of the office to those working on staff. Office clerks may also work with other personnel on individual projects, such as preparing a yearly budget or making sure a mass mailing gets out on time.

Administrative clerks assist in the efficient operation of an office by compiling business records; providing information to sales personnel and customers; and preparing and sending out bills, policies, invoices, and other business correspondence. Administrative clerks may also keep financial records and prepare the payroll. *File clerks* review and classify letters, documents, articles, and other information and then file this material so it can be quickly retrieved at a later time. They contribute to the smooth distribution of information at a company.

Some clerks have titles that describe where they work and the jobs they do. *Congressional-district aides* work for the elected officials of their U.S. congressional district. *Police clerks* handle routine office procedures in police stations, and *concrete products dispatchers* work with construction firms on building projects.

Requirements

A high school diploma is usually sufficient for beginning office clerks, although business courses covering office machine operation and bookkeeping are also helpful. Prospective clerks should have computer skills, the ability to concentrate for long periods of time on repetitive tasks, good English and communication skills, and mathematical abilities. Legible handwriting is a necessity.

High school students should take courses in English, mathematics, and as many business-related subjects, such as keyboarding and bookkeeping, as possible. Community colleges and vocational schools often offer business education courses that provide training for general office workers.

Office clerks should have an even temperament, strong communication skills, and the ability to work well with others. They should find systematic and detailed work appealing. Other personal qualifications include dependability, trustworthiness, and a neat personal appearance.

Opportunities for Experience & Exploration

Students can gain experience by taking on clerical or bookkeeping responsibilities with a school club or other organization. In addition, some school work-study programs may provide opportunities for part-time, practical on-the-job training with local businesses. Students may also be able to get a part-time or summer job in a business office by contacting businesses directly, or enlisting the aid of a guidance counselor. Training in the operation of business machinery (computers, word processors, and so on) may be available through evening courses offered by business schools and community colleges.

Methods of Entering

Those interested in securing an entry-level position should contact businesses or governmental agencies directly. Major employers include utility companies, insurance agencies, and finance, real estate, and other large firms. Smaller companies also hire office workers and sometimes offer a greater opportunity to gain experience in a variety of clerical tasks. Newspaper ads and temporary-work agencies are also good sources for finding jobs in this area.

Most companies provide on-the-job training during which time company policies and procedures are explained.

Advancement

Office clerks usually begin their employment performing more routine tasks such as delivering messages and sorting and filing mail. With experience, they may advance to more complicated assignments and assume a greater responsibility for the entire project to be completed. Those who demonstrate the desire and ability may move to other clerical positions, such as *secretary* or *receptionist*. Clerks with good leadership skills may become group managers or supervisors. To be promoted to a professional occupation such as accountant, a college degree or other specialized training is normally necessary.

The high turnover rate that exists among office clerks increases promotional opportunities. The number and kind of opportunities, however, usually depend on the place of employment and the ability, education, and experience of the employee.

Employment Outlook

About 3,111,000 people held jobs as office workers in 1996. Though employment of office clerks is expected to grow more slowly than the average through the year 2006, there will still be many jobs available due to the vastness of this field, along with a high turnover rate. With the increased use of data processing equipment and other types of automated office machinery, more and more employers are hiring people proficient in a variety of office tasks.

Because they are so versatile, office workers can find work in virtually any kind of industry, so their overall employment does not depend on the fortunes of any single sector of the economy. In addition to private companies, the federal government should continue to be a good source of jobs. Employment opportunities should be especially good for those trained in various computer skills, as well as knowledge of office machinery. Temporary and part-time work opportunities should also increase, especially during busy business periods.

Earnings

According to the *1998-99 Occupational Outlook Handbook*, beginning office clerks averaged $14,200 a year, depending on the size and geographic location of the company and the skills of the worker. Median annual earnings for full-time office clerks were $19,300, while half earned between $15,300 and $26,200 annually. The top 10 percent earned over $34,600 a year.

Experienced clerks averaged between $21,800 and $29,000 per year; the higher wages were paid to those with the greatest number of job responsibilities. The highest wages were currently found in public utilities and mining companies, while the lowest were found in the real estate, insurance, construction, and finance industries. The federal government generally offered salaries competitive with those in the private sector, about $26,350 a year.

As is the case with most office workers, office clerks work an average thirty-seven to forty-hour week. Full-time workers generally also receive paid vacations, health insurance, sick leave, and other benefits.

Conditions of Work

Clerks usually work in comfortable surroundings and are provided with modern equipment. Although clerks have a variety of tasks and responsibilities, the job itself can be fairly routine and repetitive. Clerks often interact with accountants and other office personnel and may work under close supervision.

Sources of Additional Information

OfficeTeam
2884 Sand Hill Road
Menlo Park, CA 94025
Tel: 800-804-8367

Operations Research Analysts

Definition

Operations research analysts work in the field of applied mathematics. They convert management and operational data into a mathematical model and solve problems using analytical and mathematical techniques. They might help an airline streamline its service, a retail chain determine peak shopping hours, or a restaurant decide how to price the items on its menu. By preparing the business problem in mathematical terms, they are able to find cost-effective solutions.

Nature of the Work

Operations research analysts are the people who apply mathematics to everyday situations and problems. They find practical applications for theoretical principles.

They often work as part of a research team consisting of other mathematicians and engineers, and they frequently use data-processing equipment in their research. They prepare written and oral reports of their findings for upper management officials.

These analysts can be found in a variety of industries and research settings, especially in engineering and the physical sciences. The business problems they evaluate and their specific job responsibilities vary according to the employer.

Company managers usually begin the process by describing a business problem to the analyst. For example, a bank president wants to improve the overall check processing procedure and know which type of personnel should handle specific job responsibilities. First the analyst selects the most practical and accurate method of computing all the data. He or she may use algebra, trigonometry, vector analysis, or calculus to simplify raw data into manageable terms.

After the analyst defines the problem, he or she prepares charts, tables, and diagrams to describe the flow of information or products. This involves the use of mathematical methods as analytical tools as well as various other techniques, such as cost accounting and sampling. It may also involve talking to other company personnel. Then the analyst creates a mathematical model or set of equations that explain how things happen within the represented system.

Models are simplified representations that enable the analyst to break down systems into their component parts, assign numerical values to each component, and examine the mathematical relationships between them. For example, a model for the check processing procedure might include an analysis of the network flow (who handles each check that enters the bank and what their role is in the process), the number of checks processed daily, the current error rate in the process, and the cost to the bank of operating with the current procedure.

Types of models include simulation and linear programming, which are computerized. Analysts must be able to use these programs, as well as work with computer programmers to write new programs. Analysts may need to alter existing models to determine what will happen to the system under different sets of circumstances. For some problems, there may be more than one useful approach. The analyst would probably try the model using several sets of business assumptions and experiment with several models to ensure that the most efficient model is being used.

At this point, the analyst interprets the results and translates them into terms understandable to management. He or she will usually transcribe the data into equations, flow charts, graphs, or other media. It is then up to management officials to implement a decision or ask the research analyst to develop other options. After a final decision is made, the analyst works with staff to implement it as successfully as possible. The entire process, from beginning to end, can take as little as several hours or as much as a year.

Requirements

Aspiring operations research analysts work with complex formulas and equations. It's not enough for them just to be good with numbers. These analysts should truly enjoy math and all its applications. A strong background in and aptitude for mathematics, science, or engineering is necessary. Many employers require that operations research analysts have a bachelor's degree in mathematics, business administration, operations research, or another quantitative discipline. Other employers require graduate work in one of these fields. An increasing number of employers look for graduates with degrees in computer science, information science, or data processing. Classes in statistics, economics, and quantitative mathematics are strongly recommended.

High school students interested in pursuing a career as an operations research analyst should take college-preparatory courses, such as English, history, science, and as many mathematics and statistics courses as possible. Because the computer is an important tool for the research analyst, any available computer programming courses should also be taken. Analysts may choose to earn a degree in areas other than mathematics. Many colleges offer a four-year degree in engineering technology. These programs tend to teach how to use mathematics and science in industrial research, production, or design.

Core college classes include calculus, advanced calculus, linear algebra, statistics, and computers. Analysts take courses in applied mathematics, such as linear and nonlinear programming, graph theory, discreet optimization, and combinatorics.

Increasing specialization in the field means that employers will seek out analysts who are trained to handle certain types of problems. For example, someone with a background in business administration might be asked to handle problems dealing with financial data or personnel scheduling.

Many employers also have on-the-job training for assistant analysts who have a background in mathematics. Some will even subsidize continued education for their employees.

Positions with the federal government usually require the applicant to pass a civil service examination.

Opportunities for Experience & Exploration

Because work in this field requires advanced study, it is hard to get any hands-on experience as a high school student. However, those interested in the career should seek part-time work, such as a temporary job at a bank or insurance company with an in-house operations research department. Students should also take advantage of opportunities to enroll in special summer sessions or advanced placement mathematics courses to develop their knowledge of mathematics.

In addition to job and school exploration, interested students are encouraged to talk with professionals already working in the field to get an accurate picture of the rewards and responsibilities of an operations research analyst.

Methods of Entering

College placement counselors usually help qualified graduates find business and industry opportunities. College graduates can also contact appropriate companies on their own. Major employers include manufacturers of machinery and transportation equipment, telecommunications companies, banks, insurance companies, and private management consulting firms. The federal government, especially the armed forces, also hires operations research analysts. Many of these employers recruit from colleges and technical institutes.

Most operations research analysts find jobs in private industry. Aircraft and automobile manufacturers are among some of the largest employers. Private consulting firms also frequently hire these analysts because businesses of all kinds are relying more and more on their services to help them streamline their production methods and provide the most cost-efficient service possible.

New employees usually have several months of on-the-job training in which they learn about the individual company's systems. Entry-level employees work closely with experienced personnel during this period.

Advancement

Numerous opportunities for advancement to higher-level management positions or into related areas of employment are available to operations research analysts. Skilled analysts may be promoted to the head of an operations research staff or may move to another upper-level management position within a firm. They may also choose to move to a larger company. Promotions usually go to those analysts who have computer skills, technical experience, and the ability to manage people and organize projects. Some successful analysts with a great deal of experience may choose to open their own consulting company. Those with the proper education and experience may also move into a related field, such as statistics or actuarial work.

Employment Outlook

This field is expected to experience slower than average growth through the year 2006. Despite this prediction, the need to replace retiring workers will result in good job opportunities. Those with advanced degrees in operations research, industrial engineering, or management science will be in high demand. The success of companies that have used operations research as part of a systematic approach to decision making as well as the availability of smaller, less-expensive computers have fueled this growth. There should be a demand for qualified operations research analysts throughout the country, and this demand should be greatest in the manufacturing sector and the trade and service industries. Little growth is expected in opportunities with the federal government, especially in defense-related areas.

Earnings

Earnings depend on experience, type of job, and the geographic location of the firm. As listed in the *1998-99 Occupational Outlook Handbook*, 1996 salary averages for operations research analysts were $42,400 a year. Fifty percent earned between $33,100 to $55,500; the top ten percent earned about $65,500. Those working for the federal government earned an average salary of $66,760 a year. Overall, the highest salaries will be found in the private sector.

Conditions of Work

Analysts typically work a regular forty-hour week in a comfortable office setting with computers close at hand. They may work overtime if a project is on a deadline. The work is sedentary in nature and may require long periods of close concentration on mathematical formulas and their application to specific management concerns. Diligence and attention to detail are extremely important, as is patience. Communication skills are important because all research findings must be fully explained, both in written reports and during meetings with management officials.

Sources of Additional Information

American Mathematical Society (AMS)
PO Box 6248
Providence, RI 02940
Tel: 401-455-4000
WWW: http://www.ams.org

Association for Women in Mathematics
4114 Computer and Space Sciences Building,
University of Maryland
College Park, MD 20742-2461
Tel: 301-405-7892

Mathematical Association of America
1529 18th Street, NW
Washington, DC 20036
Tel: 202-387-5200
WWW: http://www.maa.org

Society for Industrial and Applied Mathematics (SIAM)
3600 University City Science Center
Philadelphia, PA 19104
Tel: 215-382-9800
Email: siam@siam.org
WWW: http://www.siam.org

Paralegals

Definition

Paralegals, also known as *legal assistants*, assist in trial preparations, investigate facts, prepare documents such as affidavits and pleadings, and, in general, do work customarily performed by lawyers.

Nature of the Work

Paralegals perform a variety of functions to assist lawyers. Although the lawyer assumes responsibility for the paralegal's work, the paralegal may take on all the duties of the lawyer except for setting fees, appearing in court, accepting cases, and giving legal advice.

Paralegals spend much of their time in law libraries, researching laws and previous cases and compiling facts to help lawyers prepare for trial. After analyzing the laws and facts that have been compiled for a particular client, the paralegal often writes a report that the lawyer may use to determine how to proceed with the case. If a case is brought to trial, the paralegal may help prepare legal arguments and draft pleadings to be filed in court. They also organize and store files and correspondence related to cases.

Not all paralegal work centers on trials. Paralegals also draft contracts, mortgages, affidavits, and other documents. They may help with corporate matters, such as shareholder agreements, contracts, and employee benefit plans. Paralegals may also review financial reports.

Some paralegals work for the government. They may prepare complaints or talk to employers to find out why health or safety standards are not being met. They often analyze legal documents, collect evidence for hearings, and prepare explanatory material on various laws for use by the public.

Other paralegals are involved in community or public-service work. They may help specific groups, such as poor or elderly members of the community. They may file forms, research laws, and prepare documents. They may represent clients at hearings, although they may not appear in court on behalf of a client.

Many paralegals work for large law firms, agencies, and corporations and specialize in a particular area of law. Some work for smaller firms and have a general knowledge of many areas of law. Paralegals have varied duties, and an increasing number are using computers in their work.

Requirements

Requirements for paralegals vary by employer. Some paralegals start out as legal secretaries or clerical workers, and gradually are given more training and responsibility. The majority, however, choose formal training and education programs. These formal programs usually range from one to three years and are offered in a variety of educational settings: four-year colleges and universities, law schools, community and junior colleges, business schools, proprietary schools, and paralegal associations. Admission requirements vary, but good grades in high school and college are always an asset. There are over eight hundred paralegal programs, about two hundred of which have been approved by the American Bar Association.

Some paralegal programs require a bachelor's degree for admission; others do not require any college. In either case, those with a college degree usually have an edge over those without. High school students should take a broad range of subjects, including English, social studies, and languages, especially Spanish. Strong communications and research skills are crucial.

Presently, paralegals are not required to be licensed or certified. Instead, when lawyers employ paralegals, they often follow guidelines designed to protect the public from the practice of law by unqualified persons.

Paralegals may, however, opt to be certified. To do so, they may take and pass an extensive two-day test conducted by the National Association of Legal Assistants Certifying Board. Paralegals who pass the test may use the title Certified Legal Assistant (CLA) after their names. In 1996, the National Federation of Paralegal Associations established the Paralegal Advanced Competency Exam, a means for paralegals with bachelor's degrees and at least two years experience to acquire professional recognition. Paralegals who pass this exam may use the designation Registered Paralegal (RP).

Opportunities for Experience & Exploration

There are several ways interested students can explore the career of a paralegal. They may work part time as a secretary or in the mailroom of a law firm to get an idea of the nature of the work. Students may join an organization affiliated with the legal profession or talk directly with lawyers and paralegals. They can write to schools with paralegal programs or to the organizations listed at the end of this article for general information.

Methods of Entering

Although some law firms promote legal secretaries to paralegal status, most employers prefer to hire individuals who have completed paralegal programs. Those interested in becoming paralegals should consider attending paralegal school. In addition to providing a solid background in paralegal studies, most schools help graduates find jobs. Even though the job market for paralegals is expected to grow very rapidly over the next ten years, those with the best credentials will get the best jobs.

The American Association for Paralegal Education (AAPE) is a national organization that was established in 1981 to promote high standards for paralegal education and, in association with the American Bar Association, to develop an approval process for paralegal education programs. A com-

plete list of member institutions is available from the AAPE headquarters(see address listed at the end of this article).

Advancement

There are no formal advancement paths for paralegals; paralegals usually do not become lawyers or judges. There are, however, some possibilities for advancement, as large firms are beginning to establish career programs for paralegals.

For example, a person may be promoted from paralegal to a head legal assistant who supervises others. In addition, a paralegal may specialize in one area of law, such as environmental, real estate, or medical malpractice. Many paralegals also advance by moving from small to large firms.

Expert paralegals who specialize in one area of law may go into business for themselves. Rather than work for one firm, these freelance paralegals often contract their services to many lawyers. Some paralegals with bachelor's degrees obtain additional education to become lawyers.

Employment Outlook

In 1997, there were about 113,000 paralegals in the United States; most employed by private law firms. The employment outlook for paralegals through the year 2006 is excellent, representing one of the fastest-growing professions in the country. One reason for the expected growth in the profession is the financial benefits of employing paralegals. The paralegal, whose duties fall between those of the legal secretary and those of the attorney, helps make the delivery of legal services more cost effective to clients. The growing need for legal services among the general population and the increased popularity of prepaid legal plans is creating a tremendous demand for paralegals in private law firms. In the private sector, paralegals can work in banks, insurance companies, real estate firms, and corporate legal departments. In the public sector, there is a growing need for paralegals in the courts and community legal service programs, government agencies, and consumer organizations.

The growth of this occupation, to some extent, is dependent on the economy. Businesses are less likely to pursue litigation cases when profit margins are down, thus curbing the need for new hires.

Earnings

Salaries vary. The size and location of the firm and the education and experience of the employee are some factors that determine the annual earnings of the paralegal.

According to 1997 statistics from the National Federation of Paralegal Associations, beginning paralegals average about $23,800 a year. Paralegals with seven to ten years' experience make about $32,900. Top paralegals in large offices can earn as much as $40,000 a year; and paralegal supervisors, $40,000 to $50,000. Many paralegals receive year end bonuses, some averaging $1,900 or more.

Paralegals employed by the federal government averaged $44,000 annually in 1997, as reported by the U.S. Department of Labor.

Conditions of Work

Paralegals often work in pleasant and comfortable offices. Much of the work is performed in a law library. Most paralegals work a forty-hour week, although long hours are sometimes needed to meet court-imposed deadlines.

Many of the paralegal's duties involve routine tasks, so he or she must have a great deal of patience. However, paralegals may be given increasingly difficult assignments over time.

Sources of Additional Information

For information regarding accredited educational facilities, contact:

American Association for Paralegal Education
PO Box 40244
Overland Park, KS 66204
Tel: 913-381-4458

American Bar Association
750 North Lake Shore Drive
Chicago, IL 60611
Tel: 312-988-5000
WWW: http://www.abanet.org

National Association of Legal Assistants
1516 South Boston Avenue, Suite 200
Tulsa, OK 74119
Tel: 918-587-6828

National Federation of Paralegal Associations
PO Box 33108
Kansas City, MO 64114-0108
Tel: 816-941-4000
Email: info@paralegals.org
WWW: http://www.paralegals.org

Physical Therapist Assistants

Definition

Physical therapist assistants are skilled health care workers who assist physical therapists in a variety of techniques (such as exercise, massage, heat, and water therapy) to help restore physical function in people with injury, birth defects, or disease.

Physical therapist assistants work directly under the supervision of physical therapists. They instruct and assist patients in learning and improving functional activities required in their daily lives, such as walking, climbing, and moving from one place to another. The assistants observe patients during treatments, record the patients' responses and progress, and report these to the physical therapist, either orally or in writing. They fit patients for and help them learn to use braces, artificial limbs, crutches, canes, walkers, wheelchairs, and other devices. They may make physical measurements to assess the effects of treatments or to use in patient evaluations, determining the patients' range of motion, length and girth of body parts, and vital signs. Physical therapist assistants act as members of a team and regularly confer with other members of the physical therapy staff. In addition, they sometimes perform various clerical tasks in the department and order supplies, take inventories, and answer telephones.

Nature of the Work

Physical therapy personnel work to prevent, diagnose, and rehabilitate, to restore physical function, prevent permanent disability as much as possible, and help people achieve their maximum attainable performance. For many patients, this objective involves daily living skills, such as eating, grooming, dressing, bathing, and other basic movements that unimpaired people do automatically without thinking.

Physical therapy may alleviate conditions such as muscular pain, spasm, and weakness, joint pain and stiffness, and neuromuscular incoordination. These conditions may be caused by any number of disorders, including fractures, burns, amputations, arthritis, nerve or muscular injuries, trauma, birth defects, stroke, multiple sclerosis, and cerebral palsy. Patients of all ages receive physical therapy services; they may be severely disabled or they may need only minimal therapeutic intervention.

Many kinds of equipment may be used in physical therapy, including mechanical devices such as parallel bars, stationary bicycles, and weightlifting equipment. Heat may be applied to the body using a whirlpool bath, paraffin bath, infrared lamp, heating pad, or diathermy (a technique for generating heat inside body tissue using a carefully controlled small electrical current). Other equipment is needed to produce ultrasound (sound vibrations of extremely high frequency that heat body tissue). Swimming pools are often found in physical therapy facilities. Therapy may involve teaching patients how to use corrective and helpful equipment, such as wheelchairs, canes, crutches, orthotic devices (orthopedic braces and splints), and prosthetic devices (artificial limbs and other body parts).

Physical therapy personnel must often work on improving the emotional state of patients, preparing them psychologically for treatments. The overwhelming sense of hopelessness and lack of confidence that afflict many disabled patients can reduce the patients' success in achieving improved functioning. The health team must be attuned to both the physical and nonphysical aspects of patients to assure that treatments are most beneficial. Sometimes physical therapy personnel work with patients' families to educate them on how to provide simple physical treatments and psychological support at home.

Physical therapist assistants always work under the direction of a qualified physical therapist. Other members of the health team may be a physician or surgeon, nurse, occupational therapist, psychologist, or vocational counselor. Each of these practitioners helps establish and achieve realistic goals consistent with the patient's individual needs. Physical therapist assistants help perform tests to evaluate disabilities and determine the most suitable treatment for the patient; then, as the treatment progresses, they routinely report the patient's condition to the physical therapist. If they observe a patient having serious problems during treatment, the assistants notify the therapist as soon as possible. Physical therapist assistants generally perform complicated therapeutic procedures decided by the physical therapist; however, assistants may initiate routine procedures independently.

These procedures may include physical exercises, which are the most varied and widely used physical treatments. Exercises may be simple or complicated, easy or strenuous, active or passive. Active motions are performed by the patient alone and strengthen or train muscles. Passive exercises involve the assistant moving the body part through the motion, which improves mobility of the joint but does not strengthen muscle. For example, for a patient with a fractured arm, both active and passive exercise may be appropriate. The passive exercises may be designed to maintain or increase the range of motion in the shoulder, elbow, wrist, and finger joints, while active resistive exercises strengthen muscles weakened by disuse. An elderly patient who has suffered a stroke may need guided exercises aimed at keeping the joints mobile, regaining the function of a limb, walking, or climbing stairs. A child with cerebral palsy who would otherwise never walk may be helped to learn coordination exercises that enable crawling, sitting balance, standing balance, and, finally, walking.

Patients sometimes perform exercises in bed or immersed in warm water. Besides its usefulness in alleviating stiffness or paralysis, exercise also helps to improve circulation, relax tense muscles, correct posture, and aid the breathing of patients with lung problems.

Other treatments that physical therapist assistants may administer include massages, traction for patients with neck or back pain, ultrasound and various kinds of heat treatment for diseases such as arthritis that inflame joints or nerves, cold applications to reduce swelling, pain, or hemorrhaging, and ultraviolet light.

Physical therapist assistants train patients to manage devices and equipment that they either need temporarily or permanently. For example, they instruct patients how to walk with canes or crutches using proper gait and maneuver well in a wheelchair. They also instruct patients in how to apply, remove, care for, and cope with splints, braces, and artificial body parts.

In addition, physical therapist assistants may perform office duties: they schedule patients, keep records, handle inventory, and order supplies.

Requirements

A degree from an accredited physical therapist assistant program is required; programs are usually offered in community and junior colleges. These programs, typically two years long, combine academic instruction with a period of supervised clinical practice in a physical therapy department setting. In recent years, admission to accredited programs has been fairly competitive, with three to five applicants for each available opening.

Some physical therapist assistants begin their careers while in the armed forces, which operate training programs. While these programs are not sufficient for state licensure and do not award degrees, they can serve as an excellent introduction to the field for students who later enter more complete training programs.

Licensure for physical therapist assistants is currently mandatory in forty-four states. Licensure requirements vary from state to state, but all require graduation from an American Physical Therapy Association–accredited two-year associate degree program and passing a written examination administered by the state. Conditions for renewing the license also vary by state. For information about licensing requirements, candidates should consult their schools' career guidance offices or the state licensure boards.

While still in high school, prospective physical therapist assistants should take courses in health, biology, mathematics, psychology, social science, physical education, computer data entry, English, and other courses that develop communications skills. In the physical therapist assistant training program, students can expect to study general education plus anatomy, physiology, biology, history and philosophy of rehabilitation, human growth and development, psychology, and physical therapist assistant procedures such as massage, therapeutic exercise, and heat and cold therapy. Other courses in mathematics and applied physical sciences help students understand the physical therapy apparatus and the scientific principles on which therapeutic procedures are based.

Physical therapist assistants must have large amounts of stamina, patience, and determination, but at the same time they must be able to establish personal relationships quickly and successfully. They should genuinely like and understand people, both under normal conditions and under the stress of illness. An outgoing personality is highly desirable as is the ability to instill confidence and enthusiasm in patients. Much of the work of physical retraining and restoring is very repetitive, and assistants may not perceive any progress for long periods of time. At times patients may seem unable or unwilling to cooperate. In such cases, assistants need boundless patience, to appreciate small gains and build on them. When restoration to good health is not attainable, physical therapist assistants must help patients adjust to a different way of life and find ways to cope with their situation. Creativity is an asset to devising methods that help disabled people achieve greater self-sufficiency. Assistants should be flexible and open to suggestions offered by their co-workers and willing and able to follow directions closely.

Because the job can be physically quite demanding, physical therapist assistants must be reasonably strong and enjoy physical activity. Manual dexterity and good coordination are needed to adjust equipment and assist patients. Assistants should be able to lift, climb, stoop, and kneel.

Opportunities for Experience & Exploration

While still in high school, students can get experience through summer or part-time employment or by volunteering in the physical therapy department of a hospital or clinic. Also, many schools, both public and private, have volunteer assistance programs for work with their disabled student population. Students can also gain useful direct experience by working with disabled children in a summer camp.

These opportunities provide prospective physical therapy workers with direct job experience that helps them determine whether they have the personal qualities necessary for this career. Students who have not had such direct experience should make an effort to talk to a physical therapist or physical therapist assistant during career-day programs, if available. It may also be possible to arrange to visit a physical therapy department, watch the staff at work, and ask questions.

Methods of Entering

The student's school placement office is probably the best place to find a job. Alternatively, assistants can apply to the physical therapy departments of local hospitals, rehabilitation centers, extended-care facilities, and other potential employers. Openings are listed in the classified ads of newspapers, professional journals, and with private and public employment agencies. In locales where training programs have produced many physical therapist assistants, competition for jobs may be keen. In such cases, assistants may want to widen their search to areas where there is less competition, especially suburban and rural areas.

Advancement

With experience, physical therapist assistants are often given greater responsibility and better pay. In large health care facilities, supervisory possibilities may open up. In small institutions that employ only one physical therapist, the physical therapist assistant may eventually take care of all the technical tasks that go on in the department, within the limitations of his or her training and education.

Physical therapist assistants with degrees from accredited programs are generally in the best position to gain advancement in any setting. They sometimes decide to earn a bachelor's degree in physical therapy and become fully qualified physical therapists.

Employment Outlook

Employment prospects are very good for physical therapist assistants, with job growth projected around 80 percent through the year 2006. Demand for rehabilitation services is expected to continue to grow much more rapidly than the average for all occupations, and the rate of turnover among workers is relatively high. Many new positions for physical therapist assistants are expected to open up as hospital programs that aid the disabled expand and as long-term facilities seek to offer residents more adequate services.

A major contributing factor is the increasing number of Americans aged sixty-five and over. This group tends to suffer a disproportionate amount of the accidents and chronic illnesses that necessitate physical therapy services. Many from the baby boom generation are reaching the age common for heart attacks, thus creating a need for more cardiac and physical rehabilitation. Legislation that requires appropriate public education for all disabled children also may increase the demand for physical therapy services. As more adults engage in strenuous physical exercise, more musculoskeletal injuries will result, thus increasing demand for physical therapy services.

Earnings

Salaries for physical therapist assistants vary considerably depending on geographical location, employer, and level of experience. The yearly income for a recently graduated assistant is usually between $20,000 and $24,000 a year, while experienced physical therapist assistants usually earn between $25,000 and $30,000. Fringe benefits vary, although they usually include paid holidays and vacations, health insurance, and pension plans.

Conditions of Work

Physical therapy is generally administered in pleasant, clean, well-lighted, and well-ventilated surroundings, located in hospitals, rehabilitation centers, schools for the disabled, nursing homes, community and government health agencies, physicians' or physical therapists' offices, and facilities for the mentally disabled. The space devoted to physical therapy services is often large, in order to accommodate activities such as gait training and exercises and procedures requiring equipment. Some procedures are given at patients' bedsides.

In the physical therapy department, patients come and go all day, many in wheelchairs, on walkers, canes, crutches, or stretchers. The staff tries to maintain a purposeful, harmonious, congenial atmosphere as they and the patients work toward the common goal of restoring physical efficacy.

The work can be exhausting. Physical therapist assistants may be on their feet for hours at a time, and they may have to move heavy equipment, lift patients, and help them to stand and walk. Most assistants work daytime hours, five days a week, although some positions require evening or weekend work. Some assistants work on a part-time basis.

The combined physical and emotional demands of the job can exert a considerable strain. Prospective assistants would be wise to seek out some job experience related to physical therapy so that they have a practical understanding of their psychological and physical capacities. By checking our their suitability for the work, they can make a better commitment to the training program.

Job satisfaction can be great for physical therapist assistants as they can see how their efforts help to make people's lives much more rewarding.

Sources of Additional Information

American Physical Therapy Association
1111 North Fairfax Street
Alexandria, VA 22314
Tel: 800-999-2782
WWW: http://www.apta.org

Physical Therapists

Definition

Physical therapists, formerly called *physiotherapists*, are health care specialists who restore mobility, alleviate pain and suffering, and work to prevent permanent disability for their patients. They test and measure the functions of the musculoskeletal, neurological, pulmonary, and cardiovascular systems, and treat problems in these systems caused by illness, injury, or birth defect. Physical therapists practice preventive, restorative, and rehabilitative treatment for their patients.

Nature of the Work

To initiate a program of physical therapy, the physical therapist consults the individual's medical history, examines the patient and identifies problems, confers with the physician or other health care professionals involved in the patient's care, establishes objectives and treatment goals that are consistent with the patient's needs, and determines the methods for accomplishing the objectives.

Treatment goals established by the physical therapist include preventing disability, relieving pain, and restoring function. In the presence of illness or injury, the ultimate goal is to assist the patient's physical recovery and reentry into the community, home, and work environment at the highest level of independence and self-sufficiency possible.

To aid and maintain recovery, the physical therapist also provides education to involve patients in their own care. The educational program may include exercises, posture reeducation, and relaxation practices. In many cases, the patient's family is involved in the educational program by providing emotional support or physical assistance as needed. These activities evolve into a continuum of self-care when the patient is discharged from the physical therapy program.

The care physical therapists provide for many types of patients of all ages includes working with burn victims to prevent abnormal scarring and loss of movement, with stroke victims to regain movement and independent living, with cancer patients to relieve discomfort, and with cardiac patients to improve endurance and achieve independence. Physical therapists also provide preventive exercise programs, postural improvement, and physical conditioning to individuals who perceive the need to promote their own health and well-being.

Physical therapists should have a creative approach to their work. No two patients respond the same way to exactly the same kind of treatment. The challenge is to find the right way to encourage the patient to make progress, to respond to treatment, to feel a sense of achievement, and to refuse to become discouraged if progress is slow.

Many physical therapists acquire specialized knowledge through clinical experience and educational preparation in specialty areas of practice, such as cardiopulmonary physical therapy, clinical electrophysiologic physical therapy, neurologic physical therapy, orthopedic physical therapy, pediatric physical therapy, geriatric physical therapy, and sports physical therapy.

Requirements

Physical therapists attain their professional skills through extensive educational and clinical training. Either a bachelor's degree or a master's degree in physical therapy is necessary to practice physical therapy. Entry-level professional accredited education is offered in more than forty-five bachelor's degree programs, and more than one hundred master's degree programs. All accredited physical therapy programs will be at the master's level or higher by the year 2001.

High school students who plan to become physical therapists should have a strong background in the physical and biological sciences.

Upon graduating from an accredited physical therapy educational program, physical therapists must successfully complete a licensure examination and comply with the legal requirements of the jurisdiction in which they practice. These qualifications are required in all fifty states, the District of Columbia, the Virgin Islands, and the commonwealth of Puerto Rico.

Specialist certification of physical therapists, while not a requirement for employment, is a desirable advanced credential. The American Board of Physical Therapy Specialties, an appointed group of the American Physical Therapy Association, certifies physical therapists who demonstrate specialized knowledge and advanced clinical proficiency in a specialty area of physical therapy practice and who pass a certifying examination. The seven areas currently involved in this process are cardiopulmonary, clinical electrophysiology, neurology, orthopedics, pediatrics, geriatrics, and sports physical therapy. In 1995, there were 1,348 certified specialists.

Opportunities for Experience & Exploration

Students interested in exploring a career as a physical therapist might work as a counselor in a summer camp for the disabled or as an orderly or a physical therapy aide in a hospital in which there is a physical therapy program. Students also may interview or visit a physical therapist at their work.

Methods of Entering

Physical therapy graduates may obtain jobs through their college placement offices or by answering ads in any of a variety of professional journals. They can apply in person or send letters and resumes to hospitals, medical centers, rehabilitation facilities, and other places that hire physical therapists. Some find jobs through the American Physical Therapy Association. Veterans Administration hospitals and other government agencies offer another source of employment.

Advancement

In a hospital or other type of facility, one may rise from being a staff physical therapist to being the chief physical therapist and then director of the department. Administrative responsibilities are usually given to those physical therapists who have had several years of experience, plus the personal qualities that prepare them for undertaking this kind of assignment.

After serving in a hospital or other institution for several years, some physical therapists open up their own practices or go into a group practice, with both often paying higher salaries.

Employment Outlook

Physical therapy is one of the fastest-growing professions in the United States. In 1996, 115,000 physical therapists were employed in the United States, about 25 percent worked part time. The Bureau of Labor Statistics projects a occupational growth of about 75 percent through the year 2006.

One reason for this rapid growth is the fact that the median age of the American population is rising, and this older demographic group develops a higher number of medical conditions that cause physical pain and disability. Also, advances in medical technology save more people, who then require physical therapy. For example, as more newborns with birth defects and trauma victims survive, the need for physical therapists will rise. Another reason is the public's growing interest in physical fitness, which has resulted in an increasing number of athletic injuries requiring physical therapy. In industry and fitness centers, a growing interest in pain and injury prevention also has created new opportunities for physical therapists.

Employment prospects for physical therapists should continue to be excellent into the next century. Hospitals are expected to remain the largest employer (employing about two-thirds of physical therapists), with nursing homes, outpatient rehabilitation centers, and home health agencies becoming increasingly important sources of jobs. If enrollment in accredited physical therapy programs remains at the current level, there will be more openings for physical therapists than qualified individuals to fill them.

Earnings

Salaries for physical therapists depend on experience and type of employer. Physical therapists earned an annual average salary $39,364 in 1996. Fifty percent averaged between $30,004 and $54,860; the top ten percent earned over $67,288 a year. According to the American Physical Therapy Association, hospital-employed therapists earned an average of $48,000 annually.

Federally employed physical therapists are paid starting salaries of about $20,000 a year, while supervisory therapists average about $38,700. The average for all therapists working in the federal government is about $26,400 per year.

Conditions of Work

The average physical therapist works approximately forty to fifty hours each week, including Saturdays. Patient sessions may be brief or may last an hour or more. Usually, treatment is on an individual basis, but occasionally therapy may be given in groups when the patients' problems are similar.

Sources of Additional Information

The American Physical Therapy Association offers a brochure entitled A Future in Physical Therapy, *as well as other general career information.*

American Physical Therapy Association
1111 North Fairfax Street
Alexandria, VA 22314
Tel: 800-999-2782
WWW: http://www.apta.org

Physician Assistants

Definition

Physician assistants practice medicine under the supervision of licensed doctors of medicine or osteopathy, providing various health care services to patients. Much of the work they do was formerly limited to physicians.

Nature of the Work

Physician assistants, also known as PAs, help physicians provide medical care to patients. PAs may be assigned a variety of tasks; they may take medical histories of patients, do complete routine physical examinations, order laboratory tests, draw blood samples, give injections, decide on diagnoses and choose treatments, and assist in surgery. Although the duties of PAs vary by state, they always work under the supervision and direction of a licensed physician. The extent of the PA's duties depends on the specific laws of the state and the practices of the supervising physician, as well as the experience and abilities of the PA. PAs work in a variety of health care settings, including hospitals, clinics, physician's offices, and federal, state, and local agencies.

About 50 percent of all PAs specialize in primary care medicine, such as family medicine, internal medicine, pediatrics, obstetrics and gynecology, and emergency medicine. Nineteen percent of all PAs work in surgery or surgical subspecialties. In 1998, 41 states and the District of Columbia allowed PAs to prescribe medicine to patients. In California, prescriptions written by PAs are referred to as written prescription transmittal orders. Physician assistants may be known by other occupational titles such as *child health associates, MEDEX, physician associates, anesthesiologist's assistants,* or *surgeon's assistants.*

PAs are skilled professionals who assume a great deal of responsibility in their work. By handling various medical tasks for their physician employers, PAs allow physicians more time to diagnose and treat more severely ill patients.

Requirements

Most states require that PAs complete an educational program approved by the Commission on Accreditation of Allied Health Education Programs (CAAHEP). In 1998, there were 104 fully accredited PA programs, and 24 programs with provisional accreditation. Admissions requirements vary, but two years of college courses in science or health, and some health care experience, are usually the minimum requirements. More than half of all students accepted, however, have their bachelor's or master's degrees. Most educational programs last 24 to 25 months, although some last only one year and others may last as many as three years.

The first six to twenty-four months of most programs involve classroom instruction in human anatomy, physiology, microbiology, clinical pharmacology, applied psychology, clinical medicine, and medical ethics. In the last nine to fifteen months of most programs, students engage in supervised clinical work, usually including assignments, or rotations, in various branches of medicine, such as family practice, pediatrics, and emergency medicine.

Graduates of these programs may receive a certificate, an associate's degree, a bachelor's degree, or a master's degree; most programs, however, offer graduates a bachelor's degree. The one MEDEX program that presently exists lasts only eighteen months. It is designed for medical corpsmen, registered nurses, and others who have had extensive patient-care experience. MEDEX students usually obtain most of their clinical experience by working with a physician who will hire them after graduation.

PA programs are offered in a variety of educational and health care settings, including colleges and universities, medical schools and centers, hospitals and the Armed Forces. State laws and regulations dictate the scope of the PA's duties, and, in all but a few states, PAs must be graduates of an approved training program. Currently, all states—except Mississippi—require that PAs be certified by the National Commission on Certification of Physician Assistants (NCCPA). To become certified, applicants must be graduates of an accredited PA program and pass the Physician Assistants National Certifying Examination. The examination consists of three parts: the first part tests general medical knowledge, while the second section tests the PA's specialty—either primary care or surgery—while the third part tests for practical clinical knowledge. After successfully completing the examination, physician assistants can use the credential "Physician Assistant-Certified (PA-C)."

Once certified, PAs are required to complete one hundred hours of continuing medical education courses every two years, and in addition must pass a recertification examination every six years. Besides NCCPA certification, most states also require that PAs register with the state medical board. State rules and regulations vary greatly concerning the work of PAs, and applicants are advised to study the laws of the state in which they wish to practice.

Opportunities for Experience & Exploration

Those interested in exploring the profession should talk with school guidance counselors, practicing PAs, PA students, and various health care employees at local hospitals and clinics. Students can also obtain information by contacting one of the organizations listed at the end of this chapter. Serving as a volunteer in a hospital, clinic, or nursing home is a good way for students to get exposure to the health care profession. In addition, while in college, students may be able to obtain summer jobs as hospital orderlies, nurse's aides, or medical clerks. Such jobs can help students assess their interest in and suitability for work as PAs before they apply to a PA program.

Methods of Entering

PAs must complete their formal training programs before entering the job market. Once their studies are completed, the placement services of the schools may help them find jobs. PAs may also seek employment at hospitals, clinics, medical offices, or other health care settings. Information about jobs with the federal government can be obtained by contacting the Office of Personnel Management.

Advancement

Since the PA profession is still quite new, formal lines of advancement have not yet been established. There are still several ways to advance. Hospitals, for example, do not employ head PAs. Those with experience can assume more responsibility at higher pay, or they move on to employment at larger hospitals and clinics. Some PAs go back to school for additional education to practice in a specialty area, such as surgery, urology, or ophthalmology.

Employment Outlook

There were approximately 64,000 physician assistants employed in the United States in 1998. Employment for PAs, according to the U.S. Department of Labor, is expected to increase much faster than the average for all occupations. A 46.4 percent increase in the number of new jobs is projected through the year 2006. In fact, job growth is expected to outpace the number of potential employees entering this occupation by as much as 9 percent. This field was also mentioned in *U.S. News & World Report*'s recent article, "Best Jobs for the Future."

The role of the PA in delivering health care has also expanded over the past decade. PAs have taken on new duties and responsibilities, and they now work in a variety of health care settings. Most PAs, about thirty-six percent, are employed by single physicians, or group practices; three out of ten are employed by hospitals. Many areas lacking quality medical care personnel, such as remote rural areas and the inner city, are turning to PAs to meet their needs. Many hospitals and busy practices hire PAs to help alleviate the workload. PAs are assigned to routine cases or less serious patients, leaving doctors to treat more serious patient cases.

Earnings

According to the American Academy of Physician Assistants, 80 percent of PA graduates find employment as a PA in less than a year. Salaries of PAs vary according to experience, specialty, and employer. In 1998, PAs earned a starting average of $62,294 annually. Those working in hospitals and medical offices earn slightly more than those working in clinics. Experienced PAs have the potential to earn close to $100,000 a year. PAs working for the military averaged $50,320 a year. PAs are well compensated compared with other occupations with similar training requirements. Most PAs receive health and life insurance among other benefits.

Conditions of Work

PAs work in a variety of health care settings. Some work for one physician; others work in group practices. PAs work in hospitals, clinics and medical offices. They also hold jobs in nursing homes, long-term care facilities, and prisons. Most work settings are comfortable and clean, although, like physicians, PAs spend a good part of their day standing or walking. The workweek varies according to the employment setting.

A few emergency room PAs may work twenty-four-hour shifts, twice a week; others work twelve-hour shifts, three times a week. PAs who work in physicians' offices, hospitals, or clinics may have to work weekends, nights, and holidays. PAs employed in clinics, however, usually work five-day, forty-hour weeks.

Sources of Additional Information

■**American Academy of Physician Assistants**
950 North Washington Street
Alexandria, VA 22314
Tel: 703-836-2272
Email: aapa@aapa.org
WWW: http://www.aapa.org

■**Association of Physician Assistant Programs**
950 North Washington Street
Alexandria, VA 22314
Tel: 703-548-5538
Email: apap@aapa.org
WWW: http://www.apap.org

■**National Commission on Certification of Physician Assistants**
6849-B2 Peachtree Dunwoody Road
Atlanta, GA 30328
Tel: 404-493-9100
WWW:
http://www.social.com/health/nhicdata/hr1300/hr1334.html

Physicians

Definition

The *physician* diagnoses, prescribes medicines for, and otherwise treats diseases and disorders of the human body. A physician may also perform surgery and often specializes in one aspect of medical care and treatment. Physicians hold either a doctor of medicine or osteopathic medicine degree.

Nature of the Work

The greatest number of physicians are in private practice. They see patients by appointment in their offices and examining rooms, and visit patients who are confined to the hospital. In the hospital, they may perform operations or give other kinds of medical treatment. Some physicians also make calls on patients at home if the patient is not able to get to the physician's office or if the illness is an emergency.

Approximately 15 percent of physicians in private practice are *general practitioners* or *family practitioners*. They see patients of all ages and both sexes and will diagnose and treat those ailments that are not severe enough or unusual enough to require the services of a specialist. When special problems arise, however, the general practitioner will refer the patient to a specialist.

Although the major portion of this article deals with the *doctor of medicine* (M.D.), also known as a *doctor of allopathic medicine*, there is another distinct type of physician—the *doctor of osteopathic medicine* (D.O.), or *osteopathic physician*. Both treat disease and injury, but D.O.s place special emphasis on the musculoskeletal system—ligaments, muscles, nerves, and bones. Osteopathic physicians use all modern diagnostic procedures to determine the extent of a condition, and treatment may include drugs, surgery, or one of the basic treatments of osteopathic manipulative treatment. Most D.O.s are general practitioners, providing primary care; only about 36 percent are specialists.

Not all physicians are engaged in private practice. Some are in academic medicine and teach in medical schools or teaching hospitals. Some are engaged only in research. Some are salaried employees of health maintenance organizations or other prepaid health care plans. Some are salaried hospital employees.

Some physicians, often called *medical officers*, are employed by the federal government, in such positions as public health, or in the service of the Department of Veterans Affairs. State and local governments also employ physicians for public health agency work. A large number of physicians serve with the armed forces, both in this country and overseas.

More and more physicians are entering industrial medicine. Known as *industrial physicians* or *occupational physicians*, they are employed by large industrial firms for two main reasons: to prevent illnesses that may be caused by the kind of work in which the employees are engaged and to treat accidents or illnesses of employees.

Although most industrial physicians may roughly be classified as general practitioners because of the wide variety of illnesses that they must recognize and treat, their knowledge must also extend to public health techniques and to understanding such relatively new hazards as radiation and the toxic effects of various chemicals, including insecticides.

A specialized type of occupational physician is the *flight surgeon*. Flight surgeons study the effects of high-altitude flying on the physical condition of flight personnel. They place members of the flight staff in special low-pressure and refrigeration chambers that simulate high-altitude conditions and study the reactions on their blood pressure, pulse and respiration rate, and body temperature.

Another growing specialty is the field of nuclear medicine. Some large hospitals have a nuclear research laboratory, which functions under the direction of a chief of nuclear medicine, who coordinates the activities of the lab with other hospital departments and medical personnel. These physicians perform tests using nuclear isotopes and use techniques that let physicians see and understand organs deep within the body.

Both M.D.s and D.O.s may become specialists in any of the forty different medical care specialties, including those described below:

Allergist-immunologists specialize in diseases and conditions caused by allergies or related to the immune system. They treat patients with ailments such as bronchial asthma, skin disorders, diseases of the connective tissues, and impairment of the autoimmune system. They also treat those undergoing surgical transplantation to help prevent rejection of the transplanted organ.

Anesthesiologists administer anesthetics before and during surgery and other medical procedures so the patient will feel no pain. They may induce general anesthesia, rendering the patient unconscious, using drugs, gases, or vapors; or they may use a local or spinal anesthetic, which blocks pain in a specific area while the patient remains awake. Anesthesiologists also work in emergency rooms, where they may help victims of drug overdose, heart attacks, poison, electric shock, drowning, or other accidents that can interfere with breathing. Some of these specialists work in respiratory care units or help plan home care for patients with respiratory illness, and some specialize in the diagnoses and treatment of chronic pain.

Cardiologists concentrate on diseases and functions of the heart. They listen to a patient's heart with a stethoscope, make recordings of its activity with an electrocardiograph, and study X-ray photographs to determine the existence or extent of a heart disorder. They may prescribe medication and recommend special diets and exercise programs and may refer the patient to a surgeon if corrective surgery is indicated.

Dermatologists treat diseases and problems of the human skin, hair, and nails. Their patients may be troubled with something as common as warts or acne or as serious as cancer. Dermatologists may treat boils and abscesses or skin injuries or infections. They may remove lesions, cysts, birthmarks, and other growths. They also treat scars and perform hair transplants.

Gynecologists and *obstetricians* are concerned with the health of the woman's reproductive system. Whereas gynecologists specialize in treating diseases and disorders and obstetricians in providing medical care before, during, and after childbirth, physicians often handle both specialties.

Internists are specialists in internal medicine. In other words, they diagnose and treat diseases and injuries of the internal organs, such as lungs, heart and valves, glands, stomach and intestines, blood, kidneys, tumors, and joints and muscles. Internists are often an adult's primary care physician. They are not to be confused with interns, medical school graduates who practice medicine under the supervision of a hospital staff for a specified length of time to gain experience and qualify for a state license.

Naturopathic physicians treat diseases and illnesses with natural treatments, such as nutrition, acupuncture, physiotherapy, massage, homeopathy, meditation, relaxation, and herbs and vitamins. They combine natural healing methods with modern techniques and therapies. They generally try to avoid prescribing synthetic medications.

Neurologists treat disorders of the nervous system. They study the results of tests done on the patient's blood and cerebrospinal fluid and the results of electroencephalograms (brain-wave tests) and X rays. They may prescribe medications and drugs or recommend surgery, depending on the diagnosis.

Ophthalmologists are eye specialists. They examine a patient's eyes for poor vision or disease, prescribe corrective lenses or medication, and may recommend exercises to strengthen eye muscles. They perform surgery when indicated.

Otolaryngologists are ear, nose, and throat specialists. They treat patients with hearing loss or speech loss from disease or injury, prescribe medications, and may perform surgery. A physician may specialize in only one type of disorder: ear (otologist), nose (rhinologist), or throat (laryngologist).

Pathologists study the nature, cause, progression, and effects of diseases. They perform tests on body tissues, fluids, secretions, and other specimens to see if a disease is present and to determine what stage it is in. They perform autopsies to find out why people died and to study the effects of medical treatment. Pathologists often specialize in areas such as clinical chemistry, microbiology, or blood banking. They may supervise the pathology department of a medical school, hospital, clinic, medical examiner's office, or research institution.

Pediatricians give medical care to children from birth through adolescence. They provide a program of preventive health care, including inoculations and vaccinations, and treat illnesses and injuries as they arise.

Physiatrists specialize in the use of physical devices and exercise to rehabilitate patients. They determine the kind of therapy needed; prescribe exercises or treatments using light, heat, cold, or other processes; and instruct the physical therapists who administer these treatments. They also recommend occupational therapy for patients who must remain hospitalized for long periods of time or for those who must change their work because of a disability.

Physician assistants do not have M.D. or D.O. degrees, but are graduates of an accredited physician assistant program. They work under the supervision of physicians and perform routine diagnostic, therapeutic, and preventive procedures. P.A.s usually work in family practices, internal medicine, orthopedics, and surgery, where they take medical histories, do physical examinations, and order lab tests and X rays. They may make preliminary diagnoses and take care of emergencies until a physician is available.

Proctologists treat diseases and disorders of the anus, rectum, and colon. They may prescribe medication and recommend changes in the patient's living habits or may perform surgery to treat the affected region.

Psychiatrists treat persons with mental, emotional, and behavioral disorders. Using psychotherapy and sometimes medication, they help patients to understand and overcome problems that interfere with everyday living.

Radiologists use X rays and radioactive substances to treat illness. They treat internal and external tumors and growths with radiation and administer radioactive materials to patients to make their internal organs visible on X-ray films or fluoroscopic screens. Radiologists may specialize in diagnostic radiology, radiation therapy, or nuclear medicine. A director of radiology plans, organizes, and supervises the activities of a radiology department in cooperation with hospital officials and other department heads.

Sports physicians develop programs to prevent, diagnose, and treat injuries and disorders experienced by athletes.

Surgeons operate to correct deformities, repair injuries, prevent diseases, and improve the health of patients. They examine patients to see whether surgery is necessary, estimate the possible risks, and decide which procedures to use. They take into consideration the patient's general health, medical history, and reaction to drugs. General surgeons perform many kinds of operations, but some surgeons specialize in only one kind of operation. For example: Neurological surgeons, or neurosurgeons, operate on the brain, spinal cord, and other nerves of the body. Orthopedic surgeons treat broken bones and diseases of bones and joints. Plastic surgeons correct disfigurements of the face or body, whether present at birth or caused by illness or injury. Thoracic surgeons operate on lungs and other organs in the chest cavity.

Urologists treat disorders of the urinary system of both men and women and of the reproductive organs of men. They may prescribe medicines for simple ailments such as bladder infections or perform surgery for more complicated conditions such as kidney stones or enlarged prostate glands.

Requirements

The physician is required to devote many years to study before being admitted to practice. Interested high school students should enroll in a college preparatory course, and take courses in English, languages (especially Latin), the humanities, social studies, and mathematics, in addition to courses in biology, chemistry, and physics.

The student who hopes to enter medicine should be admitted first to a liberal arts program in an accredited undergraduate institution. Some colleges offer a "premedical" course, and it is advisable for the student to take such a course where it is offered. A good general education, however, with as many courses as possible in science and perhaps a major in biology, is considered adequate preparation for the study of medicine. Courses should include physics, biology, inorganic and organic chemistry, English, mathematics, and the social sciences.

College freshmen who hope to apply to a medical school early in their senior year should have adequate knowledge of the requirements for admission to one of the 125 accredited schools of medicine or 17 accredited schools of osteopathic medicine in the country. They should consult a copy of Medical School Admission Requirements, U.S. and Canada, available from the Association of American Medical Colleges, or the College Information Booklet for the D.O. Profession, published by the American Association of Colleges of Osteopathic Medicine. Both are also available in college libraries. If students read carefully the admissions requirements of the several medical schools to which they hope to apply, they will avoid making mistakes in choosing an graduate program.

Students who do not enter a premedical program may find it possible to change to a major in biology or chemistry after they have enrolled. Such majors may make them eligible for consideration to be admitted to many medical schools.

Some students may be admitted to medical school after only three years of study in an undergraduate program. There are a few medical schools that will award the bachelor's degree at the end of the first year of medical school study. This practice is becoming less common as more students seek admission to medical schools. Most premedical students plan to spend four years in an undergraduate program and to receive the bachelor's degree before entering the four-year medical school program.

During the second or third year in college, undergraduates should arrange with an advisor to take the Medical College Admission Test (MCAT). This test is given each spring and each fall at certain selected sites. The student's advisor should know the date, place, and time; or the student may write for this information to the Association of American Medical Colleges. All medical colleges in this country require this test for admission, and a student's MCAT score is one of the factors that is weighed in the decision to take or to reject any applicant. Because the test does not evaluate medical knowledge, most college students who are enrolled in liberal arts programs should not find it to be unduly difficult. The examination covers four areas: verbal facility, quantitative ability, knowledge of the humanities and social sciences, and knowledge of biology, chemistry, and physics.

Students who hope to be admitted to medical school are encouraged to apply to at least three institutions to increase their chances of being accepted by one of them. Approximately one out of every two qualified applicants to medical schools will be admitted each year. Two services are available to medical school applicants to make this step easier. The American Medical College Application Service (AMCAS) and the American Association of Colleges of Osteopathic Medicine Application Service (AACOMAS) will check, copy, and submit applications to medical schools specified by the individual student. More information about this service may be obtained from AMCAS, AACOMAS, premedical advisers, and medical schools.

In addition to the traditional medical schools, there are several schools of basic medical sciences that enroll medical students for the first two years (preclinical experience) of medical school. They offer a preclinical curriculum to students similar to that which is offered by a regular medical school. At the end of the two-year program, the student will then apply to a four-year medical school for the final two years of instruction.

Although high scholarship is considered to be a determining factor in admitting a student to a medical school, it is actually only one of the criteria upon which such a decision is based. By far the greatest number of successful applicants to medical schools are "B" students. Because admission is also determined by a number of other factors, including a personal interview, other qualities in addition to a high scholastic average are considered desirable for a prospective physician. High on the list of desirable qualities are emotional stability, integrity, reliability, resourcefulness, and a sense of service.

The average student enters medical school at age twenty-one or twenty-two. The student then begins another four years of formal schooling. During the first two years of medical school, the student learns human anatomy, biochemistry, physiology, pharmacology, psychology, microbiology, pathology, medical ethics, and laws governing medicine. Most instruction in the first two years is given through classroom lectures, laboratories, seminars, independent research, and the reading of textbook material and other types of literature. Students also learn to take medical histories, examine patients, and recognize symptoms.

During the last two years in medical school, the student becomes actively involved in the treatment process. The student who spends a large proportion of the time in the hospital becomes part of a medical team that is headed by a teaching physician who specializes in a particular area. Others on the team may be interns or residents. Students are closely supervised but learn much firsthand about techniques such as how to take a patient's medical history, how to make a physical examination, how to work in the laboratory, how to make a diagnosis, and how to keep all the necessary records.

Students rotate from one medical specialty to another, to obtain a broad understanding of each field. Students are assigned to duty in internal medicine, pediatrics, psychiatry, obstetrics and gynecology, and surgery. Students may be assigned to other specialties, too.

In addition to this hospital work, students continue to take coursework. They are expected to be responsible for assigned studies and also for some independent study.

Prospective physicians must have some plan for financing their long and costly education. They face a period of at least eight years after college when they will not be self-supporting. While still in school, students may be able to work only during summer vacations, because the necessary laboratory courses of the regular school year are so time consuming that little time is left for activities other than the preparation of daily lessons. Some scholarships and loans are available to qualified students.

After receiving the M.D. or D.O. degree, the new physician is required to take an examination to be licensed to practice. Every state requires such an examination. It is conducted through the board of medical examiners in each state. Some states have reciprocity agreements with other states so that a physician licensed in one state may be automatically licensed in another without being required to pass another examination. Because this is not true throughout the U.S., however, the wise physician will find out about licensing procedures before planning to move.

Most states require all new M.D.s to complete at least one year of postgraduate training, and a few require an internship plus a one-year residency. New D.O.s serve a one-year rotating internship during which they gain experience in surgery, pediatrics, internal medicine, and other specialties.

Physicians wishing to specialize spend from three to seven years in advanced residency training plus another two or more years of practice in the specialty. Then they must pass a specialty board examination to become a board-certified M.D. or D.O.

For a teaching or research career, physicians may also earn a master's degree or a Ph.D. in biochemistry or microbiology.

Opportunities for Experience & Exploration

One of the best introductions to a career in health care is to volunteer at a local hospital, clinic, or nursing home. In this way it is possible to get a feel for what it's like to work around other health care professionals and patients and possibly determine exactly where your interests lie. As in any career, reading as much as possible about the profession, talking with a high school counselor, and interviewing those working in the field are other important ways to explore your interest.

Methods of Entering

There are no shortcuts to entering the medical profession. Requirements are an M.D. or D.O. degree, a licensing examination, a one- or two-year internship and a period of residency that may extend as long as five years.

Upon completing this program, which may take up to fifteen years, physicians are then ready to enter practice. They may choose to open a solo private practice, enter a partnership practice, enter a group practice, or take a salaried job with a prepaid plan. Salaried positions are also available with federal and state agencies, the military, including the Department of Veterans Affairs, and private companies. Teaching and research jobs are usually obtained after other experience is acquired.

The highest ratio of physicians to patients is in the Northeast and West. The lowest ratio is in the South. Most M.D.s practice in urban areas near hospitals and universities. D.O.s tend to practice in small cities, towns, and rural areas.

Physicians can find employment in a wide variety of settings, including hospitals, nursing homes, managed-care offices, prisons, schools and universities, research laboratories, trauma centers, clinics, and public health centers.

Advancement

Physicians who work in a managed-care setting or for a large group or corporation can advance by opening a private practice. The average physician in private practice does not advance in the accustomed sense of the word. Their progress consists of advancing in skill and understanding, in numbers of patients, and in income. They may be made a fellow in a professional specialty or elected to an important office in the American Medical Association or American Osteopathic Association. Teaching and research positions may also increase a physician's status. These kinds of achievements, however, may represent a type of success that is different from the usual definition of advancement.

Employment Outlook

In the late 1990s, there are about 560,000 M.D.s and D.O.s working in the United States. Others are involved in research, teaching, administration, and consulting for insurance or pharmaceutical companies. About 70 percent of all physicians practice in offices. Others are on the staff of hospitals, or work in a variety of other health care facilities and in schools, prisons, and business firms.

This field is expected to grow faster than the average through the year 2006. Population growth, particularly among the elderly, is a factor in the demand for physicians. Another factor contributing to the predicted increase is the widespread availability of medical insurance, through both private plans and public programs. More physicians will also be needed for medical research, public health, rehabilitation, and industrial medicine. New technology will allow physicians to perform more procedures to treat ailments once thought incurable.

Employment opportunities will be good for family practitioners and internists, geriatric and preventive care specialists, as well as general pediatricians. Rural and low-income areas are in need of more physicians, and there is a short supply of general surgeons and psychiatrists.

The shift in health care delivery from hospitals to outpatient centers and other nontraditional settings, to contain rising costs, may mean that more and more physicians will become salaried employees. In 1994, for example, 39 percent of employed physicians were considered employees, rather than self-employed, up from 36 percent the previous year.

There will be considerable competition among newly trained physicians entering practice, particularly in large cities. Physicians willing to locate to inner cities and rural areas—where physicians are scarce—should encounter little difficulty.

The issue of physician oversupply has been addressed by groups such as the National Academy of Sciences Institute of Medicine and the Pew Health Professions Commission. They suggest limiting the number of future residency positions available. If so done, there will be fewer doctors vying for positions in the medical field.

Earnings

Physicians have among the highest average earnings of any occupational group. The level of income for any individual physician depends on a number of factors, such as region of the country, economic status of the patients, and the physician's specialty, skill, experience, professional reputation, and personality. Income tends to vary less across geographic regions, however, than specialties. The median income after expenses for all physicians in 1995, according to the American Medical Association, was $160,000 per year Earnings vary according to specialty, the number of years in practice, geographic region, hours worked, skill, and professional reputation. In 1995, the median income of radiologists was $230,000; general surgeons, $225,000; family practitioners, $124,000; anesthesiologists, $203,000, and emergency medicine physicians, $170,000. The AMA survey found that, for the first time since the AMA has been collecting data, physician net income actually declined in 1994.

In 1996-97, the average first year resident received a stipend of about $32,789 a year, depending on the type of residency, the size of the hospital, and the geographic area. Sixth year residents earned about $40,849 a year. If the physician enters private practice, earnings during the first year may not be impressive. As the patients increase in number, however, earnings will also increase.

Physicians who complete their residencies but have no other experience begin work with the Department of Veterans Affairs at salaries of about $44,400. In addition, those working full-time could receive other cash benefits of up to $13,000.

Conditions of Work

The offices and examining rooms of most physicians are well equipped, attractive, well lighted, and well ventilated. There is usually at least one nurse-receptionist on the physician's staff, and there may be several nurses, a laboratory technician, one or more secretaries, a bookkeeper, or receptionist.

Physicians usually see patients by appointments that are scheduled according to individual requirements. They may reserve all mornings for hospital visits and surgery. They may see patients in the office only on certain days of the week. If it is necessary to cut down on the workload, they can schedule fewer appointments.

Physicians spend much of their time at the hospital performing surgery, setting fractures, working in the emergency room, or visiting patients.

Physicians in private practice have the advantages of working independently, but most put in long hours—an average of fifty-eight per week in 1994. Also, they may be called from their homes or offices in times of emergency. Telephone calls may come at any hour of the day or night. It is difficult for physicians to plan leisure-time activities, because their plans may change without notice. One of the advantages of group practice is that members of the group rotate emergency duty.

The areas in most need of physicians are rural hospitals and medical centers. Because the physician is normally working alone, and covering a broad territory, the workday can be quite long with little opportunity for vacation. Because placement in rural communities has become so difficult, some towns are providing scholarship money to students who pledge to work in the community for a number of years.

Physicians in academic medicine or in research have regular hours, work under good physical conditions, and often determine their own workload.

Teaching and research physicians alike are usually provided with the best and most modern equipment.

Sources of Additional Information

American Academy of Family Physicians
8880 Ward Parkway
Kansas City, MO 64114
Tel: 816-333-9700

American Academy of Physician Assistants
950 North Washington Street
Alexandria, VA 22314-1552
Tel: 703-836-2272

American Association of Colleges of Osteopathic Medicine
5550 Friendship Boulevard, Suite 310
Chevy Chase, MD 20815
WWW: http://www.aacom.org

American College of Surgeons
55 East Erie Street
Chicago, IL 60611
Tel: 312-440-2740

American Medical Association
515 North State Street
Chicago, IL 60610
Tel: 312-464-5000

American Osteopathic Association
142 East Ontario Street
Chicago, IL 60611
Tel: 312-280-5800
WWW: http://am-osteo.assn.org

Association of American Medical Colleges
2450 N Street, NW
Washington, DC 20037
Tel: 202-828-0400
WWW: http://www.aamc.org

Plumbers and Pipefitters

Definition

Plumbers assemble, install, alter, and repair pipes and pipe systems that carry water, steam, air, or other liquids and gases for sanitation and industrial purposes as well as other uses. Plumbers also install plumbing fixtures, appliances, and heating and refrigerating units. Pipefitters design, install, and maintain the piping systems for steam, hot water, heating, cooling, lubricating, sprinkling, and industrial processing systems.

Nature of the Work

Because little difference exists between the work of the plumber and the pipefitter in most cases, the two are often considered to be one trade. However, many craftsworkers specialize in one field or the other, especially in large cities. Plumbers assemble, install, and repair heating, water, and drainage systems, especially those that must be connected to public utilities systems. Some of their duties include replacing burst pipes and installing and repairing sinks, bathtubs, water heaters, hot water tanks, garbage disposal units, dishwashers, and water softeners. Plumbers also may work on septic tanks, cesspools, and sewers. During the final construction stages of both commercial and residential buildings, plumbers install heating and air-conditioning units and connect radiators, water heaters, and plumbing fixtures.

Most plumbers follow set procedures in their work. After inspecting the installation site to determine pipe location, they cut and thread pipes, bend them to required angles by hand or machines, and then join them by means of welded, brazed, caulked, soldered, or threaded joints. To test for leaks in the system, they fill the pipes with water or air.

Plumbers use a variety of tools, including hand tools such as wrenches, reamers, drills, braces and bits, hammers, chisels, and saws; power machines that cut, bend, and thread pipes; gasoline torches; and welding, soldering, and brazing equipment.

Pipefitters design, install, and maintain high and low pressure pipe systems. Steamfitters, a specialized pipefitter, construct pipe systems that must withstand high amounts of pressure. Steamfitting is a skilled and demanding line of work, because careless or incomplete work could cost lives. Spinklerfitters install automatic fire sprinkler systems. Diesel engine pipefitters, ship and boat building coppersmiths, industrial-gasfitters, gas-main fitters, prefab plumbers, and pipe cutters are other pipefitting specialties.

The work of pipefitters differs from that of plumbers mainly in its location and the variety and size of pipes used. Pipe systems carry more than just water. In power plants, they carry live steam to the turbines to create electricity. At oil refineries, pipes carry raw crude oil to processing tanks, then transport the finished products, such as petroleum, kerosene, and natural gas, to storage areas. In some manufacturing plants, pneumatic (air) pipe systems are used to monitor and adjust the industrial processes in the plant. Naval ships, submarines, aircraft, food processing plants, refrigerated warehouses, nuclear power plants, and office buildings all depend heavily on pipe systems for their operation. Pipe systems are also needed in the home for natural gas, hot and cold water, and sewage.

Pipefitters work both in preexisting buildings and those under construction. When installing pipe systems in buildings under construction, the pipefitter usually works under the supervision of the general contractor for the project. The blueprints for the piping are usually drawn up by the architect and the contractor and show the type of piping needed, what kind of fixtures are required, and where valves and connectors should be placed.

DOT: 862   GOE: 05.05.03   NOC: 7251, 7252

Plumbers work primarily in residential and commercial buildings, whereas pipefitters are generally employed by a large industry such as an oil refinery, refrigeration plant, or defense establishment where more complex systems of piping are used.

Requirements

Plumbers and pipefitters learn their occupations through apprenticeship programs. These programs take four to five years to complete, combining on-the-job training with a minimum of 144 hours of related classroom instruction each year. To apply for apprenticeship programs, people must be at least eighteen years of age, in good physical condition, and have earned a high school diploma or its equivalent. Apprenticeship applicants are expected to have taken high school courses in shop, drafting, mathematics, physics, chemistry, and blueprint reading. Coursework from vocational schools and correspondence schools may supplement an apprentice's training. To measure their mechanical readiness for this profession, apprentice applicants take mechanical aptitude tests.

Apprentices sign a written agreement with the local apprenticeship committee, which is made up of members from both the union and management. This committee sets the standards for work and training that ensures apprentices gain a broad range of experience through employment with several different contractors. In their training period, they learn to cut, bend, fit, solder, and weld pipes. They also learn the proper use and care of tools and equipment, materials handling, workplace operations and safety (including the regulations of the Occupational Safety and Health Administration), and how to make cost estimates.

Plumbers and pipefitters learn related construction techniques, such as installing gas furnaces, boilers, pumps, oil burners, and radiators. They study and work on various heating and cooling systems, hot water systems, and solar and radiant heat systems. They explore industrial applications such as pneumatic control systems and instrumentation. Classroom work for apprentices includes subjects such as drafting, blueprint reading, applied math and physics, and local building codes and regulations.

Union membership often is a requirement for most plumbers and pipefitters. The main union representing this trade is the United Association of Journeymen and Apprentices of the Plumbing and Pipe Fitting Industry of the United States and Canada. In certain industries such as the aerospace or petroleum industries, plumbers and pipefitters may belong to other unions.

Though there is no national licensing requirement enforced, most cities and states prefer plumbers and pipefitters to be licensed. This requires passing a written test that covers local building and plumbing codes and offering proof of training and skills in the trade.

Interested students should like to solve a variety of problems and should not object to being called on during evenings, weekends, or holidays to perform emergency repairs. As in most service occupations, plumbers and pipefitters should be able to get along well with all kinds of people. They should be able to work alone, but also be able to direct the work of helpers and work well with those in the other construction trades.

Opportunities for Experience & Exploration

To get an idea of the type of work done by plumbers and pipefitters, students can look for jobs as construction helpers to these trades. This does not involve the commitment of an apprenticeship, and it is a good vantage point from which to consider whether one is interested in the type of work and the amount of training that the profession requires. A job as a helper is also a very good stepping-stone to apprenticeship programs.

Although opportunities for direct experience in this occupation are rare for those in high school, there are ways to explore the field. Courses in chemistry, physics, mechanical drawing, and mathematics are all helpful to the work of the plumber and pipefitter. By taking these courses in high school, students can test their ability and aptitude in the theoretical aspects of the trade.

Methods of Entering

Applicants who wish to become apprentices usually contact local plumbing, heating, and air-conditioning contractors who employ plumbers, the state employment service bureau, or the local branch of the United Association of Journeymen and Apprentices of the Plumbing and Pipe Fitting Industry of the United States and Canada. Individual contractors or contractor associations often sponsor local apprenticeship programs. Before becoming apprentices, however, prospective plumbers must have the approval of the joint labor-management apprenticeship committee. The Bureau of Apprenticeship and Training, the U.S. Department of Labor, and state employment offices are also good sources of information.

For those who do not want to commit to an apprenticeship program, local unions and contractors are the best sources for work. Both unions and contractors may hire helpers to plumbers and pipefitters. If applicants are rejected from apprenticeship programs or if the programs are filled, they may wish to enter the field as on-the-job trainees. Others pursue plumbing training through the armed forces.

Advancement

After their training, apprentice plumbers and pipefitters become journeyworkers, which means more money and more employment opportunities. They may continue to work for the same contractor or switch to a new employer. If they gain experience in all the skills of the trade, they may rise to the position of supervisor. Some plumbers and pipefitters decide to go into business for themselves as independent contractors, lining up job contracts and hiring their own employees.

Successful completion of a training program is necessary before an individual can become a qualified journeyworker plumber, and licenses are required in most communities. It takes two to four years to master most of the skills the plumber needs to perform everyday tasks.

If plumbers have certain qualities, such as the ability to deal with people and good judgment and planning skills, they may progress to such positions as supervisor or job estimator for plumbing or pipefitting contractors. If they work for a large industrial company, they may advance to the position of job superintendent.

Employment Outlook

Employment prospects for plumbers and pipefitters are expected to be slower than average through the year 2006. However, the demand is greater than the number of qualified plumbers and pipefitters entering the trade. The need to replace retiring workers will also contribute to many job openings. A total of 389,000 plumbers and pipefitters were employed in the United States in 1996; 1 out of 5 were self employed. Two-thirds of all plumbers and pipefitters were contracted by mechanical and plumbing companies working in new construction, repair, or maintenance. Industrial and commercial companies, as well as the government were other job sources.

Expansion of certain industries, such as chemical and food-processing factories and those that rely on automated production, will be an important source of employment for plumbers and pipefitters. Demand for plumbers and pipefitters will also stem from new building construction and building renovation. Legislation requiring sprinkler systems in older buildings will create many jobs. Keeping existing pipe systems in good repair will also help employment rates for many workers in the trade.

Earnings

According to the U.S. Department of Labor, plumbers and pipefitters who were not self-employed earned an average of $30,732 a year in 1995. Fifty percent earned between $21,476 and $42,224; the top ten percent earned over $54,444 annually. A recent *U.S. World & News Report* article listed average wages for plumbers between $23,000 and $49,000. Salaries for plumbers and pipefitters are among the highest in the construction trades. Wages vary, however, according to location. Plumbers working in the Midwest and West tend to earn more than others working elsewhere in the United States. Hourly pay rates for apprentices usually start at 50 percent of the experienced worker's rate, and increase by five percent every six months until a rate of 95 percent is reached. Benefits for union workers usually include health insurance, sick and vacation pay, as well as pension plans.

Conditions of Work

Plumbing and pipefitting are demanding trades. Much of their work is done in cramped quarters and uncomfortable positions. Lifting, joining, and installing heavy pipework and operating large machinery can cause fatigue and muscle strain. Other hazards include cuts from sharp tools, burns from hot pipes and welding material, and related construction injuries. However, the injury rate for plumbers and pipefitters matches the average for most construction employees. Aside from the physical strain the work requires, plumbers and pipefitters must perform very careful, conscientious, and exacting work. Flaws in their work could lead to damage to property and injury to others. They must be able not only to follow instructions but to apply judgment and experience in making decisions and directing other workers when necessary.

Most plumbers and pipefitters are employed by building contractors and perform their work at different sites every day. They may work for a few hours at one work site and then travel to another. However, the construction of a large housing or industrial complex may keep plumbers and pipefitters at the same site for several months. They work a regular forty-hour week, although they may work overtime to meet deadlines or complete assignments. Plumbers and pipefitters on the maintenance staff of large processing plants generally work from thirty-five to forty hours a week.

Plumbers and pipefitters invest a lot of time training for the profession, so relatively few workers leave the field to move into other lines of work. Work is usually available in all parts of the country.

Sources of Additional Information

■ **Mechanical Contractors Association of America**
1385 Piccard Drive
Rockville, MD 20850
Tel: 301-869-5800

■ **National Association of Plumbing-Heating-Cooling Contractors**
PO Box 6808
180 South Washington Street
Falls Church, VA 22046
Tel: 703-237-8100

■ **United Association of Journeymen and Apprentices of the Plumbing and Pipe Fitting Industry of the United States and Canada**
PO Box 37800
Washington, DC 20013
Tel: 202-628-5823

Police Officers

Definition

Police officers perform many duties relating to public safety. Their responsibilities include not only preserving the peace, preventing criminal acts, enforcing the law, investigating crimes, and arresting those who violate the law but also directing traffic, community relations work, and controlling crowds at public events. Police officers are employed at the federal, state, county, and city level.

State police officers patrol highways and enforce the laws and regulations that govern the use of those highways, in addition to performing general police work. Police officers are under oath to uphold the law twenty-four hours a day.

Nature of the Work

If police officers patrol a beat or work in small communities, their duties may be many and varied. In large city departments, their work may be highly specialized.

Depending on the orders they receive from their commanding officers, police may direct traffic during the rush-hour periods and at special events when traffic is unusually heavy. They may patrol public places such as parks, streets, and public gatherings to maintain law and order. Police are sometimes called upon to prevent or break up riots and to act as escorts at funerals, parades, and other public events. They may administer first aid in emergency situations, assist in rescue operations of various kinds, investigate crimes, issue tickets to violators of traffic or parking laws or other regulations, or arrest drunk drivers. Officers in small towns may have to perform all these duties and administrative work as well.

As officers patrol their assigned beats, either on foot, horseback, or in cars, they must be alert for any situations that arise and be ready to take appropriate action. Many times they must be alert to identify stolen cars, identify and locate lost children, and identify and apprehend escaped criminals and others wanted by various law enforcement agencies. While on patrol, they keep in constant contact with headquarters and their fellow officers by calling in regularly on two-way radios. Although their profession may at times be dangerous, police officers are trained not to endanger their own lives or the lives of ordinary citizens. If they need assistance, they radio for additional officers.

In large city police departments, officers usually have more specific duties and specialized assignments. The police departments generally are comprised of special work divisions such as communications, criminal investigation, firearms identification, fingerprint identification and forensic science, accident prevention, and administrative services. In very large cities, police departments may have special work units such as the harbor patrol, canine corps, mounted police, vice squad, fraud or bunco squad, traffic control, records control, and rescue units. A few of the job titles for these specialties are identification and records commanders and officers, narcotics and vice detectives or investigators, homicide squad commanding officers, detective chiefs, traffic lieutenants, sergeants, parking enforcement officers, public safety officers, accident-prevention squad officers, safety instruction police officers, and community relations lieutenants.

In very large city police departments, officers may fill positions as police chiefs, precinct sergeants and captains, desk officers, booking officers, police inspectors, identification officers, complaint evaluation supervisors and officers, crime prevention police officers, and internal affairs investigators, whose job is to police the police. Some officers work as plainclothes detectives in criminal investigation divisions. Other specialized police officers include police reserves commanders; police officer commanding officers III, who act as supervisors in missing persons and fugitive investigations; and police officers III, who investigate and pursue nonpayment and fraud fugitives. Many police departments employ police clerks, who perform administrative and community-oriented tasks.

A major responsibility for state police officers (sometimes known as *state troopers* or *highway patrol officers*) is to patrol the highways and enforce the laws and regulations of those traveling on them. Riding in patrol cars equipped with two way radios, they monitor traffic for troublesome or dangerous situations. They write traffic tickets and issue warnings to drivers who are violating traffic laws or otherwise not observing safe driving practices. They radio for assistance for drivers who are stopped because of breakdowns, flat tires, illnesses, or other reasons. They direct traffic around congested areas caused by fires, road repairs, accidents, and other emergencies. They may check the weight of commercial vehicles to verify that they are within allowable limits, conduct driver examinations, or give safety information to the public.

In case of a highway accident, officers take charge of the activities at the site by directing traffic, giving first aid to any injured parties, and calling for emergency equipment such as ambulances, fire trucks, or tow trucks. They write up a report to be used by investigating officers who attempt to determine the cause of the accident.

In addition to these responsibilities, state police officers in most states do some general police work. They are often the primary law-enforcement agency in communities or counties that have no police force or large sheriff's department. In those areas, they may investigate such crimes as burglary and assault. They also may assist municipal or county police in capturing lawbreakers or control civil disturbances.

Most police officers are trained in the use of firearms and carry guns. Police in special divisions, such as chemical analysis and handwriting and fingerprint identification, have special training to perform their work. Police officers often testify in court regarding cases with which they have been involved. Police personnel are required to complete accurate and thorough records of their cases.

Requirements

Police job appointments in most large cities and in many smaller cities and towns are governed by local civil service regulations. Applicants are required to pass written tests designed to measure the candidates' intelligence and general aptitude for police work. Physical examinations are required and, usually include tests of physical agility, dexterity, and strength. Candidates' personal histories, backgrounds, and character undergo careful scrutiny because honesty and law-abiding characteristics are essential traits for law-enforcement officers. An important requirement is that the prospective police officer has no arrest record.

Applicants must be at least twenty-one years of age (or older for some departments), and some municipalities stipulate an age limit of not more than thirty-five years. Candidates must have, in most cases, 20/20 uncorrected vision, good hearing, and weight proportionate to their height. Applicants must meet locally prescribed weight and height rules for their gender. Most regulations require that applicants be U.S. citizens, and many police departments have residency requirements.

The majority of police departments today require that applicants have a high school education. Although a high school diploma is not always required, related work experience is generally required. The best chance for advancement, however, is for officers with some postsecondary education, and many police departments now require a two-year or four-year degree, especially for more specialized areas of police work. There are more than 800 junior colleges and universities offering two-year and four-year degree programs in law enforcement. The armed forces also offer training and opportunities in law enforcement that can be applied to civilian police work.

High school students who are interested in pursuing this career will find the subjects of psychology, sociology, English, law, mathematics, U.S. government and history, chemistry, and physics most helpful. Because physical stamina is very important in this work, sports and physical education are also valuable. Knowledge of a foreign language is especially helpful, and bilingual officers are often in great demand. High school students interested in specialized and advanced positions in law enforcement should pursue studies leading to college programs in criminology, criminal law, criminal psychology, or related areas. Prospective police officers should enjoy working with people and be able to cooperate with others. Because of the stressful nature of much police work, police officers must be able to think clearly and logically during emergency situations, have a strong degree of emotional control, and be capable of detaching themselves from incidents.

Newly recruited police officers must pass a special training program. After training, they are usually placed on a probationary period lasting from three to six months. In small towns and communities, training may be given on the job by working with an experienced officer. Inexperienced officers are never sent out on patrol alone but are always accompanied by veteran officers.

Large city police departments give classroom instruction in laws, accident investigation, city ordinances, and traffic control. These departments also give instruction in the handling of firearms, methods of apprehension and arrest, self-defense tactics, and first-aid techniques. Both state and municipal police officers are trained in safe driving procedures and maneuvering an automobile at high speeds. Physical fitness training is a mandatory, continuing activity in most police departments, as are routine physical examinations. Police officers can have no physical disabilities that would prevent them from carrying out their duties.

Opportunities for Experience & Exploration

A good way to explore police work is to talk with various law enforcement officers. Most departments have community outreach programs and many have recruiting programs as well. Students may also wish to visit colleges offering programs in police work or write for information on their training programs.

In some cases, high school graduates can explore this occupation by seeking employment as police cadets in large city police departments. These cadets are paid employees who work part time in clerical and other duties. They attend training courses in police science on a part-time basis. When they reach the age of twenty-one, they are eligible to apply for

regular police work. Some police departments also hire college students as interns.

Methods of Entering

Applicants interested in police work should apply directly to local civil service offices or examining boards to qualify as a candidate for police officer. In some locations, written examinations may be given to groups at specified times. In smaller communities that do not follow civil service methods, applicants should apply directly to the police department or city government offices in the communities where they reside. Those interested in becoming state police officers may apply directly to their state civil service commissions or state police headquarters, which are usually located in the state capital.

Advancement

Advancement in these occupations is determined by several factors. An officer's eligibility for promotion may depend on a specified length of service, job performance, formal education and training courses, and results of written examinations. Those who become eligible for promotion are listed on the promotional list along with other qualified candidates. Promotions generally become available from six months to three years after starting, depending on the department. As positions of different or higher rank become open, candidates are promoted to fill them according to their position on the list. Lines of promotion usually begin with officer third grade and progress to grade two and grade one. Other possible promotional opportunities include the ranks of detective, sergeant, lieutenant, or captain. Many promotions require additional training and testing. Advancement to the very top-ranking positions, such as division, bureau, or department director or chief, may be made by direct political appointment. Most of these top positions are held by officers who have come up through the ranks.

Large city police departments offer the greatest number of advancement opportunities. Most of the larger departments maintain separate divisions, which require administration workers, line officers, and more employees in general at each rank level.

Officers may move into areas that they find challenging, such as criminal investigation or forensics.

Most city police departments offer various types of in-service study and training programs. These programs allow police departments to keep up-to-date on the latest police science techniques and are often required for those who want to be considered for promotion. Training courses are provided by police academies, colleges, and other educational institutions. Some of the subjects offered are civil defense, foreign languages, and forgery detection. Some municipal police departments share the cost with their officers or pay all educational expenses if the officers are willing to work toward a college degree in either police work or police administration. Independent study is also often required.

Intensive twelve-week administrative training courses are offered by the National Academy of the Federal Bureau of Investigation in Washington, DC. A limited number of officers are selected to participate in this training program.

Advancement opportunities on police forces in small communities are considerably more limited by the rank and number of police personnel needed. Other opportunities for advancement may be found in related police, protective, and security service work with private companies, state and county agencies, and other institutions.

Employment Outlook

Employment of police officers is expected to increase about as fast as the average for all occupations through the year 2006. Federal "tough-on-crime" legislation passed in the mid-1990s created a short-term increase of new jobs in police departments at the federal, state, and local levels.

The opportunities that become available, however, may be affected by technological, scientific, and other changes occurring today in police work. Automation in traffic control is limiting the number of officers needed in this area, while the increasing reliance on computers throughout society is creating demands for new kinds of police work. New approaches in social science and psychological research are also changing the methodology used in working with public offenders. These trends indi-cate a future demand for more educated, specialized personnel.

This occupation has a very low turnover rate. However, new positions will open as current officers retire, leave the force, or move into higher positions. Retirement ages are relatively low in police work compared to other occupations. Many officers retire while in their forties and then pursue a second career. In response to increasing crime rates, some police departments across the country are expanding the number of patrol officers; however, budget problems faced by many municipalities may limit growth.

In the past decade, private security firms have begun to take over some police activities such as patrolling airports and other public places. Some private companies have even been contracted to provide police forces for some cities. Many companies and universities also operate their own police forces.

Earnings

According to the U.S. Department of Labor, police officers in 1996 earned an annual average salary of $34,700; the lowest 10 percent earned less than $19,200 a year, while the highest 10 percent earned over $58,500 annually. Police officers in supervisory positions earned median salaries of $41,200 a year in 1996, with a low of $22,500 and a high of over $64,500. Sheriffs and other law enforcement officers earned median annual salaries of $26,700 in 1996. Salaries for police officers range widely based on geographic location. Police departments in the West and North generally pay more than those in the South.

Most police officers receive periodic and annual salary increases up to a limit set for their rank and length of service. Police departments generally pay special compensation to cover the cost of uniforms. They usually provide any equipment required such as firearms and handcuffs. Overtime pay may be given for certain work shifts or emergency duty. In these instances, officers are usually paid straight or time-and-a-half pay, while extra time off is sometimes given as compensation.

Because most police officers are civil service employees, they receive generous benefits, including health insurance and paid vacation and sick leave, and enjoy increased job security. In addition, most police departments offer retirement plans and retirement after twenty or twenty-five years of service, usually at half pay.

Conditions of Work

Police officers work under many different types of circumstances. Much of their work may be performed outdoors, as they ride in patrol cars or walk the beats assigned to them. In emergency situations, no consideration can be made for weather conditions, time of day or night, or day of the week. Police officers may be on call twenty-four hours a day; even when they are not on duty, they are usually required by law to respond to emergencies or criminal activity. Although they are assigned regular work hours, individuals in police work must be willing to live by an unpredictable and often erratic work schedule. The work demands constant mental and physical alertness as well as great physical strength and stamina.

Police work generally consists of an eight-hour day and a five-day week, but police officers may work night and weekend shifts and on holidays. Emergencies may add many extra hours to an officer's day or week. The occupation is considered dangerous. Some officers are killed or wounded while performing their duties. Their work can involve unpleasant duties and expose them to sordid, depressing, or dangerous situations. They may be called on to deal with all types of people under many types of circumstances. While the routine of some assigned duties may become boring, the dangers of police work are often stressful for the officers and their families. Police work in general holds the potential for the unknown and unexpected, and most people who pursue this work have a strong passion for and commitment to police work.

Sources of Additional Information

■■International Union of Police Associations
1421 Prince Street, Suite 330
Alexandria, VA 22314
Tel: 703-549-7473

The educational arm of the American Federation of Police and the National Association of Chiefs of Police, the American Police Academy compiles statistics, operates a placement service and a speaker's bureau, and offers home study programs. For more information, contact:

■■American Police Academy
1000 Connecticut Avenue, NW, Suite 9
Washington, DC 20036
Tel: 202-293-9088

The following association maintains a speaker's bureau, conducts educational programs, and offers both recognition and scholarship awards. For more information, contact:

■■National Police Officers Association of America
PO Box 22129
Louisville, KY 40252-0129
Tel: 800-467-6762

The following organization compiles statistics, operates a hotline, hall of fame, and speaker's bureau, offers children's services, and sponsors competitions and scholarships. For more information, use the toll free number, 800-533-4649, or write:

■■National United Law Enforcement Association
256 East McLemore Avenue
Memphis, TN 38106
Tel: 901-774-1118

Preschool Teachers and Child Care Workers

Definition

Preschool teachers promote the education of children under age five in all areas. They help students develop physically, socially, and emotionally, work with them on language and communications skills, and help cultivate their cognitive abilities. They also work with families to support parents in raising their young children and reinforcing skills at home. They plan and lead activities developed in accordance with the specific ages and needs of the children. Many schools and districts consider kindergarten teachers, who teach students five years of age, to be preschool teachers. For the purposes of this article, kindergarten teachers will be included in this category. Regardless of whether they teach kindergartners or younger students, it is the goal of all preschool teachers to help students develop the skills, interests, and individual creativity that they will use for the rest of their lives.

Preschool teachers are part of the larger category of *child care workers*; however, all child care workers are not preschool teachers. Child care workers include such people as day care center employees (even those who work with infants), day camp counselors, teacher aides, and before- and after-school child care programs staff, among others.

Nature of the Work

Preschool teachers design and implement activities that build on children's abilities and curiosity and aid them in developing skills and characteristics that help them grow. Attention to the individual needs of each child is vital, and teachers need to be aware of these needs and capabilities and, when possible, adapt activities to the specific needs of the individual child. Teachers should be aware of the growth and devel-

opmental stages of children and plan activities accordingly. For example, a teacher should plan activities based on the understanding that a three-year-old child has different motor skills and reasoning abilities than a child of five years of age. A teacher should also understand the psychology of a young child.

To accommodate the variety of abilities and temperaments of children enrolled in a preschool program, a teacher should develop a flexible schedule with varying amounts of time for music, art, playtime, academics, rest, and other activities. Preschool teachers should plan activities that encourage children to develop skills appropriate to their developmental needs. Preschool teachers might work with the youngest students to learn the days of the week and recognize colors, seasons, and animal names and characteristics; they might help older students with number and letter recognition and even simple writing skills. Preschool teachers need to be aware that all children develop at different rates and although one child may not be ready to recognize individual letters, another may be ready to read. A preschool teacher helps children with such simple yet important tasks as tying shoelaces and washing hands before snack time.

Self-confidence and the development of communications skills are encouraged in preschools. For example, teachers may give children simple art projects, such as finger painting and have children show and explain their finished projects to the rest of the class. Show and tell, or "sharing time" as it is often called, gives students opportunities to speak and listen to others. Preschool teachers help students develop problem-solving and social skills.

For most children, preschool is their first time away from home and family for an extended period of time. A major portion of a preschool teacher's day is often spent helping children adjust to being away from home and encouraging them to play together. This is especially true at the beginning of the school year. Preschool teachers need to be able to gently reassure children who become frightened or homesick.

A preschool teacher often has an *assistant*, also called an *aide*, to help with the children. The assistant helps the teacher manage the classroom throughout the day. Assistants might supervise nap time for the youngest children while the teacher supervises older children involved in an activity. Preschool teachers also work with the parents of each child. It is not unusual for parents to come to preschool and observe a child or go on a field trip with the class, and preschool teachers often take these opportunities to discuss the progress of each child as well as any specific problems or concerns. Scheduled meetings are available for parents who cannot visit the school during the day. Solutions to fairly serious problems are worked out in tandem with the parents, often with the aid of the director of the preschool, or in the case of an elementary school kindergarten, with the principal or headmaster.

The preschool teacher adopts many parental responsibilities while the child is in school. The teacher greets each child in the morning and supervises the child throughout the day. Often these responsibilities can be quite demanding and complicated. In harsh weather, for example, preschool teachers contend with not only boots, hats, coats, and mittens, but with the inevitable sniffles, colds, and generally cranky behavior that can occur in young children.

In both full-day and half-day programs, the teacher supervises snack time, helping children learn how to eat properly and clean up after themselves. Proper hygiene, such as hand washing before meals, is also stressed. Other activities include storytelling, music, and simple arts and crafts projects. Full-day programs involve a lunch period and at least one nap time. Programs usually have exciting activities interspersed with calmer ones. Even though the children get nap time, a preschool teacher must be energetic throughout the day, ready to face with good cheer the many challenges and demands of young children.

Because young children look up to adults and learn through example, it is especially important that a preschool teacher be a good role model. With more families putting children into child care settings, the age range in preschools can vary from two or three years old up to age five, sometimes in the same classroom. Preschool teachers must be able to work with children of all these ages.

Kindergarten teachers usually have their own classrooms, made up exclusively of five-year-olds. Although these teachers don't have to plan activities for a wide range of ages, they need to consider individual developmental interests, abilities, and backgrounds represented by the students. Kindergarten teachers usually spend more time helping students with academic skills than do other preschool teachers. While a teacher of a two-, three- and four-year-old classroom may focus more on socializing and building confidence in students through play and activities, kindergarten teachers often develop activities that help five-year-olds acquire the skills they will need in grade school, such as introductory activities on numbers, reading, and writing.

Requirements

Specific education requirements for preschool and kindergarten teachers vary from state to state and also depend on the specific guidelines of the school or district. Many schools and child care centers require preschool teachers to have a bachelor's degree in education or a related field, but others accept adults with a high school diploma and experience working with children. Preschool facilities that accept applicants with a minimum of high school diploma often offer on-the-job training to their teachers, hiring them as assistants or aides until they are sufficiently trained to work in a classroom alone.

Several groups offer on-the-job training programs for prospective preschool teachers. For example, the American Montessori Society offers a career program for aspiring preschool teachers. This program requires a three-month classroom training period followed by one year of supervised on-the-job training.

A high school student interested in pursuing a career as a preschool teacher should take courses in early childhood development, English, mathematics, art, music, and physical education. It is beneficial for a preschool teacher to be able to draw from the widest possible knowledge base and pursuing a well-rounded high school education provides an excellent foundation. A college degree program should include coursework in a variety of liberal arts subjects, including English, history, and science, as well as nutrition, child development, psychology of the young child, and sociology.

In some states, licensure may be required. Many states accept the Child Development Associate (CDA) credential or an associate's or bachelor's degree as sufficient requirements for work in a preschool facility. Individual state boards of education can provide specific licensure information. Kindergarten teachers working in public elementary schools almost always need teaching certification similar to that required by other elementary school teachers in the school. Other types of licensure or certification may be required, depending upon the school or district. These may include first-aid or CPR training.

Opportunities for Experience & Exploration

High school students can gain experience in this field by volunteering at a child care or other preschool facility. Some high schools provide internships with local preschools for students interested in working as a teacher's aide. Many guidance counselors can provide information on these opportunities. Summer day camps or Bible schools with preschool classes also hire high school students as counselors or counselors-in-training. Discussing the field with preschool teachers and observing in their classes are other good ways to discover specific job information and explore one's aptitude for this career.

Methods of Entering

Qualified individuals can contact child care centers, nursery schools, Head Start programs, and other preschool facilities to identify job opportunities. Often jobs for preschool teachers are listed in the classified section of newspapers. In addition, many school districts and state boards of education maintain job listings of available teaching positions. If no permanent positions are available at a preschool, potential teachers can often gain entry into the field by applying as a substitute teacher. Most preschools and kindergartens maintain a substitute list and refer to it frequently. Substitutes who do good work in that capacity are often hired when a permanent position becomes open, provided they meet necessary qualifications.

Advancement

Many teachers advance by becoming more skillful in what they do. Skilled preschool teachers, especially those with additional training, usually receive salary increases as they become more experienced. A few preschool teachers with administrative ability and an interest in administrative work advance to the position of director. Administrators need to have at least a master's degree in child development or a related field and have to meet any state or federal licensing regulations. Some become directors of Head Start programs or other government programs.

A relatively small number of experienced preschool teachers open their own facility. This requires not only the ability to be an effective administrator, but also the knowledge of how to operate a business. Kindergarten teachers sometimes have the opportunity to earn more money by teaching at a higher grade level in the elementary school. This salary increase is especially true when a teacher moves from a half-day kindergarten program to a full-day grade school classroom.

Employment Outlook

Employment opportunities for preschool teachers are expected to increase through the year 2006. More women than ever are part of the workforce; of those who have children, many take only an abbreviated maternity leave. More teachers are needed to meet the demand of quality child care needed by those without satisfactory home child care. Specific job opportunities vary from state to state and depend on demographic characteristics and level of government funding. Jobs should be available at private child care centers, nursery schools, Head Start facilities, public and private kindergartens, and laboratory schools connected with universities and colleges. In the past, the majority of preschool teachers were female, and although this continues to be the case, more males are becoming involved in early childhood education.

Because of low pay and often poor working conditions, there is a very high turnover of child care workers, such as preschool teachers. On the one hand, this may lead to dissatisfaction with the career, but it means there are usually positions available to those willing to accept the limitations of the job.

Earnings

Although there have been some attempts to correct the discrepancies in salaries between preschool teachers and other teachers, salaries in this profession tend to be lower than teaching positions in public elementary and high schools. Because some preschool programs are only in the morning or afternoon, many preschool teachers work only part time. As part-time workers, they often do not receive medical insurance or other benefits and may get paid minimum wage to start.

In 1996, the lowest salaries for full-time preschool teachers averaged $7,200. A mid-range salary in the field is $13,000, and the highest paid teachers earn $20,200 or more per year. Kindergarten teachers, on average, have the highest salaries in this field. In addition, earnings depend on the geographic region in which the preschool facility is located. Some preschool teachers supplement their incomes by staying after standard teaching hours or arriving early to work in school-sponsored extended-day child care programs. Others tutor or babysit in the evenings or work other part-time jobs.

Conditions of Work

Preschool teachers spend much of the day on their feet in a classroom or a playground. Facilities vary from a single room to large buildings. Class sizes also vary; some preschools serve only a handful of children, while others serve several hundred. Classrooms may be crowded.

Part-time employees generally work between eighteen and thirty hours a week, while full-time employees work thirty-five to forty hours a week. Part-time work gives the employee flexibility, and for many, this is one of the advantages of the job. Some preschool teachers teach both morning and afternoon classes, going through the same schedule and lesson plans with two sets of students. Some preschool teachers work nine months of the year (with summers off), but many others work year-round.

A preschool teacher should be able to deal with a wide variety of children and parents. Parents may sometimes be more difficult to deal with than the children, as parents have special concerns about their children and may be frustrated that they cannot spend more time with them. While a preschool or kindergarten classroom is usually an exciting place full of discovery and learning, it can also be stressful and tiring for the teachers. Teachers need the ability to be patient and calm.

Sources of Additional Information

For information on training programs, contact:

■■**American Montessori Society**
Teacher Education Program,
150 Fifth Avenue, Suite 203
New York, NY 10011-4384
Tel: 212-924-3209
Email: amspaul@aol.com

For general information on preschool teaching careers, contact:

■■**National Association for the Education of Young Children**
1509 16th Street, NW
Washington, DC 20036
Tel: 800-424-2460

■■**National Council for Accreditation of Teacher Education**
2010 Massachusetts Avenue, NW, Suite 500
Washington, DC 20036-1023
Tel: 202-466-7496

Producers

Definition

Producers organize and secure the financial backing for the production of motion pictures. They decide which scripts will be used or which books will be adapted for film. Producers also raise money to finance the filming of a motion picture; hire the director, screenwriter, and cast; oversee the budget and production schedule; and monitor the distribution of the film.

Many in the field are self-employed, or independent, producers. Others are salaried employees of film companies, television networks, and television stations.

Nature of the Work

The primary role of a producer is to organize and secure the financial backing necessary to undertake a motion picture project. The director, by contrast, creates the film from the screenplay. Despite this general distinction, the producer often takes part in creative decisions, and occasionally one person is both the producer and director. On some small projects, such as a nature or historical documentary for a public television broadcast, the producer might also be the writer and cameraman.

The job of a producer generally begins in the pre-production stage of filmmaking with the selection of a movie idea from a script, or other material. Some films are made from original screenplays, while others are adapted from books. If a book is selected, the producer must first purchase the rights from the author or his or her publishing company, and a writer must be hired to adapt the book into a screenplay format. Producers are usually inundated with scripts from writers and others who have ideas for a movie. Producers may have their own idea for a motion picture and will hire a writer to write the screenplay. Occasionally a studio will approach a producer, typically a producer who has had many commercially or artistically successful films in the past, with a project.

After selecting a project, the producer will find a director, the technical staff, and the star actor or actors to participate in the film. Along with the script and screenwriter, these essential people are referred to as the "package." Packaging is sometimes arranged with the help of talent agencies. It is the package that the producer tries to sell to an investor to obtain the necessary funds to finance the salaries and cost of the film.

There are three common sources for financing a film: major studios, production companies, and individual investors. A small number of producers have enough money to pay for their own projects. Major studios are the largest source of money and finance most of the big budget films. Although some studios have full-time producers on staff, they hire independent producers for many projects. Large production companies often have the capital resources to fund projects which they feel will be commercially successful. On the smaller end of the scale, producers of documentary films commonly approach individual donors; foundations; art agencies of federal, state, and local governments; and even family members and churches. The National Endowment for the Humanities and the National Endowment for the Arts are major federal benefactors of cinema.

Raising money from individual investors can occupy much of the producer's time. Fund-raising may be done on the telephone, as well as in conferences, business lunches, and even cocktail parties. The producer may also look for a distributor for the film even before the production begins.

Obtaining the necessary financing does not guarantee a film will be made. After raising the money, the producer takes the basic plan of the package and tries to work it into a developed project. The script may be rewritten several times, the full cast of actors is hired, salaries are negotiated, and logistical problems, such as the location of the filming, are worked out; on some projects it might be the director who handles these tasks, or the director may work with the producer. Most major motion film projects do not get beyond this complicated stage of development.

During the production phase, the producer tries to keep the project on schedule and the spending within the established budget. Other production tasks include the review of dailies, which are prints of the day's filming. As the head of the project, the producer is ultimately responsible for resolving all problems, including personal conflicts such as those between the director and an actor and the director and the studio. If the film is successfully completed, the producer monitors its distribution and may participate in the publicity and advertising of the film.

To accomplish the many and varied tasks that the position requires, producers hire a number of subordinates, such as associate producers, sometimes called coproducers, line producers, and production assistants. Job titles, however, vary from project to project. In general, *associate producers* work directly under the producer and oversee the major areas of the project, such as the budget. *Line producers* handle the day-to-day operations of the project. *Production assistants* may perform substantive tasks, such as reviewing scripts, but others are hired to run errands. Another title, *executive producer*, often refers to the person who puts up the money, such as a studio executive, but it is sometimes an honorary title with no functional relevance to the project.

Requirements

There is no minimum educational requirement for becoming a producer. Many producers, however, are college graduates, and many also have a business degree or other previous business experience. They must not only be talented salespeople and administrators but also have a thorough understanding of films and motion picture technology. Such understanding, of course, only comes from experience.

Formal study of film, television, communications, theater, writing, English literature, or art are helpful, as the producer must have the background to know whether an idea or script is worth pursuing. Many entry-level positions in the film industry are given to people who have studied liberal arts, cinema, or both.

In the United States there are more than a thousand colleges, universities, and trade schools that offer classes in film or television studies; more than 120 of these offer undergraduate programs, and more than fifty grant master's degrees. A small number of Ph.D. programs also exist.

Graduation from a film or television program does not guarantee employment in the industry. Some programs are quite expensive, costing more than $50,000 in tuition alone for three years of study. Others do not have the resources to allow all students to make their own films.

Programs in Los Angeles and New York, the major centers of the entertainment industry, may provide the best opportunities for making contacts that can be of benefit when seeking employment.

Producers come from a wide variety of backgrounds. Some start out as magazine editors, business school graduates, actors, or secretaries, messengers, and production assistants for a film studio. Many have never formally studied film.

Most producers, however, get their position through several years of experience in the industry, perseverance, and a keen sense for what projects will be artistically and commercially successful.

Opportunities for Experience & Exploration

There are many ways to gain experience in filmmaking. Some high schools have film and video clubs, for example, or courses on the use of motion picture equipment. Experience in high school or college theater can also be useful. One of the best ways to get experience is to volunteer for a student or low-budget film project; positions on such projects are often advertised in local trade publications. Community cable stations also hire volunteers and may even offer internships.

Methods of Entering

Becoming a producer is similar to becoming president of a company. Unless a person is independently wealthy and can finance whichever projects he or she chooses, prior experience in the field is necessary. Because there are so few positions, even with experience it is extremely difficult to become a successful producer.

Most motion picture producers have attained their position only after years of moving up the industry ladder. Thus, it is important to concentrate on immediate goals, such as getting an entry-level position in a film company. Some enter the field by getting a job as a *production assistant.* An entry-level production assistant may Xerox copies of the scripts for actors to use, assist in setting up equipment, or may perform other menial tasks, often for very little or even no pay. While a production assistant's work is often tedious and of little seeming reward, it nevertheless does expose one to the intricacies of filmmaking and, more importantly, creates an opportunity to make contacts with others in the industry.

Those interested in the field should approach film companies, television stations, or the television networks about employment opportunities as a production assistant. Small television stations often provide the best opportunity for those who are interested in television producing. Positions may also be listed in trade publications.

Advancement

There is little room for advancement beyond the position, as producers are at the top of their profession. Advancement for producers is generally measured by the types of projects, increased earnings, and respect in the field. At television stations, a producer can advance to program director. Some producers become directors or make enough money to finance their own projects.

Employment Outlook

Employment for producers is expected to grow faster than the average through the year 2006. The occupation of TV news producer was recently listed as a runner-up in *U.S. News & World Report*'s annual compilation of 20 hot track careers. Though opportunities may increase with the expansion of cable television and news programs, video rentals, and an increased overseas demand for American-made films, competition for jobs will be high. Live theater and entertainment will also provide job openings. Some positions will be available as current producers leave the workforce.

The greatest concentration of motion picture producers is in Hollywood and New York. Hollywood alone has more than two thousand producers.

Earnings

Producers are generally paid a percentage of the project's profits or a fee negotiated between the producer and a studio. Average yearly earnings range from about $25,000 to $70,000. Producers of highly successful films can earn as much as $200,000 or more, while those who make low-budget, documentary films might earn considerably less than the average. In general, producers in the film industry earn more than television producers. A producer for a large market news program can average from about $24,000 to $40,000 a year. Smaller markets pay less, about $17,000 a year. Entry-level production assistants can earn from less than minimum wage to $15,000 per year.

Conditions of Work

Producers have greater control over their working conditions than most other people working in the motion picture industry. They may have the autonomy of choosing their own projects, setting their own hours, and delegating duties to others as necessary. The work often brings considerable personal satisfaction. But it is not without constraints. Producers must work within a stressful schedule complicated by competing work pressures and often daily crises. Each project brings a significant financial and professional risk. Long hours and weekend work are common. Most producers must provide for their own health insurance and other benefits.

Sources of Additional Information

■**Producers Guild of America**
400 South Beverly Drive
Beverly Hills, CA 90212
Tel: 310-557-0807

Property and Real Estate Managers

Definition

Property and real estate managers plan and supervise the activities that affect land and buildings. Most of them manage rental properties, such as apartment buildings, office buildings, and shopping centers. Others manage the services and commonly owned areas of condominiums and community associations.

Nature of the Work

Most property and real estate managers are responsible for day-to-day management of residential and commercial real estate and usually manage several properties at one time. Acting as the owners' agents and advisors, they supervise the marketing of space, negotiate lease agreements, direct bookkeeping activities, and report to owners on the status of the property. They also negotiate contracts for trash removal and other services and hire the maintenance and on-site management personnel employed at the properties.

Some managers buy and develop real estate for companies that have widespread retail operations, such as franchise restaurants and hotel chains, or for companies that build such projects as shopping malls and industrial parks.

On-site managers are based at the properties they manage and may even live on the property. Most of them are responsible for apartment buildings and work under the direction of property managers. They train, supervise, and assign duties to maintenance staffs; inspect the properties to determine what maintenance and repairs are needed; schedule routine service of heating and air-conditioning systems; keep records of operating costs; and submit cost reports to the property managers or owners.

They deal with residents on a daily basis and are responsible for handling their requests for service and repairs, resolving complaints concerning other tenants, and enforcing rules and lease restrictions.

Apartment house managers work for property owners or property management firms and are usually on-site managers. They show apartments to prospective tenants, negotiate leases, collect rents, handle tenants' requests, and direct the activities of maintenance staffs and outside contractors.

Building superintendents are responsible for operating and maintaining the facilities and equipment of such properties as apartment houses and office buildings. At small properties they may be the only on-site manager and report directly to property managers; at larger properties they may report to on-site managers and supervise maintenance staffs.

Housing project managers direct the operation of housing projects provided for such groups as military families, low-income families, and welfare recipients. The housing is usually subsidized by the government and may consist of single-family homes, multiunit dwellings, or house trailers.

Condominium managers are responsible to unit-owner associations and manage the services and commonly owned areas of condominium properties. They submit reports to the association members, supervise collection of owner assessments, resolve owners' complaints, and direct the activities of maintenance staffs and outside contractors. In some communities, such as planned unit developments (PUDs), homeowners belong to associations that employ managers to oversee homeowners' own jointly used properties and facilities.

Real estate asset managers work for institutional owners such as banks and insurance companies. Their responsibilities are larger in scope. Rather than manage day-to-day property operations, asset managers usually have an advisory role regarding the acquisition, rehabilitation, refinancing, and disposition of properties in a particular portfolio, and they may act "as the owner" in making specific business decisions, such as selecting and supervising site managers, authorizing operating expenditures, reviewing and approving leases, and monitoring local market conditions.

Specialized property and real estate managers perform a variety of other types of functions. *Market managers* direct the activities of municipal, regional, or state markets where wholesale fruit, vegetables, or meat are sold. They rent space to buyers and sellers and direct the supervisors who are responsible for collecting fees, maintaining and cleaning the buildings and grounds, and enforcing sanitation and security rules. *Public events facilities rental managers* negotiate contracts with organizations that wish to lease arenas, auditoriums, stadiums, or other facilities that are used for public events. They solicit new business and renewals of established contracts, maintain schedules to determine the availability of the facilities for bookings, and oversee operation and maintenance activities.

Real estate firm managers direct the activities of the sales agents who work for real estate firms. They screen and hire sales agents and conduct training sessions. They confer with agents and clients to resolve such problems as adjusting selling prices, determining who is responsible for repairs, and for closing costs. *Business opportunity-and-property-investment brokers* buy and sell business enterprises and investment properties on a commission or speculative basis. They investigate such factors as the financial ratings of businesses that are for sale, the desirability of a property's location for various types of businesses, and the condition of investment properties.

Businesses employ real estate managers to find, acquire, and develop the properties they need for their operations and to dispose of properties they no longer need. *Real estate agents* often work for companies that operate retail merchandising chains, such as fast-food restaurants, gasoline stations, and apparel shops. They locate sites that are desirable for their companies' operations and arrange to purchase or lease them. They also review their companies' holdings to identify properties that are no longer desirable and then negotiate to dispose of them. (Real estate sales agents also may be called real estate agents, but they are not involved in property management.) *Land development managers* are responsible for acquiring land for such projects as shopping centers and industrial parks. They nego-

tiate with local governments, property owners, and public interest groups to eliminate obstacles to their companies' developments, and they arrange for architects to draw up plans and construction firms to build the projects.

Requirements

Most employers prefer college graduates for property and real estate management positions. They prefer degrees in real estate, business management, finance, and related fields, but they also consider liberal arts graduates. In some cases, inexperienced college graduates with bachelor's or master's degrees enter the field as assistant property managers. High school students interested in this field should enroll in college preparatory programs.

Many property and real estate managers attend training programs offered by various professional and trade associations. Employers often send their managers to these programs to improve their management skills and expand their knowledge of such subjects as operation and maintenance of building mechanical systems, insurance and risk management, business and real estate law, and accounting and financial concepts. Many managers attend these programs voluntarily to prepare for advancement to positions with more responsibility.

Certification or licensing is not required for most property managers. Managers who have appropriate experience, complete required training programs, and achieve satisfactory scores on written exams, however, can earn certification and such professional designations as certified property manager (CPM), accredited residential manager (ARM), real property administrator (RPA), and certified shopping center manager (CSM). (Note that CPM and ARM are registered trademarks of the Institute of Real Estate Management.) Such designations are usually looked upon favorably by employers as a sign of a person's competence and dedication.

The federal government requires certification for managers of public housing that is subsidized by federal funds. Business opportunity-and-property-investment brokers must hold state licenses, and some states require real estate managers to hold licenses.

Property and real estate managers must be skilled in both oral and written communications and adept at dealing with people. They need to be good administrators and negotiators, and those who specialize in land development must be especially resourceful and creative to arrange financing for their projects. Managers for small rental or condominium complexes may be required to have building repair and maintenance skills, as well as business management skills.

Opportunities for Experience & Exploration

High school students interested in property and real estate management positions should seek activities that help them develop management skills, such as serving as an officer in an organization or participating in Junior Achievement projects. They also should seek part-time or summer jobs in sales or volunteer for work that involves public contact.

Students may be able to tour apartment complexes, shopping centers, and other real estate developments and should take advantage of any opportunities to talk with property and real estate managers.

Methods of Entering

Students who are about to graduate from college can obtain assistance from their school placement offices in finding their first job. Persons also can apply directly to property management firms and check ads in the help wanted sections of local newspapers. Property and real estate managers often begin as on-site managers for small apartment house complexes, condominiums, or community associations.

Advancement

With experience, entry-level property and site managers may transfer to larger properties or they may become assistant property managers, working closely with property managers and acquiring experience in a variety of management tasks. Assistant managers may advance to property manager positions, where they most likely will be responsible for several properties. As they advance in their careers, property managers may be responsible for larger or more

complex operations, may specialize in managing specific types of property, or may eventually establish their own companies.

To be considered for advancement, property managers must demonstrate the ability to deal effectively with tenants, contractors, and maintenance staff. They must be capable administrators and possess business skills, initiative, good organization, and excellent communications skills. Companies may offer management service to property owners, or experienced managers may choose to invest in properties to lease or rent.

Employment Outlook

About 271,000 people in the United States were employed as property and real estate managers in 1996. Most work for real estate operators and property management firms. Others work for real estate developers, government agencies that manage public buildings, corporations with large property holdings used for their retail operations, real estate investors, and mining and oil companies. Many work as self-employed developers, apartment building owners, property management firm owners, or owners of full-service real estate businesses.

Employment of property and real estate managers is expected to increase as fast as the average for all occupations in the United States through the year 2006. Job openings are expected to occur as older, experienced managers transfer to other occupations or leave the labor force. The best opportunities will be for college graduates with degrees in real estate, business administration, and related fields.

In the next decade, many of the economy's new jobs are expected to be in wholesale and retail trade, finance, insurance, real estate, and other service industries. Growth in these industries will bring a need for more office and retail properties and for people to manage them.

In housing, there will be a greater demand for apartments because of the high cost of owning a home. New home developments also are increasingly organized with community or homeowner associations that require managers. In addition, more owners of commercial and multiunit residential properties are expected to use professional managers to help make their properties more profitable.

Earnings

Managers of residential and commercial rental real estate are usually compensated by a fee based on the gross rental income of the properties. Managers of condominiums and other homeowner-occupied properties also are usually paid on a fee basis. Site managers and others employed by a management company are typically salaried.

According to the *1998-99 Occupational Outlook Handbook,* annual earnings for all property managers in 1996 ranged from a low of $12,000 or less to a high of more than $60,700. The median annual average for property managers in 1996 was $28,500.

Property and real estate managers usually receive such benefits as medical and health insurance. On-site apartment building managers may have rent-free apartments, and many managers have the use of company automobiles. In addition, managers involved in land development may receive a small percentage of ownership in their projects.

Conditions of Work

Property and real estate managers usually work in offices, but may spend much of their time at the properties they manage. On-site apartment building managers often leave their offices to inspect other areas, check maintenance or repair work, or resolve problems reported by tenants.

Many apartment managers must live in the buildings they manage so they can be available in emergencies, and they may be required to show apartments to prospective tenants at night or on weekends. Property and real estate managers may attend evening meetings with property owners, association boards of directors, or civic groups interested in property planned for development. Real estate managers who work for large companies frequently travel to inspect their companies' property holdings or locate properties their companies might acquire.

Sources of Additional Information

■Apartment Owners and Managers Association of America
65 Cherry Plaza
Watertown, CT 06795
Tel: 860-274-2589

■Building Owners and Managers Association
720 Light Street
Baltimore, MD 21230
Tel: 410-752-3318
WWW: http://www.boma.org

■Community Associations Institute
1630 Duke Street
Alexandria, VA 22314
Tel: 703-548-8600
WWW: http://www.caionline.com

■Institute of Real Estate Management
430 North Michigan Avenue
Chicago, IL 60611
Tel: 312-329-6000
WWW: http://www.irem.org

■National Apartment Association
201 North Union Street, Suite 200
Alexandria, VA 22314
Tel: 703-518-6141

■Canadian Real Estate Association
320 Queen Street, Suite 2100,
Ottawa, ON K1R 5A3 Canada
Tel: 613-237-7111

Radiologic Technologists

Definition

Radiologic technologists, sometimes called *radiographers*, operate equipment that creates images of the body's tissues, organs, and bones for medical diagnoses and therapy. These images allow physicians to know the exact nature of a patient's injury or disease, such as the precise place a bone is broken, or the confirmation of an ulcer in a patient.

Before an X-ray examination, radiologic technologists may administer drugs or chemical mixtures to the patient to better highlight internal organs. They put the patient in the correct position between the X-ray source and the film, and protect body areas, which are not to be exposed, from radiation. After determining the proper duration and intensity of the exposure, they operate the controls to beam X rays through the patient and expose the photographic film.

They may also operate computer-aided imaging equipment that does not involve X rays and may help to treat diseased or affected areas of the body by exposing the patient to specified concentrations of radiation for prescribed times.

Nature of the Work

All radiological work is done at the request of and under the supervision of a physician. Just as a prescription is required for some kinds of drugs to be dispensed or administered, so also must a physician's request be issued before a patient can receive any kind of imaging procedure.

There are four principle disciplines in which radiologic technologists may work: radiography, which is taking X-ray pictures or radiographs; nuclear medicine; radiation therapy; and sonography. In each of these, the technologist works under the direction of a physician who specializes in interpretation of the pictures produced by X rays, other imaging techniques, or radiation therapy. Technologists can work in more than one of these areas. Some technologists specialize in a particular part of the body or a specific condition.

X-ray pictures or radiographs are the most familiar use of radiologic technology. They are used to diagnose and determine treatment for a wide variety of afflictions, including ulcers, tumors, and bone fractures. Chest X-ray pictures can determine whether a person has a lung disease. To do their job, radiologic technologists who operate X-ray equipment first help the patient prepare for the radiologic examination. After explaining the procedure, they may administer a substance that makes the part of the body being imaged more clearly visible on the film. They make sure that the patient is not wearing any jewelry or other metal that would obstruct the X rays. They position the person sitting, standing, or lying down so that the correct view of the body can be radiographed, and then they cover adjacent areas with lead shielding to prevent unnecessary exposure to radiation.

The technologist positions the X-ray equipment at the proper angle and distance from the part to be radiographed and determines exposure time based on the location of the particular organ or bone and the thickness of the body in that area. The controls of the X-ray machine must be set to produce pictures of the correct density, contrast, and detail. Placing the photographic film closest to the body part being X-rayed, the technologist takes the requested images, repositioning the patient as needed. Typically, there are standards regarding the minimal number of views that should be taken of a given body part. The film is then developed for the radiologist or other physician to interpret.

In a fluoroscopic examination, a more complex imaging procedure that examines the gastrointestinal area, a beam of X rays passes through the body and onto a fluorescent screen, enabling the physician to see the internal organs in motion. For these, the technologist first prepares a solution of barium sulfate to be administered to the patient, either rectally or orally, depending on the exam. That increases the contrast between the digestive tract and the surrounding organs, making the picture clearer. The technologist follows the physician's guidance in positioning the patient, monitors the machine's controls, and takes any follow-up radiographs as needed.

Other imaging procedures radiologic technologists may learn are computed tomography (CT) scanning, which uses X rays to get detailed cross-sectional pictures of the body's internal structures, and magnetic resonance imaging (MRI), which uses radio waves, powerful magnets, and computers to obtain body part images. These diagnostic procedures are becoming more and more common and usually require radiologic technologists to undergo additional on-the-job training to learn them.

Other specialties within the radiography discipline include mammography and cardiovascular interventional technology. In addition, some technologists may focus on radiography of joints and bones, or they may be involved in such areas as angiocardiography (visualization of the heart and large blood vessels) or neuroradiology (the use of radiation to diagnose diseases of the nervous system).

Radiologic technologists also perform a range of duties, from greeting patients and putting them at ease by explaining the procedures, to developing the finished film. Their administrative tasks include maintaining patients' records and recording equipment usage and maintenance, and they may organize work schedules and manage a radiologist's private practice or a hospital's radiology department. Some radiologic technologists teach in programs to educate other technologists.

Requirements

Students who wish to become radiologic technologists must complete an education program in radiography. Programs range in length from two to four years. Depending on length, the programs award either a certificate, associate's degree, or bachelor's degree.

Educational programs are available in hospitals, medical centers, colleges and universities, and vocational and technical institutes. It is also possible to get an education in radiologic technology in the armed forces.

To enter an accredited program, applicants must be high school graduates; some programs may require one or two years of higher education. High school courses in mathematics, physics, chemistry, biology, and photography are useful background preparation. The courses that are taught in radiologic technology education programs include anatomy, physiology, patient care, physics, radiation protection, medical ethics, principles of imaging, medical terminology, radiobiology, and pathology. For some supervisory or administrative jobs in this field, a bachelor's or master's degree may be required.

Radiologic technologists may register with the American Registry of Radiologic Technologists after graduating from an accredited program in radiography, radiation therapy, or nuclear medicine. *Sonographers* may register with the American Registry of Diagnostic Medical Sonographers. Although registration and certification are voluntary, many jobs are open only to technologists who have acquired these credentials.

In addition to being registered in the various imaging disciplines, radiologic technologists can receive advanced qualifications in each of the four radiography specializations: mammography, computed tomography (CT), magnetic resonance imaging (MRI), and cardiovascular interventional technology. As the work of radiologic technologists grows increasingly complex, and employment opportunities become more competitive, the desirability of registration and certification will also grow. An increasing number of states have licensing requirements. In 1995, licenses were needed by radiographers in thirty states.

Radiologic technologists should be responsible individuals, with a mature and caring nature. They should also be personable and enjoy interacting with many types of people, some of whom may be very ill. A compassionate attitude is important.

Opportunities for Experience & Exploration

There is no way to gain direct experience in this profession without the appropriate qualifications. However, it is possible to learn about the duties of radiologic technologists by talking with them and observing the facilities and equipment they use. It is also possible to have interviews with teachers of radiologic technology. Guidance counselors or teachers can contact local hospitals or schools with radiography programs to locate technologists who would be able to talk to interested students.

As with any career in health care, volunteering at a local hospital, clinic, or nursing home provides an excellent opportunity to test your real interest in the field. Most hospitals are eager for volunteers, and working in the setting gives a chance to see health care professionals in action as well as to have some patient contact.

Methods of Entering

With more states regulating the practice of radiologic technology, certification by the appropriate accreditation body for a given specialty is quickly becoming a necessity for employment. Persons who acquire training in schools that have not been accredited, or who learn on the job, may have difficulty in qualifying for many positions, especially those with a wide range of assignments.

Students enrolled in hospital educational programs often work for the hospital upon completion of the program. Those students who attend degree programs can get help finding jobs through their school's placement office.

Advancement

About three-quarters of all radiologic technologists are employed in hospitals, where there are opportunities for advancement to administrative and supervisory positions such as chief technologist or technical administrator. Other technologists develop special clinical skills in advanced imaging procedures such as computed tomography (CT) scanning or magnetic resonance imaging (MRI). Some radiologic technologists qualify as instructors. There is more chance of advancement for persons who hold a bachelor's degree. For those who wish to become teachers or administrators, a master's degree and considerable experience are necessary.

Employment Outlook

This field is estimated to grow faster than average for all occupations through the year 2006. A growing older population is a factor for this growth. Although enrollments in accredited schools have equalized in recent years, the demand for qualified people in some areas of the country far exceeds the supply. This shortage is particularly acute in rural areas and small towns.

In the years to come, increasing numbers of radiologic technologists will be employed in nonhospital settings, such as physicians' offices, clinics, health maintenance organizations, laboratories, government agencies, and diagnostic imaging centers. This pattern will be part of the overall trend toward holding down health care costs by delivering more care outside of hospitals. Nevertheless, hospitals will remain the major employers of radiologic technologists for the near future. Because of the increasing importance of radiologic technology in the diagnosis and treatment of disease, it is unlikely that hospitals will do fewer radiologic procedures than in the past. Instead, they try to do more on an outpatient basis, and on weekends and evenings. This should increase the demand for part-time technologists and thus open more opportunities for flexible work schedules.

At present, most of the nation's radiologic technologists are radiographers, and this is the field that will continue to employ most technologists. Radiation, either alone or in combination with surgery and chemotherapy, will continue in the near future to be an important weapon against cancer and certain other diseases. More widespread use of ultrasound testing, especially in cardiology and obstetrics/gynecology, will have a positive effect on the hiring of diagnostic medical sonographers.

Earnings

Salaries for radiologic technologists compare favorably with those of similar health care professions. According to a 1997 Hay Group Survey of acute care hospitals, the starting salary in a hospital or medical center averages about $28,800 a year for radiologic technologists. With experience, technologists earn average salaries of about $31,000 or more a year.

Technologists with specialized skills may make larger salaries. Radiation therapists earn an average salary of about $37,300. In ultrasound technology, the average pay for those with experience is about $36,000. Most technologists are covered by the same vacation and sick leave provisions as other employees in the organizations that employ them, and some receive free medical care and pension benefits.

Conditions of Work

Full-time technologists generally work eight hours a day, forty hours a week and may be on call for some night emergency duty or weekend hours, which pays in equal time off or additional compensation.

In diagnostic radiologic work, technologists perform most of their tasks while on their feet. They move around a lot and often are called upon to lift patients who need help in moving.

Great care is exercised to protect technologists from radiation exposure. Each technologist wears a badge that measures radiation exposure, and records are kept of total exposure accumulated over time. Routine pre-cautions include the use of safety devices such as individual instruments that measure radiation (badges), lead aprons, lead gloves, and other shielding. Other protections routinely taken by technologists may include the use of disposable gowns, gloves, and masks. Careful attention to safety procedures has greatly reduced or eliminated radiation hazards for the technologist.

Radiologic technology is dedicated to conserving life and health. Technologists derive satisfaction from their work, which helps promote health and alleviate human suffering. Those who specialize in radiation therapy need to be able to handle the close relationships they inevitably develop while working with very sick or dying people over a period of time.

Sources of Additional Information

■**American Society of Radiologic Technologists**
15000 Central Avenue, SE
Albuquerque, NM 87123
Tel: 505-298-4500

■**Canadian Association of Medical Radiation Technologists**
294 Albert Street, Room 601
Ottawa, ON K1P 6E6 Canada
Tel: 613-231-4361

■**Society of Diagnostic Medical Sonographers**
12770 Coit Road, Suite 508
Dallas, TX 75251
Tel: 214-239-7367

For information on accreditation, please contact:

■**American Registry of Radiologic Technologists**
1255 Northland Drive
St. Paul, MN 55120
Tel: 612-687-0048

■**American Cancer Society**
1599 Clifton Road
Atlanta, GA 30329
Tel: 404-320-3333
WWW: http://www.cancer.org

Real Estate Agents and Brokers

Definition

Real estate brokers execute instructions from buyers or sellers for the sale or rental of property. Brokers employ agents to rent or sell property for clients on a commission basis. Both of these workers are sometimes called *real estate agents*.

Nature of the Work

The primary responsibility of a real estate broker or agent is to help his or her client buy, sell, rent, or lease a piece of real estate. Real estate is a piece of land or property and all improvements attached to it. The property may be residential, commercial, or agricultural. When a person wishes to put a piece of property up for sale or rent, he or she contracts with a real estate broker to arrange the sale and to represent them in the transaction. This contract with a broker is called a "listing."

One of the broker's main duties is to solicit listings actively for the agency. They develop leads for potential listings by distributing promotional items, by advertising in local publications, and by showing other available properties in "Open Houses." They also spend a great deal of time on the phone exploring leads gathered from various sources, including personal contacts.

Once the listing is obtained, real estate brokers must analyze the property to best present it to prospective buyers. They have to recognize and promote the property's strong selling points, while also being aware of its weaknesses. The agent usually develops a description of the property to be used in ads and promotions and has the property photographed. They may also advise the owner on ways to make the property more attractive to prospective buyers.

Frequently, the broker counsels the owner about the asking price for the property. This is done by comparing it with similar properties in the area that have been sold recently to determine the property's fair market value. The owners usually sign a contract agreeing that if they sell the property, they will pay the broker a percentage of the selling price. Unless stated in the contract, the broker and any agents of the brokerage are working to obtain the best selling price for the seller. Home buyers in some states are allowed to engage a broker as a *buyer's broker*, which means the broker is committed to work for the buyer's best interests.

When the property is ready to be shown, agents in the office review their files to identify prospective buyers. Frequently, after a week or two of exclusive marketing by one broker, the property for sale is entered into a computerized multiple-listing service so that other local real estate firms may show the property. To stimulate interest in the property, the broker advertises the house in local newspapers.

As potential buyers are contacted, the agent arranges a convenient time for them to see the property. If the property is vacant, the broker usually retains the key. To adjust to the schedules of potential buyers, agents frequently show properties in the late afternoon or evening and on weekends. In many areas, Sunday afternoon Open Houses are used to provide easy access to available properties. Because a representative of the broker's firm is usually on the premises in each house, open houses are a good way to put part-time or beginning agents to work.

An agent may have to meet several times with a prospective buyer to discuss and view available properties. The successful real estate agent has to determine the style and size of property the buyer is looking for, and the price they will be able to pay. The agent will often emphasize points that might be of particular interest to the buyer. To people with young families, the agent may emphasize the convenient floor plan or the proximity of schools and shopping centers. To people looking for investment rental properties, the agent may stress available financing arrangements, the ease of finding a tenant, and factors that may contribute to the long-range value of the property. In addition to this, the agent points out features that the buyer should weigh when considering alternative purchases. The agent must also be familiar with tax rates, zoning regulations, home construction methods, and insurance needs.

When the buyer finds an affordable and desirable property, the agent must bring the buyer and seller together at terms agreeable to both. In many cases, the seller and buyer will be represented by different brokers or agents. Very often the parties must bargain over the price of the property. In such situations, good negotiating skills become very important. Both agents may have to present counteroffers to get the best possible price for the seller and buyer.

Once the contract has been signed by both parties, the broker or agent must see to it that all special terms of the contract are carried out before the closing date. For example, if the seller has agreed to a home inspection or a termite inspection, the agent must make sure that the inspection is carried out. If the seller has agreed to make any repairs, again the broker or agent must make sure that they have been made, otherwise the sale cannot be completed.

Brokers often provide buyers with information on loans to finance their purchase. They also arrange for title searches and title insurance. A broker's knowledge, resourcefulness, and creativity in arranging financing that is favorable to the buyer can mean the difference between success and failure in closing a sale. In some cases, agents assume the responsibilities of closing the sale, but in many areas this is accomplished by lawyers or loan officers.

Specialists in commercial or agricultural real estate operate in much the same fashion. Their clients usually have very established priorities about what an acceptable property must have. For example, any property that would be of interest to a trucking firm must be located near major highways. These real estate specialists often conduct extensive searches for property that meets clients' specifications, so they must study the properties more carefully. They usually make fewer sales, but receive higher commissions.

In addition to selling real estate, some brokers rent and manage properties for a fee. Some brokers combine other types of work, such as selling insurance or practicing law, with their real estate business.

Requirements

There are no standard educational requirements for the real estate field. However, most employers require at least a high school diploma. An increasing percentage of real estate agents and brokers have some college education. A good general education provides background helpful in working with the many different types of people that an agent encounters. College courses in psychology, economics, sociology, marketing, finance, business administration, architecture, and engineering are helpful. Many agents and brokers have taken formal college courses in real estate. A complete list of the hundreds of colleges and universities offering courses in real estate is available from the National Association of Realtors.

Every state and the District of Columbia requires that real estate agents and brokers be licensed. Most states ask prospective agents to complete at least thirty hours of classroom training and to pass written examinations on real estate fundamentals and state laws. Brokers must pass more extensive examinations and must usually complete at least ninety hours of classroom training. They are also often required to have sales experience of one to three years.

State licenses are usually renewed annually without examination. Agents who move to another state must qualify under the licensing laws of that state. To supplement minimum state requirements, many agents take courses in real estate principles, laws, financing, appraisal, and property development and management. These courses are often sponsored by local real estate boards that are members of the National Association of Realtors or its affiliates.

Qualified agents and brokers are usually affiliated with the National Association of Realtors through membership in one of the more than thirteen hundred local boards or its affiliated associations. Only those active members who subscribe to the N.A.R. Code of Ethics may legally use the term "Realtor." Qualified specialists may join such N.A.R. affiliates such as the Institute of Real Estate

Management, the Society of Industrial and Office Realtors, or the Farm Land Institute.

Successful brokers and agents must be willing to study the industry and improve their skills constantly. For example, those who sell or rent business property must stay abreast of the latest business and economic trends, as well as the prices being charged for competing properties in the market. Residential real estate brokers have to keep up with the latest trends in mortgage financing, construction, and community development. Real estate agents and brokers must have a thorough knowledge of the housing market in their community. They must know which neighborhoods will best fit their clients' needs and budgets. They must be familiar with local zoning and tax laws and know where buyers can obtain reasonable financing. Agents and brokers must also act as go-betweens in the price negotiations between buyers and sellers. Many real estate firms, especially the larger ones, offer formal training programs for both beginners and experienced agents.

In most cases, educational experience is less important than the right personality. Brokers want agents who possess a pleasant personality, exude honesty, and maintain a neat appearance. To be successful as an agent requires a general liking for people. Agents must work with many different types of people and inspire their trust and confidence. They must be able to express themselves well and show enthusiasm to motivate customers.

The agent must have good judgment to combine a knowledge of current real estate market values with informed predictions of future developments in the communities they serve. They should also be well organized and detail-oriented, as well as have a good memory for names, faces, and business details, such as taxes, zoning regulations, and local land-use laws.

Maturity is an asset in this profession. In fact, many successful agents enter the field in middle age. A thorough knowledge of the general geographical area will help those entering the field. To drum up new listings and prospective buyers, agents must be willing to participate in local civic and social organizations.

Agents must be tactful. Frequently, an agent receives a listing that exactly meets the specifications established by a customer. Unfortunately, after seeing the property, the customer may be indecisive about what he or she really wants. In such cases, the agent must be patient and allow cus-

tomers to make their own decisions. An agent may show one customer through dozens of properties before closing a sale.

Opportunities for Experience & Exploration

Calling on local real estate brokers and agents should provide useful information on the field. Information on licensing requirements may be obtained from local real estate boards or from the real estate departments of each state. State licensing requirements prohibit inexperienced workers from gaining sales experience. Part-time and summer employment in a real estate office, however, may provide a clearer picture of the field.

Methods of Entering

The typical entry position in this field is as an agent working for a broker with an established office. Another opportunity may be in inside-sales with a construction firm that is building a new housing development. Beginners usually apply directly to local real estate firms or may be referred through public and private employment services. Brokers looking to hire agents may run newspaper advertisements. Local real estate boards may be able to steer applicants toward offices that are hiring. People often contact firms in their own communities, where their knowledge of local neighborhoods is an advantage.

The beginning agent must choose between the advantages of joining a small or a large organization. In a small office, the newcomer will train informally under an experienced agent. The newcomer's duties will be broad and varied, and as the junior member of a small organization, they may often be menial. However, this is a good chance to learn all the basics of the business, including the use of computers to locate available properties or identify available sources of financing. In larger firms, the new agent may proceed through a more standardized training process and may specialize in one phase of the real estate field, such as commercial real estate, mortgage financing, or property management.

The first months are usually difficult for beginning agents. They need to develop a reputation for service and a clientele of satisfied customers. People who have successfully purchased or sold a home through an agent are inclined to turn to that person for help with future real estate transactions and to recommend that agent to their relatives and friends. The beginner spends a great deal of time on the telephone seeking listings of properties to sell and answering calls in response to advertisements.

Advancement

While many successful agents develop professionally by expanding the quality and quantity of their services, others seek advancement by entering management or by specializing in residential or commercial real estate.

The agent may enter management by becoming the head of a major division of a large real estate firm. Other agents purchase an established real estate business, join one as a partner, or set up their own offices. Self-employed agents must meet the state requirements for a broker's license.

Agents who wish to specialize have a number of available options. They may have to decide between residential and commercial sales. Real estate brokers may develop property management businesses. In return for approximately 5 percent of the gross receipts, property managers operate apartment houses or multiple-tenant business properties for their owners. *Property managers* are in charge of renting (including advertising, tenant relations, and collecting rents), building maintenance (heating, lighting, cleaning, and decorating), and accounting (financial recording and filing tax returns).

There are a number of professional designations available to both residential and commercial real estate agents. These designations demonstrate an advanced level of experience and knowledge, and focus on various specialty areas.

A limited number of agents may qualify for the complex role of the *appraiser*, who estimates the current market value of land and buildings.

Highly experienced agents may serve as *real estate counselors*, advising clients on the suitability of available property. Other agents may enter mortgage financing, placing real estate loans with interested financial institutions or private lenders.

Real estate brokers sometimes play a key role in land development through their cooperation in long-range plans for cities, subdivisions, housing tracts, shopping centers, and industrial sites. Some brokers engage in the business of buying and selling homes for their own account. Anticipating metropolitan expansion, they buy up lands that may appreciate in value and thus may facilitate development. Occasionally, experienced brokers may join the real estate departments of major corporations or large governmental agencies.

Employment Outlook

About 408,000 people worked as real estate agents and brokers in 1996, many of them part-time. Employment of these workers is expected to grow more slowly than the average through year 2006. But as the average age of real estate agents and brokers is considerably higher than for workers in many other occupations, many opportunities for new agents will be made available because of agents retiring or transferring to other types of work. Because of this high job turnover, tens of thousands of real estate openings are expected yearly.

The country's expanding population will create additional demand for real estate services, and growing affluence suggests that the percentage of Americans owning their own homes will increase. Continuing mobility among Americans also indicates a continued high volume of real estate transactions. People are buying their first homes later in life, but as the general age of the population increases, the overall number of property owners should continue to rise.

Increased use of technology, such as computers, faxes and databases, will help improve an agent's productivity. Computer generated images now allow agents and customers to view multiple property listings without leaving the office. Well-trained, ambitious people who enjoy selling should have the best chance for success in this field.

Employment of real estate agents and brokers is sensitive to economic swings. A downturn in the general economy usually results in a diminishing of mortgage financing and slows construction of new homes. During these periods, the earnings of agents and brokers decline, and many people work fewer hours or leave the profession.

Earnings

Compensation in the real estate field is based almost entirely upon commissions. Commissions range from 5 to 10 percent of the selling price, averaging about 7 percent. Agents usually split commissions with the brokers who employ them. The broker may take half the commission in return for providing the agent with the office space, advertising support, sales supervision, and the use of the broker's good name. When two or more agents are involved in a transaction (for example, one agent listing the property for sale and another selling it), the commission is usually divided between the two on the basis of an established formula. Agents can earn more if they both list and sell the property.

Full-time residential real estate agents earn an average of about $31,500 a year. Commercial agents usually earn $50,000 or more annually. Brokers may advance their agents (especially those new to the business) a stated amount each month against future commissions on sales. Brokers earn a median gross personal annual income (after expenses) of about $50,000 in residential real estate and about $100,000 in commercial real estate. The most successful people in the field earn much more. Brokers have a much higher gross salary, out of which they have to pay staff and office expenses, advertising costs, travel and entertainment expenses, and other costs of doing business. Agents may have to pay their own travel expenses.

Because most agents work on a commission basis, and as such are considered independent from the firms they work with, they do not usually receive standard benefits like paid vacations, health insurance, or sick leave.

Agents and brokers may supplement their income by appraising property, placing mortgages with private lenders, or selling insurance. Since earnings are irregular and economic conditions unpredictable, agents and brokers should maintain sufficient cash reserves for slack periods.

Conditions of Work

It is relatively simple to enter the real estate field. Anyone who qualifies for a license needs only a telephone number to be in business. However, a glance at the real estate advertisements in any newspaper will offer a picture of a highly competitive field. In addition to the full-time workers operating, the existence of many part-time agents increases competition for those making their entire living from the field.

Beginning agents must accept the frustration inherent in the early months in the business. All agents must begin by accepting modest listings, which they work hard to get. Building a client base and developing sales skills can take some time.

After agents become established, they can expect to work many evenings and weekends. Agents work on their own schedule and are free to take a day off when they choose. However, this also means they may be missing out on an important lead or may not be available to service their clients. Unlike some other areas of sales, real estate agents do little overnight travel. Some real estate brokers do much of their work out of their own homes. Successful agents will spend little time in an office, but will be out showing properties to potential buyers or meeting with sellers to set up a listing.

Most real estate agents and brokers work in small business establishments. Only in metropolitan areas do agents have the option of joining larger organizations. Real estate positions are found in every part of the country, but are concentrated in large urban areas and in smaller, rapidly growing communities. Regardless of the size of the community in which they work, good agents should know its economic life, the personal preferences of its citizens, and the demand for real estate.

Sources of Additional Information

For information on professional designations, real estate courses, and publications, contact:

National Association of Realtors
430 North Michigan Avenue
Chicago, IL 60611
Tel: 312-329-8200
WWW: http://www.realtor.com

For information on industrial and office real estate, contact:

Society of Industrial and Office Realtors
700 11th Street, NW, Suite 510
Washington, DC 20001
Tel: 202-737-1150

Receptionists

Definition

Receptionists—so named because they receive visitors places of business—have the important job of giving a business's clients and visitors a positive first impression. These front-line workers are the first communication sources who greet clients and visitors, answer their questions, and direct them to the people they wish to see. Receptionists also answer telephones, take and distribute messages for other employees, and make sure no one enters the office unescorted or unauthorized. Many receptionists perform additional clerical duties. *Switchboard operators* perform similar tasks but primarily handle equipment that receives an organization's telephone calls.

Nature of the Work

The receptionist is a specialist in human contact: the most important part of a receptionist's job is dealing with people in a courteous and effective manner. Receptionists greet customers, clients, patients, and salespeople, take their names, and determine the nature or their business and the person they wish to see. The receptionist then pages the requested person, directs the visitor to that person's office or location, or makes an appointment for a later visit. Receptionists often keep records of all visits by writing down the visitor's name, purpose of visit, person visited, and date and time.

Almost all types of companies hire receptionists. They work in manufacturing, wholesale, retail, real estate, insurance, medicine, advertising, government, banking, church administration, and law. Their day-to-day duties depend almost entirely on the nature of the place at which they work.

Most receptionists answer the telephone at their place of employment; many operate switchboards or paging systems. These workers usually take and distribute messages for other employees and may receive and distribute mail. Receptionists may perform a variety of other clerical duties, including keying in and filing correspondence and other paperwork, proofreading, preparing travel vouchers, and preparing outgoing mail. In some businesses, receptionists are responsible for monitoring the attendance of other employees. In businesses where employees are frequently out of the office on assignments, receptionists may keep track of their whereabouts to ensure they receive important phone calls and messages. Many receptionists use computers and word processors in performing their clerical duties.

Receptionists are partially responsible for maintaining office security, especially in large firms. They may require all visitors to sign in and out and carry visitors' passes during their stay. Since visitors may not enter most offices unescorted, receptionists usually accept and sign for packages and other deliveries.

Receptionists are frequently responsible for answering inquiries from the public about a business's nature and operations. To answer these questions efficiently and in a manner that conveys a favorable impression, a receptionist must be as knowledgeable as possible about the business's products, services, policies, and practices and familiar with the names and responsibilities of all other employees. They must be careful, however, not to divulge classified information such as business procedures or employee activities that a competing company might be able to use. This part of a receptionist's job is so important that some businesses call their receptionists *information clerks*.

A large number of receptionists work in physicians' and dentists' offices, hospitals, clinics, and other health care establishments. Workers in medical offices receive patients, take their names, and escort them to examination rooms. They make future appointments for patients and may prepare statements and collect bill payments. In hospitals, receptionists obtain patient information, assign patients to rooms, and keep records on the dates they are admitted and discharged.

In other types of industries, the duties of these workers vary. Receptionists in hair salons arrange appointments for clients and may escort them to stylists' stations. Workers in bus or train companies answer inquiries about departures, arrivals, and routes. *In-file operators* collect and distribute credit information to clients for credit purposes. *Registrars, park aides,* and *tourist-information assistants* may be employed as receptionists at public or private facilities. Their duties may include keeping a record of the visitors entering and leaving the facility, as well as providing information on services that the facility provides. Information clerks, automobile club information clerks, and *referral-and-information aides* provide answers to questions by telephone or in person from both clients and potential clients and keep a record of all inquiries.

Switchboard operators may perform specialized work, such as operating switchboards at police district offices to take calls for assistance from citizens. Or, they may handle airport communication systems, which includes public address paging systems and courtesy telephones, or serve as *answering-service operators*, who record and deliver messages for clients who cannot be reached by telephone.

Requirements

Most employees require receptionists to have a high school diploma. Some businesses prefer to hire workers who have completed post–high school courses at a junior college or business school. Applicants need a friendly, outgoing personality, excellent people skills, neat appearance, and good grasp of English and grammar. Many employers require typing, switchboard, computer, and other clerical skills, but may provide some on-the-job training as the work is typically entry level.

High school students may prepare for receptionist or switchboard operator positions by taking courses in business procedures, office machine operation, keyboarding, computers, business math, English, and public speaking. Students interested in post–high school education may find courses in basic bookkeeping and principles of accounting helpful in finding higher-paying receptionist jobs with better chances for advancement.

Good receptionists need to be well-groomed, have pleasant voices, and be able to clearly express themselves. Because receptionists sometimes deal with demanding people, a smooth, patient disposition and good judgment are important. All receptionists need to be courteous and tactful. A good memory for faces and names also proves very valuable. Most important are good listening and communications skills and an understanding of human nature.

Opportunities for Experience & Exploration

A good way to obtain experience in working as a receptionist is through a high school work-study program. Students participating in such programs spend part of their school day in classes and the rest working for local businesses. This arrangement helps students gain valuable practical experience before they look for their first job. High school guidance counselors can provide information about work-study opportunities.

Methods of Entering

High school students may be able to learn of openings with local businesses through their school guidance counselors or newspaper want ads. Local state employment offices frequently have information about receptionist work. Students should also contact area businesses for whom they would like to work; many available positions are not advertised in the paper because they are filled so quickly. Temporary-work agencies are a valuable resource for finding jobs, too, some of which may lead to permanent employment. Friends and relatives may also know of job openings.

Advancement

Advancement opportunities are limited for receptionists, especially in small offices. The more clerical skills and education workers have, the greater their chances for promotion to such better-paying jobs as *secretary*, *administrative assistant*, or *bookkeeper*. College or business school training can help receptionists advance to higher-level positions. Many companies provide training for their receptionists and other employees, helping workers gain skills for job advancement.

Employment Outlook

According to the U.S. Department of Labor, over one million people were employed as receptionists in 1996, accounting for about a third of all information clerks. Factories, wholesale and retail stores, and service providers employ a large percentage of these workers. Nearly one-third of the receptionists in the United States work in health care settings, including offices, hospitals, nursing homes, urgent care centers, and clinics. Almost one-third work part time.

This field is expected to grow faster than the average through the year 2006. Many openings will occur due to the occupation's high turnover rate. Opportunities will be best for those with wide clerical skills and work experience. Growth in jobs for receptionists are expected to be greater than for other clerical positions because automation will have little effect on the receptionist's largely interpersonal duties and because of an anticipated growth in the number of businesses providing services. In addition, more and more businesses are learning how valuable a receptionist can be in furthering their public relations efforts and helping them convey a positive image.

Earnings

Earnings for receptionists vary widely with the education and experience of the worker and type, size, and geographic location of the business. According to the U.S. Department of Labor, receptionists earned starting salaries of over $11,900 in 1996. Those with experience earned $24,250 or more.

In 1997, the federal government paid beginning receptionists salaries ranging from $18,900 to $19,200 a year; the average annual salary for experienced receptionists in the federal government was $21,240.

Receptionists are usually eligible for paid holidays and vacations, sick leave, medical and life insurance coverage, and a retirement plan of some kind.

Most receptionists work five days, thirty-five to forty hours a week. Some may work weekend and evening hours, especially those in medical offices. Switchboard operators may have to work any shift of the day if their employers require twenty-four-hour phone service, such as hotels and hospitals. These workers usually work holidays and weekend hours.

Conditions of Work

Because receptionists usually work near or at the main entrance to the business, their work area is one of the first places a caller sees. Therefore, these areas are usually pleasant and clean and are carefully furnished and decorated to create a favorable, businesslike impression. Work areas are almost always air-conditioned, well lit, and relatively quiet, although a receptionist's phone rings frequently. Receptionists work behind a desk or counter and spend most of their workday sitting, although some standing and walking is required when filing or escorting visitors to their destinations. The job may be stressful at times, especially when a worker must be polite to rude callers.

Sources of Additional Information

■Accrediting Council for Independent Colleges and Schools
750 First Street, NE, Suite 980
Washington, DC 20002
Tel: 202-336-6780

■Accrediting Council of Career Schools and College of Technology
2101 Wilson Boulevard, Suite 302
Arlington, VA 22201
Tel: 703-247-4212

■Professional Secretaries International
PO Box 20404
10502 NW Ambassador Drive
Kansas City, MO 64195-0404
Tel: 816-891-6600

Recreation Workers

Definition

Recreation workers help people, as groups and as individuals, enjoy and use their leisure time constructively. They organize and administer physical, social, and cultural programs. They also operate recreational facilities and study recreation needs.

Nature of the Work

Recreation workers plan, organize, and direct recreation activities for people of all ages, social and economic levels, and degrees of physical and emotional health. The exact nature of their work varies and depends on their individual level of responsibility.

Recreation workers employed by local governments and voluntary agencies include *recreation supervisors* who coordinate recreation center directors, who in turn supervise recreation leaders and aides. With the help of volunteer workers, they plan and carry out programs at community centers, neighborhood playgrounds, recreational and rehabilitation centers, prisons, hospitals, and homes for children and the elderly, often working in cooperation with social workers and sponsors of the various centers.

Recreation supervisors plan programs to meet the needs of the people they serve. Well-rounded programs may include arts and crafts, dramatics, music, dancing, swimming, games, camping, nature study, and other pastimes. Special events may include festivals, contests, pet and hobby shows, and various outings. Recreation supervisors also create programs for people with special needs, such as the elderly or people in hospitals. Supervisors have overall responsibility for coordinating the work of the recreation workers who carry out the programs and supervise several recreation centers or an entire region.

Recreation center directors run the programs at their respective recreation buildings, indoor centers, playgrounds, or day camps. In addition to directing the staff of the facility, they oversee the safety of the buildings and equipment, handle financial matters, and prepare reports.

Recreation leaders, with the help of *recreation aides*, work directly with assigned groups and are responsible for the daily operations of a recreation program. They organize and lead activities such as drama, dancing, sports and games, camping trips, and other recreations. They give instruction in crafts, games, and sports, and work with other staff on special projects and events. Leaders help train and direct volunteers and perform other tasks, as required by the director.

In industry, recreation leaders plan social and athletic programs for employees and their families. Bowling leagues, softball teams, picnics, and dances are examples of company-sponsored activities. In addition, an increasing number of companies are providing exercise and fitness programs for their employees.

Camp counselors lead and instruct children and adults in nature-oriented forms of recreation at camps or resorts. Activities usually include swimming, hiking, horseback riding, and other outdoor sports and games, as well as instruction in nature and folklore. Camp counselors teach skills such as wood crafting, leather working, and basket weaving. Some camps offer specialized instruction in subjects such as music, drama, gymnastics, and computers. In carrying out the programs, camp counselors are concerned with the safety, health, and comfort of the campers. Counselors are supervised by a *camp director*.

Another type of recreation worker is the *social director*, who plans and organizes recreational activities for guests in hotels and resorts or for passengers aboard a ship. Social directors usually greet new arrivals and introduce them to other guests, explain the recreational facilities, and encourage guests to participate in planned activities. These activities may include card parties, games, contests, dances, musicals, or field trips and may require setting up equipment, arranging for transportation, or planning decorations, refreshments, or entertainment. In general, social directors try to create a friendly atmosphere, paying particular attention to lonely guests and trying to ensure that everyone has a good time.

Requirements

For some recreation positions, a high school diploma or an associate degree in parks and recreation, social work, or other human service discipline is sufficient preparation. However, most full-time career positions require a bachelor's degree, and a graduate degree is often a necessity for high-level administrative posts. Acceptable majors include parks and recreation management, leisure studies, fitness management, and related disciplines. A degree in any liberal arts field may be sufficient if the person's education includes courses relevant to recreation work.

In industrial recreation, employers usually prefer applicants with a bachelor's degree in recreation and a strong background in business administration. Some jobs require specialized training in a particular field, such as art, music, drama, or athletics. Others need special certifications, such as a lifesaving certificate to teach swimming. In addition to specialized training, students interested in recreation work should get a broad liberal arts and cultural education and acquire at least a working knowledge of arts and crafts, music, dance, drama, athletics, and nature study.

Over 200 community and junior colleges offer associate degrees in parks and recreation programs, and about 300 colleges and universities have similar, but more extensive programs leading to a bachelor's, master's, or doctoral degree. In 1997, there were ninety-three parks and recreation curriculums at the bachelor's degree level accredited by the National Recreation and Park Association.

Many recreation professionals apply for certification as evidence of their professional competence. The National Recreation and Park Association, the American Camping Association, and the National Employee Services and Recreation Association award certificates to individuals who meet their standards. In the 1990s, more than forty states had adopted NRPA standards for park/recreation professionals.

The federal government employs many recreation leaders in national parks, the armed forces, the Department of Veterans Affairs, and correctional institutions. It may be necessary to pass a civil service examination to qualify for these positions.

Personal qualifications for recreation work include a desire to work with people, outgoing personality, even temperament, and ability to lead and influence others. Recreation workers should have good health and stamina, and should be able to stay calm and think clearly and quickly in emergencies.

Opportunities for Experience & Exploration

Young people interested in this field should obtain related work experience as part-time or summer workers or volunteers in recreation departments, neighborhood centers, camps, and other organizations.

Methods of Entering

College placement offices are useful in helping graduates find employment. Most college graduates begin as either recreation leaders or specialists and, after several years of experience, may become recreation directors. A few enter trainee programs leading directly to recreation administration within a year or so. Those with graduate training may start as recreation directors.

Advancement

Recreation leaders without graduate training will find advancement limited, but it is possible to obtain better-paying positions through a combination of education and experience. With experience it is possible to become a recreation director. With further experience, directors may become supervisors and eventually head of all recreation departments or divisions in a city. Some recreation professionals become consultants.

Employment Outlook

There were about 233,000 recreation workers, not counting summer workers or volunteers, in 1996. More than 50 percent worked for government agencies, mostly at the municipal or county level. Nearly 20 percent were employed by civic, social, fraternal, or religious membership organizations such as the Boy Scouts, YWCA, or Red Cross. The rest worked in social service organizations such as centers for seniors and adult day care, and residential-care facilities, such as halfway houses, institutions for delinquent youths, and group homes or commercial recreation establishments and private industry.

Employment opportunities for recreation workers are expected to increase faster than the average through the end of 2006. The expected expansion in the recreation field will result from increased leisure time and income for the population as a whole combined with a continuing interest in fitness and health and a growing elderly population in nursing homes, senior centers, and retirement communities. There also is a demand for recreation workers to conduct activity programs for special needs groups.

Two areas promising the most favorable opportunities for recreation workers are the commercial recreation and social service industries. Commercial recreation establishments include amusement parks, sports and entertainment centers, wilderness and survival enterprises, tourist attractions, vacation excursions, hotels and other resorts, camps, health spas, athletic clubs, and apartment complexes. New employment opportunities will arise in social service agencies such as senior centers, halfway houses, children's homes, and day-care programs for the mentally or developmentally disabled.

Recreation programs that depend on government funding are most likely to be affected in times of economic downturns when budgets are reduced. During such times, competition will increase significantly for jobs in the private sector.

In any case, competition is expected to be keen because the field is open to college graduates regardless of major; as a result, there are more applicants than there are job openings. Opportunities will be best for individuals who have formal training in recreation and for those with previous experience.

Earnings

Full-time recreation workers earned an average of $18,700 a year in 1996. Some earned up to $37,500 or more, depending on job responsibilities and experience. Some top level managers can make considerably more.

Salaries in industrial recreation are higher. Newly hired recreation workers in industry have starting salaries of about $18,000 to $24,000 a year. Camp directors average about $1,600 per month in municipally operated camps; in private camps, earnings are higher. Camp counselors employed seasonally are paid anywhere from $200 to $800 a month. Recreation workers in the federal government start at about $14,800 a year.

Conditions of Work

Physical conditions vary greatly from outdoor parks to nursing homes for the elderly. A recreation worker can choose the conditions under which he or she would like to work. Recreation workers with an interest in the outdoors may become camp counselors. Those who have an interest in travel may seek a job as a social director on a cruise ship. There are opportunities for people who want to help the elderly or mentally handicapped, as well as for people with an interest in drama or music.

Generally, recreation workers must work while others engage in leisure activities. Most recreation workers work forty-hour weeks. But they should expect, especially those just entering the field, some night and weekend work. A compensating factor is the pleasure of helping people enjoy themselves.

Many of the positions are part time or seasonal, and many full-time recreation workers spend more time performing management duties than in leading hands-on activities.

Sources of Additional Information

■American Association for Leisure and Recreation
1900 Association Drive
Reston, VA 22091
Tel: 703-476-3472
WWW: http://www.aalr.org

American Camping Association
5000 State Road, 67 North
Martinsville, IN 46151-7902
Tel: 317-342-8456

National Employee Services and Recreation Association
2211 York Road, Suite 207
Oak Brook, IL 60521-2371
Tel: 630-368-1280

National Recreation and Park Association
2775 South Quincy Street, Suite 300
Arlington, VA 22206
Tel: 703-820-4940
Email: info@nrpa.org
WWW: http://www.nrpa.org/nrpa

For information on placement and accreditation, write:

National Recreation and Park Association
2775 South Quincy Street, Suite 300
Arlington, VA 22206
Tel: 703-820-4940
Email: info@nrpa.org
WWW: http://www.nrpa.org

Recreational Therapists

Definition

Recreational therapists plan, organize, direct, and monitor medically approved recreation programs for patients in hospitals, clinics, and various community settings. These therapists use recreational activities to assist patients with mental, physical, or emotional disabilities to achieve the maximum possible functional independence.

Nature of the Work

Recreational therapists are professionals who employ leisure activities as a form of treatment, much as other health practitioners use surgery, drugs, nutrition, exercise, or psychotherapy. Recreational therapists strive to minimize patients' symptoms, restore function, and to improve their physical, mental, and emotional well-being. Enhancing the patient's ability to take part in everyday life is the primary goal of recreational therapy; interesting and rewarding activities are the means for working toward that goal.

Recreational therapists work in a number of different settings, including mental hospitals, psychiatric day hospitals, community mental health centers, nursing homes, adult day care programs, residential facilities for the mentally disabled, school systems, and prisons. They can work as individual staff members, as independent consultants, or as part of a larger therapeutic team. They may get personally involved with patients, or direct the work of assistants and support staff.

The recreational therapist first confers with the doctors, psychiatrists, social workers, physical therapists, and other professionals on staff to coordinate their efforts in treatment. The recreational therapist needs to understand the nature of the patient's ailment, current physical and mental capacities, emotional state, and prospects for recovery. The patient's family and friends are also consulted, to find out the patient's interests and hobbies. With this information, the recreational therapist then plans an agenda of activities for that person.

To enrich the lives of people in hospitals and other institutions, recreational therapists use imagination and skill in organizing beneficial activities. Sports, games, arts and crafts, movie screenings, field trips, hobby clubs, and dramatics are only a few examples of activities that can enrich the lives of patients.

Some therapists specialize in certain areas.

Dance therapists plan and conduct dance and body movement exercises to improve patients' physical and mental well-being.

Art therapists work with patients in various art methods, such as drawing, painting, and ceramics, as part of their therapeutic and recovery program. Therapists may also work with pets and other animals, such as horses.

Music therapists design programs for patients that can involve solo or group singing, playing in bands, rhythmic and other creative activities, listening to music, or attending concerts.

Even flowers and gardening can prove beneficial to patients, as is proved by the work of *horticultural therapists*. When the treatment team feels that regular employment would help certain patients, the industrial therapist arranges a productive job for the patient in an actual work environment, one that will have the greatest therapeutic value based on the patient's needs and abilities.

Orientation therapists for the blind work with people who have recently lost their sight, helping them to readjust to daily living and independence through training and exercise.

All of these professional therapists plan their programs to meet the needs and capabilities of patients. They also carefully monitor and record each patient's progress and report it to the other members of the medical team.

As part of their job, recreational therapists need to understand their patients and set goals for their progress accordingly. A patient having trouble socializing, for example, may have an interest in playing chess but be overwhelmed by the prospect of actually playing, since that involves interaction with another person. A therapist would proceed slowly, first letting the patient observe a number of games and then assigning a therapeutic assistant to serve as a chess partner for weeks or even months, as long as it takes for the patient to gain enough confidence to seek out other patients for chess partners. The therapist makes a note of the patient's response, modifies the therapy program accordingly, and lets other professionals know of the results. If a patient is responding more enthusiastically to the program, working more cooperatively with others, or is becoming more disruptive, the therapist must note these reactions and periodically re-evaluate the patient's activity program.

Responsibilities and elements of the job can vary, depending on the setting in which the recreational therapist works. In nursing homes, the therapist often groups residents according to common or shared interests and ability levels, and then plans field trips, parties, entertainment, and other group activities. The therapist documents residents' responses to the activities and continually searches for ways of heightening residents' enjoyment of recreational and leisure activities, not just in the facility but in the surrounding community as well. Because nursing home residents are likely to remain in the facility for months or even years, the activities program makes a big difference in the quality of their lives. Without the stimulation of interesting events to look forward to and participate in, the daily routine of a nursing home can become monotonous and depressing, and some residents are apt to deteriorate both mentally and physically. In some nursing homes, recreational therapists direct the activities program. In others, activities coordinators plan and carry out the program under the part-time supervision of a consultant who is either a recreational or occupational therapist.

The therapist in a community center might work in a day-care program for the elderly or in a program for mentally disabled adults operated by a county recreation department. No matter what the disability, recreational therapists in community settings face the added logistical challenge of arranging transportation and escort services, if necessary, for prospective participants. Coordinating transportation is less of a problem in hospitals and nursing homes, where the patients all live under one roof. Developing therapeutic recreation programs in community settings accordingly requires a large measure of organizational ability, flexibility, and ingenuity.

Recreational therapy is a relatively new field, but it is already a respected, integral part of the treatment of many elderly and disabled people. These people often need extra encouragement and support to stay active and build on the things they can, rather than can't, do. The activity programs that recreational therapists design and operate can add immeasurable enjoyment to the lives of patients. Beyond this, the activities provide opportunities for exercise and social interaction, and may also help relieve anxiety and loneliness, build confidence, and promote each patient's independence.

Requirements

A bachelor's degree is required for employment as a recreational therapist. More than 130 academic programs in this field are offered at colleges and universities in the United States. Fewer than fifty of these programs were accredited by the National Council on Accreditation as of 1996. Four-year programs include courses in both natural science, such as biology, behavioral science, and human anatomy, and social science, such as psychology and sociology. Courses more specific to the profession, include programming for special populations; rehabilitative techniques including self-help skills, mobility, signing for the deaf, and orientation for the blind; medical equipment; current treatment approaches; legal issues; and professional ethics. Students also take recreation courses and are required to serve 360 hours of internship under the supervision of a certified therapeutic recreation specialist.

Continuing education is increasingly becoming a requirement for professionals in this field. Many therapists attend conferences and seminars, and take additional university courses. Those with degrees in related fields can enter the profession by earning master's degrees in therapeutic recreation. Advanced degrees are advisable for those seeking advancement to supervisory, administrative, and teaching positions. These requirements will become more strict as more professionals enter the field.

Interested high school students should follow a college preparatory program. Recommended courses include biology and other sciences, English, speech, mathematics, psychology, physical education, art, music, and drama. Verbal and written communications skills are essential because of the interaction with people and the report writing that the job requires.

A number of states regulate the profession of therapeutic recreation. Licensing is required in Georgia and Utah; professional certification (or eligibility for certification) is required in Maryland's long-term care facilities and California's state hospitals; and titling is regulated in North Carolina. In other states, many hospitals and other employers require recreational therapists to be certified. Certification for recreational therapists is available through the National Council for Therapeutic Recreation, which awards credentials for therapeutic recreation specialists and assistants.

Several other professional organizations offer continuing education classes and additional benefits to professional members. These include the National Therapeutic Recreation Society; the American Therapeutic Recreation Association; and the American Alliance for Health, Physical Education, Recreation, and Dance. These groups also work to improve the salaries and working conditions of the people in the profession.

Opportunities for Experience & Exploration

Students interested in recreational therapy can find part-time work as a sports coach or referee, park supervisor, or camp counselor. Volunteer work in a nursing home, hospital, or care facility for disabled adults is also a good way to learn about the daily realities of institutional living. These types of facilities are always looking for volunteers to work with and visit patients. Working with people with physical, mental, or emotional disabilities can be stressful, and volunteer work is a good way for a prospective therapist to test if they can handle this kind of stress.

Methods of Entering

There are many methods for finding out about available jobs in recreational therapy. A good place to start is the job notices and want ads printed in the local newspapers, bulletins from

state park and recreation societies, and publications of the professional associations previously mentioned. State employment agencies and human service departments will know of job openings in state hospitals. College placement offices might also be able to put new recreational therapy graduates in touch with prospective employers. Internship programs are sometimes available, which offer good opportunities to find potential full-time jobs.

Recent graduates should also make appointments to meet potential employers personally. Most colleges and universities offer career counseling services. Most employers will make themselves available to discuss their programs and the possibility of hiring extra staff. They may also guide new graduates to other institutions currently hiring therapists. Joining professional associations, both state and national, and attending conferences are good ways to meet potential employers and colleagues.

Advancement

Newly graduated recreational therapists generally begin as staff therapists. Advancement is chiefly to supervisory or administrative positions, usually after some years of experience and continuing education. Some therapists teach, conduct research, or do consulting work on a contract basis; a graduate degree is essential for moving into these areas.

Many therapists continue their education but prefer to continue working with patients. For variety, they may choose to work with new groups of people or get a job in a new setting, such as moving from a retirement home to a facility for the disabled. Some may also move to a related field such as special education, or sales positions involving products and services related to recreational therapy.

Employment Outlook

Recreational therapists held more than 38,000 jobs in 1996, according to the U.S. Department of Labor. About 38 percent of these people worked in nursing homes. Hospitals, chiefly psychiatric, rehabilitation, and other specialty hospitals, were the second leading employer—about 42 percent. Other employers included community mental health centers, adult day care programs, residential facilities for the mentally disabled, and community programs for people with disabilities. About 25 percent of all therapists worked as independent consultants.

Employment for recreational therapists is expected to grow faster than the average, chiefly because of anticipated expansion of long-term care facilities and services. By 2006, the number of recreational therapists employed in the United States is expected to grow to more than forty-five thousand. Workers with a healthcare background, specifically a bachelor's degree in therapeutic recreation will be in high demand. Jobs will result from the increased life expectancies of the elderly and people with developmental disabilities such as Down syndrome. Significant growth is also projected for those who work with the mentally ill, in part because of the large number of young adults who have reached the age of peak risk for schizophrenia and other chronic mental illnesses. The incidence of alcohol and drug dependency problems is also growing.

Most openings for recreational therapists will be in nursing homes because of the increasing number of people aged sixty-five and older in the United States who require this type of therapy. There is also greater public pressure to regulate and improve the quality of life in retirement centers, which may mean more jobs and increased scrutiny of recreational therapists.

Growth in hospital jobs is not expected to be great. Many of the new jobs created will be in hospital-based adult day care programs or in units offering short-term mental health services. Because of economic and social factors, no growth is expected in public mental hospitals. Many of the programs and services formerly offered there are being shifted to community residential facilities for the disabled. Community programs for special populations are expected to expand significantly through the year 2006.

Earnings

Salaries of recreational therapists vary according to employment setting, educational background, experience, and region of the country. According to a survey by the American Therapeutic Recreation Association, in 1996, therapists earned an average of $33,000 a year. Consultants, supervisors, administrators, and educators average $42,000 annually. Those employed by the Federal government earned an average of $39,400 in 1997.

Therapists employed at hospitals, clinics, and other facilities generally enjoy a benefit package including health insurance, and vacation, holiday, and sick pay. Consultants and self-employed therapists must provide their own insurance coverage.

Conditions of Work

Working conditions vary, but generally recreational therapists work in a ward, a specially equipped activity room, or, at a nursing home, a communal room or hall. In a community setting, recreational therapists may interview subjects and plan activities in an office, but might be in a gymnasium, swimming pool, playground, or outdoors on a nature walk when leading activities. Therapists may also work on horse ranches, farms, and other outdoor facilities catering to people with disabilities.

The job may be physically tiring because therapists are often on their feet all day and may have to lift and carry equipment. Recreational therapists generally work a standard forty-hour week, although weekend and evening hours may be required. Supervisors may have to work overtime, depending on their workload.

Sources of Additional Information

■**American Therapeutic Recreation Association**
P.O. Box 15215
Hattiesburg, MS 39404-5215
Tel: 800-553-0304
WWW: http://www.atra-tr.org

■**American Association for Leisure and Recreation**
1900 Association Drive
Reston, VA 22091
Tel: 703-476-3472

■**American Dance Therapy Association**
2000 Century Plaza, Suite 108
Columbia, MD 21044
Tel: 410-997-4040

American Health Care Association
1201 L Street, NW
Washington, DC 20005
Tel: 202-842-4444

National Council for Therapeutic Recreation Certification
PO Box 479
Thiells, NY 10984-0479
Tel: 914-947-4346

National Therapeutic Recreation Society
National Recreation and Park Association
2775 South Quincy Street, Suite 300
Arlington, VA 22206-2204
Tel: 703-820-4940
Email: NTRANRPA@aol.com

Salary Range: $11,000 to $33,000 to $42,000

Registered Nurses

Definition

Registered nurses (RNs) help individuals, families, and groups to achieve health and prevent disease. They care for the sick and injured, using procedures based on knowledge, skill, and experience. They work in hospitals and other health care facilities, in physicians' offices, in private homes, in public health agencies, schools, camps, and industry. Some registered nurses are employed in private practice.

Nature of the Work

Registered nurses work under the direct supervision of nursing departments and in collaboration with physicians. Two-thirds of all nurses work in hospitals, where they may be assigned to general, operating room, or maternity room duty. They may also care for sick children or be assigned to other hospital units, such as emergency rooms, intensive care units, or out-patient clinics. There are many different kinds of nurses categorized under the term "registered nurse."

General duty nurses work together with other members of the health care team to assess the patient's condition and to develop and implement a plan of health care. These nurses may perform such tasks as taking patients' vital signs, administering medication and injections, recording the symptoms and progress of patients, changing dressings, assisting patients with personal care, conferring with members of the medical staff, helping prepare a patient for surgery, and completing any number of duties that require skill and understanding of patients' needs.

Surgical nurses oversee the preparation of the operating room and the sterilization of instruments. They assist the surgeons during operations and coordinate the flow of patient cases in the operating rooms.

Maternity nurses help in the delivery room, take care of newborns in the nursery, and teach mothers how to feed and care for their babies.

The activities of staff nurses are directed and coordinated by head nurses and supervisors. Heading up the entire nursing program in the hospital is the nursing service director, who administers the nursing program to maintain standards of patient care. The nursing service director advises the medical staff, department heads, and the hospital administrator in matters relating to nursing services and helps prepare the department budget.

Private duty nurses may work in hospitals or in a patient's home. They are employed by the patient they are caring for or by the patient's family. Their service is designed for the individual care of one person and is carried out in cooperation with the patient's physician.

Office nurses usually work in the office of a dentist, physician, or health maintenance organization (HMO). They may be one of several nurses on the staff or the only staff nurse. If the nurse is the only staff member, this person may have to combine some clerical duties with those of nursing, such as serving as receptionist, making appointments for the doctor, helping maintain patient records, sending out monthly statements, and attending to routine correspondence. If the physician's staff is a large one that includes secretaries and clerks, the office nurse will concentrate on screening patients, assisting with examinations, supervising the examining rooms, sterilizing equipment, providing patient education, and performing other nursing duties.

Occupational health nurses, or industrial nurses, are an important part of many large firms. They maintain a clinic at a plant or factory and are usually occupied in rendering preventive, remedial, and educational nursing services. They work under the direction of an industrial physician, nursing director, or nursing supervisor. They may advise on accident prevention, visit employees on the job to check the conditions under which they work, and advise management about the safety of such conditions. At the plant, they render treatment in emergencies.

School nurses may work in one school or in several, visiting each for a part of the day or week. They may supervise the student clinic, treat minor cuts or injuries, or give advice on good health practices. Examining students to detect conditions of the eye or teeth requiring attention may be a part of their job. They also assist the school physician.

Community health nurses, also called *public health nurses,* require specialized training for their duties. Their job usually requires them to spend part of the time traveling from one assignment to another. Their duties may differ greatly from one case to another. For instance, in one day they may have to instruct a class of expectant mothers, visit new parents to help them plan proper care for the baby, visit an aged patient requiring special care, and conduct a class in nutrition. They usually possess many and varied nursing skills and often are called upon to meet unexpected or unusual situations.

Administrators in the community health field include *nursing directors, educational directors,* and *nursing supervisors.* Some nurses go into nursing education and work with nursing students to instruct them on theories and skills they will need to enter the profession. *Nursing instructors* may give classroom instruction and demonstrations or supervise nursing students on hospital units. Some instructors eventually become nursing school directors, university faculty, or deans of a university degree program. Nurses also have the opportunity to direct staff development and continuing education programs for nursing personnel in hospitals.

Advanced practice nurses are nurses with training beyond that required to have the RN designation. There are four primary categories of nurses included in this category of nursing. Advanced practice nurses handle many of the duties previously restricted to the physician and in so doing free the physician to take care of more severely ill patients. The *nurse anesthetist* specializes in giving anesthesia to patients about to undergo surgery. The nurse anesthetist must be certified and possess great technical skill and theoretical knowledge, for anesthesia requires delicate judgment. The nurse anesthetist sometimes works under the supervision of an anesthesiologist, who is a physician, and sometimes under the supervision of a surgeon performing the operation.

The *nurse midwife* is yet another category of advanced practice nurse, which as a profession was not introduced in the United States until 1925. Today nurse midwives are well-educated, certified professionals who provide health care and treatment to women. *Certified nurse midwives (CNMs)* work with other CNMs and obstetricians. They examine pregnant patients and instruct and advise them about childbirth, diet, and exercise. They deliver babies, and teach new parents about the care and feeding of newborns. Nurse midwives examine nonpregnant women, performing tests for pregnancy, Pap tests for cancer, and breast examinations. They counsel patients on family planning and birth control methods and screen patients for infections and venereal disease. In case of a serious problem, major illness, or difficult labor, the nurse midwife confers with the team obstetrician.

Nurse practitioners (NPs) are an even more recent entry in the field of nursing. Nurse practitioners are registered nurses with advanced education that expands their diagnostic and decision making skills. They work in many health care settings, either on their own or as members of a team. In addition to basic nursing responsibilities, they perform many tasks formerly assigned to physicians. They treat common ailments, recommend standard medications, take patient histories, and perform patient examinations. In some states, they set simple fractures or suture minor wounds.

Clinical nurse specialists are also nurses with advanced education, usually at the master's degree level. They specialize in some field of nursing practice, such as cardiovascular nursing, working with cancer patients, or working with high-risk mothers and babies.

Some nurses are consultants to hospitals, nursing schools, industrial organizations, and public health agencies. They advise clients on such administrative matters as staff organization, nursing techniques, curriculums, and education programs. Other administrative specialists include *educational directors for the state board of nursing,* who are concerned with maintaining well-defined educational standards, and *executive directors of professional nurses' associations,* who administer programs developed by the board of directors and the members of the association.

Some nurses choose to enter the Armed Forces. All types of nurses, except private duty nurses, are represented in the military services. They provide skilled nursing care to active-duty and retired members of the armed forces and their families. In addition to basic nursing skills, *military nurses* are trained to provide care in various environments, including field hospitals, on-air evacuation flights, and onboard ships. Military nurses actively influence the development of health care through nursing research. Recent advances influenced by military nurses include the development of the artificial kidney (dialysis unit) and the concept of the intensive care unit.

Requirements

High school students interested in becoming a registered nurse should take science and mathematics courses, including biology, chemistry, and physics. English and speech courses should not be neglected because the nurse must be able to communicate well with patients.

There are three basic kinds of training programs that prospective nurses may choose to become registered nurses: associate's degree programs, diploma programs, and bachelor's degree programs. Which of the three training programs to choose depends on one's career goals. A bachelor's degree in nursing is required for most supervisory or administrative positions, for jobs in public health agencies, and for admission to graduate nursing programs. A master's degree is usually necessary to prepare for a nursing specialty or to teach. For some specialties, such as nursing research, a Ph.D. is essential.

The baccalaureate degree program is offered by colleges or universities. It requires four (in some cases, five) years to complete. The graduate of this program receives a Bachelor of Science in Nursing degree. The Associate in Arts in Nursing is awarded after completion of a two-year study program that is usually offered in a junior or community college. The student receives hospital training at cooperating hospitals in the general vicinity of the community college. The diploma program, which usually lasts three years, is conducted by hospitals and independent schools. At the conclusion of each of these programs, the student becomes a graduate nurse, but not, however, a registered nurse. To obtain this designation the graduate nurse must take and pass a licensing examination required in all states. After licensing, one has the privilege of

adding the initials "RN" to one's name and of seeking employment as a registered nurse.

In 1996, there were over 1,500 entry level nursing programs offered in the United States. In addition, there were 198 master's degree and 33 doctoral degree programs. Nurses can pursue postgraduate training that allows them to specialize in certain areas, such as emergency room, operating room, premature nursery, or psychiatric nursing. This training is sometimes offered through hospital on-the-job training programs.

All states and the District of Columbia require a license to practice nursing. To obtain a license, graduates of approved nursing schools must pass a national examination. Nurses may be licensed by more than one state. In some states, continuing education is a condition for license renewal. Different titles require different education and training levels.

Opportunities for Experience & Exploration

High school students can explore their interest in the nursing field in a number of ways. They may read books on careers in nursing and talk with high school guidance counselors, school nurses, and local public health nurses. Visits to hospitals to observe the work and to talk with hospital personnel are also valuable.

Some hospitals now have extensive volunteer service programs in which high school students may work after school, on weekends, or during vacations in order to both render a valuable service and to explore their interests. Other volunteer work experiences may be found with the Red Cross or community health services. Camp counseling jobs sometimes offer related experiences. Some schools offer participation in Future Nurses programs.

Methods of Entering

The only way to become a registered nurse is through completion of one of the three kinds of educational programs, plus passing the licensing examination. Registered nurses may apply for employment directly to hospitals, nursing homes, companies, government agencies that hire nurses. Jobs can also be obtained through school placement offices, or by signing up with employment agencies specializing in placement of nursing personnel, or through the state employment office. Other sources of jobs include nurses' associations, professional journals, and newspaper want ads.

Advancement

Increasingly, administrative and supervisory positions in the nursing field go to nurses who have earned at least the bachelor of science degree in nursing. Nurses with many years of experience but who are graduates of the diploma program may achieve supervisory positions, but requirements for such promotions have become more difficult in recent years and in many cases require at least the bachelor of science in nursing degree.

Nurses with bachelor's degrees are usually those who are hired as public health nurses. Nurses with master's degrees are often employed as clinical nurse specialists, faculty, instructors, supervisors, or administrators.

Some nurses return to school to take courses in special fields. Courses leading to the specialty practice of nurse anesthetist usually require eighteen to twenty-four months of graduate education. Once this education is completed, the nurse anesthetist may obtain a position paying a higher salary.

Employment Outlook

In 1996, there were almost two million nurses employed in the United States—making this field the largest of all health care occupations. Employment prospects for nurses look good. The U.S. Department of Labor projects registered nurses to be one of the top twenty-five occupations with fastest growth, high pay, and low unemployment. In fact, it is predicted that there will be about 425,000 additional jobs available through the year 2006.

Increasing numbers of nurses who have been attracted to the profession in recent years have, however, lessened the demand for nurses in some areas. Even so, there are still many employment opportunities for nurses, especially in the inner cities and in rural areas. Employment opportunities for nurses will be best in home health situations.

The increased number of older people and better medical technology have spurred the demand for nurses to bring complicated treatments to the patients' homes.

Employment in nursing homes is expected to grow much faster than the average. Though more people are living well into their eighties and nineties, many need the kind of long term care available at a nursing home. Also, because of financial reasons, patients are being released from hospitals sooner and admitted into nursing homes. Many nursing homes have facilities and staff capable of caring for long term rehabilitation patients, as well as those afflicted with Alzheimer's. Many nurses will also be needed to help staff the growing number of outpatient facilities, such as HMOs, group medical practices, and ambulatory surgery centers.

Two thirds of all nursing jobs are found in hospitals. However, because of administrative cost cutting, increased nurse's work load, and rapid growth of outpatient services, hospital nursing jobs will experience slower than average growth.

Nursing specialties will be in great demand. Nurses that specialize in lactation consultation, for example, were recently included in *U.S. News & World Report*'s article "Best Jobs for the Future." There are in addition many part-time employment possibilities for nurses with family responsibilities that prevent them from working full-time. Approximately thirty percent of all nurses work on a part-time basis.

Earnings

According to the *1998-99 Occupation Outlook Handbook*, registered nurses earned an average of $36,244 annually in 1996. Fifty percent earned between $29,692 and $45,136. The top ten percent made over $54,028 a year.

According to the Hay Group survey of HMOs, in 1996, nurse practitioners earned an average of $66,800; nurse midwives earned $70,100. The same survey reports that a full time nurse anesthetist earned about $82,000 in 1997. A Buck Survey found that staff RNs working in a nursing home setting earned an average of about $32,968 a year.

Entry-level positions with the Department of Veterans Affairs start at approximately $16,500 for nurses who were graduates of the diploma program or the associate's of arts program. The average annual salary for all nurses in federal government agencies is about $26,100.

The salary for nursing assistants ranges from $7,500 to $22,000 a year. Beginning aides may start at about $12,000 a year.

Salary is determined by several factors: setting, education, and work experience. Most full time nurses are given flexible work schedules, health and life insurance; some are offered education reimbursement and year-end bonuses. A staff nurse's salary is limited only by the amount of work one is willing to take on. Many nurses take advantage of overtime work and shift differentials. About ten percent of all nurses held more than one job.

Conditions of Work

Most nurses work in facilities that are clean and well lighted and where the temperature is controlled, although some work in rundown inner city hospitals in less than ideal conditions. Usually, nurses work eight-hour shifts. Those in hospitals generally work any of three shifts: 7:00 a.m. to 3:00 p.m.; 3:00 p.m. to 11:00 p.m.; or 11:00 p.m. to 7:00 a.m.

Nurses spend much of their day on their feet, either walking or standing. Handling patients who are ill or infirm can also be very exhausting. Nurses who come in contact with patients with infectious diseases must be especially careful about cleanliness and sterility. Although many nursing duties are routine, many responsibilities are unpredictable. Sick persons are often very demanding, or they may be depressed or irritable. Despite this the nurse must retain her or his composure and should be cheerful to help the patient achieve emotional balance.

Community health nurses may be required to visit homes that are in poor condition or very dirty. They may also come in contact with social problems such as family violence. Still the nurse is an important health care provider, and in many communities the sole provider.

Both the office nurse and the industrial nurse work regular business hours and are seldom required to work overtime. In some jobs, such as where nurses are on duty in private homes, they may frequently travel from home to home and work with various cases.

Sources of Additional Information

■■American Association of Colleges of Nursing
1 Dupont Circle, Suite 530
Washington, DC 20036
Tel: 202-463-6930
Email: webmaster@aacn.nche.edu
WWW: http://www.aacn.nche.edu

For information on careers in long-term care, contact:

■■American Health Care Association
1201 L Street, NW
Washington, DC 20005
Tel: 202-842-4444
Email: jmartin@ahca.org
WWW: http://www.ahca.org

For information about opportunities as an RN, contact:

■■American Nurses' Association
600 Maryland Avenue, SW, Suite 100W
Washington, DC 20024-2571
Tel: 800-274-4ANA
WWW: http://www.nursingworld.org

For information about state-approved programs and information on nursing, contact:

■■National Association for Practical Nurse Education and Service, Inc.
1400 Spring Street, Suite 310
Silver Spring, MD 20910
Tel: 301-588-2491
Email: napnes@aol.com
WWW: http://www.aoa.dhhs.gov/aoa

■■National League for Nursing
Communications Department
350 Hudson Street
New York, NY 10014
Tel: 212-989-9393
Email: nlnweb@nln.org
WWW: http://www.nln.org

Rehabilitation Counselors

Definition

The *rehabilitation counselor* provides counseling and guidance services to people with disabilities to help them resolve life problems and to train for and locate work that is suitable to their physical and mental abilities, interests, and aptitudes.

Nature of the Work

The rehabilitation counselor works with people with disabilities to identify barriers to medical, psychological, personal, social, and vocational adjustment and to develop a plan of action to remove or reduce those barriers.

People are referred to rehabilitation programs from many sources. Sometimes they seek help on their own initiative; sometimes their families bring them for help. They may be referred by a physician, hospital, or a social worker, or they may be sent by employment agencies, schools, or accident commissions. A former employer may seek help for the individual.

The counselor's first step is to determine the nature and extent of the disability and evaluate how that disability interferes with work and other life functions. This determination is made from medical and psychological reports, as well as from family history, educational background, work experience, and other evaluative information.

The next step is to determine a vocational direction and plan of services to overcome the handicaps to employment or independent living.

The rehabilitation counselor coordinates a comprehensive evaluation of a client's physical functioning abilities and vocational interests, aptitudes, and skills. This information is used to develop for the client a vocational or independent-living goal and the services necessary to reach that goal. Services that the rehabilitation counselor may coordinate or provide include physical and mental restoration, academic or vocational training, vocational counseling, job analysis, job modification or reasonable accommodation, and job placement. Limited financial assistance in the form of maintenance or transportation assistance may also be provided.

The counselor's relationship with the client may be as brief as a week or as long as several years, depending on the nature of the problem and the needs of the client.

Requirements

High school students interested in rehabilitation counseling should enroll in a college preparatory course, including sociology, biology, English, speech, mathematics, psychology, and social studies.

Although there are some positions available for people with a bachelor's degree in rehabilitation counseling, a master's degree in rehabilitation counseling, counseling and guidance, or counseling psychology is preferred for those entering the field. Six out of ten of all rehabilitation counselors have a master's degree. Preparation for a master's degree program requires an undergraduate major in behavioral sciences, social sciences, or a related field, or the completion of an undergraduate degree program in rehabilitation counseling. Such a degree is offered at more than thirty colleges and universities in the United States. Students preparing for this career should take courses in sociology, psychology, physiology, history, and statistics, as well as courses in English and communications. Several universities now offer courses in various aspects of physical therapy and special education training. Students also should consider courses in sign language and speech therapy. Foreign language skills are also helpful in this field.

The master's degree program in rehabilitation counseling is usually a two-year program, plus 600 hours of supervised clinical internship. There are graduate programs in rehabilitation counseling in many large universities. The program includes courses in medical aspects of disability, psychosocial aspects of disability, testing techniques, statistics, personality theory, personality development, abnormal psychology, techniques of counseling, occupational information, and vocational training and job placement. More than seventy-five graduate programs in rehabilitation counseling have been accredited by the Council on Rehabilitation Education.

Most state government rehabilitation agencies, which employ about 40 percent of all rehabilitation counselors, require future counselors to meet state civil service and merit system rules. The applicant must take a written competitive examination and may also have an individual interview and evaluation by a special board.

Many employers now require their rehabilitation counselors to be certified by the Commission on Rehabilitation Counselor Certification (CRCC). The purpose of certification is to provide assurance that professionals engaged in rehabilitation counseling meet acceptable standards and maintain those standards through continuing education. To become certified, counselors must pass an extensive written examination to demonstrate their knowledge of rehabilitation counseling. The CRCC requires the master's degree as the minimum educational level for certification.

In about thirty-five states, counselors in private practice must be licensed by the state. Licensing requirements vary by state; however, not all states include rehabilitation counselors under state regulatory boards.

The most important personal attribute required for rehabilitation counseling is the ability to get along well with other people. Rehabilitation counselors work with many different kinds of clients and must be able to see situations and problems from the client's point of view. They must be both patient and persistent. Rehabilitation may be a slow process, with many delays and setbacks. The counselor must maintain a calm, positive manner even when no progress is made.

Opportunities for Experience & Exploration

Students considering a career working with the disabled should seek opportunities to gain experience in this field. They may volunteer to work as a counselor at a disabled children's camp. They also may volunteer with a local vocational rehabilitation agency, or a facility such as the Easter Seal Society or Goodwill. Students may be able to read to the blind or teach a hobby to someone who has been disabled by accident or illness.

Methods of Entering

School placement offices are the best place for the new graduate to begin the career search. In addition, the National Rehabilitation Counseling Association and the American Rehabilitation Counseling Association (a division of the American Counseling Association) are sources for employment information. The new counselor may also apply directly to agencies for available positions. State and local vocational rehabilitation agencies employ about ten thousand rehabilitation counselors. The Department of Veterans Affairs employs several hundred people to assist with the rehabilitation of disabled veterans.

Many rehabilitation counselors are employed by private for-profit or nonprofit rehabilitation programs and facilities. Others are employed in industry, schools, hospitals, and other settings, while others are self-employed.

Advancement

The rehabilitation counselor will usually receive regular salary increases after gaining experience in the job. He or she may move from relatively easy cases to increasingly challenging ones. Counselors may advance into such positions as administrator or supervisor after several years of counseling experience. It is also possible to find related counseling and teaching positions, which may represent an advancement in other fields.

Employment
Outlook

The passage of the Americans with Disabilities Act of 1990 has increased the demand for rehabilitation counselors. The U.S. Department of Labor predicts about as fast as the average growth for rehabilitation counselors through the year 2006, as more local, state, and federal programs are initiated that are designed to assist people with disabilities, and as private institutions and companies seek to comply with this new legislation. This field will also have one of the largest numerical employment increases compared to other occupations that have similar education or training requirements. A factor in the projected job growth for rehabilitation counselors is the advanced medical technology available today. Many people whose lives would have been lost in the past, are surviving accidents and illnesses. However, they need much medical and therapeutic help, some of which is given by the rehabilitation counselor. Also, an increased number of older people will need the services of rehabilitation counselors as they cope with the lifestyle changes of growing older. Managed care systems allow many rehabilitation services to be covered under insurance policies, enabling many counselors to move from small agencies and schools into group practices.

Some areas of this occupation are directly affected by the health of the economy. Budget pressures may serve to limit the numbers of new rehabilitation counselors hired by government agencies.

Earnings

Salaries for rehabilitation counselors will vary widely according to each state and community. According to the *1998-99 Occupational Outlook Handbook,* starting salaries for educational and vocational counselors in 1996 averaged around $35,800 per year. Fifty percent earned between $25,600 and $48,500 a year; the top ten percent earned around $60,100. Counselors in supervisory and administrative positions can earn well over $60,000 per year. Self-employed counselors with an established practice generally earn the highest salaries. Salaries for federal government workers vary according to the region of the country in which they work. Those working in areas with a higher cost of living receive additional locality pay.

Counselors employed by government and private agencies and institutions generally receive health insurance, pension plans, and other benefits, including vacation, sick, and holiday pay. Self-employed counselors must provide their own benefits.

Conditions
of Work

Rehabilitation counselors work approximately forty hours each week and do not usually have to work during evenings or weekends. They are usually given annual vacation and sick leave. Most counselors enjoy the benefits of retirement plans, group insurance, and other related advantages.

Rehabilitation counselors work both in the office and in the field. Depending on the type of training required, they may have or use lab space and workout or therapy rooms. They must usually keep detailed accounts of their progress with clients and write reports. They may spend many hours traveling about the community to visit employed clients, prospective employers, trainees, or training programs.

Sources of
Additional Information

The following is a professional organization for rehabilitation counselors and interested professionals and students:

American Rehabilitation Counseling Association
c/o American Counseling Association
5999 Stevenson Avenue
Alexandria, VA 22304
Tel: 703-823-9800
Email: aca@counseling.org

Commission on Rehabilitation Counselor Certification
520 North Michigan Avenue
Chicago, IL 60611

National Rehabilitation Counseling Association
8807 Sudley Road, Suite 102
Manassas, VA 22110-4719
Tel: 703-361-2077
Email: nrcaoffice@aol.com

Respiratory Therapists and Technicians

Definition

Respiratory therapists, or *respiratory care practitioners*, evaluate, treat, and care for patients with deficiencies or abnormalities of the cardiopulmonary (heart/lung) system, either providing temporary relief from chronic ailments or administering emergency care where life is threatened.

Working under a physician's direction, these workers set up and operate respirators, mechanical ventilators, and other devices. They monitor the functioning of the equipment and the patients' response to the therapy, and maintain the patients' charts. They also assist patients with breathing exercises, and inspect, test, and order repairs for respiratory therapy equipment. They may demonstrate procedures to trainees and other health care personnel.

Nature of the Work

Respiratory therapists treat patients with various cardiorespiratory problems. They may provide care that affords temporary relief from chronic illnesses such as asthma or emphysema, or they may administer life-support treatment to victims of heart failure, stroke, drowning, or shock. These specialists often mean the difference between life and death in cases involving acute respiratory conditions, as may result from head injuries or drug poisoning. Adults who stop breathing for longer than three to five minutes rarely survive without serious brain damage, and an absence of respiratory activity for more than nine minutes almost certainly means death. Respiratory therapists carry out their duties under a physician's direction and supervision. They set up and operate special devices to treat patients who need temporary or emergency relief from breathing difficul-

ties. The equipment may include respirators, positive-pressure breathing machines, or environmental control systems. Aerosol inhalants are administered to confine medication to the lungs. Patients who have undergone surgery are often treated by these workers because anesthesia depresses normal respiration, and the patients need some support to restore their full breathing capability and to prevent respiratory illnesses.

In evaluating patients, therapists test the capacity of the lungs and analyze the oxygen and carbon dioxide concentration and potential of hydrogen (pH), a measure of the acidity or alkalinity level of the blood. To measure lung capacity, therapists have patients breathe into an instrument that measures the volume and flow of air during inhalation and exhalation. By comparing the reading with the norm for the patient's age, height, weight, and sex, respiratory therapists can determine whether lung deficiencies exist. To analyze oxygen, carbon dioxide, and pH levels, therapists draw an arterial blood sample, place it in a blood gas analyzer, and relay the results to a physician.

Respiratory therapists watch the equipment gauges and maintain prescribed volumes of oxygen or other inhalants. Besides monitoring the equipment to be sure it is operating properly, they observe the patient's physiological response to the therapy and consult with physicians in case of any adverse reactions. They also record pertinent identification and therapy information on each patient's chart and keep records of the cost of materials and the charges to the patients.

Therapists instruct patients and their families on how to use respiratory equipment at home, and they may demonstrate respiratory therapy procedures to trainees and other health care personnel. Their responsibilities include inspecting and testing equipment. If it is faulty, they either make minor repairs themselves or order major repairs.

Respiratory therapy workers include therapists, technicians, and assistants. The duties of therapists and technicians are essentially the same, although therapists are expected to have a higher level of expertise, and their responsibilities often include teaching and supervising other workers. Assistants clean, sterilize, store, and generally take care of the equipment but have very little contact with patients.

Requirements

Formal training is necessary for entry to this field. Training is offered at the postsecondary level by hospitals, medical schools, colleges and universities, trade schools, vocational-technical institutes, and the armed forces. Some programs prepare graduates for jobs as respiratory therapists; other, shorter programs lead to jobs as respiratory therapy technicians. In 1996, 210 programs for respiratory therapists were accredited by the Commission on Accreditation of Allied Health Education Programs (CAAHEP). Another 158 programs offered CAAHEP-accredited preparation for respiratory therapy technicians.

To be eligible for these programs, applicants must have graduated from high school. High school courses that will best prepare a student for further education in this field include health, biology, mathematics, chemistry, and physics.

Accredited programs in respiratory therapy combine both theory and clinical work and last from two to four years. A bachelor's degree is awarded to students who successfully complete the four-year program. Students who complete shorter programs may earn an associate's degree. The program for technicians runs approximately one year and results in a certificate. The areas of study for both therapists and technicians cover human anatomy and physiology, chemistry, physics, microbiology, and mathematics. Technical courses cover procedures, equipment, and clinical tests.

There are no standard hiring requirements for assistants. The individual department head who is doing the hiring sets the standards and may require only a high school diploma.

Forty-seven states license respiratory care personnel. The National Board for Respiratory Care (NBRC) offers voluntary certification and registration to graduates of CAAHEP-accredited programs. Two credentials are awarded to respiratory care practitioners who satisfy the requirements: Certified Respiratory Therapy Technician (CRTT) and Registered Respiratory Therapist (RRT). All graduates—those from two- and four-year programs in respiratory therapy, as well as those from one-year technician programs—take the CRTT examination first. CRTTs who meet education and experience requirements can take a separate examination, leading to the award of the RRT.

Those with a four year nonrespiratory degree can become a CRTT after completing an American Medical Association accredited program, usually lasting one to two years. College level courses in anatomy, physics, mathematics, physiology, biology, and chemistry, among others, are prerequisites.

Most employers require that applicants for entry-level or generalist positions hold the CRTT or are eligible to take the certification examination. Supervisory positions and those in intensive care specialties usually require the RRT (or RRT eligibility).

Respiratory therapists must enjoy working with people. They must be sensitive to their patients' physical and psychological needs because they will be dealing with people who may be in pain or who may be frightened. The work of this occupational group is of great significance. Respiratory therapists are often responsible for the life and well-being of people already in critical condition. They must pay strict attention to detail, be able to follow instructions and work as part of a team, and remain cool in emergencies. Mechanical ability and manual dexterity are necessary to operate much of the respiratory equipment.

Opportunities for Experience & Exploration

High school students may prepare for a career in respiratory therapy by taking courses in health, biology, mathematics, physics, and bookkeeping. Those considering advanced study may obtain a list of accredited educational programs in respiratory therapy by writing to the American Association for Respiratory Care (AARC) at the address listed at the end of this article. Formal training in this field is available in hospitals, vocational-technical institutes, private trade schools, and other noncollegiate settings as well. Local hospitals can provide information on training opportunities. School vocational counselors may be a source of additional information about educational matters and may be able to set up interviews with or lectures by a respiratory therapy practitioner from a local hospital.

Hospitals are excellent places to obtain part-time and summer employment. They have a continuing need for helpers in many departments. Even though the work may not be directly related to respiratory therapy, the student will gain knowledge of the operation of a hospital and may be in a position to get acquainted with respiratory therapists and observe them as they carry out their duties. If part-time or temporary work is not available, students may wish to volunteer their services.

Methods of Entering

Graduates of CAAHEP-accredited respiratory therapy training programs may have the school's placement service to aid them in finding a job. Otherwise, they may apply directly to individual local health care facilities.

High school graduates may apply directly to local hospitals for jobs as respiratory therapy assistants. If their goals are to become therapists or technicians, however, they would do better to enroll in a formal respiratory therapy educational program.

Advancement

Many respiratory therapists start out as assistants or technicians. With appropriate training courses and experience, they advance to the therapist level. Respiratory therapists with sufficient experience may be promoted to assistant chief or chief therapist. With graduate education, they may be qualified to teach respiratory therapy at the college level.

Employment Outlook

There were 82,000 respiratory therapists employed in the United States in 1996. Most of them, about 90 percent, worked in hospitals in the respiratory therapy, anesthesiology, or pulmonary medicine departments. The rest were employed by oxygen equipment rental companies, ambulance services, nursing homes, and home health agencies.

Employment growth for respiratory therapists is expected to be much faster than the average for all occupations through the year 2006, even though efforts to control rising health care costs have resulted in a reduction of job opportunities in hospitals.

The demand for therapists will be greater because of several factors. The fields of neonatal care and gerontology are growing. Also, there is a greater incidence of cardiopulmonary and AIDS-related diseases, coupled with more advanced methods of diagnosing and treating them.

Employment opportunities for therapists should be very favorable in the rapidly growing field of home health care, although this area accounts for only a small number of respiratory therapy jobs. In addition to jobs in home health agencies and hospital-based home health programs, there should be numerous openings for respiratory therapists in equipment rental companies and in firms that provide respiratory care on a contract basis.

Earnings

According to a 1996 Hay Group Survey, full time respiratory therapists earned an average salary of $32,500 a year. Fifty percent of all therapists earned an average of $29,300 to $35,000. Hospital workers receive benefits that include health insurance, paid vacations and sick leave, and pension plans. Some institutions provide additional benefits such as uniforms and parking and offer free courses or tuition reimbursement for job-related courses.

Conditions of Work

Respiratory therapists generally work in extremely clean, quiet surroundings. They usually work forty hours a week, which may include nights and weekends because hospitals operate twenty-four hours a day, seven days a week. The work requires long hours of standing and may be very stressful during emergencies.

A possible hazard is that the inhalants these employees work with are highly flammable. The danger of fire is minimized, however, if the workers test equipment regularly and are strict about taking safety precautions. As with many health occupations, respiratory therapists run a risk of catching infectious diseases. Careful adherence to proper procedures minimizes the risk.

Sources of Additional Information

For information on accreditation, please contact:

■American Association for Respiratory Care (AARC)
11030 Ables Lane
Dallas, TX 75229
Tel: 214-243-2272

■Commission on Accreditation of Allied Health Education Programs (CAAHEP)
515 North State Street, Suite 7530
Chicago, IL 60610
Tel: 312-464-4625

■National Board for Respiratory Care, Inc. (NBRC)
8310 Nieman Road
Lenexa, KS 66214
Tel: 913-599-4200

■Joint Review Committee for Respiratory Therapy Education (JRCRTE)
1701 West Euless Boulevard, Suite 300
Euless, TX 76040
Tel: 817-283-2835

Restaurant and Food Service Managers

Definition

Restaurant and food service managers are responsible for the overall operation of businesses that serve food. Food service work includes the purchasing of a variety of food, selection of the menu, preparation of the food, and, most importantly, maintenance of health and sanitation levels. It is the responsibility of managers to oversee staffing for each task in addition to performing the business and accounting functions of restaurant operations.

Nature of the Work

Restaurant and food service managers work in restaurants ranging from elegant hotel dining rooms to fast-food restaurants. They also may work in food service facilities ranging from school cafeterias to hospital food services. Whatever the setting, these managers coordinate and direct the work of the employees who prepare and serve food and perform other related functions. They are responsible for buying the food and equipment necessary for the operation of the restaurant or facility. They may help with menu planning. Periodically they inspect the premises to ensure the maintenance of health and sanitation regulations. They perform many clerical and financial duties, such as keeping records, directing payroll operations, handling large sums of money, and taking inventories. Their work usually involves much contact with customers and vendors, such as taking suggestions, handling complaints, and creating a friendly atmosphere. Restaurant managers generally supervise any advertising or sales promotion for their operation.

In some very large restaurants and institutional food service facilities, the manager is assisted by one or more *assistant managers* and an *executive chef* or *food manager*. These specially trained assistants oversee service in the dining room and other areas of the operation and supervise the kitchen staff and preparation of all foods served.

Restaurant and food service managers are responsible for the success of their establishment. They continually analyze every aspect of its operation and make whatever changes are needed to guarantee its profitability.

These duties are common, in varying degrees, to both owner-managers of relatively small restaurants and to nonowner-managers who may be salaried employees in large restaurants or institutional food service facilities. The owner-manager of a restaurant is more likely to be involved in service functions, sometimes operating the cash register, waiting on tables, and performing a wide variety of tasks.

Requirements

Educational requirements for restaurant and food service managers vary greatly. In many cases, no specific requirements exist and managerial positions are filled by promoting experienced food and beverage preparation and service workers. However, as more colleges offer programs in restaurant and institutional food service management—programs that combine academic work with on-the-job experience—more restaurant and food service chains are seeking individuals with this training.

In the 1990s, more than 160 colleges and universities offer four-year programs leading to a bachelor's degree in restaurant and hotel management or institutional food service management. Some individuals qualify for management training by earning an associate degree or other formal award below the baccalaureate from one of the more than 800 community and junior colleges, technical institutes, or other institutions that offer programs in these fields. Students hired as management trainees by restaurant chains and food service management companies undergo vigorous training programs.

Experience in all areas of restaurant and food service work is an important requirement for successful managers. Managers must be familiar with the various operations of the establishment: food preparation, service operations, sanitary regulations, and financial functions.

One of the most important requirements for restaurant and food service managers is to have good business knowledge. They must possess a high degree of technical knowledge in handling business details, such as buying large items of machinery and equipment and large quantities of food. Desirable personality characteristics include poise, self-confidence, and an ability to get along with people. Managers may be on their feet for long periods, and the hours of work may be both long and irregular.

Opportunities for Experience & Exploration

Practical restaurant and food service experience is usually easy to get. In colleges with curriculum offerings in these areas, summer jobs in all phases of the work are available and, in some cases, required. Some restaurant and food service chains provide on-the-job training in management.

Methods of Entering

Many restaurants and food service facilities provide self-sponsored, on-the-job training for prospective managers. There are still cases in which people work hard and move up the ladder within the organization's workforce, finally arriving at the managerial position. More and more, people with advanced education and specialized training move directly into manager-trainee positions and then on to a managerial position.

Advancement

In large restaurants and food service organizations, promotion opportunities are frequent for employees with a knowledge of the overall operation. Experience in all aspects of the work is an important consideration for the food service employee who desires advancement. The employee with a knowledge of kitchen operations may advance from pantry supervisor to food manager, assistant manager, and finally to restaurant or food service manager. Similar advancement is possible for dining room workers with a knowledge of kitchen operations.

Advancement to top executive positions is possible for managers employed by large restaurant and institutional food service chains. A good educational background and some specialized training are increasingly valuable assets to employees who hope to advance.

Employment Outlook

The industry is rapidly growing and employs about 493,000 professional managers. Opportunities for well-qualified restaurant and food service managers appear to be excellent through the year 2006, especially for those with bachelor's or associate degrees. New restaurants are always opening to meet increasing demand. It has been estimated that at least 25 percent of all of the food consumed in the United States is eaten in restaurants and hotels.

Many job openings will arise from the need to replace managers retiring from the workforce. Also, population growth will result in an increased demand for eating establishments, and in turn, a need for managers to oversee them. As the elderly population increases, managers will be needed to staff dining rooms located in hospitals and nursing homes.

Economic downswings have a great effect on eating and drinking establishments. During a recession, people have less money to spend on luxuries such as dining out, thus hurting the restaurant business. However, with more women working outside the home, eating out, or purchasing carry out food from a restaurant is quickly becoming a necessity.

Earnings

The earnings of salaried restaurant and food service managers vary a great deal, depending on the type and size of the establishment. According to a 1995 salary survey conducted by the National Restaurant Association, manager-trainees earned an average salary of $21,000 a year. Those working in larger restaurants and food service facilities received about $30,000. In addition, most trainees earn annual bonuses or incentive payments ranging from $1,000 to $3,000. Experienced managers receive an average of approximately $30,000 a year. Those in charge of the largest restaurants and institutional food service facilities often earn over $50,000. Managers of fast-food restaurants average about $21,000 a year. In addition to a base salary, most managers receive bonuses based on profits, which can range from $2,000 to $7,500 a year.

Conditions of Work

Work environments are usually pleasant. There is usually a great deal of activity involved in preparing and serving food to large numbers of people, and managers usually work forty to forty-eight hours a week. In some cafeterias, especially those located within an industry or business establishment, hours are regular, and little evening work is required. Many restaurants serve late dinners, however, necessitating the manager to remain on duty during a late evening work period.

Many restaurants furnish meals to employees during their work hours. Annual bonuses, group plan pensions, hospitalization, medical, and other benefits may be offered to restaurant managers.

Sources of Additional Information

■Council on Hotel, Restaurant, and Institutional Education
1200 17th Street, NW
Washington, DC 20036-3097
Tel: 202-331-5990
Email: alliance@access.digex.net

■Educational Foundation of the National Restaurant Association
250 South Wacker Drive, Suite 1400
Chicago, IL 60606

■Canadian Restaurant and Food Services Association
316 Bloor Street, West
Toronto, ON M5S 1W5 Canada
Tel: 416-923-8416
Email: 102477.3104@compuserve.com

Retail Sales Workers

Definition

Retail sales workers assist customers with purchases by identifying their needs, showing or demonstrating merchandise, receiving payment, recording sales, and wrapping their purchases or arranging for their delivery. They are sometimes called *sales clerks*, *retail clerks*, or *salespeople*.

Nature of the Work

Salespeople work in more than one hundred different types of retail establishments in a variety of roles. Some, for example, work in a small specialty shop where, in addition to waiting on customers, they might check inventory, order stock from sales representatives (or by telephone or mail), place newspaper display advertisements, prepare window displays, and rearrange merchandise for sale.

Other salespeople work in a specific department, such as the furniture department, of a large department store. The employees in a department work in shifts to provide service to customers six or seven days a week. To improve their sales effectiveness and knowledge of merchandise, they attend regular staff meetings. The work of retail salespeople is supported by advertising, window decorating, sales promotion, buying, and market research specialists.

Whatever they are selling, the primary responsibility of retail sales workers is to interest customers in the merchandise. This might be done by describing the product's features, demonstrating its use, or showing various models and colors. Some retail sales workers must have specialized knowledge, particularly those who sell such expensive, complicated products as stereos, appliances, and personal computers.

In addition to selling, most retail sales workers make out sales checks; receive cash, check, and charge payments; bag or package purchases; and give change and receipts. Depending on the hours they work, retail sales workers might have to open or close the cash register. This might include counting the money in the cash register; separating charge slips, coupons, and exchange vouchers; and making deposits at the cash office. The sales records they keep are normally used in inventory control. Sales workers are often held responsible for the contents of their registers, and repeated shortages are cause for dismissal in many organizations.

Sales workers must be aware of any promotions the store is sponsoring and know the store's policies and procedures, especially on returns and exchanges. Also, they often must recognize possible security risks and know how to handle such situations.

Consumers often form their impressions of a store by its sales force. To stay ahead in the fiercely competitive retail industry, employers are increasingly stressing the importance of providing courteous and efficient service. When a customer wants an item that is not on the sales floor, for example, the sales worker might be expected to check the stockroom and, if necessary, place a special order or call another store to locate the item.

Requirements

Employers generally prefer to hire high school graduates for most sales positions. Such subjects as English, speech, and mathematics provide a good background for these jobs. Many high schools and two-year colleges have special programs that include courses in merchandising, principles of retailing, and retail selling.

In retail sales, as in other fields, the level of opportunity tends to coincide with the level of a person's education. In many stores, college graduates enter immediately into on-the-job training programs to prepare them for management assignments. Successful and experienced workers who do not have a degree might also qualify for these programs. Useful college courses include economics, business administration, and marketing. Many colleges offer majors in retailing. Executives in many companies express a strong preference for liberal arts graduates, especially those with some business courses or a master's degree in business administration.

The retail sales worker must be in good health. Many selling positions require standing most of the day. The sales worker must have stamina to face the grueling pace of busy times, such as weekends and the Christmas season, while at the same time remaining pleasant and effective. Personal appearance is important. Salespeople should be neat and well-groomed and have an outgoing personality.

A pleasant speaking voice, a natural friendliness, tact, and patience are all helpful personal characteristics. The sales worker must be able to converse easily with strangers of all ages. In addition to interpersonal skills, sales workers must be equally good with figures. They should be able to add and subtract accurately and quickly and operate cash registers and other types of business machines.

Most states have established minimum standards that govern retail employment. Some states set a minimum age of fourteen, require at least a high school diploma, or prohibit more than eight hours of work a day or forty-eight hours in any six days. These requirements are often relaxed for those people employed during the Christmas season.

Opportunities for Experience & Exploration

Because of its seasonal nature, retailing offers numerous opportunities for temporary or part-time sales experience. Most stores add extra personnel for the Christmas season. Vacation areas may hire sales employees, usually high school or college students. Fewer sales positions are available in metropolitan areas during the summer, as this is frequently the slowest time of the year.

Many high schools and junior colleges have developed "distributive education" programs that combine courses in retailing with part-time work in the field. The distributive education student may receive academic credit for this work experience in addition to regular wages. Store owners cooperating in these programs often hire students as full-time personnel upon completion of the program.

Methods of Entering

If they have openings, retail stores usually hire beginning salespeople who come in and fill out an application. Major department stores maintain extensive personnel departments, while in smaller stores the manager might do the hiring. Occasionally, sales applicants are given an aptitude test.

Young people might be hired immediately for sales positions. Often, however, they begin by working in the stockroom as clerks, helping to set up merchandise displays or assisting in the receiving or shipping departments. After a while they might be moved up to a sales assignment.

Training varies with the type and size of the store. In large stores, the beginner might benefit from formal training courses that discuss sales techniques, store policies, the mechanics of recording sales, and an overview of the entire store. Programs of this type are usually followed by on-the-job sales supervision. The beginner in a small store might receive personal instruction from the manager or a senior sales worker, followed by supervised sales experience.

College graduates and people with successful sales experience often enter executive training programs (sometimes referred to as "flying squads" because they move rapidly through different parts of the store). As they rotate through various departments, the trainees are exposed to merchandising methods, stock and inventory control, advertising, buying, credit, and personnel. By spending time in each of these areas, trainees receive a broad retailing background designed to help them as they advance into the ranks of management.

Advancement

Large stores have the most opportunities for promotion. Retailing, however, is a mobile field, and successful and experienced people can readily change employment. This is one of the few fields where, if the salesperson has the necessary initiative and ability, advancement to executive positions is possible regardless of education.

When first on the job, sales workers develop their career potential by specializing in a particular line of merchandise. They become authorities on a certain product line, such as sporting equipment, women's suits, or building materials. Many good sales workers prefer the role of the senior sales worker and remain at this level. Others might be asked to become supervisor of a section. Eventually they might develop into a department manager, floor manager, division or branch manager, or general manager.

People with sales experience often enter related areas, such as buying. Other retail store workers advance into support areas, such as personnel, accounting, public relations, and credit.

Young people with ability find that retailing offers the opportunity for unusually rapid advancement. One study revealed that half of all retail executives are under thirty-five years of age. It is not uncommon for a person under thirty-five to be in charge of a retail store or department with an annual sales volume of over $1,000,000. Conversely, the retail executive who makes bad merchandising judgments might be quickly out of a job.

Employment Outlook

In 1996, about 4,522,000 people were employed as sales workers in retail stores of all types and sizes. The employment of sales personnel should grow about as fast as the average for all occupations through the year 2006. Turnover among sales workers is much higher than average. Many of the expected employment opportunities will stem from the need to replace workers. Other positions will result from existing stores' staffing for longer business hours or reducing the length of the average employee workweek.

Several factors—the full effects of which have yet to be measured—might reduce the long-range demand for sales personnel. As drug, variety, grocery, and other stores rapidly convert to self-service operations, they will need fewer sales workers. In contrast, many other stores are trying to stay competitive by offering better customer service and more sales staff attention.

At the same time, many products (such as stereo components, electrical appliances, computers, and sporting goods) do not lend themselves to self-service operations. These products require extremely skilled sales workers to assist customers and explain the benefits of various makes and models. On balance, as easy-to-sell goods will be increasingly marketed in self-service stores, the demand in the future will be strongest for sales workers who are knowledgeable about particular types of products.

During economic recessions, sales volume and the resulting demand for sales workers generally decline. Purchases of costly items, such as cars, appliances, and furniture, tend to be postponed during difficult economic times. In areas of high unemployment, sales of all types of goods might decline. Since turnover of sales workers is usually very high, however, employers often can cut payrolls simply by not replacing all those who leave.

There should continue to be good opportunities for temporary and part-time workers, especially during the holidays. Stores are particularly interested in people who, by returning year after year, develop good sales backgrounds.

Earnings

Most beginning sales workers start at the federal minimum wage, which is currently $5.15 an hour. Wages vary greatly, depending primarily on the type of store and the degree of skill required. Businesses might offer higher wages to attract and retain workers. Some sales workers make as much as $12 an hour or more.

Department stores or retail chains might pay more than smaller stores. Higher wages are paid for positions requiring a greater degree of skill. Many sales workers also receive a commission (often 4 to 8 percent) on their sales or are paid solely on commission. According to the *1998-99 Occupational Outlook Handbook*, sales workers earned the following average annual salaries: motor vehicles and boats, $30,836; apparel, $13,780; furniture and home furnishings, $20,956; and various door-to-door sales, $19,344.

Salespeople in many retail stores are allowed a discount on their own purchases, ranging from 10 to 25 percent. This privilege is sometimes extended to the worker's family. Meals in the employee cafeterias maintained by large stores might be served at a price that is below cost. Many stores provide sick leave, medical and life insurance, and retirement benefits. Most stores give paid vacations.

Conditions of Work

Retail sales workers generally work in clean, comfortable, well-lighted areas. Those with seniority have reasonably good job security. When business is slow, stores might curtail hiring and not fill vacancies that occur. Most stores, however, are able to weather mild business recessions without having to release experienced sales workers. During periods of economic recession, competition among salespeople for job openings can become intense.

With nearly two million retail stores across the country, sales positions are found in every region. An experienced salesperson can find employment in almost any state. The vast majority of positions, however, are located in large cities or suburban areas.

The five-day, forty-hour workweek is the exception rather than the rule in retailing. Most salespeople can expect to work some evening and weekend hours, and longer than normal hours might be scheduled during Christmas and other peak periods. In addition, most retailers restrict the use of vacation time between Thanksgiving and early January. Most sales workers receive overtime pay during Christmas and other rush seasons. Part-time salespeople generally work at peak hours of business, supplementing the full-time staff. Because competition in the retailing business is keen, many retailers work under pressure. The sales worker might not be directly involved but will feel the pressures of the industry in subtle ways. The sales worker must be able to adjust to alternating periods of high activity and dull monotony. No two days—or even customers—are alike. Because some customers are hostile and rude, salespeople must learn to exercise tact and patience at all times.

Sources of Additional Information

National Retail Federation
325 7th Street, NW, Suite 1000
Washington, DC 20004
Tel: 202-783-7971

Secretaries

Definition

Secretaries perform a wide range of jobs that vary greatly from business to business. However, most secretaries key in documents, manage records and information, answer telephones, handle correspondence, schedule appointments, make travel arrangements, and sort mail. The amount of time secretaries spend on these duties depends on the size and type of the office as well as on their own job training.

Nature of the Work

Secretaries perform a variety of administrative and clerical duties. The goal of all their activities, however, is to assist their employers in the execution of their work and to help their companies conduct business in an efficient and professional manner.

Secretaries' work includes processing and transmitting information to the office staff and to other organizations. They operate office machines and arrange for their repair or servicing. These machines include computers, typewriters, dictating machines, photocopiers, switchboards, and fax machines. These secretaries also order office supplies and perform regular duties such as answering phones, sorting mail, managing files, taking dictation, and composing and keying in letters.

Some offices have word processing centers that handle all of the firm's typing. In such a situation, *administrative secretaries* take care of all secretarial duties except for typing and dictation. This arrangement leaves them free to respond to correspondence, prepare reports, do research and present the results to their employers, and otherwise assist the professional staff. Often these secretaries work in groups of three or four so that they can help each other if one secretary has a workload that is heavier than normal.

In many offices, secretaries make appointments for company executives and keep track of the office schedule. They make travel arrangements for the professional staff or for clients, and occasionally are asked to travel with staff members on business trips. Other secretaries might manage the office while their supervisors are away on vacation or business trips.

Secretaries take minutes at meetings, write up reports, and compose and type letters. They often will find their responsibilities growing as they learn the business. Some are responsible for finding speakers for conferences, planning receptions, and arranging public relations programs. Some write copy for brochures or articles before making the arrangements to have them printed or microfilmed. Or, they might use desktop publishing software to create the documents themselves. They greet clients and guide them to the proper offices, and often supervise and train other staff members and newer secretaries, especially in computer software programs.

Some secretaries perform very specialized work. *Legal secretaries* prepare legal papers including wills, mortgages, contracts, deeds, motions, complaints, and summonses. They work under the direct supervision of an attorney or paralegal. They assist with legal research by reviewing legal journals and organizing briefs for their employers. They must learn an entire specialized vocabulary that is used in legal papers and documents.

Medical secretaries take medical histories of patients, make appointments; prepare and send bills to patients, as well as track and collect them; process insurance billing, maintain medical files; and pursue correspondence with patients, hospitals, and associations. They assist physicians or medical scientists with articles, reports, speeches, and conference proceedings. Some medical secretaries are responsible for ordering medical supplies. They, too, need to learn an entire specialized vocabulary of medical terms and be familiar with laboratory or hospital procedures.

Technical secretaries work for engineers and scientists preparing reports and papers that often include graphics and mathematical equations that are difficult to format on paper. The secretaries maintain a technical library and help with scientific papers by gathering and editing materials.

Social secretaries, often called *personal secretaries*, arrange all of the social activities of their employers. They handle private as well as business social affairs, and may plan parties, send out invitations, or write speeches for their employers. Social secretaries are often hired by celebrities or high-level executives who have busy social calendars to maintain.

Many associations, clubs, and non profit organizations have *membership secretaries* who compile and send out newsletters or promotional materials while maintaining membership lists, dues records, and directories. Depending on the type of club, the secretary may be the one who gives out information to prospective members and who keeps current members and related organizations informed of upcoming events.

Education secretaries work in elementary or secondary schools or on college campuses. They take care of all clerical duties at the school. Their responsibilities may include preparing bulletins and reports for teachers, parents, or students, keeping track of budgets for school supplies or student activities, and maintaining the school's calendar of events. Depending on the position, they may work for school administrators, principals, or groups of teachers or professors. Other education secretaries work in administration offices, state education departments, or service departments.

Requirements

Secretaries must have a high school education. They need good office skills that include rapid and accurate keyboarding skills, good spelling and grammar, and they should enjoy handling details. Some positions require typing a minimum number of words per minute, as well as shorthand ability. Knowledge of word processing, spreadsheet, and database management is important, and many employers require it. Some of these skills can be learned in business education courses taught at vocational and business schools. Courses that are helpful include business, communications, English, keyboarding, and computers.

Personal qualities are important for secretaries. They often are the first employees of a company that clients meet, and therefore must be friendly, poised, and professionally dressed. Because they must work closely with others, they should be personable and tactful. Discretion, good judgment, organizational ability, and initiative are also important. These traits will not only get them hired, but will also help them advance in their careers.

Some employers encourage their secretaries to take advanced courses and to be trained to use any new piece of equipment in the office. Requirements vary widely from company to company.

Opportunities for Experience & Exploration

High school guidance counselors can give interest and aptitude tests to help students assess their suitability to a career as a secretary. Local business schools often welcome visitors, and sometimes offer courses that can be taken in conjunction with a high school business course. Work-study programs also provide students with an opportunity to work in a business setting to get a sense of the work performed by secretaries.

Part-time or summer jobs as receptionists, file clerks, and office clerks are often available in various offices. These jobs are the best indicator of future satisfaction in the secretarial field. Students who are computer-literate may find part-time jobs. Cooperative education programs arranged through schools and "temping" through an agency also are valuable ways to acquire experience. In general, any job that teaches basic office skills is helpful.

Methods of Entering

Most people looking for work as secretaries find jobs through the newspaper want ads or by applying directly to local businesses. Both private employment offices and state employment services place secretaries, and business schools help their graduates find suitable jobs. Temporary-help agencies also are an excellent way to find jobs, many of which may turn into permanent ones.

Advancement

Secretaries often begin by assisting executive secretaries and work their way up by learning the way their business operates. Initial promotions from a secretarial position are usually to jobs such as secretarial supervisor, office manager, or administrative assistant. Depending on other personal qualifications, college courses in business, accounting, or marketing can help the ambitious secretary enter middle and upper management. Training in computer skills can also lead to advancement. Secretaries who become proficient in word processing, for instance, can get jobs as instructors or as sales representatives for software manufacturers.

Qualifying for the designation Certified Professional Secretary (CPS) rating is increasingly recognized in business and industry as a consideration for promotion as a senior level secretary. The examinations required for this certification are given by Professional Secretaries International. Secretaries with limited experience can become an Accredited Legal Secretary (ALS) by obtaining certification from the Certifying Board of the National Association of Legal Secretaries. Those with at least three years of experience in the legal field can be certified as a Professional Legal Secretary (PLS) from this same organization. Board Certified Civil Trial Legal Secretaries have five or more years of experience in litigation and probate, and have passed an examination given by Legal Secretaries International. Many legal secretaries, with additional training and schooling, become paralegals. Secretaries in the medical field can advance into the fields of Radiological and Surgical Records or Medical Transcription.

Employment Outlook

There were 3.4 million secretaries employed in 1996, making this profession one of the largest in the United States. Of this total, 284,000 specialized as legal secretaries and 239,000 worked as medical secretaries. Good job growth is expected for secretaries who specialize in legal (about as fast as the average employment growth) or medical (faster than the average growth) fields. Those secretaries who do not specialize can expect job opportunities to decline through the year 2006.

Industries such as computer and data processing, public relations, and personnel supply may create some new jobs to offset this decline. As common with large occupations, the need to replace retiring workers will generate many openings.

Computers, fax machines, electronic mail, copy machines and scanners are some technological advancements that have greatly improved the work productivity of secretaries. Company downsizing and restructuring, in some cases, have redistributed traditional secretarial duties to other employees. There has been a growing trend in assigning one secretary to assist two or more managers, adding to this field's decline. Though more professionals are using personal computers for their correspondence, some administrative duties will still need to be handled by secretaries. The personal aspects of the job and responsibilities such as making travel arrangements, scheduling conferences, and transmitting staff instructions have not changed.

Many employers currently complain of a shortage of capable secretaries. Those with skills and experience will have the best chances for employment. Specialized secretaries should attain certification in their field to stay competitive.

Earnings

Salaries for secretaries vary widely by region; type of business; and the skill, experience, and level of responsibility of the secretary. Medical secretaries, according to a survey conducted by the state of Minnesota, earned a starting average of $7.96 an hour, or $16,556 a year in 1996. Those with experience had an average hourly rate of at least $10.05, or $20,904 or more annually.

As reported by Abbott, Langer & Associates, experienced legal secretaries averaged an annual salary of over $30,000. Ten percent earned a low average of $22,204; ten percent averaged over $39,450. The Pacific states pay the highest, about $37,000 a year for legal secretaries with at least three year of experience; though states such as California and Hawaii have a higher cost of living. An attorney's rank in the firm will also affect the earnings of a legal secretary; secretaries who work for a partner will earn higher salaries than those who work for an associate.

In other industries, secretaries with limited experience earned an average of $19,700 annually, as reported in the *1988-99 Occupational Outlook Hand-*

book. Those with experience averaged about $40,600 a year; some with executive titles earned considerably more. Secretaries employed by the federal government earned a starting salary of $17,400 a year; with experience, $27,900.

Secretaries, especially those working in the legal profession, earn considerably more if certified. Most secretaries receive paid holidays and two weeks' vacation time after a year of work, as well as sick leave. Many offices provide benefits including health and life insurance, pension plans, overtime pay, and tuition reimbursement.

Conditions of Work

Most secretaries work in pleasant offices with modern equipment. Office conditions vary widely, however. While some secretaries have their own offices and work for one or two executives, others share crowded workspace with other workers.

Most office workers work thirty-five to forty hours a week. Very few secretaries work on the weekends on a regular basis, although some may be asked to work overtime if a particular project demands it.

The work is not physically strenuous or hazardous, although deadline pressure is a factor and sitting for long periods of time can be uncomfortable. Many hours spent in front of a computer can lead to eyestrain or repetitive-motion problems for secretaries. Most secretaries are not required to travel. Part-time and flexible schedules are easily adaptable to secretarial work.

Sources of Additional Information

For information on the Certified Professional Legal Secretary and the Accredited Legal Secretary designations, contact:

■**National Association of Legal Secretaries**
2448 East 81st Street, Suite 3400
Tulsa, OK 74137-4238
Tel: 918-493-3540
WWW: http://www.nals.org

■**National Association of Secretarial Services**
3637 Fourth Street North, Suite 330
St. Petersburg, FL 33704-1336
Tel: 813-823-3646

■**Office and Professional Employees International Union**
265 West 14th Street, Suite 610
New York, NY 10011
Tel: 212-675-3210

■**OfficeTeam**
2884 Sand Hill Road
Menlo Park, CA 94025
Tel: 800-804-8367

For information on the Certified Professional Secretary Designation, contact:

■**Professional Secretaries International**
PO Box 20404
10502 NW Ambassador Drive
Kansas City, MO 64195-0404
Tel: 816-891-6600
WWW: http://www.giv.net/psi

Security Consultants and Technicians

Definition

Security consultants and technicians are responsible for protecting public and private property against theft, fire, vandalism, illegal entry, and acts of violence. They may work for commercial or governmental organizations or private individuals.

Nature of the Work

A security consultant is engaged in protective service work. Anywhere there is valuable property or information, or public figures at risk, a security consultant may be called in to devise and implement security plans that offer protection. Security consultants may work for a variety of clients, including large stores, art museums, factories, laboratories, data processing centers, and political candidates. They are involved in preventing theft, vandalism, fraud, kidnapping, and other crimes. Specific job responsibilities depend on the type and size of the client's company and the scope of the security system required.

A security consultant always works closely with company officials or other appropriate individuals in the development of a comprehensive security program that will fit the needs of the individual client. After discussing goals and objectives with the relevant company executives, the consultant studies and analyzes the physical conditions and internal operations of a client's operation. Much is learned by simply observing day-to-day operations.

The size of the security budget also influences the type of equipment ordered and methods used. For example, a large factory that produces military hardware may fence off its property and place electric eyes around the perimeter of the fence. They may also install perimeter alarms and use passkeys to limit access to restricted areas. A smaller company may only use entry control mechanisms in specified areas. The consultant may recommend sophisticated technology, such as closed circuit surveillance or ultrasonic motion detectors, alone or in addition to security personnel. Usually, a combination of electronic and human resources is used.

Security consultants not only devise plans to protect equipment but also recommend procedures on safeguarding and possibly destroying classified material. Increasingly, consultants are being called on to develop strategies to safeguard data processing equipment. They may have to to develop measures to safeguard transmission lines against unwanted or unauthorized interceptions.

Once a security plan has been developed, the consultant oversees the installation of the equipment, ensures that it is working properly, and checks frequently with the client to ensure the client is satisfied. In the case of a crime against the facility, a consultant investigates the nature of the crime (often in conjunction with police or other investigators) and then modifies the security system to safeguard against similar crimes in the future.

Many consultants work for security firms that have several types of clients, such as manufacturing and telecommunications plants and facilities. Consultants may handle a variety of clients or work exclusively in a particular area. For example, one security consultant may be assigned to handle the protection of nuclear power plants and another will be assigned to handle data processing companies.

Security consultants may be called on to safeguard famous individuals or persons in certain positions from kidnapping or other type of harm. They provide security services to presidents of large companies, media personalities, and others who want their safety and privacy protected. These consultants, like bodyguards, plan and review client travel itineraries and usually accompany the client on trips, checking accommodations and appointment locations along the way. They often check the backgrounds of people who will interact with the client, especially those who see the client infrequently.

Security consultants are sometimes called in for special events, such as sporting events and political rallies, when there is no specific fear of danger, but just a need for overall coordination of a large security operation. The consultants oversee security preparation, such as the stationing of appropriate personnel at all points of entry and exit, and then direct specific responses to any security problems.

Security officers develop and implement security plans for companies that manufacture or process material for the federal government. They ensure that their clients' security policies comply with federal regulations in such categories as the storing and handling of classified documents and restricting access to nonauthorized personnel only.

Security guards have various titles, depending on the type of work they do and the setting in which they work. They may be referred to as *patrollers*, *merchant patrollers*, *bouncers* (people who eject unruly people from places of entertainment), *golf-course rangers* (who patrol golf courses), or *gate tenders* (who work at security checkpoints). They may work as *airline security representatives* in airports or as *armored-car guards and drivers*.

Many security guards are employed during normal working hours in public and commercial buildings and other areas with a good deal of pedestrian traffic and public contact. Others patrol buildings and grounds outside of normal working hours, such as at night and on weekends. Guards usually wear uniforms and may carry a nightstick. Guards who work in situations where they may be called upon to apprehend criminal intruders are usually armed. They may carry a flashlight, whistle, two-way radio, and a watch clock, which is used to record the time at which they reach various checkpoints.

Guards in public buildings may be assigned to a certain post or they may patrol an area. In museums, art galleries, and other public buildings, guards answer visitors' questions and give them directions; they also enforce rules against smoking, touching art objects, and so forth. In commercial buildings, guards may sign people in and out after hours and inspect packages being carried out of the building. Bank guards observe customers carefully for any sign of suspicious behavior that may signal a possible robbery attempt. In department stores, security guards often work with undercover detectives to watch for theft by customers or store employees. Guards at large public gatherings such as sporting events and conventions keep traffic moving, direct people to their seats, and eject unruly spectators. Guards employed at airports limit access to boarding areas to passengers only. They make sure people entering passenger areas have valid tickets and observe passengers and their baggage as they pass through X-ray machines and metal detection equipment.

After-hours guards are usually employed at industrial plants, defense installations, construction sites, and transport facilities such as docks and railroad yards. They make regular rounds on foot or, if the premises are very large, in motorized vehicles. They check to be sure that no unauthorized persons are on the premises, that doors and windows are secure, and that no property is missing. They may be equipped with walkie-talkies to report in at intervals to a central guard station. Sometimes guards perform custodial duties, such as turning on lights and setting thermostatic controls.

In a large organization, a security officer is often in charge of the guard force; in a small organization, a single worker may be responsible for all security measures. As more businesses purchase advanced electronic security systems to protect their properties, more guards are being assigned to stations where they monitor perimeter security, environmental functions, communications, and other systems. In many cases, these guards maintain radio contact with other guards patrolling on foot or in motor vehicles. Some guards use computers to store information on matters relevant to security such as visitors or suspicious occurrences during their time on duty.

Security technicians work for government agencies or for private companies hired by government agencies. Their task is usually to guard secret or restricted installations in this country or in foreign countries. They spend much of their time patrolling areas, which they may do on foot, horseback, or in automobiles or aircraft. They may monitor activities in an area through the use of surveillance cameras and video screens. Their assignments usually include detecting and preventing unauthorized activities, searching for explosive devices, standing watch during secret and hazardous experiments, and other routine police duties within government installations.

Security technicians are usually armed and may be required to use their weapons or other kinds of physical force to prevent some kinds of activities. They are usually not, however, required to remove explosive devices from an installation. When they find such devices, they notify a bomb disposal unit, which is responsible for removing and then defusing or detonating the device.

Requirements

Most companies prefer to hire security consultants who have at least a college degree. An undergraduate or associate's degree in criminal justice, business administration, or related field is best. Coursework should be broad and include business management, communications, computer courses, sociology, and statistics. As the security consulting field becomes more competitive, many consultants chose to get a master's in business administration (MBA) or other graduate degree.

Although there are no specific educational or professional requirements, many security consultants have had previous experience with police work or other forms of crime prevention. It is helpful if a person develops an expertise in a specific area. For example, if a person wants to work devising plans securing data processing equipment, it is helpful if the consultant has had previous experience working with computers. Many security consultants are certified by the Certified Protection Professionals. To be eligible for certification, a consultant must pass a written test and have ten years' work and educational experience in the security profession. Information on certification is available from the American Society for Industrial Security, a professional organization to which many security consultants belong.

There are no specific educational requirements for security guards, although most employers prefer to hire high school graduates. General good health (especially vision and hearing), alertness, emotional stability, and the ability to follow directions are important characteristics for this job. Military service and experience in local or state police departments are assets. Prospective guards should have clean police records.

Some employers require applicants to take a polygraph examination or a written test that indicates honesty, attitudes, and other personal qualities. Most employers require applicants and experienced workers to submit to drug screening tests as a condition of employment.

For some hazardous or physically demanding jobs, guards must be under a certain age and meet height and weight standards. For top-level security positions in facilities such as nuclear power plants or vulnerable information centers, guards may be required to complete a special training course. They may also need to fulfill certain relevant academic requirements.

Guards employed by the federal government must be U.S. armed forces veterans, have some previous experience as guards, and pass a written examination. Many positions require experience with firearms. In many situations, guards must be bonded.

Virtually every state has licensing or registration requirements for those guards who work for contract security agencies. Registration generally requires that a person newly hired as a guard be reported to the licensing authorities, usually the state police department or special state licensing commission. To be granted a license, individuals generally must be eighteen years of age, have no convictions for perjury or acts of violence, pass a background investigation, and complete classroom training on a variety of subjects, including property rights, emergency procedures, and capture of suspected criminals.

Security technicians are required to be high school graduates. In addition, they should expect to receive from three to six months of specialized training in security procedures and technology. While in high school, they should take mathematics courses to ensure that they can perform basic arithmetic operations with different units of measure, compute ratios, rates, and percentages, and interpret charts and graphs. They should take English courses to develop their reading and writing skills and be able to read manuals, memos, textbooks, and other instructional materials and write reports with correct spelling, grammar, and punctuation. They should also be able to speak to small groups with poise and confidence.

Security technicians need good eyesight and should be in good physical shape, able to lift at least fifty pounds, climb ladders, stairs, poles, and ropes, and maintain their balance on narrow, slippery, or moving surfaces. They should be able to stoop, crawl, crouch, and kneel with ease.

Opportunities for Experience & Exploration

Part-time or summer employment as a clerk with a security firm is an excellent way to gain insight into the skills and temperament needed to become a security consultant. Discussions with professional security consultants are another way of exploring career opportunities in this field. Young people may find it helpful to join a safety patrol at school.

Those interested in a particular area of security consulting, such as data processing, for example, can join a club or association to learn more about the field. This is a good way to make professional contacts.

Opportunities for part-time or summer work as security guards are not generally available to high school students. Students may, however, work as lifeguards, safety patrols, and school hallway monitors, which can provide helpful experience.

Methods of Entering

People interested in a career in security services generally apply directly to security companies. Some jobs may be available through state or private employment services. People interested in security technician positions should apply directly to government agencies.

Beginning security personnel receive varied amounts of training. Training requirements are generally increasing as modern, highly sophisticated security systems become more common. Many employers give newly hired security guards instruction before they start the job and also provide several weeks of on-the-job training. Guards receive training in protection, public relations, report writing, crisis deterrence, first aid, and drug control.

Those employed at establishments that place a heavy emphasis on security usually receive extensive formal training. For example, guards at nuclear power plants may undergo several months of training before being placed on duty under close supervision. Guards may be taught to use firearms, administer first aid, operate alarm systems and electronic security equipment, handle emergencies, and spot and deal with security problems.

Many of the less strenuous guard positions are filled by older people who are retired police officers or armed forces veterans. Because of the odd hours required for many positions, this occupation appeals to many people seeking part-time work or second jobs.

Most entry-level positions for security consultants are filled by those with a bachelor's or associate's degree in criminal justice, business administration, or a related field. Those with a high school diploma and some experience in the field may find work with a security consulting firm, although they usually begin as a security guard and become a consultant only after training.

Because many consulting firms have their own techniques and procedures, most require entry-level personnel to complete an on-the-job training program, where company policy is introduced.

Advancement

In most cases, security guards receive periodic salary increases, and guards employed by larger security companies or as part of a military-style guard force may increase their responsibilities or move up in rank. Guards with outstanding ability, especially those with some college education, may move up to the position of chief guard, gaining responsibility for the supervision and training of an entire guard force in an industrial plant or department store, or become director of security services for a business or commercial building. A few guards with management skills open their own contract security guard agencies; other guards become licensed private detectives. Experienced guards may become bodyguards for political figures, executives, and celebrities or choose to enter a police department or other law enforcement agency. Additional training may lead to a career as a corrections officer.

Increased training and experience with a variety of security and surveillance systems may lead security guards into higher-paying security consultant careers. Security consultants with experience may advance to management positions or they may start their own private consulting firms. Instruction and training of security personnel is another advancement opportunity for security guards, consultants, and technicians.

Employment Outlook

Security services is one of the largest employment fields in the United States. About 995,000 persons are employed as security guards in the United States. Industrial security firms and guard agencies, also called contract security firms, employ over 50 percent of all guards, while the remainder are in-house guards employed by various establishments.

The demand for guards and other security personnel is expected to increase faster than the average through the year 2006, as crime rates rise with the overall population growth. The highest estimates call for more than 1.25 million guards to be employed by the year 2006. Many job openings will be created as a result of the high turnover of workers in this field.

A factor adding to this demand is the trend for private security firms to perform duties previously handled by police officers, such as courtroom security and crowd control in airports. Private security companies employ security technicians to guard many government sites, such as nuclear testing facilities. Private companies also operate many training facility for government security technicians and guards, as well as provide police services for some communities.

Earnings

Earnings for security consultants vary greatly depending on the consultant's training and experience. Entry-level consultants with a bachelor's degree commonly start at $26,000 to $32,000 per year. Consultants with graduate degrees begin at $34,000 to $41,000 per year, and experienced consultants may earn $50,000 to $100,000 per year or more. Many consultants work on a per-project basis, with rates of up to $75 per hour.

Average starting salaries for security guards and technicians vary according to their level of training, experience, and the location of where they work. Starting salaries generally range between $5.50 and $11.73 per hour in 1996, according to the U.S. Department of Labor. Experienced security guards average as high as $35,600 per year, with those employed in manufacturing facilities receiving the highest wages. Entry-level guards working for a contract agency may receive little more than the minimum wage, however. In-house guards generally earn higher wages and have greater job security and better advancement potential.

Security guards and technicians employed by federal government agencies earned starting salaries of $15,500 or $17,500 per year, and average $22,900 per year with experience. Location of the work also affects earnings, with higher pay in locations with a higher cost of living. Government employees typically enjoy good job security and generous benefits. Benefits for positions with private companies vary significantly.

Conditions of Work

Consultants usually divide their time between their offices and a client's business. Much time is spent analyzing various security apparati and developing security proposals. The consultant talks with a variety of employees at a client's company, including the top officials, and discusses alternatives with other people at the consulting firm. A consultant makes a security proposal presentation to the client and then works with the client on any modifications. A consultant must be sensitive to budget issues and develop a security system that the client can afford.

Consultants may specialize in one type of security work (nuclear power plants, for example) or work for a variety of large and small clients, such as museums, data processing companies, and banks.

Although there may be a lot of travel and some work may require outdoor activity, there should be no strenuous work. A consultant may oversee the implementation of a large security system but is not involved in the actual installation process. Consultants may have to confront suspicious people but they are not expected to do the work of a police officer.

Security guards and technicians may work indoors or outdoors. In high-crime areas and industries vulnerable to theft and vandalism, there may be considerable physical danger. Guards who work in museums, department stores, and other buildings and facilities remain on their feet for long periods of time, either standing still or walking while on patrol. Guards assigned to reception areas or security control rooms may remain at their desks for the entire shift. Much of their work is routine and may be tedious at times, yet guards must remain constantly alert during their shift. Guards who work with the public, especially at sporting events and concerts, may have to confront unruly and sometimes hostile people. Bouncers often confront intoxicated people and are frequently called upon to intervene in physical altercations.

Many companies employ guards around the clock in three shifts, including weekends and holidays, and assign workers to these shifts on a rotating basis. The same is true for security technicians guarding government facilities and installations. Those with less seniority will likely have the most erratic schedules. Many guards work alone for an entire shift, usually lasting eight hours. Lunches and other meals are often taken on the job, so that constant vigilance is maintained.

Sources of Additional Information

International Security Officers' Police and Guard Union
321 86th Street
Brooklyn, NY 11209
Tel: 718-836-3508

International Association of Security Service
PO Box 8202
Northfield, IL 60093
Tel: 847-973-7712

International Union of Security Officers
2404 Merced Street
San Leandro, CA 94577
Tel: 510-895-9905

For information on certification procedures, please contact:

American Society for Industrial Security
1655 North Fort Myer Drive, Suite 1200
Arlington, VA 22209
Tel: 703-522-5800

Services Sales Representatives

Definition

Services sales representatives sell a variety of services, from furniture upholstery and graphic arts to pest control and telephone communications systems. In general, they try to find potential clients, describe or demonstrate the services to them, answer any questions they might have, and attempt to make the sale. Services sales representatives usually telephone their customers or travel to their homes or places of business. Some, however, work out of an office and meet clients who come to them.

Nature of the Work

Although specific job responsibilities depend on the type of service being sold, all services sales representatives have a variety of duties in common. For example, most contact prospective clients, try to determine the clients' needs and describe or demonstrate the pertinent services. It is vital that sales representatives understand and be able to discuss the services provided by their company. For example, a services sales representative who works for a shipping company must be familiar with shipping rates, import and export regulations, industry standards, and a host of other factors affecting packaging and handling.

The sales procedure usually begins with developing lists of prospective clients. A sales representative might be able to form a list from telephone and business directories, by asking existing customers and other business associates for leads, or by receiving inquiries from potential customers. The representative can then call the potential clients and either begin the sales pitch over the phone or set up a meeting. Sales pitches are typically made in person, as they often require the use of literature or a demonstration of the service. Sales representatives also try to analyze their clients' specific needs and answer any questions they might have.

Keeping in constant touch with customers and potential customers is another important component of the job. If they fail to make a sale to a potential customer, for example, the services sales representative might follow up with more visits, letters, and phone calls. Periodic contact with customers can encourage the continued use of the services and increases the likelihood that a customer will recommend the services to friends or business acquaintances.

Job responsibilities vary with the size of the company. Those working for large companies generally have more specialized responsibilities and are assigned to specific territorial boundaries. Those who work for small companies might have public relations and administrative tasks in addition to their sales responsibilities.

There are many specialized jobs within the services sales field. These include *sales-service promoters*, who create goodwill for companies by attending appropriate conventions and advising other sales representatives on ways to increase sales of a particular service. Sales representatives sell warehouse space and services to manufacturers and others who need it.

Data-processing services sales representatives sell various complex services, such as inventory control and payroll processing, to companies using computers in their business operations. *Travelers' checks sales representatives* visit banks, consumer groups, and travel agencies to explain the benefits of travelers' checks. *Business services sales agents* sell business services, such as linen supply and pest control services, usually within a specified territory.

Financial-report service sales agents sell such services as credit and insurance investigation reports to stores and other business establishments. *Communications consultants* discuss communications needs with residential and commercial customers and suggest services that would help clients meet those needs.

Telephone services sales representatives visit commercial customers to review their telephone systems, analyze their communications needs, and recommend additional telecommunication services, if necessary.

Public utilities sales representatives visit commercial and residential customers to promote an increased or more economical use of gas, electricity, or telephone service. They quote rates for changes in service and installation charges.

Advertising sales representatives sell advertising space or broadcast time to advertising firms or to other companies that maintain their own advertising departments.

Hotel services sales representatives contact business, government, and social groups to solicit conference and convention business for their hotel.

Group-sales representatives work for sports teams or other entertainment organizations and promote group ticket sales or season ticket sales. They might also arrange for group seating and special activities on the day of the event.

Sales-promotion representatives visit retail outlets and encourage the use of display items, such as posters, that can increase retail sales.

Education courses sales representatives recruit students for technical or commercial training schools. They inform prospective applicants of enrollment requirements and tuition fees.

Psychological tests and industrial relations sales agents sell programs of psychological, intelligence, and aptitude tests to businesses and schools. They aid in integrating the programs into the school or business operation and help in the administration, scoring, and interpretation of the tests.

Other sales representatives have job titles that define who they work for and what services they sell. These include pest control service sales agents, franchise sales representatives, herbicide service sales representatives, shipping services sales representatives, graphic art sales representatives, signs and displays sales representatives, printing sales representatives, signs sales representatives, audiovisual program productions sales representatives, electroplating sales representatives, elevators, escalators, and dumbwaiters sales representatives, dancing instruction sales representatives, and television cable service sales representatives.

Requirements

For most positions, a college degree is required, though some companies of nontechnical services hire high school graduates. The more complex a service, the greater the likelihood of it being sold by a college-trained person. For example, a company that markets advertising services would likely seek a sales representative with an undergraduate degree in advertising or a master's degree in business administration. A company that sells laundry services might accept applications from high school graduates.

High school students should take college-preparatory courses, including English, speech arts, mathematics, and history. College programs will vary depending on the student's particular area of interest but might include coursework in psychology, marketing, public relations, finance, and business law.

It is important for salespeople to work well with others. A successful salesperson usually is cheerful, optimistic, sociable with both acquaintances and strangers, sincere, and tactful. They must be able to make a good first impression and maintain it while working repeatedly with the same customers.

Many services sales representatives work without direct supervision and make their own schedules. Thus, they must be efficient and well organized and have sufficient self-motivation to continue to go after potential customers even after a long day or a series of setbacks.

Opportunities for Experience & Exploration

Because many services require that salespeople have specialized knowledge, untrained workers have few opportunities to explore the field directly. Students, however, can measure their abilities and interest in sales work by finding a part-time sales job in a store. In addition, some school work-study programs offer opportunities with local businesses for part-time, practical on-the-job training. It might also be helpful to read periodicals, such as *Selling Magazine* and *Personal Selling Power*, that publish articles on the sales field.

Methods of Entering

Because maturity and the ability to work independently are so important, many employers prefer to hire people who have achieved success in other jobs, either in sales or in a related field. Small companies in particular are reluctant to hire applicants without previous sales experience. In contrast, extremely large companies sometimes prefer applicants who are recent college graduates.

For those entering the job market just out of college, school placement offices might be helpful in supplying job leads. In addition, those interested in securing an entry-level position can contact appropriate companies directly. Jobs might also be located through help wanted advertisements.

Most new sales representatives must complete a training period before receiving their first sales assignment. Large companies might use formal training classes that last several months, while smaller organizations might emphasize supervised sales experience.

Selling highly technical services, such as communications or computer systems, usually involves more complex and lengthy sales training. In these situations, sales representatives usually work as part of a team and receive technical assistance from support personnel. For example, those who sell telecommunications equipment might work with a communications consultant.

Advancement

The primary form of advancement for services sales representatives is an increase in the number and size of accounts they handle and, possibly, an increase in their sales territory. Some experienced representatives with leadership ability become branch office managers and supervise other sales representatives. A few representatives advance to top management positions or become partners in their companies. Some go into business for themselves.

It is not unusual for someone to begin as a sales representative and then enter a related position with a company. For example, a successful sales representative might become a purchasing agent or a marketing executive.

Employment Outlook

Services sales representatives held 694,000 jobs in 1996. Over half work for firms providing business services, including computer and data processing, advertising, personnel, equipment rental, mailing, printing, and stenographic services.

As a result of the continued demand for services in general, employment opportunities for services sales representatives are expected to grow much faster than the average through the year 2006. Future opportunities, however, will vary greatly depending on the service involved. For example, the continued growth in office automation should lead to greatly increased opportunities for data-processing services sales representatives, while only average growth is expected in the number of advertising sales representatives. Employment growth for education course sales representatives will probably be slower than average. Some businesses, to offset expenses, have increased in-house sales, sometimes contracting temporary help for outside sales.

As with other sales occupations, the high turnover among services sales representatives will lead to many new job openings each year, especially for those who sell nontechnical services. Those with a college education, training, and sales experience will have the best job opportunities. Workers without a college degree, but with a proven sales record, will equally be in demand.

Earnings

Earnings depend on a number of variables, including sales skills, the quality of the services, geographic location, the number of potential customers and their need for the services, and the health of the economy. A beginning services sales representative, according to a Dartnell Corporation Sales Compensation Survey, can earn an average of $36,000 a year. Middle level sales representatives averaged $46,000 annually; senior representatives, $63,000. Some successful sales representatives, especially those in the technical field, can earn over $100,000. Those who work for large companies receive considerably better salaries. Experienced sales workers often earn more than their branch managers. It is important to realize, however, that the amount of sales in almost every industry is directly affected by the overall economy. Because sales can go up and down frequently, earnings can fluctuate widely.

Sales representatives work on different types of compensation plans. Some get a straight salary; others are paid commissions based on the total volume of sales. Most sales representatives are paid a combination of salary, commission, and bonuses. Bonuses, might be based on the increase in number of new clients brought to the company or an increase in overall sales. Bonuses or incentive pay can equal up to 25 to 75 percent of a base salary. Some companies also provide expense accounts and company cars for their outside sales representatives. Trips and other prizes are often awarded to those that meet or exceed a set sales quota.

Conditions of Work

Services sales representatives work long and irregular hours. Sales workers with large territories frequently spend all day calling on customers in one city and then travel to another city to make calls the next day. Many sales representatives spend at least several nights a month away from home. Those sales workers with limited territories might have less overnight travel, but, like all sales workers, they might have to spend many evenings preparing reports, writing up orders, and entertaining customers and potential customers. Some representatives who sell primarily by phone spend the majority of their time in the office.

Although most services sales representatives work long hours and make appointments to fit the convenience of customers, they usually have a considerable amount of flexibility. They can set their own schedules as long as they meet their company's goals.

Sales work is physically demanding. Sales representatives might spend most of the day on their feet. Many travel constantly from one place to another. Sales workers also face competition from other representatives and the possibility that their customers might switch their business to another organization. This, coupled with the uncertainty of sales during tough economic times, can add greatly to the stress of the job.

Sources of Additional Information

■■Sales and Marketing Executives International
6600 Hidden Lake Trail
Brecksville, OH 44141
Tel: 800-999-1414

Social Workers

Definition

Social workers help people and communities solve problems. These problems include poverty, racism, discrimination, physical and mental illness, addiction, and abuse. They counsel individuals and families, they lead group sessions, they research social problems, and they develop policy and programs. Social workers are dedicated to empowering people and helping people to preserve their dignity and worth.

Nature of the Work

After months of physical abuse from her husband, a young woman has taken her children and moved out of her house. With no job, no home, and fearing for her safety, she looks for a temporary shelter for herself and her kids. Once there, she can rely on the help of social workers who will provide her with a room, food, and security. The social workers will offer counseling and emotional support to help her address the problems in her life. They'll involve her in group sessions with other victims of abuse. They'll direct her to job training programs and other employment services. They'll set up interviews with managers of low-income housing. And while the woman makes efforts to improve her life, the shelter will provide day care for the children. Because the social work profession has long been committed to empowering people and improving society, all these resources exist.

The social worker's role extends even beyond the shelter. If the woman has trouble getting the help she needs from other agencies, the social worker will serve as an advocate, stepping in to assure she gets the aid she's entitled to. The woman may also qualify for long-term assistance from the shelter, such as a second-step program in which a social worker may offer counseling and other support over several months. Also, the woman's individual experience will help in the social worker's research of the problem of domestic violence; with that research, the social worker can help the community come to a better understanding of the problem and can direct society toward solutions. Some of these solutions may include the development of special police procedures for domestic disputes, or court-ordered therapy groups for abusive spouses.

Theories and methodologies of social work have changed over the years, but the basis of the profession has remained the same: helping people and addressing social problems. But as society changes, so do its problems, calling for redefinition of the social work profession. The first three fields of formal social work were defined by setting: medical social work; psychiatric social work; and child welfare. Later, practice was classified by different methodologies: casework; group work; and community organization. Most recently, the social work profession has been divided into two areas—direct practice and indirect practice. These changes reflect the need for social work professionals to adjust to the times, to incorporate new knowledge and new client groups.

Direct practice is also known as clinical practice. As the name suggests, direct practice involves working directly with the client by offering counseling, advocacy, information and referral, and education. Indirect practice concerns the structures through which the direct practice is offered. Indirect practice (a practice consisting mostly of social workers with Ph.D.s) involves program development and evaluation, administration, and policy analysis. Of the 134,200 members of the National Association of Social Workers, 69 percent work in direct service roles and 19 percent in indirect roles (according to a recent survey conducted by the NASW).

Because of the number of problems facing individuals, families and communities, social workers find jobs in a variety of settings and with a variety of client groups. Some of these areas are discussed in the following paragraphs:

Health/mental health care. Mental health care has become the lead area of social work employment. These jobs are competitive and typically go to more experienced social workers. Settings include community mental health centers, where social workers serve persistently mentally ill people and participate in outreach services; state and county mental hospitals, for long-term, inpatient care; veterans administration, involving a variety of mental health care for veterans; and private psychiatric hospitals, for patients who can pay directly. Social workers also work with patients with physical illnesses. They help the individual and the family adjust to the facts of illness and the changes that illness may bring to their lives. They confer with the physician and with other members of the medical team to make plans about the best way in which to be of service to the patient. They explain the treatment and its anticipated outcome to both the patient and the family. They help the patient adjust to the prospect of long hospitalization and isolation from the family.

Child care/family services. Efforts are being made to offer a more universal system of care which would incorporate child care, family services, and community service. Child care services are composed of day care homes, child care centers, and Head Start centers. Social workers in this setting attempt to address all the problems children face from infancy to late adolescence. They work with families to detect problems early and intervene when necessary. They research the problems children and families are confronted with, and they establish new services or adapt existing services to address these problems. They provide parenting education to teenaged parents, which can involve living with a teen mother in a foster-care situation, teaching parenting skills, and caring for the baby while the mother attends school. Social workers alert employers to employees' needs for daytime child care.

Social workers in this area of service are constantly required to address new issues; in recent years, for example, social workers have developed services for families composed of different cultural backgrounds and services for children with congenital disabilities resulting from the mother's drug use and disabilities related to HIV.

Gerontological social work. Within this field, social workers provide individual and family counseling services in order to examine the older person's needs and strengths. Social workers help older people locate transportation and housing services. They also offer adult day care services or adult foster care services that match older people with families. Adult protective services protect older people from abuse and neglect, and respite services allow family members time off from the care of an older person. Not so well known is the fact that AIDS is also a growing problem for older people; 10 percent of all AIDS patients are aged fifty or over.

School social work. In schools, social workers serve students, their families, teachers, administration, and other school staff members. Education, counseling, and advocacy are important aspects of school social work. With education, social workers attempt to prevent alcohol and drug abuse, teen pregnancy, and the spread of AIDS and other sexually transmitted diseases. They provide multicultural and family life education. They counsel students who are discriminated against because of their sexual orientation, or their racial, ethnic, or religious backgrounds. They also serve as advocates for these students, bringing issues of discrimination before administrators, school boards, and student councils.

A smaller percentage of social workers are employed in the areas of social work education (a field composed of the professors and instructors who teach and train students of social work); group practice (in which social workers facilitate treatment and support groups); and corrections (providing services to inmates in penal institutions). Social workers also offer counseling, occupational assistance, and advocacy to those with addictions and disabilities, to the homeless, and to women, children, and the elderly who have been in abusive situations.

Client groups expand and change as societal problems change. Social work professionals must remain aware of the problems affecting individuals and communities in order to offer assistance to as many people as possible.

Computers have become important tools for social workers. Client records are maintained on computers, allowing for easier collection and analysis of data. Interactive computer programs are used in training social workers, as well as to analyze case histories (such as for an individual's risk of HIV). And the Internet allows for better links to the larger community.

Requirements

Social work requires great dedication. As a social worker, you have the responsibility of helping whole families, groups, and communities, as well as focusing on the needs of individuals. Your efforts won't always be supported by the society at large; sometimes you must work against a community's prejudice, disinterest, and denial. And you must remain sensitive to the problems of your clients, offering support and not moral judgment or personal bias. The only way to effectively address new social problems and new client groups is to remain open to the thoughts and needs of all human beings. Assessing situations and solving problems requires a clarity of vision, and a genuine concern for the well-being of others.

With this clarity of vision, your work will be all the more rewarding. You'll have the satisfaction of making a connection with other people and helping them through difficult times. But along with the rewards, the work can provide a great deal of stress. Hearing repeatedly about the deeply troubled lives of prison inmates, the mentally ill, abused women and children, and others can be depressing and defeating. Trying to convince society of the need for changes in laws and services can be a long, hard struggle. You must have perseverance to fight for your clients against all odds.

To prepare for social work, you should take courses in high school that will improve your communications skills, such as English, speech, and composition. On a debate team, you could further develop your communications skills, as well as your research and analysis skills. History, social studies, and sociology courses are important in understanding the concerns and issues of society. Though some work is available for those with only a high school diploma or associate's degree (jobs as a social work aide, or social services technician), the most opportunities exist for people with degrees in social work.

The Council on Social Work Education requires that five areas be covered in accredited bachelor's degree social work programs: human behavior and the social environment; social welfare policy and services; social work practice; research; and field practicum. Most programs require two years of liberal arts study, followed by two years of study in the social work major. Also, students must complete a field practicum of at least four hundred clock hours. Graduates of these programs can find work in public assistance or they can work with the elderly or with people with mental retardation or developmental disabilities.

Though no clear lines of classification are drawn in the social work profession, most supervisory and administrative positions require at least a master's degree in social work (MSW). Master's programs are organized according to fields of practice (such as mental health care), problem areas (substance abuse), population groups (the elderly), and practice roles (practice with individuals, families, or communities). They are usually two-year programs, with at least nine hundred hours of field practice. Most positions in mental health care facilities require an MSW. Doctoral degrees are also available and prepare students for research and teaching. Most social workers with doctorates go to work in community organization.

Licensing, certification, or registration of social workers is required by all states. To receive the necessary licensing, a social worker will typically have to gain a certain amount of experience and also pass an exam. Five voluntary certification programs help to identify those social workers who have gained the knowledge and experience necessary to meet national standards.

Opportunities for Experience & Exploration

As a high school student, you may find openings for summer or part-time work as a receptionist or file clerk with a local social agency. If there is no opportunity for paid employment, you could work as a volunteer. Good experience is also provided by work as a counselor in a camp for children with disabilities or mental retardation. Your local YMCA may need volunteers for group recreation programs, including programs designed for the prevention of delinquency. By reporting for your high school newspaper, you'll have the opportunity to interview people, conduct surveys and research social change, all important aspects of the social work profession.

You could also volunteer a few afternoons a week to read to people in retirement homes or to the blind. Work as a tutor in special education programs is sometimes available to high school students.

Methods
of Entering

Most students of social work pursue a master's degree, and in the process, learn about the variety of jobs available. They also make valuable connections through faculty and other students. Through the college's job placement service, or an internship program, a student will learn about job openings and potential employers.

A social work education in an accredited program will provide you with the most opportunities, and the best salaries and chances for promotion, but practical social work experience can also earn you full-time employment. A part-time job, or volunteer work, will introduce you to social work professionals who can provide you with career guidance and letters of reference. Agencies with limited funding may not be able to afford to hire social workers with MSWs and will therefore look for applicants with a great deal of experience and lower salary expectations.

Advancement

The attractive and better-paying jobs tend to go to those with more years of practical experience. Dedication to your job, an extensive resume, and good references will lead to advancement in the profession. Also, many social work programs offer continuing education workshops, courses, and seminars. These refresher courses help practicing social workers to refine their skills and to learn about new areas of practice, and new methods and problems. These courses are intended to supplement your social work education, not substitute for a bachelor's or master's degree. These continuing education courses can lead to job promotions and salary increases.

Employment
Outlook

The field of social work is expected to grow faster than the average for all occupations through the year 2006. The greatest factor for this growth is the increased number of older people who are in need of social services. Social workers that specialize in gerontology will find many job opportunities in nursing homes, hospitals, and home health agencies. The needs of the future elderly population are likely to be different from those of the present elderly. Currently, the elderly appreciate community living, while subsequent generations may demand more individual care.

Schools will also need more social workers to deal with issues such as teen pregnancies, children from single parent households, and any adjustment problems recent immigrants may have. The trend to integrate disabled students into the general school population will require the expertise of social workers to make the transition smoother. However, job availability in schools will depend on funding given by state and local sources.

To help control costs, hospitals are encouraging early discharge for some of their patients. Social workers will be needed by hospitals to help secure patients with human service care at home. There is also a growing number of people with physical disabilities or impairments staying in their own homes, requiring home health care workers.

Increased availability of health insurance funding, and the growing number of people able to pay for professional help will create opportunities for those in private practice. Many businesses hire social workers to help in employee assistance programs, many on a contractual basis.

Poverty is still a main issue addressed by social workers. Families are finding it increasingly challenging to make ends meet on wages just barely above the minimum. The problem of "deadbeat dads"—fathers who don't make their court-ordered child support payments—force single mothers to work more than one job or rely on welfare. An increased awareness of domestic violence has also alerted us to the fact that many of our homeless and unemployed are women who have left abusive situations. Besides all this, work with the poor is often considered unattractive, leaving many social work positions in this area unfilled.

Competition for jobs in urban areas will remain strong. However, there is still a shortage of social workers in rural areas; these areas usually can't offer the high salaries or modern facilities that attract large numbers of applicants.

The social work profession is constantly changing. The survival of social service agencies, both private and public, depends on shifting political, economic, and workplace issues.

Social work professionals are worried about the threat of declassification. Because of budget constraints and a need for more workers, some agencies have lowered their job requirements. When unable to afford qualified professionals, they hire those with less education and experience. This downgrading raises questions about quality of care and professional standards. Just as in some situations low salaries push out the qualified social worker, so do high salaries. In the area of corrections, attractive salaries (up to $40,000 for someone with a two-year associate's degree) have resulted in more competition from other service workers.

Liability is another growing concern. If a social worker, for example, tries to prove that a child has been beaten, or attempts to remove a child from his or her home, the worker can potentially be sued for libel. At the other extreme, a social worker can face criminal charges for failure to remove a child from an abusive home. More social workers are taking out malpractice insurance.

Earnings

The higher your degree, the more you can make in the social work profession. Earnings are also determined by your area of practice. The areas of mental health, group services, and community organization and planning provide higher salaries, while elderly and disabled care provide lower. Salaries also vary among regions; social workers on the East and West coasts earn higher salaries than those in the Midwest. Earnings in Canada vary from province to province, as well. And during the first five years of practice, your salary will increase faster than in later years.

The median salary range for social workers in the United States is approximately $35,000 for those with a master's degree in social work. Those who hold a bachelor's degree earn about $25,000 a year. Social workers employed by the U.S. government earn an average annual salary of about $46,900. Average salaries in Canada are higher, with a median range of $40,000 to $45,000.

Though women make up a large percentage of the profession, only 2.2 percent of female social workers in the United States received over $60,000, as opposed to 6.3 percent of male social workers.

Conditions of Work

Social workers do not always work at a desk. When they do, they may be interviewing clients or writing reports or conferring with other staff members. Depending on the size of the agency, office duties such as typing letters, filing, and answering phones may be performed by an aide or volunteer. Social workers employed at shelters or halfway houses may spend most of their time with clients, tutoring, counseling, or leading groups.

Some social workers have to drive to remote areas to make a home visit. They may go into inner city neighborhoods, schools, courts, or jails. In larger cities, domestic violence and homeless shelters are typically located in rundown, sometimes dangerous areas. Most social workers are involved directly with the people they serve, and must carefully examine the client's living conditions and family relations. Though these living conditions can be pleasant and demonstrate a good home situation, they can also be squalid and depressing.

Advocacy involves work in a variety of different environments. Though much of this work may require making phone calls and sending faxes and letters, it also requires meetings with clients' employers, directors of agencies, local legislators, and others. It may sometimes require testifying in court as well.

Sources of Additional Information

For information on educational programs, contact:

■**Council on Social Work Education**
1600 Duke Street
Alexandria, VA 22314
Tel: 703-683-8080

■**Canadian Association of Schools of Social Work**
30 Rosemount Avenue, Suite 100-B
Ottawa, ON K1Y 1B4 Canada

For job listings and information about careers and education, contact:

■**National Association of Social Workers**
Information Center
750 First Street, NE
Washington, DC 20002
Tel: 202-408-8600

■**Canadian Association of Social Workers**
383 Parkdale Avenue, Suite 402
Ottawa, ON K1Y 4R4 Canada

Salary Range: $25,000 to $40,000 to $60,000+

Software Engineers

Definition

Software engineers are responsible for customizing existing software programs to meet the needs and desires of a particular business or industry. First, they spend considerable time researching, defining, and analyzing the problem at hand. Then, they develop software programs to resolve the problem on the computer. Software engineering work is done in many fields, including medical, industrial, military, communications, aerospace, scientific, and other commercial businesses.

Nature of the Work

Every day, businesses, scientists, and government agencies encounter difficult problems that they cannot solve manually, either because the problem is just too complicated or because it would take too much time to calculate the appropriate solutions. For example, astronomers receive thousands of pieces of data every hour from probes and satellites in space as well as telescopes here on earth. If they had to process the information themselves, that is, compile careful comparisons with previous years' readings, look for patterns or cycles, and keep accurate records of the origin of the various data, it would be so cumbersome and lengthy a project as to make it next to impossible. They can, however, process the data, but only thanks to the extensive help of computers. Computer software engineers define and analyze specific problems in business or science and help develop computer software applications that effectively solve them. The software engineers that work in the field of astronomy are well versed in its concepts, but many other kinds of software engineers exist as well.

The basic structure of computer engineering is the same in any industry. First, software engineers research specific problems and investigate ways in which computers can be programmed to perform certain functions. Then, they develop software applications customized to the needs and desires of the business or organization. For example, many software engineers work with the federal government and insurance companies to develop new ways of reducing paperwork, such as income tax returns, claims forms, and applications. There are currently several independent but major form automation projects taking place throughout the United States. As software engineers find new ways to solve the problems associated with form automation, more and more forms are completed online and less on paper.

Software engineers specializing in a particular industry, such as a particular science, business, or medicine, are expected to demonstrate a certain level of proficiency in that industry. Consequently, the specific nature of their work varies from project to project and industry to industry. Software engineers also differ by the nature of their employer. Some work for consulting firms, who complete software projects for different clients on an individual basis. Others work for large companies that hire engineers full time to develop software customized to their needs. Software engineering professionals also differ by level of responsibility. Software engineering technicians assist engineers in completing projects. They are usually knowledgeable in analog, digital, and microprocessor electronics and programming techniques. Technicians know enough about program design and computer languages to fill in details left out by engineers or programmers, who conceive of the program from a large-scale perspective. Technicians might also test new software applications with special diagnostic equipment.

Software engineering is extremely detail-oriented work. Since computers do only what they are programmed to do, engineers have to account for every bit of information with a programming command. Software engineers are thus required to be very well organized and precise. In order to achieve this, they generally follow strict procedures in completing an assignment.

First, they interview clients and colleagues in order to determine exactly what they want the final program to be able to do. Defining the problem by outlining the goal can sometimes be difficult, especially when clients have little technical training. Then, they evaluate the software applications already in use by the client to understand how and why they are failing to fulfill the needs of the operation. After this period of fact-gathering, the engineers use methods of scientific analysis and mathematical models to develop possible solutions to the problems. These analytical methods allow them to predict and measure the outcomes of different proposed designs.

When they have developed a good notion of what type of program is required to fulfill the client's needs, they draw up a detailed proposal which includes estimates of time and cost allocations. Management must then decide if the project will meet their needs, is a good investment, and whether or not it will be undertaken.

Once a proposal is accepted, both software engineers and technicians begin work on the project. They verify with hardware engineers that the proposed software program is completed with existing hardware systems. Typically, the engineer writes program specifications and the technician uses his or her knowledge of computer languages to write preliminary programming. Engineers focus most of their effort on program strategies, testing procedures, and reviewing technicians' work.

Software engineers are usually responsible for a significant amount of technical writing, including projects proposals, progress reports, and user manuals. They are required to meet regularly with the clients in order to keep project goals clear and learn about any changes as quickly as possible.

When the program is completed, the software engineer organizes a demonstration of the final product to the client. Supervisors, management, and users are generally present. Some software engineers may offer to install the program, train users on it, and make arrangements for ongoing technical support.

Requirements

A high school diploma is the a minimum requirement for software engineering technicians. A bachelor's or advanced degree in computer science or engineering is required for most software engineers. High school students interested in pursuing this career should take as many computer, math, and science courses as possible, since they provide fundamental math and computer knowledge and teach analytical thinking skills. Classes that rely on schematic drawing and flowcharts are also very valuable. English and speech courses help students improve their communications skills, which is very important for software engineers who must make formal business presentations and interact with people having different levels of computer expertise. The qualities developed by these classes, plus an ability to work well under pressure, are key to success in software engineering.

There are several ways to enter the field of software engineering, although it is becoming increasingly necessary to pursue formal postsecondary education. Individuals without an associate's degree may first be hired in the quality assurance or technical support departments of a company. Many complete associate degrees while working and then are promoted into software engineering technician positions. As more and more well-educated professionals enter the industry, however, it is becoming more important for applicants to have at least an associate's degree in computer engineering or programming. Many technical and vocational schools offer a variety of programs that prepare students for jobs as software engineering technicians.

Interested students should consider carefully their long-range goals. Being promoted from a technician's job to that of software engineer often requires a bachelor's degree. In the past, the computer industry has tended to be fairly flexible about official credentials; demonstrated computer proficiency and work experience has often been enough to obtain a good position. This may hold true for some in the future. The majority of young computer professionals entering the field for the first time, however, will be college educated. Therefore, those with no formal education or work experience will have less chance of employment.

Obtaining a postsecondary degree in computer engineering is usually considered challenging and even difficult. In additional natural ability, students should be hard working and determined to succeed. Software engineers planning to work in specific technical fields, such as medicine, law, or business, should receive some formal training in that particular discipline.

Another option for individuals interested in software engineering is to pursue commercial certification. These programs are usually run by computer companies that wish to train professionals in working with their products. Classes are challenging and examinations can be rigorous. New programs are introduced every year.

Opportunities for Experience & Exploration

Interested high school students should try to spend a day with a working software engineer or technician in order to experience firsthand what a typical day is like. School guidance counselors can help arrange such visits. They may also talk to their high school computer teacher for more information.

In general, students should be intent on learning as much as possible about computers and computer software. They should learn about new developments by reading trade magazines and talking to other computer users. They also can join computer clubs and surf the Internet for information about working in this field.

Methods of Entering

Most software engineers work for computer companies or consulting firms. Individuals with work experience and perhaps even an associate's degree are sometimes promoted to software engineering technician positions from entry-level jobs in quality assurance or technical support. Those already employed by computer companies or large corporations should read company job postings to learn about promotion opportunities. Employees who would like to train in software engineering, either on the job or through formal education, can investigate future career possibilities within the same company and advise management of their wish to change career tracks. Some companies offer tuition reimbursement for employees who train in areas applicable to business operations.

Technical, vocational, and university students of software engineering should work closely with their schools' placement offices, as many professionals find their first position through on-campus recruiting. Placement office staff are well trained to provide tips on resume writing and interviewing techniques, and locating job leads.

Individuals not working with a school placement office can check the classified ads for job openings. They also can work with a local employment agency that places computer professionals in appropriate jobs. Many openings in the computer industry are publicized by word of mouth, so interested individuals should stay in touch with working computer professionals to learn who is hiring. In addition, these people may be willing to refer interested job seekers directly to the person in charge of recruiting.

Advancement

With additional education and work experience, software engineering technicians may be promoted to software engineer. Software engineers who demonstrate leadership qualities and thorough technical know-how may become project team leaders who are responsible for full-scale software development projects. Project team leaders oversee the work of technicians and engineers. They determine the overall parameters of a project, calculate time schedules and financial budgets, divide the project into smaller tasks, and assign these tasks to engineers. Overall, they do both managerial and technical work.

Software engineers with experience as project team leaders may be promoted to a position as software manager, running a large research and development department. Managers oversee software projects with a more encompassing perspective; they help choose projects to be undertaken, select project team leaders and engineering teams, and assign individual projects. In some cases, they may be required to travel, solicit new business, and contribute to the general marketing strategy of the company.

Many computer professionals find that their interests change over time. As long as individuals are well qualified and keep up-to-date with the latest technology, they are usually able to find positions in other areas within the computer industry.

Employment Outlook

The field of software engineering is expected to be one of the fastest growing occupations through the year 2006. Demands made on computers increase every day and from all industries. The development of one kind of software sparks ideas for many others. In addition, users rely on software programs that are increasingly user-friendly.

Since technology changes so rapidly, software engineers are advised to keep up on the latest developments. While the need for software engineers will remain high, computer languages will probably change every few years and software engineers will need to attend seminars and workshops to learn new computer languages and software design. They also should read trade magazines, surf the Internet, and talk with colleagues about the field. These kinds of continuing education techniques help ensure that software engineers are best equipped to meet the needs of the workplace.

Earnings

Software engineering technicians usually earn beginning salaries of $24,000. Software engineers with college degrees can expect to start in the high twenties or low thirties. They generally earn more in geographical areas where there are clusters of computer companies, such as the Silicon Valley in northern California.

Mid-level salaries for technicians with some experience average about $34,000 per year. High-end salaries for technicians usually do not exceed $30,000 per year; such salaries are reserved for technicians with experience and an associate's degree. Software engineers can earn over $76,000 a year. When they are promoted into management, as project team leaders or software managers, they earn even more.

Most software engineers work for companies who offer extensive benefits, including health insurance, sick leave, and paid vacation. In some smaller computer companies, however, benefits may be limited.

Conditions of Work

Software engineers usually work in comfortable office environments. Overall, they usually work forty-hour weeks, but this depends on the nature of the employer and expertise of the engineer. In consulting firms, for example, it is typical for engineers to work long hours and frequently travel to out-of-town assignments.

Software engineers generally receive an assignment and a time frame within which to accomplish it; daily work details are often left up to the individuals. Some engineers work relatively lightly at the beginning of a project, but work a lot of overtime at the end in order to catch up. Most engineers are not compensated for overtime. Software engineering can be stressful, especially when working to meet deadlines. Working with programming languages and intense details is often frustrating. Therefore, software engineers should be patient, enjoy problem-solving challenges, and work well under pressure.

Sources of Additional Information

American Software Association
c/o ITAA
1616 North Fort Meyer Drive, Suite 1300
Arlington, VA 22209-9998
Tel: 703-522-5055

American Society of Information Science
8720 Georgia Avenue, Suite 501
Silver Spring, MD 20910-3602
Tel: 301-495-0900

IEEE Computer Society
1730 Massachusetts Avenue, NW
Washington, DC 20036
Tel: 202-371-0101
WWW: http://www.ieee.org

Special Interest Group on Software Engineering
c/o Association for Computing Machinery
1515 Broadway
New York, NY 10036-5701
Tel: 212-869-7440

Special Education Teachers

Definition

Special education teachers teach students, aged three through twenty-one, with a variety of disabilities. They design individualized education plans and work with students one-on-one to help them learn academic subjects and lifeskills.

Nature of the Work

Special education teachers instruct students who have a variety of disabilities. Their students may have physical disabilities, such as vision, hearing, or orthopedic impairment. They may also have learning disabilities or serious emotional disturbances. Although less common, special education teachers sometimes work with students who are gifted and talented, children who have limited proficiency in English, children who have communicable diseases, and children who are neglected and abused.

In order to teach special education students, these teachers design and modify instruction so that it is tailored to individual student needs. Teachers collaborate with school psychologists, social workers, and occupational, physical, and speech-language therapists to develop a specially-designed program—called an Individualized Education Program (IEP)—for each one of their students. The IEP sets personalized goals for a student, based upon his or her learning style and ability, and outlines specific steps to prepare him or her for employment or postsecondary schooling.

Special education teachers teach at a pace that is dictated by the individual needs and abilities of their students. Unlike most regular classes, special education classes do not have an established curriculum that is taught to all students at the same time. Because student abilities vary widely, instruction is individualized and it is part of the teacher's responsibility to match specific techniques with a student's learning style and abilities. They may spend much time working with students one-on-one or in small groups.

Working with different types of students requires a variety of teaching methods. Some students may need to use special equipment or skills in the classroom in order to overcome their disabilities. For example, a teacher working with a physically handicapped student might use a computer that is operated by touching a screen or by voice commands. To work with hearing impaired students, the teacher may need to use sign language. With visually impaired students, he or she may use teaching materials that have Braille characters or large, easy-to-see type. Gifted and talented students may need extra challenging assignments, a faster learning pace, or special attention in one curriculum area, such as art or music.

In addition to teaching academic subjects, special education teachers help students develop both emotionally and socially. They work to make students as independent as possible by teaching them functional skills for daily living. They may help young children learn basic grooming, hygiene, and table manners. Older students might be taught how to balance a checkbook, follow a recipe, or use the public transportation system.

Special education teachers meet regularly with their students' parents to inform them of their child's progress and offer suggestions of how to promote learning at home. They may also meet with school administrators, social workers, psychologists, various types of therapists, and students' general education teachers.

The current trend in education is to integrate disabled students into regular classrooms to the extent that it is possible and beneficial to them. This is often called "mainstreaming." As mainstreaming becomes increasingly common, special education teachers frequently work with general education teachers in general education classrooms. They may help adapt curriculum materials and teaching techniques to meet the needs of disabled students and offer guidance on dealing with students' emotional and behavioral problems.

In addition to working with students, special education teachers are responsible for a certain amount of paperwork. They document each student's progress and may fill out any forms that are required by the school system or the government.

Requirements

The requirements for becoming a special education teacher are similar to those for becoming an elementary or secondary school teacher.

All states require that teachers have at least a bachelor's degree and that they complete a prescribed number of subject and education credits. It is increasingly common for special education teachers to complete an additional fifth year of training after they receive their bachelor's degree. Many states require special education teachers to get a master's degree in special education.

All states also require that special education teachers be licensed, although the particulars of licensing vary by state. In some states, these teachers must first be certified as elementary or secondary school teachers, then meet specific requirements to teach special education. Some states offer general special education licensure; others license several different sub-specialties within special education.

Some states allow special education teachers to transfer their license from one state to another, but many still require these teachers to pass licensing requirements for that state.

There are approximately 700 colleges and universities in the United States that offer programs in special education—including undergraduate, master's and doctoral programs. These programs include general and specialized courses in special education, including educational psychology, legal issues of special education, child growth and development, and knowledge and skills needed for teaching students with disabilities. The student typically spends the last year of the program student teaching in an actual classroom, under the supervision of a licensed teacher.

Some college programs offer a specialization, such as teaching children with specific learning dis-

abilities. Others offer generalized special education degrees.

High school students who are considering a career as a special education teacher should focus on courses that will prepare them for college. These classes include, natural and social sciences, mathematics, and English. Speech classes would also be a good choice for improving one's communication skills. Finally, classes in psychology might be helpful both to help prospective teachers understand the students they will eventually teach, and prepare them for college level psychology coursework.

Special education teachers need to have many of the same personal characteristics as regular classroom teachers—the ability to communicate, a broad knowledge of the arts, sciences, and history, and a love of children. In addition, these teachers need a great deal of patience and persistence. They need to be creative, flexible, cooperative, and accepting of differences in others. Finally, they need to be emotionally stable and consistent in their dealings with students.

Opportunities for Experience & Exploration

There are a number of ways for the interested high school student to explore the field of special education. One of the first and easiest might be to approach a special education teacher at his or her school and ask to talk about the job. Perhaps the teacher could provide a tour of the special education classroom, or allow the student to visit while a class is in session.

Students might also become acquainted with special needs students at their school, or become involved in a school or community mentoring program for these students. There may also be other opportunities for volunteer work or part-time jobs in the school, communities agencies, camps, or residential facilities that allow students to work with disabled persons.

Methods of Entering

The majority of special education teachers work in public school systems. The next largest group are employed by local education agencies, and a minority of others work in colleges and universities, private schools, and state education agencies. Because public school systems are by far the largest employers of special education teachers, this is where the beginning teacher should focus his or her job search.

Since the special education teacher must have at least a bachelor's degree, he or she should have access to his or her college's career placement center. This may prove a very effective place to begin. The student may also write to the state department of education for information on placement and regulations, or contact state employment offices to enquire about job openings. Applying directly to local school systems can sometimes be effective. Even if a school system does not have an immediate opening, it will usually keep applicant resumes on file, should a vacancy occur.

Finally, job seekers should check local newspapers for classified ads from schools seeking special education teachers.

Advancement

Advancement opportunities for special education teachers, as for regular classroom teachers, are fairly limited. It may take the form of higher wages, better facilities, or more prestige. In some cases, these teachers do advance to become supervisors or administrators, although this may require continued education on the teacher's part.

Another option is for special education teachers to earn advanced degrees and become instructors at the college level.

Employment Outlook

The field of special education is expected to grow much faster than the average. As projected by the U.S. Bureau of Labor Statistics, about 300,000 new jobs will be created by the year 2006. This demand is caused partly by the growth in the number of special education students needing services. Medical advances resulting in more survivors of illness and accidents, the rise in birth defects, especially in older pregnancies, as well as general population growth, are also significant factors for strong demand. Because of the rise in the number of disabled youths under the age of twenty-one, the government has given

approval for more federally funded programs. Growth of jobs in this field has also been influenced positively by legislation emphasizing training and employment for individuals with disabilities and a growing public awareness and interest in our disabled population.

Finally, there is a fairly high turnover rate in this field, as special education teachers find the work too stressful and switch to mainstream teaching or change jobs altogether. Many job openings will arise out of a need to replace teachers who have left their positions. There is a shortage of qualified teachers in rural areas and in the inner city. Jobs will also be plentiful for teachers that specialize in speech and language impairments, learning disabilities, and early childhood intervention. Bilingual teachers with multicultural experience will be in high demand.

Earnings

In some school districts, salaries for special education teachers follow the same scale as general education teachers. According to the National Education Association, the average salary for special education teachers in 1996 was $37,900. Public secondary schools paid an average of $38,600; elementary schools, $37,300. Private school teachers usually earn less as compared with their public school counterparts. Teachers can supplement their annual salaries by becoming an activity sponsor, or by summer work.

Other school districts pay their special education teachers on a separate scale, which is usually higher than that of general education teachers.

Regardless of the salary scale, special education teachers usually receive a complete benefits package, which includes health and life insurance, paid holidays and vacations, and a pension plan.

Conditions of Work

The special education teacher usually works from 7:30 or 8:00 a.m. to 3:00 or 3:30 p.m. Like most teachers, however, he or she typically spends several hours in the evening grading papers, completing paperwork, or preparing lessons for the next day. Altogether, most special education teachers work more than the standard 40 hours per week.

Although some schools offer year-round classes for students, the majority of special education teachers work the traditional ten-month school year, with a two-month vacation in the summer. Many teachers find this work schedule very appealing, as it gives them the opportunity to pursue personal interests or additional education during the summer break. Teachers typically also get a week off at Christmas and for spring break.

Special education teachers work in a variety of settings in schools, including both ordinary and specially-equipped classrooms, resource rooms, and therapy rooms. Some schools have newer and better facilities for special education than others. Although it is less common, some teachers work in residential facilities or tutor students who are homebound or hospitalized.

Working with special education students can be very demanding, due to their physical and emotional needs. Teachers may fight a constant battle to keep certain students, particularly those with behavior disorders, under control. Other students, such as those with mental impairments or learning disabilities, learn so slowly that it may seem as if they are making no progress. The special education teacher must deal daily with frustration, setbacks, and classroom disturbances.

These teachers must also contend with heavy workloads, including a great deal of paperwork to document each student's progress. In addition, they may sometimes be faced with irate parents who feel that their child is not receiving proper treatment or an adequate education.

The positive side of this job is in helping students overcome their disabilities and learn to be as functional as possible. For a special education teacher, knowing that he or she is making a difference in a child's life can be very rewarding and emotionally fulfilling.

Sources of Additional Information

Council of Administrators of Special Education
615 16th Street NW
Albuquerque, NM 87104
Tel: 505-243-7622
Email: thomason@apsicc.aps.edu

National Clearinghouse for Professions in Special Education, Council for Exceptional Children
1920 Association Drive
Reston, VA 20191
Tel: 800-328-0272
Email: ericec@cec.sped.org
WWW: http://www.cec.sped.org

National Resource Center for Paraprofessionals in Education and Related Services
25 W. 43rd Street
New York, NY 10036
Tel: 212-642-2948

Speech-Language Pathologists and Audiologists

Definition

Speech-language pathologists and audiologists help people who have speech and hearing defects. They identify the problem, then use tests to further evaluate it. Speech-language pathologists and audiologists also try to improve the speech and hearing defect by treating the patient. Some speech-language pathologists and audiologists take their expertise to the classroom to teach others, or they may investigate what causes certain speech and hearing defects through research.

Speech-language pathologists specialize in problems with speech disorders; audiologists work with hearing disorders. It's not uncommon for patients to require assistance in both areas, so the specialists may work together to help the patient.

Nature of the Work

Even though the two professions seem to blend together at times, speech-language pathology and audiology are very different from one another. However, because both speech and hearing are related to one another, a person competent in one must have familiarity with the other. Most speech-language pathologists and audiologists work in public schools. Colleges and universities employ the next largest number in classrooms, clinics, and research centers. Other speech-language pathologists and audiologists work in hospitals, rehabilitation and community speech and hearing centers, state and federal government agencies, industry, and private practice.

The duties performed by speech-language pathologists and audiologists differ depending on how much education and experience are attained and where one works. In a clinical capacity (such as a community clinic or rehabilitation center),

speech pathologists and audiologists find and evaluate speech and hearing disorders using prescribed diagnostic procedures. The initial treatment is usually followed by an organized program of therapy, with help from other specialists in psychology, social work, and physical therapy. In a research environment, speech pathologists and audiologists investigate communicative disorders and their causes and ways to improve clinical services. Those teaching in colleges and universities instruct students on the principles and bases of communication, communication disorders, and clinical techniques used in speech and hearing.

Requirements

Most states require a master's degree in speech-language pathology or audiology for a beginning job in either profession. Undergraduate study in speech-language pathology and audiology should include courses in anatomy, biology, physiology, physics, and other related areas, such as linguistics, semantics, and phonetics. It's also helpful to have some exposure to child psychology. There are many opportunities for graduate work in speech-language pathology and audiology. About 230 universities and colleges in the United States offer graduate programs in speech-language pathology; about 120 colleges and universities offer graduate programs in audiology. Coursework involves extensive training in the fundamental areas of speech and hearing, such as acoustics, the psychological aspects of communication, the nature of hearing and speech disorders, and analysis of speech and auditory processes.

Speech pathologists and audiologists working in the public schools are required to be certified teachers and must meet special state requirements if treating disabled children.

In most states, one must be licensed to offer speech-language pathology or audiology services in other than a school setting—in private practice or in a clinic, for example. The American Speech-Language-Hearing Association offers speech-language pathologists the Certificate of Clinical Competence in Speech-Language Pathology (CCC-SLP), and audiologists the Certificate of Clinical Competence in Audiology (CCC-A). To apply for certification, applicants must have earned a graduate degree in speech-language pathology or audiology and 375 hours of supervised clinical experience, and have completed a postgraduate clinical fellowship. An examination must also be passed. Some states may have additional requirements.

Opportunities for Experience & Exploration

Although the specialized nature of the work makes it difficult for those interested in speech-language pathology and audiology to get an informal introduction to either profession, there are opportunities to be found. Official training must begin at the college or university level, but it is possible for interested students to volunteer in clinics and hospitals. Prospective speech-language pathologists and audiologists also can learn sign language, or volunteer their time in speech, language, and hearing centers.

Methods of Entering

If you want to work in the public school systems, the college placement office can help you with interviewing skills. Professors sometimes know of job openings and may even post these openings on a centrally located bulletin board. It may be possible to find employment by contacting a hospital or rehabilitation center. To work in colleges and universities as a specialist in the classroom, clinic, or research center, it is almost mandatory to be working on a graduate degree. Many scholarships, fellowships, and grants for assistants are available in colleges and universities giving courses in speech-language pathology and audiology. Most of these and other assistance programs are offered at the graduate level. The U.S. Rehabilitation Services Administration, the Chil-

dren's Bureau, the U.S. Department of Education, and the National Institutes of Health allocate funds for teaching and training grants to colleges and universities with graduate study programs. In addition, the Department of Veterans Affairs provides stipends (a fixed allowance) for predoctoral work.

Advancement

Advancement in speech-language pathology and audiology is based chiefly on education. Individuals who have completed graduate study will have the best opportunities to enter research and administration areas, supervising other speech-language pathologists or audiologists either in developmental work or in public school systems.

Employment Outlook

There were about eighty seven thousand speech-language pathologists and audiologists employed in 1996, almost one half of whom were employed in education, from elementary school to the university level. Others worked in speech, language, and hearing centers; hospitals; nursing homes; and physicians' offices. A small but growing number of speech-language pathologists and audiologists were in private practice, generally working with patients referred to them by physicians and other health practitioners.

Population growth, lengthening life spans, and increased public awareness of the problems associated with communicative disorders indicate a highly favorable employment outlook for well-qualified personnel. This field is expected to grow much faster than the average through the year 2006. Much depends on economic factors, further budget cutbacks by health care providers and third-party payers, and legal mandates requiring services for the disabled.

Nearly half of the new jobs emerging through the end of the decade are expected to be in speech and hearing clinics, physicians' offices, and outpatient care facilities. Speech-language pathologists and audiologists will be needed in these places, for example, to carry out the increasing number of rehabilitation programs for stroke victims and patients with head injuries.

Substantial job growth has already occurred in elementary and secondary schools because of the Education for All Handicapped Children Act of 1975. Such laws guarantee special education and related services to minors with disabilities.

Many new jobs will be created in hospitals, nursing homes, rehabilitation centers, and home health agencies; most of these openings will probably be filled by private practitioners employed on a contract basis. Opportunities for speech-language pathologists and audiologists in private practice should increase in the future. There should be a greater demand for consultant audiologists in the area of industrial and environmental noise as manufacturing and other companies develop and carry out noise control programs.

Earnings

According to a 1997 salary survey conducted by the American Speech-Language-Hearing Association, full time certified speech-language pathologists earned an average salary of $44,000; audiologists averaged $43,000. Pathologists, with one to three years experience, earned a median salary of $38,000, according to this survey. Beginning audiologists earned $32,000. Experienced pathologists, averaged $52,000 annually; audiologists earned $55,000. Geographic location and type of facility are important salary variables.

Conditions of Work

Most speech-language pathologists and audiologists work forty hours a week. Speech pathologists and audiologists who focus on research, however, may work longer hours. Almost all employment situations provide fringe benefits such as paid vacations, sick leave, and retirement programs.

Sources of Additional Information

■**American Auditory Society**
1966 Inwood Road
Dallas, TX 75235
Tel: 602-789-0755

■**American Speech-Language-Hearing Association**
10801 Rockville Pike
Rockville, MD 20852
Tel: 301-897-5700
WWW: http://www.asha.org

■**National Student Speech, Language, and Hearing Association**
10801 Rockville Pike
Rockville, MD 20852
Tel: 301-897-5700

Sports Instructors and Coaches

Definition

Sports instructors demonstrate and explain the skills and rules of particular sports, like golf or tennis, to individuals or groups. They help beginners learn basic stances, grips, movements, and techniques of a game. Sports instructors often help experienced athletes to sharpen their skills.

Coaches work with a single, organized team or individual, teaching them the skills associated with that sport. A coach prepares her or his team for competition, and during the competition, continue to give instruction from a vantage point near the court or playing field.

Nature of the Work

The specific job requirements of sports instructors and coaches varies according to the type of sport and who they teach. For example, an instructor teaching advanced skiing at a resort in Utah will have different duties and responsibilities than an instructor teaching beginning swimming at a municipal pool. Nevertheless, all instructors and coaches are teachers. They must be very knowledgeable about rules and strategies for their respective sports, but without an effective teaching method that reinforces correct techniques and procedures, their students or players won't be able to share that valuable knowledge. Also, instructors and coaches need to be aware of and open to new procedures and techniques. Many attend clinics or seminars to learn more about their sport or even how to teach more effectively. Many are members of professional organizations that deal exclusively with their sport.

Safety is a primary concern for all coaches and instructors. Coaches and instructors make sure their students have the right equipment and know its correct use. A major component of safety is helping students feel comfortable and confident with their abilities. This entails teaching the proper stances, techniques, and movements of a game, instructing students on basic rules and answering any questions.

While instructors may tutor students individually, or in small groups, a coach works with all the members of a team. Both use lectures and demonstrations to show students the proper skills, and both point out the mistakes or deficiencies of individuals.

Motivation is another key element in sports instruction. Almost all sports require stamina, and most coaches will tell you that psychological preparation is every bit as important as physical training.

Coaches and instructors also have administrative responsibilities. College coaches actively recruit new players to join their team. Professional coaches attend team meetings with owners and general managers to determine which players they will draft the next season. Sports instructors at health and athletic clubs schedule classes, lessons and contests.

Requirements

Training and educational requirements vary, depending on the specific sport and the ability level of students being instructed. Most coaches who are associated with schools have bachelor's degrees. Many middle and high school coaches are also teachers within the school. Most instructors need to combine several years of successful experience in a particular sport with some educational background, preferably in teaching. A college degree is becoming more important as part of an instructor's background.

To prepare for college courses, high school students should take courses that teach them human physiology; biology, health and exercise classes would all be helpful. Courses in English and speech are also important to improve or develop communication skills.

There is no substitute for developing an expertise in a sport. If you can play the sport well, and effectively explain to other people how they might play as well as you, you will most likely be able to get a job as a sports instructor. The most significant source of training for this occupation is gained while on the job.

Many facilities require sports instructors to be certified. Information on certification is available from any organization that deals with the specific sport in which one might be interested.

Opportunities for Experience & Exploration

Interested individuals should gain as much experience as possible in all sports and a specific sport in particular. It is never too early to start. High school and college offer great opportunities to participate in sporting events either as a player, manager, trainer or in intramural leagues.

Most communities have sports programs such as Little League baseball or track and field meets sponsored by the Recreation Commission. Students interested in a future coaching career can volunteer as a coach, umpire, or starter.

Discussions with sports instructors already working in the field are also a good way discovering specific job information and finding out about career opportunities.

Methods of Entering

People with an expertise in a particular sport, who are interested in becoming an instructor, should apply directly to the appropriate facility. Sometimes a facility will provide training.

For those interested in coaching, many colleges offer positions to *graduate assistant coaches*. Graduate assistant coaches are recently graduated players who are interested in becoming coaches. They receive a stipend and gain valuable coaching experience.

Advancement

Advancement opportunities for both instructors and coaches depend on the individual's skills, willingness to learn, and work ethic. A sports instructor's success can be measured by caliber of play and number of students. Successful instructors may become well known enough to open their own schools or camps, and write books, or produce how-to videos.

A coach's success is often measured in the win/loss column. For professional coaches, that could, arguably, be their only criteria. However coaches in the scholastic ranks have other responsibilities and other factors that measure success. High school and college coaches must make sure their players are getting good grades, and middle school coaches can be successful if they produce a team who competes in a sportsmanlike fashion regardless of whether they win or lose.

Successful coaches are often hired by larger schools. High school coaches may advance to become college coaches and the most successful college coaches often are given the opportunity to coach professional teams. Former players sometimes land assistant or head coaching positions.

Employment Outlook

Americans have more leisure time than ever and many have decided that they are going to put this time to good use by getting in, or staying in, shape. This fitness boom has created employment opportunities for many people employed in sports-related occupations.

Health clubs, community centers, parks and recreational facilities, and private business, now employ sports instructors who teach everything from tennis and golf to scuba diving.

According to the U.S. Department of Labor, this occupation will grow much faster than the average through the year 2006. There were 303,000 sports instructors and coaches employed in the United States in 1996. By the year 2006, a projected 125,000 additional jobs will be available for instructors and coaches.

Job opportunities will be greatest in urban areas, where population is the most dense. Health clubs, adult education programs, and private industry will be hiring competent, dedicated instructors.

Those with the most training, education, and experience will have the best chance for employment.

Coaching jobs at the high school or amateur level will be plentiful as long as the public continues its quest for a healthier and more active lifestyle. The creation of the Women's National Basketball Association (WNBA) and the expansion of current professional leagues will open new employment opportunities for professional coaches. There will also be openings as other coaches retire, or are terminated. However, there is very little job security in coaching, unless you can consistently produce a winning team.

Earnings

Earnings for sports instructors vary considerably depending on the sport and to whom the lesson is being presented. The coach of a Wimbledon champion commands much more an hour than the swimming instructor for the tadpole class at the municipal pool.

Much of the work is part-time and part-time employees generally do not receive paid vacations, sick days, or health insurance. Instructors who teach group classes for beginners through park districts or at city recreation centers can expect to earn around $6.00 per hour. A hour-long individual lesson through a golf course or tennis club averages $75. Many times, coaches for children's teams work as volunteers.

Many sports instructors work in camps teaching swimming, archery, sailing and other activities. These instructors generally earn between $1,000 and $2,500, plus room and board, for a summer session.

Full time fitness instructors at gyms or health clubs can expect to earn between $13,000 and $22,000 per year. Instructors with many years of experience and college degree have the highest earning potential.

Most coaches who work at the high school level or below also teach within the school district. Besides their teaching salary and coaching fee—either a flat rate or a percentage of their annual salary—school coaches receive a benefits package that includes paid vacations and health insurance.

According to *American Almanac of Jobs and Salaries 1997,* college head football coaches generally earn an average of $50,000. Head coaches of men's college basketball teams average $69,400 annually, while coaches of women's teams average consid-

erable less at $42,200 a year. Many larger universities pay more. Coaches for professional teams often earn between $125,000 and $500,000. Some top coaches can command million-dollar-salaries. Many popular coaches augment their salaries with personal appearances and endorsements.

Conditions of Work

An instructor or coach may work indoors, in a gym or health club, or outdoors, perhaps at a swimming pool. Much of the work is part time. Full time sports instructors generally work between thirty-five and forty hours per week. During the season when their teams compete, coaches can work sixteen hours each day, five or six days each week.

It's not unusual for coaches or instructors to work evenings or weekends. Instructors work then because that is when their adult students are available for instruction. Coaches work nights and weekends because those are the times their teams compete.

One significant drawback is the lack of job security. A club may hire a new instructor on very little notice, or may cancel a scheduled class for lack of interest. Athletic teams routinely fire coaches after losing seasons.

Sports instructors and coaches should enjoy working with a wide variety of people. They should be able to communicate clearly and possess good leadership skills to effectively teach complex skills. They can take pride in the knowledge that they have helped their students or their players reach new heights of achievement and training.

Sources of Additional Information

■■■**American Alliance for Health, Physical Education, Recreation and Dance**
1900 Association Drive
Reston, VA 20191
Tel: 703-476-3400
Email: webmaster@aahperd.org
WWW: http://www.aahperd.org

American Baseball Coaches Association
108 South University Avenue, Suite 3
Mount Pleasant, MI 48858-2327
Tel: 517-775-3300

American Sports Education Institute
200 Castlewood Drive
North Palm Beach, FL 33408
Tel: 561-842-4100

Surgical Technologists

Definition

Surgical technologists, also called surgical technicians or operating room technicians, are members of the surgical team who work in the operating room with surgeons, nurses, anesthesiologists, and other personnel before, during, and after surgery. They perform functions that ensure a safe and sterile environment for surgical procedures at all times. To prepare a patient for surgery, they may wash, shave, and disinfect the area where the incision will be made. They arrange the equipment, instruments, and supplies in the operating room according to the preference of the surgeons and nurses. During the operation, they adjust lights and other equipment as needed. They assist by counting sponges, needles, and instruments used during the operation, by handing instruments and supplies to the surgeon, and by holding retractors and cutting sutures as directed. They maintain specified supplies of fluids such as saline, plasma, blood, and glucose and may assist in administering these fluids. Following the operation, they may clean and restock the operating room and wash and sterilize the used equipment using germicides, autoclaves, and sterilizers, although in most larger hospitals these tasks are done by other central service personnel.

Nature of the Work

In general, the work responsibilities of surgical technologists may be divided into three phases: preoperative (before surgery), intraoperative (during surgery), and postoperative (after surgery). Surgical technologists may work as the scrub person, circulator, or surgical first assistant.

In the preoperative phase, surgical technologists prepare the operating room by selecting and opening sterile supplies such as drapes, sutures, sponges, electrosurgical devices, suction tubing, and surgical instruments. They assemble, adjust, and check nonsterile equipment to ensure that it is in proper working order. Surgical technologists also operate sterilizers, lights, suction machines, electrosurgical units, and diagnostic equipment.

When patients arrive in the surgical suite, surgical technologists may assist in preparing them for surgery by providing physical and emotional support, checking charts, and observing vital signs. They properly position the patient on the operating table, assist in connecting and applying surgical equipment and monitoring devices, and prepare the incision site by cleansing the skin with an antiseptic solution.

During surgery, surgical technologists have primary responsibility for maintaining the sterile field. They ensure that all members of the team adhere to aseptic technique so the patient does not develop a postoperative infection. As the scrub person, they most often function as the sterile member of the surgical team who passes instruments, sutures, and sponges during surgery. After "scrubbing," which involves the thorough cleansing of the hands and forearms, they put on a sterile gown and gloves and prepare the sterile instruments and supplies that will be needed. After other members of the sterile team have scrubbed, they assist them with gowning and gloving and applying sterile drapes around the operative site.

Surgical technologists must anticipate the needs of surgeons during the procedure, passing instruments and providing sterile items in an efficient manner. Checking, mixing, and dispensing appropriate fluids and drugs in the sterile field are other common tasks. They share with the circulator the responsibility for accounting for sponges, needles, and instruments before, during, and after surgery. They may hold retractors or instruments, sponge or suction the operative site, or cut suture material as directed by the surgeon. They connect drains and tubing and receive and prepare specimens for subsequent pathologic analysis.

Surgical technologists most often function as the scrub person, but may function in the nonsterile role of circulator. The *circulator* does not wear a sterile gown and gloves, but is available to assist the surgical team. As a circulator, the surgical technologist obtains additional supplies or equipment, assists the individual providing anesthesia, keeps a written account of the surgical procedure, and assists the scrub person in counting sponges, needles, and instruments before, during, and after surgery.

Surgical first assistants, those technologists with additional education or training, provide aid in retracting tissue, controlling bleeding, and other technical functions that help surgeons during the procedure.

After surgery, surgical technologists are responsible for preparing and applying dressings, including plaster or synthetic casting materials, and for preparing the operating room for the next patient. They may provide staffing in postoperative recovery rooms where patients' responses are carefully monitored in the critical phases following general anesthesia.

Some of these responsibilities vary depending on the size of the hospital and department in which the surgical technologist works; they also vary based on geographic location and health care needs of the local community.

Requirements

Surgical technology education is available through postsecondary programs offered by community and junior colleges, vocational and technical schools, the military, universities, and structured hospital programs in surgical technology. A high school diploma is required for entry into any of these programs. During their high school years, prospective technologists should take courses that develop their basic skills in mathematics, science, and English. They also should take all available courses in health and biology.

About 145 of these programs are accredited by the Commission on Accreditation of Allied Health Education Programs (CAAHEP). The accredited programs vary from nine to twelve months for a diploma or certificate, to two years for an associate's degree. Students can expect to take courses in medical terminology, communications, anatomy,

physiology, microbiology, pharmacology, medical ethics, and legal responsibilities. Students gain a thorough knowledge of patient preparation and care, surgical procedures, surgical instruments and equipment, and principles of asepsis (how to prevent infection). In addition to classroom learning, students receive intensive supervised clinical experience in local hospitals, which is an important component of their education.

Surgical technologists may earn a professional credential by passing a nationally administered certifying examination. Those who become certified are granted the designation of Certified Surgical Technologist (CST). Increasing numbers of hospitals are requiring certification as a condition of employment. To take the examination, an individual must be currently or previously certified or be a graduate of a formal educational program or its equivalent (starting in March 2000, only graduates of CAAHEP-accredited programs will be eligible to take the test). The Liaison Council on Certification for the Surgical Technologist (LCC-ST), an independent affiliate of the Association of Surgical Technologists, is the certifying agency for the profession. Those who become certified demonstrate a commitment to maximum performance and quality patient care. To renew the six-year certificate, the CST must earn continuing education credits or retake the certifying examination. The LCC-ST also offers an advanced credential for surgical first assistants; this exam awards the designation of CST certified first assistant (CST/CFA).

Surgical technologists should have a strong sense of responsibility for their patients, be highly organized, and have the ability to integrate a number of tasks at the same time. They need good manual dexterity to handle awkward surgical instruments with speed and agility. In addition, they need physical stamina to stand through long surgical procedures.

Opportunities for Experience & Exploration

It is difficult for interested students to gain any direct experience on a part-time basis in surgical technology. The first opportunities for direct experience generally come in the clinical and laboratory phases of their educational programs. However, interested students can explore some aspects of this career in several ways. They or their teachers can arrange a visit to a hospital, clinic, or other surgical setting in order to learn about the work. They also can visit a school with a CAAHEP-accredited program. During such a visit, a student can discuss career plans with the admissions counselor. Volunteering at a local hospital or nursing home can also give students insight into the health care environment and help them to evaluate their aptitude to work in such a setting.

Methods of Entering

Graduates of surgical technology programs are frequently offered jobs in the same hospital in which they received their clinical training. Programs generally cooperate closely with hospitals in the area, which are usually eager to employ technologists educated in local programs. Openings are also advertised in newspaper classified ads.

Advancement

Most surgical technologists are employed in hospital operating rooms. They also work in delivery rooms, cast rooms, emergency departments, ambulatory care areas, and central supply departments. With experience, surgical technologists can serve in management roles in surgical services departments and may work as central service managers, surgery schedulers, and materials managers. The role of surgical first assistant on the surgical team requires additional training and experience and is considered an advanced role. Technologists may also be employed directly by surgeons as private scrubs or as surgical first assistants or they may work in clinics and surgicenters.

Surgical technologists function well in a number of diverse areas. Their multicompetency is demonstrated by their employment in organ and tissue procurement/preservation, cardiac catheterization laboratories, medical sales and research, and medical-legal auditing for insurance companies. A number are instructors and directors of surgical technology programs.

Employment Outlook

In 1996, there were 49,000 surgical technologists employed in the United States. Job opportunities for competent surgical technologists far exceed the supply. According to the U.S. Bureau of Labor Statistics, the field of surgical technology is projected to experience faster than average growth through the year 2006. Population growth and increasing longevity, and improvement in medical and surgical procedures have all contributed to a growing demand for surgical services and hence for surgical technologists. As long as the rate at which people undergo surgery continues to increase, there will continue to be a need for this profession. Also, as surgical methods become increasingly complex, using technological advances such as fiber optics and laser technology, more surgical technologists will be needed.

Hospitals will continue to be the primary employer of surgical technologists. However, much job growth is expected from doctors' offices and clinics, as well as ambulatory surgical centers.

Staffing patterns are also changing in response to the need to control costs. Hospitals are changing their staffing ratios of registered nurses to other health care workers and are employing more allied health professionals such as surgical technologists who can provide cost-effective care. On the other hand, hospitals are also increasing their use of multiskilled workers who can handle a wide variety of tasks in different areas of the hospital. A number of health care workers, including surgical technologists, are being asked by their employers to participate in training programs to become multiskilled.

Earnings

Salaries vary greatly in different institutions and localities. According to a 1996 membership survey conducted by the Association of Surgical Technologists, starting salaries averaged about $20,900 annually. The median salaries for all surgical technologists was about $25,000 a year; experienced technologists averaged $28,000.

Most surgical technologists are required to be periodically on call—available to work on short notice in cases of emergency—and can earn overtime from such work.

Graduates of educational programs usually receive salaries higher than technologists without formal education. In general, technologists working on the East and West coasts earn more than surgical technologists in other parts of the country. Surgical first assistants and private scrubs employed directly by surgeons tend to earn more than surgical technologists employed by hospitals.

Conditions of Work

Surgical technologists naturally spend most of their time in the operating room. Operating rooms are cool, well lighted, orderly, and extremely clean. Technologists are often required to be on their feet for long intervals during which their attention must be closely focused on the operation.

Members of the surgical team, including surgical technologists, wear sterile gowns, gloves, caps, masks, and eye protection. This surgical attire is meant not only to protect the patient from infection but also to protect the surgical team from any infection or bloodborne diseases that the patient may have. Surgery is usually performed during the day; however, hospitals, clinics, and other facilities require twenty-four-hour-a-day coverage. Most surgical technologists work regular forty-hour weeks, although many are required to be periodically on call.

Surgical technologists must be able to work under great pressure in stressful situations. The need for surgery is often a matter of life and death, and one can never assume that procedures will go as planned. If operations do not go well, nerves may fray and tempers flare. Technologists must understand that this is the result of stressful conditions and should not take this anger personally.

In addition, surgical technologists should have a strong desire to help others. Surgery is performed on people, not machines. Patients literally entrust their lives to the surgical team, and they rely on them to treat them in a dignified and professional manner. Individuals with these characteristics find surgical technology a rewarding career in which they can make an important contribution to the health and well-being of their community.

Sources of Additional Information

Association of Surgical Technologists (AST)
7108-C South Alton Way, Suite 100
Englewood, CO 80112-2106
Tel: 303-694-9130
WWW: http://www.ast.org

Teacher Aides

Definition

Teacher aides perform a wide variety of duties to help teachers run a classroom. The work they do helps free the teachers' time so they can concentrate on instructing their pupils. Teacher aides may prepare instructional materials, help students with classroom work, and supervise students in the library, on the playground, and at lunch. They may perform administrative duties such as photocopying, keeping attendance records, and grading papers.

Nature of the Work

Teacher aides work in public, private, and parochial preschools and elementary and secondary schools. Their duties vary depending on the classroom teacher, school, and school district. Teacher aides often help a classroom run more smoothly by copying, compiling, and handing out class materials, setting up and operating audiovisual equipment, arranging field trip, and typing or word processing materials. They may organize classroom files, including grade reports, and attendance and health records. They may also obtain library materials and order classroom supplies.

Many teacher aides are in charge of keeping order in classrooms, school cafeterias, libraries, hallways, and playgrounds. Often, they wait with preschool and elementary students coming to or leaving school and make sure that all students are accounted for. When a class leaves its room for such subjects as art, music, physical education, or computer lab, the teacher aide may go with them to help the teachers of these other subjects.

Another responsibility of teacher aides is correcting and grading homework and tests, usually for "objective" work—assignments and tests that require specific correct answers. Teacher aides often use answer sheets to mark students' papers and examinations and keep records of students' scores. In some large schools, an aide may be called a *grading clerk* and be responsible only for scoring objective tests and computing and recording test scores. Often using an electronic grading machine or computer, the grading clerk totals errors found and computes the percentage of questions answered correctly. The worker then records this score and averages students' test scores to determine their grade for the course.

Under the teacher's supervision, some teacher aides work directly with students in the classroom. They may listen to a group of young students read aloud or involve the class in a special project such as a science fair, art project, or drama production. With older students, teacher aides may provide review or study sessions prior to exams or give extra help with research projects or homework.

Some teacher aides work with individual students in a tutorial setting, helping in areas of special need or concern. Teacher aides may work with the teacher to prepare lesson plans, bibliographies, charts, and maps. They may help to decorate the classroom, design bulletin boards and displays, and arrange work stations. They may even participate in parent-teacher conferences to discuss students' progress.

Some teacher aides specialize in one subject and some work in a specific type of school setting. These settings include bilingual classrooms, gifted and talented programs, classes for learning disabled students and those with unique physical needs, and multi-age classrooms. They conduct the same type of classroom work as other teacher aides, but may provide more individual assistance to students.

Requirements

Education and certification requirements for teacher aides depend on the school or school district and the kinds of responsibilities the aides have. In districts where aides perform mostly clerical duties, applicants may need only to have high school diploma or the equivalent, Graduation Equivalency Degree (GED). Those who work in the classroom may be required to take some college courses and attend in-service training and special teacher conferences and seminars. Some schools and districts help teacher aides pay some of the costs involved in attending these programs. Often community and junior colleges offer courses that prepare teacher aides for classroom work.

High school courses in English, history, social studies, mathematics, art, drama, physical education and the sciences provide teacher aides with a broad base of knowledge in a wide variety of areas. This enables them to help students learn in these same subjects. Knowledge of a second language can be an asset to teacher aides, especially those who work in schools with bilingual student, parent, or staff populations. Courses in child care, home economics, and psychology are also valuable for this career.

High school students interested in this field should try to gain some experience working with computers, as students at many elementary schools and even preschools now do a large amount of computer work, and computer skills may be important to teacher aides as they perform clerical duties.

Newly hired aides participate in orientation sessions and formal training at the school. In these sessions, aides learn about the school's organization, operation, and philosophy. They learn how to keep school records, operate audiovisual equipment, check books out of the library, and administer first aid.

Many schools prefer to hire teacher aides who have some experience working with children and some schools prefer to hire workers who live within the school district. Some schools may require teacher aide applicants to pass a physical examination. All teacher aides must be able to work effectively with both children and adults and should have good verbal and written communications skills.

Teacher aides must enjoy working with children and be able to handle their demands, problems, and questions with patience and fairness. A teacher aide must be willing and able to follow instructions, but should also be able to take initiative in projects. Flexibility, creativity, and a cheerful outlook are definite assets for anyone working with children.

Students interested in becoming teacher aides should find out the specific job requirements from the school, school district, and state department of education where they would like to work. Requirements vary from school to school and state to state. It is important to remember that an aide who is qualified to work in one state, or even one school, may not be qualified to work in another.

Opportunities for Experience & Exploration

High school students who wish to become teacher aides can get experience in working with children by volunteering to help with religious education classes at their church, synagogue, or other place of worship. They may volunteer to help with scouting troops or work as counselors at summer camps. Often high school students can volunteer to help coach a children's athletic team or work with children in after-school programs at community centers. Babysitting is common way to gain experience in working with children and learn about different stages of child development. College students can obtain experience by working in schools as aspiring teacher aides who help with real classes while earning course credit.

Methods of Entering

Once they have fulfilled certification requirements, most workers apply directly to school district or schools for teacher aide positions. College students may contact their school placement offices for information about openings. Many school districts and state departments of education maintain job listings, or bulletin boards and hot lines that list available job openings. Teacher aide jobs are often advertised in the classified section of the newspaper.

Advancement

Teacher aides usually advance only in terms of increases in salary or responsibility, which come with experience. Aides in some districts may receive time off to take college courses. Some teacher aides choose to pursue bachelor's degrees and fulfill the licensing requirements of the state or school to become teachers.

Some aides, who find that they enjoy the administrative side of the job, may move into school or district office staff positions. Others get more training and then work as resource teachers, tutors, guidance counselors, or reading, mathematics, or speech specialists. Some aides go into school library work or become media specialists. While it is true that most of these jobs require additional training, the job of teacher aide is a good place to begin.

Employment
Outlook

According to the U.S. Department of Labor, there were 981,000 teacher aide or aide-related jobs in the United States in 1996. Ninety percent of the jobs were found in elementary and secondary schools, mainly in the lower grade levels. Growth in this field is expected to be much faster than the average through the year 2006 because of an expected increase in the number of school-age children. As the number of students in a school or district increases, new schools and classrooms will be added and more teachers and teacher aides will be hired. Recent school reforms will create a strong demand for aides to help provide individual instruction between teacher and student. Opportunities for teacher aides may be better in the South or West than in the Northeast and North Central regions of the country.

The field of special education—working with students with specific learning, emotional, or physical concerns or disabilities—is expected to grow rapidly, and more aides will be needed in these areas. Teacher aides who want to work with young children in day care or extended day programs will have a relatively easy time finding jobs because more children are attending these programs while their parents are at work.

This job has a high turnover rate. Many aides leave to return to school or pursue other careers. In fact, most openings in the field are to replace workers who leave. It is important to note, however, that school funding is highly dependent on the health of the economy and the budgets of states, municipalities, and federal government programs. When education expenditures are reduced, teacher aides may be among the first to be laid off.

Earnings

Teacher aides are usually paid on an hourly basis and usually only during the nine or ten months of the school calendar. Salaries vary depending upon the school or district, region of the country, and the duties the aides perform. Some teacher aides may earn as little as minimum wage while others earn up to $15.00 an hour. According to a survey conducted by the Educational Research Service, hourly wages average about $9.04 an hour for aides involved in teaching activities. Non-teaching aides average about $8.52 an hour.

Benefits such as health insurance and vacation or sick leave may also depend upon the school or district as well as the number of hours an aide works. Many schools employ aides only part time and do not offer such benefits. Other teacher aides may receive the same health and pension benefits as the teachers in their school and be covered under collective bargaining agreements. About thirty percent of all teacher aides belong to unions such as the American Federation of Teachers and the National Education Association.

Conditions
of Work

Teacher aides may work in either well-kept schools or those needing painting and repairs and having unpredictable heating or cooling systems. Teacher aides may work outdoors in good weather. Those in elementary schools may spend some time kneeling, while all aides do a great deal of standing and walking. Although this work is not physically strenuous, working closely with children can be stressful and tiring.

Because schools close during summer months, most aides work about ten months out of the year. They may, however, use this time to continue their own education or find other jobs for extra income. Some private and religious schools and day care centers hire teacher aides to work in summer programs, day camps, and Bible schools.

Sources of Additional Information

American Federation of Teachers, Paraprofessionals and School-Related Personnel
555 New Jersey Avenue, NW
Washington, DC 20001
Tel: 202-879-4400

For a brochure on careers in childhood education, send a self-addressed, stamped envelope to:

Association for Childhood Education International
11501 Georgia Avenue, Suite 315
Wheaton, MD 20902-1924

National Resource Center for Paraprofessionals in Special Education
CASE-SUNY
25 West 43 Street, Room 620
New York, NY 10036
Tel: 212-642-2948

Technical Support Specialists

Definition

Technical support specialists investigate and resolve problems in computer functioning. They listen to customer complaints, walk them through possible solutions, and write technical reports based on the event. Specialists differ in two ways—whom they assist and what they fix. Regardless of specialty, all technical support specialists must be very knowledgeable about the products they work with and be able to communicate effectively with users from different technical backgrounds. They must be patient with frustrated users and be able to perform well under stress. Technical support is basically like solving mysteries, so support specialists should enjoy the challenge of problem solving and have strong analytical thinking skills.

Nature of the Work

It is relatively rare today to find a business that does not rely on computers for at least something. Some use them heavily and in many areas, from daily operations, like employee time clocks; to monthly projects, like payroll and sales accounting; to major reengineering of fundamental business procedures, like form automation in government agencies, insurance companies, and banks. Once employees get used to performing their work on computers, they soon can barely remember how they ever got along without them. As more companies become increasingly reliant on computers, it becomes increasingly critical that they function properly all the time. Any computer down time can be extremely expensive, in work left undone and sales not made, for example. When employees experience problems with their computer system, they call technical support for help. Technical support specialists investigate and resolve problems in computer functioning.

Technical support can generally be broken up into at least three distinct areas, although these distinctions vary greatly with the nature, size, and scope of the company. The three most prevalent areas are user support, technical support, and microcomputer support. Most technical support specialists perform some combination of the tasks explained below.

Technical support specialists vary in two ways—whom they assist and what they fix. Some specialists exclusively help private users, others are on call to a major corporate buyer. Some work with computer hardware and software, while others help with printer, modem, and fax problems. *User support specialists*, also known as *help desk specialists*, work directly with users themselves, who call when they experience problems. The support specialist listens carefully to the user's explanation of the precise nature of the problem and the commands entered that seem to have caused it. Some companies have developed complex software that allows the support specialist to enter a description of the problem and wait for computer suggestions about what the user should do.

The initial goal is to isolate the source of the problem. If user error is the culprit, they explain procedures related to the program in question, whether graphics, database, word processing, or printing. If the problem seems to lie in the hardware or software, they ask the user to enter certain commands in order to see if the computer makes the appropriate response. When it doesn't, the support specialist is closer to isolating the cause. The support specialist consults supervisors, programmers, and others in order to outline the cause and possible solutions.

Some technical support specialists who work for computer companies are mainly involved with solving problems whose cause has been determined to lie in the computer system's operating system, hardware, or software. They make exhaustive use of resources, whether colleagues or books, and try to solve the problem through a variety of methods, including program modifications and the replacement of certain hardware or software.

Technical support specialists employed in the information systems department of large corporations do this kind of troubleshooting as well. They also oversee the daily operations of the various computer systems in the company. Sometimes they compare the system's work capacity to the actual daily workload in order to determine if upgrades are needed. In addition, they might help out other computer professionals in the company with modifying commercial software for their company's particular needs.

Microcomputer support specialists are responsible for preparing computers for delivery to a client, including installing the operating system and desired software. After the unit is installed at the customer's location, the support specialists might help train users on appropriate procedures and answer immediate questions they have. They help diagnose problems as they arise, transferring major concerns to other technical support specialists.

All technical support work must be well documented. Support specialists write detailed, technical reports on each and every problem they work on. They try to tie together different problems on the same software, so programmers can make adjustments that address all of them. Record keeping is crucial because designers, programmers, and engineers use technical support reports to revise current products and improve future ones. Some support specialists help write training manuals. They are often required to read trade magazines and company newsletters in order to keep up-to-date on their products and the field in general.

Requirements

A high school diploma is a minimum requirement for technical support specialists. Any technical courses, like computer science, schematic drawing, or electronics can help students develop the logical and analytical thinking skills necessary to be successful in this field. Courses in math and science are also valuable for this reason. Since technical support specialists have to deal with both computer programmers on the one hand and computer users who may not know anything about computers on the other, interested high school students should take English and

speech classes to improve their communications skills, both verbal and written.

Technical support is a field as old as computer technology itself, so it might seem odd that post-secondary programs in this field are not more common or standardized. The reason why not is relatively simple—formal education curricula cannot keep up with the changes, nor can they provide specific training on individual products. Some large corporations might consider educational background, both as a way to weed out applicants and to insure a certain level of proficiency. Most major computer companies, however, look for energetic individuals who demonstrate a willingness and ability to learn new things quickly and who have general computer knowledge. These employers count on training new support specialists themselves.

Individuals interested in pursuing a job in this field should first determine what area of technical support appeals to them the most and then honestly assess their level of experience and knowledge. Large corporations often prefer to hire people with an associate's degree and some experience. They may also be impressed with commercial certification in a computer field, like networking. However, if they are hiring from within the company, they will probably weigh experience more heavily than education when making a final decision.

Employed individuals looking for a career change may want to commit themselves to a program of self-study in order to be qualified for technical support positions. Many computer professionals learn a lot of what they know by playing around on computers, reading trade magazines, and talking with computer professionals. Self-taught individuals should prepare themselves for how to effectively demonstrate knowledge and proficiency on the job or during an interview. Besides self-training, employed individuals should investigate the tuition reimbursement programs offered by their company.

High school students with no experience should seriously consider earning an associate's degree in a computer-related technology. The degree shows the prospective employer that the applicant has attained a certain level of proficiency with computers and has the intellectual ability to learn technical processes, a promising sign for success on the job.

There are many computer technology programs that lead to an associate's degree. A specialization in PC support and administration is very applicable to technical support.

Most computer professionals eventually need to go back to school to earn a bachelor's degree in order to keep themselves competitive in the job market and prepare themselves for promotion to other computer fields.

Technical support specialists should be patient, enjoy challenges of problem solving, and think logically. They should work well under stress and demonstrate effective communications skills. Working in a field that changes rapidly, they should be naturally curious and enthusiastic about learning new technologies as they are developed.

Opportunities for Experience & Exploration

Interested high school students should try to organize a career day with an employed technical support specialist. Local computer repair shops that offer technical support service might be a good place to look. Otherwise, students should contact major corporations, computer companies, and even the central office of their school system.

Students interested in any computer field should start working and playing on computers as much as possible; many working computer professionals became computer hackers at a very young age. Students can surf the Internet and other on-line services. They can read computer magazines and join school or community computer clubs.

Students might also attend a computer technology course at a local technical/vocational school. This would give them hands-on exposure to typical technical support training. In addition, if students experience problems with their own hardware or software, they should call technical support, paying close attention to how the support specialist handles the call and asking as many questions as he or she has time to answer.

Methods of Entering

Most technical support positions are considered entry-level. They are found mainly in computer companies and large corpora-

tions. Individuals interested in obtaining a job in this field should scan the classified ads for openings in local businesses and may want to work with an employment agency for help finding out about opportunities. Since many job openings are publicized by word of mouth, it is also very important to speak with as many working computer professionals as possible. They tend to be aware of job openings before anyone else and may be able to offer a recommendation to the hiring committee.

If students of computer technology are seeking a position in technical support, they should work closely with their school's placement office. Many area employers inform placement offices of openings before they run ads in the paper. In addition, placement office staff are generally very helpful with resume and interviewing techniques.

If an employee wants to make a career change into technical support, he or she should contact human resources or speak directly with appropriate management. In companies that are expanding their computing systems, it is often helpful for management to know that current employees would be interested in growing in a computer-related direction. They may even be willing to finance additional education.

Advancement

Technical support specialists who demonstrate leadership skills and a strong aptitude for the work may be promoted to a supervisory position within the technical support department. Supervisors are responsible for the more complicated problems that arise, as well as some administrative duties like scheduling, interviewing, and job assignments.

Further promotion requires additional education. Some technical support specialists may opt to become commercially certified in computer networking so that they can install, maintain, and repair computer networks. Others may prefer to pursue a bachelor's degree in computer science, either full-time or part-time. The range of careers available to college graduates is widely varied. *Software engineers* analyze industrial, business, and scientific problems and develop software programs to handle them effectively. *Quality assurance engineers* design automated quality assurance tests for new software applications. *Systems analysts* study the broad computing picture for a company or a group of companies in order to determine the best way to organize the computer systems.

There are limited opportunities for technical support specialists to be promoted into managerial positions. This would require additional education in business, but would probably also depend on the individual's advanced computer knowledge.

Employment Outlook

The U.S. Department of Labor predicts that technical support specialists will be one of the fastest growing of all occupations through the year 2006. The U.S. Department of Labor forecasts huge growth—about 115 percent—of additional support jobs through the year 2006. Every time a new computer product is released on the market or another system is installed, there will unavoidably be problems, whether from user error or technical difficulty. Therefore, there will always be a need for technical support specialists to solve the problems. Since technology changes so rapidly, it is very important for these professionals to keep up-to-date on advances. They should read trade magazines, surf the Internet, and talk with colleagues in order to know what is happening on the cutting edge.

Since some companies stop offering technical support on old products or applications after a designated time, the key is to be technically flexible. This is important for another reason as well. While the industry as a whole will require more technical support specialists in the future, it may be the case that certain computer companies go out of business. It can be a volatile industry for start-ups, or young companies dedicated to the development of one product. So technical support specialists interested in working for computer companies should consider living in those areas where many such companies are clustered. In this way, it will be easier to find another job if necessary.

Earnings

Technical support specialist jobs are plentiful in areas where clusters of computer companies are located, such as Northern California and Seattle, Washington. According to the Robert Half International, Inc, the average techni-

cal support specialists earns between $25,000 to $36,500 a year. Those with more education, responsibility, and expertise, have the potential to earn much more.

Most technical support specialists work for companies that offer a full range of benefits, including health insurance, paid vacation, and sick leave. Smaller service or start-up companies may hire support specialists on a contractual basis.

Conditions of Work

Technical support specialists work in comfortable business environments. They generally work regular, forty-hour weeks. For certain products, however, they may be asked to work evenings or weekends or at least be on call during those times in case of emergencies. If they work for a service company, they may be required to travel to the client's site and log in overtime hours.

Technical support work can be stressful since specialists often deal with frustrated users who may be difficult to work with. Communication problems with people less technically qualified may also be a source of frustration. Patience and understanding are essential to avoiding these problems.

Technical support specialists are expected to work quickly and efficiently and be able to perform under pressure. The ability to do this requires thorough technical expertise and keen analytical ability.

Sources of Additional Information

For information about technical support careers, contact:

The Association for Computing
1515 Broadway
New York, NY 10036
Tel: 212-869-7440
Email: acmhelp@acm.org
WWW: http://www.info.acm.org/

IEEE Computer Society
1730 Massachusetts Avenue, NW
Washington, DC 20036
Tel: 202-371-0101
WWW: http://www.ieee.org

Tour Guides

Definition

Tour guides plan and oversee travel arrangements and accommodations for groups of tourists. They assist travelers with questions or problems and may provide travelers with itineraries of their proposed travel route and plans. Tour guides research their destinations thoroughly so that they can handle any unforeseen situation that may occur.

Nature of the Work

Acting as knowledgeable companions and chaperons, tour guides escort groups of tourists to different cities and countries. Their job is to make sure that the passengers in a group tour enjoy an interesting and safe trip. To do this, they have to know a great deal about their travel destination and about the interests, knowledge, and expectations of the people on the tour.

One basic responsibility of tour guides is handling all the details of a trip prior to departure. They may schedule airline flights, bus trips, or train trips, as well as book cruises, house boats, or car rentals. They also research area hotels and other lodgings for the group and make reservations in advance. If anyone in the group has unique requirements, such as a specialized diet or a need for wheelchair accessibility, the tour guide will work to meet these requests.

Tour guides plan itineraries and daily activities, keeping in mind the interests of the group. For example, a group of music lovers visiting Vienna may wish to see the many sites of musical history there, as well as attend a performance by that city's orchestra. In addition to sight-seeing tours, guides may make arrangements in advance for special exhibits, dining experiences, and side trips. Alternate outings are sometimes planned in case of inclement weather conditions.

The second major responsibility of tour guides is, of course, the tour itself. Here, they must make sure all aspects of transportation, lodging, and recreation meet the itinerary as it was planned. They must see to it that travelers' baggage and personal effects are loaded and handled properly. If the tour includes meals and trips to local establishments, the guide must make sure that each passenger is on time for the various arrivals and departures.

Tour guides provide the people in their groups with interesting information on the locale and alert them to special sights. Tour guides become familiar with the history and significance of places through research and previous visits and endeavor to make the visit as entertaining and informative as possible. They may speak the native language or hire an interpreter so as to get along well with the local people. They are also familiar with local customs so their group will not offend anyone unknowingly. They see that the group stays together so that they do not miss their transportation arrangements or get lost. Guides may also arrange free time for travelers to pursue their individual interests, although time frames and common meeting points for regrouping are established in advance.

Even with thorough preparation, unexpected occurrences can arise on any trip and threaten to ruin everyone's good time. Tour guides must be resourceful to handle these surprises, such as when points of interest are closed or accommodations turn out to be unacceptable. They must be familiar with an area's resources so that they can help in emergencies such as an ill passenger or lost personal items. They often intercede on their travelers' behalf when any questions or problems arise regarding currency, restaurants, customs, or necessary identification.

Requirements

Although tour guides do not need a college education, they should at least have a high school diploma. Courses such as speech, communications, art, sociology, anthropology, political science, and literature often prove beneficial. Some tour guides study foreign languages and cultures, as well as geography, history, and architecture.

Some cities have professional schools that offer curricula in the travel industry. Such training may take nine to twelve months and offer job placement services. Some two- and four- year colleges offer tour guide training that lasts from six to eight weeks. Community colleges may offer programs in tour escort training. Programs such as these often may be taken on a part-time basis. Classes may include world geography, psychology, human relations, and communication courses. Sometimes students go on field trips themselves to gain experience. Some travel agencies and tour companies offer their own training so that their tour guides may receive instruction that complements the tour packages the company offers.

Tour guides are outgoing, friendly, and confident people. They are aware of the typical travelers' needs and the kinds of questions and concerns they might have. Tour guides are comfortable being in charge of large groups of people and have good time-management skills. They need to be resourceful and able to adapt to different environments. They are also fun-loving and know how to make others feel at ease in unfamiliar surroundings. Tour guides should enjoy working with people as much as they enjoy traveling.

Opportunities for Experience & Exploration

One way to become more familiar with the responsibilities of this job is to accompany local tours. Many cities have their own historical societies and museums that offer tours, as well as opportunities to volunteer. To appreciate what is involved with speaking in front of groups and the kind of research that may be necessary for leading tours, students may prepare speeches or presentations for class or local community groups.

Methods of Entering

A person interested in a career as a tour guide may begin as a guide for a museum or state park. This would be a good introduction to handling groups of people, giving lectures on points of interest or exhibits, and developing confidence and leadership qualities. Zoos, theme parks, historical sites, or local walking tours often need volunteers or part-time employees to work in their information centers, offer visitors directions, and answer a variety of inquiries. When openings occur, it is common for part-time workers to move into full-time positions.

Travel agencies, tour bus companies, and park districts often need additional help during the summer months when the travel season is in full swing. Societies and organizations for architecture and natural history, as well as other cultural groups, often train and employ guides. Students interested in working as tour guides for these types of groups should submit applications directly to the directors of personnel or managing directors.

Advancement

Tour guides gain experience by handling more complicated trips. Some workers may advance through specialization, such as tours to specific countries or to multiple destinations. Some tour guides choose to open their own travel agencies or work for wholesale tour companies, selling trip packages to individuals or retail tour companies.

Some tour guides become *travel writers* and report on exotic destinations for magazines and newspapers. Other guides may decide to work in the corporate world and plan travel arrangements for company executives. With the further development of the global economy, many different jobs have become available for people who know foreign languages and cultures.

Employment Outlook

Because of the many different travel opportunities for business, recreation, and education, there will be a significant need for tour guides through the year 2006. This demand is due in part to the fact that when the economy is strong—which it is currently—people earn more and are able to spend more on travel.

Tours for special interests, such as to ecologically significant areas and wilderness destinations, continue to grow in popularity. Although certain seasons are more popular for travel than others, well-trained tour guides can keep busy all year long.

Another area of tourism that is on the upswing is inbound tourism. Many foreign travelers view the United States as a dream destination, with tourist spots such as Hollywood, Disney World, and Yellowstone National Park drawing millions of foreign visitors each year. Job opportunities in inbound tourism—guiding foreign visitors through famous American tourist sites—will likely be more plentiful than those guiding Americans in foreign locations. The best opportunities in inbound tourism are in large cities with international airports and in areas with a large amount of tourist traffic. Opportunities will also be better for those guides who speak foreign languages.

Aspiring tour guides should keep in mind that this field is highly competitive. Tour guide jobs, because of the obvious benefits, are highly sought after, and the beginning job seeker may find it difficult to break into the business. It is also important to remember that the travel and tourism industry is affected by the overall economy. When the economy is depressed, people have less money to spend and, therefore, travel less.

Earnings

Tour guides may find that they have peak and slack periods of the year that correspond to vacation and travel seasons. Many tour guides, however, work eight months of the year. Salaries range from $9.75 to $20.00 an hour. Experienced guides with managerial responsibilities can earn up to $65,000 a year, including gratuities. According to *U.S. News & World Report*, the average salary for an entry-level inbound tour guide is $20,000, with average mid-level earnings approximately $35,000 per year. The most experienced guides can earn as much as $75,000 annually.

Guides receive their meals and accommodations free while conducting a tour, as well as a daily stipend to cover their personal expenses. Salaries and benefits vary depending upon the tour operators that employ guides and the location they are employed in. Generally, the Great Lakes, Mid-Atlantic, Southeast, and Southern regions of the country offer the highest compensation.

Tour guides very often receive paid vacations as part of their fringe benefits package; some may also receive sick pay and health insurance as well. Some companies may offer profit sharing and bonuses. They often receive discounts from hotels, airlines, and transportation companies in appreciation for repeat business.

Conditions of Work

The key word in the tour guide profession is variety. Most tour guides work in offices while they make travel arrangements and handle general business, but once on the road they experience a wide range of accommodations, conditions, and situations. Tours to distant cities involve maneuvering through busy and confusing airports. Side trips may involve bus rides, train transfers, or private car rentals, all with varying degrees of comfort and reliability. Package trips that encompass seeing a number of foreign countries may require the guide to speak a different language in each city.

The constant feeling of being on the go, plus the responsibility of leading a large group of people, can sometimes be stressful. Unexpected events and uncooperative people have the capacity to ruin part of a trip for everyone involved, including the guide. However, the thrill of travel, discovery, and meeting new people can be so rewarding that all the negatives can be forgotten (or eliminated by pre-planning on the next trip).

Sources of Additional Information

American Society of Travel Agents
1101 King Street, Suite 200
Alexandria, VA 22314
Tel: 703-739-2782
Email: kristil@astahq.com
WWW: http://www.astanet.com

For general information on the career of tour guide, as well as a listing of tour operators who are members of the association, contact:

National Tourism Foundation & National Tour Association
546 East Main Street
Lexington, KY 40508
Tel: 800-682-8886
WWW: http://www.ntaonline.com

For information regarding its certification program and other general information concerning a career as a tour guide, contact:

The Professional Guides Association of America
2416 South Eads Street
Arlington, VA 22202
Tel: 703-892-5757

Travel Educational Center
One Westbrook Center, Suite 200
Westchester, IL 60154
Tel: 800-945-2220
Email: tec@ultranet.com

Travel Agents

Definition

Travel agents assist individuals or groups who will be traveling, by planning their itineraries, making transportation, hotel, and tour reservations, obtaining or preparing tickets, and performing related services.

Nature of the Work

The travel agent may work as a salesperson, travel consultant, tour organizer, travel guide, bookkeeper, or small business executive. If the agent operates a one-person office, he or she usually performs all of these functions. Other travel agents work in offices with dozens of employees, which allows them to specialize in certain areas. In such offices, one staff member may become an authority on sea cruises, another may work on trips to the Far East, and a third may develop an extensive knowledge of either low-budget or luxury trips. In some cases, travel agents are employed by national or international firms and can draw upon very extensive resources.

As salespeople, travel agents must be able to motivate people to take advantage of their services. Travel agents study their customers' interests, learn where they have traveled, appraise their financial resources and available time, and present a selection of travel options. Customers are then able to choose how and where they want to travel with a minimum of effort.

Travel agents consult a variety of published and computer-based sources for information on air transportation departure and arrival times, air fares, and hotel ratings and accommodations. They often base their recommendations on their own travel experiences or those of colleagues or clients. Travel agents may visit hotels, resorts, and restaurants to rate their comfort, cleanliness, and quality of food and service.

As travel consultants, agents give their clients suggestions regarding travel plans and itineraries, information on transportation alternatives, and advice on the available accommodations and rates of hotels and motels. They also explain and help with passport and visa regulations, foreign currency and exchange, climate and wardrobe, health requirements, customs regulations, baggage and accident insurance, traveler's checks or letters of credit, car rentals, tourist attractions, and welcome or escort services.

Many travel agents only sell tours that are developed by other organizations. The most skilled agents, however, often organize tours on a wholesale basis. This involves developing an itinerary, contracting a knowledgeable person to lead the tour, making tentative reservations for transportation, hotels, and side trips, publicizing the tour through descriptive brochures, advertisements, and other travel agents, scheduling reservations, and handling last-minute problems. Sometimes tours are arranged at the specific request of a group or to meet a client's particular needs.

In addition to other duties, travel agents may serve as tour guides, leading trips ranging from one week to six months to locations around the world. Agents often find tour leadership a useful way to gain personal travel experience. It also gives them the chance to become thoroughly acquainted with the people in the tour group, who may then use the agent to arrange future trips or recommend the agent to friends and relatives. Tour leaders are usually reimbursed for all their expenses or receive complimentary transportation and lodgings. Most travel agents, however, arrange for someone to cover for them at work during their absence, which may make tour leadership prohibitive for self-employed agents.

Agents serve as bookkeepers to handle the complex pattern of transportation and hotel reservations that each trip entails. They work directly with airline, steamship, railroad, bus, and car rental companies. They make direct contact with hotels and sight-seeing organizations or work indirectly through a receptive operator in the city involved. These arrangements require a great deal of accuracy, because mistakes could result in a client being left stranded in a foreign or remote area. After reservations are made, agents write up or obtain tickets, write out itineraries, and send out bills for the reservations involved. They also send out confirmations to airlines, hotels, and other companies.

Travel agents must promote their services. They present slides or movies to social and special interest groups, arrange advertising displays, and suggest company-sponsored trips to business managers.

Requirements

Travel courses are available from certain colleges, private vocational schools, and adult education programs in public high schools. Some colleges and universities grant bachelor's and master's degrees in travel and tourism. Although college training is not required for work as a travel agent, it can be very helpful and is expected to become increasingly important for these workers in the future. It is predicted that in the future most agents will be college graduates. Travel schools provide basic reservation training and other training related to travel agents' functions, which is helpful but not required.

A liberal arts or business administration background is recommended for college students interested in this field. Useful liberal arts courses include foreign languages, geography, English, history, anthropology, political science, art and music appreciation, and literature. Pertinent business courses include transportation, business law, hotel management, marketing, office management, and accounting. As in many other fields, computer skills are increasingly important. High school students desiring to enter the field of travel should study English, social studies, business mathematics, typing, computers, and foreign languages.

To be able to sell passage on various types of transportation, a travel agent must be approved by the conferences of carriers involved. These are the Airlines Reporting Corporation, the International Air Transport Association, Cruise Lines International Association, and the Rail Travel Promotion

Agency. To sell tickets for these individual conferences, the agent must be clearly established in the travel business and have a good personal and business background. Not all travel agents are authorized to sell passage by all of the above conferences. Naturally, those who wish to sell the widest range of services should seek affiliation with all four.

Currently, travel agents are not required to be federally licensed, except in the state of Rhode Island. However, Ohio, California, and Hawaii do require their travel agents to be registered. In California, agents not approved by a corporation must be licensed. The American Society of Travel Agents (ASTA) certifies those agents who complete a travel and tourism course at Baruch College.

The primary requisite for success in the travel field is a sincere interest in travel. An agent's knowledge of and travel experiences with major tourist centers, various hotels, and local customs and points of interest make that person a more effective and convincing source of assistance. Yet the work of travel agents is not one long vacation. They operate in a highly competitive industry.

Travel agents must be able to make quick and accurate use of transportation schedules and tariffs. They must be able to handle addition and subtraction quickly. Almost all agents make use of computers to get the very latest information on rates and schedules and to make reservations.

Most travel agents work with a wide range of personalities, so their skills in psychology and diplomacy are always in use. They must also be able to generate enthusiasm among their customers and be resourceful in solving any problems that might arise. A knowledge of foreign languages is useful, because many customers come from other countries and agents are in frequent contact with foreign hotels and travel agencies.

Opportunities for Experience & Exploration

Any type of part-time experience with a travel agency would be helpful for those interested in this career. A small agency may welcome help during peak travel seasons or when an agent is away from the office. If their high school or junior college arranges career conferences, students may be able to invite a speaker from the travel industry. Visits to local travel agents also provide helpful information.

Examining the various travel magazines should provide a broader picture of the field and some of its current issues and newest developments. Students who are able to travel will, of course, learn some of the joys and problems of travel.

Methods of Entering

Young people seeking careers in the travel field usually begin by working for a company involved with transportation and tourism. Fortunately, a number of positions exist that are particularly appropriate for young people and those with limited work experience. Airlines, for example, hire flight attendants, reservation agents, and ticket clerks. Railroads and cruise line companies also have clerical positions; the rise in their popularity in recent years has resulted in more job opportunities. Those with travel experience may secure positions as tour guides. Organizations and companies with extensive travel operations may hire employees whose main responsibility is making travel arrangements.

Since travel agencies tend to have relatively small staffs, most openings are filled as a result of direct application and personal contact. In evaluating the merits of various travel agencies, job seekers may wish to note whether the agency's owner belongs to ASTA. This trade group may also help in several other ways. It sponsors adult night school courses in travel agency operation in some metropolitan areas. It also offers a fifteen-lesson travel agency correspondence course. Also available, for a modest charge, is a travel agency management kit containing information that is particularly helpful to people considering setting up their own agencies. ASTA's publication Travel News includes a classified advertising section listing available positions and agencies for sale.

Advancement

Advancement opportunities within the travel field are limited to growth in terms of business volume or extent of specialization. Successful agents, for example, may hire additional employees or set up branch offices. A travel agency worker who has held his or her position for a while may be promoted to become a travel assistant. Travel assistants are responsible for answering general questions about transportation, providing current cost of hotel accommodations, and providing other valid information.

Travel bureau employees may decide to go into business for themselves. Agents may show their professional status by belonging to ASTA, which requires its members to have three years of satisfactory travel agent experience and approval by at least two carrier conferences.

In addition to the regular travel business, a number of travel jobs are available with oil companies, automobile clubs, and transportation companies. Some jobs in travel are on the staffs of state and local governments seeking to encourage tourism.

Employment Outlook

About 142,000 people are currently employed as travel agents. About one in ten travel agents is self-employed. Although future prospects in the travel field will depend to some degree on the state of the economy, the travel industry is expected to expand rapidly as more Americans travel for pleasure and business. New travel agencies will open and existing ones will expand, causing employment of these workers to grow faster than the average for all occupations through the year 2006. The U.S. Department of Labor estimates that the number of travel agents will increase by at least 77,000 by the year 2006. Many of the expected job openings will result from workers leaving the field due to retirement or other reasons.

Certain factors may hinder growth for travel agents. On-line computer systems now enable people to make their own travel reservations. Electronic ticketing and a reduction on commissions paid to travel agencies by the airline industry may also hinder the growth of the travel industry. Since these innovations are recent, their full effect on travel agents has not yet been determined.

Earnings

Travel agencies earn their income from commissions from airlines, cruise lines, car rental companies, hotels, and other entities with whom agencies do business. The rate of commission varies, depending on the type of sale, from 8 to 10 percent of the cost to the customer. Air travel commissions vary on both domestic and international flights. Cruise lines pay a commission on a sliding scale depending upon the season. Bus tours, sight-seeing trips, and resort hotels often pay a commission of 10 percent or higher. From these commissions, travel agencies pay employee salaries and overhead costs.

The enterprising agency will be able to supplement transportation and hotel sales by offering automobile rentals, travel books, baggage forwarding, currency exchange, gift services, house rentals, insurance, letters of credit, prepaid meals, traveler's checks, and transfers. Many of the companies supplying such services also offer commissions.

Employed travel agents may be hired either on a regular salary, paid entirely on a commission basis, or receive a salary plus a modified commission or bonus. Salaries of travel agents ranged from $16,400 to $32,600, with an average of $24,500 in 1996, according to the Bureau of Labor Statistics. Those with five years of experience earn an average of $22,300. Managers with ten years of experience may earn from $26,300 to over $32,600 annually. In addition to experience, location also determines agent salaries, with those operating in large cities earning more.

In addition to income, travel agents receive a number of attractive opportunities for personal travel. Major airlines and cruise lines, knowing that agents who have used their services may recommend them more highly, offer some trips to agents at only 25 percent of the usual cost. Occasionally, the opening of a new hotel, airline route, or resort area leads to free trips for agents, as these companies encourage agents to recommend them to customers. If they organize tours, agents may be able to take advantage of the fact that transportation carriers and hotels usually offer one free trip for every fifteen to twenty paid members of a travel group.

Conditions of Work

While this is an interesting and appealing occupation, the job of the travel agent is not as simple or glamorous as might be expected. Travel is a highly competitive field. Since almost every travel agent can offer the client the same service, agents must depend upon repeat customers for much of their business. Their reliability, courtesy, and effectiveness in past transactions will determine whether they will get repeat business.

Travel agents also work in an atmosphere of keen competition for referrals. They must resist direct pressure or indirect pressure from travel-related companies that have provided favors in the past (free trips, for example) and book all trips based only on the best interests of clients.

Most agents work a forty-hour week, although this frequently includes working a half-day on Saturday or an occasional evening. During busy seasons (typically from January through June) overtime may be necessary. Agents may receive additional salary for this work or be given compensatory time off.

As they gain experience, agents become more effective. One study revealed that 98 percent of all agents had more than three years' experience in some form of the travel field. Almost half had twenty years or more in this area.

Small travel agencies provide a smaller-than-average amount of fringe benefits such as retirement, medical, and life insurance plans. Self-employed agents tend to earn more than those who work for others, although the business risk is greater. Those who own their own businesses may experience large fluctuations in income because the travel business is extremely sensitive to swings in the economy.

Sources of Additional Information

■American Society of Travel Agents
1101 King Street, Suite 200
Alexandria, VA 22314
Tel: 703-739-2782

For information regarding certification, contact:

■The Institute of Certified Travel Agents
PO Box 812059
48 Linden Street
Wellesley, MA 02181-0012
Tel: 617-237-0280

■Society of Travel Agents in Government
6935 Wisconsin Avenue
Bethesda, MD 20815-6109

Truck Drivers

Definition

Truck drivers generally are distinguished by whether they drive a certain area or travel longer distances. *Local drivers*, also known as *short-haul drivers* or *pickup and delivery drivers*, operate trucks that transport materials, merchandise, and equipment within a limited area, usually a single city or metropolitan area. Local drivers may be responsible for loading and unloading their trucks. Sometimes, they are expected to make minor mechanical repairs in order to keep their trucks in working order.

Over-the-road drivers, also known as *long-distance drivers* or *tractor-trailer drivers*, haul freight over long distances in large trucks and tractor-trailer rigs that are usually diesel-powered. Depending on the specific operation, over-the-road drivers also load and unload the shipments and make minor repairs to vehicles.

Nature of the Work

Truckers drive trucks of all sizes, from small straight trucks and vans to tanker trucks and tractors with multiple trailers. The average tractor-trailer rig is no more than 102 inches wide, excluding the mirrors, and is 13 feet 6 inches tall and just under 70 feet in length. The engines in these vehicles range from 250 up to 600 horsepower.

Local truck drivers generally operate the smaller trucks and transport a variety of products. They may travel regular routes or routes that change as needed. Local drivers include delivery workers who supply fresh produce to grocery stores and drivers who deliver gasoline in tank trucks to gas stations. Other local truck drivers, such as those who keep stores stocked with baked goods, may sell their employer's products as well as deliver them to customers along a route. These drivers are known as route drivers or route-sales drivers.

Often local truck drivers receive their assignments and delivery forms from dispatchers at the company terminal each day.

Some drivers load goods or materials on their trucks, but in many situations dockworkers have already loaded the trucks in such a way that the unloading can be accomplished along the route with maximum convenience and efficiency.

Local drivers must be skilled at maneuvering their vehicles through the worst driving conditions, whether they are traffic-congested streets or rutted roads. The abilities to pull into tight parking spaces, negotiate narrow passageways, and back up to loading docks are essential.

Some drivers have helpers who travel with them and assist in unloading at delivery sites, especially if the loads are heavy or bulky or when there are many deliveries scheduled. Drivers of some heavy trucks, such as dump trucks and oil tank trucks, operate mechanical levers, pedals, and other devices that assist with loading and unloading cargo. Drivers of moving vans generally have a crew of helpers to aid in loading and unloading customers' household goods and office equipment.

Once a local driver reaches his or her destination, he or she sometimes obtains a signature acknowledging that the delivery has been made and may collect a payment from the customer. Some drivers serve as intermediaries between the company and its customers by responding to customer complaints and requests.

Each day, local drivers have to make sure that their deliveries have been made correctly. At the end of the day, they turn in their records and the money they have collected. Local drivers may also be responsible for doing routine maintenance on their trucks to keep them in good working condition. Otherwise, any mechanical problems are reported to the maintenance department for repair.

Over-the-road drivers operate tractor-trailers and other large trucks that are often diesel-powered. These drivers generally haul goods and materials over long distances and frequently drive at night. Whereas many other truck drivers spend a considerable portion of their time loading and unloading materials, over-the-road drivers spend most of their working time in actual driving.

At the terminal or warehouse where they receive their load, drivers get ready for long-distance runs by checking over the vehicle to make sure all the equipment and systems are functioning and that the truck is loaded properly and has on board the necessary fuel, oil, and safety equipment.

Some over-the-road drivers travel the same route repeatedly and on a regular schedule. Other companies require drivers to do unscheduled runs and work when dispatchers call with an available job. Some long-distance runs are short enough that drivers can get to the destination, remove the load from the trailer, replace it with another load, and return home all in one day. Many runs, however, take up to a week or longer, with various stops. Some companies assign two drivers to long runs, so that one can sleep while the other drives. This method ensures that the trip will take the shortest amount of time possible.

In addition to driving their trucks long distances, over-the-road drivers have other duties. They must inspect their vehicle before and after trips, prepare reports on accidents, and keep a daily log. They may load and unload some shipments or hire workers to help with these tasks at the destination. Drivers of long-distance moving vans, for example, do more loading and unloading work than most other long-haul drivers. Drivers of vehicle-transport trailer trucks move new automobiles or trucks from manufacturers to dealers and also have additional duties. At plants where the vehicles are made, transport drivers drive new vehicles onto the ramps of transport trailers. They secure the vehicles in place with chains and clamps to prevent them from swaying and rolling. After driving to the destination, the drivers remove the vehicles from the trailers.

Over-the-road drivers must develop a number of skills that differ from the skills needed for operating smaller trucks. Because trailer trucks vary in length and number of wheels, skilled operators of one type of trailer may need to undergo a short training period if they switch to a new type of trailer. Over-the-road drivers must be able to maneuver and judge the position of their trucks and must be able to back their huge trailers into precise positions.

Over-the-road and local drivers may be employed by either private carriers or for-hire carriers. Food store chains and manufacturing plants that transport their own goods are examples of private carriers. There are two kinds of for-hire carriers: trucking companies serving the general public (common carriers) and trucking firms transporting goods under contract to certain companies (contract carriers).

Drivers who work independently are known as owner-operators. They own their own vehicles and often do their own maintenance and repair work. They must find customers who need goods transported, perhaps through personal references or by advertising their services. There is now an "Internet truckstop" on the world wide web where drivers can advertise their services and companies can post locations of loads they need transported. Some independent drivers establish long-term contracts with just one or two clients, such as trucking companies.

Requirements

Truck drivers must meet federal requirements and any requirements established by the state where they are based. All drivers must obtain a state commercial driver's license. Applicants for commercial driver's licenses must pass tests of their knowledge and driving ability, and they must not have had a previous license suspended or revoked.

Truck drivers involved in interstate commerce must meet requirements of the U.S. Department of Transportation. They must be at least twenty-one years old and pass a physical examination that requires good vision and hearing, normal blood pressure, and normal use of arms and legs (unless the applicant qualifies for a waiver).

In addition to meeting standards set by the state and federal governments, drivers must learn skills appropriate for the kind of driving they do. In some companies, new employees can learn these skills informally from experienced drivers. They may ride with and watch other employees of the company or they may take a few hours of their own time to learn from an experienced driver. For jobs driving some kinds of trucks, companies require new employees to attend classes that range from a few days to several weeks. During this time, potential drivers learn company policies and procedures, as well as how to load, unload, and operate the trucks.

One of the best ways to prepare for a job driving large trucks is to take a tractor-trailer driver training course. These courses are offered at many vocational and technical schools and include instruction in driving under various road and traffic conditions, complying with laws and regulations, and inspecting trucks and freight. However, programs vary in the amount of actual driving experience they provide. Programs that are certified by the Professional Truck Driver Institute of America meet established guidelines for training and generally provide good preparation for drivers. Another way to determine whether programs are adequate is to check with local companies that hire drivers and ask for their recommendations. Completing a certified training program helps potential drivers learn specific skills, but it does not guarantee a job.

Vehicles and the freight inside trucks can represent a large investment to companies that employ truck drivers. Therefore, they seek to hire responsible and reliable drivers in order to protect their investment. For this reason many employers set various requirements of their own that exceed state and federal standards. For example, employers may require a high school diploma, several years of driving experience, a minimum age of twenty-five, the ability to lift heavy weights, annual physical examinations, and periodic screenings for drug use.

High school students who think that they are interested in working as a truck driver should take courses in driver training and automobile mechanics. In addition, some bookkeeping, mathematics and business courses will help a truck driver learn methods that help in keeping accurate records of customer transactions.

Many drivers work with little supervision, so they need to have a mature, responsible attitude toward their job. In jobs where drivers deal directly with company customers, it is especially important for the drivers to be pleasant, courteous, and able to communicate well with people. Helping a customer with a complaint can mean the difference between losing and keeping a client.

Many truck drivers are members of the International Brotherhood of Teamsters, Chauffeurs, Warehousemen and Helpers of Americas.

Opportunities for Experience & Exploration

High school students interested in becoming truck drivers may be able to gain experience by working as drivers' helpers during summer vacations or in part-time delivery jobs. Many people get useful experience in driving vehicles while they are serving in the armed forces. It may also be helpful to talk with employers of local or over-the-road truck drivers or with the drivers themselves.

The Internet provides a forum for prospective truck drivers to explore their career options. *Road King* a magazine for truckers, has a World Wide Web site at WWW: http://www.roadking.com, with a chat group called "the driver's lounge." Feature articles about the lives of truck drivers are posted regularly. There is also a truck driver's news group, WWW: misc.transport.trucking, where potential truck drivers can pose questions.

Methods of Entering

Most truck drivers hold other jobs before they become truck drivers. Some local drivers start as drivers' helpers, loading and unloading trucks and gradually taking over some driving duties. When a better driving position opens up, helpers who have shown they are reliable and responsible may be promoted. Members of the armed forces who have gained appropriate experience may get driving jobs when they are discharged.

Job seekers may apply directly to firms that use drivers. Listings of specific job openings are often posted at local offices of the state employment service and in the classified ads in newspapers. Many jobs, however, are not posted. Looking in the yellow pages under trucking and moving and storage can provide names of specific companies to solicit. Also, large manufacturers and retailing companies sometimes have their own fleets. Many telephone calls and letters may be required, but can lead to a potential employer. Personal visits, when appropriate, sometimes get the best results.

Prospective over-the-road drivers can gain commercial driving experience as local truck drivers and then attend a tractor-trailer driver training program. Driving an intercity bus or dump truck is also suitable experience for aspiring over-the-road truck drivers. Many newly hired long-distance drivers start by filling in for regular drivers or helping out when extra trips are necessary. They are assigned regular work when a job opens up. Some companies provide in-house training.

Advancement

Local truck drivers can advance by learning to drive specialized kinds of trucks or by switching to better schedules or other job conditions. Some may move into positions as dispatchers and, with sufficient experience, eventually become supervisors or terminal managers. Other local drivers decide to become over-the-road drivers to receive higher wages. A few local truck drivers with business ability and sufficient capital establish their own independent local trucking companies.

Many over-the-road drivers look forward to going into business for themselves by acquiring their own tractor-trailer rigs. This step requires a significant initial investment and a continuing good income to cover expenses. Like many other small business owners, independent drivers sometimes have a hard time financially. Those who are their own mechanics and have formal business training are in the best position to do well.

Some over-the-road drivers who stay with their employers advance by becoming safety supervisors, driver supervisors, or dispatchers.

Employment Outlook

The employment of truck drivers is expected to increase as fast as the average for all other occupations through the year 2006. This increase will be related to overall growth in the nation's economy and in the volume of freight moved by trucks, both locally and over long distances. Currently, there is a shortage of both local and over-the-road drivers. There were 3,050,000 truck drivers employed in 1996.

The need for trucking services is directly linked to the growth of the nation's economy. During economic downturns, when the pace of business slows, some drivers may receive fewer assignments and thus have lower earnings or they may be laid off. Truck drivers who are self employed suffer the most during these times. Drivers employed in some vital industries, such as food distribution, are less affected by an economic recession. Even though our rail system is a popular choice in transporting goods across the country, perishable items, such as fruits and vegetables, are best delivered by refrigerated trucks.

A large number of driver jobs become available each year. Most openings develop when experienced drivers transfer to other fields or leave the workforce entirely. Beginners are able to get many of these jobs. Some positions offer much better pay, hours, and working conditions than others. Competition is expected to remain strong for the more desirable jobs, and people who have the best training and experience will have an advantage.

Earnings

Wages of truck drivers vary according to their employer, size of the truck they drive, product being hauled, geographical region, and other factors.

Although some local truck drivers are guaranteed minimum or weekly wages, most are paid an hourly wage and receive extra compensation for overtime work. In contrast, long-distance drivers are usually paid by the mile at rates that depend on their employer, number of miles driven in a pay period, seniority, and type of truck they drive.

On average, truck drivers can expect earnings at least in the range of $8.56 to $14.64 per hour. Drivers who are employed by for-hire carriers have higher earnings than those who work independently or for private carriers. In 1996, the U.S. Department of Labor's Bureau of Labor Statistics reported a median hourly rate of $13.39. Tractor-trailer drivers usually have the highest earnings; average hourly pay generally increases with the size of the truck. Drivers in the South have lower earnings than those in the Northeast and West. The annual earnings of long-distance drivers can range from about $20,000 to well over twice that amount. Owner-operators have average earnings between $20,000 and $25,000 per year, after subtracting expenses.

In addition to their wages, the majority of truck drivers receive benefits, many of which are determined by agreements between their unions and company management. The benefits may include health insurance coverage, pension plans, paid vacation days, and work uniforms.

Conditions of Work

Although there is work for truck drivers in even the smallest towns, most jobs are located in and around larger metropolitan areas. About a third of all drivers work for for-hire carriers, and another third work for private carriers. Less than 10 percent are self-employed.

Even with modern improvements in cab design, driving trucks is often a tiring job. Although some local drivers work forty-hour weeks, many work eight hours a day, six days a week, or more. Some drivers, such as those who bring food to grocery stores, often work at night or very early in the morning. Drivers who must load and unload their trucks may do a lot of lifting, stooping, and bending.

It is common for over-the-road truck drivers to work at least fifty hours a week. However, federal regulations require that drivers cannot be on duty for more than sixty hours in any seven-day period. Furthermore, after drivers have driven for ten hours, they must be off duty for at least eight hours before they can drive again. Drivers often work the maximum allowed time to complete long runs in as little time as possible. In fact, most drivers drive ten to twelve hours per day and make sure they have proper rest periods. A driver usually covers between 550 and 650 miles daily. The sustained driving, including at night, can be fatiguing, boring, and sometimes very stressful, as when traffic or weather conditions are bad.

Local drivers may operate on schedules that easily allow a social and family life, but long-distance drivers often find that difficult. They may spend a considerable amount of time away from their homes and families, including weekends and holidays. After they try it, many people find they do not want this way of life.

On the other hand, some people love the lifestyle of the over-the-road driver. Many families are able to find ways to work around the schedule of a truck driving spouse. In some cases, the two people assigned to a long-distance runs are a husband and wife team. Although the romantic notion of a truck driver being master of his or her own destiny is far from the reality of everyday life, the allure of the open road and the opportunity to see the country make this career attractive and satisfying to many.

Sources of Additional Information

For further information and literature about a career as a truck driver, contact the following organizations:

■**American Trucking Associations**
Office of Public Affairs
2200 Mill Road
Alexandria, VA 22314
Tel: 703-838-1700
WWW: http://www.trucking org

■**International Brotherhood of Teamsters, Chauffeurs, Warehousemen, and Helpers of America**
25 Louisiana Avenue, NW
Washington, DC 20001
Tel: 202-624-6800

■**Professional Truck Driver Institute of America, Inc.**
8788 Elk Grove Boulevard
Elk Grove, CA 95624
Tel: 916-686-5146

Veterinarians

Definition

The *veterinarian*, or *doctor of veterinary medicine*, diagnoses and controls animal diseases, treats sick and injured animals medically and surgically, prevents transmission of animal diseases, and advises owners on proper care for pets and livestock. Veterinarians are dedicated to the protection of the health and welfare of all animals and to society as a whole.

Nature of the Work

Veterinarians ensure a safe food supply by maintaining the health of food animals. They also protect the public from residues of herbicides, pesticides, and antibiotics in food. Veterinarians are involved in wildlife preservation and conservation, and use their knowledge to increase food production through genetics, animal feed production, and preventive medicine.

In North America, about 80 percent of veterinarians are in private clinical practice. Although some veterinarians treat all kinds of animals, about half limit their practice to companion animals such as dogs, cats, and birds.

Of the veterinarians in private practice, about 11 percent work mainly with horses, cattle, pigs, sheep, goats, and poultry. Today, a veterinarian may be treating llamas, catfish, or ostriches as well. Others are employed by wildlife management groups, zoos, aquariums, ranches, feed lots, fish farms, and animal shelters.

Twenty percent of veterinarians work in public and corporate sectors. Many veterinarians are employed by city, county, state, provincial, or federal governmental agencies that investigate, test for, and control diseases in companion animals, livestock, and poultry that affect both animal and human health.

Veterinarians are utilized by pharmaceutical and biomedical research firms to develop, test, and supervise the production of drugs, chemicals, and biological products such as antibiotics and vaccines that are designed for human and animal use. Some veterinarians are employed in management, technical sales and services, and marketing in agribusiness, pet food companies, and pharmaceutical companies. Still other veterinarians are engaged in research and teaching at veterinary and human medical schools, working with racetracks or animal-related enterprises, while others work within the military, public health corps, and space agencies.

Other veterinarians in private clinical practice become specialists in surgery, anesthesiology, dentistry, internal medicine, ophthalmology, or radiology. Many veterinarians also pursue advanced degrees in the basic sciences such as anatomy, microbiology, physiology, and a parasitology. Veterinarians who seek specialty board certification in one of the twenty specialty fields must complete a two- to five-year residency program and must pass an additional examination. Some veterinarians combine their degree in veterinary medicine with a degree in business (MBA) or law (JD).

Veterinarians are employed in various branches of federal, state, provincial, county, or city government. The U.S. Department of Agriculture has opportunities for veterinarians in the food safety inspection service and the animal and plant health inspection service, notably in the areas of food hygiene and safety, animal welfare, animal disease control, and research. Agencies in the U.S. Department of Agriculture utilize veterinarians in positions related to research on diseases transmissible from animal to human beings and on acceptance and the use of drugs for treatment or prevention of diseases. Veterinarians also are employed by the Environmental Protection Agency to deal with public health and environmental risks to the human population.

Requirements

All states and the District of Columbia require that veterinarians be licensed to practice private clinical medicine. To obtain a license, applicants must have a doctor of veterinary medicine (D.V.M.) degree from an accredited or approved college of veterinary medicine. They must also pass one or more national examinations and an examination in the state in which they are applying.

A veterinarian does not have to complete an internship in order to practice clinical medicine. Some states issue licenses without further examination to veterinarians already licensed by another state. Approximately half of the states require veterinarians to attend continuing education courses in order to maintain their licenses. Veterinarians may be employed by a government agency (such as the U.S. Department of Agriculture) or at some academic institution without having a state license. For positions in research and teaching, a master's degree or Ph.D. is usually required.

The D.V.M. degree requires a minimum of six years of college after graduation from high school, consisting of at least two years of preveterinary study that emphasizes physical and biological sciences and a four-year veterinary program. It is possible to obtain preveterinary training in a junior college. Most preveterinary students, however, enroll in four-year colleges. In addition to academic instruction, veterinary education includes clinical experience in diagnosing disease and treating animals, performing surgery, and performing laboratory work in anatomy, biochemistry, and other scientific and medical subjects.

In 1997, all twenty-seven colleges of veterinary medicine in the United States were accredited by the Council of Veterinary Medicine of the American Veterinary Medical Association (AVMA). Each college of veterinary medicine has its own preveterinary requirements, which typically include basic language arts, social sciences, humanities, mathematics, chemistry, and the biological and physical sciences.

Application for admission to a school of veterinary medicine should be filled out well in advance of April 1 of the year in which the prospective student hopes to enroll. Admission is highly competitive. Applicants usually must have grades of "B" or better, especially in the sciences. Applicants must take the Veterinary Aptitude Test, Medical College Admission Test, or the Graduate Record Examination. Fewer than half of the applicants to schools of veterinary medicine may be admitted, due to small class sizes and limited facilities. Most colleges give preference to candidates with animal- or veterinary-related experience. Colleges usually give preference to in-state applicants because most colleges of veterinary medicine are state-supported. There are regional agreements in which states without veterinary schools send students to designated regional schools. The veterinary medicine program involves many hours of study, which makes outside employment to handle expenses difficult for students with limited financial resources. There are, however, various scholarship programs offered to qualified students who need financial help.

For the high school student who is interested in admission to a school of veterinary medicine, a college-preparatory course with a strong emphasis on science is a wise choice.

Individuals who are interested in veterinary medicine should have an enquiring mind and keen powers of observation. Aptitude and interest in the biological sciences are important. Veterinarians need a lifelong interest in scientific learning as well as a liking and understanding of animals. Veterinarians should be able to meet, talk, and work well with a variety of people. An ability to communicate with the animal owner is as important in a veterinarian as are diagnostic skills of observation.

Veterinarians use state-of-the-art medical equipment, such as electron microscopes, laser surgery, radiation therapy, and ultrasound, to diagnose animal diseases and to treat sick or injured animals. Although manual dexterity and physical stamina are often required, especially for farm vets, important roles in veterinary medicine can be adapted for veterinarians with disabilities.

Veterinarians may have to euthanize (that is, "humanely kill") an animal that is very sick or severely injured and cannot get well. When an animal such as a beloved pet dies, the veterinarian must deal with the owner's grief and loss.

Opportunities for Experience & Exploration

High school students interested in becoming veterinarians may find part-time or volunteer work on a farm, in small-animal clinics, pet shops, animal shelters, or research laboratories. Participation in extracurricular activities such as 4-H are good ways to learn about the care of animals. Such experience is important because, as already noted, many schools of veterinary medicine have established experience with animals as a criterion for admission to their programs.

Methods of Entering

The only way to become a veterinarian is through the prescribed degree program, and vet schools are set up to assist their graduates in finding employment. Veterinarians who wish to enter private clinical practice must have a license to practice in their particular state before opening an office. Licenses are obtained by passing the state's examination.

Advancement

New graduate veterinarians may enter private clinical practice, usually as employees in an established practice, or become employees of the U.S. government as meat and poultry inspectors, disease control workers, and commissioned officers in the U.S. Public Health Service or the military. New graduates may also enter internships and residencies at veterinary colleges and large private and public veterinary practices or become employed by industrial firms.

The veterinarian who is employed by a government agency may advance in grade and salary after accumulating time and experience on the job. For the veterinarian in private clinical practice, advancement usually consists of an expanding practice and the higher income that will result from it, or by becoming an owner of several practices.

Those who teach or do research may obtain a doctorate and move from the rank of instructor to that of full professor, or advance to an administrative position.

Employment Outlook

In 1996, about 70 percent of the more than 58,000 veterinarians were employed in private clinical practice. The federal government employed about 2,000, mostly in the Department of Agriculture and the Public Health Service. Approximately 30 percent of veterinarians were self-employed as private practice owners. The remainder were employees of private clinical practices, industry, or schools and universities.

Employment of veterinarians is expected to grow faster then the average through the year 2006. The number of pets is expected to increase slightly because of the rising incomes and an increase in the number of people in the thirty-four- to fifty-nine-year age group, where pet ownership has been highest in the past. Single adults and senior citizens have come to appreciate animal ownership. Pet owners also may be willing to pay for more elective and intensive care than in the past. In addition, emphasis on scientific methods of breeding and raising livestock, poultry, and fish and continued support for public health and disease control programs will contribute to the demand for veterinarians. The number of jobs stemming from the need to replace workers will be equal to new job growth.

The outlook is good for veterinarians with specialty training. Demand for specialists in toxicology, laboratory animal medicine, and pathology is expected to increase. Most jobs for specialists will be in metropolitan areas. Prospects for veterinarians who concentrate on environmental and public health issues, aquaculture, and food animal practice appear to be excellent because of perceived increased need in these areas of veterinary medicine. Positions in small animal specialties will be competitive. Opportunities in large animal specialties will be better since most such positions are located in remote, rural areas.

Despite the availability of additional jobs, competition among veterinarians is likely to be stiff. First-year enrollments in veterinary schools have increased slightly and the number of students in graduate-degree and board-certificate programs has risen dramatically. New graduates could choose to work in salaried retail positions.

Earnings

According to the American Veterinary Medical Association, newly graduated veterinarians employed by the federal government start at salaries of about $35,800 a year. The average yearly salary of veterinarians working for the federal government is about $57,600. For those in industry, the average yearly salary for veterinarians is about $44,500.

The earnings of veterinarians in private clinical practice varies according to practice location, type of practice, and years of experience. New graduates employed in the established private clinical practices of other veterinarians generally are paid an average of $29,900 a year. The average income of veterinarians in private clinical practice was $57,500 in 1995. Owners of private clinical practices must operate their practices as a small business. The average starting income for practice owners specializing in large animal care was $39,500 compared with an average income of $31,900 for veterinarians specializing in small animal care.

Conditions of Work

Veterinarians usually treat companion and food animals in hospitals and clinics. Those in large animal practice also work out of well-equipped trucks or cars and may drive considerable distances to farms and ranches. They may work outdoors in all kinds of weather. The chief risk for veterinarians is injury by animals; however, modern tranquilizers and technology have made it much easier for men and women to work on all types of animals.

Most veterinarians work fifty or more hours per week; however, about a fifth work forty hours per week. Although those in private clinical practice may work nights and weekends, the increased number of emergency clinics has reduced the amount of time private practitioners have to be on call. Large animal practitioners tend to work more irregular hours than do those in small animal practice, industry, or government. Veterinarians who are just starting a practice tend to work longer hours.

Sources of Additional Information

American Veterinary Medical Association
1931 North Meacham Road, Suite 100
Schaumburg, IL 60173-4360
Tel: 800-248-2862
WWW: http://www.avma.org

U.S. Department of Agriculture
Food Safety and Inspection Service
Animal and Plant Health Inspection Service
Butler Square West, 4th Floor
100 North Sixth Street
Minneapolis, MN 55403

Canadian Veterinary Medical Association
339 Booth Street
Ottawa, ON K1R 7K1 Canada
Tel: 613-236-1162
Email: mmcvma@magi.com

Visual Artists

Definition

Visual artists convey thoughts, opinions, and ideas through their work—be it a realistic painting, a piece of pottery, or abstract sculpture. They use different mediums, such as clay, paint, metal, or computer technology, to accomplish this. The field of visual arts is usually separated into two categories—graphic art or design, and fine art. The majority of visual artists are self employed.

Nature of the Work

Visual artists use their creative abilities to produce original works of art. *Graphic artists* produce art as a commercial service for their clients, such as an advertising agency, publishing house, or a retail store. The artists covered in this article, however, are generally classified as fine artists rather than commercial artists because they are responsible for selecting the theme, subject matter, and medium of their artwork. Their main purpose for creating art is for self expression. As fine artists, *painters and sculptors* create works to be viewed and judged for aesthetic content. Visual art can take as many forms as the people who create them.

Ceramic artists—also known as *potters, ceramists, sculptors,* and *clay artists*—work with clay to make both functional and purely aesthetic objects. They blend basic elements (such as clay and water) and more specialized components (such as texture fillers, colorants, and talc) and form the mixture into shapes; they then use glazing and firing techniques to finish their pieces. Depending on the artist's individual inclinations, they use either manual techniques or wheel throwing techniques to create such things as functional pottery (like coffee cups and vases), beads, tiles, architectural installations, and sculptures. Although each artist works the clay in a unique way, there are some basic methods that can be used to define the nature of an artist's work. Some ceramic artists build their objects almost completely by hand, not using a potter's wheel; others use a wheel to mold their forms; others make molds and pour clay into them.

Sculptors use a combination of media and methods to create three-dimensional works of art. They may carve objects from stone, plaster, concrete, or wood. They may use their fingers to model clay or wax into objects. Some sculptors create forms from metal or stone, using various masonry tools and equipment. Others create works from found objects, whether parts of a car, branches of a tree, or other objects. Like painters, sculptors may be identified with a particular technique or style. Their work can take monumental forms or they may work on a very small scale.

Painters use different mediums to paint a variety of subjects, including landscapes, people, and objects. They work with oil paint, acrylic paint, tempera, watercolors, pen and ink, pencil, charcoal, crayon, pastels, but may also use such non-traditional media as earth, clay, cement, paper, cloth, and any other material that allows them to express their artistic ideas. They use brushes, palette knives, and other artist's tools to apply color to canvas or other surfaces. Painters develop line, space, color, and other visual elements to produce the desired effect. They may prefer a particular style of art, such as realism or abstraction, and they may be identified with a certain technique or subject matter. Many artists develop a particular style and apply that style across a broad range of techniques, from painting to etching to sculpture.

Some artists, such as *printmakers*, create and engrave their designs on wood, stone, or metal. These designs are then transferred, or printed, on paper. Printmakers can also create their art using computer data; the information is then printed using high quality color printers.

The preservation and restoration of aged, faded, or damaged art is done by *painting restorers*. This is a tedious and detailed process using solvent and cleaning agents that are applied to the art. Painting restorers are usually experts in their field.

Illustrators paint or draw pictures for a variety of publications such as books and magazines, even greeting cards. Medical illustration is a specialized field combining artistic talent with a knowledge of anatomy and medical procedures.

Art directors read and lay out information and photos so it will be easy to read as well as be attractive and pleasing to the reader. Art directors are employed by newspapers, magazine, and by organizations that have a presence on the Internet.

Other artists concentrate on specific niches in which they enjoy producing objects considered both functional and artful. Or one might go through phases, working as a potter for a while, then sculpting, then exploring other creative inclinations. Bead making, tile making, and making architectural ceramics are a few examples of creative endeavors.

Sculptors creating large works, especially those that will be placed outdoors and in public areas, usually work under contract or commission. Most artists, however, create works that express their personal artistic vision and then hope to find someone to purchase them. Artists generally seek out a gallery to display their work and function as the sales agent for the work. The gallery owner and artist set the prices for pieces of art, and the gallery owner receives a commission on any work that sells. The relationship between the gallery owner and artist is often one of close cooperation, and the gallery owner may encourage the artist to explore new techniques, styles, and ideas, while helping to establish a reputation for the artist. As an artist becomes well known, selling his or her work often becomes easier, and many well-known artists receive commissions for their art.

There is no single way to become or to be an artist. As with other areas of the arts, painting and sculpting usually are intensely personal endeavors. If it is possible to generalize, most painters and sculptors are people with a desire and need to explore visual representations of the world around them or the world within them, or both. Throughout their careers, they seek to develop their vision and the methods and techniques that allow them to best express themselves. Many artists work from or within a tradition or style of art. They may develop formal theories of art or advance new theories of

visual presentation. Many artists, of course, combine both elements of painting and sculpture in their art. They may also combine techniques of music, dance, photography, and even science, engineering, mechanics, and electronics in their work. As film, video, and computer technology has developed, the work of painters and sculptors has expanded into new forms of expression. The recently developed three-dimensional computer animation techniques in particular often blur the boundaries between painting, sculpture, photography, and cinema. Artists are usually aware of the art that has come before them as well as the work of their contemporaries.

Every artist has his or her way of working. Many work in studios, often separate from their homes, where they can produce their work in privacy and quiet. Many artists, however, work outdoors. Most artists probably combine both indoor and outdoor work during their careers. An artist may choose complete solitude to work; others thrive on interaction with other artists and people. Artists engaged in monumental work, particularly sculptors, often have helpers who assist in the creation of a piece of art, working under the artist's direction. They may contract with a foundry to cast the finished sculpture in bronze, iron, or another metal.

The work of an artist usually continues throughout his or her lifetime. Creating fine art is rarely a career choice but rather a way of life, a following of a desire or need that may exhibit itself at an extremely early age. Visual artists use their work to communicate what they see, feel, think, believe, or simply are in a form other than language. For some, this may be the only way they feel they can truly communicate.

Requirements

There are no formal educational requirements for becoming a visual artist. However, most artists benefit from training, and many—about 90 percent—attend art schools or programs in colleges and universities. Twenty percent of all artists major in fine arts, according to the American Institute of Graphic Arts, and of those, 20 percent have at least a master's degree. There are also many workshops and other ways for artists to gain instruction, practice, and exposure to art and the works and ideas of other artists. The artist should learn a variety of techniques, be exposed to as many media and styles as possible, and gain an understanding of the history of art and art theory. By learning as much as possible, the artist is better able to choose the appropriate means for his or her own artistic expression.

Medical illustrators, because of the nature of their work, are required to have biological training besides artistic talent. Medical or *scientific illustrators* have not only a four-year degree in art with an emphasis in pre-medical courses, but most have a master's in medical illustration. Only a few schools in the United States offer this specialized coursework.

The most important requirement for a career as an artist is ability. Of course, this is entirely subjective, and it is perhaps more important that artists believe in their ability, or in their potential. Apart from being creative and imaginative, artists should exhibit such traits as patience, persistence, determination, independence, and sensitivity.

Because earning a living as a fine artist is very difficult, especially when one is just starting out, many artists work at another job. With the proper training and educational background, many artists are able to work in art-related positions, such as art teachers, art directors, or graphic designers, while pursuing their art activities independently. For example, many art teachers hold classes in their studios.

Opportunities for Experience & Exploration

Experience drawing, painting, and even sculpting can be had at a very early age, even before formal schooling begins. Most elementary, middle, and high schools offer classes in art. Aspiring painters and sculptors can undertake a variety of artistic projects at school or at home. Many art associations and schools also offer beginning classes in various types of art for the general public.

Students interested in pursuing art as a career are encouraged to visit museums and galleries to view the work of other artists. In addition, they can learn about the history of art and artistic techniques and methods through books, videotapes, the Internet, and other sources. The New York Foundation for the Arts sponsors a toll-free hotline, 800-232-2789, that offers quick information on programs

and services and answers to specific questions on visual artists. The hotline is open Monday through Friday, between 2:00 and 5:00 p.m., Eastern Standard Time.

Methods of Entering

Artists interested in exhibiting or selling their products should investigate potential markets. Reference books, such as *Artist's Market,* may be helpful, as well as library books that offer information on business and tax law, and related issues. Local fairs and art shows often provide opportunities for new artists to display their work. Art councils are a good source of information on upcoming fairs in the area. A portfolio, a collection of the artist's work, is an essential tool when looking for work. An artist's portfolio should be organized and showcase a wide variety of the artist's talent and capabilities.

Some artists sell their work on consignment. When a painter or sculptor sells work this way, a store or gallery displays an item; when the item is sold, the artist gets the price of that item minus a commission that goes to the store or gallery. Artists who sell on consignment should read contracts very carefully.

Many art schools and universities have placement services to help students find jobs. Although fine artists are generally self-employed, many need to work at another job, at least initially, to support themselves while they establish a reputation.

Advancement

Fine artists are largely self-employed; thus, the channels for advancement are not as well defined as they are at a company or firm. An artist may become increasingly well known, both nationally and internationally, and as an artist's reputation increases, he or she can command higher prices for his or her work. The success of the fine artist depends on a variety of factors, including talent, drive, and determination. However, luck often seems to play a role in many artists' successes, and some artists do not achieve recognition until late in life, if at all. Artists with business skills may open galleries to display their own and others' work. Those with the appropriate educational backgrounds may become art teachers, agents, or critics.

Employment Outlook

Employment for visual artists is expected to grow faster than the average. The U.S. Department of Labor projects an additional 90,000 new art jobs to be available by the year 2006. However, because they are usually self-employed, much of their success depends on the amount and type of work created, the drive and determination in selling the artwork, and the interest or readiness of the public to appreciate and purchase the work. Continued population growth, higher incomes, and increased appreciation for fine art will create a demand for visual artists.

Success for an artist, however, is difficult to quantify. Individual artists may consider themselves successful as their talent matures and they are better able to present their vision in their work. This type of success goes beyond financial considerations. Few artists enter this field for the money. Financial success depends on a great deal of factors, many of which have nothing to do with the artist or his or her work. Artists with good marketing skills will likely be the most successful in selling their work. Although artists should not let their style be dictated by market trends, those interested in financial success can attempt to determine what types of artwork are wanted by the public.

It often takes several years for an artist's work and reputation to be established. Many artists have to support themselves through other employment. There are numerous employment opportunities for commercial artists in such fields as publishing, advertising, fashion and design, and teaching. Artists should consider employment in these and other fields. They should be prepared, however, to face strong competition from others who are attracted to these fields. Freelancers may have difficulty selling their work until they establish their artistic reputation. Artists skilled in computer techniques will have an edge.

This occupation may be affected by the amount of funding granted by the government. The National Endowment of the Arts, for example, awards grants and funding to help talented artists hone their craft.

Earnings

The amount of money earned by visual artists varies greatly. Most are self-employed—about 60 percent—a figure seven times greater compared to other occupations. As freelancers, artists can set their hours and prices. Those employed by businesses usually work for the motion picture and television industries, wholesale or retail trades, or public relation firms. According to the *1998-99 Occupational Outlook Handbook,* salaried, full time artists in 1996 earned an average of $27,100 annually. Fifty percent earned between $20,000 and $36,400; the top ten percent earned over $43,000. Some internationally known artists may command millions of dollars for their work.

However, the majority of artists often work long hours and earn little, especially when they are first starting out in the business The price they charge is up to them, but much depends on the value the public places on their work. A particular item may sell for a few dollars, a few hundred, or a few thousand or tens of thousands of dollars and more. Often, the value of an artwork may increase considerably after it has been sold. An artwork that may have earned an artist only a few hundred dollars may earn many thousands of dollars the next time it is sold. Some artists obtain grants that allow them to pursue their art; others win prizes and awards in competitions. Most artists, however, have to work on their projects part-time while holding down a regular, full-time job. Many artists teach in art schools, high schools, or out of their studios.

Conditions of Work

There were 276,000 visual artists employed in the United States in 1996. Most painters and sculptors work out of their homes or in studios. Some work in small areas in their apartments; others work in large, well-ventilated lofts. Occasionally, painters and sculptors work outside. In addition, artists often work at fairs, shops, museums, and other places where their work is being exhibited.

Artists often work long hours, and those who are self-employed do not receive paid vacations, insurance coverage, or any of the other benefits usually offered by a company or firm. However, artists are able to work at their own pace, set their own prices, and make their own decisions. The energy and creativity that go into an artist's work brings feelings of pride and satisfaction. Most artists genuinely love what they do.

Sources of Additional Information

American Society of Artists
PO Box 1326
Palatine, IL 60078

National Art Education Association
1916 Association Drive
Reston, VA 20191-1590
Tel: 703-860-8000
Email: naea@dgs.dgsys.com
WWW: http://www.naea-reston.org

National Council on Education for the Ceramic Arts
PO Box 1677
Bandon, OR 97411
Tel: 800-99-NCECA
WWW: http://www.arts.ufl.edu/nceca

National Endowment for the Arts
Nancy Hanks Center
Arts and Education
Education and Access Division
1100 Pennsylvania Avenue, NW
Washington, DC 20506-0001
Tel: 202-682-5426

Sculptors Guild
The Soho Building
110 Greene Street
New York, NY 10012
Tel: 212-431-5669
WWW: http://www.artincontext.com

For information on a scholarship offered for a specific summer workshop in Maine, contact:

Haystack Mountain School of Crafts
Deer Isle, ME 04627
Tel: 207-348-2306
WWW: http://www.craftweb.com/org/haystack

Webmasters

Definition

Webmasters design, implement, and maintain World Wide Web sites for corporations, educational institutions, not-for-profit organizations, government agencies, or other institutions. Webmasters should have working knowledge of network configurations, interface, graphic design, software development, business, writing, marketing, and project management. Because the function of a webmaster encompasses so many different responsibilities, in a large organization, the position is often held by a team of individuals, rather than a single person.

Nature of the Work

Because the idea of designing and maintaining a Web site is relatively new, there is no complete, definitive job description for a webmaster. Many of their job responsibilities depend upon the goals and needs of the particular organization for which they work. There are, however, some basic duties that are common to almost all webmasters.

The webmaster, specifically site managers, first secures space on the Web for the site he or she is developing. This is done by contracting with an Internet service provider. The provider serves as a sort of storage facility for the organization's on-line information, usually charging a set monthly fee for a specified amount of megabyte space. The webmaster may also be responsible for establishing a URL (Uniform Resource Locator) for the Web site he or she is developing. The URL serves as the sites on-line "address," and must be registered with InterNIC, the Web URL registration service.

The webmaster is responsible for developing the actual Web site for his or her organization. In some cases, this may involve actually writing the text content of the pages. More commonly, however, the webmaster is given the text to be used, and is merely responsible for programming it in such a way that it can be displayed on a Web page. In larger companies webmasters specialize in content, adaptation, and presentation of data.

In order for text to be displayed on a Web page, it must be formatted using HyperText Markup Language (HTML). HTML is a system of coding text so that the computer that is "reading" it knows how to display it. For example, text could be coded to be a certain size or color or to be italicized or boldface. Paragraphs, line breaks, alignment, and margins are other examples of text attributes that must be coded in HTML.

Although it is less and less common, some webmasters code text manually, by actually typing the various commands into the body of the text. This method is time-consuming, however, and mistakes are easily made. More often, webmasters use a software program that automatically codes text. Some word processing programs, such as WordPerfect, even offer HTML options.

Along with coding the text, the webmaster must lay out the elements of the Web site in such a way that it is visually pleasing, well organized, and easy to navigate. He or she may use various colors, background patterns, images, tables, or charts. These graphic elements can come from image files already on the Web, software clip art files, or images scanned into the computer with an electronic scanner. In some cases, when an organization is using the Web site to promote its product or service, the webmaster may work with a marketing specialist or department to develop a page.

Some Web sites have several directories or "layers." That is, an organization may have several Web pages, organized in a sort of "tree," with its home page connected, via hypertext links, to other pages, which may in turn be linked to other pages. The webmaster is responsible for organizing the pages in such a way that a visitor can easily browse through them and find what he or she is looking for. Such webmasters are called *programmers* and *developers;* they are also responsible for creating Web tools and special Web functionality.

For webmasters who work for organizations that have several different Web sites, one responsibility may be making sure that the "style" or appearance of all the pages is the same. This is often referred to as "house style." In large organizations, such as universities, where many different departments may be developing and maintaining their own pages, it is especially important that the webmaster monitor these pages to ensure consistency and conformity to the organization's requirements. In almost every case, the webmaster has the final authority for the content and appearance of his or her organization's Web site. He or she must carefully edit, proofread, and check the appearance of every page.

Besides designing and setting up Web sites, most webmasters are charged with maintaining and updating existing sites. Most sites contain information that changes regularly. Some change daily, or even hourly. Depending upon his or her employer and the type of Web site, the webmaster may spend a good deal of time updating and remodeling the page. He or she is also responsible for ensuring that the hyperlinks contained within the Web site lead to the sites they should. Since it is common for links to change or become obsolete, the webmaster usually performs a link check every few weeks.

Other job duties vary, depending upon the employer and the position. Most webmasters are responsible for receiving and answering email messages from visitors to the organization's Web site. Some webmasters keep logs and create reports on when and how often their pages are visited and by whom. Depending on the company, Web sites count anywhere from 300 to 1.4 billion visits, or "hits," a month. Some create and maintain order forms or on-line "shopping carts" that allow visitors to the Web site to purchase products or services. Some may train other employees on how to create or update Web pages. Finally, webmasters may be responsible for developing and adhering to a budget for their departments.

Requirements

High school students who are interested in becoming a webmaster should take as many computer science classes as they can. Mathematics classes are also helpful.

Finally, because writing skills are important in this career, English classes are good choices.

As of today, there is no set advanced educational path or requirement for becoming a webmaster. While many have bachelor's degrees in computer science, liberal arts degrees, such as English, are not uncommon. There are also webmasters who have degrees in engineering, mathematics, and marketing. Not all webmasters have bachelor's degrees, however; some have two-year degrees, or a high school education only. Currently, most webmasters do not have formal, specific training in how to design Web sites. According to a *Web Week* survey, most webmasters are self taught in the basics of building Internet sites.

There is strong debate within the industry regarding certification. Some, mostly corporate CEOs, favor certification. They view certification as a way to gauge an employees skill and Web mastery expertise. Others argue, however, that is nearly impossible to test knowledge of technology that is constantly changing and improving. Despite the split of opinion, webmaster certification programs are available at many colleges, universities, and technical schools throughout the United States. Programs vary in length, anywhere from three weeks, to nine months or more; topics covered include client/server technology, Web development, programs, and software and hardware. The International Webmasters Association also offers a voluntary certification program.

Should webmasters be certified? Though it's currently not a prerequisite for employment, certification can only enhance a candidate's chance at landing a webmaster position.

What most webmasters have in common is a strong knowledge of computer technology. Most people who enter this field are already well-versed in computer operating systems, programming languages, computer graphics, and Internet standards. When considering candidates for the position of webmaster, employers usually require at least two years of experience with World Wide Web technologies. In some cases, employers require that candidates already have experience in designing and maintaining Web sites. It is, in fact, most common for someone to move into the position of webmaster from another computer-related job in the same organization.

Webmasters should be creative. It is important for a Web page to be well designed in order to attract attention. Good writing skills and an aptitude for marketing are also excellent qualities for anyone considering a career in Web site design.

Opportunities for Experience & Exploration

One of the easiest ways to learn about what a webmaster does is to spend time "surfing" on the World Wide Web. By examining a variety of Web sites to see how they look and operate, high school students can begin to get a feel for what goes into a home page.

An even better way to explore the career is for a student to design his or her own personal Web page. Many Internet servers offer their users the option of designing and maintaining a personal Web page for a very low fee. A personal page can contain virtually anything that the individual wants to include, from snapshots of friends to audio files of favorite music to hypertext links to other favorite sites. The student who is interested in designing Web sites as a career can easily start by becoming the "webmaster" for his or her own personal page.

Associations offer a wealth of information and experience for interested students. The National Association of Webmasters, for example, holds "Web fairs" as a way to introduce teenagers interested in Web careers to those already in the industry—webmasters, teachers, and other workers in the technological field. Local libraries and on-line sources should have a wealth of information on Web site design.

Methods of Entering

Most people become webmasters by moving into the position from another computer-related position within the same company. Since most large organizations already use computers for various functions, they may employ a person or several people to serve as computer "specialists." If these organizations decide to develop their own Web sites, they frequently assign the task to one of these employees who is already experienced with the computer system. Often, the person who ultimately becomes an organization's webmaster at first just takes on the job in addition to his or her other, already-established duties.

Another way that individuals find jobs in this field is through on-line postings of job openings. Many companies post webmaster position openings on-line because the candidates they hope to attract are very likely to use the Internet for a job search. Therefore, the prospective webmaster should use the World Wide Web to check job-related newsgroups. He or she might also use a Web search engine to locate openings.

Advancement

Experienced webmasters employed by a large organization may be able to advance to a supervisory position in which he or she directs the work of a team of webmasters. Others might advance by starting their own business, designing Web sites on a contract basis for several clients, rather than working exclusively for one organization.

Opportunities for webmasters of the future are endless due to the continuing development of on-line technology. As understanding and use of the World Wide Web increase, there may be new or expanded job duties for individuals with expertise in this field. People working today as webmasters may be required in a few years to perform jobs that don't even exist yet.

Employment Outlook

There can be no doubt that computer—and specifically on-line—technology will continue its rapid growth for the next several years. Likewise, then, the number of computer-related jobs, including that of webmaster, should also increase. The World Organization of Webmasters projects an explosion of jobs available through the year 2006—well over 8 million. The majority of webmasters working today are full time employees—about 86 percent according to the 1998 Webmaster Study, conducted by Collaborative Marketing. The newness of this job is reflected in the age demographics of webmasters—35 percent are between the ages of 26 and 35 (1998 Webmaster Study); and according to *Web Week,* 72 percent are in their first webmaster position. This indicates the attraction of the young to the Internet, and to better tap that market, a company's desire to fill webmaster positions with young computer-savvy individuals.

The 1998 Webmaster Study found this field to be currently male-dominated. However, there is great opportunity for women in this field. Many large companies, such as Wal-Mart, are looking for talented individuals who, according to a Wal-Mart webmaster (yes, female) "can combine a lot of technical knowledge with the ability to cooperate with people who don't know a lot of technology. Women can often be very good at that."

As more and more businesses, not-for-profit organizations, educational institutions, and government agencies choose to "go on-line," the total number of Web sites will grow, as will the need for experts to design them. Companies are starting to view Web sites as more than a temporary experiment, but rather an important and necessary business and marketing tool. Growth will be largest with content developers——webmasters responsible for the information displayed on a Web site. The 1998 Webmaster Study predicts content developers will become more sophisticated with their techniques and will significantly surpass the growth of the technical segment of webmasters.

One thing to keep in mind, however, is that when technology advances extremely rapidly, it tends to make old methods of doing things obsolete. If current trends continue, the role and role of webmaster will be carried out by a group or department instead of a single employee, in order to keep up with the demands of the position. It is possible that in the next few years, changes in technology will make the Web sites we are now familiar with a thing of the past. Another possibility is that, like desktop publishing, user-friendly software programs will make Web site design so easy and efficient that it no longer requires an "expert" to do it well. Webmasters who are concerned with job security should be willing to continue learning and using the very latest developments in technology, so that they are prepared to move into the future of on-line communication, whatever it may be.

Earnings

According to *U.S. News & World Report,* salaries for the position of webmaster range from $50,000 to $100,000 per year. The demand for webmasters is so great that some companies are offering stock options, sign-on bonuses and other perks, in addition to salaries from $80,000

to $110,000. While this may be true for those who are hired into an organization specifically to fill the position, it is not representative of the many webmasters who have merely moved into the position from another position within their company or have taken on the task in addition to other duties. These employees are often paid approximately the same salary they were already making. According to the 1998 Webmaster Survey, the majority of webmasters earn under $50,000. Nineteen percent of all webmasters earned from $25,000 to $40,999 annually; seventeen percent earned less than $25,000.

Depending upon the organization for which they work, webmasters may receive a benefits package in addition to salary. A typical benefits package would include paid vacations and holidays, medical insurance, and perhaps a pension plan.

Conditions of Work

Webmasters who are employed by a business, school or university, not-for-profit organization, or government agency, or other institution are likely to spend almost all of their time in an office at a computer monitor. Although not physically demanding, full days of computer work can be tiring and hard on one's eyes.

Although much of the webmaster's day may be spent alone, it is nonetheless important that he or she be able to communicate and work well with others. Depending upon the organization for which he or she works, the webmaster may have periodic meetings with graphic designers, marketing specialists, writers, or other professionals who have input into the Web site development. In many larger organizations, there is a team of webmasters, rather than just one. Although each team member works alone on his or her own specific duties, the members may meet frequently to discuss and coordinate their activities.

Because technology changes so rapidly, this job is constantly evolving. Webmasters must spend time reading and learning about new developments in on-line communication. They may be continually working with new computer software or hardware. Their actual job responsibilities may even change, as the capabilities of both the organization and the World Wide Web itself expand. It is important that these employees be flexible and willing to learn and grow with the technology that drives their work.

Because they don't deal with the general public, most webmasters are allowed to wear fairly casual attire and to work in a relaxed atmosphere. In most cases, the job calls for standard working hours, although there may be times when overtime is required.

Sources of Additional Information

Association of Internet Professionals (AIP)
9200 Sunset Boulevard, Suite 710
Los Angeles, CA 90069
Tel: 800-JOIN-AIP
Email: info@association.org

For information on its newsletter, Webreference Update, *and information regarding its voluntary certification program, contact:*

International Webmasters Association
WWW: http://www.iwanet.org

National Association of Webmasters
9580 Oak Avenue Parkway, Suite 7-177
Folsom, CA 95630
Tel: 916-929-6557
WWW: http://www.naw.org

For information on the career of webmaster, contact:

Webmaster Magazine
492 Old Connecticut Path
PO Box 9208
Framingham, MA 01701
Tel: 800-788-4605
WWW: http://www.web-master.com/

Webmasters' Guild
WWW: http://www.webmaster.org/

World Organization of Webmasters
9580 Oak Avenue Parkway, Suite 7-177
Folsom, CA 95630
Tel: 916-929-6557
Email: info@world-webmasters.org

Index